W9-AEX-263

Gift
Farjan, 10/84

The Great Asian Religions

Kansas School of Religion
At the University of Kansas
Smith Hall, Rm. 109, Library
Lawrence, Kansas 66045-2164

The Great Asian Religions

AN ANTHOLOGY

COMPILED BY Wing-tsit Chan

Isma'īl Rāgī al Fārūqī

Joseph M. Kitagawa

P. T. Raju

MACMILLAN PUBLISHING CO., INC.
NEW YORK

COLLIER MACMILLAN PUBLISHERS
LONDON

© Copyright 1969, Macmillan Publishing Co., Inc.

All rights reserved. No part of this book may be reproduced or transmitted in any form or by any means, electronic or mechanical, including photocopying, recording or by any information storage and retrieval system, without permission in writing from the Publisher.

Library of Congress catalog card number: 69–10182

MACMILLAN PUBLISHING CO., INC.
866 THIRD AVENUE, NEW YORK, NEW YORK 10022

COLLIER-MACMILLAN CANADA, LTD., TORONTO, ONTARIO

Printed in the United States of America

PRINTING 12131415 YEAR 23456789

Acknowledgments

We wish to acknowledge our indebtedness to the following publishers for their kindness in permitting us to use the material indicated:

Wm. H. Allen and Co., London, for Ernest Trumpp, *The Holy Scripture of the Sikhs*, 1877, pp. 6, 74, and 126.

George Allen and Unwin Ltd., London, for S. Radhakrishnan, *An Idealist View of Life*, 1932, pp. 343–45; S. Radhakrishnan and J. H. Muirhead, ed., *Contemporary Indian Philosophy*, 2nd ed., 1952, p. 21; and Rabindranath Tagore, *The Religion of Man*, 1931, pp. 205–6.

The International Aryan League, New Delhi, for Dayānanda Sarasvati, *Satyārthaprakāśa, The Light of Truth*, tr. by Chirañjiva Bhāradwāja, 1932, pp. 190–91 and 223.

YMCA Publishing House, New Delhi, for F. Kingsbury and G. E. Phillip, *Hymns of the Tamil Śaivaite Saints*, 1921, hymns 18 and 24.

Śrī Aurobindo Asram, Pondicherry, India, for Śrī Aurobindo, *The Divine Life*, 1949, pp. 247–48.

Bobbs-Merrill Co., Inc., Indianapolis, for *The Way of Lao Tzu*, tr. with introductory essays, comments and notes, by Wing-tsit Chan, copyright © 1963, by the Bobbs-Merrill Company, Inc., reprinted by permission of the Liberal Arts Press Division, chs. 1, 2, 6, 7, 10, 14, 16, 19, 21, 25, 28, 31, 33, 34, 40, 42, 43, 51, 55, 57, 59, and 73.

Columbia University Press, New York, for Wm. Theodore de Bary, comp., *Sources of Indian Tradition*, 1960, pp. 610–11; de Bary, Wing-tsit Chan, and Burton Watson, comp., *Sources of Chinese Tradition*, 1960, pp. 298–304 (passages from the *Pao-p'u tzu*), pp. 391 and 392–95 (3 verses and secs. 13, 16–19, 30 from the *Platform Scripture*), pp. 632–35 (the *Treatise of the Most Exalted One on Moral Retribution*), pp. 635–38 (the *Silent Way of Recompense*), and pp. 641–49 (*Questions and Answers on the Way of Pervading Unity*).

Krishnamurti Writings, Inc., Ojai, California, for J. Krishnamurti, *Education and the Significance of Life*, 1953, pp. 37–39.

Philosophical Library, New York, for Edward Conze, *Buddhist Texts through the Ages*, 1954, pp. 42, 130–31.

Princeton University Press, Princeton, New Jersey, for Wing-tsit Chan, tr. and comp., *A Source Book in Chinese Philosophy*, 1963, pp. 7–8 (2 odes from the *Book of Odes*), pp. 11–13 (passages from the *Tso chuan*), selected passages from pp. 19–48 (*Analects*, 1:2, 8, 11; 2:3–5, 24; 3:3, 4, 12, 13, 17; 4:3, 15; 5:11, 12; 6:20, 25, 26, 28; 7:19, 20, 22, 24, 34; 9:1, 3, 5, 6; 11:8, 11; 12:1, 2, 5; 14:36, 37; 15:23, 28; 16:8; 17:19, and 19:6), selected passages from pp. 62–83 (*Book of Mencius*, 2A:2, 6; 4A:2; 5A:5; 6B:15; 7A:1–2, 4, 13; and 7B:24, 25, 33), selected passages from pp. 101–12 (*Doctrine of the Mean*, chs. 1, 14, 16, 19, 21, 22, 24, 25, part of 26, and 29), pp. 116–18 (passages from "On Nature" of the *Hsün Tzu*), pp. 181, 196–98 (passages from the *Chuang Tzu*), selected passages from pp. 612–14, 634–46 (*Complete Works of Chu Hsi*, secs. 31–32, 34, 36, 100, 102–3, 107, 109, 123, 129, 131, and 133).

Sri Ramakrishna Math, Mylapore, Madras, for Swami Tyāgīsananda, *Nārada Bhaktisūtras*, 1955, chs. 1 and 4.

Ramakrishna-Vivekananda Center, New York, for Swami Nikhilananda, *Ramakrishna: Prophet of New India*, 1948, pp. 166–67.

St. John's University Press, New York, for Hui-neng, *The Platform Scripture, the Basic Classic of Zen Buddhism*, tr. by Wing-tsit Chan, from Asian Institute Translation, No. 3, Copyright 1963, St. John's University, secs. 34–36.

Preface

This anthology offers essential materials for a beginning course on Asian, comparative, or world religions. Although limited in quantity to what one volume will hold, the selections are indispensable for the understanding and evaluation of the religious systems of Asia.

With the exception of Islām, Asian religions are greatly different from Christianity and Judaism and contrast even more among themselves. Because of this, our presentation does not follow any Western standard or any uniform pattern. The four compilers of this book were free to choose and treat their material according to their own judgments. It was felt that any prescribed uniformity would falsify the varying nature of the religions and reinforce the impression—long held, happily declining, but still lingering—that all Asian religions are alike. As the reader will see, Indian religions are presented doctrinally, with concentration on their teachings; Chinese and Japanese religions are presented historically; and the Islāmic religion topically, as the Muslim consciousness has seen and continues to see it. None of these may be the "best" way to deal with the subject, but we hope that they will at least be helpful.

The anthology is not geared to any particular text or course but is arranged in such a manner that it can be used in a variety of ways in any semester- or year-long course, inasmuch as each chapter, of manageable length, forms a unit and can be read independently. We wish all minor religions and all aspects of the major religious systems could have been included. Because space is limited, certain lesser religions, such as Zoroastrianism, had to be left out with much regret. The omission of Moism in China will raise some eyebrows. But although its doctrines of universal love and obedience to the will of Heaven have attracted considerable attention among Western students of China because of their counterparts in Christianity, Moism has actually exercised little, if any, influence on the religious life or thought of the Chinese people. We wish, too, that space had allowed us to treat all traditions fully so that none would occupy fewer pages than others, but different religions have different claims on space, whether the standard is their number of followers, length of history, the number of their subdivisions, the number of countries they cover, or the amount of literature they have produced. We have arbitrarily treated Islām by religion but the others by country. It is felt that although Islām prevails in many countries, its character has remained essentially the same, despite its many changes in India and China; therefore, it seems logical to set it apart. Although Buddhism is a major religion with many distinguishing features, it has so intimately intermingled with the religious life of China and Japan that it is meaningful to paint it as part of the total religious picture in those countries. Whatever the space allotment and arrangement, we hope the fundamental concepts, doctrines, and issues have been clearly brought out so that although the basket does not hold all the eggs, it contains basic and healthful rations.

New features presented in this book include the key controversies in Chinese religious history, Neo-Confucian religious thought, and the long tradition of the harmony of the Three Religions. In the case of Islām, materials on each major topic are given on two levels: that of scripture, which is unquestionably normative for its followers past and present, and that of civilization, where the Islāmic content is interpreted, elaborated, analyzed, and discussed. Hinduism is traced through its doctrinal developments from classical comparative commentaries to Radhakrishnan, including the nature of devotion and the yoga of music. For Japan, the case of Zen has been built around its central focus, Dōgen, who more than anyone else embodies the spirit of Japanese Zen.

All the compilers were born and brought up in the milieu of the religions they portray. Very naturally, almost inevitably, they have looked at these religions from within. On the other hand, all of them have taught for a number of years in American institutions of higher learning, and may be said to look at the religions also from without. With a few minor exceptions, they have translated all the materials especially for this anthology.

To help the reader understand and to stimulate further interest, explanatory comments are supplied between source materials, and the use of foreign words reduced to a minimum. All Asian titles are translated or explained, and the English rendering of Asian terms is consistent. We hope the ideas are clear and the reading interesting.

Throughout the text, we use brackets for extraneous material, parentheses for simple explanation and identification and, unless otherwise indicated, footnotes are our own. Chinese and Japanese personal names are given according to the East Asian custom, that is, the family name first, except in the case of contemporary Asians who, like two of the compilers, prefer to follow the Western custom. The Chinese and Japanese traditional lunar calendar year is equated with the Western calendar year, although the two do not exactly coincide.

Thanks are due the Aspen Institute for Humanistic Studies for granting me a U.S. Steel Scholar-in-Residence fellowship, which enabled me to bring this project to completion; Mr. Ben Cooper of the Institute, for editorial advice on Part Two; Misses Robin Rourke and Hilary Knight-Revel, also of the Institute, for typing the manuscript of the same; and Mr. Alan L. Miller, Professor Kitagawa's research associate, for making many stylistic improvements of the professor's translations in Part Three. Most of all, I thank my three colleagues who have been most co-operative and most patient with my ignorant suggestions and uninformed queries.

Chatham College **Wing-tsit Chan**

Contents

Part Two: Religions of China

Part Three: Religions of Japan

Part Four: Islām

The act of offering is the Brahman, the oblation is the Brahman, the sacrificial fire is the Brahman, the sacrificer is the Brahman. In the *samādhi* (concentration) of the activity of the Brahman, the destination (purpose) is the Brahman . . . .

Lord Kṛṣṇa, in the *Bhagavad-gītā*, 4: 24

This, O monks, is the Aryan truth of the way. It is the way that leads to the cessation of pain. This is the eight-fold way of right views, right aims, right words, right deeds, right profession, right effort, right mindfulness, and right *samādhi*.

Gotama Buddha, Sermon on the Four Aryan Truths

The superior man stands in awe of three things. He stands in awe of the Mandate of Heaven; he stands in awe of great men; and he stands in awe of the words of the sages.

Confucian *Analects*, 16: 8

O People of the Book! Let us now come to agreement upon a noble principle common to all of us, namely, that we shall not worship aught but God, that we shall not associate anyone with Him, and that we shall not take one another for lords beside God.

Qur'ān, 3: 64

Chronology

		India	China
B.C.	4000–3000	Pre-Aryan religion	
	2000–1500	*Ṛgveda* (other Vedas a little later)	
	9th cent.	First Upaniṣads	*Books of Odes* and *History*
	6th cent.	Mahāvīra, founder of Jainism	Lao Tzu, beginning of Taoism (?)
		Gotama (Buddha), founder of Buddhism	Confucius, 551–479 B.C.
	5th cent.	*Vedānta Aphorisms*	Confucian *Doctrine of the Mean* (?)
	4th cent.	Patañjali's *Yoga Aphorisms*	Mencius, 372–289 B.C.? Idealistic Confucianism
		Manu's Ethical Code (?)	Chuang Tzu, b. 369 B.C.? Taoist philosopher
	3rd cent.	*Bhagavad-gītā*	Hsün Tzu, 313–238 B.C.? Rationalistic Confucianism
	2nd cent.		Han dynasty, 206 B.C.–A.D. 220 Confucian institutional developments
	1st cent.		*Book of Rites; Classic of Filial Piety* (?)
			Buddhism known in China, 2 B.C.
A.D.	1st cent.		Official introduction of Buddhism, 67 A.D.
	2nd cent.		Founding of Taoist religion, 143 A.D.
			42 Chapter Scripture: Settling of Doubts
	3rd cent.		Taoist Ko Hung (Pao-p'u Tzu), 284–363
	4th cent.		Issue between Church and State, Hui-yüan, 334–417
	5th cent.		Kumārājiva's trans. of *Lotus Scripture*, 406
	6th cent.		Fan Chen on the destructibility of the soul, 502
			Pure Land Buddhism flourished
	7th cent.		Fa-tsang, 643–712, founder of Hua-yen Buddhism
			Hui-neng, 638–713, 6th Patriarch of Ch'an (Zen) Buddhism; *Platform Scripture*
	8th cent.	Śaṅkara, greatest exponent of non-dualism	Ch'an Buddhism prevalent

Japan	Islām		
		4000–3000	B.C.
		2000–1500	
		9th cent.	
		6th cent.	
		5th cent.	
		4th cent.	
		3rd cent.	
		2nd cent.	
		1st cent.	
		1st cent.	A.D.
		2nd cent.	
		3rd cent.	
Gradual development of Shintō		4th cent.	
		5th cent.	
Buddhism introduced, 538 (or 552)		6th cent.	
Prince Regent Shōtoku, 573–621	1st revelation of Muḥammad in Makkah, 612 622: Islāmic calendar began; The Prophet emigrated to Madīnah; Islāmic community began Muḥammad died, 632. Islām spread outside Arabia Qur'ānic text collected and published, 645–647 Islāmization of Middle East and North Africa, 634–661	7th cent.	
Nara period, 710–781 *Records of Ancient Matters; Chronicles of Japan; Collection of a Myriad Leaves; Provincial Records; Chronicles Continued*, 797	Islāmization of Spain, Central Asia, and India, 711 Golden Age of Baghdad; victory of the Arabic language and literature, 786	8th cent.	

	India	China
8th cent. (*cont.*)		
9th cent.		Discussions on Heaven (Nature, God), 814 fl.
10th cent.		
11th cent.	Rāmānuja, greatest exponent of qualified nondualism	
12th cent.		Chu Hsi, 1130–1200, greatest Neo-Confucianist
13th cent.	Madhva, greatest exponent of dualism	
14th cent.		
15th cent.	Kabīr, 1440–1518 (religion of love of God)	
16th cent.	Nānak, 1449–1538, founder of Sikhism	
17th cent.		
18th cent.		
19th cent.	Tyāgarāja, 1767–1847, exponent of music for salvation Roy, 1772–1833, founder of Brāhmo Samāj D. Tagore, 1817–1905, exponent of the religion of Brāhmo Samāj Sarasvati, 1824–1883, founder of Ārya Samāj Rāmakrishna, 1836–1886, mystic saint	
20th cent.	Rabindranath Tagore, 1861–1941 Mahandas K. Gandhi, 1869–1948 Aurobindo Ghose, 1872–1950 Jiddu Krishnamurti, 1885– S. Radhakrishnan, 1888–	Way of Pervading Unity Sect flourished Harmony and Unity of Three Religions continue

Japan	Islām	
	Translation from Greek, Syriac, Persian, Sanskrit; 4 schools of Jurisprudence elaborated; critical research into the Traditions, 740–850	8th cent. (*cont.*)
Gleanings from Ancient Sources, 807 Saicho, 767–822, founder of Tendai Buddhism Kūkai, 774–835, founder of Shingon Buddhism	Orthodoxy's battles for crystallizing doctrinal teaching, 813 The Traditions of the Prophet arranged in the six *Sahihs*, 850–915	9th cent.
Institutes of the Engi Period, 927 Genshin's *Essentials of Salvation*, 985		10th cent.
		11th cent.
Hōnen, 1133–1212, founder of Pure Land Buddhism Eisai, 1141–1215, founder of Rinzai Zen Buddhism	Death of al Ghazzālī, 1111	12th cent.
Shinran, 1173–1262, founder of True Pure Land Dōgen, 1200–1253, founder of Soto Zen Buddhism Nichiren, 1222–1282, founder of Nichiren Buddhism	Golden Age of Islāmic Spain, 750–1250 Fall of Baghdad under the Tartars, 1258	13th cent.
	Death of Ibn Taymiyah, 1st Muslim Reformer, 1328	14th cent.
Ichijō Kanera, 1402–1481, apologist of Shintō		15th cent.
		16th cent.
Kumazawa Banzan, 1619–1691, Neo-Confucianist		17th cent.
Motoori Norinaga, 1730–1801, Shintō scholar	Death of Muḥammad ibn 'Abd al Wahhab, founder of the reformist, modernist, activist, and puritanist movements in the Near East, 1792	18th cent.
Hirata Atsutane, 1776–1843, led Neo-Shintō Nakayama Miki, 1798–1887, founded Tenri-kyō Meiji Restoration, 1868		19th cent.
		20th cent.

PART ONE

Religions of India

P. T. Raju

Introduction to Hinduism: A Summary Account

1. The word *Hinduism*, although it refers to one of the great religions of the world, cannot and perhaps should not be defined except as the religion of those people who claim to be and do not mind being classified as Hindus. Christianity is the religion of those who claim to follow the teachings of Christ and Islam that of those who claim to follow the teachings of Moḥammad. But there is no such single founder of Hinduism. The word *Hindu* was not used by the Indo-Aryans who were responsible for the evolution and unification of the doctrines of so-called Hinduism. They called themselves *Aryans* and their religion the Aryan Way (*ārya-dharma*). When the Vedas, their sacred texts, shaped themselves, the same Aryans called their religion the Vedic Way also. But the early Iranians, who conquered Sindh, pronounced the word *Sindhu* (the Sanskrit name for the river Indus) as *Hindu* and this corruption of the word engendered all the words, *Hindus*, *Hinduism*, *Indus*, *India*, and *Indians*. Further mistaken uses have resulted in calling the original inhabitants of the North, Central, and South Americas by the name Indians.

2. If we are to adopt the term originally used by the Indo-Aryans, their religion should be called Arya Dharma (the Aryan Way of Life). Gotama Buddha (sixth century B.C.) did not know of Hinduism. He called the truths he taught the Aryan Truths. His contemporary, Vardhamāna (Mahāvīra, Jina), the founder of Jainism, must have thought that he also was teaching the true Aryan Way. In fact, the Jaina encyclopaedia[1] defines the Aryan as one who is a vegetarian, observes noninjury (*ahiṁsā*), and follows the true teachings of Vardhamāna. The aim of all these religions was to make man lead what they considered to be the true Aryan Way of Life directed towards other living beings and to the transcendental in man's existence. This high teaching may or may not have percolated to the lower, illiterate, and uneducated strata of society and their traditional ways of life and belief. But the aim of the religious leaders was to place the Aryan ideal before all and to *aryanize* the life of all. The word *Aryan* lost its racial meaning.

3. It is such a complex of life's activity and ideals that was called by the general name *Hinduism* by the early foreigners. But later foreigners began distinguishing Buddhism and Jainism from the residue which they called Hinduism. Hence the difficulty in giving a positive definition of the word. Rightly understood from the point of view of inner growth, Hinduism may be described as the way of life lived and then brought to conscious self-reflection by the Indo-Aryans, who then taught the truth they discovered to the earlier settlers. How effective their teachings have been or could have been on all levels of society is a different question. The difference of Hinduism from revealed religions such as Judaism, Christianity, and Islam lies in this, viz., that whereas in the case of the latter religions it is accepted that the truths were revealed by God to a particular person at a particular time and place, in the case of Hinduism the realization of the truths and their expressions were the result of a gradual process of reflection by many individuals through centuries. Furthermore, in Hinduism the individuals as historical persons are not so important as the truths they discovered. They are no longer regarded as privileged mediators between the Divine and man. Their truths cannot properly be called revelations, but insights into and intuitions of the depths of man's life and existence. For revelation is associated with the ideas of the revealer (God), the undeniability of the truth revealed, and the particular person to whom the truth is revealed, who could not have been any other person. But in Hinduism, any one or all these ideas may be rejected.

THE GROWTH OF HINDUISM

4. Much has to be said in explanation of the word *Hinduism*, because the beginner tends to look in Hinduism for some historical revelation, a historical founder, and an undeniable dogma and book. There are indeed some narrations of what may be considered to be revelations like those to Manu, the author of *Manu-dharma śāstra* (Manu's ethical code); they are found in other places also like the Tantric Āgamas (sacred books). But these ideas of revelation are not taken seriously and, if one sect of Hinduism accepts them, many reject them. The practice of such texts to give their teachings as revelations of Śiva to his consort and so forth is a mere means to confer prestige on the texts. That is why Hinduism is called a natural religion, a metaphysical religion, and a reflective religion.

5. Taking both geography and history into account, it is now the practice of writers to trace Hinduism to the Mohenjo-daro civilization (4000–3000 B.C.), an adequate picture of which is still not easy to give. All that is assertable in a general way is that the civilization very likely knew some form of yogic meditation, that it had some form of Śakti (Mother Goddess) worship, and that it had the cult of animal worship also. The Aryan tribes began invading India sometime between 2000 and 1500 B.C., conquered the early settlers, driving them toward the South, and then conquered the South also. At the same time they began to superimpose their own religion on the religions of the conquered, which were many, as the different tribes followed their different religions and worshiped different gods and goddesses. In this process of superimposition, the religion of the Aryans themselves began to be transformed. The gods of the non-Aryans, like Śiva, became identified with the gods of the Aryans, like Rudra,[2] through similarity of forms and functions.

But the original Vedic gods continued to occupy a higher place than those of the non-Aryans. When the Aryans finally established their monotheism of the Brahman, this pure demythologized religion was given the place of the highest prestige, and all the other forms of worship, both meditative and ritualistic, were interpreted as subsidiary to the worship and realization of the Brahman.

6. The evolution of the worship of the Brahman reveals an interesting development of the religious life and thought of the Indo-Aryans. They were first polytheists, worshiping through sacrifices (not necessarily animal sacrifices) gods such as the Fire-god, Wind-god, the god of death, the Dawn, Varuṇa the god of the Waters enveloping the world and ruling in the highest heaven, the god of clouds called Indra, and so on. The Aryans were what are philosophically called hylozoists, consubstantialists[3] who made no distinction between spirit and matter, or animatists who worshiped the natural forces as living, thinking beings like themselves without distinguishing between the animating and thinking spirit and the body. This religion may be called animatism as distinct from animism, in which man distinguishes between spirit and body and worships the former. Both animatism and animism are forms of polytheism. But the latter, when the spiritual conception is enlarged, elaborated, and developed into that of the Brahman, can become monotheism or even monism. The idea of the anima in a body is found in the concept of presiding deity or simply deity of the earth, sound, eye, and so on of the Upaniṣads.[4]

7. Next, as a logical development of religious thought and practice, we find what Max Müller called *henotheism* or the worship of each one of some of the gods as the highest and supreme. This tendency shows the Indo-Aryan mind wavering between one god and another in the attempt finally to fix one as the Supreme. Such gods are Varuṇa, Prajāpati,[5] and so on. From this henotheism the Indo-Aryan mind advanced to the monotheistic conception of the Brahman, which was taken by some religious thinkers like Gauḍapāda (*c.* sixth century), and Śaṅkara (eighth century), as nonpersonal and monistic.

8. However, this impersonalistic monism can be traced back to some later Ṛgvedic hymns themselves like the Hymn to Creation[6] or even the Hymn to Prajāpati.[7] The two hymns indicate that we cannot describe God, the Creator, and so we cannot even treat him as a person, although he exists. But this impersonalistic monism can be challenged by the Hymn to Person,[8] in which the Supreme Creator is called Puruṣa,[9] who created the Cosmic Person (Virat, the Logos) through a kind of self-sacrifice, who in his turn created man through a similar sacrifice. The highest Puruṣa later became the Brahman. Should we call the Brahman then personal or impersonal? The answer depends on the philosophical inclinations of the commentator.

9. The cult of the early Indo-Aryans was a cult of sacrifices. As the Hymn to Person and the Upaniṣadic conception of sacrifice show,[10] these Aryans understood creation and every form of creativity as a sacrifice. The philosophy of sacrifice was worked out by the early Mīmāṁsā School,[11] which did not care to give a place even to the creator God. We find in later *Brāhmaṇas* meditations on sacrifice,[12] in which the sacrificial altar and the horse sacrificed are to be meditated upon as the universe itself so that what man sacrifices becomes the universe itself. After everything is sacrificed, only the soul or spirit performing the sacrifice remains. The meditations show that the idea that all sacrifice is meant for the realization of one's spirit was

already dawning on the mind of the Indo-Aryans and the philosophy and religion for which the Mīmāṁsā fought had its rival in seed. But sacrifice meant action and so the idea of the transcendence of action must also have been dawning. Thus arose the philosophy of spirit-realization, of meditation on the *ātman* (spirit), which engaged the minds of the Upaniṣadic thinkers from the time of the *Bṛhadāraṇyaka Upaniṣad* (ninth century B.C.). Thus arose the split between the two Vedic philosophies and religions, the Mīmāṁsā School and the Vedānta School (the Upaniṣads being called the Vedānta because they come at the end of the Vedic texts).

10. Whereas for the man of understanding sacrifice meant some spiritual activity, the common man took it in its external aspects as the ceremonial killing and offering of animals to gods. In protest against this common man's religion, dominated by ritualistic priesthood, Jainism and Buddhism arose in the sixth century B.C., opposed sacrifices and the Vedas which taught sacrifices, and preached that the ultimate aim of man is to realize what he essentially is and can be and that the right action for realizing this aim is not the performance of sacrifices, but self-discipline and self-control. Both these sects, particularly Jainism—at the time they were born they were branches of the Aryan Way of Life—taught more the importance of self-realization than the activity necessary for a healthy and vigorous life. The result was that people lost zest for life in this world and India became an easy prey for the foreign invader.

11. Both Jainism and Buddhism are called heterodox religions—they were actually two protestantisms—for not accepting the scriptural authority of the Vedas. Their phenomenal expansion in India produced (seventh or eighth century) revolts against them, staged particularly by Kumārila from the side of the Mīmāmsā and by Śaṅkara from the side of the Vedānta. Buddhism, even as a religion, was absorbed by making Buddha a member of the orthodox pantheon. By the fifteenth century Buddhism as a separate religion more or less disappeared from India except in the frontiers. Or one may say that it lives in its spirit in entire India, although it has lost its hold on the people, as a distinct institution. Jainism has survived in a few regions of Western India and has made a number of compromises with the orthodox religion. Some Jainas intermarry with the Vaiśyas (trader caste) and a few of them have become Vaiṣṇavas (followers of Vaiṣṇavism).

12. Islam, as a religion, made itself felt in India from about the tenth century, although Indian contacts with Islam were earlier. Moḥammad Kasim invaded Sindh in the seventh century and there were quite a few forcible conversions. The contact with Islam, which was militant rather than persuasive in its conversions, did not produce much change in the spiritual content of Hinduism, which, however, reacted to it, as it did to Jainism and Buddhism, by attempting to absorb whatever was good in Islam. From Jainism, orthodox Hinduism took over monasticism, noninjury, and vegetarianism, the last two of which imply respect for all life, not merely for human life. From Buddhism, it adopted monasticism, certain well-defined concepts like *māyā* (appearance, illusion), *avidyā* (ignorance), *advaya* (the nondual), suffering, and the idea that the meaning of existence is not to be found in this world, but outside it. But it should be added that the orthodox sects modified these ideas in their own ways. From Islam Hinduism adopted the ideas that caste system should be abolished, that idol worship should be discarded, and that religion

should be defended, if not propagated, by the sword. Sikhism, a reformed Hindu religion founded by Guru Nānak (1449–1538), is the most outstanding example. It has to be noted that these adaptations and adoptions were not done by every sect of orthodox Hinduism. But those that did so became new sects.

13. The advent of the missions of Christianity (sixteenth century) made peaceful reforms possible. Christianity was persuasive, not militant. The exceptions were the forcible conversions of Hindus and Muslims by the Portuguese. Islam was communal-minded and was in constant tension and conflict with other communities. But because of Christ's teaching of love, Christianity in general theory and practice was humanity-minded and, with its educational and medical institutions, created a strong favorable impression on the Hindu mind, which felt that Hinduism, while retaining and sticking to its own essential spiritual teachings, should incorporate all that was humanly true and good in Christianity. Hence started reform movements such as the Brāhmo Samāj, founded by Rājā Rām Mohan Roy (1772–1833) and the Ārya Samāj, founded by Dayananda Sarasvati (1824–1883).[13]

THE SECTS OF HINDUISM

14. In the preceding section we have seen how some of the sects came into existence. But there are many more. The earliest division was not into sects, but into branches of the Vedic tradition, different families of the Brahmins (priests) belonging to different branches. Although there was no prohibition of intermarriage among the branches, the sects would not intermarry. Even during the later Ṛgvedic period, there seems to exist the worship of Śiva, Viṣṇu, Śrī (the goddess of wealth) and so on, as shown by the so-called *khila* additions to the hymns. But there is no evidence that the worshipers were sectarian. However, by about the first century B.C. or A.D. or about the time of the beginnings of the Āgama literature (texts handed down by traditions), different sects such as the Smārtas, the Śaivas, the Vaiṣṇavas, and the Śāktas may have been formed. There are others like the Gāṇapatyas (worshipers of Gaṇapati, the elephant-headed god), which are not so important as the foregoing. The Smārtas are found only among the Brahmins. They accept only the Vedas (*śrutis* or what are heard) as interpreted by the *smṛtis* (remembered texts). There is of course much controversy about which texts are true *smṛtis*. The Supreme God of the Smārtas is the Brahman only. The other three accept their respective Āgamas also as of equal importance with the Vedas. The Śaivas identify Śiva with the Brahman of the Vedas, and the Vaiṣṇavas, Viṣṇu. The Śāktas on the whole identify *śakti* (energy) with the energy or power of Śiva, whom they identify with the Brahman. These sects became so separate that intermarriage and in some cases interdining were stopped. In the case of Śaivism and Vaiṣṇavism, the sectarian differences obtain not only among the Brahmins, but also among the other castes, thus giving rise to subcastes. The Śāktas, particularly those who adopt the prohibited left-handed worship—using wine, women, and meat—ignore caste differences in their worship. Members of the right-handed worship may be found among all the castes. Śāktism, on the whole, is a kind of appendage to the other sects and may be found here and there in all sects; for God, whatever be his name, has the creative energy (*śakti*), which is also an object of worship, whatever be the form of worship.

15. The next important sects, at least in the beginning, were Jainism and Buddhism. It is difficult to say whether they should be called sects or religions. Whatever be the opinion, it should not be forgotten that even Brahmins joined these religions in those days and changed from one to another to find out which contained the final truth about life and death. The phenomenon was like a Christian changing nowadays from one sect to another. It was only later, when the sects became separatist, that they became rigid.

16. Sikhism came into existence as a reconciliation of Hinduism and Islam and was founded by Guru Nānak. The influence of Islam was felt even on Jainism and Śaivism. The two main sects of Jainism are the Digambaras (the space-clad, because their monks are not clad at all) and the Śvetāmbaras (the white-clad, so called because their monks wear white clothing). The Sthānikavāsi sect was formed from the latter and gave up idol worship. One sect of Śaivism, called the Heroic Śaivism gave up caste distinctions and idol worship. It also used the sword in defense of its religion, though for a short time in history.

17. The main sects of Buddhism in India are first the Hīnayāna (the Small Vehicle) and the Mahāyāna (the Great Vehicle). The followers of the former do not like the term *Small Vehicle*. Some scholars think that the word *Theravāda* ("doctrine of the elders") should be used instead. There is a real difficulty here for any author who does not wish to offend either. But the Theravādins themselves were a sect of the so-called Hīnayāna in India. Southern Buddhism and Northern Buddhism are perhaps better alternatives. In India itself there were about eighteen schools or sects of the former and three of the latter and quite a few crossings of one another. The Hīnayāna schools are regarded as closer to Buddha's original teachings than the Mahāyāna, which are closer to the Vedānta teachings than the Hīnayāna.

18. The reform sects like the Brāhmo Samāj and the Ārya Samāj are fading out, as their teachings are being accepted and practiced to a large extent by the orthodox people also. Besides, the government has enacted laws incorporating all the social reforms advocated by the reform movements. Legally, there is now no caste system in India, no prohibition of widow remarriages, no untouchability, and no opposition to the education of girls. Even informal sentiment and practice favor the education of girls.

THE CASTES AND STAGES OF LIFE

19. Much has been written on the caste system. The selection from *Manu's Code*[14] gives an idea of it. It was not originally a preplanned institution, but was brought into existence by the circumstances of color (race) and occupation. Historically, it was an accidental feature of Hinduism as a religion, even though it has outlived its usefulness. It was first a differentiation of color (*varṇa*, now meaning caste), the whites comprising the three higher castes—the Brahmins (priests, the knowers of the Brahman or the Supreme Being), the Kṣatriyas (warriors comprising kings and soldiers), and the Vaiśyas (traders, owners of property including lands). The colored people, the Śūdras, were the pre-Aryan settlers and were given the profession of labor like agriculture and service. But it should be noted that many pre-Aryan Indians were very expert in trade and commerce, as shown by the

Mohenjo-daro excavations, and in South India even today many trader castes do not have Aryan features. The people not belonging to the four castes were the outcastes or untouchables. Through the intermingling of the castes several sub-castes were born, each of which was again given a distinct profession. The Śūdras were not allowed to read the Vedas, but to understand their teachings through subsidiary works like the *Smṛtis*, epics, etc. Many of them like king Kāṭayavema[15] became great scholars; and some like Sūta[16] and Vidura[17] taught about divine knowledge even to Brahmins. Thus divine knowledge was allowed to be the common property of all. It may be mentioned that the practice of not teaching the Vedas to the Śūdras is not recognized now in educational institutions and all, including Muslims and Christians, can read the Vedas if they want.

20. The institution of stages of life (*āśramas*) is very significant, although it was not allowed to the Śūdras by the orthodoxy. These stages are four in number—the stage of the student, of the householder, of the forest-dweller, and of the renouncer (*sannyāsa*, ascetic life) of the world. The first two are obligatory and the other two are recommended. The duty of the student is to acquire knowledge by studying at the feet of a teacher. That of the householder consists of paying back what are called the three debts—the debt to the forefathers, which is paid back by having children, particularly a male who will continue the family line; the debt to the teachers, which is paid back by transmitting to the next generation the learning one obtained from one's teachers; and the debt to gods, which is paid back by performing sacrifices. It is significant that these obligations are called debts; for they are unconditional obligations by fulfilling which one contributes to the welfare of the world but obtains no special merit, but by not fulfilling which one obtains sin. The duty of the forest-dweller is to retire to the forest with his wife and reflect over the values of life. But one can become a forest-dweller only after seeing the face of one's own grandson, as recommended by Manu.[18] In the third stage, if one finds that no pleasure in the world has any attraction, one is asked to send back the wife to one's son, enter the fourth stage, and become an ascetic or renouncer. But there seem to be many ignoring the conditions laid by Manu and this has been mainly due to the influence of Buddhism and Jainism.

THE VALUES OF LIFE

21. Hinduism recognizes four main values of life—wealth, enjoyment (desire, love, pleasure), ethical merit (*dharma*, duty), and liberation (*mokṣa*). The reader will see in the selection from Manu that he mentions the first three, although he discusses the fourth also. Wealth is required not for wealth's sake, but for the sake of enjoyment. Enjoyment is not meant for enjoyment's sake and it is not to be chaotic. One should spend one's wealth in paying back the three debts, in keeping guests and living beings satisfied, and in the enjoyment of one's senses and desires according to the laws procuring ethical merit. And ethical merit ought to be so chosen and aimed at as to lead to final salvation. Ethical merit is conceived as a potency that is creative of man's future, including future lives. It is, however, recommended, although not commanded, that man should aim at that ethical merit which leads to salvation, but not future lives. As the last is recommended, but not mandatory, Manu gives particular importance to the first three.

THE MAIN SCHEMATA OF HINDUISM

22. One may see by now that Hinduism is a great complex,[19] but not a confusion, of several sects. It is a great assemblage of sects, each one of which respects the others for the spiritual truths they contain. The followers of one may consult the followers of another for spiritual insights. Or they may criticize one another for unorthodoxy or inadequacy in understanding the essential truths. For instance, the Sikhs formed a separate sect or a separate religion. Yet the sect founded by Sri Chand, Guru Nānak's son, follows Śaṅkara's nondualism (*advaita*). And there are many so-called *kacca* (nonripe) Sikhs who visit both Hindu and Sikh temples. In South India some followers of Madhva (*c.* 1199–*c.* 1278) intermarry with followers of the Smārta sect. Similarly some followers of Rāmānuja (eleventh century) intermarry with the Smārtas. There are similar intermarriages between some subsects of the Smārtas and those of the Śaiva sect. In all these happenings, there are mild and strong protests, which also have to be recognized. But what should interest the student of Hinduism is not only the enormous sect complexity that is Hinduism, but also that which unifies all these sects, viz., the answer to the question: How can I obtain liberation from the world of becoming (*saṁsāra*), which, as becoming, contains suffering, or at least anxiety and fear? Is there a way to transcend the cycle of birth and death to an existence beyond them? These questions are those of salvation, redemption. But they cannot be separated from other questions. We may briefly express the main schemata of Hinduism through the following:

(1) Inasmuch as the world contains suffering, is there a happy existence undiluted by suffering?

(2) If such an existence is called the state of salvation, what is the nature of its transcendence of this world?

(3) Can I reach the state of salvation with my body? Otherwise, what is it in me that obtains salvation? Who and what am I really if I can have an existence without this body?

(4) Does the concept of salvation have a truth value? Who guarantees its truth? What is the relation of my true self to that guarantor and granter of salvation (God, Brahman)?

(5) How are God and my self related to the world?

(6) Is salvation possible in this life or only after death?

(7) What am I to do to obtain salvation? Shall I follow the way of ethical action (*karma-mārga*, way of action) as found in the doctrine of debts and also as prescribed by the ethical codes? Or discarding the way of action, shall I attempt, shall I pursue knowledge of the self (*ātman*) and the Brahman (*jñāna-mārga*, way of knowledge)? Or realizing my own finitude and weakness and not relying on my own powers to follow the way of action or of knowledge, shall I completely surrender myself to God, take refuge in him, and cultivate love of him and devotion to him (*bhakti-mārga*, way of devotion)?

(8) What is the form of worshiping God for communion with him? Is it silent meditation, singing his glory individually or in a congregation, or offering flowers, fruit, or cooked food to the idol in the house or temple? How are these to be done ritually?

(9) In the light of man's relation to God, how is the former to conduct himself towards other men, towards other living beings, and towards the material world?

23. It is with questions like the foregoing that the Hindu sects are primarily concerned. Although the answers are not unanimous in all detail, there is an underlying unity in the answers which the sects try to find in the Vedas and the Āgamas. The sacred books for the Buddhists are the *Tripiṭaka* ("three baskets of books"), and the Mahāyāna accepts the Prajñāpāramitās (prefection of wisdom literature) in addition. The Jainas in the beginning had no book, but later composed their own scripture and other works. The sacred book of the Sikhs is called the *Ādi Granath* (Original book). But in all, the influence of Vedic ideas is evident. Some of the lectures of Jaina saints which I attended made confirmatory references to the *Bhagavadgītā* and the Upanisads, thereby showing that they had something in common with the orthodox spiritual life. In India it is not necessary for a religion to be called religion that it should accept the existence of God (cf. Jainism) or of the *ātman* or spirit in man (cf. Buddhism).

24. To the *first* question cited previously all the Indian religions give an affirmative answer (provided we do not call the materialism of the Cārvāka School by the name religion, although it was a philosophy of life). Even the early Mīmāṁsā School thinks that we can have undiluted happiness, if we perform only right actions; but it would add that such an existence is not beyond the world of becoming as there can be nothing, according to this school, beyond it. The *second* question concerns man's self-transcendence. Just as the I can transcend the body, the mental states, one's profession—one may compare Sartre's idea here—it can transcend the ego. But according to Śaṅkara, it can transcend the I-consciousness also and be one with the Supreme Spirit (Brahman). But his view is not accepted by the other Vedāntic religious leaders. It is at this point, viz., of self-realization that the schools of Śaṅkara's nondualism, Madhva's dualism, and Rāmānuja's nondualism of the qualified Brahman have their relevance.

25. To the *third* question all except the early Buddhists and the Mādhyamikas (The Middle Doctrine School)[20] answer that there is something other than the psychophysical body, and only that something obtains salvation. The early Buddhists and the Mādhyamikas say that the I is merely an appearance and its disappearance in infinite quietude (*nirvāna*) is salvation. To the *fourth* question all, except the Buddhists, Jainas, and early Mīmāsakas and the nontheistic Sāṅkhya School, answer that it is the Supreme Spirit, personal or impersonal, that grants salvation. The differences in understanding the relation between the natures of the finite and the Supreme Spirits concern Śaṅkara, Madhva, and Rāmānuja. For Śaṅkara, they are in essence identical. For Madhva, they are essentially different. For Rāmānuja, the finite spirit constitutes a part of the body of the Supreme and as such is both identical with and different from the latter.

26. The answer to the *fourth* question depends on the nature of the spirit's embodiment and of the creative act of God. Śaṅkara understood both embodiment and creation as due to Māyā, which is an inexplicable creative power of the Brahman and is neither different from nor identical with the Brahman. Madhva understood the body and the world as different from both the finite spirit and the Supreme. The spirit is somehow made to assume a physical body, which is a part of the material world, by the Lord, who makes the material world evolve its variety of forms. For

Rāmānuja, both the spirits and the material world are distinct from one another and from the Brahman. Yet they constitute his body. We owe to the Brahman that our own embodiment and the evolution of the material world take place.

27. The answer given by the Vedāntins to the *fifth* question is found in part in their answers to the fourth. As the Supreme Spirit has the power (*śakti*) to create the world, it has control over the world and can make salvation possible for the man who strives for it. This question, as we can see, does not arise for the early Mīmāṁsā School, which did not accept the existence of anything beyond the world of becoming. For Buddhism, Jainism, and the Sāṅkhya School, only man's own effort can obtain salvation for him.

28. Śaṅkara and Madhva answer the *sixth* question, accepting that salvation is possible in this life. Rāmānuja rejects their view and says that it is possible only after death. The *seventh* question concerns the three main ways. The differences of view are due to differences of emphasis. For Śaṅkara, Buddhism, and Jainism, the way of knowledge is primary, the two others being secondary. For the later Mīmāṁsā School, the way of action is primary. For Rāmānuja, Madhva, and a large number of other sects including Sikhism, the way of devotion and love is primary. This third group accepts the idea of the descent of grace also. There are some religious thinkers like Madhusūdana (tenth century) who give equal importance to all the three. There are other ways than the three, such as the yoga of merging in the infinite, the yoga of drugs, and the psychophysical yoga. But they are considered to be less important than the three previously mentioned.

29. In answer to the *eighth* question it should be said that worship takes various forms, of which individual meditation is said to be the highest. It is meant for the realization of the macrocosm within the microcosm, of the Supreme Spirit within the finite. It is not necessary that the two spirits should be regarded as identical—that depends on the philosophy one accepts. What is necessary is the acceptance of the truth that the macrocosm is represented in the microcosm in a kind of intimate correlation and can be realized inwardly within the latter. The Logos resides in our own consciousness, God resides in our hearts. So the meditator first symbolically places all the gods of the macrocosm within himself. Then meditation goes deeper and deeper, making man transcend himself. Forms of worship other than meditation have their differences according to the sects. On the whole, congregational worship is less characteristic of Hinduism than of Christianity and Islam. It is, however, present in group singing, musical narratives of the lives of gods and incarnations, recitations and explanations of the holy epics like the *Rāmāyaṇa*, (Career of Rāma), and so on. Individuals and families go separately to temples. And gods are worshiped in homes also.

30. The general answer to the *ninth* question given by all Hindu religions and sects is that all life should be respected. There are differences in the practice of eating meat. The attitudes to the material world are various. With only the early Mīmāṁsā School can conquest, subjugation, and enjoyment of the material world be consistent. With the others, the attitude is either that of transcendence of the world or flight from matter. The latter exists mainly in theory and among the monks. For the orthodox, on the whole, the attitude towards the world is expressed in the doctrine of three debts. Welfare of the world, including gods and ancestors, is an absolute obligation. We should not forget that the world of the early Aryans included gods and ancestors.

THE PRIMACY OF THE RELIGIOUS POINT OF VIEW

31. It is difficult to give an adequate picture of Hinduism in a short introductory account. Hinduism is not a simple straight religion like Islam or even Christianity, even when we consider its elemental forms. Very often the presentation in part may amount to misrepresentation, as it allows the reader to think that what has not been presented does not exist. The choice of what ought to be presented in a few pages is a difficult one to make. I have, however, given what I consider to be important for obtaining the central ideas of what is called Hinduism. In studying alien religions it is nowadays a common practice to approach them from the anthropological, ethnological, sociological, linguistic, and such other points of view. These studies are very useful in clarifying and explicating the human situation in which religions exist. But they cannot tell us what a religion in itself is. However, there is another point of view, viz., that of religion itself, which ought to be treated as primary. This point of view concerns the problems of man's existence, its needs and values. They are existential problems or, simply expressed, they are problems of life and death, of life after death and immortality, of the sense of being bound to the world of becoming and of the possibility of freedom from such bondage, of evil and suffering, of salvation and the Supreme Spirit, and of the secondary problems which these involve. All the great religions have given answers to most of these problems and they have become great by evolving a consciousness of these problems and by offering answers fairly consistent with one another.

NOTES

1. *Abhidhānarājendra* (Great king of names).
2. See N. Venkataramanayya, *Rudra-Śiva* (On the gods Rudra and Śiva).
3. See H. Frankfort, *et al.*, *Before Philosophy*, pp. 71–78.
4. See ch. 2, selection 7. This distinction between animatism and animism seems to me to be important, as the latter contains the idea of the embodiment of a spirit or deity. It is at least important for the Upanisadic philosophy and for the distinction between the psychological and physical sense.
5. See ch. 1, selections 7 and 13.
6. Ch. 1, selection 14.
7. Ch. 1, selection 13. If we accept *Ka* (Who) as the name of the unnameable and inconceivable God, then we have here the worship of the unknown God, Who, like the worship of the Jewish YWH.
8. Ch. 1, selection 15.
9. Purusa in literary language means man as opposed to woman. It means also person. In philosophical language, it means spirit and is used in the Upaniṣads as a synonym for *ātman*.
10. Ch. 2, selection 8.
11. This is one of the Six Systems or philosophical schools that developed about B.C. 400, namely, the Nyāya School which emphasizes logic, the Vaiśeṣika School which emphasizes analysis of nature, the Sāṅkhya School which is realistic pluralism, the Yoga School which concentrates on mental discipline, the Mīmāṁsā School whose object is ascertainment of duty, and the Vedānta School which sets forth the philosophy of the Upaniṣads consistently.
12. Ch. 2, selection 10.
13. See chs. 8 and 9.
14. See ch. 4.

15. He (perhaps between the eighth and tenth centuries A.D.) is the best-known commentator on Kālidāsa's dramas.
16. He, an epical figure, taught the great seers (*maharṣis*) like Śaunaka.
17. An epical figure of the *Mahābhārata* (The Great Bharata people).
18. See ch. 4.
19. These complications cannot easily be seen by foreign observers.
20. We cannot enter into the finer differences here for want of space.

CHAPTER 1

The Vedas: Hymns and Ritual Texts

□ The Vedas constitute the basic sacred literature of Hinduism. Their composition may have started before 2000 B.C., even before the Aryans entered India, and continued up to about the sixth century A.D. They are four in number: *Ṛgveda* (knowledge of hymns), *Yajur-veda* (knowledge of rites), *Sāma-veda* (knowledge of chants), and *Atharva-veda* (knowledge given by the sage, Atharva). Of the four, the *Ṛgveda* is the earliest. Again, each Veda has four parts: Hymns (*saṁhitās*), Ritual Texts (*brāhmaṇas*), Forest Treatises (*āraṇyakas*), and Upaniṣads. The last deal with philosophy. The Hymns give us an idea of the earliest form of the Aryan religion. For additional information, see "Introduction to Hinduism: A Summary Account." ¶5–9. □

1. Hymn to Fire (Agni)

1. With praises we worship you, O Fire, king of sacrifices, long-tailed like a horse.[1]

2. May you, O son of strength, be propitious and bountiful to us in your great way.

3. May you, who moves everywhere, O Fire, protect us from mortals far and near who seek to harm us.

4. May you, O Fire, convey our offering of praise to the gods.

5. May we obtain the food of the upper world and the middle world; give us the wealth of this world.

6. O Fire, with variegated colors, you distribute wealth to those who make their offerings to you, as the river its waters to the cultivators.

7. O Fire, the mortal whom you protect and encourage in battle receives continuous strength.

8. Never does exist a conqueror of the man, O conqueror Fire, who sacrifices to you and is devoted to you.

9. May Fire, approached by all men, enable them to win the battle with horses. May Fire, satisfied along with the priests, be the giver of rewards.

10. O Fire, invoked through praises, enter the sacrifice, favor it and complete it. The sacrificer praises you in appropriate terms, lest you should be angry.

11. May he, the great, the unlimited, the smoke-bannered Fire, make us find pleasure and strength in sacrifice.

12. May he, like a king his bards, hear us with our hymns, he who is the ruler of men, and is the associate and banner of gods.

13. Salutations to the great, salutations to the small, salutations to the youth, salutations to the old. Let us sacrifice to the gods as much as we can. O gods, may I not interrupt the continuous hymn addressed to the important god. (*Ṛgveda*, 1:27)

2. Hymn to Fire (Agni)

□ In this hymn Fire is regarded as the priest of gods. He can make the gods come and attend the sacrifice. Besides, by consuming the sacrificial offerings he carries them to the respective gods. He is himself a god and his function is conceived in this hymn as that of the priest of gods. He is here invited to act as the priest of the earthly sacrifice also, so that it can become the most effective. □

1. Put on the robes of light, O Fire, worthy of sacrifice, and perform our sacrifice, O lord of power.

2. O Fire, be here, most youthful, chosen as our priest, worshiped by words of glory, full of splendors signifying your presence.

3. O most excellent, like a father, grant me, your son, my desire by performing this sacrifice A father performs the sacrifice for his son, a kinsman for a kinsman, a friend for a friend.

4. Here may Varuṇa, Mitra, and Aryaman, the destroyer of foes, sit on the sacred grass like men.

5. O ancient priest be pleased for the sake of this sacrifice and for our sake, and hearken to our words of praise.

6. Whatever offering is made in this eternal way to this or that god—that is offered to you.

7. O lord of men, sacrificer, pleasant and excellent priest, be pleased with us; may we be with auspicious Fire and be dear to him.

8. The auspicious and glorious priests hold our excellent oblations. Thus associated with you, auspicious Fire, we beg of you.

9. O immortal Fire, let the praises at the end of sacrifice be said by us both, we telling the sacrificer that the sacrifice is well done and you telling him that it is accepted.

10. O son of strength, be pleased in all your different forms with this our sacrifice and with this our praise, and give us strength. (*Ṛgveda*, 1:26)

3. Hymn to Wind (Vāyu)

1. Come, O beautiful Wind, for you these *soma*[2] drinks are prepared. Drink them.

2. O Wind the hymn-singers who know the days prescribed for the different sacrifices are glorifying you with the *uktha*[3] implements in hand.

3. O Wind, your voice, loudly proclaiming the virtues of the *soma* drink, reaches the sacrificer who has laid the drink for you.

4. O Indra[4] and Wind, this *soma* juice is pressed for you both and is being offered along with other foods by us. Come, they are yearning for you both.

5. O Wind and Indra, look at these pressed *soma* drinks. Be present in the sacrificial food, come soon.

6. O Wind and Indra, approach the *soma* that purifies the sacrificer pressing it; the purification becomes complete when you come.

7. I invoke Mitra, the possessor of holy power and I invoke Varuṇa, the destroyer of dangerous enemies, to work for rain.

8. O Mitra and Varuṇa, increasers of rain, right (*ṛta*), sacrifice by means of law (*ṛta*), and the necessary fruit (*kratu*) of sacrifice, be present at this sacrifice.[5]

9. O Mitra and Varuṇa, who are wise and born for helping the many and who reside in many places, vouchsafe us our sacrifice and strength (*Ṛgveda*, 1:2)

4. Hymn to Indra

□ Indra is the name of the god wielding the thunderbolt and seems to correspond to Odin of Scandinavian mythology. He is the god of clouds and rain and is worshiped for obtaining rain. In the mythology of the epics, he is the ruler of heaven, but sometimes falls in love with the wives of mortals. In the Upaniṣads, he is represented variously as the wisest god, as the Supreme Being, and so on.

A key concept here is *ṛta*, which means according to Śāyana, water, practical truth (right), and sacrifice (rite). It means also the necessary fruit, the inexorable result, of ethical action including sacrifice. It is derived from the verbal root $\sqrt{ṛ}$ meaning to move, to go. The waters from the celestial regions move; rivers move; the potencies (forces) move in producing or creating their fruit; the ethical potencies (merit and demerit) of actions move in producing their fruit. And all move along fixed paths of moral law and its necessity. So all, including their paths, are called *ṛtas*, "they that go." One should note that at the time of the *Ṛgveda* no distinction was made by man between ethical paths (laws) and the paths of natural forces (natural laws). □

1. O Indra, in the past the sages of old bore your Indra-power. This one (power) is on the earth and is of the form of fire; the other in the form of the sun dwells in the heavens. Both are one like two banners.

2. Indra held the earth menaced by the demons. He fixed it and then expanded it. He killed the demons with the bolt, smote the clouds with it, and made the waters (rain) come out of them from the sky. He struck down Ahi, the serpent demon; he rent Rauhiṇa (the demon of draught) to death and slaughtered Vyamsa (another name for Vṛtra,[6] a demon) in fight.

3. With trust in his prowess, he roams shattering the cities of the Dāsas[7] with his bolt. O wielder of the bolt, O wise one, throw your weapons at the Dasyus (the aborigines), our enemies, and increase the might and glory of the Aryans.

4. The power directed at the enemies is, for the singing sacrificer, really worth praising. With that power, Maghavan (Indra) has created the aeons known to men. The wielder of the bolt, coming out of his abode, bears the name of Vajrin (wielder of the bolt) for the destruction of the enemies.

5. O sacrificing men, look at this, the power of Indra has grown and immensely expanded. Respect and trust that power. By it has Indra restored the cows and horses stolen by the Paṇis[8] and revived plant life on earth.

6. We prepare *soma* to offer him, the author of many great deeds, the Bull,[9] worthy of the *soma* drink. He, the hero, takes the wealth of those who do not perform the sacrifice to give it to those who perform it.

7. O Indra, you performed the heroic deed that has become famous. You awakened through your power the intoxicated Ahi[10] (the demon named Vṛtra) who was overjoyed to fight with you. At the death of Ahi, the divine damsels and other gods rejoiced.

8. After Indra destroyed the four demons Suṣṇa, Pipru, Kuyava, and Vṛtra—he razed Śambara's fort to the ground. May Mitra, Varuṇa, Aditi, Pṛthivī (earth), and Dyau (sky) grant this prayer of ours. (*Ṛgveda*, 1:103)

5. Hymn to Varuṇa

□ Varuṇa corresponds to the Greek god Ouranos and is the god of waters enveloping the world and of heaven. The word is derived from the root $\sqrt{vṛ}$, meaning to surround. It was believed that the waters surrounded the world and were controlled by Varuṇa. These waters are mythological and do not seem to be the waters of the earth's oceans. Later, Varuṇa lost the supreme status and became the god of the earth's oceans. □

1. This sacrifice is offered to Varuṇa, the self-effulgent, wise, Āditya.[11] May the sacrificer (hymn-singer)[12] obtain power over all the worlds from Varuṇa, and may Varuṇa be pleased with him. I beg renown of Varuṇa.

2. May we have high fortune, O Varuṇa, singing your praises with pious mind in this sacrifice.[13] This sacrifice is meant for you. At the approach of brilliant dawn, when preparing the fires, may we shine every day singing your praises.

3. O leader of the whole world, Varuṇa, lord of many heroes, may we be in your happy abode. May the sons of Aditi,[14] never harmed by enemies, pardon our sins and make us your friends.

4. Varuṇa, son of Aditi, broke the dam of waters by means of *ṛta* (truth, right) and made the rivers flow full. Because of his *ṛta* (truth, waters), rivers flow and are not tired of flowing. They do not stop and are ever the same. They go swiftly like birds and fall on the earth.

5. O Varuṇa, loosen me, as from a bond (rope, fetter), from sin committed from nonperformance of duties. May we reach the river Khā (a heavenly river) full of your *ṛta*. May my thread of the continuous series of (religious and ethical) actions be not broken. May not my action (*karma*) be broken before completion.

6. O sovereign, holder of *ṛta*, be gracious to me. O Varuṇa, remove fear from me, as the milker removes the cord from the calf

that goes to its mother. No other than you can control even the eyelid's movements.

7. O Varuṇa, ignored by sinners, strike us not with those weapons which, O Asura,[15] destroy the men who destroy the order of your sacrificial rites. May we not be removed from the light of home. Scatter the men who injure our life.

8. O Varuṇa, we said in the past, "Salutations to you." We say them now. O the omnipresent, we shall say them in the future. For in yourself, as on the summit of a mountain, are fixed infallible sacrificial rites.

9. O Varuṇa, wipe out the debts contracted by my forefathers and also by myself. O king, may I not live by the wealth acquired by others. For many a dawn has gone by, but not for me always thinking of debts. In such dawns, O Varuṇa, be the guide to us, living beings.

10. O king, if an ancestor, friend, or kinsman frightens me in sleep, if a robber or wolf fain would harm us—protect us from all of them.

11. O Varuṇa, may I not know the poverty of those belonging to a friend, wealthy, great, and charitable. O king, may I not be deprived of rightly earned riches. We, the sons of good men, sing this hymn in the house of sacrifice. (*Ṛgveda*, 2:28)

6. Hymn to Waters

1. May the goddesses Waters, with their chief, the Sea, coming always from the middle of the sky and purifying everything in their way dug by Indra, the Bull, protect me.

2. The goddesses Waters, pure and purifying, dug by a spade or flowing by themselves, come down here, though divine, towards the sea. May they protect me.

3. Amidst them goes king Varuṇa, watching *ṛta* (truth, right, rite) and *anṛta* (the opposite of *ṛta*) of men. May the goddesses Waters, dripping honey, pure and purifying, protect me.

4. May the goddesses Waters, in whom Varuṇa, Soma (Moon), Viśvedevas (all gods of the universe) drink nourishment, into whom the Vaiśvānara[16] Fire entered, protect me. (*Ṛgveda*, 7:49)

7. Dethronement of Varuṇa

1. Come to this, our sacrifice, O Fire; you have been built up by the sacrificer and the four priests[17] with the three offerings[18] and seven threads.[19] Come and be the carrier of our offerings, be our leader, and walk in front. You have slept in thick darkness leaving us for a long time.

Fire says:

2. I, a god, invited by gods, having come from the godless cave and having seen the sacrificial offerings spread out for me, become immortal. I leave a shining, auspicious sacrifice at its end in an unshining (invisible) form, and in the form of a horse reach the friendly Araṇi[20] that binds me to another (sacrifice).

3. Seeing the earth, my abode, and its heavenly guest, the Sun, I have founded my abodes of *ṛta*.[21] Then I sing the praises of the Father, Asura (Varuṇa) living in the heavens, for his happiness.[22] So I leave the place where sacrifices cannot be offered for places where they can be.

4. I live many a year in this altar. Choosing Indra, I leave the Father.[23] When I leave the gods and hide in the cave, then those gods—Fire,[24] Soma, and Varuṇa—fall from their kingdom.

5. The demons lose their magical sway over this place when I come. O Varuṇa, if you want me, destroy the untruth of magic. O king, establish truth (*ṛta*) through my activities, and become the lord of the kingdom established by me.

Indra says:

6. O Soma, these are the heavens and have become desirable. Look at the sky with its brilliance spread. Now we shall both kill Vṛtra. So go forth and return. We shall offer you the drink that is worthy of you.

7. The seer Mitra, through his wisdom, attained his heavenly brilliance. Varuṇa with a little effort let loose rain from the clouds. The rains become flowing rivers and follow Varuṇa, like women-folk following and doing good to their men, and bear the pure shining color of Varuṇa.

8. The waters obtain the energy (sperm) of old Varuṇa. They enjoy the sacrificial offering, go to Varuṇa, but cannot approach

him from fear, as Vṛtra constrains them.[25]

9. The Sun[26] is called the friend of the afraid. He is the friend of those in the heavens. The sages, with their hymns, worship Indra, the worshipful, who acts according to the hymns. (*Ṛgveda*, 10:125)

8. Hymn to Dawn

1. There comes the light, the greatest of all lights. Expanding, she wonderfully reveals everything hidden in darkness. As Night is born of the Sun, so is Dawn born of Night.

2. The mother of the shining Sun, she arrives shining white. Then the Dark Night goes to her abode. Night and Dawn are mutual friends of the Sun. In the form of time, they go in succession every day.

3. The two sisters, Night and Dawn, taught by the shining Sun, have the same endless path to go. The two auspicious creators, though of opposed characters (darkness and light), are of the same mind, and do not clash and do not tarry.

4. We behold her, Dawn, the creator of glad sounds. Of various hues, she reveals to us things at a distance veiled in darkness. She reaches the world and reveals its riches to us. She belches, as it were, all the worlds from her mouth.

5. Rich Dawn, she awakens man from sleep. She sends one after enjoyment, another to perform sacrifice, and another after wealth. She belches out, as it were, all beings whose vision is limited by darkness, by spreading her light.

6. O Dawn, you send one to high sway, one for food, one to greatness, and another to his own gain. You send all in pursuit of their respective livelihoods. O Dawn, you have as though belched out from your mouth all the worlds swallowed by darkness.

7. The daughter of the heavens, young maiden,[27] white-robed, Dawn is seen dispelling darkness. O sovereign of the riches of the whole earth, auspicious Dawn, dispel darkness now from this sacrificial house of the gods.

8. The Dawn of today follows the path of the heavens as did the Dawns of old. And she is the first of the Dawns to be. Rending darkness, she urges forth many living beings who are as though dead in their sleep.

9. O Dawn, of all the gods you have done the best. For you have caused Fire to be kindled in the morn, removed darkness from the light of the Sun, and pushed up men from out of darkness for performing sacrifices.

10. When does Dawn approach and when does she pass? She is endless. She longs for the Dawns of the past, and meets the Dawns of the future.[28]

11. The men who saw the earliest Dawn rising are all gone. Now she is seen by us clearly. The men who will see her in the future Nights will arrive. She lives in the past, present, and future.

12. Chaser of enemies,[29] protector of *ṛta*, born for the sake of *ṛta*, full of joy, truthful, waker of the voices of living beings, the auspicious,[30] supporter of sacrifice longed for by gods, shine here, now, in this sacrificial place.

13. O Dawn, in the days past you dispelled darkness. Now, O lady of riches, you do the same; and you will do the same in the future. You live in your eternal glory, never old, always the same, immortal.

14. Dawn shines with her luster in all directions of the sky. The goddess has thrown off her black veil. She comes in her chariot drawn by shining red horses, awakening all those asleep.

15. Bringing all desirable, life-sustaining riches, Dawn rules all the world, proclaiming herself through banners, her rays, and appropriating the whole world through her spreading light. She is an instance of all Dawns that are gone and is the first of those that will come.

16. O men, leave your bed and rise. The light-giver of our bodies has come. Darkness has been dispelled. The light of our body, our soul, has appeared. It clears the way of the Sun. We shall go there where food (life) is growing.

17. Fire is the carrier of hymns. The shining Dawn, singing, reveals the serial Uktha hymns. O rich Dawn, remove the darkness now from the sight of the man who is praising you with his hymns. Grant life (nourishment) to us also with our children and grandchildren.

18. For him who is offering sacrifices to you, O Dawns, with numerous cows and heroes, remove darkness. May the sacrificer, who has extracted the *soma* juice, have, after his hymns, the Dawns, the givers of horses. His hymns are truthful and swift like horses.

19. O Dawn, you are the mother of gods.[31] You are the image of Aditi, the mother of gods. Shine as the banner of sacrifice. Say that the hymn is well sung and come to listen to our Brahman (prayer). Establish us, O worship-worthy of all, as the great among men.

20. Whatever wonderful wealth the Dawns bring will be auspicious to the man who worships with oblations and hymns. May the gods Mitra, Varuṇa, Aditi, Sindhu,[32] Earth, and Sky grant whatever we ask for through these hymns. (*Ṛgveda*, 1:113)

9. Hymn to the Sun

1. The wonderful cluster of gods has arisen, the eye of Mitra, Varuṇa, and Fire. He fills the earth and the sky with his light. He is the soul (*ātman*) of the moving and nonmoving.

2. The Sun follows the beautiful goddess Dawn like a man a woman. In all ages man worships the Sun and performs the sacrificial ceremonies after Dawn. We offer prayers to the Sun, the auspicious, for prosperity.

3. Auspicious are the yellow horses of the Sun; they change their hues on the way. Worshipped by us, they reach the zenith (back of the sky) and then circle fast the earth and sky.

4. This is the godliness and power of the Sun. When he sets, man leaves his work in the middle, even though unfinished.[33] When he drives his yellow horses away from the earth and keeps them in another place, Night spreads out her dark garment.

5. For showing the world to Mitra and Varuṇa, the Sun shows his form in the middle of the sky. His yellow horses (rays) create the white light over all the world by their presence and create the black light by their withdrawal.

6. O gods, now when the Sun has risen, may the horses of the Sun deliver us from sin and protect us. May Mitra, Varuṇa, Sindhu, Earth, and Sky grant us our prayer. (*Ṛgveda*, 1:115)

10. Hymn to the Sky and Earth

1. In the face of impediments, I worship Heaven and Earth,[34] worthy of sacrifice, with rites and praises. To them, the great parents of gods, was assigned precedence by sages singing in the past.

2. O singers with newest hymns, set the ancient parents in the *ṛta* (order) of precedence. O Heaven and Earth, come to us with all your celestial people to grant us wealth, for which we pray.

3. O Heaven and Earth, you have in your possession many a treasure for the sacrificer. What you give us is not little. Protect us always, you gods. (*Ṛgveda*, 7:54)

11. Hymn to the God of Death (Yama)

1. O sacrificer, honor the king of our ancestors with oblations. He, the son of Vivasvān,[35] Yama, whom all men reach, has led all men of good deeds along the path to their respective places without trouble.

2. Yama, the first, knows our merits and demerits. None can mislead him. By whichever path our ancestors went, by that path all those born will go.

3. Mātali[36] prospers there with the sages, Yama with Aṅgirases,[37] and Bṛhaspati with Ṛkvas.[38] These gods exalt the ancestors and the ancestors the gods. Indra and other gods are pleased with the *svāhā*[39] oblations and the ancestors with the *svadhā*[40] oblations.

4. O Yama, accompanied by these fathers and Aṅgirasas, be seated in this sacrificial place. May the texts recited by the priests reach you. O king, favor the sacrificer and be pleased with the oblations.

5. O Yama, come with the Aṅgirases who have many forms. Favor the sacrificer who is inviting your father Vivasvān. May he also be seated on this grass and favor the sacrificer.

6. O fathers, Aṅgirasas, Atharvans, and Bhṛgus have newly arrived. All deserve *soma*. We intend to sacrifice to them and shall be in pleasant mood.

7. O father, go the way by which our forefathers went. See the two kings, Yama and Varuṇa, who are pleased with the *svadhā* oblations.

8. O father, be united with your fathers, with Yama, and with the merit of ethical and religious deeds and be in heaven. Through your merit, leave back your sins and reach the Vriyamāna house in heaven. Be united then with your own shining body.[41]

9. Go away, you devils, from this sacrificial cremation plot. By Yama's command, the fathers have provided this place for this dead father. Besides, Yama has purified this place by water day and night.

10. O Fire, avoiding Yama's two four-eyed dogs, offspring of Saramā (a heavenly dog), of variegated colors, take the soul along a good path. Go to the fathers who are enjoying with Yama, and entrust the soul to them.

11. O King Yama, protect this soul from your dogs who, with their four eyes, guard your house and the path leading to it and who are extolled by the poets. Give this soul happiness and health.

12. May the two messengers of Yama, the dogs, with their long tongues and immense strength, relishing the lives taken out of others, grant us our life so that we can see the Sun in this ritual.

13. O priests, prepare *soma* for Yama and offer it in Fire who conveys it. The sacrifice for which Fire is the messenger goes to Yama.

14. O priests, make the oblation of clarified butter to Yama and serve it to him. May Yama grant us life among gods.

15. O priests, offer the sweetest offering to King Yama. Here we salute the sages who were born in the beginning, our forefathers, our forerunners who created the path for us.

16. Yama comes to the three sacrifices[42] to protect them. He comes to the six[43] worlds to inspect the performance and nonperformance (of ethical and religious deeds). The whole world is the realm ruled by Yama. The meters, Triṣṭubh, Gāyatrī, and so on, are all founded by Yama. (*Ṛgveda*, 10:14)

12. Hymn to the Fathers

1. May the highest among the Fathers receive the highest oblation; may the middle among them obtain it; and may the lowest also receive it. May all be favorable to us. Those among them who are not like wolves know *ṛta*. May they protect us in our sacrifices.

2. Now, salutations be to our Fathers, those who were born before the sacrificer, those who are born after him, and those who have come as relatives[44]—to all who have come and sit in this place.

3. I have before me the Fathers who know my devotion to them. I know the procedure of the growing sacrifice.[45] The Fathers who have come and are seated on the grass[46] are taking the pressed *soma* juice with Svadhā.

4. O seaters on the grass, Fathers, protect us, born after you. We have prepared these offerings for you. Receive them and meet us with a pleasant mind and protect us. Grant us happiness without sin.

5. The Fathers, gracious because of the dear, rich, and worthy oblations, are invoked. May they come and listen to our hymns at this sacrifice. May they approve of it and protect us.

6. O Fathers, come to this earth and sit on my left. Say that this ceremony is well done. If, as human beings, we committed errors in this ceremony, do not punish us.

7. Sitting near the Aruṇis,[47] grant wealth to the man who is making these oblations; bless his sons with wealth. In this ceremony itself, keep great wealth.

8. Our ancient Fathers, covering themselves with cloths, pressed the *soma* drink and offered it to gods and ancestors in the order. May Yama, living with the Fathers who are enjoying the offerings with him, partake of these offerings, choosing what he likes.

9. The Fathers, who by stages have become divine and who knew well the sacrificial rites and the *soma* libations, are now satisfied. O Fire, come to us with these Fathers, who are truthful and holding the warm sacrificial food.

10. O Fire, come with the Fathers, truthful, and eating and drinking the

sacrificial offerings. You are adored by thousands of hymns by the Fathers of ancient and bygone days. Those Fathers travel with Indra and other gods in the same chariot.

11. O Fathers, Fire has consumed the oblations. Come here, well inclined towards us, and take your respective seats. Eat the offerings spread out on grass. Then grant us wealth and progeny.

12. O Fire, the all-knower, praised by us, you have carried our offerings, making them smell sweet, and have given them to the Fathers. May they eat them with Svadhā. May you eat them. They are prepared with great effort.

13. You, all-knowing Fire, know all the Fathers, those whom we know and those whom we do not know. May you enjoy the offerings of this sacrifice. With Svadhās[48] they are procured and well done.

14. O Fire, along with those Fathers who were cremated and those who were not cremated, shape this divine body, the soul of my father, as you wish. (*Ṛgveda*, 10:15)

13. Hymn to Prajāpati (Lord of Living Beings)

□ Note the questions asked in the first nine verses. The Sanskrit word *ka* (who, which) is used to mean a question. The interpretation also is given that the nature of the Supreme Being, who and what he is, is a question mark, meaning thereby that he is unthinkable and indescribable. □

1. Hiraṇyagarbha[49] existed in the beginning. Being the only being when born, he became the lord of all that was. He held the earth and heaven. What god shall we adore with oblations?

2. He is the giver of life[50] and strength. All beings and gods acknowledge his commands. Immortality is his shadow, so also is death. What god shall we adore with oblations?

3. Being without a second, he became the king of everything that breathes and twinkles. He rules the two-footed and the four-footed. What god shall we adore with oblations?

4. These mountains manifest his greatness. The sages say that the oceans with the rivers are his great splendor. The regions (East, and so on) are his arms. What god shall we adore with oblations?

5. By him is the sky spread, the earth stabilized, heaven fixed, and water created on high. What god shall we adore with oblations?

6. Earth and Heavens, stabilized by him and shining and roaring, see him with their mind. Supported by him, the rising Sun shines. What god shall we adore with oblations?

7. The great waters spread over the whole world and became the womb bearing Prajāpati, and so Fire and all else. From the waters then was born Prajāpati, the one life of all gods. What god shall we adore with oblations?

8. He surveyed with his power the waters that created all the objects of sacrifice and held him, containing the creation, in themselves. He is the god of gods and none exists beside him. What god shall we adore with oblations?

9. May he not harm us—he who has created the earth, the law of which is *ṛta*, he who is the author of heaven and other worlds, and he whom the great and pleasant waters created. What god shall we adore with oblations?

10. O Prajāpati, none else than you comprehends all these worlds that are born. With whatever desire we offer our sacrifice to you, may it be granted. May we be the lords of wealth. (*Ṛgveda*, 10:121)

14. Hymn to Creation

□ The Hymn to Creation is the famous *nāsádīya* hymn, regarded as the earliest philosophical utterance of the Aryan race. Śāyana gives it a full philosophical interpretation in terms of his nondualistic philosophy. He says that the deity addressed by this hymn is the Supreme Spirit itself and the seer or sage (*ṛṣi*) of the hymn is no other than Prajāpati himself. One may not go all the way with Śāyana in his philosophical interpretation. Yet the hymn cannot be intelligible without his commentary.

A number of ultimate questions are raised in this great hymn. For example, what is time, or *karma* (action-potency), or *jīva* (individual soul)? In the beginning there was no time even (stanza 2), as the sun and the moon were not created as yet to differentiate day and night, fortnight and month. Time cannot exist without such differentiation. The world of being is bound to that of nonbeing (4), that is, bound by the potencies of ethical activities, rites, and so on. Multiplicity is due to the multiplicity of these potencies, which also are called *karmas*. But how the first *karma* or potency appeared cannot be explained by any one. It is a wonder. Just as the sun, when he rises (5), spreads his rays over the world, action (*karma*), when it first appears, makes the multiplicity manifest. But how did it first arise? No one can answer. The seed-holders of the world are the individual souls. They are called seed-holders because the world is born and continues to exist as a result of their deeds, which produce creative potencies. These potencies are held by the souls. But if the souls are part of the world, how and why were they first born? No one can answer, except perhaps the Supreme Spirit. The last question in (7), according to Śāyana, means that, if the Supreme Spirit does not know it, none else can. That is, the Supreme Spirit alone knows the truth. □

1. Then in the beginning there was no nonbeing; neither was there being. There was neither the earth, nor the sky, nor anything beyond. What surrounded the world[51] then, what could be surrounded, and for what purpose? How could the unfathomed, deep waters[52] exist then?

2. There was then neither death nor immortality. There was no difference between night and day. There breathed the One, breathless, by his own Svadhā.[53] Beside it there was none.

3. Before creation all was concealed in darkness. All this was unknowable, covered by water,[54] the empty,[55] and the One, and was born through the power of desire (will).[56]

4. Then arose desire, the seed (sperm) in mind. The sages, thinking with their minds, see in them the world of being bound to nonbeing.

5. Were the rays of all this, the world of action, spread first transversely or from above (vertically)? There existed only the seed-holders and their power.[57] Svadhā (nourishment)[58] is the lower, and the agent[59] the higher.

6. Who knows this truth? Who can explain it? From what does this multiformed world come forth? Who created it? Even the gods are created after the first creation. Then how can they know about the first creation before them? Then how can any one know it?

7. Who knows from whom the world comes out or whether he forms it or does not form it? He who resides in the highest heaven perhaps knows it. Or does he also not know it? (*Ṛgveda*, 10:129)

15. Hymn to Puruṣa (Person)

□ *Puruṣa* literally means man, but in religion and philosophy the word means person, soul, or spirit. The first spirit, the origin of the world, is the Supreme Spirit. The world is the result of his self-sacrifice. Mythology knows no logic and introduces gods as sacrificing Puruṣa. The atmosphere of this hymn is that of sacrificial religion that has begun to attain spiritual inwardness. If everything could be obtained (produced) through sacrifice, the world also could be so obtained. But the recognition of the existence of spirit made the Aryans think that the world was created through the self-sacrifice of the Supreme Spirit. □

1. A thousand heads has Puruṣa, a thousand eyes, and a thousand feet. He pervades the whole world and is far beyond it, which is his ten fingers[60] wide.

2. All this is the Puruṣa, and all that which is past and that which is future. He is the lord of immortality and manifests himself through the food enjoyed.[61]

3. All this world is his power (greatness). Puruṣa is greater than this. All the world of creatures are one fourth of him. His three fourths is the immortality in heaven.

4. The three-fourths Puruṣa went up and the one fourth came here (to become this), and spread out as the eating (living) and the noneating (nonliving).

5. From him the first Puruṣa, Virāt[62], was born, and from Virāt another Puruṣa.[63] He

became different from Virāt. Then was born the earth, and then the bodies of creatures.

6. Then gods performed the sacrifice of Puruṣa, making him the victim.[64] The spring season was the clarified butter,[65] summer its fuel, and autumn the sacrificial gift.

7. The gods sprinkled holy water on the first-born Puruṣa,[66] the sacrificial animal, in grass. The gods, the Sādhyas,[67] and the sages performed the sacrifice.

8. From that sacrifice in which the All (Puruṣa) was sacrificed, Pṛṣadājya (sacrificial butter) was procured. The Puruṣa formed those that live by air, the beasts of the forests, and the animals of villages.

9. From that sacrifice of the All, were born the *Ṛgvedic* hymns and the hymns of the *Sāma-veda.* From it were born the meters (of verses) and from it the *Yajurveda.*[68]

10. From that sacrifice were born the horses and others who have two rows of teeth (up and down). From it were born the cattle and from it the goats and sheep.

11. The gods divided the Puruṣa. Into how many parts did they divide it? Which is his face (mouth), which are his arms, which thighs and which feet?

12. The Brahmins were his face (mouth), his arms were the Kṣatriyas (warriors), the Vaiśyas (traders) were his thighs, and the Śūdras (manual workers) were created out of his feet.

13. The moon was born of his mind, the sun from his eyes, Indra and Agni from his mouth, and Vāyu (wind) from his breath.

14. The mid-air came out of his navel, from his head the sky, from his feet the earth, from his ears the directions (East, and so on). Thus the gods formed the worlds.

15. The gods made seven boundaries[69] for that sacrifice and three times seven fuel sticks when they bound the Puruṣa as the sacrificial animal.

16. The gods sacrificed through this ceremony. These acts were the first important ordinances. These mighty ones attained heaven, where the earliest Sādhyas, the gods of old, live. (*Ṛgveda,* 10:90)

16. Hymn to Śrī

1. O Fire, bring me Lakṣmī,[70] the golden colored, who is like a deer,[71] has garlands of gold and silver, and is beautiful like the moon, and is full of gold.

2. O Fire, invoke Lakṣmī who will not depart. May we obtain gold, cattle, horses, and many children from her.

3. She has horses going in front and chariots in the middle. She is known by the sounds of elephants. I invoke the goddess Śrī. May she favor me.

4. I invoke Śrī, the Kā (Who)[72] smiling, surrounded by gold, wet from the milky ocean (in which she was born), brilliant, satisfied, worshiped, standing on the lotus flower, the lotus-colored.

5. I take refuge in Śrī, beautiful like the moon, shining in fame and worshiped by gods in the world so that my poverty may disappear. O Śrī, I beg of you.

7. May the famous Kubera (the god of wealth) come to me with Maṇibhadra, his treasurer, and bring precious stones. I am born in this kingdom. Grant me fame and wisdom.

8. I shall overcome your elder sister,[73] dark with hunger and thirst. Remove poverty and meagerness of means from my house. (*Ṛgveda,* Khila, 2:6)

17. Hymn to Viśvakarman (Maker of the Universe)

□ Viśvakarman was once regarded during the *Ṛgvedic* times as the Supreme God. He is supposed to have performed a sacrifice in which he made himself the sacrificial victim for becoming gods, men, lower animals, and the worlds. He was thus the father, the creator of beings, and also, as the created beings, the son (of himself). This myth avoids the man-woman relationship for creating the world. Later, when he fell from the supreme position, he became the god of carpenters, blacksmiths, goldsmiths, and so on, in some parts of India. Tvaṣṭā, another Supreme God, is said to correspond to Vulcan of Greek mythology. □

1. The sage, the sacrificing priest, our father, offered all the worlds in sacrifice. Longing for prosperity, he entered the

worlds in sacrifice. Longing for prosperity, he entered the worlds, which were first hidden from Fire, and offered himself through them.[74]

2. What then was the place at which the sacrifice was done? How could it be done? And what could be the procedure? Standing at which place did the all-seeing Viśvakarman create the earth and heaven through his power?

3. The all-seeing Viśvakarman, the one God, with his face on all sides, with arms at every place, with feet everywhere, created the earth and heaven with his hands and feet.

4. You men of thought, ask your minds the question: What was the forest from which the tree was cut to build up the earth and heaven? And what is the place, standing on which the Lord holds the worlds?[75]

5. O Viśvakarman, teach me about the sacrificial offering for you, your highest abodes (bodies), your middle abodes, and your lowest abodes.[76] I am your friend and you grow your three bodies with your sacrificial food.

6. O Viśvakarman, exalted by my oblations, you yourself sacrifice earth and heaven. Let other men (not performing sacrifices) be deluded. Here may a rich man sponsor our sacrifice.

7. Let us today invoke Viśvakarman, the lord of words (speech), who is swift like thought (mind) to receive these oblations. May he enjoy our offerings. He is the happiness of the worlds and one of good deeds. (*Ṛgveda*, 10:81)

18. Hymn to Viṣṇu

1. Shining all-glorious, worshipful with butter, protector, be our Mitra,[77] O Viṣṇu. The wise sacrificer is to worship you with hymns in this sacrifice.

2. He who brings offerings to Viṣṇu, the creator, ancient and ever new, the self-created, and he who praises the created world with the greatness manifest of the great, goes with fame to the place where every one has to go.

3. O singers of hymns, so long as you please Viṣṇu, you will know yourselves the ancient one, the womb of *ṛta*. Sing that he is the destiny of all men. O Viṣṇu, we worship your great and good heart (mind).

4. King Varuṇa and the Aśvins wait on the sacrifice performed by this sacrificer, the wise one among the winds (priests). Viṣṇu holds the best potent power that leads to heaven and, along with his friends, he removes the hindrance from the clouds.

5. Viṣṇu, the greatest among gods, comes to the sacrificer singing beautiful hymns. May Viṣṇu, occupying the three places (worlds), satisfy the sacrificer and come to grant this Aryan the fruit of sacrifice. (*Ṛgveda*, 1:156)

19. Hymn to Time (Kāla)

□ Time runs like a perfectly trained horse on which a pot filled with water to the brim is placed, without spilling even a drop. That is, nothing—past, present, or future—is lost in Time but exists in it, as Time is one and the same all through. The Sanskrit word *kāla* is derived from the root √*kal* meaning to collect, to count. Time is the collector, the gatherer of everything past, present, and future. □

1. Time, the horse, rushes with seven reins (rays). It has a thousand eyes, it is ageless, and is full of seed (creative potencies). The sages with spiritual ideas can mount him. All the worlds are his wheels.

2. Time rides with seven wheels, It has seven names. Its axle is immortality. He conveys all beings there. Time, the first god, marches onward.

3. A vessel completely full is placed on Time. We see him in many forms. He carries away all the beings. They name him Time in the highest heaven.

4. Indeed, Time brought all the worlds here. Indeed, he encompassed all the worlds. He is their father and yet their son. Verily, there is no power other than he.

5. Time created yonder heaven and also all these worlds. Whatever was and whatever will be spreads out urged by Time.

6. Time created the earth; the Sun scorches in Time. All the beings exist in Time. The eye sees in Time.

7. Mind is founded in Time; breath and names are founded in him. The creatures are happy when Time arrives.

8. Penance is founded in Time; even the highest is fixed in it. Brahma is stabilized in Time. Time is the father of Prajāpati and is the lord of everything.

9. The universe is pushed forth by Time. It was born of him and founded in him. Time becoming Brahma supports the highest lord (Parameṣṭin).

10. Time created whatever is born and even Prajāpati in the beginning. Kaśyapa, the self-existing, and penance were born from Time. (*Atharva-veda*, 19:53)

20. Hymn to Fire Altar

□ Although called a hymn, the Hymn to Fire Altar is actually a meditation in which the performer of the sacrifice is asked to meditate on the fire altar as the whole universe, in which he is sacrificing to obtain spiritual knowledge. This hymn is very significant in that it indicates the transition from the religion of sacrifices to that of self-realization taught by the Upaniṣads. The similarities drawn in the hymn look farfetched, but the spirit of the hymn can be understood. □

1. Indeed, the Fire Altar built here is this world. Its enclosing stones are the waters. Its Yajuṣmati bricks are the men. The cattle are its Sūdadohas (a kind of drink of immortality). The plants and trees are its cement (between bricks), oblations, and fuel. Fire (the physical) is its joining brick. So does this make up the whole Fire (divine). The whole Fire pervades space. Whoever knows this becomes the whole Fire, the pervader of space.

2. Yet, verily, the Fire Altar is the air also. The horizon is its enclosing circle of bricks. . . . The birds are its Yajuṣmati bricks. . . .

3. Yet, verily, the Fire Altar is the sky also. . . .

4. Yet, verily, the Fire Altar is the Sun also. . . .

5. Yet, verily, the Fire Altar is the stars also. . . .

7. Yet, verily, the Fire Altar is the meters (of verses) also. . . .

10. Yet, verily, the Fire Altar is the year also. . . .

12. Yet, verily, the Fire Altar is the body also. . . .

14. Yet, verily, the Fire Altar is all beings and all gods. All beings, all gods are the waters, and the Fire Altar is the same as the waters.

16. In this context the verse runs:

They ascend through knowledge to the place where desires vanish.
Neither sacrificial gifts go there, nor do the zealous performers of sacrifices without knowledge.
He who is ignorant of this truth does not go to that world by sacrificial gifts and devout practices.
It belongs to those with knowledge.

(*Śatapada Brāhmaṇa* [Ritual text of hundred feet] 10:5, 4)

21. Manu and the Flood

1. They brought water to Manu for washing, as it is now usual to bring it for washing hands. When he was washing, a fish came into his hands.

2. It said to him in words, "Bring me up, I shall save you." "From what will you save me?" "A flood will carry away all the creatures. I shall save you from that flood." "How can I bring you up?"

3. "Fish swallow fish. So long as we remain small, destruction awaits us. Keep me first in a jar. When I outgrow it, dig a pond and keep me in it. When I outgrow that also, take me to the sea. Then I shall be beyond danger."

4. It quickly became a Jhaṣa (a large fish), which becomes the largest (of all fish). Then it said, "The flood will come in such and such a year. Take my advice then, and build a ship. Enter it when the flood rises, and I shall save you from the flood."

5. After rearing the fish thus, Manu took it to the sea. In the year indicated to him by the fish, he acted according to the advice of the fish and built a ship. When the flood rose, he entered it. The fish then swam to him. He tied the rope of the ship to the horn of the fish and thus reached swiftly the Northern Mountain (Himalaya) there.

6. The fish then said, "I have saved you. Tie the ship to a tree and do not let the water leave you stranded when you are on

the mountain. Descend as the water subsides." Thus gradually he descended, hence that slope of the Northern Mountain is called "Manu's Descent." The flood carried off all the creatures, Manu alone survived.

7. Wishing for progeny, he began to worship and do penance. Then he performed a sacrifice of cooked meal. In the waters he offered melted butter, buttermilk, whey, and curd as oblations. In a year, a woman was created out of them. She rose dripping, melted butter collected at her footprints.

10. Wishing for progeny, he continued to worship and perform penance along with her. Through her this race was generated by him. This is the race of Manu. Whatever blessings he desired through her were all conferred on him. (*Śatapada Brāhmaṇa*, 1:8)

22. Hymn to Rudra[78]

1. O priests, sing the praises of god Rudra who, with swift flying arrows, holds his bow firm, who is strong, unconquered, and ever defeating his enemies, and whose weapons are sharp. May he hear our praises.

2. He knows, through his power, the earth-born and the heaven-born. O Rudra, protect our people who are singing your praises, and come to our abodes and remove our sicknesses.

3. O Rudra, may your lightning arrow shot by you from heaven avoid us. O Apivāta (giver of knowledge), give us the thousand medicines you have, and do not harm our sons and progeny.

4. O Rudra, do not kill us, do not neglect us. May we not be caught in your noose when you are angry. Make us partake in the sacrifice desired by all living beings. (*Ṛgveda*, 7:46)

23. Hymn to Śiva

1. May my mind meditate on Śiva, the consciousness that is unthinkable, immeasurable, beyond the manifest and the unmanifest, subtler than the subtlest.

2. He is and yet, destroying everything, is not. Still he is eternal. He is the middle between being and nonbeing. May my mind meditate on him.

3. This contradiction is there that he is and is not. That all this is and is not, is a secret (mystery). He is beyond being and nonbeing. May my mind meditate on him.

4. That which is beyond the beyond and beyond that also—that beyond the beyond is unknowable. May my mind meditate on him.

5. That which is beyond the beyond is Brahmā; beyond him is Hari (Viṣṇu); and beyond Hari is Śiva. May my mind meditate on him.

6. He has cows, riches, life, strength, people, and cattle. He is the first plenitude. May my mind meditate on him.

7. To the man who seeks the eternal, supreme, the highest Puruṣa, the Omkāra,[79] he is the Praṇava.[80] May my mind meditate on him. (*Ṛgveda*, Khila 11)

24. Hymn to Divine Knowledge

□ The Hymn to Divine Knowledge may be called the Hymn to Vāk or Word also. Śāyana says that Bṛhaspati praises knowledge of the Supreme Spirit through this hymn. Bṛhaspati, as the following verses indicate, seems to be wondering how divine knowledge is conveyed through word-sound heard by the ear. The context of the hymn is still sacrifice. Śāyana says that Bṛhaspati is here addressing himself as the inner self. □

1. O Bṛhaspati, the first and earliest Vāk (Word, Speech), holding names, urges babies to speak[81] and is the best and is without sin. It is hidden, and manifests itself through love.

2. As man cleans the corn flour (for cooking), the learned clean[82] the words in assemblies by thought. There the friends (words) know their friendships (relations). In Vāk lies auspiciousness and sacredness.

3. They obtain the path of Vāk from sacrifice. They know it as existing in the sages. Taking her, they spread her in many lands. The seven meters (of verses), sounding like flying birds, enter her.

4. Though seeing, one does not see Vāk; though hearing, one does not hear her. Yet to another, she shows her body like a well-dressed wife to her husband.

5. In the assembly, they call one strongly

drunk (with knowledge). Some do not understand (the words) spoken in it. In it, some are in Māyā, listening to Vāk without flowers and fruit.[83]

6. He who leaves the friend (teacher of the Veda), the knower of friendship, can have no part in Vāk. If he hears, he hears in vain. He does not know the path that is good.

7. All friends (members of the assembly) are equal in having eyes and ears, but they are unequal in having spiritual knowledge. Some are like tanks running with water reaching the mouth, some like those with water reaching the waist, but others are like tanks not fit to bathe.

8. O Vāk, where many friendly Brahmins of the assembly determine and establish the intellectually knowable (merits and defects in interpreting the Vedic texts), there they leave you (Vāk, sacred word) and go after those (secular words) they wish to know. But some roam in you.[84]

9. These ignorant men, who do not move with the knowers of the Brahman in this world or with gods in the other, are after neither the meaning[85] of the Vedas nor the performance of sacrifices. They, having obtained the vulgar, sinful words and remaining ignorant, become tillers of the earth and carry on ploughing.

10. All the friends of the assembly are happy with the famous *soma* that has come to the sacrifice. This *soma* is the destroyer of sin, the giver of food and gifts and, when placed in the dishes in the sacrifice, is capable of strengthening our senses.

11. One of the priests, the Hotā,[86] recites the several hymns in the prescribed order; a second, the Udgātā, sings the Gāyatra (Sāma) with Sakvarī hymns;[87] and third, the Brahmā, sings the verses ordaining the different rites at the various stages; and the fourth, the Adhvaryu, fixes the various acts (rites) in their order at the sacrifice. (*Ṛgveda*, 10:71)

NOTES

1. Śāyana (thirteenth century), the great commentator on the Vedas, says that as the horse drives away flies and other insects with its tail, the Fire-god drives away the enemies of the sacrificers. It seems also that the smoking flame of a rushing fire is imagined to be like the tail of a running horse. In translating the selections from the Vedas, Śāyana's commentary is especially used. He lived Hinduism, observed and performed sacrifices, and was acquainted with the meanings of the passages given by the great scholars of the time. The Advaita (nondualism) leaning of his commentary, however, is avoided.
2. *Soma* is a kind of fermented juice from a plant known at that time.
3. Śāyana explains *uktha* as the chariot shafts that were used for pressing *soma*. The word means also certain hymns.
4. See following hymn to Indra.
5. The sacrifice here is that of *soma.*
6. Vṛtra was the name of the demon that prevented the clouds from raining. Indra killed him with his thunderbolt and released rain from the clouds.
7. Dāsas are the aboriginals, also called Dasyus. *Dāsa* in the literary language means the servant and *dasyu* the thief.
8. A class of demons called serpents. It is thought that these aboriginals were worshipers of serpents, which were their totems.
9. Śāyana explains that the word *bull* means the best of gods. Even in classical Sanskrit, *vṛṣabha* (bull) is used in the sense of the best, the greatest.
10. *Ahi* also means serpent. The worshipers of serpents were called Ahis and Paṇis.
11. Varuṇa is said to be the son of Aditi and is, therefore, called Āditya.
12. Hymns also were regarded as offerings in sacrifice.
13. The Sanskrit word *vrata* means any ceremony including sacrifice.
14. Aditi had many sons including Sūrya, Mitra, and Varuṇa.
15. It is intriguing that Varuṇa is called Asura, which generally means a demon. Commentàtors try to explain it by splitting up the word. Perhaps he was originally an Assyrian god.

16. The Vedic people believed that one form of Fire called Vaiśvānara (the universal man) resides in water. This Fire is also said to be the heat that digests our food.
17. The four priests are Adhvaryu, Udgātā, Hotā, and Brahma.
18. The three offerings are cooked food, butter, and the *soma* juice.
19. The seven threads are the seven priests—Hotā, Poṣṭā, Neṣṭā, Agnidh, Praśāsta, Adhvaryu, and Brahma.
20. Śāyana explains Araṇi as Aśvattha, which is the name of a tree also. Perhaps the word has something to do with Fire being called a horse, which is tied to the tree and is, therefore, its friend.
21. *Ṛta* means water also, as explained in selection 4. Water is the abode of Fire, and so Fire establishes waters wherever he is present. As *ṛta* means rite also, the sacred Fire establishes rites also.
22. This is a farewell.
23. The use of the word *Father* indicates that Varuṇa has become old or elderly and is to be retired.
24. Fire here is the physical fire, not fire as the Fire-god, the priest of the gods.
25. This verse indicates that Varuṇa has become too old and Vṛtra, the preventor of rain (Waters), the imprisoner of Waters, was not yet destroyed. Indra killed him and became the respected successor of Varuṇa with Fire's help.
26. *Hamsa* (the sun) means also the swan. The sun is compared to the bird flying across the sky.
27. The Sanskrit word *yuvati* is explained by Śāyana as the giver of rewards and blessings.
28. The meaning is that all the dawns are alike. We may note that the hymn sometimes uses the singular to denote that all the dawns are the same.
29. When the dawn begins to shine, the enemies run away. They are, therefore, called the night-wanderers. Sacrifices were possible only after dawn, as the enemies of the Aryans used to pollute and destroy the ceremonies stealthily in darkness. For the pre-Aryan inhabitants of India, the sacrificial religion of the Aryans was a harmful magic against them.
30. The word *sumaṅgalī* means a woman whose husband is alive. She is considered to be auspicious unlike the widow. In this verse Dawn is said to be born for protecting *ṛta*, as all religious and ethical activities are possible after dawn without hindrance from enemies who work in the dark.
31. She is called the mother of gods because man remembers his duties to gods after he wakes up at dawn. In his sleep, the gods do not exist, as it were. Further, as the daughter she resembles her mother, Aditi.
32. Sindhu is the name of the river now called Indus. Śāyana says that the hymn invokes the god residing in the river.
33. It was the practice of cultivators to leave their work, even though unfinished, at sunset.
34. The Sanskrit word is translated both as "Sky and Earth" and "Heaven and Earth." In Vedic mythology, the celestial heaven is beyond the sky and is inhabited by Varuṇa and the highest gods. But often the sky also is called heaven.
35. Vivasvān is the name of the Sun, said to be the father of Yama, who is, therefore, called Vaivasvān.
36. Mātali is the name of Indra's charioteer. So Indra is called Mātalī.
37. Aṅgirasas are a class of ancestors.
38. Ṛkvas is the name of some spirits who sing praises of Bṛhaspati.
39. *Svāhā* is a kind of oblation and the word is generally uttered when the oblation is made to gods.
40. *Svadhā* is another kind of oblation and the word is generally uttered when the oblation is offered to the ancestors.
41. After death the soul is said to assume a brilliant body in heaven.
42. The three sacrifices are called *jyoti* (light), *gau* (cow), and *āyus* (span of life). The cow is not killed, but given as a gift to some one.
43. The six worlds are the heaven, earth, water, plants, hymns, and truth (morality, righteousness).
44. That is, those who are ancestors of relatives. It is believed that people who die without male children to offer oblations visit the ceremonies performed by relatives.

45. Even the funeral and ancestral ceremonies are regarded as sacrifices. At these rites, there is no killing of animals.
46. *Barhi* is a kind of long grass considered to be sacred and used on such occasions.
47. Śāyana explains that *aruṇi* is either the red flame of fire or gods who shine like fire.
48. The word is used also when procuring and preparing the offerings.
49. Literally means the "golden womb" or the "womb that bears the golden egg," i.e., the womb, origin of all conscious beings. Consciousness shines like gold.
50. The word used is *ātman*. He is the *ātman* of all living beings. The word may be interpreted as life, breath, soul, or spirit.
51. If there is nothing to be surrounded, there can be no surrounder.
52. The mythological historians say that waters surrounded the world and that originally everything was water (cf. Thales), out of which the gods and the world rose. But if there was nothing to support the waters at the bottom, how could they exist? Even Varuṇa could not have existed then, as the waters themselves could not exist. The water myth, that everything came out of water, seems to be common to the early mythological thought of many lands of the time. This hymn questions the truth of the myth.
53. Svadhā is explained by Śāyana here as that which supports (*dhā*) oneself (*sva*), i.e., as one's nature. That is, the One did not breathe with the help of external air.
54. The word used is *salila* meaning water. Śāyana says that originally the multiplicity of the world was one massive darkness and had no distinctions, as there are no separate bits of water that can be distinguished in the massive water of the ocean. He accepts also the view of mythological waters as an alternative explanation.
55. The word used is *tuccha*. It means the low, the insignificant, because it cannot be fixed or determined as being or nonbeing. As a nondualist, Śāyana says that it is *māyā*, which is neither being nor nonbeing.
56. The Sanskrit word *tapas* means fervor, penance, warmth. Perhaps the warmth or fervor of desire is said to have turned the waters into the world (cf. Thales again). This is the will, which the moment it arises, creates the object willed.
57. The power is the potency of the ethical and religious activities of the souls.
58. Śāyana says that *svadhā* here means food and so all that is to be enjoyed. This verse means that, whatever was the origin of the world, it first divided itself into the enjoyer and the enjoyed.
59. The agent is the soul that performs actions.
60. The world is only as big as the width of the ten fingers of the Puruṣa, who is far greater than the world.
61. The food enjoyed is the object of enjoyment obtained through sacrifices, and means the world of sacrificial and ethical actions. The world is taken as meant for enjoyment.
62. Virāt is the first derivative Puruṣa and is the Cosmic Person or the Cosmos conceived as a Person. One may compare this idea to that of the Logos.
63. This Puruṣa, the third, is the finite person, man. Gods also may be considered as coming under this third class of Puruṣas, as they also are after enjoyment.
64. He is not actually burnt. Śāyana says that this is only a mental sacrifice or a spiritual sacrifice, not a physical sacrifice. It is a transformation of the will, which is a part of the Puruṣa.
65. There was no sacrificial butter, fuel, and food at that time. So no ordinary physical sacrifice was possible. The means or instruments of sacrifice were only the seasons—which means that time was there, for the finite man implies that he was born into time.
66. That the gods sprinkled water on the grass, not on the Puruṣa (Virāt) himself, shows that the sacrifice was a mental one. This interpretation supports the view that the world was created through will (desire). Every creative, productive, act was a sacrifice for the Aryans of the time.
67. Sādhyas are a kind of divine beings.
68. The *Atharva-veda*, which consists of hymns of sacrifice, is not mentioned because sacrifice is the source of all the other Vedas.
69. The seven here means the seven meters of verse in the sacrificial hymns. The three times seven

are the fuel sticks used for keeping the fire. There are generally twenty-one kinds of offerings placed in fire with those sticks.

70. Lakṣmī is another name of Śrī and is regarded as the goddess of wealth. The word is used also for everything man desires in life. In Indian mythology, she is the wife of Viṣṇu. This hymn does not belong to the original *Ṛgveda*, but seems to be current even at that time. It is said to be one of the *khilas* (hearsays) added to the *Ṛgveda* as an additional hymn.
71. A woman is generally compared to the deer, as she has large, timid (shy), attractive eyes.
72. This goddess is conceived to be indescribable like the Supreme Spirit and is called Kā (feminine Who), whereas the Supreme Spirit is called Ka (masculine Who).
73. In mythology, Poverty was first born and then Śrī. So the former is called Jyeṣṭā, the elder, or the elder sister.
74. Through self-sacrifice this Supreme God created the world.
75. Cf. the hymn to Prajāpati and that to Creation (selections 13–14) in which the unknowability and inexplicability are expressed.
76. The three bodies—the highest, the middle, and the lowest—are the bodies of gods, men, and lower animals.
77. *Mitra* means friend also.
78. Rudra means the howler, the roaring destruction of natural forces. He came to be identified later with Śiva, one of the Hindu Trinity, the others being Brahmā and Viṣṇu.
79. The sacred syllable *Om* ($a+u+m$).
80. Praṇava is another name for Oṁkāra.
81. The reference is to the sounds like "tātā," "māmā," "dādā," and so on, which babies utter. They learn other words later.
82. Cleaning the words means fixing their meanings and grammatical forms. This work was done in conferences (assemblies, councils) of the learned or men of knowledge. At every sacrifice, it was the practice to set apart a place for the assembly of the learned who carried on discussions on the Vedas and spiritual knowledge. As the meditations of the *Brāhmaṇas* show, the spiritual knowledge of the Upaniṣads originated in such discussions and in such assemblies and was further developed by the sages of the forests.
83. The obvious and the deeper meanings of words and sentences.
84. The stanza refers to the distinction between the so-called textual criticism with the help of grammar and etymology and the deeper spiritual meanings of the texts. In most of the assemblies of the learned, the center of interest was the former. Yet a few were interested in the latter. These few roam (swim) in the ocean of spiritual knowledge.
85. There are people who attend the sacrificial ceremonies, but do not understand the meaning of the Vedic texts repeated in the sacrifices. This verse refers to such people, who are like the tillers of the earth and have neither spiritual knowledge nor knowledge of sacrificial rites. Indirectly, it refers also to men who are not desirous of either knowledge. This verse seems to contain the roots of the distinction between higher and lower knowledge.
86. In this verse, the names and functions of the four classes of priests (*ṛtviks*) are given. Brahmā here is the name of one of the priests, not that of the god Brahmā (one of the Trinity, Brahmā, Viṣṇu, and Śiva) or of the Brahman (Supreme Spirit).
87. Sakvarī hymns extol Indra as having the power to kill the demon, Vṛtra.

CHAPTER 2

The Upaniṣads

□ The Upaniṣads (secret doctrines) constitute the fourth part of the Vedas and are generally philosophical in character. At present more than two hundred Upaniṣads are available. Of these some eleven are treated as the earliest and the most important. The earliest of the Upaniṣads is the *Bṛhadāraṇyaka*, which is generally assigned to the ninth century B.C. The composition of the Upaniṣads seems to have continued up to the sixth century A.D. or even later. For additional information, see "Introduction to Hinduism: A Summary Account," ¶5, 6, 8. □

1. *Īśāvāsya Upaniṣad*[1]

□ It should be noted that the Upaniṣads constitute the fourth part of the Veda, the third being the *Araṇyakas* (Forest Treatises). If the *Araṇyakas* are the buds, the Upaniṣads are the flowers of the Vedānta. "That" here is the unseen Supreme Spirit, whereas "this" is the finite spirit or the world. Ignorance is not necessarily the *māyā* of Śaṅkara. It means the actions (like the ethical and ritual) performed by men who are ignorant of the Supreme Spirit. Knowledge is not the knowledge in "the way of knowledge," but the *upāsanā* (worship and meditation) of this or that god. Immortality is only the relative immortality of the god worshiped and meditated upon. The teaching of this Upaniṣad is that this world, including ourselves, should live and enjoy its values, performing the prescribed ethical duties and religious rites. □

Om, that is full, and this is full. The latter has arisen taking the fullness of the former, and is, therefore, full. Om. Peace, Peace, Peace.

1. Om, the world, whatever it is as the universe, is pervaded and surrounded by the Lord. So enjoy life in surrender (to the Lord). Desire not for another's wealth.

2. Wish for a hundred-year life, performing actions. If you are such a man—there is no other way—the (result of) action does not pollute you.

4. Without moving, it is faster than mind. The gods do not know that which existed prior to them. Standing, it overtakes other runners. In it are held waters and wind.

5. It moves and does not move; it is far and yet near. It is inward to all this; yet it is beyond all this.

8. He pervades everthing; he is the pure (white) sperm (seed); he is bodiless, without wounds, without veins, pure, sinless; he is the all-knower, all-pervading, self-created who created the things in their order.

9. Those who worship ignorance (*avidyā*) enter blinding darkness; those who worship knowledge (*vidyā*) enter a thicker darkness.

10. We heard from those learned men who taught us that the fruit of the worship of ignorance is one thing and that of the worship of knowledge another.

11. He who knows both ignorance and knowledge overcomes death through ignorance and obtains immortality through knowledge.

2. *Kena Upaniṣad*[2]

□ The *Kena Upaniṣad* shows that the Brahman is the Supreme Power, the Supreme God, and the Supreme Spirit. Until the gods obtained this realization, they were thinking that by themselves they possessed their respective powers.

The word *brahman* is not a proper name but is like the word *Absolute*. Etymologically it means "ever growing" (*bṛh* = to grow, to expand). For this reason it is right to put the definite article before it as before *Absolute*. □

Ch. 1, 1. Directed by whom does the mind work? Commanded by whom does this life-principle, the foremost, function? Initiated by whom do they utter words (*vāk*)? And which god directs the eye and the ear?

2. The wise obtain immortality after death by leaving back their identity (with the senses). For the Lord is the ear of our ear, the mind of mind, the speech of speech, life of life, and eye of the eye.

3. The eye does not go there (to the Supreme Being), nor does speech or mind. We do not know it (through the senses); and we do not know it through our intellect. Thus it is taught: It is different from the known, it is different from the unknown. So we have heard from the men of old who explained it to us.

4. That is the Brahman (Supreme Spirit), not this[3] which is worshiped.

14. The Brahman obtained victory for the gods; but they thought that the victory was theirs and was due to their powers.

15. The Brahman came to know of it and manifested himself as a form. But they could not know what that adorable spirit was.

16. They said to Fire, "O Fire, find out what this spirit is." He said, "Yes."

17. He approached it. The spirit asked, "Who are you?" He replied, 'I am Fire, Jātaveda."

18. The spirit asked, "What is your power?" He said, "I can burn everything here on earth."

19. The spirit placed a straw before him and said, "Burn it." He approached it with all speed, but could not burn it. He returned and said, "I could not know what that spirit was."

20. Then the gods asked Wind to find out what that spirit was. He consented.

21. He approached it and was asked, "Who are you?" He replied, "I am Wind, I am Mātariśvan."

22. Then the spirit asked, "What is your power?" He said, "I can carry off everything on earth."

23. Then the spirit placed a straw in front of him and asked him to lift it. He approached it with all speed but could not move it. He returned and said, "I could not know what the spirit was."

24. Then the gods asked Indra to find out what the spirit was. He approached it and it vanished from him.

25. Then in the sky, he saw a very beautiful lady by name Umā,[4] the daughter of the Himalayas. He asked her, "Who is the spirit?"

26. She said, "It is the Brahman; through its victory, you obtained your lordship." Then Indra understood that it was the Brahman.

3. *Kaṭha Upaniṣad*[5]

□ The *Kaṭha Upaniṣad* is one of the principal Upaniṣads and its spiritual teachings center in the story of a boy named Naciketas. The boy's father, Āruṇi, performed a sacrifice in which he had to give away everything he had. But instead of making a gift of his son also, he gave a few old cows. The boy became curious and questioned his father, who, disturbed, got angry and said, "I give you to Yama, the god of death." So the boy went to the palace of Yama. But the latter was absent from his house and the boy remained for three days without being received. Yama returned and was horrified to find a Brahmin guest without any reception. So he gave the boy three boons. As the first boon, the boy asked that his father, when he would meet him again, should receive him without anger, but with peace and affection. As a second boon, the boy asked Yama to teach about the heavenly fire. Yama taught him about the fire and in commemoration of the boy's visit, named the fire Naciketas. As the third boon, the boy asked Yama about what happens to man after death. Yama was reluctant at first to tell the truth to the boy and wanted to tempt him with wealth, sovereignty of the earth, and so forth, if he did not insist on the answer. But the boy remained adamant and so Yama taught him about the *ātman*, which never dies, but which ordinary men think dies at death of the body. □

Ch. 1 § 2, 14. Naciketas asked Yama: "Tell me what you see beyond merit and demerit, beyond cause and effect, and beyond what has been and what will be.

15. Yama said, "Succinctly I shall tell you that which all the Vedas teach, all the penances aim at, and desiring which they (the sages) observe continence: It is Om.

16. "This letter is indeed the Brahman, it is the supreme letter. Whoever knows it obtains what he wants.

17. "This is the best support (of life), this is the supreme support. Knowing this support, man enjoys in the Brahmā-world.

18. "The eternal conscious Self is not born, never dies; it does not come from anywhere, nothing is born from it. Unborn, eternal, everlasting, the ancient one is not destroyed when the body is destroyed.

19. "If the destroyer intends to destroy and the destroyed thinks of being destroyed, then neither knows the truth. This (*ātman*) does not destroy and is not destroyed.

20. "The *ātman* of all living creatures is smaller than the smallest and greater than the greatest. It is hidden in the hearts (caves, *buddhis*). One who does not perform sacrifices with desires and is free from grief, sees it and its majesty through the purity of mind and senses."

Ch. 1. § 3, 1. Drinking the *ṛta*[6] of their ethical deeds, there exists the Two (*jīva*, the finite self, and the Lord, the Supreme Self) in the Supreme Ether,[7] the abode of the Supreme, in this world. They are different like light and shade. Thus declare the knowers of the Brahman, the five fires,[8] and the three Naciketa fires.[9]

2. We know the Naciketa fire, which is the bridge for the sacrificers to cross over sorrow. It is the imperishable supreme Brahman in which fear does not exist for those who desire to cross over.

3. Know that the *ātman* is the rider of the chariot, the body is the chariot, reason (*buddhi*)[10] is the charioteer, and the mind (*manas*) is the reins.

4. The senses are called the horses, objects are the destinations. The wise say that the enjoyer is the *ātman* joined to the mind.

5. If one is foolish and does not hold the mind firmly, then one's senses go beyond control like the bad horses of a charioteer.

6. If one is wise and holds the mind firmly, then one's senses remain under control like the good horses of a charioteer.

7. If one is foolish without control of mind and is impure, then one can never reach the goal, but enters *saṁsāra* (the world of becoming, of birth and death).

8. If one is wise with mind fully controlled and is pure, one reaches the goal and will not be born again.

9. He reaches the end of the path, the supreme abode of Viṣṇu, if his charioteer is reason and his reins the mind.

10. Beyond the senses are the objects (goals); mind is beyond the objects; reason (*buddhi*) is beyond the mind; and the Mahān Ātmā[11] is beyond reason.

11. The Unmanifest (*Avyakta*) is beyond the Mahān Ātmā; and the Puruṣa[12] is beyond the Avyakta. Beyond the Puruṣa there is nothing. He is the final rest of everything, he is the destination of the path.

12. This hidden *ātman* does not shine in all the objects. It is seen by the subtle-minded with their subtle and sharp reason.

13. The wise should withdraw speech into mind, mind into reason, reason into the Mahān Ātmā and that into the *ātman* of peace.

14. Arise, awake, go to the sages and learn. The wise say that the path is sharp like the edge of a razor, hard to walk on, and difficult to obtain.

15. It is soundless, intangible, formless, inexhaustible. Likewise, it is tasteless, eternal and odorless. It is beginningless, endless, beyond the great, and unchanging. Knowing it, one escapes the jaws of death.

16. The wise man who has heard and narrates the ancient story of Naciketas and

the teachings of Death goes to the Brahmā-world and prospers.

17. He who, with self-control, relates the supreme secret in the assembly that discusses the Brahman or on the occasion of a death ceremony obtains endless rewards and endlessness.

Ch. 2. § 4, 1. Yama said: "The self-born forged the senses by directing them outwards (towards external objects). So man sees external objects, but not his inner *ātman*. But some steady-minded one, desiring immortality, turns his senses in the reverse direction and sees the inner *ātman*.

2. "Children (ignorant men) go after outward pleasures. They enter the net of death spread everywhere. But the steady-minded ones, knowing immortality, do not seek the permanent in the impermanent.

3. "One knows color, taste, smell, sounds, and touches, and sexual pleasures only through this (*ātman*). What else remains to be known? This verily is That.[13]

4. "That through which man knows all that is in dream and waking states is the great all-pervading *ātman*. Knowing it the wise man does not grieve. This is verily That.

5. "He who knows the *ātman*, which is the nearest to the *jīva* that enjoys the fruit of actions, and which is the lord of the past and the future, is never afraid later. This is verily That.

6. "He who knows him (Prajāpati) who was born through penance along with the other elements out of the waters, who dwells in the heart (cave), and who is known by the elements—This verily is That.

7. "He is Aditi who was born as Life and who was full (pregnant) with the deities, and who enters the heart with the elements. This verily is That.

8. "Fire exists hidden in the fire sticks, safely held like a child by the womb of the mother. He is worshiped thus by enlightened men with oblations. This verily is That.

9. "From him arises the sun and into him he sets. In him are all gods fixed, and none can be separated from him. This verily is That.

10. "What is here in this world is there in that world (of the *ātman*). One who sees many here goes from death to death.

11. "That there is no multiplicity can be known only by the mind. One goes from death to death, if one sees many here.

12. "The Lord of the past and future, Puruṣa, only of the size of the thumb, resides within the *ātman* (the body). Knowing him, one loses all fear. This verily is That.

13. "The Lord of the past and the present, the Puruṣa, is of the size of the thumb and is like fire without smoke. He is today and he will be tomorrow. This verily is That.

14. "Just as the rain, falling from the summit of a mountain, flows down the many hills, even so the man who sees all the different forms as merely different goes after them.

15. "Just as pure water poured into pure water becomes like it, so also, O Gautama,[14] does the *ātman* of the silent sage."

4. *Muṇḍaka Upaniṣad*[15]

□ The *Muṇḍaka Upaniṣad* is famous for its two doctrines, that of the two kinds of knowledge and that of the two birds. Of the two kinds of knowledge, the higher is that of the Ultimate, the ultimate ground of one's own being as an "I." The lower is the knowledge of good and evil, right and wrong, of sacrifice, of language, in short, of what we generally call arts and sciences. Of the two birds, the higher is the higher self or Spirit, which is unaffected by the good and evil of ethical actions. The lower is the finite soul, the *jīva*, the ethical and psychical person. □

Ch. 1. § 1, 3. Śaunaka, a great householder, approached Aṅgirasa with propriety and asked, "Sir, upon knowing which does all this become understood?"

4. He answered, "There are two kinds of knowledge; thus we have heard from the knowers of the Brahman teaching. They are the higher and the lower.

5. The lower is *Ṛgveda*, *Yajur-veda*, *Sāma-veda*, *Atharva-veda*[16], phonetics, ritual, grammar, etymology, meter, and

astronomy. The higher knowledge is that by which the undecaying (eternal) is known.

6. By the higher knowledge, the wise know that which is imperceptible, the ungraspable, that which has not descended from anything else, and which is without color, eyes, ears, hands, and feet; the eternal, the great, the all-pervading, the subtle, the undecaying, and the origin of everything.

7. Just as the spider creates (its web) and withdraws it (into itself), the plants arise from the earth, and the hair grows from the head and body of the living man, even so the world is born from the imperishable.

8. Through penance (desire), the Brahman expands. From it comes forth matter, life, mind, truth, the words, and the immortal fruit of actions.

Ch. 3. § 1, 1. Two birds (the Supreme and finite spirits), friends, always united, cling to the same tree (body). One of them eats the sweet fruit of the *pippala* tree (the fruit of actions); the other looks on without eating.

2. Entangled in the same tree, man (*puruṣa*) grieves powerless and bewildered. But when he sees the other, the Lord, and his power, worshiped by all, he gives up his grief.

3. When he sees Puruṣa, the shining Lord, the creator, the womb of Brahmā, then the wise man wipes out good and evil and, being pure, becomes similar to the Supreme.

5. *Aitareya Upaniṣad*[17]

□ The following passages of the *Aitareya Upaniṣad* are important for many reasons. They show, firstly, that man is a copy, an image, of the Cosmic Person from whom the gods came out; secondly, that the so-called gods have an objective, cosmic function and an individual function, i.e., a macrocosmic and a microcosmic function, the latter by being the functions of our senses and organs; thirdly, that whatever we call our enjoyment of our senses is their enjoyment also; and fourthly, that the I-consciousness of man is a replica of the Ātman. Our senses and organs cannot function without the I, just as the different deities cannot exist without the Ātman. This Upaniṣad exemplifies the inwardization of the original external, polytheistic gods by relating them to our senses, and clearly explains, although in semi-mythological terms, the trend towards an inward, spiritual monotheism and monism. The macrocosm-microcosm idea, used in ritual worship and meditation, is also distinct in this Upaniṣad. □

Ch. 1. §1, 1. In the beginning the Ātman alone existed, nothing blinked. He wanted to create the worlds.

2. He created the worlds—*ambhas* (mythological waters), *marīcī* (rays), *māra* (of death), *āpas* (ordinary waters). *Ambhas*[18] is that beyond the heavens, the seat of gods; *marīcī* is the heavens (sky); *māra* is the earth; that below it is *āpas*.

3. He said, "I have created the worlds. Let me create the rulers (protectors) of the worlds." From the waters (elements), he lifted a form[19] and made it concrete (solid).

4. He fixed his mind on it (willed, warmed it). Thus fixed upon, its mouth burst open and from the mouth came Speech (Vāk) and from Speech Fire. Its nostrils burst open; from its nostrils came Life and from Life Wind. Its eyes burst open; from the eyes Vision came out and from Vision the Sun. Its ears burst open; from its ears issued Audition and from Audition the Regions (East, and so on). Its skin burst; from skin Hair came out and from Hair Herbs and Plants. Its heart burst; from it Mind came out and from Mind Moon. Its navel burst; from the navel came Apāna[20] (the down going wind in the body) and from Apāna Death. Its penis burst; from the penis came Sperm and from Sperm Waters.

Ch. 1. § 2, 1. The deities thus created fell into this vast ocean and approached the Ātman in hunger and thirst. They said to him, "Give us an abode living in which we can obtain nourishment.

2. He brought them a cow. But they said, "It is not enough (adequate)." He brought them a horse. They said, "It is not enough."

3. He brought them a man. They said,

"Well done." Man is the well-done. The Ātman said to them, "Enter man in order."

4. Fire became Speech and entered the mouth. Wind became Life and entered the nostrils. The Sun became Vision and entered the eyes. The Regions became Audition and entered the ears. Herbs and Plants became Hair and entered the skin. The Moon became Mind and entered the heart. Death became Apāna and entered the navel. Waters became Sperm and entered the penis.

5. Hunger and Thirst said to the Ātman, "Think of an abode for us also." He said, "I shall make you partakers of the same deities." So if an offering is made to any deity, Hunger and Thirst become its partakers.

Ch. 1. § 3, 1. The Ātman thought, "These are the worlds and these are the rulers of the worlds. I shall create nourishment (food) for them."

2. He fixed his mind (concentrated his will) on the waters (elements). From the waters on which his mind was fixed upon, a form arose. That was food.

3. This food was placed before the gods, but it wanted to run away. The deities tried to catch it through Speech, but failed. Had the deities succeeded in catching food through Speech, then men could have eaten by uttering, "Food."

4. Then the deities tried to catch the food through Life, but failed. If they succeeded, then men could have eaten by merely smelling.

5. Then they wanted to catch it through Vision, but failed. Had they succeeded, then men could have eaten by merely looking.

6. Then they tried through the ear, but in vain. Had they succeeded, then men could have eaten by hearing about food.

7. Then they tried through Touch and failed. Had they succeeded, then men could have eaten by merely touching.

8. Next they tried through Mind and failed. Had they succeeded, men could have eaten by thinking of food.

9. They tried with penis and failed. Had they succeeded, they could have eaten by ejecting food.

10. Then they tried with Apāna and succeeded in getting it. This is the catcher of food, this Wind, the life of which is food.

11. Then the Ātman thought, "How can the deities exist without me? By which path should I enter the body? If Speech is the diety of speaking, if Wind is the deity of breathing, if the eye performs the function of seeing, if the ear hears, the skin touches, the mind thinks, Apāna carries food inside, and the penis ejects, then what shall I become (what function shall I perform)?"

12. Then he made a hole at the top of the skull and entered through it. So this hole is called Vidṛti (hole), the blissful.[21] It has three places and three dreams (experiences).[22] This, this, and this are its places.[23]

6. *Taittirīya Upaniṣad*[24]

□ The reader may note that in the selections from this Upaniṣad, there are (1) advice to the students after their education, (2) a description of the different levels of the *ātman*, and (3) the teaching that the Brahman is the most blissful, and its bliss more intense than any bliss which men and gods can have. Also note that charity (giving) is important. The best form of it is that done with divine knowledge. One should give because one has faith in religion or is without such faith, or one has a lot of wealth and is giving anyway, or because he is ashamed of not giving when others are giving, or because he understands the cosmic significance of giving. □

Ch. 1. § 8, 1. The Brahman is Om. All this is Om. This Om is said in consent, as when they say it when they mean, "Let us hear," and hear. Saying Om, they sing the Sāma hymns. Saying Om Som, they sing weapon-like hymns. Saying Om, the Adhvaryu priest utters every word. Saying Om, the Brahma priest sprinkles (sacred water). Saying Om, the kindling of the sacrificial fire is sanctioned. The Brāhmaṇa starts his study with Om, hoping to attain the Brahman. He attains the Brahman.

Ch. 1. § 9. *Ṛta* and reading and explaining; truth and reading and explaining; penance and reading and explaining; self-control and reading and explaining;

endurance and reading and explaining; keeping the five fires and reading and explaining; guests and reading and explaining; oblations in the Āhita fire and reading and explaining; human activities[25] and reading and explaining; nuptial ceremonies and reading and explaining; procreative activities and reading and explaining; births and reading and explaining: all these have to be performed. Of all these, the truth-speaking Rāthītara says, truth is the highest; for the teacher Pauriśiṣṭi, engaged perpetually in penance, the highest is penance; Nāka, the son of Mudgala says that the highest is reading and explaining. That verily is penance, That verily is penance.

Ch. 1. § 11. 1. After instructing the Veda, the teacher commands the student:

"Speak truth, Do the right. Do not neglect studies. Bring pleasing gifts to the teacher and do not break the family line. Do not violate truth. Do not neglect right conduct. Do not fall from happiness. Do not ignore prosperity. Do not neglect reading and explaining. Do not forget the rites to gods and ancestors.

2. "Treat your mother as a god. Treat your father as a god. Treat your teacher as a god. Treat your guest as a god. Perform only those actions that are unreproachable, but not the others. Whatever be the deeds done by us (teachers), do only those (from among them) that are good, but not the others.

3. "Offer seat and rest to those Brāhmaṇas among us who are the best. Give with faith. Give even without faith. Give because of wealth. Give because of shame. Give because of fear. Give with knowledge.

4. "If you have doubts about a particular act (rite) or a particular ethical act (right in society), act like those Brāhmaṇas who are critical minded, skilled, and unwavering, never lose their temper, and who always desire the true law (*dharma*).

5. "In dealing with men with whom you ought to have no dealings, deal with them, as the Brāhmaṇas who are critical minded, skilled, unwavering, and who never lose their temper and are desirous of the true law, do.

6. "This is the command; this is the commendation. This is the essence of the Upaniṣads. This is the divine command. This has to be followed. This has to be acted upon."

Ch. 2. 1. He who knows the Brahman obtains the Supreme. This is said: The Brahman is Truth, Consciousness, and Infinity. He who knows that which is hidden in the cave (heart), the Supreme Ether, obtains all his desires along with the all-knowing Brahman.

From it, this Ātman, ether is born, from ether wind, from wind fire, from fire water, and from water earth. From earth are born plants, from plants is born food, from food sperm, and from sperm man (*Puruṣa*). This man is made up of food and water.

Of the food-born Puruṣa, this is the head, this is the right side, this is the left side. This (between the right and left sides, viz., the body) is the *ātman*.

2. All beings living on the earth are born of food. They live by food. At the end they enter food.

Food is the highest of the elements. It is, therefore, the medicine of all. The elements are born of it; having been born, they grow by it. It is called food because it is eaten and eats all beings.

Inward to this, which is made of food and drink, is a different *ātman*, that which is the life-principle (vital principle). The former is filled with (pervaded by) the latter. It is really like man (*Puruṣa*). Its form is like (but not the same as) the human form of the former (physical human form).

Its head is *prāṇa*.[26] Its right side is *vyāna*. Its left side is *apāna*. Ether is its *ātman*. Earth is its tail (hind part) and base. This is the verse:

> 3. The gods depend on Prāṇa,[27] so also men and beasts live. Prāṇa is the life of beings. So it is called the life of all, a life of hundred years.

They obtain a whole life who worship the Brahman as Prāṇa. Prāṇa is the life of beings and is, therefore, called whole-life. This is the *ātman* of the previous *ātman*.

Inward to this, the vital *ātman*, is another *ātman*, the mind-*ātman*. The former is pervaded by the latter. This is like man, following the likeness of the former to man. Its head is *Yajur-veda*; its right side is the *Ṛgveda*; its left side is the *Sāma-veda*. Commands (the *Brāhamaṇa* texts) are its *ātman*. The *Atharva-veda* (*atharvāṅgirasa*) is its tail and base. So runs the verse:

4. He who knows the bliss of the Brahman, unable to reach which all words along with mind return, never fears.

Of this, the previous one, this is the *ātman*. Inward to this, the mind-*ātman*, is another, the reason-*ātman*. The former is filled with the latter. This is like man, in the likeness of the former to man. Its head is faith (decision), *ṛta* is its right side, Truth is its left side. Yoga (steadiness of *buddhi*, *citta*) is its *ātman*. Mahas[28] is its tail and base. Thus runs the verse:

5. Reason (*vijñāna*, *buddhi*) spreads the sacrifice and all its activities. All gods worship Reason, the Brahman, the eldest. If one knows that Reason is the Brahman, one never lapses and, leaving back the sins of the body, obtains all the desires.

Of the previous *ātman*, this is the *ātman*. Inward to this reason-*ātman*, there is another *ātman*, the blissful. The former is filled with the latter. It is like man, in the likeness of the former to man. Its head is the pleasure derived from seeing desired objects. Its right side is the pleasure from obtaining the desired objects. Bliss is its *ātman*. The Brahman is its tail and base. Thus runs the verse:

6. He who knows (thinks) the Brahman as nonbeing becomes nonbeing. If he knows that the Brahman is being, then the wise know such a knower as a being (as not nonexistent).

Of the previous *ātman*, this is the *ātman*. Here the questions arise: Where does the man who is ignorant of the Brahman go after death? Or does he not go anywhere? What does he become after death? Or does he not become anything?

The Ātman desired to become many through creation. He performed penance. Then he created all this, whatever this is. After creating it, he entered it.

Entering it, he became the visible (earth, water, fire) and the invisible (air and ether) elements, the determinate and the indeterminate, the supported and the unsupported, the sensient and the insensient, truth and untruth, the ultimate Truth and whatever this is. All this is called the Truth. Thus runs the verse:

7. All this was nonbeing at first. Out of it was born being. It created itself out of itself. So it is called the good creator.

That which is well done is verily pleasure. This world obtains it and become blissful. If it is not bliss residing in our heart, who will care to inhale and exhale? The same bliss-*ātman* makes one happy. When man obtains his abode in the invisible, bodiless, unexplained, abodeless, fearless, he attains fearlessness.

If he acknowledges the smallest difference, he will have fear. That is the fear of the learned who merely thinks.[29] Thus runs the verse:

8. Afraid of him, the wind blows; afraid of him the Sun rises, Indra and Agni (Fire) are afraid of him, and Death, the fifth, runs away.

Now comes the discussion on bliss.

(a) Let there be a youth, a good youth, a teacher, or a leader, well-built and strong. Let the whole world be filled with riches for him. His bliss is the human bliss.

(b) Hundred such human blisses are equal to one bliss of the man who has become a Gandharva[30] or of the man learned in the Veda and not spoiled by passions.

(c) Hundred such blisses of the man who has become a Gandharva are equal to one bliss of a divine Gandharva or of the man learned in the Veda and not spoiled by passions.

(d) Hundred such blisses of a divine Gandharva are equal to one bliss of the ancestor residing in the long-lasting worlds or of the man learned in the Veda and not spoiled by passions.

(e) Hundred blisses of such an ancestor residing in the long-lasting worlds are equal to one bliss of a god born in heaven or of the man learned in the Veda and not spoiled by passions.

(f) Hundred blisses of such a god are equal to one bliss of the man who reaches the higher gods through actions (the man who has become a god through ethical and religious actions) or of the man who is learned in the Veda and not spoiled by passions.

(g) Hundred blisses of such a man are equal to one bliss of a god (god by birth) or of the man who is learned in the Veda and not spoiled by passions.

(h) Hundred blisses of a god are equal to one bliss of Indra or of the man who is learned in the Veda and not spoiled by passions.

(i) Hundred blisses of Indra are equal to one bliss of Bṛhaspati (the priest of gods) or of the man who is learned in the Veda and not spoiled by passions.

(j) Hundred blisses of Bṛhaspati are equal to one bliss of Prajāpati (Virāt, whose body is the three worlds) or of the man who is learned in the Veda and not spoiled by passions.

(k) Hundred blisses of Prajāpati are equal to one bliss of the Brahman or of the man who is learned in the Veda and not spoiled by passions.

(l) He who is in man and he who is in the Sun are the same. He who knows this, after leaving this world, goes out of this *ātman* made of food; he goes out of the *ātman* constituted by the vital principle; he goes out of the *ātman* that is reason; he goes out of the *ātman* that is bliss. Thus runs the verse:

He who knows the bliss of the Brahman, whom words cannot reach and so return (disappointed) along with mind, fears nothing. The question, "What good have I left undone, what sin have I committed?" does not torment him. The wise man reaches the Ātman.

He who knows this sees both (merit and demerit) as the Ātman itself. This is the great secret.

7. *Praśna Upaniṣad*[31]

□ The selection also shows that the gods are being inwardized, made psychological and spiritual, and that the very ancient polytheism is being transformed into a spiritual monotheism and monism. The shining senses, mind, and so on, functions that make men conscious and act, are gods and the shining (appearing to consciousness) cosmic elements also are gods. □

Ch. 2. 1. Then Vaidarbhī Bhārgava asked Pippalāda, "How many gods support the creature? How many illumine the body (make it conscious)? Which among them is the greatest?"

2. Pippalāda replied, "The gods are Ether, Wind, Fire, Water, Earth, Speech, Mind, Eye (Vision), Ear (Audition), and so forth (i.e., Nose, Tongue, Skin). After illumining it, they say, "We shall support this body and act."

3. The highest of them, Prāṇa, said, "Do not be deluded. Verily, dividing myself into five parts,[32] I support the body and act."

4. They were not convinced. From pride, he (Prāṇa) rose up. When he rose up, all the others also rose up. When he settled down, all the others settled down. This is like the bees that fly up when the king (queen) bee flies up, and settle down when he settled down. Likewise, Speech, Mind, Vision, Audition, and so on, were satisfied; they praised Prāṇa:

He is Fire, he is the Sun that warms.
He is the cloud, he is Maghavan (Indra).
He is Wind, He is Earth, he is the shining god, Moon.
He is all that is being, nonbeing, and immortality.

8. *Chāndogya Upaniṣad*[33]

□ The selection shows not only how, according to the Vedic sages, man is born, but also how the idea of sacrifice was transformed. Every creative act is a sacrifice; without something sacrificing itself, nothing can be born. Death means going back to the origins and becoming one with the creative process, which is the Cosmic Sacrifice. We should trace back this idea to the Hymn to Puruṣa (see Ch. 1, selection 15). We should note that it is a mistake to dismiss sacrificial religion as ritualism and its philosophy as a philosophy of mere ritualism. The idea of sacrifice was developed into one of grand religious and philosophical significance. The Aryan awareness of this significance seems to be at least as old as the Hymn to Puruṣa. □

Ch. 5, pt. 3, § 4, 1. O Gautama, that (the highest world) is the sacrificial Fire; its fuel is the Sun; the rays are the smoke; the day is the flame; the Moon is the coals; the stars are the sparks.

2. The gods sacrifice faith (*śrāddhā*, will, conviction) into that Fire. King Soma is born from this oblation.

§ 5, 1. The cloud, O Gautama, is the sacrificial Fire; Wind is its fuel; the sky is the smoke; lightning is the flame; thunderbolt is the coals; the roars are the sparks.

2. In this sacrificial Fire, the gods, sacrifice king Soma. Rain is born from this oblation.

§ 6, 1. O Gautama, Earth is the sacrificial Fire. In it year is the fuel. Space is the smoke. Night is the flame. Quarters (East, and so on) are the coals. Intermediate quarters are the sparks.

2. In this Fire, the gods sacrifice rain. From this oblation food is born.

§ 7, 1. Man, O Gautama, is the Fire. Speech is the fuel. *Prāṇa* is the smoke. Tongue is the flame. Vision is the coals. Audition is the sparks.

2. In this Fire, the gods sacrifice food. From this oblation sperm is born.

§ 8, 1. Woman, O Gautama, is the sacrificial Fire. Her sexual organ is the fuel. Indicating to her is the smoke. Womb is the flame. Inserting is the coals. Pleasure is the sparks.

2. In this fire, the gods sacrifice semen. From this oblation is born the embryo.

§ 9, 1. Thus in this fifth oblation, waters become human words. The embryo, thus surrounded by the foetus for nine or ten months and sleeping inside, becomes full (of organs) and is born.

2. Being born, he lives his span of life. When he dies, they carry him to the allotted place for the Fire, from which he was born.

9. *Bṛhadāraṇyaka Upaniṣad*[34]: Bālāki and Ajātaśatru

□ The selection shows that the Brahman is the Truth of all truths and also that the gods, mistaken by the Aryans of the earlier times for the Brahman, were by the time of the Upaniṣads acknowledged as the deities or the persons residing in the various elements, senses, and so on. The elements were not then taken as gods, but as the bodies or manifestations of gods. □

Ch. 2, § 1, 1. The proud Bālāki, a descendant of the Gargas, a teacher, told Ajātaśatru, king of Kāśī, that he would teach the Brahman. The king said, "I shall give a thousand (cows) for these words. Why do people run there, saying, 'O Janaka, O Janaka'?"[35]

2. Bālāki said, "The Person (Puruṣa) seen in the sun—him I worship as the Brahman." Ajātaśatru said, "No, no, I do not discuss him. I know him. I worship him as the king, the forehead of all beings. He who worships him as such becomes the forehead, king, of all beings."

3. Bālāki said, "The Person in the moon—him I worship as the Brahman." Ajātaśatru said, "No, no, I do not discuss him. I know him. I worship him as the great king, Soma, with his white robes. For him who worships the moon as such, the Soma juice will be pressed everyday; for him food never decreases."

4. Bālāki said, "The Person in the lightning—him I worship as the Brahman." Ajātaśatru said, "No, no, I do not discuss him. I know him. I worship him as the brilliant. He who worships him as such—the descendants of such a person will be brilliant."

5. Bālāki said, "The Person in space—him I worship as the Brahman." Ajātaśatru said, "No, no, I do not discuss him. I know him. I worship him as the Full, the Unmoving. He who worships him as such will have offspring and cattle to his satisfaction and they do not leave this world."

6. Bālāki said, "The Person in the wind—him I worship as the Brahman." Ajātaśatru said, "No, no, I do not discuss him. I know him. I worship him as Indra, the unconquerable, the unconquered army. He who worships him as such becomes the conqueror, the unconquered, the conqueror of every one born of another.

7. Bālāki said, "The Person in the fire—him I worship as the Brahman." Ajātaśatru said, "No, no, I do not discuss him. I know him. I worship him as the digester of poison. He who worships him as such becomes the digester of poison, his progeny becomes the digester of poison (also meaning the killer of enemies).

8. Bālāki said, "The Person in water—him I worship as the Brahman." Ajātaśatru said, "No, no, I do not discuss him. I know him. I worship him as the reflection. He who worships him as such will be the reflection of the sacred teachings, not a distortion; and a similar reflection will be his progeny."

9. Bālāki said, "The Person in the mirror—him I worship as the Brahman." Ajātaśatru said, "No, no, I do not discuss him. I know him. I worship him as the shining one. He who worships him as such becomes a shining one. His progeny will be shining ones. And they outshine all with whom they come into contact."

10. Bālāki said, "The sound that rises following a man walking—that I worship as the Brahman." Ajātaśtru said, "No, no, I do not discuss it. I worship it as life. He who worships him thus goes through his whole life in this world. His life will not leave him before time."

11. Bālāki said, "The Person in the quarters (East, etc.,)—him I worship as the Brahman." Ajātaśatru said, "No, no, I do not discuss him. I worship him as the inseparable Dyad (the inseparable gods, Aśvins, who are two). He who worships him as such becomes an accompanied one (i.e., one who is never alone, lonely, unprotected). From him the crowd (of relations and servants) never parts."

12. Bālāki said, "The Person constituted by the shadow—him I worship as the Brahman." Ajātaśatru said, "No, no, I do not discuss him. I worship him as death. He who worships him as death obtains all his life in this world. Death does not approach him before time.

13. Bālāki said, "The Person in the *ātman* (the body)—him I worship as the Brahman." Ajātaśatru said, "No, no, I do not discuss him. I worship him as the embodied. He who worships as such will be embodied. His progeny will be embodied." Then Bālāki kept silent.

14. Ajātaśatru asked, "Only so far?" Bālāki answered, "Indeed, only so far. Now I want you to instruct me."

15. Ajātaśatru said, "It is contrary to law that a Brāhmaṇa approaches a Kṣatriya for instruction about the Brahman. Yet I shall make you know him." Taking Bālāki by hand, he rose up. They went to a person sleeping. They called him, "Oh great-robed Soma, O king." He did not get up. Ajātaśatru then shook the man with his hand and woke him up. He rose up.

16. Ajātaśatru asked, "This man who was asleep and who had been a conscious person—where was he then (in sleep) and whence has he come?" Bālāki did not know the answer.

17. Ajātaśatru said, "This conscious person, when he was asleep, taking the consciousness of all the *prāṇas* by means of his own consciousness, sleeps in this space (*ākāśa*) within the heart (*buddhi*, reason).[36] When this person (*puruṣa*) takes away (withdraws) the senses (inwards), it is said that he sleeps. Then smell is taken away, speech is taken away, vision is taken away, hearing is taken away, mind is taken away.

18. "When he goes dreaming, those worlds are his. He becomes, as though, a great king or a great and holy Brahmin, or he has a fall. Just as a great king, taking his people, goes as he likes in his kingdom, this person also, taking his *praṇas*, roams in his own body.

19. "When this person falls into deep (dreamless) sleep and sees nothing, he sleeps in the pericardium, having crept out from the heart to it through the 72,000 arteries (veins) called *hitas*. Just as a body, a great king, or a great Brahmin sleeps with the greatest delight (bliss), this person also sleeps.

20. "As a spider moves by its threads, as small sparks issue out of fire, even so do all the *prāṇas*,[37] all the worlds, all gods, all elements, come from the *ātman*. Its sacred teaching is, 'It is the Truth of Truth.' The *prāṇas* are the Truth, this (the *ātman*) is its Truth."

10. *Bṛhadāraṇyaka Upaniṣadṣ:* Meditation on the Sacrificial Horse

□ The horse sacrifice was one of the most important for the ancient Aryans of India and was performed by emperors to establish their title. But this passage asks the sacrificer to think of the horse as the cosmos and then sacrifice it. He is thus to sacrifice the cosmos, and is, therefore, greater than the cosmos sacrificed. In another sense, he sacrifices, gives up, the world for the sake of the Supreme Spirit. We see here also that the idea of sacrifice for the sake of worldly values is being transformed and spiritualized. We should relate this meditation on the sacrificial horse to the meditation on the Sacrificial Altar (Fire Altar). Such meditations are found in the *Brāhmaṇas* also. This meditation on the sacrificial horse occurs also in *Śatapada Brāhmaṇa*, 10:6, 4. □

Ch. 1. § 1, 1. Om verily, the head of the sacrificial horse is the dawn. The sun is its eye. Wind is its *prāṇa* (life principle). Its open mouth is the *vaiśvānara* (cosmic) fire. The year is its body. Heaven is its back. The sky is its stomach. The earth is its hoofs. The quarters are its sides. The intermediate quarters are its ribs. The seasons are its limbs. Months and fortnights are its joints. Days and nights are its feet. Stars are its bones. Atmosphere is its flesh. Sands are its food (not yet digested in the stomach). Rivers are its arteries. Mountains are its breasts. Plants and herbs are its hair. Its forepart (from the navel) is the sun rising and its hind part is the sun setting. When it yawns, it illuminates. When it shakes, it thunders. When it urinates, it rains. Speech is its voice.

2. Verily, the day with its power arose in front of the horse for its sake. Its origin is the eastern sea. The night with its power arose behind the horse for its sake. Its origin is the western sea. Verily, the day and night arose on both sides of the horse, the great power. As the *haya* (one kind of horse), it carried the gods. As the *vāji* (a second kind of horse), it carried the Gandharvas. As the *arva* (a third kind of horse), it carried the demons. And as the *aśva* (a fourth kind of horse), it carried men. Its relative is the ocean; its origin is the ocean.

11. *Bṛhadāraṇyaka Upaniṣad:* Creation by the Ātman

Ch. 1. § 4, 1. In the beginning all this was the Ātman in the form of a person. He looked around and saw none else. He said first, "I am." From this is born the name (word), "I." So when called, man first says, "It is I." Then he gives whatever name he has. He is a person (*puruṣa*) because he burnt up all the sins (*pur* = formerly, *uṣ* = burn) before all this (was born). He who knows this burns him who wants to be his superior.

2. He was afraid. So one who is alone is afraid. He thought, "Why am I afraid when there is none other?" Then his fear left him. From whom is one afraid? Only from a second.

3. But he was not happy. So one who is alone is not happy. He wanted a second. He was like a man and a woman in the unity of embrace. He divided such a self of his into two. Then husband and wife were born. Then like Yājñavalkya, he said, "This, my body, is like a half fragment." This is empty space, which is filled by the woman. He copulated with her. Men were born from it.

4. Then she thought, "How can he have intercourse with me after producing me from himself? I shall conceal myself." She became a cow; the other became a bull and had intercourse with her. From it all cows and bulls were born. She became a mare and he became a stallion. She became a female ass and he became a male ass. He had intercourse with her. Therefrom were born the single-hoofed. She became a female goat and he became a he-goat. She became a ewe and he became a ram. He copulated with her. Therefore goats and sheep were born. Thus he created all the couples down to the ants.

5. He then knew, "I am the creation. I have created all this." So the name of creation arose. He who knows this will be in this creation.

17. In the beginning all this was only the Ātman. He wished, "Let there be a wife for me so that I can procreate. Let there be

wealth for me so that I can perform (ethical and religious) actions." Such is desire. Greater than this, none can obtain even if he desires. So even now when one is lonely, one wishes, "May I have a wife for procreating, may I have wealth for performing actions." So long as one does not get any of these, one considers himself incomplete. His completeness lies here: mind is the Ātman, speech his wife, Prāṇa his progeny. Vision is his human wealth, as he obtains wealth through it. His audition is his divine wealth (knowledge), for he gets it by hearing (the Veda). His body is his action, for he performs actions with it.

This is the fivefold sacrifice. The animal (sacrificed) is fivefold.[38] The person sacrificing is fivefold. The whole world, whatever it is, is fivefold. He who knows this obtains all this.

12. *Bṛhadāraṇyaka Upaniṣad:* Maitreyī and Yājñavalkya

Ch. 2. § 4, 1. "O Maitreyī," said Yājñavalkya, "I am going above this present (householder's) stage. Now I shall settle between you and Kātyāyanī."[39]

Maitreyī said, "Can I become immortal, Sir, if the whole earth filled with riches is mine?" Yājñavalkya said, "No, your life will be like that of those who have every means. There is no hope of immortality through riches."

3. Maitreyī said, "What shall I do with that by which I cannot get immortality? Sir, whatever you know, please tell me."

4. Yājñavalkya said, "You are dear to me. You speak what is dear. Come and sit down, I shall explain. Fix your mind on what is explained."

5. He said, "Behold, the husband is dear to the wife not for the husband's sake, but for the sake of her self. Nor is the wife dear to the husband for her sake, but for the sake of his own self. The sons are dear not for their sake, but for the sake of one's self. Riches are dear not for their sake, but for the sake of one's self. Kṣatrahood (heroism) is dear not for its own sake, but for the sake of one's self. The worlds are dear not for their own sake, but for the sake of one's self. The gods are dear not for their own sake, but for the sake of one's self. The elements are dear not for their sake, but for the sake of one's self. Hence this self (*ātman*) has to be seen, reflected upon, and meditated upon. O Maitreyī, all this becomes known by seeing this self, by hearing it, reflecting upon it, and meditating upon it.[40]

6. "Brahmaṇhood (being a Brahmin) leaves him who knows it in anything different from the *ātman*. Kṣatrahood deserts him who knows it in anything different from the *ātman*. The worlds desert him who knows them in anything different from the *ātman*. The gods desert him who knows them as anything different from the *ātman*. The elements desert him who knows them as anything different from the *ātman*. Everything leaves him who sees it in anything different from the *ātman*.

7. "Just as when a drum is beaten, one cannot catch its external sounds, but catches them by catching the drum or its beats;

8. "Just as, when a conch shell is being blown, one cannot catch its external sounds, but catches them by catching the conch shell or the blower;

9. "Just as when a *vīna* (a stringed musical instrument) is played, one cannot catch its external sounds, but catches them by catching the *vīna* or the player of the *vīna*;

10. "Just as from fire lit by damp fuel smokes separate themselves and come out; even so all this is verily the breath of the great Being. All these, *Ṛgveda*, *Yajur-veda*, *Sāma-veda*, *Atharvāṅgirasa* (*Atharva-veda*), history, epic, science, Upaniṣads, verses (meters), aphorisms, explanations, commentaries, are the breathings of this (*ātman*).

11. "Just as the ocean is the single abode of all waters; the sense of touch is the single abode of all touches (cool, and so on); the sense of taste is the single abode of all tastes; the sense of smell is the single abode of all smells; the sense of vision is the single abode of all colors; the sense of audition is the single abode of all sounds; mind (*manas*) is the single abode of all intentions; the heart (*buddi*, reason) is the single abode of all sciences; the hands

are the single abode of all actions; the sex organ is the single abode of all pleasures; the excretory organ is the single abode of all excretions; the feet are the single abode of all paths; speech is the single abode of all the Vedas.

12. "Just as a lump of salt thrown in water dissolves in it and cannot be picked up again and whatever is taken out is salty, even so, O Maitreyī, the great Being, endless and limitless, is massive consciousness. This, O Maitreyī, I tell you." Thus spoke Yājñavalkya.

13. Maitreyī said, "Sir, herein, in saying that there is no consciousness after death, you bewilder me." But he said, "I speak nothing bewildering. This is sufficient for the understanding.

14. "Where there is duality as it were, there one smells another; one sees another; one hears another; one speaks to another; one thinks of another; one knows another. But when all become one's *ātman*, then who smells what, who sees what, who hears whom, who thinks of whom, who knows whom? Through whom one knows all this—through whom can he be known? O Maitreyī, how can one know the knower?"[41]

13. *Bṛhadāraṇyaka Upaniṣad:* Janaka and Yājñavalkya

Ch. 4. § 3, 1. Yājñavalkya went to king Janaka of Videha. He thought, "I shall not speak of anything (spiritual)." But when they were carrying on a discussion in connection with a sacrificial fire, Yājñavalkya gave Janaka a boon; and Janaka asked permission to raise any question he liked. The other granted it. Then the king asked a question.

2. "O Yājñavalkya, what is the light of the person (*puruṣa*)?" "The sun is the light, O King. With the sun, indeed, as the light, he sits, moves, does his work, and returns." "It is so, Yājñavalkya."

3. "O Yājñavalkya, when the sun sets, what is the light of the person?" "The moon is his light. With moon as his light, he sits, moves, does his work, and returns." "It is so, Yājñavalkya."

4. "O Yājñavalkya, when the sun sets and when the moon goes down, what is the light of the person?" "Fire is his light. With fire as his light, he sits, moves, does his work, and returns." "It is so, Yājñavalkya."

5. "O Yājñavalkya, when the sun and moon set and when fire is extinguished, what is the light of the person?" "Speech is his light. With speech as his light, he sits, moves, does his work, and returns. For this reason, O King, one does not see one's hand in darkness; but if a voice is raised, one goes there straight." "It is so, Yājñavalkya."

6. "O Yājñavalkya, when the sun and moon set, when fire is extinguished and speech is silent, what is the light of the person?" "The *ātman* is his light. With the *ātman* as his light, he sits, moves, does his work, and returns."

7. "Which is the *ātman*?" "It is he among the *prāṇas*, is made up of consciousness, the light shining in the heart (*buddhi*), and who coincides (identifies himself) with it and moves in both the worlds, as though, thinking and doing the functions (of senses and organs). He becomes the dream and leaves this world containing the forms of Death (i.e., the forms of becoming, birth and death).

8. "The person, being born and obtaining a body, is touched by sins. Departing at death, he leaves back his sins.

9. "There are only two places (states) for this person, this and the place in the other (next birth). The third, the intermediate place, is dream. Staying in this intermediate place, he sees both the places, this and the other (of next birth). When the other place is there, according to his merits and demerits, he holds it and sees his joys and evils. When this person dreams, he takes a small part (impressions only) of this world that is full, leaves himself (the body of the waking state), creates himself (dream body), and sleeps by his own luster, by his own light. He himself becomes the light.

10. "There are no chariots there, no horses, no roads. He creates chariots, horses, and roads. There are no blisses, no pleasures, no delights. He creates blisses, pleasures, and delights. There are no lakes, no tanks, and no rivers. He creates

lakes, tanks and rivers. He is the agent (creator).

19. "As a fatigued kite or falcon in the sky, having descended in various ways, folding its wings, enters its nest, this person hastens to the state, in which, asleep, he desires nothing and sees no dreams.

21. "That indeed is his form without desire, sin, and fear. As a man, embraced by his beloved, knows nothing outside and nothing within, even so this person embraced by the *ātman* of massive consciousness knows nothing outside and nothing inside. That verily is his form of gratified desires, the form in which the *ātman* is the desired, the form of no desires and of no fears.

22. "There a father is no father, a mother no mother, the worlds no worlds, the gods no gods, the Vedas no Vedas. There a thief is no thief, the embryo-destroyer is no embryo-destroyer, a *cāṇḍāla* (a son born of a Śūdra father and a Brahmin mother) no *cāṇḍāla*, a *paulkasa* (a son of a Śūdra father and a Kṣatriya mother) no *paulkasa*, a mendicant no mendicant, an ascetic no ascetic. He is not followed by merit, he is not followed by sin. He becomes one who has gone beyond the sorrows of the heart.

23. "Indeed, although he does not see, seeing he does not see. There can be no losing of seeing for a seer by nature, for he is imperishable. There is no second there so that he could see something separate (from himself).

31. "Where there is as though another, then one sees another, one smells another, one tastes another, one hears another, one thinks of another, one touches another, one knows another.

32. "He, the world of the Brahman, the knower, becomes the single nondual ocean, O King." Thus Yājñavalkya instructed him. This is the supreme destiny, his supreme wealth, his supreme world, his supreme bliss. The other beings live only with a part of this bliss.

34. Having enjoyed this state of deep sleep, having seen merit and sin, he hastens in the reverse order, in the reverse origination (from deep sleep to dream and from dream to the waking state) to the waking state.

35. As a cart, fully loaded, goes creaking, so this *ātman* (man), mounted by the *ātman* of massive consciousness, goes out groaning, when the person breathes up (i.e., dies).

36. When he becomes small (weak), either through old age or disease, just as a mango, fig, or berry loosens itself from its bond, so this person free himself from these (body's) limbs, hastens in the respective order to the respective wombs for life (new births).

37. Just as noblemen, executive officers, charioteers, and village officials wait with food, drinks, and lodgings for an arriving king, so all the elements provide for this person and say, "He is coming, he is arriving, this Brahman is coming, this Brahman is arriving."

38. Just as noblemen, executive officers, charioteers, and village officials collect around a king departing, so all the *prāṇas* gather round the person at the end when he breathes his last.

Ch. 4. § 4, 1. When this *ātman* becomes weak, it becomes insensible (unconscious) as it were. Then the *prāṇas* gather around him. Then he takes his psychic parts and enters his heart (*buddhi*). When this person with the activity of vision (eye) withdraws and goes inwards, he becomes unconscious of the forms (colors, and so on).

2. They say: He becomes an integrality (unity) and does not see. He becomes an integrality and does not smell. He becomes an integrality and does not taste. He becomes an integrality and does not speak. He becomes an integrality and does not hear. He becomes an integrality and does not think. He becomes an integrality and does not touch. He becomes an integrality and does not know. Then the peak of his heart (*buddhi*) shines. With its light, the *ātman* leaves. After him, who may leave through the eye, the upper part of the skull, or any other part of the body, Prāṇa leaves. After Prāṇa leaves, other *prāṇas* leave. He becomes one with consciousness. His knowledge and actions (good and evil)

and the potencies thereof accompanying him, he is conscious.

3. Just as the caterpillar, reaching the end of one blade of grass and placing its forepart on another, draws the hind part, even so this *ātman*, destroying this body, crossing *avidyā* (the unconscious) and occupying another abode (body), withdraws itself (from the previous body).

5. Indeed, the *ātman* is the Brahman, made up of reason (*vijñāna*, rational consciousness), mind, Prāṇa, vision, audition, earth, water, wind, ether, fire, nonfire, desire, nondesire, anger, nonanger, merit, demerit, and everything. He becomes as he did, and as he conducted himself. The doer of good becomes good, the doer of evil becomes evil. He becomes meritorious by meritorious actions, he becomes sinful by sinful actions. So they say, "The person is made up of desires." He becomes as he desires. By whatever fruit of actions he is made, that kind of action he performs. Whatever actions he does, that (kind of fruit, good or evil) he obtains.

6. Thus runs the verse:

He is immersed in that action (*karma*) in which his subtle mind is stuck.
Reaching the end of the fruit of actions he has performed here.
He who desires (pleasures) comes again to this world to perform actions.
But he who does not desire anything, who is without desires, the roots of whose desires are destroyed,
Who has obtained all he desired, who desires the *ātman*—
His *prāṇa* does not leave (he becomes immortal). He being the Brahman attains the Brahman.

22. Verily he is the great, unborn *ātman*, the conscious among the *prāṇas* (senses, and so on) and sleeps in the space (*ākāśa*, ether) in the heart (*buddhi*). He is the controller of all, ruler of all, lord of all. He does not increase by good actions and does not decrease by the evil ones. He is the ruler of all, he is the lord of all elements, he is the protector of all elements. He is the dam to separate these worlds. The Brahmins desire to know him by learning the Vedas and through sacrifice, charity, penance, and fasting. Knowing him, they become silent. Desiring him as their destiny, the wanderers (wandering monks) wander. It is this that made the ancient learned men not to desire progeny, saying, "What shall we, whose world is this *ātman*, do with progeny?" Leaving the desire for progeny, wealth, and the world, they live by begging. The desire for progeny is the desire for wealth; the desire for wealth is the desire for the world. All this is not the *ātman*, all this is not the *ātman* (*neti*, *neti*). The unseizable cannot be seized, the indestructible cannot be destroyed, the unattachable cannot be attached. The unbound does not suffer, it is not hurt. The two do not encompass him: "I have committed sin" and "I have done good." These are the two. He transcends them. The committed and the uncommitted do not hurt him.[42]

14. *Māṇḍūkya Upaniṣad*

1. This syllable, Om, is all this. Its explanation is: All that is past, present, and future is the syllable Om. That which is beyond the three times is also the syllable Om only.

2. All this is the Brahman. The *ātman* is the Brahman. This *ātman* has four parts (states).

3. That in the waking state, with consciousness turned outwards,[43] with seven limbs,[44] with nineteen gates,[45] the enjoyer of the gross (elements), is the first state and is called *vaiśvānara* (the world man or person).

4. That in the dream, with consciousness within, with seven limbs, with nineteen gates, the enjoyer of the subtle (elements), is the second state and is called *taijasa* (the person made up of psychic energy).

5. Where he is asleep, does not desire anything, does not see any dream, is deep sleep. That which is deep sleep, is integrated, is only a mass of consciousness, is full of bliss and enjoys bliss, and whose gate is consciousness, is the third state and is called *prājña* (that which is made up of consciousness).

6. He is the lord of all, he is the knower of all, he is the inner pervader, he is the womb (source of waking and dream

experiences). All beings originate in him and enter him.

7. They consider the fourth (state) as neither inward consciousness, not outward consciousness, nor both, nor massive consciousness, nor knowing, nor unknowing. It is unseen, undealable, ungraspable, uncharacterized, unthinkable, unnameable; it is the essence of the cognition of the one *ātman*, the cessation of the world, the tranquil, the benign, the nondual. That is the *ātman*, that has to be known.

15. Identity Statements

□ The Identity Statements, called the Great Statements (sentences, *mahāvākyas*), teach the essential identity of the world, the *ātman*, and the Brahman. Here is the teaching of the identity of the microcosmos with the macrocosmos. The fully developed microcosmos is man, in and by whom this identity can be fully realized. □

1. Verily, *all this is the Brahman* (*sarvam khalu idam brahma*). In peace worship and meditate on it as that from which all this is born and into which it enters. Man is made up of will (*kratu*).[46] Whatever will he has developed in this birth—that he will be in the next. Let him develop the will. (*Chāndogya Upaniṣad*, 3:14, 1)

2. All this was originally the Brahman. It knew itself only and said, "I am the Brahman." Then he became all. Whoever among the gods knew this became this. So also among the sages and men. Realizing this, the sage Vāmadeva came to know that he was Manu and the sun. So whoever knows, "*I am the Brahman*" (*aham brahma asmi*), becomes all this. Even the gods cannot prevent him from becoming all this; for he becomes their very *ātman*. Whoever worships another deity, thinking, "He is one and I am another," does not know that he is like a sacrificial animal to gods. As the many animals are for the enjoyment of man, so every man is for the enjoyment of gods. Even if one animal is taken away, it becomes unpleasant, not to speak of many being taken away. So it is not liked by gods that man should know this (secret). (*Bṛhadāraṇyaka Upaniṣad*, 1:4, 10)

3. This verily is the honey that Dadhyañc Athavāṇa taught the Aśvins. Observing this, the sage said:

He became the corresponding form to every form.
This corresponding form is meant for explaining.
Indra,[47] with his mysterious powers (*māyās*) assumes many forms.
Yoked are his ten thousand horses.[48]

This (*ātman*) itself is the horses (in the form of the different senses and organs). They are ten, and thousands, many and infinite. This Brahman is unprecedented, unequalled, without an inside and without an outside. *This ātman is the Brahman* (*ayam ātmā brahma*), *the omniscient:*—this is the instruction. (*Ibid.*, 2:5, 19)

4. *All this is the Brahman* (*sarvam hi etat brahma*). *This ātman is the Brahman*[49] (*ayam ātmā brahma*). He, this *ātman*, has four states. (*Māṇḍūkya Upaniṣad*, 2)

5. That which is subtlety belongs to the *ātman*. This, all this truth, belongs to the *ātman*. *That thou art* (*tat tvam asi*), O Śvetaketu. (*Chāndogya Upaniṣad*, 6:8, 7)

16. Other Identity Statements

□ The identity statements are quite many and some of them are descriptive also. The five given in selection 15 are considered to be the most important. Here a few more are given. The Upaniṣads repeat the identity statements more often and emphatically than the difference statements. □

1. *All this is indeed the ātman* (*ātmaiava idam sarvam*). (*Ibid.*, 7:15, 2)

2. *All this is from the ātman* (*ātmata eva idam sarvam*). (*Ibid.*, 7:16, 1)

3. *This ātman residing in my inner heart* (*buddhi*)—*this is the Brahman* (*eṣa me ātmā antarhṛdaya etat brahma*). (*Ibid.*, 3:14, 4)

4. *All this, whatever it is, is the ātman* (*sarvam yadayamātmā*). (*Bṛhadāraṇyaka Upaniṣad*, 2:4, 6)

5. *That which the ātman is the Brahman* (*sa vā ayam ātmā brahma*). *Ibid.*, 4:14, 3 and 5)

6. *Consciousness and bliss are the Brahman* (*vijñānam ānandam brahma*). (*Ibid.* 3:9, 28)

7. *Massive consciousness is the Brahman* (*prajñānam brahma*). (*Aitareya Upaniṣad*, 3:3)

8. *The Brahman is Truth, Consciousness, and Infinity* (*satyaṁ jñānam anantaṁ brahma*). (*Taittirīya Upaniṣad*, 2:1)

17. Difference Statements

1. The form of this Person (Puruṣa) is like the golden colored robe, like the wool of a white sheep, like the Indragopa beetle (a red shining beetle), like the flame of fire, like the white lotus flower, like the sudden lightning. The glory of the man who knows this will be like the sudden lightning flash. Now, the instruction is: *Not this, not this* (*neti, neti*). The meaning is: There is nothing other than the Brahman. The Brahman is not the other. Its name is the Truth of Truth. The *prāṇas* (living beings) are the Truth; it is their Truth. (*Bṛhadāraṇyaka Upaniṣad*, 2:3, 6)

2. "Where do you and your *ātman*[50] dwell?"
"In the *Prāṇa*."
"Where is *Prāṇa* established?"
"In *apāna*."
"Where is *apāna* founded?"
"In *vyāna*."
"Where is *vyāna* based?"
"On *vyudāna*."
"Where is *vyudāna* founded?"
"In *samāna*."

"The *ātman*[51] is *not this, not this* (*neti, neti*). It is ungraspable, and is not grasped; it is indestructible, and is not destroyed; it is unstickable and does not stick; it is unbound and does not suffer. These are the eight bases, these are the eight worlds (realms, spheres), these are the eight gods, these are the eight persons.[52] I ask you about the Person of the Upaniṣads, who, moving all these persons and withdrawing them (into himself) transcends them." (*Ibid.*, 3:9, 26)

3. Of his (the Cosmic Person), the eastern quarters are the eastern *prāṇas* (breaths); the southern quarters are the southern *prāṇas*; the western quarters are the western *prāṇas*; the northern quarters are the northern *prāṇas*; the upper quarters are the upper *prāṇas*; the lower quarters are the lower *prāṇas*; all quarters are all his *prāṇas*. The *ātman* is *not this, not this*, (*neti, neti*). (*Ibid.*, 4:2, 4)

4. (*Ibid.*, 4:4, 22) (see selection 13)

5. Where it becomes like duality, then one sees another; one smells another; one tastes another; one speaks to another; one hears another; one thinks of another; one touches another; one knows another. But when all this becomes his *ātman*, then by what will one see another; by what will one smell another; by what will one taste another; by what will one speak to another; by what will one hear another; by what will one think of another; by what will one touch another; by what will one know another? By what will one know that which knows all this? The ātman is *not this, not this* (*neti, neti*). It is ungraspable and is not grasped. (*Ibid.*, 4:5, 15)

NOTES

1. Or the secret doctrine of the world of the abode of God.
2. Or the secret doctrine of by whom is the world created and sustained.
3. "This" here refers to the lower gods who are worshiped and meditated upon.
4. Umā is said to be the wife of Śiva. Here she is made the personification of divine knowledge.
5. Or the secret doctrine of the Kaṭha branch of the Vedas.
6. It should be noted that *ṛta* here means the fruit (merit and demerit) of man's ethical actions. Note the meanings given earlier.
7. This ether is *ākāśa*, which is an abbreviation of *hṛdayākāśa* (the ether of the heart), not the physical.
8. The five fires—*gārhaspatya, dakṣiṇāgni, āvahanīya, sabhya*, and *āvasathya*—are the fires that had to be kept day and night by every Brahmin in his house.
9. The Naciketas fires are three, lighted one after another, and are supposed to lead man to heaven.

10. *Buddhi* is often translated as intellect and understanding. But these words are not appropriate. As this Upaniṣad itself teaches, it is higher than mind, just as Reason in Plato's philosophy is higher than the other two parts. It has its own ontological status. The appropriate translation is "reason." The use of this word makes it easy for a non-Indian to understand the Sanskrit word better.
11. The term *Mahān Ātmā* is often translated as the "Great Ātman," which is misleading. It makes one wonder how it can be great, while the *ātman* itself does not have such an adjective. The former is the Mahat, the Great, explained as the integrated *buddhis* (reasons) of all the souls, and corresponds to the Logos of the Stoics. It is the higher rational soul common to all the finite souls. It is called Ātmā (Ātman) because, as the *Taittirīya Upaniṣad* explains, the body, the life-principle, mind, finite reason, etc., are all *ātmans* but at lower and higher stages of the same "I." Cf. also the Stoic and Neo-Platonic view that our reason partakes of the Logos, the Cosmic Reason.
12. Puruṣa is he who dwells in the body (*puri śete iti puruṣah*, he who lives in the fort is called Puruṣa). The fort here is the body made up of the physical and psychological factors. Puruṣa and *ātman* are interchangeably used in this Upaniṣad.
13. *Etat vai tat*. We should note that in this and the following stanzas, some of the early gods, regarded as the Supreme God in different hymns, are being identified with the *ātman*, the innermost Universal Spirit for every man.
14. Gautama is another name of Naciketas.
15. Or secret doctrine of the Shaved Heads.
16. For the four Vedas, see ch. 1, introduction.
17. Or the secret doctrine of the sage, Aitareya.
18. This refers us to the waters of Indian mythology. In them were born Varuṇa, Prajāpati, etc., who made them their abode, and ruled the world from there. Āpas, also meaning water, is the water of the earth's oceans, rivers, etc., and is conceived to be below the earth.
19. This form is said to be that of the Cosmic Person.
20. Apāna is believed to be the wind that takes the food down from the mouth through the stomach and intestines to the excreting organ. The life of ordinary mortals at death is believed to go that way. Such mortals may go to heaven, but do not obtain salvation.
21. This hole at the top of the head is noticeable in babies. Concentration at that spot, it is said, enables one to realize the Ātman and leads one to heavenly bliss.
22. From the Ātman's point of view, all experiences—waking, dream, and deep sleep—are experiences within the Ātman, just as dream is an experience within the mind, which creates the dream objects. Hence the use of the word *dream* for the three experiences: waking, dream, and deep sleep.
23. Here the teacher points out the three places, It is believed that, during the waking state the Ātman lives in the eye, during the dream state at the neck, and during the deep, dreamless sleep in the heart.
24. Or secret doctrine of the sage, Tittira.
25. Activities pertaining to human beings as members of society, such as birth and death ceremonies, initiation ceremonies, marriage ceremonies.
26. The vital principle, which is sometimes identified with Wind, is called *prāṇa*. It is of five kinds, one of which is, again, called *prāṇa*. This *prāṇa* is said to reside in the heart and make one breathe. The second, *apāna*, resides at the navel (anus according to some writers), takes the food down, and excretes it. The third, *samāna*, exists at the navel (or heart) and maintains the heat of the body and the metabolic processes. The fourth, *udāna*, is at the throat and controls the functions of speech, etc., belonging to the upper parts. The fifth, *vyāna*, pervades the whole body and coordinates its functions. In this place, only three are mentioned. The functions of all the five are not exactly the same in all texts.
27. The five parts just mentioned are parts of this Prāṇa, the vital principle that makes life possible.
28. Mahas here is the Mahat and the Mahān Ātmā, the Cosmic Reason, Logos. It is called the tail

and base of finite reason because it is behind the latter and is its support. We sit on our hind part, which becomes our support. Finite reason is founded in (partakes of) the Cosmic Reason. Cf. the Stoic conception.

29. Thought, reflective knowledge, works only with the distinction between the thinker and the object thought about. But spiritual knowledge presupposes that this distinction is overcome, that the knower becomes the object known or at least like it. Cf. the implications of the Socratic dictum, "Virtue is knowledge."
30. Gandharvas are celestial musicians, dancers, etc., all those who carry on the profession of fine arts.
31. Or secret doctrine of questions.
32. These are the five vital principles referred to in n. 26. Without the universal vital principle, Prāṇa, neither can the cosmic elements be coordinated nor can the parts of man do their work.
33. Or secret doctrine of the Chāndogya (a branch of the Vedas). *Chanda* means meter. The Upaniṣad is capable of being recited in metrical style.
34. Or secret doctrine of the Great Forest Treatise.
35. Janaka was the name of a king famed throughout India for his spiritual knowledge. He used to invite sages and wise men to discuss spiritual matters and to reward them well. Ajātaśatru says that he also can give the same rewards.
36. The word heart (*hṛdaya*) means not only the physical heart but also its spiritual counterpart, *buddhi* (reason, the rational center of our conscious being), which is given an ontological status by the Upaniṣads. Sometimes the word *ākāśa* (meaning both space and ether) also is used. The word has to be translated according to the context. It is interesting to compare the idea of the integrated conscious being lying in sleep with the view of Heraclitus that the Logos in its fullness is found in deep sleep.
37. In the semi-mythological and semiphilosophical parts of the Upaniṣads, the word *prāṇa* has many meanings. It means the vital principle, the biological reality, performing the involuntary functions of the body. It is said also that the voluntary functions of the senses and other organs are its parts and are dependent on it. As mentioned already, it is sometimes identified with wind and assigned the function of keeping the cosmic parts together. It is, however, a derivative of the Ātman or the Brahman, although often addressed as the Brahman because of its importance and of its being a near derivative of the Supreme, as the teaching of Ajātaśatru shows.
38. Because in the sacrificial victims and also in the sacrificer, there exist the five—mind, speech, Prāṇa, vision, and audition, or the body of the sacrificer, wife, progeny, wealth, and sacred texts.
39. The second wife of Yājñavalkya, who wanted to renounce the world.
40. This is not to be interpreted as a kind of subjectivism or worship of the subject. It is somewhat like the Socratic teaching: Know thyself. If without the self, there are no sense activities, no mental activities, no pleasures, then what is this self? By knowing it alone, all else can be known.
41. This knower is the ultimate knower, not the mere subject of ordinary knowledge. Within the ultimate knower, there is no duality.
42. Many consider this passage to be a very important spiritual teaching of Yājñavalkya, who describes the three states—waking, dream, and deep sleep—of the *ātman*, the nature of the transmigration of the unredeemed soul, and the nature of the redeemed soul. It indicates also where the light of the *ātman*, which does not merely reveal but also creates its objects, can be found.
43. "Outwards" means towards objects existing outside oneself. Objects existing inside the mind are the objects of mind.
44. The seven limbs are differently interpreted, depending on whether the person concerned is the finite or the cosmic person. In the case of the former, the seven are head, eyes, *prāṇa*, trunk, pelvis, feet, and face. In the case of the latter, they are heaven, sun-and-moon, wind, fire,

ether, water, and earth. What the Upaniṣad says applies to both the persons because of the macrocosmos-microcosmos relationship.

45. The nineteen gates through which man enjoys are (1) the five sense organs (eye, ear, nose, tongue, skin); (2) the five organs of action (mouth, hands, generative organ, anus, and feet); (3) the five *prāṇas*, as explained earlier (see n. 26); and (4) the four parts of the inner sense, or *antaḥkaraṇa* (*manas* or mind, *ahaṁkāra* or ego, *buddhi* or reason, and *citta* or apperceptive reason or synthetic reason). The Cosmic Person also is supposed to have all these nineteen gates.

46. The word *kratu* means sacrifice (*yajña*). The commentary explains it as will, determination (*adhyavasāya*). Through activity, sacrificial and otherwise, man strengthens his will according to the nature of his activity. This will is *karma* (action itself) in its state of potency and creates the conditions of the next birth. So man is called *karma-maya* (made up of *karma*) and also *kratu-maya* (made up of will, sacrifice). Man's personality is what it is in accordance with the nature of the sacrifice he makes of himself in the cosmic sacrifice.

47. Indra here is identified with the Supreme Being itself.

48. The horses are metaphorical for senses and other organs, which lead man in different directions.

49. The Brahman in its microcosmic aspect is the *ātman* and the *ātman* in its macrosmic aspect is the Brahman. Commentators, like Śaṅkara and Rāmānuja, interpret the relation in different ways such as identity, similarity, body-mind relationship, identity-in-difference, etc.

50. *Ātman* here means the heart, not spirit.

51. *Ātman* here means spirit. The lower self dwells in all these different kinds of Prāṇa (see n. 26), but the higher self is yet different and transcends them all.

52. The eight bases are earth, desire, forms like colors, ether, darkness, forms like reflections, water, and sperm. The eight worlds are fire, heart, vision, audition, ignorance (also called heart), reflection (as in a mirror), heart (*buddhi*), and heart (sperm). We should note that the word *heart* is here used in four senses: the physical heart, rational consciousness, ignorance, and sperm, which was perhaps supposed to run along with blood through the heart. The eight gods are elixir (immortality), woman, Truth, quarters, Death, Prāṇa, Varuṇa, and Prajāpati. The eight persons are the physical (bodily) person, the desiring person, the person in the sun, the person in the echo, the person in the shadow, the person in the mirror, the person in waters, and the person in the son (progeny). The whole passage purports to say that the Supreme Person (Puruṣa) taught by the Upaniṣads is none of these.

CHAPTER 3

Bhagavad-gītā

□ The *Bhagavad-gītā* (The Lord's song) or simply called the *Gītā* (although there are other *Gītās*) is a small part of the great epic *Mahābhārata* (The Great Bhārata race). The Lord here is Kṛṣṇa, who is practically, but not theoretically, regarded as the incarnation of Viṣṇu, one of the Trinity. The context of this teaching is the battlefield in which the rival armies of the Pāṇḍavas and Kauravas were arrayed. The Pāṇḍavas and Kauravas were cousins, being the sons of two brothers, Pāṇḍu and Dhṛtarāṣṭra. Arjuna, one of the Pāṇḍavas, had Kṛṣṇa as his charioteer and felt dejected when he saw that he had to kill his own kith and kin in the battle. He wanted, therefore, to retire from life and adopt the path of nonaction. Kṛṣṇa dissuaded him from giving up action, which was of course his duty to perform. He explained to Arjuna the nature of right action, nonaction, and evil action and said that action done without egoistic desire, but not for the purpose of enjoying its fruit, was really nonaction, as it was done with the spirit of "O God, let thy will be done, not mine." Thus action done according to the cosmic law (duty for duty's sake) and without involvement of egoism is nonaction. The same done with the involvement of egoism is action. Evil action is that which violates the law of the cosmos, understood here as the Cosmic Person (*Viśva-rūpa*). Kṛṣṇa explains also that the ways of knowledge, devotion, and action should not be separated. Action has to be done with knowledge and knowledge should be accompanied by right action (the nonegoistic). The difficulties of either way are overcome through devotion and self-surrender. □

1. The Dejection of Arjuna

Ch. 1. 26–30. Standing there (on the battlefield), Pārtha (Arjuna) saw his fathers, grandfathers, teachers, maternal uncles, brothers, sons, grandsons, friends, paternal uncles, well-wishers in both armies. He, a son of Kunti, saw closely all of them, his relations.

He was overcome by sorrow, felt dejected, and said, "Seeing my own men gathered and ready for battle, my limbs give way and mouth dries up, my body trembles and hairs stand on end. My Gāṇḍīva (name of his bow) slips from my hand, and my skin burns. I am unable to stand and my mind whirls."

35–39. "Even if they (the enemies), whose mind is struck by greed, do not see the sin in destroying the family (*kula*, tribe, race) and in being unfaithful to friends, why should it be not known by us that we should avoid this sin?"

46. "If the sons of Dhṛtarāṣṭra, with weapons in their hands, kill me who is without weapons in hand and who does not retaliate in this battle, it will be better for me."

2. The Steady Rational Mind

Ch. 2. 9. So saying to Hṛṣīkeśa (Kṛṣṇa), Guḍākeśa (Arjuna), the conqueror of the enemy, told Govinda (Kṛṣṇa) that he would not fight and kept silent.

11–13. Kṛṣṇa said "You grieve over the

ungrievable and yet utter, as though, wise words. But the wise do not grieve over the dead or the living. As boyhood, youth, and old age are to the embodied, even so is obtaining another body to it. The steady-minded is not befooled by it (this process).

16–18. "Nonbeing does not become being and being does not become nonbeing. The knowers of truth have seen the bounds of both. Know that which pervades all this (body and world) is imperishable. All these bodies, which have an end, belong to the embodied, the eternal, the indestructible, the immeasurable. So, O Bhārata (Arjuna, a descendant of the Bhārata clan), fight.

22. "As a man leaves his old clothes and puts on new ones, even so the embodied leaves its old bodies and takes to other new ones.

28. "All beings are the unmanifest in the beginning, they are manifest in the middle, and become the unmanifest at the end. What is there to grieve about?"

41. "Reason (*buddhi*) is one and by nature it is decision (resolution, determination). The reasons of the undecided are endless and have many branches.

49–50. "Action done for a reward is far lower than that done in wisdom (reason). Take refuge in reason. Wretched are those who act for selfish ends.

"He who acts in the yoga of reason (*buddhi*) leaves merit and demerit here. So strive for yoga. Yoga is skill (rightness) in action."

54. Arjuna asked "O Keśava (Kṛṣṇa), what is the language of the man whose reason (*buddhi*, rational conscious being) is steady and who abides in *samādhi*?[1] What does he say, where does he exist, and where does he go?"

55. Kṛṣṇa said, "He who gives up all the desires latent in his mind and whose spirit is contented with itself is called the man of steady reason.

56. "His mind is unagitated by sorrows. He is not attached to pleasures, though in their midst. He is devoid of attachment, fear, and anger. He is silent and is called the man of steady reason.

57. "He has no ties to anything, anywhere. He neither rejoices when good comes nor dislikes evil when it visits. The reason of such a man is stable.

58. "As a tortoise withdraws his limbs, he withdraws his senses from their objects. The reason of such a man is steady.

59. "The objects recede from the embodied when he does not enjoy them. His sense of taste is without taste, it vanishes when it sees the Supreme.

67. "Mind accompanies the senses when they operate. It then carries away reason like wind a boat on water.

69. "In that which is night for all (other) beings, the self-controlled is awake. That in which all (other) beings are awake is the night for the knowing, silent man.

71. "The man who gives up all desires and lives without attachment and who is without egoism and the sense of 'mine' obtains peace.

72. "O Pārtha (Kṛṣṇa), this is the state called *brāhmī* (characteristic of the Brahman). Having reached it, none will be deluded. Remaining in it, one obtains at death the *nirvāṇa* of the Brahman."

3. The Way of Action

Ch. 3. 4. "By not doing the works, man does not obtain actionlessness. By merely renouncing the world, man does not obtain the supreme attainment.

5. "Stopping the organs of action, if a man sits remembering their objects (pleasures), such a deluded person will be called a man of false conduct.

6. "But the man who, controlling the senses by his mind, performs works with his organs of action, is different.

7. "Do the prescribed works. Action is higher than nonaction. Even the maintenance of the body is not possible for the man of nonaction.

22. "O Pārtha (Arjuna), for me there is no duty in the three worlds.[2] There is nothing to be obtained and not yet obtained. Yet I engage myself in works.

23. "If I do not untiringly occupy myself with activities, all men, O Pārtha, will follow my path.

24. "These worlds will then come to an end, if I do not perform my work. I shall become the author of confusion and destruction of all men.

30. "Surrendering all your actions to me, renouncing everything with a spiritual mind, free yourself from selfish desires and egoism, and fight sinless (without anxiety)."

4. Knowledge and Surrender of Action

Ch. 4. 6. "I am unborn, my self is inexhaustible, I am the lord of all beings. Yet I am born by entering Prakṛti (Nature, Matter) through my mysterious power (*māyā*).

7. "Whenever there is danger to righteousness (virtue) and there is rise of unrighteousness, then I create (incarnate) myself.

13. "The four castes (*varṇas*, colors) were created by me according to character and profession. Know me as their author, although I am infintie and never an agent.

14. "He who knows that works do not pollute him and that he has no attachment to works is not bound by them.

15. "Realizing this, works were done by the ancients who desired salvation. So perform actions; they were done by the ancients.

16. "Even the wise are puzzled by the question: What is action and what is nonaction? That I shall explain to you. Knowing it, you will be free from evil.

17. "Action has to be understood; evil action has to be understood; and nonaction has to be understood. The nature of action is very profound.

18. "He who sees action in nonaction and nonaction in action is the rational (wise) among men. Through this yoga he performs all his actions.

19. "The wise call him the man of knowledge, whose actions are all willed without egoistic desire and whose actions (i.e., their fruit) are burnt in the fire of knowledge.

20. "Giving up all attachment to the fruit of his actions, always contented, and without (the sense of) possession, the man who is engaged in actions verily does not perform any action.

21. "Without desiring anything for himself, with mind controlled, refusing to accept any rewards, he who performs actions relating to his bodily existence does not commit sin.

22. "Contented with whatever comes by the way, beyond all duties, without pride, even-tempered in success and failure, he who performs his works is not bound.

23. "All action vanishes from him who has no attachment, who is liberated, whose mind is fixed in knowledge (wisdom), even if he perfomrs actions for the sake of sacrifice.[3]

24. "The act of offering is the Brahman, the oblation is the Brahman, the sacrificial fire is the Brahman, the sacrificer is the Brahman. In the *samādhi* of the activity of the Brahman, the destination (purpose) is the Brahman."

5. The Supreme in the Mundane

Ch. 7. 3. "One out of a thousand men tries for the attainment of knowledge. One out of such a thousand who try, knows me as I am.

4. "Earth, water, fire, air, ether, mind, reason, ego—into these eight is my Prakṛti (Nature, *pnysis*) divided.

5. "There is another Prakṛti of mine, different from the foregoing. It has become the (cosmic) Soul, O long-armed one, and holds this world. Know this.

6. "All beings have this as their origin (womb). Know this. I am the origin of this whole world and also its dissolution.

7. "There is nothing above me, O Dhanañjaya (Arjuna). All this is fixed in me like precious stones in a thread (through it).

8. "I am the taste in water. I am the light of the sun and the moon. I am the Om in the Vedas, and sound in ether.

9. "I am the pure fragrance in the earth, I am the brightness of fire, life in all beings, and the penance of the ascetics.

10. "I am the ancient seed of all beings, reason in the rational, and majesty in the majestic.

11. "Of the strong, I am the strength devoid of selfishness and attachment. O the best of the Bhāratas, in all beings I am the desire (enjoyment) that is not opposed to righteousness (cosmic law)."

6. The Way of Devotion

Ch. 12. 6. "They who surrender all their actions to me are devoted to me, and through this single yoga, meditate on me and worship me.

7. "I lift such people whose mind is fixed on me from the ocean of the world of death.

8. "Fix your mind on me, enter your reason in me. There is no doubt that afterwards you will live in me.

9. "If you cannot fix your mind steadily on me, try to attain me, O Dhanañjaya, through the yogic practice (of Patañjali).

10. "If you are incapable of going through even that practice, then go through the works (activities) of mine (i.e., ethical and religious). Even doing your duties for my sake, you will obtain spiritual success.

11. "If you are incapable of even this, then practicing self-control and relying on my yoga, renounce the fruit of all actions.

12. "Knowledge is superior to practice, meditation is superior to knowledge, renunciation[4] of the fruit of all actions is superior to meditation, and superior to renunciation is the peace that follows."

NOTES

1. The word *samādhi* means the state of unity with the object meditated upon. Here this unity is the identification of one's actions and purposes with the actions and purposes of the Cosmic Person.
2. The upper or heaven, the middle or earth, and the lower or underworld.
3. The sacrifices to gods referred to here are meant to support the universe, but not for any selfish purpose. We have already seen in the Hymn to Person (see ch. 1, selection 15) that the birth and growth of the universe is through the self-sacrifice of the Puruṣa, and then the sacrifice of the Cosmic Puruṣa, from whom the gods emanate and sustain the universe. Man should sustain these gods through his own sacrifices and thus contribute to the sustenance of the universe. Such sacrificial acts are not egoistic.
4. This renunciation is not becoming static by not doing any action, but the surrender, through devotion, of all the fruit of action to God and is, therefore, considered to be superior to meditation. This renunciation, as the eleventh verse says, is not possible without absolute reliance on the yoga (the yogic power) of God, through which he is said to create and control the world and grant salvation to men.

CHAPTER 4

The Ethical Code of Manu

□ The following is a free translation of *Manusmṛti* (also called *Manu-dharma śāstra* or Manu's ethical code) with the help of the commentary of Kullūka. Manu, whose date may be as early as 300 B.C. or as late as A.D. 300, is by tradition the first lawgiver to man. He is said also to be the originator of man. The English word *man*, like the Sanskrit word *mānava*, can etymologically be traced to the word *manu*, which is itself derived from the verbal root √*man* (to think). Thus *man* will etymologically mean a thinking being. But Manu thought not about the ways of thinking, but about those of right conduct. Then as a descendant of Manu, man will be a thinking ethical being.

Manu's ethics are based on castes and stages of life. However, it is primarily individualistic. The individual has to work up and work out his individual destiny through the caste structure. The implication that society represents the body of Brahmā is there, however, as a kind of mythological explanation of the caste structure. To say this is not to criticize Manu. Perhaps nothing better could have been done than what Manu did, in the situation present at that time. It should be noted that contemporary India has far outgrown much of the teaching of Manu. (See "Introduction to Hinduism: A Summary Account," ¶4, 19–21, for further information.) □

Ch. 1. 31. For the growth of the worlds, (Brahmā) created [the four castes of] Brahmaṇas (Brahmins), Kṣatriyas (warriors), Vaiśyas (traders), and Śūdras (manual workers) from his face, arms, thighs, and feet respectively.

32. He, the Lord, divided himself into two and became man through one part and woman through the other. He created Virāt (Cosmic Person) in her.

33. This Person, Virāt, himself performed penance and what he thereby created was myself (Manu), the creator of all this (society of men). Know this, O the best of the twice-born.[1]

34. Wishing to create men, I performed a very difficult penance. I created first the ten great sages, the Prajāpatis (lords of men).

35. They are: Marīci, Atri, Aṅgiras, Pulastya, Pulaha, Kratu, Pracetasa, Vaśiṣṭha, Bhṛgu, and Nārada.

36. They created seven other Manus of great splendor, gods and their abodes, and the great sages with unlimited power.

61. The other six Manus belong to the six families[2] of this (first) Manu, Svāyambhuva.[3] These noble souls of great power created their own living beings.

62. They are Svārociṣa, Uttama, Tāmasa, Raivata, Cākṣuṣa of great powers, and Vaivaśvata.

63. These seven Manus—Svāyambhuva, and so on—had great power. In their periods, every one of them created all this moving and nonmoving (world of beings) and ruled it.

64. Eighteen movements of the eyelid are called Kāṣṭā, Kalā is thirty Kāṣṭās, thirty Kalās constitute a Muhūrta, and thirty Muhūrtas make a day and night.

65. The night and day are divided by the sun for men and gods. The night is meant for the sleep of beings and the day for their work.

66. The night and day of ancestors (of the abode of the souls of ancestors) is one month of men. Its black fortnight is meant for their (ancestors') action and the white for their sleep.

67. The night and day of gods is the year of men. Its division again is into the summer solstice as the day and the winter solstice as the night.

68. Now, understand the night and day of Brahmā and their duration, and also of each of the aeons in succession.

69. The Kṛta (also called Satya) aeon consists of 4,000 years. Four hundred years before and four hundred after are the intervening times for this aeon.

70. In the case of the other three aeons with their prior and posterior twilights, the number of thousands and hundreds is to be less and less by one.

71. The aeon of the gods is said to be 12,000 times the four aeons counted previously.

72. One thousand times the aeon of gods is the day Brahmā. His night also is as long.

73. The knowers of day and night call the day of Brahmā, which is 1,000 aeons long, the auspicious day. His night also is such.

74. At the end of the night of his day, Brahmā wakes up from his sleep. Waking up, he creates (makes up) his mind, made up of being and nonbeing (to create the world).

81. All the four parts of *dharma* (righteousness, ethical law, order that supports mankind and the world)[4] are complete along with truth in the Kṛta aeon.

82. In the other aeons, *dharma* is deprived of one part after another in succession. *Dharma* thus disappears by degrees through stealing, falsehood, and cheating.

85. In the Kṛta, Tretā, Dvāpara, and Kali aeons, the virtues of men are different.

86. In the Kṛta aeon, penance is the dominant virtue; in the Tretā, knowledge; in the Dvāpara, sacrifice; and in the Kali, charity.

87. For preserving his creation in full, Brahmā of great light created separate duties (activities) from his face, arms, thighs, and feet.

88. For the Brahmaṇas (Brahmins) he created teaching, studying, sacrifice, officiating at sacrifice, giving gifts, and accepting gifts.

89. For the Kṣatriya, he created in short the protection of people, giving gifts, performing sacrifices, studying, and nonattachment to sense pleasures.

90. For the Vaiśya, he created the protection of cattle, charity, performance of sacrifices, studying, trading, lending on interest, and agriculture.

91. The Lord created only one profession for the Śūdra: service without envy of the above three castes.

Ch. 2. 1. Understand *dharma* (morality, law, ethical law), which is practised by good and learned men who are always without hate and attachment and who have known *dharma* directly.

6. The basis of all *dharma* is the whole Veda. So also are the Smṛtis (sacred texts remembered and handed down by traditions) and virtue (character).[5] Besides, the conduct of good men and what gives pleasure to oneself are such bases.[6]

12. The Veda, the Smṛti, the conduct of good men, and one's own pleasure are said to be the direct determinants of *dharma*.[7]

67. After initiating the student, the teacher should first teach him purity (cleanliness), the ways of conduct, the preparation of the sacrificial fire, and worship at the joints of time (sunrise, midday, and sunset).

88. The learned (student), like the controller of horses, should attempt to control his senses that go the wrong way and drag one towards pleasures.

177. He (the student) should give up wine, flesh, scents, garlands, tastes, women, fermented and stale foods, and injury of living beings.

224. Some teachers say that virtue (*dharma*, merit, duty) and wealth are the highest values; some assert that enjoyment and wealth are the best; some maintain that virtue alone is the best; and others say that the best is wealth. But the truth is that the three constitute the highest triad.[8]

225. The teacher, father, elder brother—

these should not be disrespected even by one in danger. This rule applies particularly to the Brahmin.

226. The teacher is the form of the Brahman, father the form of Prajāpati, mother of the goddess Earth, and elder brother of one's inner *ātman.*

Ch. 3. 1. One should devote to a life of Vedic study with a teacher a period of thirty-six years, or half of it, or one fourth of it, or until the Vedas are finished.

2. After studying all the Vedas, or two of them, or one of them,[9] one, with celibacy unbroken, should take to the life of the householder.

4. After obtaining the permission of the teacher, the twice-born should bathe, dress himself according to his family traditions, and marry a girl, beautiful and belonging to his own caste.

21. There are eight types of marriage—*brāhma*, *daiva*, *ārṣa*, *prājāpatya*, *āsura*, *gāndharva*, *rākṣasa*, and *piśāca*. The last is the lowest.

23. The first six belong to the Brahmin, and the last four to the Kṣatriya. To the Vaiśya and Śūdra belong the same four except the *rākṣasa* (i.e., only three).

24. The wise know the first four of the Brahmin as the best; so also is the *rākṣasa* for the Kṣatriya, and the *asura* for the Vaiśya and the Śūdra.

25. Of the last five, three are meritorious for this Smṛti (of Manu). The *paiśāca* and *āsura* marriages should never be practised.

27. The *brāhma* marriage consists in giving the bride, well-dressed and adorned, to the bridegroom with good character and well versed in the Veda, after oneself inviting him.

28. The *daiva* marriage is that in which one, after properly getting the sacrifice ready, gives one's daughter with jewels to the Ṛtvik (one of the priests) who is performing the rites.

29. That is called the *ārṣa* marriage in which one takes ceremoniously a cow and a bull or one of the two[10] from the bridegroom and gives the bride with propriety.

30. The *prājāpatya* marriage is known as that in which the girl is worshiped and given away in marriage to the bridegroom, with the words: "You both live with each other according to duty (*dharma*)."

31. If a man, of his will, gives money to a kinsman of the bride (father, and so on) and also to the bride according to his own ability and takes the bride, it is called an *āsura* marriage.

32. The *gāndharva* marriage is known as that in which the girl and the groom have intercourse because of desire (passion). It is the result of sex intercourse and lust.

33. That is called the *rākṣasa* marriage in which the groom carries away the weeping and screaming girl by force after beating (her parents, and so on) or hurting (them) or breaking (their walls, and so on).

34. The *paiśāca* marriage is the lowest, meanest, and the most sinful of the marriages. It occurs when a man has sex intercourse secretly with a girl who is fast asleep, intoxicated, or drunk.

69. The great sages have created five great sacrifices to be performed every day by the householder.

70. Teaching is the sacrifice to the Brahman. Oblations of water are the sacrifice to the ancestors. Offerings in fire are the sacrifice to the gods. Offering food is the sacrifice to beings. Hospitality is the sacrifice to men.

77. Just as all animals live depending on air, all the people of all stages of life live depending on the householder.

78. The people of all the other stages of life are supported by the householder through (the supply of) knowledge and food. Hence the stage of life of the householder is the best of all.

Ch. 4. 1. The first one fourth of the span of life[11] should be lived by the twice-born with his teacher. The second one fourth should be lived in one's own house with his wife.

Ch. 5. 147. Even at home nothing should be done independently by a woman, whether she is a young girl, a youthful maiden, or an old lady.

148. When young, she should be in the control of her father and in her youth of her husband. When the husband dies, she should be in the protection of her sons. She should not love independence.

149. She should never desire separation

from her father, husband, or children. Separated from them, she brings bad name to both the families (i.e., of the husband and of her father).

Ch. 6. 1. The twice-born, having lived the stage of the householder according to prescribed rules, should take his bath and live in the forest with control of his senses as usual.

2. When the householder observes wrinkles on his skin and white hair on his head, and sees also a son to his son, then he should take refuge in a forest.

3. Leaving the vulgar food and all his external appendage (like clothing, attendants, and so on), he should go to the forest either with his wife or after entrusting her to his son.

5. There he should continue performing the five great sacrifices as prescribed, and live on the different kinds of pure food of the hermits or with leafy vegetables or fruit.

23. (For increasing his capabilities of penance) he should sit amidst the five fires (four fires around him and the sun above) in summer, under the sky in the rainy season, and with wet clothes in winter. Thus he should increase his penance.

33. Having spent the third part of his life in this way, one should give up all associations (duties and responsibilities) and renounce the world (become a wanderer) for the fourth part.

34. He who has gone from one stage of life to another, who has made all the oblations with controlled senses, and who is satisfied with whatever is obtained by begging, prospers after death, by entering the stage of the life of renunciation.

35. Having paid back the three debts,[12] one should fix one's mind on salvation. One devoted to salvation without having paid back the debts goes down (will fall from his path).

36. Having studied and taught the Vedas according to rules, having procreated sons according to law, and having performed sacrifices to one's ability, one should aim at liberation.

38. The Brahmin should leave home (renounce the world) after performing the *prājāpatya* sacrifice in which one should give away all one possesses. He should also place all fires[13] in his *ātman* itself.

43. He is without fire, without an abode. He approaches a village only for food. He is detached and is of a steady, fixed mind. He is silent and enters the Brahman in meditation.

49. He finds joy in the *ātman*, he is detached and beyond temptation. Pursuing happiness, he wanders in the world with the help of his *ātman*.

87. Student, householder, forest-dweller, and ascetic (*sannyāsin*, renouncer)—these four are separate stages of life and all originate in the householder.

88. All these, when followed in succession according to the sacred texts, takes the Brahmin who acts in the prescribed way to the supreme destiny.

89. Of all these, according to the way of the Vedas and the Smṛtis, the householder is the greatest. He supports the (other) three.

90. As the rivers and their tributaries reach their rest in the ocean, all the men of these stages of life are established in the householder.

91. The twice-born of all these four stages should follow the tenfold law (of virtue) with effort.

92. The ten characteristics of virtue are pleasantness (steadiness), patience (forgiveness), control of mind, nonstealing, purity, control of senses, intelligence (understanding the sacred texts), knowledge (of the Brahman), truthfulness, and nonirritability (control of anger).

93. The Brahmins who learn these ten characteristics of virtue, and having learned them follow them, reach the supreme end.

94. Following the virtue of ten characteristics with a fixed mind and listening to the Vedānta as prescribed, the twice-born without the (three) debts should renounce the world.

95. Having renounced[14] all activities and having removed (expiated) the sins of (past) actions, one may, studying the Vedas according to rules, live on the prosperity (wealth) of his son (in his house).

96. Renouncing all actions in that way, being without any attachment, and having destroyed one's sin through renunciation,

one should be devoted to his own aim. One then obtains the supreme end.

Ch. 7. 2. Having gone through the education of the Brahman (i.e., the stage of the student) with its rules and sacraments, he (the king, Kṣatriya) should protect all this (world of men) according to law.

3. When this world without a king was shaken by fear, God created the king to protect all this,

4. By combining the eternal (essential) factors (parts) of the gods: Indra, Wind, Yama (god of death and punisher of sins), Sun, Fire, Varuṇa, Moon, and Kubera (god of riches).

5. As the king is constituted by the parts of these gods, he overpowers (surpasses) all beings by his power.

35. The king is created to protect all who are engaged in their respective duties belonging to the different castes and stages of life.

37. The king, rising up every morning, should worship the knowers of the Brahman (Brahmins), the masters of the three Vedas, and experts in justice, and should obey them.

38. He should respect the elders, the Brahmins who are pure and know the Vedas. The respecter of elders is always worshiped even by the Rākṣasas (demons).

39. He should always learn humility from them, even if he is already modest. The king who is always a man of humility is never destroyed.

110. As the cultivator plucks out grass and weeds and protects rice plants, the king protects his kingdom and kills the wicked.

111. The king who, through indiscrimination (between the good and the wicked) oppresses his own kingdom will, with all his relatives, be deprived of his kingdom and life.

112. As life decreases in living beings when the body is weakened, even so the life of kings decreases when their kingdom is weakened.

113. Always follow this principle in preserving the kingdom: The king increases his happiness in his kingdom if it is well governed.

151. The king should reflect on morality, enjoyment, and wealth (the three values of life), either alone or with his ministers every midday or midnight[15] with peace and without fatigue.

Ch. 8. 18. One fourth of the sin (of the evil person) goes to the agent, one fourth to the witness, one fourth to the assembly (that judges the case like the jury), and one fourth to the king.

318. Even if a man commits sin, he becomes pure if he receives punishment for it from the king. He will go to heaven like the meritorious.

Ch. 9. 2. Women should be made dependent by their men day and night. They should be kept under one's control even when devoted to the various pleasures of life.

3. The woman does not deserve independence. The father protects her when young, the husband in her youth, and the sons in her old age.

4. The father is to blame if he does not marry her away in time, the husband if he does not have intercourse with her in her periods, and the son if he does not protect her after her husband's death.

6. This is the best virtue of men of all castes, who know. Even the weak husbands try to protect their wives.

7. If a man with every effort protects his wife, he protects himself, his children, his caste, and his virtue.

26. Women are meant for children. They are for the good and light of home. They are to be worshiped. In a home there is no difference between a woman on the one side and wealth, beauty, and splendor on the other.

45. The measure of man is this: His self is his wife; he is complete only with children. The wise said thus: "He who is a husband implies the woman."

94. A man, when he enters the stage of the householder, if he is thirty years of age, should marry a girl of twelve whom he likes. A man of twenty-four may marry a girl of eight.

326. The Vaiśya (trader), having gone through the sacraments, and having accepted a wife, should engage himself in trade and in the protection of cattle.

327. Prajāpati created the cattle and

gave them to the Vaiśya. To the Brahmin and Kṣatriya he gave all men.

328. It should never be the wish of a Vaiśya that he should not protect the cattle. When he wishes to protect them, no other should protect them.

333. He should engage himself with every effort in increasing wealth according to law. And with every effort he should give food to all beings.

334. Of the Śūdra the duty that leads to the supreme end is the service of the Brahmins versed in the Vedas and of the householders with a good name.

335. He (the Śūdra) will obtain the highest caste if he is pure, does his service, is soft-worded, nonegoistic, and dependent on the Brahmin and other castes.

Ch. 10. 1. The three twice-born castes should study the Vedas without giving up their respective duties. But the Brahmin alone should teach them, certainly not the other two.

2. The Brahmin should know the forms of livelihood of all as prescribed. He should teach them to others, but himself perform his own duties.

3. By superiority (of his caste), by nature, by the strictness of the rules he maintains, and by the peculiarity of his sacraments, the Brahmin is the lord of all the castes.

4. The Brahmin, Kṣatriya, and Vaiśya are the twice-born. The fourth, the Śūdra, is only once-born. There is no fifth.[16]

63. Manu said that noninjury, truth, nonstealing, purity, and control of senses are together the virtues common to the four castes.

75. Teaching, studying, sacrifice, officiating at sacrifice, giving gifts, and acceptance of gifts—these are the six duties of the highest born (Brahmin).

76. Of the six, three constitute his livelihood. They are officiating at sacrifice, teaching, and acceptance of gifts from men of pure life.

77. The Kṣatriya has the following three less than the Brahmin: officiating at sacrifices, teaching, and acceptance of gifts.

78. Regarding the Vaiśya, the same as for the Kṣatriya holds. Manu and Prajāpati did not allow the three to him.

80. Study of the Veda for the Brahmin, protection of people for the Kṣatriya, and trade for the Vaiśya are the most important duties.

Ch. 11. 54. The murder of a Brahmin, drinking wine, stealing, and sexual intercourse with the wife of a teacher, or even association with any of them are called the great sins.

55. Falsehood for raising one's status, slandering another for the favor of the king (court intrigue), and falsely abusing one's teacher are equal to the murder of a Brahmin.

56. Forgetting the Brahman (Supreme Spirit), blaming the Vedas, false witness, murder of a friend, eating what is disgusting, and eating what is not to be eaten—these six are equal to the drinking of wine.

57. Stealing whatever is entrusted (e.g., deposits), such as men, horses, silver, land, diamonds, and other precious stones, is equal to the stealing of gold.

58. Leaving one's sperm in those born to one's mother, in daughters, in the women of Cāṇḍāla caste (outcaste) and in the wives of friends and sons is equal to polluting the bed of one's teacher.

59. Killing cows, officiating at sacrifices performed by those who are not entitled, intimacy with another person's wife, sale of oneself, abandoning the teacher, father, mother, study, the sacred fires, and sons,

60. Marrying before an elder brother, marrying the youngest brother before the younger is married, giving a daughter to them, officiating at their sacrifices,

61. Teasing unmarried girls, usury, ignoring the ceremonies, selling of water tanks, hermitages, one's wife, and one's son,

62. Nonperformance of the initiation ceremony of one's sons, abandoning one's relatives, teaching by receiving fees, studying for the sake of livelihood, and selling what is forbidden,

63. Obtaining supervision over mines,[17] managing great machines (like dams),[18] injuring medical plants, running brothels, black magic, enticing women, and so on, through charms and incantations,

64. Felling living trees for fuel, per-

forming sacrifices, and so on, for selfish purposes, eating prohibited food,

65. Not continuing the sacred fires, petty thefts, nonpayment of the three debts, reading false sacred texts, devotion to fine arts (dance, and so on),

66. The theft of paddy, of nonprecious metals, and of cattle, intercourse with drunken women, murder of women, of Śūdras, of Vaiśyas, and Kṣatriyas, atheism —all these are sins of the second class.[19]

227. One can be freed from his sin by open confession, by repentance, by penance, and by study (of sacred texts). Similarly one is freed from sin committed in danger[20] by making the gift of a cow.

257. If a man is polluted by one of the great sins, he should live with cows for a year controlling his mind, studying sacred texts, taking the name of God and repeating it constantly. He should live only by begging. Then he will be purified.[21]

258. Or he is freed from his sins, when he is purified by three fasts[22] and reads the *saṁhitās*[23] for three weeks in a forest.

Ch. 12. 3. Action (conduct) has happy and unhappy results and belongs to mind, speech, and body. The destinies of men are the result of actions and are of three kinds: the highest, the middle, and the lowest.

4. Know that the mind is the initiator of the actions of the embodied (man). Action is of the aforesaid three kinds and also of ten kinds.

5. Mind's (sinful) action is of three kinds—thinking of another's wealth, wishing to commit sins, and attachment to (faith in) false views.[24]

6. Speech's (sinful) actions are four kinds—harshness, falsehood, backbiting, and irrelevant talk.

7. Body's (sinful) actions are three—taking away things not given, unlawful injury, and devotion to another's wife.

8. One enjoys or suffers the fruit of good or evil actions thus—the fruits of mental activity through mind, those of speech activities through speech, and those of bodily activities through the body.

9. Man obtains the life of motionlessness (of plants, and so on) as a result of the evil committed by the body, the life of birds and beasts because of the evil committed by speech, and the life of the lowest born because of the evil committed by mind.

If a man performs only good actions, he will be born a god; if he performs mixed actions, he will be born a man; and if he performs only evil actions, he will be born a bird or an animal. The result of evil speech is the destruction of knowledge; that of evil mind is the loss of the supreme destiny; and that of the evil body is the loss of the worlds. So let one protect the three in every way. The punishment prescribed for evil speech is silence; that for evil mind is fasting; and that for evil action is breath control.[25]

10. The man in whom the control of speech, mind, and body are fixed is called the three-controller.[26]

83. Constant study of the teachings of the Vedas and their practice, knowledge of the *ātman*, control of the senses, noninjury, and service of the spiritual teacher are the means for the highest destiny.

85. Of all these (means), knowledge of the *ātman* is the highest. Of all the studies, the study of the *ātman* is the highest. One obtains immortality from it.

86. Of all the forms of action, either here or after death, know that action in accordance with the Vedas always leads man to the highest destiny.

87. All these means[27] are absorbed without remainder by the Vedic yoga of action in this or that procedure or order.

88. There are two kinds of Vedic action (*karma*); activity for results in the external world (*pravṛtti*) leading to the increase of pleasure and that for the supreme happiness or bliss (*nivṛtti*).[28]

89. That action which is for the satisfaction of desires here and hereafter is called *pravṛtti-karma*; but the action performed without desire and preceded by (due to) knowledge is called *nivṛtti-karma.*

90. One devoted to *pravṛtti-karma* becomes equal to the gods. But one devoted to *nivṛtti-karma* rises above the five elements (i.e., obtains salvation).

NOTES

1. The first three castes were allowed initiation when they first entered the life of the student. This initiation is called *upanayana* into *brahma-carya*, initiation into the life of the Brahman (Supreme Being). Before the initiation, they are only children and are said to have no caste. At the initiation they are said to have a second birth, the first being the natural one. So the first three castes are called the twice-born.
2. According to tradition, there are seven Manus, the originators and lawgivers of men. The first of them was born to Brahmā, the creator. The other six Manus are descendants of the first in succession.
3. The first Manu is called Svāyambhuva, being the son of Svayambhū, the self-born, i.e., Brahmā.
4. The Sanskrit word *pada* means foot. Kulluka, the commentator, says that *dharma* is a bull with four feet—penance, knowledge, sacrifice, and charity. In the Kṛta aeon, this bull walks on all the four feet.
5. The word used is *śīla*, which is translated also as character. Here it means virtue, which is of thirteen kinds: devotion to the Brahman (Supreme Spirit), devotion to gods and ancestors, pleasant-mindedness, sympathy (suffering at the suffering of others), envylessness, softness (kindness), noncruelty, friendliness, pleasant speech, gratitude, sheltering (the oppressed), mercy, and peacefulness.
6. Here the five origins or sanctions of good conduct are mentioned. Whenever there is a conflict between a former and a latter, the former is said to prevail.
7. Here also the former prevails over a latter, if there is conflict. But only four are given.
8. That is, the student should know about the three values of life. It may be noted that Manu does not mention the fourth, salvation. But he seems to include it in *dharma*, as he speaks of the supreme destiny and knowledge of the Brahman. Whether salvation is a *dharma*, whether it is an obligation to obtain salvation became a point of controversy among later philosophers.
9. The alternatives refer to the traditions of studying all the three Vedas (the fourth, the *Atharva* is not mentioned here), or two of them, or only one. There were families of Brahmins belonging to the three traditions.
10. The commentary explains this acceptance of the bull etc., not as taking the marriage price—which is a sin—but as accepting them for the sake of completing the sacrifice. A cow or bull or both have to be given away as a sacrificial gift. This marriage, like the foregoing, seems to be performed at the time of sacrifice.
11. The average span of life at the time of Manu was taken to be one hundred years.
12. The three debts are those to gods, to ancestors, and to teachers. They are absolute obligations to every man. They are paid back by performing sacrifices, by having children, and by teaching the next generation.
13. This is symbolic of the idea that from the spiritual point of view, all is sacrificed ultimately to the *ātman* by the *ātman*.
14. This is a second kind of *sannyāsa* (renunciation). The first kind of renouncer is a wanderer and leaves home, sons, etc. But this one lives in the son's house, still with the same detachment.
15. Because at that time, the king is relatively free from mental worries and bodily troubles. It should be noted that the king has not only to protect law, but also follow it.
16. There is in fact a fifth caste, who until recently were the untouchables of India and whom Gandhi renamed the Hrijans (men of God). At the time of Manu, it seems, they were outside the caste system, the Aryan social fold. Manu knew them, he refers in his Code to them as Cāṇḍālas, etc.
17. As there are plenty of opportunities and temptations to steal metals.
18. As the temptation to take bribes is very great in the distribution of water to the farmers.
19. Manu could not have meant that all the sins mentioned here are on the same level. For instance, homicide and devotion to fine arts are not of equal sin. Manu wanted to classify

sins into two general classes, the first and the second, the latter not being as great as the former. We may also note that Manu mixes up what we call religious or spiritual sins, moral sins, social crimes, and legal crimes. He regards also devotion to situations with temptations as sins.

20. Manu seems to realize that man is obliged to violate some ethical laws in moments of danger. Even then, atonement is necessary for which a cow has to be given away.
21. This is called secret atonement i.e., without openly declaring the sin.
22. *Parāka*. A *parāka* is a fast of twelve days. A sinner should observe three such *parākas*.
23. *Saṁhitās* are the hymn portions of the Vedas.
24. Such as that there is no other world, no objective ethical law (*dharma*), no life after death, and no God. Actions mentioned here and in the following verses are the sinful ones. Their opposites are the meritorious ones.
25. It is believed that exercises in breath control increase our ability to control our bodily movements that may have become habits. These verses, though given as part of the original text, seem to be interpolations according to the commentary.
26. The Sanskrit word used is *tridaṇḍin* or one who holds three *daṇḍas*. *Daṇḍa* means punishment, check, and also a kind of cane. One class of ascetics carry three canes twisted and bound together to indicate that their aim is the three kinds of control. Manu explains the spiritual meaning of carrying the three canes.
27. The means referred to do not seem to be merely the six mentioned in verse 83 of this chapter, but all those mentioned in different places by Manu. Manu holds the view that the way of action (*karma-mārga*) includes all the other ways and surpasses all.
28. It should be noted that Manu regards *nivṛtti* also as a part of the way of action enjoined by the Veda. Śaṅkara and many of his followers would not regard *nivṛtti* as a way of action at all. But Manu has his point here: all activity aiming at salvation is also activity like any activity directed towards the values of this world. The Veda has prescribed methods for both types of activity. Thus according to Manu, the Veda teaches the way of action. It is left to the choice of man whether he wants the values of this world or salvation. According to his choice, he has to follow one or the other type of action. Verses 88, 89, and 90 make his idea clear.

CHAPTER 5

The Yoga of Patañjali

☐ The following is a free translation from the *Patañjala-yoga sūtras* (Aphorisms of Patañjali's yoga) with the help of the commentaries of Vyāsa (*c.* fourth century A.D.), Bhoja (*c.* seventh century A.D.), and Vācaspati (*c.* ninth century A.D.). For understanding the Yoga of Patañjali (fourth century B.C.?), one should have some knowledge of the Sāṅkhya School also, which is utilized by Patañjali. The world according to the Sāṅkhya is due to the reflection of the Puruṣa (spirit), which is pure consciousness, in Prakṛti, which is insentient by nature. The latter is made up of three attributes (*guṇas*), *sattva*, *rajas*, and *tamas*. *Sattva* is purity, transparency; in it the reflection of the Puruṣa is pure, unagitated, and undistorted. *Rajas* is dynamism, activity. *Tamas* is darkness, staticity, lethargy, muddiness. When the Puruṣa's reflection is thrown into Prakṛti, the latter becomes agitated and begins to evolve the multiplicity of the world. The process is as follows:

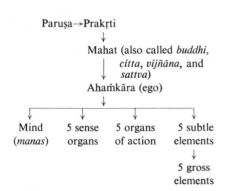

Paruṣa→Prakṛti
↓
Mahat (also called *buddhi*, *citta*, *vijñāna*, and *sattva*)
↓
Ahaṁkāra (ego)
↓

Mind (*manas*)	5 sense organs	5 organs of action	5 subtle elements ↓ 5 gross elements

The five sense organs are eye, ear, nose, tongue, and skin in their psychological aspects, not in their physical aspects. The five organs of action are hands, feet, mouth (speech, tongue standing for taste), the generative organ, and the excretory organ. The five elements, both subtle and gross, are Ether, Air, Fire, Water, and Earth.

The word *citta*, although generally translated by the word *mind*, cannot be properly understood without understanding its peculiar significance to the Yoga, Sāṅkhya, and Vedānta religious thought. It is a technical term and is derived from the verbal root √*ci* meaning "to gather", "to collect." It is that in which all our experiences are collected, remain in an integrated state, and out of which they originate and function. Thus they become functions of the same *citta*. It is an original apperceptive unity of everything and functions as apperception also in integrating our worldly experiences. It corresponds to the rational part of the soul in Plato's psychology and performs also the function of apperception in Leibniz's philosophy. Its original nature is pure and truthful consciousness. In that state, the attribute *sattva* dominates over the attribute *rajas* and the attribute *tamas*.

The difference from Plato lies here. He does not say what happens to the highest part of the soul, if it is polluted. But the Yoga and the Sāṅkhya use the same word to denote it even when it is polluted. As the commentaries say, when in this *citta* the *rajas* attribute dominates, the former aspires for power and enjoyment in the world.

When the *tamas* attribute dominates, it becomes immoral, ignorant, false, full of attachment to the objects, and runs after the petty, low, and mean.

The foregoing explanation of *citta* given by commentators leads me to translate this word (*buddhi* is its synonym) by the word *reason* with the significance that was given to the word by Plato and the Stoics. What these philosophers and the Sāṅkhya and Yoga want to signify is that there is a higher, though finite, self within us, and that is the rational part of the soul or reason for the Greeks and *citta* for the Sāṅkhya and Yoga. As the higher self, it is ontological. But for the Sāṅkhya and Yoga, it is more than merely the rational part of the self; it is the originator of the multiplicity of our experiences as well as their integrator. In it the functions of the Logos as the origin of the world of experience and of reason as the integrator of those experiences are combined. Translating the word as "intellect," "understanding," and so on leaves the concept misty in many of its contexts to the Western students. Purifying the *citta* does not mean merely developing a keen intellect; it has also the spiritual significance of self-development.

The means of valid cognition accepted by Patañjali are sense perception, inference, and scriptural authority. It should be noted that Patañjali does not condemn the three as necessarily false; he means only that the cognition obtained through them involves the functioning of *citta* and that, so long as the functioning lasts, the seer cannot assume his original form.

It should be noted that sleep is not the absence of all functions, according to Patañjali, but one of the functions of the *citta*. The *citta*, in its pure, undisturbed, nonfunctioning state, is the pure reflection of the Puruṣa, and is the undisturbed consciousness of Being.

With regard to meditation, Patañjali does not prescribe any particular posture. What suits one man many not suit another. Even lying down like a dead man, provided one can concentrate one's mind without falling asleep, is accepted. This posture has a technical name *śavāsana* (corpse posture).

It seems that the word *samādhi* is better left untranslated. It is generally translated as "trance", "ecstacy," "rapture," and so on. But these words are misleading. What Patañjali means is that in *samādhi*, only the object meditated upon remains in the meditating consciousness and that this consciousness as though vanishes. In other words, the meditating *citta* becomes as though the object meditated upon. This is *citta*'s self-identification with the object. If, for example, Christ is meditated upon, the meditating Christian yogi lives the life of Christ, but as though only. Yet he can be conscious of all the depths of the life of Christ in a true way, as though he were Christ. As explained by Patañjali in latter *sūtras* (aphorisms), there will be a transition in the consciousness of the Christian yogi thus: "I am conscious of the form of Christ"—"I am the form of Christ"—"The form of Christ am." The third statement is ungrammatical, but expresses the nature of that experience. Thus would a yogi explain the exhortation: "Realize God through Christ," "Become one with God through Christ or by becoming the body of Christ," and so on. *Samādhi* is self-transformation into and self-identification with the object meditated upon. The nature of the object makes the difference between the good and the evil ideal. Patañjali says that knowledge of the object thus obtained is not imaginary, but true (full of *ṛta* or truth). □

Ch. 1. 2. Yoga is the stopping of the functions of *citta*.

3. Then the seer (the subject of knowing, seeing) is established in his real form (assumes it, becomes as it were his original self, becomes the undistorted reflection of the Puruṣa).

4. Otherwise (when the functions are not stopped), he assumes the forms of the functions (identifies himself with them).

6. The means of cognition, false knowledge (illusions and hallucinations), cognitive distortions,[1] sleep, and memory (are the functions).

12. The functions can be stopped

through practice (of yoga) and nonattachment (to objects and pleasures).

23. Or through meditation on the Supreme Spirit.

Ch. 2. 29. The eight limbs of yoga are self-control, rules regulating life, postures of bodily restfulness (generally called sitting postures), breath control, withdrawal of senses from the objects, fixing the mind on an object, meditation (*dhyāna*), and *samādhi* (establishing oneself in the object meditated upon).

30. Noninjury, nonlying, nonstealing, celibacy, and nonacceptance[2] of gifts—these are self-controls.

31. Purity, pleasant-mindedness (contentment), penance, study (and teaching of scriptures), and meditation on the Supreme Spirit—these are the regulations of daily life.

46. A bodily posture is that which makes a man steady and comfortable.

49. After the posture is established, the breaking of the process of inhaling and exhaling is called breath control.

54. When the senses are detached from their respective objects, they assume the form as though of the *citta*—this is withdrawal of the senses.

Ch. 3. 1. Tying the *citta* to some place (by fixing it on some object) is fixing (*dhāraṇa* literally meaning holding).

2. There, when the cognition is continuous, is meditation.

3. The same (meditation), when the aspect (form) of the process of meditating (the subjective aspect of the cognitive situation) becomes as though void (*śūnya*), is *samādhi*.

NOTES

1. These are artificial and unreal concept formations, hypostatizations of concepts artificially built up with the help of words such as "the circular square," "the falling of the sky," "the highest point of the sky," "the son of a barren women," and so on.
2. Nonacceptance here may sound strange, when the ascetic is allowed food by begging only. What is meant is that nothing more should be accepted than what is absolutely necessary for keeping the body and soul together. This warning to the ascetic is necessary in view of the fact that householders like to make many presents to the yogis for obtaining blessings of prosperity and the yogi then becomes the owner of wealth and property.

CHAPTER 6

Jainism

1. The *Niyamasāra* (Essence of Regulations)

□ The following is a free translation of parts from Kunda Kunda Āchārya's (first century B.C.?) *Niyamasāra*. The selections describe the nature of the soul, vows, measures, and protections, as preached by Jainism.

The Jainas do not accept God or the Supreme Spirit as the creator and controller of the world. Every soul can be a supreme spirit and there can be an infinite number of supreme spirits. Also, they do not generally differentiate between the *ātman* (self, soul) and the *jīva* (soul) and use the two words as synonyms. They say that the *jīva* is the *ātman* in bondage and the *ātman* is the *jīva* liberated. But here Kunda Kunda Āchārya draws the distinction, saying that the *ātman* has to be realized and the *jīva* given up. But here and there he ignores this technical distinction in his work.

The Jainas look upon *karma* (actions) as a kind of material dust that sticks to the pure *ātman* and pollutes it, thereby limiting its original powers and glory. They make vows, the first of which is the vow of non-injury (*ahiṁsā*), which has been made famous by Gandhi and is applied in different ways in national and international politics. This virtue is predominantly Jaina, although it is found in the Vedas also.

Verse 68 may refer to the practice of self-immolation or bodily exercise. At any rate, Jaina asceticism is the most rigorous of all asceticisms in India. For further information, see "Introduction to Hinduism: A Summary Account," ¶11–12, 15. □

2. It is said in the Jaina scripture that there is a way and there is a destination. The way is the means of liberation, its destination is *nirvāṇa* (unagitated state, salvation).

5. Rightness results from belief in credible persons, scriptures, and principles (categories). A credible person is one who is devoid of all defects and is full of good qualities.

7. The supreme soul (spirit) is without any residue of defects and possesses the splendors of unaided (by senses, mind, and so on) knowledge, and so on. Any other cannot be the supreme soul.

8. The word coming from his mouth and without any prior and posterior defects is pure and is called the scripture. The principles of reality are taught by it.

9. Souls, bodies, the medium of motion, the medium of rest, time, and space—these are the principles together with their qualities and modifications.

38. The *ātman* has to be attained by one and all, the eternal principle which is like our soul (*jīva*). It is different from the qualities and modifications produced by the limiting *karmas*.

45. Color, taste, smell, and touch, the modifications like the three genders, structure, and compositeness—all these do not belong to the soul.

56. The first vow of man is to know the presence of souls (*jīvas*) in collections, wombs, living beings, things in which striving (search) is present, and places; and then to change his conduct (action, activity) towards and away from them.

57. The second vow is to give up lying in attachment, hatred, or delusion (infatuation). This becomes the second vow[1] of the good man who never speaks falsehood.

58. The third vow is giving up even the idea of accepting gifts, when one, desirous of ultimate truth, goes in a village, city, or forest.

59. The fourth vow is the transformation (of one's mind) into that which is devoid (of any idea) of sex intercourse. Longing should disappear when one sees the form of a woman.

60. The fifth vow is that of the man (carrier) of right conduct (a saint) who renounces the knots (of attachment) and is accompanied by a detached state of mind.

61. The measure (measuredness, measured conduct, carefulness) in walking belongs to the saint who moves forward only after watching a distance of one *yuga*[2] in day and making sure that there are no living beings on the path.

62. The measure in speech is speaking what is good for oneself and for another, without backbiting, ridiculing, harshness, self-praise, and blaming of others.

63. The measure in eating is the eating of what is cooked by another (i.e., by begging) without praising the other for what was done by him, provided that the food is pure and does not include animal food.

64. The measure of lifting and laying down of books, drinking vessels, and so on, is the carefulness (in not destroying life in such acts).

65. The measure of disposing lies in disposing excretions, etc., without inconvenience to others, in hidden places containing no life.

66. From the practical point of view, the protection of mind[3] lies in the weeding out of impurities such as passions, infatuation (delusion), animal feelings, attachment, and hatred.

67. The protection of speech lies in avoiding gossip about women, kings, thieves, foods, etc., which is a cause of sin, and also in refraining from telling falsehoods, and so on.

68. The protection of the body is said to lie in giving up bodily activities like binding (tying), cutting, beating, contracting, expanding.

69. Know that as the protection of the mind which is the removal of attachment, and the like, and that as the protection of speech which is freeing it from falsehood, etc.

70. Finally, bodily protection[4] is that which is withdrawn from all bodily movements and nonattachment to the body; or it is the avoidance of injury and so on.

2. The *Tattvārtha sūtra*

☐ The following is translated from Umāsvāti's (third century A.D.) *Tattvārtha sūtra* (Aphorisms on the meaning of truth) with the help of the commentary by Bhāskaranandi (thirteenth or fourteenth century).

Yoga here does not mean what Patañjali means by the term, but the contact (joining) of the pure *ātman* with action (*karma*). This contact is established by the flowing in of actions into the pure *ātman* and is therefore called inflow also.

Kevala (purity) is a technical term in Jainism. After the *ātman* regains its omniscience, it is alone without its body, senses, mind, family, and friends. The word *kevala* indicates also that knowledge at that stage is pure, absolutely direct, independent, and unaided and unaccompanied by senses and mind. The knowledge of one who attains this stage is called *kevalajñāna* or knowledge without the aid of mind and senses.

When the *jīva* gets liberated no new *karmas* enter it and old ones are exhausted. The greatest stress is laid by the Jainas on freedom from *karmas* and all types of activity. For them the fall of the soul is a result of action. Other Indian religions also accept this idea, but along with those of cosmic ignorance or the Unconscious, the will of God, and so on, and make the idea look as though of secondary importance. ☐

Ch. 1. 4. The categories (principles) are (the seven): soul (*jīva*), nonsoul (*ajīva*), inflow, bondage, damming, exhausting, and liberation (*mokṣa*).

Ch. 6. 1. Yoga (joining, sticking) is the activity of the body, speech, and mind.

2. The same is called the inflow.

Ch. 8. 1. The causes of bondage are false knowledge, nonwithdrawal (from objects and pleasures), lapse (from truth and righteousness), impurities (passions), and contact (with *karma*).

2. Because of passions (desires), the soul (*jīva*) takes on bodies through contact with actions (*karmas*)—this is bondage.

21. The ripening (fructifying) of actions is experience (of pleasures and pains).

23. From it (experience) results exhausting (of *karmas*).

Ch. 9. 1. The obstruction of inflow is damming.

2. That is produced by (1) the protections, (2) the measures, (3) righteousness, (4) understanding the truth about the body, and so on, (5) the conquest of hunger, thirst, and so on, and (6) good conduct.

3. And through penance,[5] exhausting is effected.

Ch. 10. 1. After delusion is destroyed and the clouds and obstacles of true knowledge are removed, there is the aloneness (purity).

2. Liberation is absolute freedom from the totality of actions through the absence of the causes of bondage and through exhaustion (of past *karmas*).

NOTES

1. This vow requires giving up lying even when one's family and friends are concerned. Besides, one should not tell falsehood to hurt a man he hates or in cases of infatuation through love.
2. Four arms length.
3. The word *monogupti* means hiding, controlling, ruling.
4. Verses 56–60 give the five vows, 61–65 the five measures, and 66–70 the three protections.
5. The commentary says that penance is a part of righteousness, an absolute obligation. Yet it is mentioned again as it is very important for damming the inflow of new actions and also for exhausting the old actions.

CHAPTER 7

Buddhism

□ Buddhism was originally an Indian religion and still lives in some parts of India. But it has more adherents outside than in India, although it underwent several modifications outside. In the beginning it was a branch of the Aryan Way of life and its ideas have continued to have a tremendous influence on the way of life of the Indians. Some of its teachings are, therefore, also found in Hinduism. For further information, see "Introduction to Hinduism: A Summary Account," ¶10–12, 15, 17.

1. The Four Aryan Truths

Although Buddha called the truths he taught the Aryan Truths, the term has no racial meaning. The word *ārya* in literature is a term of respect, meaning noble. Right view means authentic, earnest, and true views about the nature of reality and man's life. Right livelihood means that one should not take to any profession, e.g., that of a thug or bank robber, under the pretext that it is a livelihood. Right effort is to warn those who do not make adequate ethical effort. Right mindfulness means constant nonforgetfulness of one's aim of life and is meant to prevent lapses. □

1. This, O monks, is the Aryan[1] truth of pain. Birth, old age, disease, and death are all painful. Grief, lament, dejection, despair are painful. Disappointment in not getting what is wanted is painful. In short, the five classes of grasping (i.e., by the five senses) are painful.

2. This, O monks, is the Aryan truth of the cause of pain. The craving that leads to birth after birth, associated with pleasure and lust, the craving that finds pleasure here and there, in other words, the craving for passion, for existence, for nonexistence —this is the cause of pain.

3. This, O monks, is the Aryan truth of the cessation of pain. It is a cessation without any vestige of craving, an abandonment, giving up, release, nonattachment.

4. This, O monks, is the Aryan truth of the way. It is the way that leads to the cessation of pain. This is the eight-fold way of right views, right aims, right words, right deeds, right profession, right effort, right mindfulness, and right *samādhi* (concentration). (*Saṁyutta-nikāya* [Combined collection], 5: 420)

2. Conditioned Origination

□ The Sanskrit word for conditioned origination is *pratītya-samutpāda*, which means a peculiar causal view of the Buddhists. According to it, the cause does not remain in the effect, but dies out before it is born. So the cause is only a necessary condition, a necessary occasion for the origination of the effect.

It is to be noted that ignorance (*avidyā*, nescience, unconscious) is not the ignorance of anybody, because that somebody comes into being as the third link (consciousness, *vijñāna*) of the chain of causation. He is not the condition of ignorance, but ignorance is the condition of that somebody. Consciousness here means the conscious particular, the conscious seed of individuality, the seed or root consciousness, the embryonic consciousness. Activities (*samskāras*) means, particularly in Buddhism, the germinative forces of the individual. They are prior to the individual and originate in *avidyā* (Nescience, which may be written with the capital *N*), produce the individual, and are modified and increased by the activities of the individual. *Samskāras* is sometimes translated as habit-energies, habits that are also energies or forces. They are not merely those of the individual, but are also transindividualistic or cosmic. The nature of the individual is constituted not only by the psychological forces (energies) acquired by his present and past actions, but also by the cosmic forces rooted in *avidyā*. They include cosmic and individual instincts, habits, and impressions. This peculiar significance of the word has to be kept in mind.

Nāma-rūpa (name-and-shape) is interpreted as mind (*nāma*) and matter (*rūpa*), i.e., the psychophysical individual. Out of the embryonic consciousness emerges the psychophysical individual. In literary language, *nāma* means name and *rūpa* means form, shape. The name-and-shape sense refers to all the six senses. According to the Buddhists, mind also is a sense. The six together constitute the sensorium.

Becoming (*bhāva*) has a special meaning in Buddhism. It means birth, decay, and death.

All misery is ultimately to be traced to ignorance. This succinct theory of causation forms the central idea of the appearance of the world (creation for the theistic schools) for the Buddhists. Buddhism is a nontheistic, but spiritual religion in India. □

1. Conditioned by ignorance, activities come to pass; conditioned by activities consciousness, conditioned by consciousness name-and-shape, conditioned by name-and-shape sense, conditioned by sense contact, conditioned by contact feeling, conditioned by feeling craving, conditioned by craving grasping, conditioned by grasping becoming, conditioned by becoming birth, conditioned by birth old age-and-death, grief, lamenting, suffering, sorrow, despair, come to pass. Such is the uprising of the entire mass of ill. This, brethren, is called (causal) happening.

2. But from the utter fading away and ceasing of ignorance (comes) ceasing of activities; from ceasing of activities ceasing of consciousness; from ceasing of consciousness ceasing of name-and-shape; from ceasing of name-and-shape ceasing of sense; from ceasing of sense ceasing of contact; from ceasing of contact ceasing of feeling; from ceasing of feeling ceasing of craving; from ceasing of craving ceasing of grasping; from ceasing of grasping ceasing of becoming; from ceasing of becoming ceasing of birth; from ceasing of birth old age-and-death, grief, lamenting, suffering, sorrow, despair cease. Such is the ceasing of the entire mass of ill. (*Saṁyutta-nikāya*, 22:90; in Mrs. Rhys Davids, *Kindred Sayings*, vol. 2., p. 32)

3. The Fire Discourse

□ The discourse is also called "The Fire Sermon." It may be noted that the word *fire* indicates passion, the burning of passion, and also the constant change, flow, of everything. It is the passion to enjoy, to love, to hate, the passion that is never satisfied once and for all, goes on shifting and changing, and is the cause of entanglement in further passion and rebirth, that the Buddha has in mind. This is an impassioned sermon of the Buddha. □

Buddha stayed in Uruvela for a long time and from there proceeded to Gayāśirṣa with a great following of monks, a thousand of them, who were previously following the traditional asceticism. There he addressed the brethren thus: "O monks, all things are on fire. How is it so? The eye and its objects are on fire. The feelings of pleasure and pain from its sensations are on fire. How is it so? They are on the fire of passion, hate, illusions, birth, old age, death, sorrow, laments, pain, dejection, and despair. This I say. The ear is on fire, the sounds are on fire. . . . The nose is on fire, smells are on fire. The tongue and its tastes are on fire. The mind, its congnitions, and its objects, pleasure and pain, are on fire. How is it so? They are on the fire of passion, hate, illusion, birth, old age, death, sorrow, laments, pain, dejection, and despair.

"The noble among you who are endowed with wisdom, O monks, realize this and develop detachment from the eye, its objects, its processes, and from the accompanying feelings, pleasure and pain. They develop detachment from the ear and sounds, from the nose and smells, from the tongue and tastes, from the body and its touch, from the mind and its congnitions and pleasures and pains.

"Becoming detached, they become free from passion; being free from passion, they become liberated. Then arises the realization: 'I am liberated.' Then there will be no rebirth, but only living a holy life. Then one knows that one has performed one's duty and that nothing remains to be done after realization."

After hearing this sermon, the minds of all the monks became free from passion, and all became liberated. (*Mahāvagga* [Great classification], 1: 21)

4. The Arhat

□ *Arhat* in Sanskrit means one who is worthy, the respectful person. Here it means the person who is worthy of salvation, Nirvāṇa. The Pāli form is *arahant*.

Although the Small Vehicle (Hīnayāna) does not accept that all can become Buddha, it treats the arhats as the sons of the Buddha. One may say that they are his spiritual sons. The goal of the arhat is Nirvāṇa. The Buddhists use the word *Brahma*, *Brahma-state*, and so on, meaning by them ultimate freedom, Nirvāṇa. We should keep in mind that Buddhism arose and thought in the Upaniṣadic atmosphere.

The arhat understands that the ego is but a compound of five groups. These are the five *skandhas*, also translated as the five aggregates that constitute the person who says, "I am." They are the aggregate of matter, that of feelings, that of ideas, that of *saṁskāras* (instincts, habits, potencies, and so on), and that of bits (series) of consciousness (*vijñāna*). Consciousness for the early Buddhists is not one, but a series, each following upon another. When personality is analyzed away into these aggregates, nothing is said to remain in residue. The arhat realizes this truth. There is a further division of these aggregates. □

Ah, happy indeed the arhats! In them no craving's found.
The "I am" conceit is rooted out; confusion's net is burst.
Lust-free they have attained; translucent is the mind of them.
Unspotted in the world are they, Brahma-become, with out-flows none.
Comprehending the five groups, pasturing in their seven own mental states,[2]
Worthy of praise, the true men, own sons of the Buddha.
Endowed with the seven-fold gem,[3] trained in the three trainings,[4]
These great heroes follow on, fear and dread overcome,
Endowed with the ten factors,[5] great beings concentrated,
Indeed, they are best in the world; no craving's found in them.
Possessed of the adept's knowledge, this compound[6] is their last.
In that pith of the Brahma-faring, they depend not on others.
Unshaken by the triple modes,[7] well freed from again-becoming,
Attained to the stage of "tamed," they are victorious in the world.
Above, across, below, no lure in them is found.
They roar the lion's roar: "Incomparable are Buddhas in the world."

Saṁyatta-nikāya, 3:83–84, in Edward Conze, *Buddhist Texts Through the Ages*, p. 42.

5. The Bodhisattva

□ Just as the arhat is the ideal saint of the Hīnayāna, the bodhisattva is the ideal saint of the Mahāyāna. The word means one whose being (*sattva*) is knowledge (*bodhi*, enlightenment). Knowledge here is the ultimate knowledge, the highest, and has ontological significance like the Logos, Reason.

The arhats also have enlightenment (*bodhi*) and as such are called Buddhas also, as the last line in the preceding selection shows. But the word *Buddha* is applied to them only figuratively. They do not aspire to become one with the Buddha himself and the Hīnayāna believes that they cannot become one with him. But a bodhisattva can become the original Buddha himself in his transcendental state.

As the bodhisattva attains the formless state, he leaves back in his consciousness the world in which discrimination of the different forms of the world is made. He has gone beyond the worldly but is not out of this world. He is comparable to the lotus. The lotus flower and the lotus leaf have a peculiar surface. Like a waxed surface, they do not absorb water which stays on them like pearls and falls without making the surface wet. This simile is generally used to convey the idea of noncontamination, dispassion. Thus, himself all purity, the bodhisattva remains in the world to teach and uplift others. As there are different men with different attitudes, aptitudes, and levels of maturity, the bodhisattva selects different means or methods to educate different types of men. □

69. Although the son of Jina[8] has penetrated into the immutable true nature of dharmas (entities),[9]
Yet he appears like one of those who are blinded by ignorance, subject as he is to birth, and so on. This is truly wonderful.
70. It is through his compassionate skill in means for others that he is tied to the world,
And that, though he attained the state of a saint, yet he appears to be in the state of an ordinary person.
71. He has gone beyond all that is worldly, yet he has not moved out of the world;
In the world he pursues his course for the world's weal, unstained by worldly taints.
72. As a lotus flower, though it grows in water, is not polluted by water,
So he, though born in the world, is not polluted by worldly dharmas.[10]
73. Like a fire, his mind constantly blazes up into good works for others;
At the same time he always remains merged in the calm of the trances[11] and formless attainments.[12]
74. Through the power of his pervious penetration (into reality), and because he left all discrimination behind,
He again exerts no effort when he brings living beings to maturity.
75. He knows exactly who is to be educated, how, and by what means,
Whether by his teaching, his physical appearance, his practices, or his bearing.
76. Without turning towards anything, always unobstructed in his wisdom,
He goes along, in the world of living beings, boundless as space, acting for the weal of beings.
77. When a bodhisattva has reached this position, he is like the Tathāgatas (Buddhas).[13]
In so far as he is in the world for the sake of saving beings.
78. But as a grain of sand compares with the earth, or a puddle in a cow's footprint with the ocean,
So great still is the distance of the bodhisattvas from the Buddha.

Ratnagotravibhāga [Division of the lineage of gems], I, in Edward Conze, *Buddhist Texts through the Ages*, pp. 130–31.

6. The Highest Virtues (*Pāramitās*)

□ In the Mahāyāna Buddhism, we find the six great virtues (*pāramitās*) extolled. *Pāramitā* means that which has gone to the other shore. It is etymologically explained differently, but finally means a virtue that is carried to its perfection, beyond limits. By implication, one shore is that at which one starts cultivating the virtue and the other is that at which it ends up in perfection. Here Prajñākaramati (fourth century) shows how they are related, each leading to the next, and finally all ending up in the virtue of the highest knowledge (*prajñā*). These virtues are generally said to be six, but some add four more making the number ten. The additional four are skillfulness in spiritually educating the different types of men, ability to pray, strength of mind and body, and knowledge (different from *prajñā*, the highest virtue). The following selections from chapters 2 and 5 explain the virtues of charity and character, those from chapter 6 the virtue of forbearance, those from chapter 7 the virtue of vigor, those from chapter 8 the virtue of meditation, and those from chapter 9 the virtue of the highest, ultimate knowledge. □

Ch. 2. 9. (The bodhisattva says:) I shall be the inexhaustible treasure of all the needy. I shall be in the vanguard with all kinds of means (for them).

10. I shall give up all enjoyments, in which by nature the ego is involved. I shall give up the merit that leads to all the three worlds[14] (paths) and I shall do so for fulfilling the desires of all beings and without expecting any return.

11. Nirvāṇa is the renunciation (negation) of everything. My mind desires Nirvāṇa. If everything is to be given up by me, it is better that I make a gift of everything to living beings.

12. I am the light for those who need light; the bed for those who need a bed; and the servant of those who need service. I am all these to all.[15]

Ch. 5. 1. He who desires to maintain discipline (of oneself) should with effort protect his mind (enlightened mind, *citta*). It is not easy to protect discipline (character, *śīla*), for mind, uncontrolled, is fickle.

8. The sage (Buddha) told of everything that issues from the sinful mind. There is nothing more awful than mind.

9. If the virtue of charity can remove poverty from the world, why is there poverty still in the world? This (phenomenon) does not go to the credit of the earlier enlightened ones (who taught this virtue only).

10. That is called the virtue of charity which is the giving up by mind (*citta*) of every bit of property. So this virtue is mind itself (i.e., a transformation of mind, not the physical act of the body).

11. Where can the fish, and so on (other edible living beings) be removed so that (when they are taken away from this world) I can have no possibility to kill them? So the virtue of character is the acquisition by the mind (of the attitude, disposition) of reluctance and indifference (to kill).

17. They go about in vain in space to destroy misery and obtain happiness. But they forget the hidden (secret) mind that is full of these attributes.

18. So the mind presided over by me has to be made well protected by myself. What is the use of all the vows and rites, if the vow of the protection of mind is left out?

23. I fold my hands (salute) before those men who desire to safeguard their mind. Protect mindfulness[16] and the consciousness accompanying all activities.[17]

24. As a man suffering from illness is not capable of doing any of his actions, even so the mind diseased in these two (*smṛti* and *samprajanya*, mindfulness and consciousness accompanying all activities) is not competent for any action.

Ch. 6. 2. There is no sin equal to hatred and there is no penance equal to forbearance (the virtue of patience, endurance, and so on). So by all means cultivate forbearance.

3. Mind does not obtain peace, pleasure, or happiness, it cannot sleep or be steady so long as the bone (bit) of hate remains in the heart.

9. Pleasantness of my mind is not to be disturbed even when the worst evil visits me. There is nothing desirable in a bad mood of mind. Otherwise, happiness decreases.

10. What is the use of the mood (of anger) if injury can be avenged; and what is its use if injury cannot be avenged?

11. Nobody becomes voluntarily angry, saying "Let me be angry." And anger does not rise, saying "Let me rise."

Ch. 7. 1. Such endurance becomes vigor (*vīrya*, enthusiasm, energy). For enlightenment is founded (stands) on vigor. As there is no movement without wind, there is no merit without vigor.

2. What is vigor? It is enthusiasm[18] for the *summum bonum*. What is its opposite called? It is laziness, attachment to evil, dejection of mind, depreciation of oneself.

Ch. 8. 1. Thus increasing one's vigor, let man establish mind in *samādhi*. He whose mind is agitated still remains within the teeth of sorrow.

2. Agitation does not occur when one distinguishes between body and mind. So

leaving the (material) world, give up all agitation (disturbing ideas).

87. Walking where one likes and as long as one likes, one lives without any anticipation and freely in some empty temple, under a tree, or a cave without the bother of attendants and protection.

88. His abode is where he walks (lives) freely (uninhibited); bound to nothing and to none, he enjoys the happiness of complete contentment, which is not attainable even by Indra (the king of heaven).

89. Then after the distinctions are quieted by meditating on the qualities of enlightenment through their various forms, let one meditate on the mind of enlightenment.

90. Let one meditate longingly (affectionately) on the sameness of *parātman.* All the pains and pleasures of others should be regarded as one's own.[19]

107. This series (of meditation), whose pleasantness is the same as that of the pains[20] of others, enters the waveless (disturbanceless, unagitated) like the swans entering the forest (garden) of lotuses.

108. One is happy with the oceans of happiness present in the creatures being liberated. Of what use is salvation that is without any aesthetic pleasure?[21]

Ch. 9. 1. All this instrumentality was told by the sage (Buddha) for the sake of enlightenment (the virtue of knowledge, wisdom, *bodhi*). So produce enlightenment with the desire to remove misery.

2. Truth is of two kinds, the limited (*saṁvṛti*, the surrounded, the bounded, pragmatic, empirical) and the ultimate (*paramārtha*). The (ultimate) Truth is beyond the mind (*buddhi*, reason). Mind is called *samvṛti.*

3. Then the world is seen in two ways, that of the yogi and that of the ordinary man. The world of the ordinary man is sublated (negated) by that of the yogi.

8. There is no error in (seeing) the world for the knowers of the truth, merely because of the (contradiction between) yogi and *samvṛti* forms of knowing. Otherwise, if one says that a lady is polluted, he can never be true in this world.

9. If merit from Jina (Buddha) is real, how can it be so if he is an illusion? And if the beings are illusory, why are they reborn after death?

34. If that about which it is said, "It is not there," is never obtained, then if negation has no basis (with reference to which it is true), how can it then appear before our mind?[22]

35. When neither being (the positive) nor nonbeing (the negative) stands before our mind, then because of no other alternative it settles into quietude as it has no object.

36. Then man becomes like *cintāmaṇi*[23] and *kalpataru*[24] and has all his desires fulfilled. Through discipline and meditation, he sees then the prototype of Jina (Buddha).[25]

49. Without Voidness (*śūnyatā*), mind becomes again bound (to the positive and the negative). So meditate upon Voidness in the formless *samādhi.* (Prajñākaramati, *Bodhicaryāvatārapañjikā* [Exposition of the conduct of the awakened], ed. by Louis de la Vallée Pousin.)

NOTES

1. Although Buddha called the truths he taught the Aryan Truths, the term has no racial meaning. The word *ārya* in literature is a term of respect, meaning noble. For further explanation, see *Idealistic Thought of India*, by P. T. Raju (London: Allen & Unwin, 1953).
2. They are faith, shame, fear of blame, truth, the output of vigor, mindfulness, and wisdom.
3. They are the seven limbs of enlightenment: mindfulness, investigation of mental states, vigor, tranquility, rapture, concentration, and even-mindedness. All together constitute enlightenment, which is called seven-fold.
4. Morality, concentration, and wisdom.
5. The ten abilities (powers) of Buddha. They are (a) understanding the causal occasion and its distinction from the noncausal occasion; (b) understanding the result of the causal occasion and the cause for taking on *karma*; (c) understanding the way leading to all destinations, (d)

understanding the world and its elements; (e) understanding the inclinations, tendencies of things; (f) understanding the abilities, virtues, of other beings; (g) understanding how meditation, concentration, and deliverance are defiled or purified; (h) remembering all previous births; (i) comprehending how beings are born and are dying and the effects of their *karma* on them; and (j) checking the outward going senses and mind and remaining, with the highest wisdom, in ultimate absolute freedom.

6. The person that is an aggregate of aggregates.
7. These modes are the states resulting in calling oneself better, equal, and worse when compared with others.
8. *Jina* means the conqueror and here he signifies spiritual conquest. The word is generally used for the founder of Jainism.
9. In Buddhist literature, *dharma* has many meanings. Here it means objects, entities that constitute reality.
10. Here *dharmas* mean the worldly objects, their temptations, actions and their merits and demerits.
11. *Samādhis*.
12. They are the attainments of *śūnya* (void), the original *vijñāna* (pure consciousness), etc., which are without form and are indescribable.
13. See ch. 17, n. 21.
14. The past, present, and future worlds.
15. The bodhisattva who practices the virtue of charity does not refuse to serve any need of any one, even if he knows that it is socially unacceptable.
16. That is, one should remember constantly the truths one has attained and the vows one has taken to avoid lapses through forgetfulness.
17. *Samprajanya* is a difficult word to translate. A man has *samprajanya* if he is conscious of his sitting when he is sitting, if he is conscious of his speaking when he is speaking, if he is conscious of his anger when he is angry. It is constant awareness of one's thought, speech, action. Such consciousness enables man to check and control himself and avoid thinking, speaking, and acting unconsciously as a matter of habit or as merely a result of psychophysical urges.
18. It is difficult to give an exact English word for *vīrya*. It is enthusiastic vigor shown, e.g., by Florence Nightingale, the founder of the Red Cross, for her cause. Similar vigor can be found in fighting soldiers also. According to the context, it means courage, bravery, enthusiasm, heroism, etc. Cf. Carlyle's *Hero and Hero-worship*. It is often found also in charismatic individuals.
19. The commentary separates the two sentences of this stanza (90). *Parātman* in the first line means the over-individual self that is common to all persons. The commentary says that the second means that the bodhisattva regards the pains and pleasures of all as his own.
20. The wording of this stanza does not give its intention clearly. What is meant is that at the highest stage of enlightenment, I experience my own pleasures as I experience the pains of others. If another has a toothache, I may suffer from sympathy, but do not have a toothache. Similarly the bodhisattva experiences his own pains and pleasures as not his own.
21. The bodhisattva experiences greater joy from the happiness of those obtaining salvation than in his own entering Nirvāṇa. To see others happy gives an emotional, aesthetic satisfaction, not found in one's own entering Nirvāṇa.
22. *Prajñā* is the consciousness one becomes when one transcends the opposites of being and nonbeing. It is the *bodhi*, the final enlightenment. It is often translated as knowledge and wisdom—which is not wrong, but does not bring out the full significance of the Buddhist idea.
23. A kind of precious stone that gives what one prays for.
24. A heavenly tree that grants all we desire.
25. Here Buddha is identified with *prajñā* and is compared to the prototype of the reflection or image, which is the ectype. The physical sun, for instance, is the prototype of its image in water. We have here the *imago-dei* idea modified by a different context.

CHAPTER 8

Later Developments

A. ŚAṄKARA, RĀMĀNUJA, AND MADHVA

☐ The orthodox religious thought of India is contained primarily in the Vedas (including the Upaniṣads), and secondarily in the *Brahma sūtras* of Bādarāyaṇa (fourth century B.C.) and the *Bhagavad-gīta* of Vyāsa. These three are called the *prasthānatrayī* (the basic three). All the Vedāntic sects accept the three as basic. The Mīmāṁsā or sacrificial religion accepts the first two parts of the Veda, the *Saṁhitās*, and the *Brāhmaṇas*, as basic; has its own aphorisms called the *Mīmāṁsā sūtras* composed by Jaimini; rejects Bādarāyaṇa's work; and does not care for the *Bhagavad-gītā*. Later Mīmāsakas adopted a different attitude.

In his work, Bādarāyaṇa attempts to systematize the views of the Upaniṣads and is, therefore, accepted as the authority by all the Vedāntins, who differ from one another in interpreting him. The aphorism given as follows is the most important from the spiritual point of view, as here the commentators give their understanding of the relation between the *ātman* and the Brahman. Most of the commentators accept that the finite *ātman* ("I am") is incomplete and finds its completion in the Supreme Ātman ("I am"). One may compare this position with the God of Judaism and Christianity, who says that He is "I am that I am" or only "I am." The relation between God and the finite *ātman* is that between two "ams," but not between an "am" and an "are" or between "I am" and "You are." The present aphorism says that the Lord is to be experienced as an infinite "am" completing and perfecting the finite "am." Then only can the former become the ground of the being of the latter. This seems to be the view of many of the commentaries, which differ, however, in interpreting this completion.

Śaṅkara (eighth century) and Rāmānuja (eleventh century) were the greatest commentators on Hindu scriptures who developed Hindu thought to a high degree. There is much similarity in their commentaries on the passage, but the latter does not accept even the essential identity of the soul and the Lord, as Śaṅkara does.

Besides the commentary from which the following selection has been made, Madhva (thirteenth century) wrote another commentary called *Aṇubhāṣya* (Atomic commentary). Both the commentaries are very short and uncritical, unlike those of Śaṅkara and Rāmānuja. In his commentary on this aphorism, Madhva relies on the epics, not on the Upaniṣads. He interprets the aphorism thus: "Ātman (Viṣṇu) is to be meditated on as the Lord; for the wise who know Him and contemplate Him as such, instruct (their pupils accordingly)."

Here Madhva identifies the *ātman* with Viṣṇu (one of the Trinity) and does not interpret the word as self or finite spirit, although the Upaniṣads use the word often in the latter sense. In his *Aṇubhāṣva*, Madhva explains the word *ātman* as *ādātā*, one who receives, takes (the Lord who receives the souls and takes them to his abode). The word *brahman* is explained as the great (*bṛhat*) and the perfect. For Madhva the words, *ātman* and *brahman*, denote adjectives, properties of Viṣṇu. Other commentators regard his interpretation as artificial.

As referring to an attribute of Viṣṇu, the word *ātman* is made to stand for Viṣṇu, the Lord. Madhva accepts complete difference between the Lord and the finite spirit (*ātman*). The idea of difference is not discussed at all by Madhva in his commentary on this aphorism, but is implied. Rāmānuja retains the element of identity, but interprets it as that between body and soul. □

They (the teachers) realize the Brahman verily as the ātman (self, spirit) and they teach us to grasp it as the ātman. (Bādarāyaṇa, *Brahma sūtras*, [Aphorisms on the Brahman], 4:1, 3)

Śaṅkara's Commentary: It is now to be discussed whether the Supreme Ātman, whose characteristics are given by the scripture, is to be grasped as "I" or as different from myself. It may be asked: How can there be this doubt when the word *ātman* meaning the inner self is heard? This is the reply: This word, *ātman*, can be understood as primary, only if there is no difference between the *jīva* (soul)[1] and the Lord. Otherwise, it has to be understood as having a subsidiary meaning. What then is the result? It has to be grasped as "not-I." The quality of being devoid of sin, cannot be grasped as its opposite cannot be grasped as the quality of being devoid of sin. The Supreme Lord is the one having the quality of being devoid of sin; the embodied (soul) is the one having the opposite quality. If the Lord is identical with the worldly (soul), he cannot have lordship. Then the scripture will be useless.[2] Even if the worldly soul is identical with the Lord, the scripture becomes useless as there will now be no need of it. Besides, such identity will contradict our perception, etc.[3] It is said that, even though the two (the *ātman* and the Lord) are different,[4] their oneness has to be perceived like the oneness of Viṣṇu, with the idol. May that be so.[5] But we should not reach the conclusion that primarily the *ātman* of the worldly (soul) is the Lord.

In answer to such an objection,[6] we say: The Supreme Lord has to be known as the *ātman*. Thus in the worship of the Supreme Lord, the Jābālas realize him as the *ātman*. "O magnificent God, verily you are I (myself) and verily I am you, O magnificent God."[7] Similarly, other statements like "I am the Brahman,"[8] and the like, are to be understood as the realizing of one's *ātman*. The sentences of the Upaniṣads such as "This, your *ātman*, is immanent in everything,"[9] "This, your *ātman*, is inward and immortal,"[10] "That is the truth, that is the *ātman*, thou art that,"[11] and so on make us grasp the Lord as the *ātman*. The observation that this (oneness) is to be imagined like the similarity between Viṣṇu and his idol, is false. For then this aphorism would teach what is of secondary importance. Further, it is opposed to the very wording. Where similarity is intended, the word is uttered only once as in "Mind is the Brahman,"[12] "The sun is the Brahman.'[13] But here it is said, "I am you and you are I." As this case is different from similarity statements, one understands nondifference. Furthermore, the perception of difference is forbidden. "He who worships another diety, saying he is one and I am another, does not know";[14] "He who sees many in the world goes from death to death";[15] "Everything will leave him who sees it as different from the *ātman*":[16] such innumerable Vedic statements prohibit the perception of difference. It is said that entities having opposed qualities (*ātman* and the Lord) can never be identical. But this is no objection. For the opposition between the qualities can be false. And what has been objected to on the ground that the Lord will then have to be denied is false; for the authority (validity) of the scriptures is there and, besides, such a conclusion does not follow. We do not advocate that the Lord becomes the worldly (soul). What then? What is advocated is that the worldly (soul), by giving up its worldliness, becomes the *ātman* of the Lord. Then the conclusion is that the Lord has the quality of being devoid of sin, and so on, and that it is false that the worldly (soul) has (essentially) the opposite quality. It is objected that then (if the two are nondifferent) there will be no one desiring salvation and that this is opposed to our perception (experience). But this objection is wrong. Before the dawn of (the highest) knowledge, worldliness is accepted. The activities of perception, and so on, belong to it (the worldly state). "Where all becomes the *ātman* for him (the liberated), then who perceives by what?"[17] Through such statements, the scripture shows that there is no perception, and so on, in the state of (the highest) knowledge (enlightenment). If it is objected that, in the absence of perception, and so on, even the scripture also will be absent, this will be no objection. For our position is the same. Beginning with "There a father becomes no-father,"[18] it is said, "The Veda becomes no-Veda."[19] Because of these words, we accept the absence of the scripture after (the highest) knowledge dawns. Then for whom is this rising of knowledge meant (if the *ātman* is the same as the Lord)? It is meant for you who are asking this question.

The scripture says "The I is the Lord." If one is enlightened thus, then there can be no nonenlightenment for anybody. Some advance the objection: As the *ātman* with *avidyā* is the second (another) to existence (Brahman), the nondifference (between the *atman* and the Brahman) becomes impossible. To them also the answer is the same (viz., after enlightenment there can be no duality). Hence fix your mind on the Lord as your very *ātman*. (*Brahma-sūtra-śaṅkara-bhāsyam* [Śaṅkara's commentary on the *Brahma Aphorisms*])

Rāmānuja's Commentary:[20] Now it is thought: Should the Brahman which is to be meditated upon be meditated upon as different from the meditator or as the *ātman* of the meditator? Which is correct? As different from the meditator. Why? Because the meditator is different from the inward *ātman*. That the two are different is shown by passages such as "It is more, because of the pointing out of difference,"[21] "From the teaching of the more,"[22] "No, another because of unavailability,"[23] and so on. The Brahman is to be worshiped (meditated upon) as it is. If it is worshiped in a form that does not belong to it, then the realization will be false. The rule is: "As a man does in this world, he becomes so after death."[24] Hence the Brahman is to be worshiped as an other.

Anticipating this, it is said, "They realize the Brahman ——." *Verily* (*tu*) means certainty. The Brahman is to be meditated upon as the *ātman* itself of the meditator. Just as the meditator is the inward *ātman* of his own body, the Supreme Brahman is the *ātman* of one's own *ātman*. Thus should one meditate. Why? The previous meditators realized thus: "I verily am you, O magnificent God, and you are verily I."[25] To answer how the Brahman, different from the meditators, is realized by them as "I," it (the aphorism) says, "They teach us to grasp it as the *ātman*." The scripture makes the meditators grasp this meaning, which is uncontradicted. The meaning is that the scriptures (Rāmānuja interprets *they* as scriptures) teach them thus. "He who resides in the *ātman* is inward to the *ātman*; he whom the *ātman* does not know, whose body is the *ātman*, and who controls the *ātman* from within—that *ātman* is immanent and immortal."[26] "O good one (Śvetaketu), for all the creatures being is the root, being is their field, in being they are established; that being is the *ātman* of all this."[27] "Verily, all this is the Brahman, is born from it, goes back to it, is maintained by it,"[28] and is, therefore, controlled by it, is its body. So this Brahman is the *ātman* of everything. Hence it is your *ātman*. So as the inner *ātman* is the *ātman* with reference to one's body, one thinks: "I am a god," "I am a man," As the Supreme Ātman of one's inner *ātman*, it is proper that the former also has to be sought as the "I." As all minds (*buddhis*) are founded in the unitary Brahman, all the worlds are also founded in the same unitary Brahman. So the scriptures propound (the relation) in opposite directions: "I verily am you, O magnificent God, you verily are I, O magnificent God."[29] "He who meditates on a deity as different, saying, 'He is one, I am another,' does not know."[30] "Meditate on this (finite) *ātman* as incomplete."[31] "Everything leaves him who thinks that it is other than the *ātman*."[32]

All such passages prohibit the seeking of anything as not one's *ātman*. But passages like "Having known the *ātman*, the initiator, as different"[33] teach seeking the *ātman* as different. But there is no opposition between these two teachings. As the "I" is sought as one's *ātman*, the prohibition of the seeking of it as another is defended. The seeking of it as different also is defended, because just as one's own *ātman* is to be understood as greater than one's body, the Supreme Ātman is to be understood as greater than one's *ātman*. As the greater one, the Brahman is the *ātman* of one's inner *ātman*. As the latter is the body of the Brahman, it is said in the prohibitory (of identity) sentence, "He (the finite *ātman*) is incomplete." Thus it stands that the Brahman is to be meditated upon as the *ātman* of the meditator. (*Śrī Bhāṣya* [Rāmānuja's commentary])

Madhva's Commentary: It is indispensable that those who seek release should by all means instruct their pupils that Ātman is the Lord and they (themselves) meditate on Him as such; for the wise understand Him thus: "I shall not think of another, I would know Ātman only, I contemplate Ātman; for Ātman is my Lord." They instruct their pupils thus: "Meditate on Ātman only as the Lord; know him only as the Lord; do not think of any other thing; for He is (thy) Lord." This is said in the *Bhaviṣyat Purāṇa*: "By those that seek release the contemplation of Ātman as the Lord should by all means be practiced. A person should not forget at least this to do, though he may be beset with various difficulties." "The meditation that Viṣṇu is the Lord should be practiced by all seeking release, and the instruction also should be similar. Abandoning this, no one can obtain release." (*Pūrṇaprajña-darśana* [Philosophy of Madhva], adapted from S. Subbarao, tr. *The Vedāntasūtras with the Commentary of Śrī Madhvāchārya*)

B. THE KALI AGE (YUGA)

□ According to Hindu mythology, there are four ages (aeons) that succeed one another in a cycle: Kṛta, Tretā, Dvāpara, and Kali. In these aeons the virtues of men are different. As said in the ethical code of Manu, 1:81–86 (see chapter 4), in the first age, penance is the dominant virtue; in the second, knowledge; in the third, sacrifice; and in the Kali age, charity. □

The observance of caste, stages of life, and their laws will not obtain in the Kali age. The ceremonial enjoined by the Ṛg, Yajus, and Sāma Vedas will not be observed. In this age marriages do not take place with sacred ceremonies. The rules that bind the disciple to the spiritual teacher will not obtain. The laws regulating the conduct of wife and husband will be neglected. No oblations will be offered to gods with fire. Whatever be the family, the man of wealth and power gets the right to marry from any tribe. . . . Every book will be scripture because people think so. . . . In the Kali age, fasting, penance, charity will be righteousness, even when practiced whimsically. . . . Men's minds will be preoccupied with the acquisition of wealth, which will be spent solely on selfish gratifications. Women follow their inclinations and will be fond of only pleasure. . . . Verily, there will be no abundance in the Kali age and men cannot be happy. They will take their food without washing and bathing, without worshiping fire, god, and without offering oblations to ancestors. Women will be fickle, short, and fond of eating. They will have many children without the means to support them. They scratch their heads with both hands, and disobey their parents and husbands. . . . They will be scolds and liars, indecent and immoral, and will attach themselves to dissolute men. . . .

Oppressed by famine and taxation, men will leave their native lands for those growing rough grains. The Vedic way of life will be destroyed, men will become heretics, iniquity will be rampant, and the duration of life will be smaller. As a result of dreadful penances not belonging to the scriptures, as a result of the vices of the rulers, there will be infant mortality. Girls will give birth to babies at the age of five, six, or seven. Men beget them at the age of eight, nine, or ten. Man will be gray at twelve. No one lives longer than twenty.

In the Kali age, men corrupted by unbelievers stop worshiping Viṣṇu, the lord of sacrifice and everything. They ask: "Why are the Vedas the authority? Who are these gods and Brahmins? What is the need for purification with water?" Then the clouds give little rain; there will be little corn in the ear; the crop will be poor with little kernal. . . . Endowed with little sense, men, with the infirmities of mind, speech, and body, will commit sins daily. Everything that afflicts beings, everything vicious, impure, and wretched will be produced during the Kali age. Then in some lands, a separate way of life will be followed, which will be unrelated to the holy scriptures, without oblations to fire, and hymns to gods. It is then, in the Kali age, that man acquires by the smallest exertion as much eminence in virtue as hard penance in the pure Kṛta age. (*Viṣṇu purāṇa* [Epic of Viṣṇu], bk. 4, ch. 1; adapted from H. H. Wilson, tr., *The Viṣṇu Purāṇa*)

C. ŚAṄKARA'S HYMN TO ŚAKTI (GODDESS)

□ The following is a free translation of ten verses from the *Saundaryalaharī* (Wave of beauty) attributed to Śaṅkara. Scholars doubt whether this Śankara is the same as the Advaitin Śaṅkara (see foregoing section A) who condemned every tradition except the Vedic. But the traditionalists themselves say that the two are the same. This hymn is addressed to Śakti, the wife of Śiva. Here Śaṅkara shows that by nondualism he does not mean consciousness without power or energy and that ultimately the two are identical. This position agrees with that of Kasmir Śaivism, of which he is accepted as the reviver. It also supports the opinion that he was a worshiper of Śakti also and that his family had that tradition of worship, indeed, in its right-handed form, viz., without the five M's—wine (*madya*), flesh (*māṁsa*), fish (*matsya*), symbolic gestures of moods (*mudrā*), and sex intercourse (*maidhuna*). The left-handed form observes them literally, but the right-handed one makes symbolic substitutes. See "Introduction to Hinduism: A Summary Account," ¶14, for further information. □

1. Only when united to Śakti, Śiva has power to create;
   Otherwise, the god can have no power even to move.
   Of adoration worthy are you for Hara (Śiva), Hari (Viṣṇu), and Viriñci (Brahmā).
   How can one without merit be able to salute or praise you?
2. Viriñci created all the worlds in full
   Obtaining a tiny speck of dust from your lotus-feet;
   Śauri (Viṣṇu) supports these worlds somehow with his thousand heads;
   And Hara (Śiva) reduces them to ashes and besmears himself with them.
3. You are the sun illuminating the darkness of the ignorant.
   For the insentient, you are the sprouting honey of the bud of consciousness.
   For the poor, you are the rosary of wishing stones.
   For those sunk in the ocean of births, you are the tusk of the boar,[34] Muraripu (Viṣṇu).
4. Other gods grant desires and freedom from fear by the gesture of their hands;
   You alone do not exhibit openly the granting of freedom from fear.
   To protect from fear and to grant more than prayed for,
   Your able feet are the refuge for the worlds.
5. Once upon a time, Hara (Viṣṇu), having worshiped you, the giver of prosperity to the devotees,
   Became a woman[35] and stirred the mind of even Śiva, the destroyer of the three cities.[36]
   Cupid also, having saluted you with his body charming to the eyes of Rati[37]
   Becomes powerful enough to infatuate the minds of even sages.
6. His bow is made of flowers, his bow string of honey bees and his five arrows (of flowers).

Spring is his charioteer, the Malaya (south) wind is his chariot.
Yet he conquers alone the whole world, O daughter of the Himalayas,[38]
Obtaining a little of favor from the side glance of your eyes.

7. May that figure of yours be ever before us—a figure
With the waist band (a gold ornament) rattling (with little bells),
With breasts like the two sides of the head of a baby elephant[39] and with thin waist,
With face like the full moon in autumn, and with bow, arrows, noose, and goad in its (four) hands.

8. Some fortunate men worship you, the wave of consciousness and bliss,
As lying on the cot in the form of Śiva,[40] reclining on the cushion of Parama Śiva,[41]
In the house of Cintāmaṇi[42] with its pools and gardens,
In the island of gems, surrounded by forests of heavenly trees,
In the middle of the ocean of nectar.

9. Having crossed the whole path of Kula[43] with the earth principle in the Mūlādhara[44] plexus,
The Water principle in the Maṇipūra plexus, and the Fire principle in the Svādhiṣṭhāna,
The Air principle in the heart, and the Ether principle above it,
The Mind principle between the eye brows, you are now playing hidden in the Sahasrāra lotus with your husband (Śiva).

10. Sprinkling the whole world with the essences out of the springs
Of your nectar issuing out of your two feet,
You return with your great, glorious nectar to your original abode
And like the coiled serpent you sleep in the depths of the Kulakuṇḍa (Mūlādhāra plexus).[45]

D. NATURE OF DEVOTION

□ Devotion is love of God. It is one of the ways to salvation, as explained in the previous account of Hinduism. □

Ch. 1. 1. Now, we shall explain devotion.

2. Its nature is the supreme love of Him (God).

3. Its intrinsic nature is immortality (nectar).

4. Obtaining which, man becomes the realized, the immortal, and satisfied.

5. Obtaining which, he desires nothing, grieves of nothing, hates nothing, is not pleased with anything, and does not go after anything.

6. Knowing which, he becomes intoxicated, loses all movement; for him his *ātman* becomes the pleasure garden.

15. Its definitions are given, because of many view points.

16. Parāśara says that devotion is love of worship, and so on.

17. Garga says that it is love of divine stories and spiritual discussions.

18. Śāṇḍīlya says that it is all the foregoing but without prejudice to delight in the *ātman*.

19. Nārada says that it is the surrender of all activities to him (God) and extreme anguish in forgetting him.

Ch. 4. 51. The nature of love is indescribable.

52. Like the dumb man's enjoyment of taste.

53. It appears in one deserving.

54. It is an experience without qualities, without being characterized by desire, increasing every moment, continual, and very subtle.

55. Obtaining it, man sees it only, hears it only, (speaks of it only), and thinks of it only.

56. Secondary devotion is of three kinds because of the difference in qualities or because of the differences among the devotees accordingly as they are in distress, or desire some worldly reward, or are inquisitous.

57. Each preceding one is higher than the succeeding one. (*Nārada bhakti sūtras* [Nārada's aphorisms on devotion], adapted from Swami Tyāgīsananda, tr., *Nārada bhakti sūtras*)

E. SIKHISM: *THE ĀDI GRANTH*

□ *The Ādi Granth* means the original book. It is the holy book of the Sikhs (learners or disciples). The following three songs have been selected from it.

For a general introduction to Sikhism, see "Introduction to Hinduism: A Summary Account," ¶1, 12, 16, and 22. □

1.

(There are) innumerable (silent) repetitions (of the name of God), innumerable reverences.
Innumerable worships, innumerable austerities.
Recitations of innumerable books and of the Veda with the mouth,
Innumerable jogs[46] (of those who) remain secluded in their heart,
Innumerable devotees, reflecting on the comprehension of his qualities.
Innumerable truthful ones, innumerable bountiful ones.
Innumerable heroes, eating iron in the face.
Innumerable apply continual meditation in silence.
What is (thy) power? What (thy) thought? I cannot be sacrificed (to it) one time.
What is pleasing to thee, that is good work. Thou art always in safety, O Formless!

(Ernest Trumpp, tr., *The Holy Scripture of the Sikhs*, p. 6)

2.

(1) Speaking, speaking (my) heart is proclaiming (his qualities), as is known (to my heart), so it proclaims (them).
He, who is proclaimed, how great is he, in which place is he?
As many as are telling (his qualities), all having told (them) continue meditating (upon them).
Pause
O father, he (Hari) is invisible, inaccessible, infinite!
True is the preserver of a pure name, of a pure place.
(2) It is not known how much thy command is, no one knows to write it down.
If a hundred poets be assembled, not a moment they cause to arrive (at it), though they weep.
His value has been obtained (found out) by no one, all tell it by hearsay.
(3) Pīrs, prophets, Saliks, Sadiqs and martyrs
Shekhs, Mullas, Darveshes: a great blessing has come upon them, who continually read (his) salutations.
(4) Without asking (anybody) he makes, without asking he pulls down, without asking he gives and takes.
His own power he himself knows, he himself produces the (primary) causes.
He, looking on, sees all; to whom he pleases, he gives.
(5) The name of (his) place is not known nor how great his name is.
How great is that place, where my king dwells?
None can arrive there, to whom shall I go to ask?
(6) Castes and no-castes do not please (him), if he makes one great.
In the hand of the great one are the greatnesses (honors), to whom he pleases, he gives.
By his own order he adorns (a man), not a moment he delays.
(7) Every one recites much (his qualities) in the thought of taking much (from him).
What a great donor shall he be called? His gifts are not counted.
O Nānak! There is no deficiency coming forth, thy storerooms are from age to age.

(*Ibid.*, p. 74)

3.

The mother thinks that her son is getting big (growing).
She does not know so much that day by day his life-time is getting less.
Saying, "Mine," "mine" (thou art), she fondles him excessively, Yam Rāu,[47] looking on, laughs
Thus the world is misled by thee in error!

How shall it understand when it is deluded by *māyā* (illusion)?
Kabīr[48] says: Give up the pleasure of the world, in this society (thou) must certainly die!
Mutter him, who is omnipresent, O man, (it is) the word of another life, in this wise wilt thou cross the ocean of the world.
When it is pleasing to him, then faith springs up.
Error and mistake depart from within.
Understanding and knowledge (of the Supreme Being) are produced, the mind is wakeful.
By the favor of the Guru[49] deep meditation settles in the heart.
In this society (thou wilt) not die.
If thou knowest his order, thou wilt be united with the Lord.
(*Ibid.*, p. 126)

F. THE YOGA OF MUSIC

□ The yoga of music is directly related to devotion. Devotion is inner attachment, love. Without this psychological and spiritual attitude, music cannot lead to salvation. Music is not regarded by its philosophers in India as a means of diversion and pleasure, but as a path to God-realization and is called *nāda-brahma-yoga* or the Yoga of the Brahman as Sound. This Brahman is regarded by the philosophers of grammar as the Word. Music enables man to get merged in the peace and bliss of the spiritual aspect of sound. The sense of music, when developed, enables us, like the moral sense, intuitively to distinguish between harmony and disharmony, right and wrong, to realize the discordance of the worlds with ideal reality or existence, and the havoc caused by anger, and so on, on our being.

Tyāgarāja (or Tyāgarāju, 1767–1847) wrote his songs in the Telugu language and there are many editions of his songs. The four selected here are translated from the *Tyāgarāja hṛdayamu* (Heart of Tyāgarāja), p. 291, part I, and the *Tyāgarāja-kīrtana-hāramu* (Garland of Tyāgarāja's songs), p. 64. □

1. Knowledge of music without devotion to God:
O mind, can it be the right path?
Upon this knowledge have meditated Bhṛgu
Nateśa, Hanumān, Agastya (Ghaṭaja), Mataṅga,
Nārada[50] and other knowers. Through it
Are known the right and wrong, that the worlds
Are full of *māyā*, and the purpose of conquering
The six enemies (anger, etc.) born of the body, and so forth.
All this is known to Tyāgarāja.
2. O mind, devotion accompanied by the nectar of the basic sound[51] and mood[52]
Leads to heaven and salvation.
Why do you walk like a crane or leap[53] like a frog on the lotus called the Supreme Bliss?
To grasp that original sound[54] issuing from the Mūlādhāra plexus[55] is the blissful salvation.
That is salvation which is to discriminate the seven notes (of the octave) in the uproar.
Is there pleasure in beating the drum without knowing (the order of) beats and their movement?
Singing the praise of the Lord without a pure mind is (like) the action (sound) of a pig, O mind!
Salvation is to obtain enlightenment after many lives.
O mind, the liberated is he who, with inborn devotion, knows the moods.
The secrets of the ocean of notes (of the octave) revealed by Śiva to his wife
Are known to this blessed Tyāgarāja.
Have faith and learn them from him.
3. He exists for those who say that he exists.
Will the words of those who cry aloud that he exists be false today?
Why do you not come to me? I long to see your sweet face with smooth cheeks.
You, praised by Tyāgarāja, are the merciful Lord protecting the devotees

Who sing your praises, giving up sleep, delicately taking
The tambura,[56] with exact intonation of the notes, and with pure mind.

4. O mind, knowledge of the science of music gives similarity (to the Supreme) and bliss,
When accompanied by the pleasure from the story of Rāma,
Which is full of aesthetic moods[57] such as love and so forth.
This knowledge obtained by the skilful Tyāgarāja[58]
Produces love and devotion, affection of good men,
The grace of the Lord, and the bounty of vows,
Their observance, glory, and wealth.

G. TAMIL ŚAIVISM

☐ Śaivism is very strong in the Tamil-speaking South and produced a number of saints. It went into some conflict with Buddhism and Jainism. The conflict between Śaivism and Jainism was a little violent at times. These verses are from the Tamil Saiva Saint, Sambandār, whose house, it seems, was set on fire by the Jainas. ☐

18. Those Buddhists and mad Jains may slander speak.
Such speech befits the wanderers from the way.
But he who came to earth and begged for alms,
He is the thief who stole my heart away.
The raging elephant charged down at Him;
O marvel! He but took and wore its hide;
Madman, men think of Him, but He is the Lord
Who in great Brahmāpuram does abide

24. Blest the Brahmans pure, the heavenly ones and kine,
Cool rain fall on the earth! May the king's glory shine!
Perish all forms of ill! Let Hara's name resound!
May sorrow pass away, from earth's remotest bound!

(F. Kingsbury and G. E. Phillip, tr., *Hymns of the Tamil Śaivaite Saints*)

NOTES

1. The *jīva* (soul) is the *ātman* (spirit) circumscribed by and carrying the potencies of previous *karmas* (actions). It is limited by reason (*buddhi*), mind (*manas*), senses, and *prāṇa* (vital principle), is still unenlightened, and transmigrates.
2. Because there is no point in exhorting the finite soul to become something more, as it is already the same as the Lord.
3. Our perception, ordinary experience, shows that the individual soul does not have the qualities of the Lord.
4. This is an objection from the Vedānta School. Some Vedāntins who prefer difference to identity say that the identity passages are meant to teach similarity or imitation. According to them, this aphorism exhorts man to imitate the Lord. Cf. imitation of Christ. Śaṅkara does not accept their view.
5. This is not the answer of Śaṅkara, but of the propounders of difference, who say that just as there is some likeness between Viṣṇu and his idol in the temple, there can be a likeness between the soul and the Lord, and that we should not reach the conclusion that the two are identical.
6. Most of the commentators of the *Brahma sūtras* start with an anticipatory objection or a view which they do not hold and give their view as a criticism of the anticipated, unacceptable view. Now begins Śaṅkara's own view.
7. *Bṛhadāraṇyaka*, *Mādhyandinaśākha*, 5:7, 22.
8. *Bṛhadāraṇyaka Upaniṣad*, 1:4, 20.
9. *Ibid.*, 3:4, 1.
10. *Ibid.*, 3:7, 3.

11. *Chāndogya Upaniṣad*, 6:8, 7.
12. *Ibid.*, 3:18, 1.
13. *Ibid.*, 3:19, 1.
14. *Bṛhadāraṇyaka Upaniṣad*, 3:4, 10.
15. *Kaṭha Upaniṣad*, 4:11 and *Bṛhadāraṇyaka Upaniṣad*, 4:4, 11.
16. *Bṛhadāraṇyaka Upaniṣad*, 6:5, 7.
17. *Ibid.*, 2:4, 14 and 4:5, 15.
18. *Ibid.*, 4:3, 22.
19. *Ibid.*
20. Rāmānuja wrote more than one commentary. The following is a translation from his main commentary called *Śrī Bhāṣya* (Rāmānuja's commentary).
21. *Brahma sūtras* 2:1, 22.
22. *Ibid.*, 3:4, 8.
23. *Ibid.*, 1:1, 7.
24. *Chāndogya Upaniṣad*, 3:14, 1.
25. See n. 7.
26. Same as n. 10, and also 3:7, 9.
27. *Chāndogya Upaniṣad*, 6:8, 4.
28. *Ibid.*, 3:14, 1.
29. See n. 7.
30. *Bṛhadāraṇyaka Upaniṣad*, 3:4, 10.
31. Quotation not traceable.
32. *Bṛhadāraṇyaka Upaniṣad*, 6:5, 7.
33. *Śvetāśvatara Upaniṣad*, 1, 6.
34. This refers to the incarnation of Viṣṇu as a wild boar.
35. This refers to a mythological story. Viṣṇu having worshiped Śakti, became a very beautiful woman and became a temptress of Śiva himself because of his own austerities.
36. Śiva is said to have destroyed the three cities of the demons, perhaps enemies of the Indo-Aryans.
37. The wife of Cupid. He is called Smara, Manmatha, etc.
38. Śakti, the wife of Śiva, is in mythology the daughter of the mountain, Himalaya.
39. This common simile need not be interpreted to mean that the breasts of a beautiful woman are as big as the two protruding sides of the head of a baby elephant, but only as clearly and separately showing and massive.
40. Śakti in the process of creation becomes distinct from the consciousness that is Śiva. Mythology and popular religion represent Śakti as a woman, beautiful and horrible at once, walking on Śiva. The meaning is that then consciousness and activity become separated from each other.
41. The highest form of Śiva himself.
42. A gem that grants every desire.
43. *Kula* in literary language means tribe, race, family, etc. But in the Tāntric religious literature, in which this work of Śaṅkara is included, it is a technical term. Lakṣmidhara explains it thus: *Ku* means the Earth principle, and *kula* means that principle in which the Earth principle is merged (*līyate*). It is thus the name of the *Ādhāra* plexus. By convention and figure of speech, it has come to mean the path of the *suṣumṇā* nerve that is said to run from the bottom of the trunk to the brain.
44. These plexuses are said to be six, found at centers from the bottom of the spinal chord reaching up to the highest part of the brain. These centers (*cakras*, circles) are well explained in the *Ṣāṭcakrānirūpaṇi*, translated with notes and commentary by Arthur Avalon with the title, *The Serpent Power*. The names of the centers beginning from the bottom are Mūlādhāra (or merely Ādhāra), Maṇipūra, Svādhiṣṭhāna, Anāhata, Viśuddha, and Ājña. These are the sources or means of all experiences right up to and including mind. Above all lies the seventh, Sahasrāra (the thousand-petalled plexus), at which the finite consciousness becomes one with

Śiva himself. His energy, which is Śakti and which is nondifferent from him, roams up and down through the six plexuses. Of the six plexuses the respectively corresponding elements of experience are Earth, Water, Fire, Air, Ether, and Mind. The object of experience in the Sahasrāra is the divine. The word *element* here should not be interpreted in the sense of the elements of physics. They are *tattvas* (Thats, Thatnesses) or *bhūtas* (those that "have become" or the "have-becomes").

45. *Kulakuṇḍa* is a technical term in Tāntric literature and means the Mūlādhāra center. This is located between the generative and excretory organs and is the primary principle of pleasure. In normal human beings, it generally lies dormant and is excited only as Freud says. The right-handed Tāntric school says that it can and ought to be excited through the pure spiritual practices and worship and then made to pass through the higher centers until it reaches the Sahasrāra. Through this practice man transcends his physical being and, obtaining higher levels, acquires supernatural control over the levels transcended. However, doubts have been expressed about the possibility of identifying the Tāntric centers with physiological nervous centers. Arthur Avalon is the most important of the westerners who believe in the truth of this doctrine.
46. *Jog* means yoga in the Punjabi language.
47. Yam Rāu means Yama, the king, or the king of the world of the dead.
48. Kabīr (1440–1518) was Nānaks's predecessor. The following song belongs to him and is incorporated into the Holy Book of the Sikhs.
49. A *guru* is a spiritual teacher.
50. These are the names of famous mythological and semihistorical persons who realized God through the practice of music and some of them are regarded as the founders of Indian music.
51. Sound (*svara*) is the basic musical note with which the several combinations of notes are to be harmonized. Generally, it is represented by the sound of a drone.
52. These harmonies are determined by the different aesthetic moods (*rāgas*) according to which the different notes are combined without jarring.
53. Just as the aesthetic mood is disturbed by a jarring note and man is stirred up by a kind of pain, the ocean of bliss is disturbed by the irregular leaps of mind, by its fickleness.
54. *Nāda* (original sound) is still prior, psychologically and metaphysically, to *svara*. The musicians make any of the notes, depending on the nature of their own voice, the basic note and follow the resulting octave. Thus *svara* is relative. But *nāda* is more basic and deeper than *svara*.
55. *Nāda* is said to originate directly from the Mūlādhāra plexus, explained in the previous selection from *Wave of Beauty*.
56. *Tambura* is a stringed instrument playing the *svara* and corresponds to the drone.
57. It is difficult to translate the word *rasa* (aesthetic mood). It is aesthetic pleasure derived from any of the moods—love, humor, pathos, wonder, heroism, terror, disgust, and anger. These moods are made to rise by particular permutations and combinations of notes and then merge in the *svara*, when aesthetic pleasure arises. This pleasure is called *rasa* and is classified according to the moods from which it is derived. Its classifications also bear the same names. In music, a *rāga* is the mood expressed by a combination of notes. In psychology, the same is called *bhāva* and can be expressed in the different fine arts and poetry.
58. Tyāgarāja devoted his life to the worship of Rāma, the hero of the great epic, *Rāmāyaṇa* (Career of Rāma), regarded as an incarnation of Viṣṇu. The yoga he practiced is called the yoga of the Sound-Brahman. He is called the Beethoven of Indian music. He was a saint and had all his senses intact. In all his songs he mentions his name, as though God will otherwise forget him. But such is the practice of many composers of devotional songs in India.

CHAPTER 9

Recent Tendencies

A. THE BRĀHMO SAMĀJ

□ The Brāhmo Samāj is one of the reform movements in India and was started by Rājā Rām Mohun Roy (1772–1833). It emphasized monotheism, and preached abolition of the caste system and encouraged postpuberty marriage of girls, widow remarriages, women's education, and so forth.

The following passage is taken from the *Autobiography* of Devendranāth Tagore (1817–1905), father of the poet, Rabindranath Tagore. For the Brāhma Society, see "Introduction to Hinduism: A Summary Account," ¶13 and 18. □

We are worshipers of Brahma, the Supreme Being. In this we are at one with Orthodox Hinduism, for all our shastras (scriptures) declare with one voice the supremacy of the worship of Brahma, enjoining image worship for the help of those who are incapable of grasping the highest Truth.

Our first point of distinction is in the positive aspect of our creed wherein worship is defined as consisting in "Loving Him and doing the work He loveth"—this at once differentiates us from all religions and creeds which postulate a special or verbal revelation or wherein definite forms, rites, or ceremonials are deemed essential one way or the other.

The negative aspect of our creed which prohibits the worship of any created being or thing as the Creator further distinguishes from all who are addicted to the worship of avatars or incarnations or who believe in the necessity of mediators, symbols, or idols of any description.

We base our faith on the fundamental truths of religion, attended by reason and conscience and refuse to permit man, book, or image to stand in the way of the direct communion of our soul with the Supreme Spirit.

This message of the Brāhmo Samāj in the abstract does not materially differ from the doctrines of the pure theistic bodies all the world over. Viewed historically and socially, however, the Brāhmo Samāj has the further distinction of being the bearer of this message to the Hindu people. This was the idea of its founder, Rām Mohun Roy, and this points to the duty incumbent upon all Brahmos today, and will serve as the guiding principle in the selection of texts, forms, and ceremonials as aids to the religious life.

We are in and of the great Hindu community and it devolves upon us by example and precept to hold up as a beacon the highest truths of the Hindu shastras. In their light must we purify our heritage of customs, usages, rites, and ceremonies and adapt them to the needs of our conscience and our community. But we must beware of proceeding too fast in matters of social change, lest we be separated from the greater body whom we should guide and uplift.

While we should on no account allow any consideration of country, caste, or kinship to prevent our actions being consistent with our faith, we must make every allowance for, and abstain from, persecuting or alienating those who think differently from us. Why should we needlessly wound the feelings of our parents and elders by desecrating an image which they regard with the highest reverence, when all that our conscience can demand of us is to refrain from its adoration?

The steering point of this middle course is by no means an easy task, but during my long experience I have been led greatly to hope for a brighter future by the sympathetic response of our orthodox brethren to the ideal held up before them. The amount of conformity nowadays expected by even the most orthodox, demands so little of us that a little tact and common sense will in most cases be sufficient to obviate all friction.

Nevertheless, great as are the claims of our land and our people, we must never forget that we are Brahmos first, and Indians and Hindus afterwards. We must on no account depart from our vow of renouncing the worship of images and incarnations, which is of the essence of our religion. It is a sound policy on our part to sink our minor differences, but on matters of principle no compromise is possible. Our Motherland is dear to us, but Religion is dearer, Brahma is dearest of all, dearer than son, dearer than riches, supreme over everything else. (Tagore, *Autobiography*, pp. 152–53)

B. THE ĀRYA SAMĀJ

1. The True Veda

□ The Ārya Samāj is a reform movement started by Dayānanda Sarasvati (1824–1883), with practically the same ideals as those of the Brāhmo Samāj. However, it accepts caste divisions, although not by birth but by profession. Its ideal society and religion belong to the early Vedic times. Dayānanda is regarded as a revivalist, as he preached "going back to the Vedas." □

Objection: What books are called the Vedas?

Answer: The books called the *Ṛgveda*, the *Yajur-veda*, the *Sāma-veda*, and the *Atharva-veda*[1]—the *Mantra Saṁhitās*[2] only and no others.

Objection: But the sage Kātyāyana says, "Both *Mantra Samhitās* and the *Brāhmaṇas* together constitute the Veda."

Answer: You must have noticed that in the beginning of every *Mantra Saṁhitā* and at the end of each of its chapters it has always been the practice from time immemorial to write the word *veda*, but is never done so in the case of the *Brāhmaṇas.* We read in the *Nirukta*:[3] "This is in the Veda, this is in the *Brāhmaṇa*"; in the same way we read in the Pāṇini[4]: "In the *Chanda* (Veda) and the *Brāhmaṇa*, etc." It is clear from these quotations that the Veda is the name of books distinct from the *Brāhmaṇas.* The Veda is what is called the *Mantra Saṁhitā* or a collection of *mantras.* Those who want to know more about this subject can consult our book called *An Introduction to the Exposition of the Vedas*, wherein it is proved on the authority of various kinds of evidence that the above quotation quoted as Kātyāyana's could never be his. Because if we believe that the Veda (between 400 and 600 A.D.) could never be eternal, as in the *Brāhmaṇas* there are biographies of various *ṛṣis* (seers of truth) and sages, kings and princes; but since biographies of persons can only be written after their birth, the *Brāhmaṇas* that contain those biographies must have been written after the birth of those *ṛṣis* and kings, etc., and, therefore, cannot be eternal. The Veda does not contain the biography of any person; on the other hand in it only those words are used by which knowledge is made known. There is no mention of any proper names or stories of any particular event or individual in the Veda.

Objection: How many branches are there in the Vedas?

Answer: Eleven hundred and twenty-seven.

Objection: What are the branches?

Answer: The expositions are called branches. (Dayānanda Sarasvati, *Light of Truth* [*Satyārthaprakāśa*], tr. by Chīrañjīva Bhāradwāja, p. 223)

2. God and the Veda

Objection: There are more gods than one mentioned in the Vedas. Do you believe this or not?

Answer: No, we do not; as nowhere in all the four Vedas there is written anything that could go to show that there are more gods than one. On the other hand, it is clearly said in many places that there is only one God.

Objection: What is meant by the mention of the various *devatās* in the Vedas then?

Answer: Whatsoever and whosoever possesses useful and brilliant qualities is called *devatā*, as the earth for instance; but it is nowhere said that it is God or is the object of our adoration. Even in the above *mantra*[5] it is said that He, who is the sustainer of all *devatās*, is the adorable God, and is worthy of being sought after. They are greatly mistaken who take the word *devatā* to mean God. He is called *devatā of devatās*—greatest of all *devatās* because He alone is the author of Creation, Sustenance, and Dissolution of the Universe, the great Judge and Lord of all. The Vedic text, "The Lord of all, the Ruler of the Universe, the Sustainer of all, holds all things by thirty-three *devatās*," has been explained as follows in the fourteenth chapter of the *Śatapada Brāhmaṇa*: (1) Heated cosmic bodies, (2) planets, (3) atmosphere, (4) supra-terrestrial space, (5) suns, (6) rays of ethereal space, (7) satellites, (8) stars: these eight are called *vasus*, because they are the abode of all that lives, moves or exists. The eleven *rudras* are the ten *prāṇas*[6]—nervauric forces—enlivening the human body and the eleventh is the human spirit. These are called *rudras*, because when they desert the body, it becomes dead and the relations of the deceased, consequently, begin to weep. The twelve months of the year are called *ādityas*, as they cause the lapse of the term of existence of each object or being. The (all-pervading) electricity is called *indra*, as it is productive of great force. *Yajña* is called *prajāpati* because it benefits mankind by the purification of air, water, rain and vegetables and because it aids the development of various arts, and because in it the honor is accorded to the learned and wise.

These thirty-three aforesaid entities are called *devatās* by virtue of possessing useful properties and actions. Being Lord of all and greater than all, the Supreme Being is called the thirty-fourth *devatā* who alone is to be worshiped. The same thing is written in the other *Shāstras*. Had people consulted these books, they would not have fallen into this error, viz., the belief that there are more gods than one in the Vedas. (*Ibid.*, pp. 190–191)

C. ŚRĪ RĀMAKRISHNA'S ADVICE

□ Śrī Rāmakrishna (1836–1886) was one of the great saints of India. His teachings were propagated by one of his disciples, the well-known Swami Vivekananda (1863–1902), throughout India and the world. Philosophically Śrī Rāmakrishna was a follower of Śaṅkara's Advaita (nondualism). In practice, he was a worshiper of Śakti (Mother-goddess) and combined everything that he considered good in every religion including Islam and Christianity. He placed mystical religious experience above intellectualized doctrines.

The following is the advice given by Śrī Rāmakrishna to his disciples who hesitate to plunge into communion with God, but only talk about it. He is here giving his own experiences. The remarks are recorded in a diary kept by a disciple in Bengali. □

Gather all the information and then plunge in. Suppose a pot has dropped in a certain part of a lake. Locate the pot and then dive there.

One should learn the essence of the scriptures from the guru (spiritual teacher, teacher of sacred scriptures) and then practice *sādhanā* (spiritual discipline).[7] If one rightly follows spiritual discipline, then one directly sees God. The discipline is said to be rightly followed only when one plunges in. What will a man gain by merely reasoning about the words of the scriptures? Ah, the fools! They reason themselves to death over information about the path. They never take the plunge. What a pity!

God made me pass through the disciplines of various paths. First according to the *Purāṇa* (epic),[8] then according to the *Tantra* (devotion literature). I also followed the disciplines of the Vedas. At first I practiced *sādhanā* in Panchavati. I made a grove of tulsi-plants[9] and used to sit inside it and meditate. Sometimes I cried with a longing heart, "Mother! Mother!"[10] Or again, "Rāma! Rāma!"[11]

I practiced the discipline of Tantra under the bel-tree.[12] At that time I could see no distinction between the sacred *tulasī* and any other plant. Sometimes I rode on a dog and fed him with *luchi*,[13] also eating part of the bread myself. I realized that the whole world was filled with God alone.

While practicing the discipline of the Vedas I became a *sannyāsi* (ascetic). I used to lie down in the chāndni (portico)[14] and say to Hriday, "I am a *sannyāsi*. I shall take my meals here."[15]

I vowed to the Divine Mother that I would kill myself if I did not see God. I said to her, "O Mother, I am a fool. Please teach me what is contained in the Vedas, the *Purāṇas*, the *Tantras*, and the other scriptures." The Mother said to me, "The essence of the Vedānta is that Brahman alone is real and the world illusory." The essence of the *Gītā*[16] is what you get by repeating the word ten times. It is reversed into *tāgi*, which refers to renunciation.

After the realization of God, how far below lie the Vedas, the Vedānta, the *Purāṇa*, the *Tantra*! (To Hazra) I cannot utter the word "Om" in *samādhi* (identification of the meditating subject with the object of meditation).[17] Why is that? I cannot say "Om" unless I come down very far from the state of *samādhi*.

I had all the experiences that one should have, according to the scriptures, after one's direct perception of God. I behaved like a child, like a madman, like a ghoul, and like an inert thing.

I saw the visions described in the scriptures. Sometimes I saw the universe filled with sparks of fire. Sometimes I saw all the quarters glittering with light, as if the world were a lake of mercury. Sometimes I saw the world as if made of liquid silver. Sometimes, again, I saw all the quarters illumined as if with the light of Roman candles. So you see my experiences tally with those described in the scriptures.

It was revealed to me further that God himself has become the universe and all its living beings and the twenty-four[18] cosmic principles. It is like the process of evolution and involution.[19]

Oh, what a state God kept me in at that time! One experience would hardly be over before another overcame me.

I would see God in meditation, in the state of *samādhi*, and I would see the same God when my mind came back to the outer world. When looking at this side of the mirror I would see Him alone, and when looking on the reverse side I saw the same God. (Swami Nikhilananda, *Ramakrishna: Prophet of New India*, pp. 166–67)

D. JIDDU KRISHNAMURTI'S VIEW

□ Krishnamurti (1885–) originally belonged to the Theosophical Society. Mrs. Annie Besant introduced him to the world as an incarnation. But later he gave up all claim to being an incarnation and gave up his connections with the Theosophical Society. He is at least a religious genius and had strong influence over many educated minds of the world. The Theosophical Society also had a strong influence over the educated minds of India. Its main contribution to India's religious life lies in narrowing the differences among the religions existing in India. Its members came from all religious denominations.

Krishnamurti is a kind of iconoclast and preaches against frigidity in spiritual search. He is opposed to dogmas, gurus, denominations, and so forth. Spiritual realization is self-realization and it can be done only by the self, but not by anything external to it. □

What we call religion is merely organized belief, with its dogmas, rituals, mysteries and superstitions. Each religion has its own sacred book, its mediator, its priests and its ways of threatening and holding people. Most of us have been conditioned to all this, which is considered religious education; but this conditioning sets man against man, it creates antagonism, not only among the believers, but also against those of other beliefs. Though all religions assert that they worship God and say that we must love one another, they instil fear through their doctrines of reward and punishment, and through their competitive dogmas they perpetuate suspicion and antagonism.

Dogmas, mysteries and rituals are not conducive to a spiritual life. Religious education in the true sense is to encourage the child to understand his own relationships to people, to things and to nature. There is no existence without relationship; and without self-knowledge, all relationship, with the one and with the many, brings conflict and sorrow. Of course, to explain this fully to a child is impossible; but if the educator and the parents deeply grasp the full significance of relationship, then by their attitude, conduct and speech they will surely be able to convey to the child, without too many words and explanations, the meaning of spiritual life.

Our so-called religious training discourages questioning and doubt, yet it is only when we inquire into the significance of the values which society and religion have placed about us that we begin to find out what is true. It is the function of the educator to examine deeply his own thoughts and feelings and to put aside those values which have given him security and comfort, for only then can he help his students to be self-aware and to understand their own urges and fears.

True religion is not a set of beliefs and rituals, hopes and fears; and if we can allow the child to grow up without these hindering influences, then perhaps, as he matures, he will begin to inquire into the nature of reality, of God. That is why, in educating a child, deep insight and understanding are necessary.

Most people who are religiously inclined, who talk about God and immortality, do not fundamentally believe in individual freedom and integration; yet religion is the cultivation of freedom in the search for truth. There can be no compromise with freedom and it will never bring peace.

Religion is not a form of conditioning. It is a state of tranquillity in which there is reality, God; but that creative state can come into being only when there is self-knowledge and freedom. Freedom brings virtue, and without virtue there can be no tranquillity. The still mind is not a conditioned mind, it is not disciplined or trained to be still. Stillness comes only when the mind understands its own ways, which are the ways of the self.

Organized religion is the frozen thought of man, out of which he builds temples and churches; it has become a solace for the fearful, an opiate for those who are in sorrow. But God or truth is far beyond thought and emotional demands. Parents and teachers who recognize the psychological processes which build up fear and sorrow should be able to help the young to observe and understand their own conflicts and trials. (J. Krishnamurti, *Education and the Significance of Life*, pp. 37–39)

E. ŚRĪ AUROBINDO

☐ Aurobindo Ghose (1872–1950) was an England-educated Bengali nationalist, patriot, and revolutionary, who went into exile in the then French Pondicherry in South India. Even during his political activities he turned to yoga, to which he later devoted himself exclusively. He was a great mystic and combined in theory and practice Vedānta, Śaivism, Śāktism, evolutionism, and the doctrine of the Superman. But his Superman, unlike Nietzsche's, is a yogin and surrenders himself completely to the Supreme Being. As an educated writer, Aurobindo influenced a large number of educated Indians. He believed that evolution is destined, of course, through man's own efforts, including yogic practice, to produce Superman.

In the following passages Aurobindo gives the evolutionary descent and ascent of man from the Supreme Existence (Being). In Indian religious thought, the levels of evolution from the Supreme Spirit are variously understood. Aurobindo takes them to be eight. The highest destiny of man is to ascend to the source from which he came. On the way man becomes the Superman, who is not the Superman of Nietzsche, but a man completely spiritualized and transcending his psychophysical nature. □

We may, therefore, if we will, pose eight principles instead of seven, and then we perceive that our existence is a sort of refraction of the divine existence, in inverted order or ascent and descent, thus ranged—

Existence	Matter
Consciousness-Force	Life
Bliss	Psyche
Supermind	Mind

The Divine descends from pure existence through the play of consciousness force and Bliss and the creative medium of Supermind into cosmic being; we ascend from Matter through a developing life, soul and mind and the illuminating medium of supermind towards the divine being. The knot of the two, the higher and the lower hemisphere, is where mind and supermind meet with a veil between them. The rending of the veil is the condition of the divine life in humanity; for by that rending, by the illuminating of the descent of the higher into the nature of the lower being and the forceful ascent of the lower being into the nature of the higher, mind can recover its divine light in the all-comprehending supermind, the soul realizes its divine self in the all-possessing all-blissful *Ananda*[20], life reposes its divine power in the play of omnipotent Conscious-Force and Matter open to its divine liberty as a form of the divine Existence. And if there be any goal to the evolution which finds here its present crown and head in the human being, other than an aimless circling, if the infinite potentiality of this creature, who alone here stands between Spirit and Matter with the power to mediate between them, has any meaning other than an ultimate awakening from the delusion of life by despair and disgust of the cosmic effort and its complete rejection, then even such a luminous and puissant transformation and emergence of the Divine in the creature must be that high-uplifted goal and that supreme significance. (Śrī Aurobindo, *The Divine Life*, pp. 243–44.)

It follows that wherever Cosmos is, there, even if only one principle be initially apparent, even if at first that seem to be the sole principle of things and everything else that may appear afterwards in the world seems to be no more than its forms and results and not in themselves indispensable to cosmic existence, such a front presented by being can only be an illusory mask or appearance of its real truth. Where one principle is manifest in Cosmos, there all the rest must be not merely present and passively latent, but secretly at work. In any given world its scale and harmony of being may be openly in possession of all seven at a higher or lower degree of activity; in another they may all be involved in one which becomes the initial or fundamental principle of evolution in that world, but evolution of the involved there must be. The evolution of the sevenfold power of being, the realization of its septuple Name, must be the destiny of any world which starts apparently from the involution of all in one power. Therefore the material universe was bound in the nature of things to evolve from its hidden life apparent life, from its hidden mind apparent mind, and it must in the same nature of things evolve from its hidden Supermind apparent Supermind and from the concealed Spirit within it the triune glory of Sat-çhit-ānanda.[21] The only question is whether the earth is to be the scene of that emergence or the human creation on this or any other material scene, in this or any other cycle of the large wheelings of Time, its instrument and vehicle. The ancient seers believed in this possibility for man and held it to be his divine destiny; the modern thinker does not even conceive of it or, if he conceived, would deny or doubt. If he sees a vision of the Superman, it is in the figure of increased degrees of mentality or vitality; he admits no other emergency, sees nothing beyond these principles, for these have traced for us up till now our limit and circle. In this progressive world, with his human creature in whom the divine spark has been kindled, real wisdom is likely to dwell with the higher aspiration rather than with the denial of aspiration or with the hope that limits and circumscribes itself within those narrow walls of apparent possibility which are only our intermediate house of training. In the spiritual order of things, the higher we project our view and our aspiration, the greater the Truth that seeks to descend upon us, becuse it is already there within us and calls for its release from the covering that conceals it in manifested Nature. (*Ibid.*, pp. 247–48)

F. RABINDRANATH TAGORE

□ Tagore (1861–1941), the renowned poet and philosopher, was a member of the Brāhmo Samāj, a monotheist, and a personalist. For him, God is personal, not impersonal, as the Advaitins (nondualists) following Śaṅkara assert. Religion being the religion of man and not of an impersonal being has to be personalistic. God also, for the same reason, has to be personalistic. Man cannot understand God and worship him otherwise, even if many sages and saints say that he is impersonal consciousness. There are sages and saints who say that he is personal also. Such is the view of Tagore. □

According to some interpretations of the Vedānta Doctrine, Brahman is the absolute Truth, the impersonal It, in which there can be no distinctions of this and that, the good and the evil, the beautiful and its opposite, having no other quality except its ineffable blissfulness in the eternal solitude of its consciousness utterly devoid of all things and all thoughts. But as our religion can only have its significance in this phenomenal world comprehended by our human self, this absolute conception of the Brahman is outside the subject of my discussion. What I have tried to bring out in this book is the fact that whatever name may have been given to the divine Reaility, it has found its highest place in the history of our religion owing to its human character, giving meaning to the idea of sin and sanctity, and offering an eternal background to all the ideals of perfection which have their harmony with man's own nature.

We have the age-long tradition in our country, as I have already stated, that through the process of *yoga* man can transcend the utmost bounds of his humanity and find himself in a pure state of consciousness of his undivided unity with Parabrahman. There is none who has the right to contradict this belief; for it is a matter of direct experience and not of logic. It is widely known in India that there are individuals who have the power to attain temporarily the state of *Samādhi* (calmness), the complete merging of the self in the infinite, a state which is indescribable. While accepting their testimony as true, let us at the same time have faith in the testimony of others who have felt a profound love, which is the intense feeling of union, for a Being who comprehends in himself all things that are human in knowledge, will and action. And he is God, who is not merely a sum total of facts, but the goal that lies immensely beyond all that is comprised in the past and the present. (Rabindranath Tagore, *The Religion of Man*, pp. 205–6)

G. SARVAPALLI RADHAKRISHNAN

□ S. Radhakrishnan (1888–), most outstanding contemporary Indian philosopher and former president of India, is a follower of Śaṅkara, but is not prepared to assert that the world and personal God are complete illusions without human worth. In this passage Radhakrishnan is showing how the views of Śaṅkara and Rāmānuja have both a place in the philosophy of religion pertinent to human thought. □

While the Absolute is pure consciousness and pure freedom and infinite possibility, it appears to be God from the point of view of the one specific possibility which has become actualized. While God is organically bound up with the universe, the Absolute is not. The world of pure being is not exhausted by the cosmic process which is only one of the ways in which the Absolute reality which transcends the series reveals itself. The Absolute is the foundation and *prius* of all actuality and possibility. This universe is for the Absolute only one possibility. Its existence is an act of free creation. Out of the infinite possibilities open to it, this one is chosen. When we analyze our sense of freedom, we find that it consists in accepting or rejecting any one of a number of possibilities to choose from, which are all determined by its nature. It has the power of saying yes or no to any one of them. While the possible is determined by the nature of the Absolute, the actual is selected out of the total amount of the possible, by the free activity of the Absolute without any determination whatsoever. . . .

God, who is the creator, sustainer and judge of this world, is not totally unrelated to the Absolute. God is the Absolute from the human end. When we limit down the Absolute to its relation with the actual possibility, the Absolute appears as supreme Wisdom, Love and Goodness. The eternal becomes the first and the last. The abiding "I am," the changeless center and the cause of all change is envisaged as the first term and the last in the sequence of nature. He is the creative mind of the world, with a consciousness of the general plan and direction of the cosmos, even before it is actualized in space and time. He holds the successive details in proper perspective and draws all things together in bonds of love and harmony. He is the loving saviour of the world. As creator and saviour, God is transcendent to the true process, even as realization is transcendent to progress. This internal transcendence of God to the true process gives meaning to the distinctions of value, and makes struggle and effort real. We call the supreme the Absolute, when we view it apart from the cosmos, God in relation to the cosmos. The Absolute is the pre-cosmic nature of God, and God is the Absolute from the cosmic point of view. (S. Radhakrishnan, *An Idealist View of Life*, pp. 343–45)

H. MOHANDAS KARAMCHAND GANDHI

□ The following is the most concise and direct statement of the Mahatma Gandhi's (1869–1948) view on religion in its relation to truth, nonviolence, and social service. □

I have been asked by Sir S. Radhakrishnan to answer the following three questions:

1. What is your Religion?
2. How are you led to it?
3. What is its bearing on social life?

My religion is Hinduism which, for me, is the Religion of humanity and includes the best of all the religions known to me.

I take it that the present tense in the second question has been purposely used instead of the past. I am being led to my religion through Truth and Nonviolence, i.e., love in the broadest sense. I often describe my religion as Religion of Truth. Of late, instead of saying that God is Truth I have been saying that Truth is God, in order more fully to define my religion. I used, at one time, to know by heart the thousand names of God which a booklet in Hinduism gives in verse form and which perhaps tens of thousands recite every morning. But nowadays nothing so completely describes my God as Truth. Denial of God we have known. Denial of Truth we have not known. The most ignorant among mankind have some truth in them. We are all sparks of Truth. The sum total of these sparks is indescribable, as-yet-Unknown-Truth, which is God. I am being daily led nearer to It by constant prayer.

The bearing of this religion on social life is, or has to be, seen in one's daily social contact. To be true to such religion one has to lose oneself in continuous and continuing service of all life. Realization of Truth is impossible without a complete merging of oneself in, and in identification with, this limitless ocean of life. Hence, for me, there is no escape from social service, there is no happiness on earth beyond and apart from it. Social service here must be taken to include every department of life. In this scheme there is nothing low, nothing high. For, all is one, though we *seem* to be many. (S. Radhakrishnan and J. H. Muirhead, ed., *Contemporary Indian Philosophy*, p. 21)

NOTES

1. For the four Vedas, see ch. 1, introduction.
2. *Mantra Samhitās* are the collections of hymns (*mantras*) and form the first of the four parts of the Veda or each of the four Vedas. According to Dayānanda, the founder of the Ārya Samāj, only the *mantras* constitute the Veda. A few Mīmāsakas also say so, but many of them maintain that both the *mantras* and the *Brāhmaṇas* are equally important and together they are more important than the other two parts of the *Veda*. The Vedāntins maintain that the Upaniṣads are the most important part of the Veda and together with the *Āraṇyakas*, they are primary.
3. *Nirukta* is the name of the Vedic lexicon written by Yāska (between eighth and fifth century B.C.), the oldest lexicographer.
4. Pāṇini (*c.* seventh century B.C.) is the first grammarian of Sanskrit.
5. The *mantra* referred to is from *Ṛgveda*, I:164, 39. "They are atheists and of weak intellect, and continually remain sunk in the depths of misery and pain, who do not believe in, know, and commune with Him who is Resplendent, All-glorious, All-holy, All-knowledge, sustainer of the sun, the earth and other planets, Who pervades all and is above all *devatās*. It is by the knowledge and contemplation of God alone that all men attain true happiness." This quotation also is from Bhāradwāja's book.
6. It is usually accepted that the *prāṇas* are five. For the *Śatapada Brāhmaṇa* (Ritual text of 100 feet), see ch. 1, selection 20.
7. The spiritual discipline refers to the practice involved in the various kinds of yoga.
8. *Purāṇa* is generally translated as epic. In Indian literature it is regarded as teaching the same truth as taught by the Veda, but in a way understandable by immature intellects.
9. A kind of plant considered to be auspicious and sacred to Viṣṇu.
10. Mother-goddess. Srī Rāmakrishna worshiped the mother-goddess called Kāli, regarded as the wife of Śiva.
11. The hero of the epic *Rāmāyaṇa*, who is regarded as an incarnation of Viṣṇu.
12. A kind of tree the leaves and the fruit of which are said to be sacred to Śiva and his wife.
13. A kind of food made of wheat flour.
14. In Bengal, it is an open portico in a temple garden with steps descending to the river Ganges.
15. Ascetics, if they observe strict discipline, are not to take their food under a roof, but under the sky, the roof provided by God.
16. If the word *Gītā*, which is a shortened form of *Bhagavad-gītā*, with a short "i" as in Gitā is repeated several times, then the syllables get reversed and the word becomes *tāgi*, which is a Bengali pronunciation of the Sanskrit word *tyāgī*, one who renounces (the world), one whose nature is to give up.
17. See Ch. 5, introduction.
18. This refers to the Sāṅkhya philosophy, which enumerates its principles. See ch. 5, introduction. If we include the *puruṣa*, they will be twenty-five; otherwise, only twenty-four.
19. Evolution is the creation or throwing out of all the lower categories by *prakṛti* and involution is withdrawing them into itself.
20. Bliss.
21. Being-Intelligence-Bliss or Reality-Knowledge-Bliss.

PART TWO

Religions of China

Wing-tsit Chan

CHAPTER 10

Pre-Confucian Elements

☐ As part of a folk culture, ancient Chinese religion is essentially similar to those in other lands. It was founded, as in most cases, in the belief in all sorts of gods, in the spirits of ancestors, in a supreme power called the Lord on High or Heaven, and in the existence of the soul. Heaven was regarded as anthropomorphic in character and spiritual beings could bring blessings or calamities in their mysterious ways. The soul was divided into *hun* (heavenly component) and *p'o* (earthly component),[1] definitely reflecting the early doctrine of yin (negative cosmic force) and yang (positive cosmic force), the interaction of which produces all possible objects, events, and situations. Ancestors could "match" Heaven (see B, 2).

The most remarkable development in the religion of the Three Dynasties,[2] however, was the early and persistent growth in the emphasis on virtue. When the Chou conquered the Shang in 1111 B.C., somehow it did not choose to claim the prerogative to rule on the basis of divine right or power but on virtue. The decisive factor was undoubtedly the growth of humanism. China was entering upon the iron age. New tools, utensils, trades, and towns appeared, and along with them new problems that only man could solve. Hence the new emphasis on man, on his ability, and ultimately on his virtue.

It was in this situation that the doctrine of the Mandate of Heaven developed. The Hsia dynasty was replaced by the Shang and later the Shang by the Chou, it was claimed, because their last rulers sinned against their people and therefore the mandate was taken away from them. Obviously for the Chou to continue to enjoy the trust of the mandate, the only sure way was to cultivate virtue. The conviction was that Heaven, and even spiritual beings, favored only the virtuous (C, 2). In this sense the mandate was neither constant nor reliable (B, 2–3), for it depended on man's moral effort. The point was reached when a poet sang, "Don't mind your ancestors! Cultivate your virtue" (B, 2).

It is a mistake, however, to think that this humanism meant the rejection of the belief in the most supreme being or reality. Heaven remained as august and powerful as ever, but his mandate, and rewarding good and punishing evil by Heaven or by spiritual beings, were determined by man's own conduct. Heaven ceased to be anthropomorphic and became a moral being or rather Reality, and the source of the Moral Law. It reigns but does not rule.

Several things have followed from this belief. First, the most important thing in man was considered to be his moral character. Heaven has endowed him with a "constant nature," which is basically moral (A, 2). The first task of the Chou conquerors was to "regulate the nature" of the defeated rulers (A, 4). This was the beginning of the persistent and central stress on human nature in the history of Chinese thought. Secondly, as already indicated, retribution was understood to be essentially moral in nature. Man's behavior could even affect the span of a dynasty as well as his own life. Thirdly, sacrifice was to be performed primarily for its ethical significance. Though the chief object was still blessing, it was to be achieved not through magic but through moral endeavor. Finally, whereas common folk continued to believe in the immortality of the soul, a belief later to be enhanced by the Taoist belief in immortals and the Buddhist promise of Paradise, the enlightened were convinced that immortality consisted of everlasting virtue, accomplishment, and wisdom (C, 4). Thus there are several important features of Chinese religion that have remained prominent throughout the ages, namely, the belief in Heaven, the moral interpretation of retribution, the idea of the immortality of virtue and good work, and the stress on the moral efficacy in religious sacrifice—these are deeply rooted in the apparently primitive and shamanistic religion of ancient times. □

A. THE *BOOK OF HISTORY*[3]

1. When Kao-tsung[4] repeated the sacrifice to his father on the second day, suddenly a crowing pheasant (an unlucky omen) appeared. (Virtuous minister) Tsu-i said, "It is necessary first to make the king correct before rectifying this [abnormal] affair." He therefore admonished the king, saying, "Heaven inspected the people below. Heaven's basic consideration is that of their righteousness. The span of life bestowed on them may be long or short. It is not that Heaven cuts short their span. Instead, it is the people themselves who, in the middle course of their span, terminate what Heaven has decreed. Some people do not comply with virtue and do not acknowledge their crimes. Heaven has already given the order for them to be correct in virtue. But now they say, 'What is this to us?' Alas! the king's fundamental duty is to attend to the affairs of the people. [All previous kings] were sons of Heaven. In correct sacrifices, there should be nothing extra in the sacrifice to one's father." (*Book of History*, "Kao-tsung Repeated the Sacrifice on the Second Day")

2. When King T'ang returned from the conquest of Hsia and reached (the capital) Po, he grandly announced to the feudal lords of the myriad regions, "Ah, you people of the myriad regions, listen clearly to what I, only one man, have to tell you. The august Lord on High has bestowed a moral character on the people below. When one follows his constant nature, one can be secure in one's way of life. But the ruler of Hsia destroyed his moral character and exercised his oppressive power so as to spread oppression over you people in the myriad regions. You people in the myriad regions suffered great injuries and could no longer endure the bitterness and poison. Together you voiced your innocence to the spiritual beings above and below. The way of Heaven is to give blessings to the good and misfortunes to evildoers. Heaven has sent down calamities on the ruler of Hsia in order to make clear his sins. I, the little child, following the Mandate of Heaven which gave me clear power, did not dare to forgive him. The criminal was finally degraded and subjugated. The Mandate of Heaven is always correct. The multitude are now surely flourishing as brilliantly as grass and plants. . . .

Each of you should adhere to your moral standards and thereby receive the blessings from Heaven. If you have any good point, I shall not dare conceal it. If any sin lies in my own person, I shall not dare excuse myself. I shall only examine what is in the mind of the Lord on High. If you in the myriad regions commit any sin, the fault is with me, only one man, but if I, only one man, commit any sin, I shall not involve you in the myriad regions. Ah, let us all be truthful so that [we shall all] prevail to the end." (*Ibid.*, "Announcement of T'ang")

3. The king[5] spoke thus: Ho! this is to announce to you, [lords of] the many states, and you, my ministers. It is a great misfortune that Heaven has sent calamity to our House (of Chou)[6] so that [King Wu's reign] could not continue any longer. Ah, I, a young person, have inherited the infinitely great destiny and dominions. I have not exercised wisdom to lead people to peace. How can I say that I am able to reach [the spiritual beings above] and to know the Mandate of Heaven? Ah, I am

but a little child, feeling as if I am traveling in deep waters. I only seek to do what I can accomplish, extensively carry out good governmental measures, and extend the Mandate (of Heaven) received by my predecessors. In this way (their) great accomplishments will not be obliterated. . . . (*Ibid.*, "The Great Announcement")

4. Alas! The Lord on High in august heaven has abolished the mandate given to the principal ruler of the great Yin dynasty. Now our king[7] has received this mandate. It carries with it infinite blessing but also infinite worry. Oh! How can he afford not to be serious? . . . Let our king first bring under his influence the administrators of the affairs of Yin and place them in the midst of the administrators of the affairs of Chou. Their natures will thus be regulated, and they will improve daily. Let our king be serious in what he does. He should not neglect to be serious with virtue. We should not overlook the lesson from the Hsia dynasty. Nor should we overlook the lesson from the Yin dynasty.

Now Heaven is about to give us the mandate of wisdom, fortune or misfortune, or a long span of dynastic life [all of which we are not sure]. Ah, we have now just conquered (the Yin dynasty) and are living in the new city. Therefore let our king take the quickest step to be serious with virtue. Let the king exercise virtue and thus pray to Heaven infinitely to extend the mandate. . . . (*Ibid.*, "Announcement of Duke Shao")

B. THE *BOOK OF ODES*[8]

1. The admirable, amiable prince
   Displayed conspicuously his excellent virtue.
   He put his people and his officers in concord.
   And he received his emolument from Heaven.
   It protected him, assisted him, and appointed him king.
   And Heaven's blessing came again and again.

   (Ode no. 249)

2. King Wen[9] is on high;
   Oh, he shines in Heaven.
   Although Chou is an ancient state,
   The mandate it has received from Heaven is new.
   Isn't Chou illustrious?
   Isn't the mandate of the Lord timely?
   King Wen's ascends and descends
   Are on the Lord's left and right.

   The (descendants of Yin) became subject to Chou.
   Heaven's mandate is not constant. . . .

   Don't you mind your ancestors!
   Cultivate your virtue.
   Always strive to be in harmony with Heaven's Mandate.
   Seek for yourself the many blessings.
   Before Yin lost its army,
   Its kings were able to be counterparts to the Lord on High.
   In Yin you should see as in a mirror
   That the great mandate is not easy [to keep].

   (Ode no. 235)

3. The Lord on High said to King Wen:
   "I cherish your brilliant virtue,
   Which makes no great display in sound or appearance,
   Nor is changed with age.
   Without any manipulation or deliberation,
   you followed the principle of the Lord."

   (Ode no. 241)

4. Mighty is the Lord on High,
   Ruler of the people below.
   Terrible and powerful is the Lord on High,
   His decrees are various.
   Heaven produces the multitude,
   His decrees can not be relied on.
   All have the proper beginning,
   But few can continue to the end.

   (Ode no. 255)

5. Respect the anger of Heaven.
   Don't you make sport of things or be idle.
   Respect the changing moods of Heaven.
   Don't you dare drive fast (anywhere you please).
   The Vast Heaven is very clear

About where you go.
The Vast Heaven is very clear
About your laxity and indulgence.
(Ode no. 254)

6. Bright is the milky way,
Brilliantly moving around in the sky.
The king[10] said: Alas!
What sins have the people committed now,
So that Heaven has sent down destruction and disorder,
And there have been famines again and again?
There is no god to whom I have not made sacrifices.
I have never kept to myself the sacrificial animals.
I have exhausted my jades.
Has (Heaven) still not heard me?
(Ode no. 258)

7. In the midst of the field are the huts;
Along the boundaries are melons.
They are peeled and pickled,
And offered to the great ancestors,
So the distant descendants may live long,
And receive blessings from Heaven.
(Ode no. 210)

C. LATER DOCUMENTS

1. In the fifteenth year (of King Hui, 662 B.C.), a spiritual being descended and appeared in Hsin. The king asked his minister Kuo, saying, "Why is this? Is there such a thing?"

Kuo replied, "Yes. When a state is about to rise, its ruler is solemn, illustrious, sincere, and correct. He is discriminating, pure, kind, and affable. His virtue is sufficient to make his fragrant offerings manifest, and his kindness is sufficient to unify the people. As the spiritual beings enjoy his offerings and the people listen to him, neither the people nor the spiritual beings have any complaint. Therefore brilliant spiritual beings descend in his state, see the evidence of the virtue of the government, and spread blessings everywhere. When the state is about to perish, its ruler is greedy, reckless, depraved, and perverted. He is lewd, indolent, negligent, and lazy. He is vulgar and cruel. Because his government has a disgusting odor, his offerings do not rise [to reach the spiritual beings]. And because his punishments are imposed on the basis of treachery and slander, his people desert him and divert their loyalty elsewhere. The brilliant spiritual beings no longer give him purification and his people want to leave him.[11] Both the people and the spiritual beings blame him and hate him, and there is nothing in him for them to cling to. The spiritual beings likewise go to such a state, see the evidence of oppression and evil, and send down calamity." (*Kuo-yü* [Conversations of the states], 1:11a–12b).

2. The Marquis of Chin (in 655 B.C.) again borrowed a way through Yü to attach Kuo. (Great Officer) Kung Chih-ch'i remonstrated with him. . . . The marquis said, "My sacrificial offerings have been abundant and pure. Spiritual beings will comfort me."

Kung Chih-ch'i replied, "I have heard that spiritual beings are not endeared to man as such but cleave only to virtue. Therefore, it is said in the 'Book of Chou' that 'August Heaven has no affections; it helps only the virtuous.'[12] It further says, 'It is not the millet that has the fragrance [which attracts spiritual beings]. Illustrious virtue alone has the fragrance.'[13] It also says, 'People have not slighted the things, but it is virtue that makes things acceptable.'[14] Therefore, if a ruler acts against virtue, his people will not be attached to him and spiritual beings will not accept his offerings. It is virtue that the spiritual beings will adhere to." (*Tso-chuan* [Tso's commentary on the *Spring and Autumn Annals*], Duke Hsi, 5th year)

3. (In 535 B.C.) the people of Cheng frightened one another about Po-yu (who was a drunkard), crying, "Po-yu has arrived!" They all ran off, not knowing where they were going. In the second month of the year when the criminal code was cast, someone dreamed that Po-yu walked by him in armor and said, "In the year *jen-tzu* I will kill Tai and the next year, the year *jen-yin*, I will kill Tuan."

When Ssu Tai did die in the year *jen-tzu*, the terror of the pople increased. Then when in the year *jen-yin*, in the month that Ch'i and Yen states made peace, Kung-sun Tuan died, the terror of the people increased further. It did not stop until the next month when (Prime Minister) Tzu-ch'an (d. 522 B.C.) appointed Kung-sun Hsieh and (Po-yu's son) Lian-chih (as successors to their fathers) in order to pacify them. Tzu Ta-shu asked him for the reason. Tzu-ch'an replied, "When spiritual beings have a place to return to, they will not become malicious. I have given them a place to return to . . ."

When Tzu-ch'an went to Chin, Chao Ching Tzu asked him, "Can even Po-yu become a spiritual being?" Tzu-ch'an answered, "Yes, he could. In man's life the first transformations are called the earthly component of the soul (*p'o*). After *p'o* has been produced, that which is strong and positive is called the heavenly component of the soul (*hun*). If he had an abundance in the use of material things and subtle essentials, his *hun* and *p'o* will become strong. From this are developed essence and understanding until there are spirit and intelligence. When an ordinary man or woman dies a violent death. the *hun* and *p'o* are still able to keep hanging about men and do evil and malicious things. How much more would be the case of Po-yu, a descendant of Duke Mu,[15] the grandson of Tzu-liang, the son of Tzu-erh, all ministers of our state, who engaged in government for three generations! Cheng is not a great state but a small, insignificant one; nevertheless, because his family had administered the government for three generations, his use of material things must have been extensive and his enjoyment of subtle essentials abundant. Furthermore, his clan is large and there was much to which he could cling. Is it not proper that having died a violent death he should become a spiritual being?" (*Ibid.*, Duke Chao, 7th year)

4. In the spring of the twenty-fourth year (of Duke Hsiang, 546 B.C.), Mu-shu (great officer of Lu) went to Chin. Fan Hsüan Tzu met him, saying, "The ancients had the saying, 'Dead but immortal.' What does it mean?"

Before Mu-shu replied, Hsüan Tzu went on to say, "Anciently, the ancestors of our Fan family, from the time of Emperor Shun[16] and earlier, were the princes of T'ao and T'ang. In the time of Hsia, the ancestors were the lords of Yü-lung. In the time of Shang, they were the lords of Shih-wei. And in the beginning of Chou, they were the lords of T'ang and Tu. Now Chin has achieved the control of the great alliance and become the lord of Fan. Is this (unbroken heritage) what is meant by immortality?"

Mu-shu said, "According to what I have heard, this is called hereditary rank and emolument, not immortality. There was a former great officer of Lu by the name of Tsang Wen-chung. After his death his words remained established. This is what the ancient saying means. I have heard that the best course is to establish virtue, the next best is to establish achievement, and still the next best is to establish words. When these are not abandoned with time, it may be called immortality. As to the preservation of the family name and bestowment of membership in the clan branch in order to preserve ancestral sacrifice uninterrupted from age to age, no state is without these practices. But even those with great emolument cannot be said to be immortal." (*Ibid.*, Duke Hsiang, 24th year).

NOTES

1. As generally understood, *hun* is the spirit of man's vital force, which is expressed in man's intelligence and power of breathing, whereas *p'o* is spirit of man's physical nature, which is expressed in bodily movements.
2. Hsia (2183–1752 B.C.?), Shang, (1751–1112 B.C.), and Chou (1111–249 B.C.).
3. A collection of documents in 58 chapters; not all of them authentic, covering the period from the third millennium B.C. to early Chou. The traditional theory that Confucius edited the

book has been rejected by modern scholars. Our selections are from the authentic sections. For English translation, see James Legge, tr., *Shoo King, The Chinese Classics*, vol. 3.

4. Wu-ting (r. 1339–1281 B.C.).
5. King Ch'eng (r. 1104–1068 B.C.).
6. Referring to the death of King Wu (r. 1121–1116 B.C.), King Ch'eng's father.
7. King Ch'eng.
8. A collection of 305 songs sung in religious and official functions and popular songs in Chou times (except five from the Shang period). Most scholars no longer believe that Confucius selected and edited the odes. For an English translation, see Arthur Waley, tr., *The Book of Songs*.
9. Ken Wen (r. 1171–1122 B.C.) was the founder of the Chou dynasty and has been idealized by Chinese historians as a sage-king.
10. King Hsüan of Chou (r. 827–782 B.C.).
11. Another interpretation: to rebel against him.
12. *Book of History*, "Charge to Chung of Ts'ai."
13. *Ibid.*, "Prince Ch'en."
14. *Ibid.*, "Hounds of Lü."
15. He reigned from 659 to 619 B.C.
16. Legendary sage-emperor of the third millennium B.C.

CHAPTER 11

Ancient Confucian Philosophers

A. CONFUCIUS[1]

☐ It is often asked whether Confucianism is a religion. It is certainly not if one thinks of religion as an organized church with holy scriptures, a clergy, and so on, for there is none of these things in the Confucian tradition. But it is unmistakably religious because, first of all, Confucius (551–479 B.C.) and his followers have always affirmed the reality of a purposive and powerful Heaven; secondly, Confucianism has promoted traditional rites such as sacrifice to Heaven and Earth, sacrifice to ancestors, and so on; thirdly, it has exercised an influence and control on Chinese society as religion has done in other countries; and finally, its Classics have served as the fountain of truth as religious scriptures have done elsewhere.

As to Confucius himself, there have been two grave misunderstandings in the West. One is that he taught only the "negative golden rule," for, it is claimed, he told us not to do to others what one does not do to oneself (*Analects*, 5:11). This is true, but Confucius also taught the doctrine of humanity (*jen*, love, benevolence). According to his teaching, the man of *jen* establishes other people's character as well as his own and wants others to be successful and prominent as he wants to be so himself (6:28). The concept of *jen* consists of both conscientiousness, which means the full development of oneself, and altriusm, which means treating others as one treats oneself. This is the "central thread" running through the entire Confucian system (4:15).

The other grave misunderstanding is that Confucius was interested only in man and not in religion, because he seldom talked about fate (9:1), avoided discussing spiritual beings (7:20), kept silent on the Way of Heaven (5:12), and turned aside questions on serving spiritual beings and on death (11:11). But we must not forget that he glorified Heaven (8:18), believed that he knew the Mandate of Heaven (2:4), and was convinced that his own career as well as the course of culture depended on Heaven (7:22, 9:5). Heaven cannot be cheated and it is useless for one who has sinned against Heaven to pray (3:13, 9:11). There is no contradiction in Confucius' position. His discussions were primarily concerned with human character and social affairs but he never forgot that they are rooted in Heaven. He was essentially a religious man. More than that, he raised certain Chinese religious ideas and beliefs to a much higher level than before.

The Chinese belief in Heaven underwent radical change in Confucius. Heaven ceased to be an anthropomorphic being ("Heaven does not speak" 17:19). In the *Analects*, the terms *Ti* (Lord) and *Shang-ti* (Lord on High) are not used at all. Instead, the term *T'ien* is employed. This word is not easy to translate, for it means not only Nature, a person, or a principle, but all of them. At any rate it is real, purposive, powerful, and the source of the Moral Law. It does not rule but reigns, leaving the Moral Law to operate by itself. Confucius did not say all of this explicitly but all his followers have believed that he at least implied it.

In spite of the statement in the *Analects* that he seldom talked about *ming* (fate, destiny, Heaven's mandate or decree), Confucius discussed it many times. To him, life and death, are not within our control and are therefore dependent on fate, but the Mandate of Heaven is no unpredicable order from an unpredicable power but a rational and obvious moral law. When he said that he knew the Mandate of Heaven at fifty (2:4) and that a superior man stands in awe of the Mandate of Heaven (16:8), he meant that a moral man knows what the moral course and moral order are and acts accordingly.

With regard to spiritual beings, Confucius departed radically from the past. He did not deny their existence but he preferred not to talk about them because he did not want people to rely on spiritual beings to solve their problems. Ancestors should be respected as they were respected when alive but the respect should be an expression of filial piety and not a bargain for blessing. This is the meaning of his saying, puzzling to many, "Respect spiritual beings and keep them at a distance" (6:20).

Once we understand the type of humanism Confucius advocated, we understand the significance of religious rites in the Confucian tradition. To Confucius, the significance is basically moral and social. Ancestral rites are to be performed not for any magical effect but as an expression of one's feeling for and remembrance of one's ancestors. He himself insisted on performing rites personally and he wanted to feel as if the spiritual beings were actually present (3:12). In religious rites, it is the feeling that counts.

The following selections are made from the *Lun-yü* (*Analects*),[2] a collection of 499 passages in twenty "books" on Confucius' words and deeds and those of his pupils. □

1:2. Yu-Tzu[3] said, "Few of those who are filial sons and respectful brothers will show disrespect to superiors and there has never been a man who is not disrespectful to superiors and yet creates disorder. A superior man is devoted to the fundamentals (the root). When the root is firmly established, the moral law (Tao) will grow. Filial piety and brotherly respect are the root of humanity (*jen*)."

1:7. Tzu Hsia[4] said, "If a man highly exalts the worthy instead of beautiful women, does all he can in serving his parents, devotes his whole life in serving the ruler, and in dealing with friends utters words that are truthful, even if he has not learned, I will certainly say that he has."

1:8. Confucius said, "If the superior man is not grave, he will not inspire awe, and his learning will not be on firm foundation. Hold loyalty and faithfulness to be fundamental. Have no friends who are not as good as yourself. When you have made mistakes, don't be afraid to correct them."

1:9. Tseng Tzu[5] said, "When people are careful about the end (funeral rites to parents) and keep on thinking of them (by sacrificing to them) when they are far gone, their virtue will be increasingly rich."

1:11. Confucius said, "When a man's father is alive, look at the bent of his will. When his father is dead, look at his conduct. If for three years (of mourning) he does not change from the way of his father, he may be called filial."

2:3. Confucius said, "Lead the people with governmental measures and regulate them by law and punishment, and they will avoid wrongdoing but will have no sense of honor or shame. Lead them with virtue and regulate them by the rules of propriety (*li*), and they will have a sense of shame and, moreover, set themselves right."

2:4. Confucius said, "At fifteen my mind was set on learning. At thirty my character had been formed. At forty I had no more perplexities. At fifty I knew the Mandate of Heaven. At sixty I was at ease with whatever I heard. At seventy I could follow my heart's desire without transgressing moral principles."

2:5. Meng I Tzu[6] asked about filial piety. Confucius said, "Never disobey." (Later,) when Fan Ch'ih[7] was driving him, Confucius told him, "Meng-sun asked me about filial piety, and I answered him, 'Never disobey'" [the parents, the ruler of propriety, or moral principles].[8] Fan Ch'ih said, "What does that mean?" Confucius said, "When parents are alive, serve them according to the rule of propriety. When they die, bury them according to the rules of propriety and sacrifice to them according to the rules of propriety."

2:24. Confucius said, "It is flattery to offer sacrifice to ancestral spirits other than one's own. To see what is right and not to do it is cowardice."

3:3. Confucius said, "If a man is not humane (*jen*), what has he to do with ceremonies (*li*)? If he is not humane, what has he to do with music?"

3:4. Lin Fang[9] asked about the foundation of ceremonies. Confucius said, "An important question indeed! In rituals or ceremonies, be thrifty rather than extravagant, and in funerals, be deeply sorrowful rather than shallow in sentiment."

3:12. When Confucius offered sacrifice to his ancestors, he felt as if his ancestral spirits were actually present. When he offered sacrifice to other spiritual beings, he felt as if they were actually present. He said, "If I do not participate in the sacrifice, it is as if I did not sacrifice at all."

3:13. Wang-sum Chia[10] asked, "What is meant by the common saying, 'It is better to be on good terms with the God of the Kitchen (who cooks our food) than with the spirits of the shrine (ancestors) at the southwest corner of the house'?" Confucius said, "It is not true. He who commits a sin against Heaven has no god to pray to."

3:15. When Confucius entered the grand temple,[11] he asked about everything. Someone said, "Who will say that the son of the man of Tsou[12] knows the rules of propriety? When he enters the grand temple, he asks about everything!" When Confucius heard about it, he said, "This is according to the rule of propriety."

3:17. Tzu-kung[13] wanted to do away with the sacrificing of a lamb at the ceremony in which the beginning of each month is reported to ancestors. Confucius said, "Tz'u! You love the lamb but I love the ceremony."

3:26. Confucius said, "When one occupies a high position but is not liberal, when one performs ceremonies without reverence, and when one approaches a funeral without sorrow, I cannot bear to see him."

4:3. Confucius said, "Only the man of humanity knows how to love people and hate people."[14]

4:15. Confucius said, "Ts'an, there is one thread that runs through my doctrines." Tseng Tzu said, "Yes." After Confucius left, the disciples asked him, "What did he mean?" Tseng Tzu replied, "The Way of our Master is none other than conscientiousness and altruism."

5:11. Tzu-kung said, "What I do not want others to do to me, I do not want to do to them." Confucius said, "Ah, Tz'u! That is beyond you."

5:12. Tzu-kung said, "We can hear our Master's (views) on culture and its manifestation,[15] but we cannot hear his views on human nature and the Way of Heaven [because these subjects are beyond the comprehension of most people]."

5:15. Confucius said of Tzu-ch'an[16] that he had four of the moral qualities of the superior man—that in conducting himself, he was humble; in serving his superiors, he was reverent; in nourishing the people, he was kind; and in employing the people, he was just.

6:8. Po-niu was ill. Confucius went to see him. He took hold of his hand through the window and said, "It is killing him. It is the order (*ming*) (of Heaven). Alas! That such a man should have such a sickness. That such a man should have such a sickness."[17]

6:20. Fan Ch'ih asked about wisdom. Confucius said, "Devote yourself earnestly to the duties due to men, and respect spiritual beings but keep them at a distance. This may be called wisdom." Fan Ch'ih asked about humanity. Confucius said, "The man of humanity first of all considers what is difficult in the task and then thinks of success. Such a man may be called humane."

6:25. Confucius said, "The superior man extensively studies literature and restrains himself with the rules of propriety. Thus he will not violate the Way."

6:26. When Confucius visited Nan-tzu

(the wicked wife of Duke Ling of Wei, r. 533–490 B.C.) [in an attempt to influence her to persuade the duke to effect political reform], Tzu-lu was not pleased. Confucius swore an oath and said, "If I have said or done anything wrong, may Heaven forsake me! May Heaven forsake me!"[18]

6:28. Tzu-kung said, "If a ruler extensively confers benefit on the people and can bring salvation to all, what do you think of him? Would you call him a man of humanity?" Confucius said, "Why only a man of humanity? He is without doubt a sage. Even (sage-emperors) Yao and Shun[19] fell short of it. A man of humanity, wishing to establish his own character, also establishes the character of others, and wishing to be prominent himself, also helps others to be prominent. To be able to judge others by what is near to ourselves may be called the method of realizing humanity."

7:9. When Confucius ate by the side of a mourner, he never ate to the full. When he wept (at a funeral), he would not sing on the same day.

7:19. Confucius said, "I am not one who was born with knowledge; I love ancient [teaching] and earnestly seek it."

7:20. Confucius never discussed strange phenomena, physical exploits, disorder, or spiritual beings.

7:22. Confucius said, "Heaven produced the virtue that is in me. What can Huan T'ui[20] do to me?"

7:24. Confucius taught four things: culture, conduct, loyalty, and faithfulness.

7:34. Confucius was very ill. Tzu-lu asked that prayer be offered. Confucius said, "Is there such a thing?" Tzu-lu replied, "There is. A eulogy says, 'Pray to the spiritual beings above and below.'" Confucius said, "My prayer has been for a long time [that is, what counts is the life that one leads]."

8:19. Confucius said, "Great indeed was Yao as a ruler. How majestic was he! Heaven alone is grand, and only Yao modeled after him."

9:1. Confucius seldom talked about profit, destiny (*ming* or the Mandate of Heaven), and humanity.

9:3. Confucius said, "The linen cap is prescribed by the rules of ceremony but nowadays a silk one is worn. It is economical and I follow the common practice. Bowing below the hall is prescribed by the rules of ceremony, but nowadays people bow after ascending the hall. This is arrogant, and I follow the practice of bowing below the hall though that is opposed to the common practice."

9:5. When Confucius was in personal danger in K'uang,[21] he said, "Since the death of King Wen,[22] is not the course of culture (*wen*) in my keeping? If it had been the will of Heaven to destroy this culture, it would not have been given to a mortal (like me). But if it is the will of Heaven that this culture should not perish, what can the people of K'uang do to me?"

9:6. A great official asked Tzu-kung, "Is the Master a sage? How is it that he has so much ability [in practical, specific things]?" Tzu-kung said, "Certainly Heaven has endowed him so liberally that he is to become a sage,[23] and furthermore he has much ability." When Confucius heard this, he said, "Does the great official know me? When I was young, I was in humble circumstances, and therefore I acquired much ability to do the simple things of humble folk. Does a superior man need to have so much ability? He does not." His pupil Lao said, "The Master said, 'I have not been given official employment and therefore I [acquired the ability] for the simple arts.'"

9:8. Confucius said, "The phoenix has not come and no chart (indications of a sage)[24] has emerged from the river. It is all over with me!"

9:10. Yen Yüan[25] sighed heavily and said, "When I look up to his doctrines, they seem to become higher, and when I try to drill into them, they seem to become more firm. I look at them before me, and suddenly they seem to be behind. Our Master, by orderly method, skillfully leads people on. He broadens me with literature and restrains me with the rules of propriety. I cannot stop in these pursuits even if I wished to. After I have exhausted all my ability, there still seems to be something outstanding before me. Although I wish to follow it up, there is really no way to do so."

9:11. Confucius was very ill. Tzu-lu[26] told his pupils to be ministers to him [as if Confucius was an official]. During a remission of his illness, he said, "Long has the conduct of Yu been deceitful. By pretending to have ministers when I don't have any, whom do I cheat? Should I cheat Heaven? Moreover, I would rather die in the hands of several of you than in the hands of ministers. And although I cannot have a great burial [with public honor], shall I die on the roadside?"

9:28. Confucius said, "The man of wisdom has no perplexity; the man of humanity has no worry; the man of courage has no fear."

11:8. When Yen Yüan died, Confucius said, "Alas, Heaven is destroying me! Heaven is destroying me!"

11:11. Chi-lu (Tzu-lu) asked about serving the spiritual beings. Confucius said, "If we are not yet able to serve man, how can we serve spiritual beings?" "I venture to ask about death." Confucius said, "If we do not yet know about life, how can we know about death?"

12:1. Yen Yüan asked about humanity. Confucius said, "To master[27] oneself and return to propriety is humanity.[28] If a man (the ruler) can for one day master himself and return to propriety, all under heaven will return to humanity.[29] To practice humanity depends on oneself. Does it depend on others?" Yen Yüan said, "May I ask for the detailed items?" Confucius said, "Do not look at what is contrary to propriety, do not listen to what is contrary to propriety, do not speak what is contrary to propriety, and do not make any movement which is contrary to propriety." Yen Yüan said, "Although I am not intelligent, may I put your saying into practice."

12:2. Chung-kung[30] asked about humanity. Confucius said, "When you go abroad, behave to everyone as if you were receiving a great guest. Employ the people as if you were assisting at a great sacrifice.[31] Do not do to others what you do not want them to do to you. Then there will be no complaint against you in the state or in the family (the ruling clan)." Chung-kung said, "Although I am not intelligent, may I put your saying into practice."

12:5. Ssu-ma Niu,[32] worrying, said, "All people have brothers but I have none."[33] Tzu-hsia said, "I have heard (from Confucius) this saying: 'Life and death are the decree (*ming*) of Heaven; wealth and honor depend on Heaven. If a superior man is reverential (or serious) without fail, and is respectful in dealing with others and follows the rules of propriety, then all within the four seas (the world)[34] are brothers.'[35] What does the superior man have to worry about having no brothers?"

14:36. Someone said, "What do you think of repaying hatred with virtue?" Confucius said, "In that case what are you going to repay virtue with? Rather, repay hatred with uprightness and repay virtue with virtue."

14:37. Confucius said, "Alas! No one knows me!" Tzu-kung said, "Why is there no one that knows you?" Confucius said, "I do not complain against Heaven. I do not blame men. I study things on the lower level but my understanding penetrates the higher level.[36] It is Heaven that knows me."

14:38. Kung-po Liao[37] slandered Tzu-lu before Chi-sun.[38] Tzu-fu Ching-po[39] told Confucius about it, saying, "Our master (Chi-sun) is of course deceived by Kung-po Liao to some extent, but I am still powerful enough to cut Kung-po Liao up to pieces and expose him in the market."

Confucius said, "If (my) Way is to prevail, it is (Heaven's) Mandate (*ming*). If it is to be stopped, it is (Heaven's) Mandate. What can Kung-po Liao do about (Heaven's) Mandate?"

15:5. Tzu-chang[40] asked about conduct. Confucius said, "If one's words are loyal and faithful and his actions earnest and serious, they will do even in barbarian countries. If his words are not loyal or faithful and his actions are not earnest or serious, will they do even in his own neighborhood?[41] When he is standing, let him see his faithful words and serious action in front of him. When he is riding, let him see them attached to the yoke. Then he will do." Tzu-chang wrote the Master's words on his sash.

15:21, Confucius said, "The superior man is grave and reverent but is not contentious. He mixes with others but is not partisan."

15:23. Tzu-kung asked, "Is there one word which can serve as the guiding principle for conduct throughout life?" Confucius said, "It is the word *altruism*. Do not do to others what you do not want them to do to you."

15:28. Confucius said, "It is man that can make the Way great, and not the Way that can make man great."

16:8. Confucius said, "The superior man stands in awe of three things. He stands in awe of the Mandate of Heaven; he stands in awe of great men,[42] and he stands in awe of the words of the sages. The inferior man is ignorant of the Mandate of Heaven and does not stand in awe of it. He is disrespectful to great men and is contemptuous toward the words of the sages."

17:19. Confucius said, "I do not wish to say anything." Tzu-kung said, "If you do not say anything, what can we little disciples ever learn to pass on to others?" Confucius said, "Does Heaven (*T'ien*, Nature) say anything? The four seasons run their course and all things are produced. Does Heaven say anything?"

17:21. Tsai Wo[43] asked about the three years' mourning (for parents) and said, "One year is long enough. If the superior man abstains from ordinary ceremonies for three years, they will decline. If he abstains from music for three years, it will be ruined. [Within a year,] the old grain is used up, the new grain has sprung up, and whirling drills have made new fires. After a year, it should be all right for the mourning to stop."

Confucius said, "If [after a year] you eat good rice and wear silk brocade, do you feel comfortable?"

"Yes."

"If you feel comfortable, go ahead and do it. But a superior man, while he lives in mourning, does not feel the good taste if he eats delicious food. He does not enjoy if he hears music. And he does not feel at ease in his abode. Therefore he does not do (as you say)."

After Tsai Wo went out, Confucius said, "How inhumane is Yu! It is three years since a child is born before it leaves the arms of its parents. The three years' mourning is universally observed throughout the world. Didn't Yu enjoy three years of love from his parents?"

19:1. Tzu-chang said, "When a scholar sees danger [to his country], he is ready to sacrifice his life. When he sees opportunity for gain, he thinks of righteousness. In sacrificing, he thinks about reverence. And in mourning, he thinks about being sorrowful. That is all we can desire."

19:6. Tzu-hsia said, "To study extensively, to be steadfast in one's purpose, to inquire earnestly, and to reflect on what is at hand [that is, what one can put into practice]—humanity consists in these."

19:14. Tzu-yu[44] said, "When grief is carried to the highest degree, mourning should stop."

20:3. Confucius said, "Without knowing the Mandate (of Heaven), it is impossible to be a superior man. Without knowledge of the rules of propriety, it is impossible for one's character to be established. And without understanding [people's feelings from their] words, it is impossible to know men."

B. MENCIUS

☐ The two main doctrines of Mencius (372–289 B.C.)[45] are the original goodness of human nature and that man being the most important element in the state, has the right to revolt. In religion, he reaffirmed the teachings of Confucius that Heaven is purposive and most powerful and that the will of Heaven is demonstrated in human affairs. As he said, sincerity is the way of Heaven but it is man who can make sincerity real (*The Book of Mencius*, 4A:12). Like Confucius, he stressed the importance of serving parents when they are dead as they were served when alive (4B:13). And he insisted that only a good man can serve the Lord on High (4B:25).

The impression that he did not make much of an imprint on Chinese religion is wrong. In two areas he carried Chinese religious thought a great step forward, namely, in its mystical element and in an extremely significant and highly influential theory on *ming* (fate, Heaven's mandate or decree, destiny, life). Both of these are derived from his doctrine of innate goodness.

Mencius maintained that man is born with the "Four Beginnings" of humanity, righteousness, propriety, and wisdom (2A:6) and that man possesses the innate knowledge of the good and the innate ability to do good (7A:15). When this goodness is fully realized, one becomes a sage and then a "man of the spirit" (7B:25), and when a superior man extends his influence on others, his transforming influence "forms the same current above and below with that of Heaven and Earth" (7A:13). Here he laid a solid foundation for the perennial Chinese doctrine of unity of man and Heaven.

Much has been said about Chinese fatalism. Undeniably there has been very much, altogether too much, of it among the uneducated. But for the enlightened, although life and death, and certain other things in life, are definitely beyond one's control, man's duty is to cultivate his moral life and let fate (or Heaven's order) take its own course. In the normal course of events, the Moral Law prevails. Good will be rewarded and evil punished, not by order of spiritual beings but in one's happiness or guilty conscience. The reason for cultivating the moral life is simply that it is the natural dictate of one's original goodness. One should do good not because it is his fate but because it is his nature (7B:24). Whether one succeeds or fails may be due to fate, but one's only concern should be whether one's action is in accord with moral principles (5A:8). If one dies in the course of doing his duty, it is fate, but if one foolishly stands by a dangerous wall and gets killed, that is not fate (7A:2). Let us "preserve our mind and nourish our nature," he urged, for that is "the way to serve Heaven," and let us "cultivate our person and wait for fate to take its own course," for that is the "the way to fulfill one's *ming*" (7A:1).

These quotations are from perhaps the most important passage in the *Book of Mencius* so far as religion is concerned. Heaven is to be served, but the way to do so is through the fulfillment of human nature. Similarly, destiny is to be fulfilled (literally "established") by living a good moral life. The element of unpredictability is not ignored, but it should not affect one's moral course. Do good and wait and see what happens, if the unpredictable happens at all. This doctrine of "waiting for fate" has been the unflinching belief of the enlightened Chinese throughout the centuries. As in the case of Confucius, it is humanism, but it is humanism rooted in Heaven.

The following selections are from the *Book of Mencius*[46] in which his doctrines have been recorded. □

2A:2. (Kung-sun Ch'ou) asked, "May I venture to ask, sir, how you maintain an unperturbed mind and how Kao Tzu[47] maintains an unperturbed mind. May I be told?" Mencius answered, "Kao Tzu said, 'What is not attained in words is not to be sought in the mind, and what is not attained in the mind is not to be sought in the vital force (*ch'i*).[48]' It is all right to say that what is not attained in the mind is not to be sought in the vital force, but it is not all right to say that what is not attained in words is not to be sought in the mind. The will is the leader of the vital force, and the vital force pervades and animates the body. The will is the highest; the vital force comes next. Therefore I say, 'Hold the will firm and never do violence to the vital force.'"

Ch'ou said, "You said that the will is the highest and that the vital force comes next. But you also say hold the will firm and never to do violence to the vital force. Why?"

Mencius said, "If the will is concentrated, the vital force [will follow it] and become active. If the vital force is concentrated, the will [will follow it] and become active. For instance, here is a case of a man falling or running. It is his vital force that is active, and yet it causes his mind to be active too." Ch'ou asked, "May I venture to ask, sir, in what you are strong?"

Mencius replied, "I understand [people's

feelings from their] words.[49] And I am skillful in nourishing my strong, moving power."

"May I ask what is meant by the strong, moving power?"

"It is difficult to describe. As power, it is exceedingly great and exceedingly strong. If nourished by uprightness and not injured, it will fill up all between heaven and earth. As power, it is accompanied by righteousness and the Way. Without them, it will be devoid of nourishment. It is produced by the accumulation of righteous deeds but is not obtained by incidental acts of righteousness. When one's conduct is not satisfactory to his own mind, then one will be devoid of nourishment. I therefore said that Kao Tzu never understood righteousness because he made it something external."

"Always be doing something without expectation.[50] Let the mind not forget[51] its objective, but let there be no artificial effort to help it grow. Do not be like the man of Sung. There was a man of Sung who was sorry that his corn was not growing, and so he pulled it up. Having been tired out he went home and said to his people, 'I am all tired. I have helped the corn to grow.' When his son ran to look at it, the corn had already withered."

2A:6. Mencius said, "All men have the mind which cannot bear [to see the suffering of] others. The ancient kings had this mind and therefore they had a government that could not bear to see the suffering of the people. When a government that cannot bear to see the suffering of the people is conducted from a mind that cannot bear to see the suffering of others, the government of the empire will be as easy as making something go round in the palm.

"When I say that all men have the mind which cannot bear to see the suffering of others, my meaning may be illustrated thus: Now, when men suddenly see a child about to fall into a well, they all have a feeling of alarm and distress, not to gain friendship with the child's parents, nor to seek the praise of their neighbors and friends, nor because they dislike the reputation [of lack of humanity if they did not rescue the child]. From such a case, we see that a man without the feeling of commiseration is not a man; a man without the feeling of shame and dislike is not a man; a man without the feeling of deference and compliance is not a man; and a man without the feeling of right and wrong is not a man. The feeling of commiseration is the beginning of humanity; the feeling of shame and dislike is the beginning of righteousness; the feeling of deference and compliance is the beginning of propriety; and the feeling of right and wrong is the beginning of wisdom. Men have these Four Beginnings just as they have their four limbs. Having these Four Beginnings but saying that they cannot develop them is to destroy themselves. When they say that their ruler cannot develop them, they are destroying their ruler. If anyone with these Four Beginnings in him knows how to give them the fullest extension and development, the result will be like fire beginning to burn or a spring beginning to shoot forth. When they are fully developed, they will be sufficient to protect all people within the four seas (the world). If they are not developed, they will not be sufficient even to serve one's parents."

4A:12. Mencius said, "If those occupying inferior positions do not have the confidence of their superiors, they will not be able to govern the people. There is a way to have the confidence of the superiors. If one is not trusted by his friends, he will not have the confidence of his superiors. There is a way to be trusted by one's friends. If one's service to his parents does not give them pleasure, he will not be trusted by his friends. There is a way to please one's parents. If one examines himself and finds himself to be insincere, he cannot please his parents. There is a way to be sincere with himself. If one does not understand what is good, he will not be sincere with himself. Therefore sincerity is the way of Heaven, and to think how to be sincere is the way of man.[52] There has never been a person who was completely sincere and yet did not move others. Nor has there been a person who was not sincere and yet could move others."

4B:13. Mencius said, "The nourishment of parents when they are living is not enough to be considered a great thing. Only [the performance of funeral rites] to send them off when they die can be considered a great thing."

4B:25. Mencius said, "If (famous beauty) Lady Hsi[53] had been covered with filthy things, all people would have stopped their noses in passing her. But although a man may be ugly looking,[54] if he performs (the religious rites of) fasting and bathing, he may sacrifice to the Lord on High."

5A:5. Wan Chang[55] asked, "Is it true that Yao gave the empire to Shun?"[56] Mencius replied, "No. The emperor cannot give the empire to another person." "Yes, but Shun had the empire. Who gave it to him?" Mencius said, "Heaven gave it to him." "By Heaven's giving it to him, do you mean that Heaven gave it to him in so many words?" "No. Heaven does not speak. It simply shows its will by (Shun's) personal character and his conduct of affairs."

"May I ask how Heaven showed its will by (Shun's) character and his conduct of affairs?" Mencius said, "The emperor can recommend a person to Heaven, but he cannot make Heaven give that man the empire. A feudal lord can recommend a person to the emperor, but he cannot make the emperor make that man a feudal lord. A great officer can recommend a person to a feudal lord, but he cannot make the feudal lord make that man a great officer. In ancient times, Yao recommended Shun to Heaven, and Heaven accepted him. He showed him to the people, and the people accepted him. I therefore say that Heaven did not speak, but that it simply indicated its will by his character and his conduct of affairs."

"May I ask how it was that Yao recommended him to Heaven and Heaven accepted him, and that he showed him to the people and the people accepted him?" Mencius said, "He had him preside over the sacrifices, and all the spiritual beings enjoyed them. This means that Heaven accepted him. He had him preside over the conduct of affairs, and the affairs were well managed, and the people felt satisfied. This means that the people accepted him. It was Heaven that gave the empire to him. It was the people that gave the empire to him. Therefore I said, 'The emperor cannot give the empire to another person.' Shun assisted Yao for twenty-eight years. This was more than a man could do; it was Heaven that did it. After the death of Yao, when the three-year mourning was completed, Shun withdrew from the son of Yao to the south of the South River. The feudal lords of the empire, however, going to court, went not to the son of Yao but to Shun, litigants went not to the son of Yao but to Shun, and singers sang not to the son of Yao but to Shun. Therefore I said, 'Heaven [gave the empire to him].' Only then did he go to the Middle Kingdom (China) and take the emperor's seat. If he had occupied the place of Yao and applied pressure to his son, it would have been an act of usurpation, and not a gift of Heaven. The 'Great Declaration' said, 'Heaven sees as my people see; Heaven hears as my people hear.'[57] This is the meaning."

5A:6. Mencius said, ". . . When Heaven gives the empire to the worthy, (the retiring ruler) will give it to the worthy. When Heaven gives it to his son, he will give it to his son. In the old days Shun recommended Yü[58] to Heaven. Seventeen years later, Shun died. When the three-year mourning was over, Yü withdrew to Yang-ch'eng[59] in deference to the son of Shun, but the people of the empire followed him there, just as when Yao died, the people followed Shun instead of Yao's son. Yü recommended (his minister) I (pronounced "yi") to Heaven. Seven years later, Yü died. When the three years' mourning was over, I withdrew to the northern slope of Mount Chi[60] in deference to the son of Yü, but those who went for imperial audience or litigation did not go to I but went to (Yü's son) Ch'i saying, 'He is the son of our sovereign.' Singers did not sing of I but sang of Ch'i, saying, 'He is the son of our sovereign.' (Yao's son) Tan-chu was unworthy and Shun's son was also unworthy. Shun assisted Yao and Yü assisted Shun for many years, and for a long time they conferred benefits on the people. Ch'i was worthy and could reverently inherit the way of Yü. I, however, assisted Yü only for several years and did not confer benefits on the people for very long. The facts that Shun, Yü, and I differed in their length of service and that the son (of Yü) was worthy but the sons of (Yao and Shun) were not, are all due to Heaven and were not things that man could do anything about. That which is done without man's doing is Heaven. That which happens without man's causing it to happen is the Mandate of Heaven. For a private individual to become sovereign of an empire, his virtue must be comparable to that of Shun and Yü and he must also be recommended by the Son of Heaven. For this reason, Chung-ni (Confucius) did not have the empire . . . "

5A:8. Wan Chang asked, "Some say that when Confucius was in Wei, he stayed with (the eunuch) Yung-chü[61] and when he was in Ch'i he stayed with the attendant, Chi-huan. Is that true?"

Mencius said, "No, it is not true. Those are stories invented by trouble makers. When he was in Wei, he stayed with Yen Ch'ou-yu. The wives of Mei Tzu[62] and Tzu-lu[63] were sisters. Mei Tzu said to Tzu-lu, 'If Confucius stays with me, he may become a high official in Wei.' Tzu-lu told Confucius about it. Confucius said, 'There is the Mandate (of Heaven).' Confucius advanced according to rules of propriety and withdrew according to moral principles. Whether he obtained office or not, he said that 'There is the Mandate (of Heaven).' If he had stayed with Yung-chü or the attendant, Chi-huan, that means he would ignore moral principles or the Mandate (of Heaven). . . ."

6B:15. Mencius said, ... "When Heaven is about to confer a great responsibility on any man, it will exercise his mind with suffering, subject his sinews and bones to hard work, expose his body to hunger, put him to poverty, place obstacles in the paths of his deeds, so as to stimulate his mind, harden his nature, and improve wherever he is incompetent." . . . .

7A:1. Mencius said, "He who exerts his mind to the utmost knows his nature. He who knows his nature knows Heaven. To preserve one's mind and to nourish one's nature is the way to serve Heaven. Not to allow any double-mindedness regardless of longevity or brevity of life, but to cultivate one's person and wait for [destiny (*ming*, fate, Heaven's decree or mandate) to take its own course] is the way to fulfill one's destiny."[64]

7A:2. Mencius said, "Everything is destiny. A man should accept obediently what is correct [in one's destiny]. Therefore, he who knows destiny does not stand beneath a precipitous wall. Death sustained in the course of carrying out the Way to the limit is due to correct destiny. But death under handcuffs and fetters is not due to correct destiny."

7A:4. Mencius said, "All things are already complete in oneself. There is no greater joy than to examine oneself and be sincere. When in one's conduct one vigorously exercises altruism, humanity is not far to seek but right by him."

7A:13. Mencius said, "Under a despot, the people look brisk and cheerful [only temporarily and superficially, for the despot's kindness is selfishly motivated]. Under a true king, however, the people feel magnificent and at ease with themselves. Though he punishes them by death, they do not complain, and when he benefits them, they do not think of their merit. From day to day they make progress toward the good without knowing who makes them do so. Whenever the superior man passes through, transforming influence follows. Wherever he abides, spiritual influence remains. This forms the same current above and below with that of Heaven and Earth. Is this a small help?"

7B:24. Mencius said, "It is due to our nature that our mouths desire sweet taste, that our eyes desire beautiful colors, that our ears desire pleasant sounds, that our noses desire fragrant odors, and that our four limbs desire ease and comfort. But there is also fate (*ming*) [whether these desires are satisfied or not]. The superior man does not say they are man's [and insist on satisfying them]. The virtue of humanity in the relationship between father and son, the virtue of righteousness in the relationship between ruler and minister, the virtue of propriety in the relationship between guests and host, the virtue of wisdom in the worthy and the sage in regard to the Way of Heaven—these are [endowed in people in various degrees] according to fate. But there is also man's nature. The superior man does not [refrain from practicing them and] say they are matters of fate."

7B:25. Hao-sheng Pu-hai asked, "What sort of man is Yo-cheng?"[65] Mencius said, "He is a good man and a true man." "What is a good man? And what is a true man?" Mencius said, "One who commands our liking [because of his virtue] is called a good man. One who is sincere with himself is called a true man. He [whose goodness] is extensive and solid is called a beautiful man. He [whose goodness] is abundant and is brilliantly displayed is called a great man. When one is great and is completely transformed [to be goodness itself], he is called a sage. When a sage is beyond our knowledge, he is called a man of the spirit."

7B:33. Mencius said, "With Yao and Shun it was their nature. With T'ang and Wu,[66] it was their effort to return [to their nature]. When all movements and expressions are exactly proper according to the rules of propriety, that shows the highest degree of eminent virtue. The sorrow in weeping for the dead is not for the sake of the living. The regular practice of virtue without any deviation is not to seek emolument. And words should always be sincere not because of any conscious desire to do what is right. The superior man practices principle (Natural Law) and waits for destiny (*ming*, Mandate of Heaven) to take its own course."

C. THE *DOCTRINE OF THE MEAN*

☐ There is a great deal of similarity between the *Doctrine of the Mean*[67] and Mencius. Like Mencius, *The Mean* teaches us to do good and "wait for fate" (ch. 14), to know Heaven (ch. 29), to be sincere (ch. 25), and to follow our nature (ch. 1). In the first two doctrines, Mencius was more emphatic and elaborate. In the latter two, however, *The Mean* shows great developments.

So far as man himself is concerned, Mencius had carried the doctrine of the fulfillment of nature to a very high degree, but *The Mean* has added that one who fully develops his nature can develop the nature of other people and then develop the nature of things until he can assist in the transforming and nourishing process of Heaven and Earth and thus form a trinity with Heaven and Earth (ch. 22). The idea of unity of man and Heaven is here clearly stated and firmly established. With regard to the concept of sincerity, its meaning of being genuine and real is forcefully put forth. A sincere man "completes" (*ch'eng*) others as well as himself (ch. 25), says *The Mean*. Sincerity is unceasing (ch. 26), combines beginning and end as one (ch. 25), and therefore the future may be predicted (ch. 24). The upshot is that a man of perfect sincerity forms a unity with the universe.

In this Classic is also found the definite statement that man's nature is imparted to man by Heaven (ch. 1), a doctrine that has remained a cardinal one throughout the history of Chinese thought. Equally influential has been its description of *kuei* and *shen*. They are neither seen nor heard, says *The Mean*, but they form the substance of (or enter into) all things and nothing can be without them (ch. 16). They are ordinarily understood as spiritual beings (who can enter into everything). Later, however, Neo-Confucianists interpreted them as cosmic spiritual forces (see ch. 13, B, f). In any case, in both its concept of man forming a triad with Heaven and Earth in its concept of *kuei* and *shen*, the Classic has intensively broadened the spiritual and mystical dimension of Confucianism. In the matter of religion, too, it has provided concrete expressions with reference to temples, ceremonies, and so on. All of this is beside its central teaching of the Mean as the synthesis of extremes and opposites and of its idea of harmony prevailing throughout the universe. No wonder Neo-Confucianists of the eleventh century singled it out of the *Book of Rites* of which it is a chapter, and Chu Hsi (1130–1200) grouped it with the *Analects*, the *Book of Mencius*, and the *Great Learning* as the Four Books. As such they have been the basis of Chinese thought for the last 750 years. ☐

Ch. 1. What Heaven (*T'ien*, Nature) imparts to man is called human nature. To follow[68] our nature is called the Way (Tao). Cultivating the Way is called education. The Way cannot be separated from us for a moment. What can be separated from us is not the Way. Therefore the superior man is cautious over what he does not see and apprehensive over what he does not hear. There is nothing more visible than what is hidden and nothing more manifest that what is subtle. Therefore the superior man is watchful over himself when he is alone.

Before the feelings of pleasure, anger, sorrow, and joy are aroused it is called equilibrium (*chung*, centrality, mean). When these feelings are aroused and each and all attain due measure and degree, it is called harmony. Equilibrium is the great foundation of the world, and harmony its universal path. When equilibrium and harmony are realized to the highest degree, heaven and earth will attain their proper order and all things will flourish.

Ch. 14. The superior man does what is proper to his position and does not want to go beyond this. If he is in a noble station, he does what is proper to a position of wealth and honorable station. If he is in a humble station, he does what is proper to a position of poverty and humble station. If he is in the midst of barbarian tribes, he does what is proper in the midst of barbarian tribes. In a position of difficulty and danger, he does what is proper to a position of difficulty and danger. He can find himself in no situation in which he is not at ease with himself. In a high position he does not treat his inferiors with contempt. In a low position he does not court the favor of his superiors. He rectifies himself and seeks nothing from others, hence he has no complaint to make. He does not complain against Heaven above or blame men below.[69] Thus it is that the superior man lives peacefully and at ease and waits for his destiny (*ming*, Mandate of Heaven, fate), while the inferior man takes to dangerous courses and hopes for good luck. Confucius said, "In archery we have something resembling the Way of the superior man. When the archer misses the center of the target, he turns around and seeks for the cause of failure within himself."

Ch. 16. Confucius said, "How abundant is the display of power of spiritual beings! We look for them but do not see them. We listen to them but do not hear them. They form the substance of all things[70] and nothing can be without them. They cause all people in the world to fast and purify themselves and put on the richest dresses to perform sacrifices to them. Like the spread of overflowing water they seem to be above and to be on the left and the right. The *Book of Odes* says, 'The coming of spiritual beings cannot be surmised. How much less can we get tired of them?'[71] Such is the manifestation of the subtle. Such is the impossibility of hiding the real (*ch'eng*)."

Ch. 19. Confucius said, "King Wu and Duke Chou were indeed eminently filial. Men of filial piety are those who skillfully carry out the wishes of their forefathers and skillfully carry forward their undertakings. In spring and autumn they repaired their ancestral temple, displayed their ancestral vessels and exhibited the ancestral robes, and presented the appropriate offerings of the season. The ritual of the ancestral temple is in order to place the kindred on the left or on the right according to the order of descent. This order in rank is meant to distinguish the more honorable or humbler stations. Services in the temple are arranged in order so as to give distinction to the worthy [according to their ability for those services]. In the pledging rite the inferiors present their cups to their superiors, so that people of humble stations may have something to do. In the concluding feast, honored places were given people with white hair, so as to follow the order of seniority. To occupy places of their forefathers, to practice their rites, to perform their music, to reverence those whom they honored, to love those who were dear to them, to serve the dead as they were served while alive, and to serve the departed as they served while still with us: this is the height of filial piety.

"The ceremonies of sacrifices to Heaven and Earth are meant for the service of the

Lord on High, and the ceremonies performed in the ancestral temple are meant for the service of ancestors. If one understands the ceremonies of the sacrifices to Heaven and Earth and the meaning of the grand sacrifice and the autumn sacrifice to ancestors, it would be as easy to govern a kingdom as to look at one's palm."

Ch. 21. It is due to our nature that enlightenment results from sincerity. It is due to education that sincerity results from enlightenment. Given sincerity, there will be enlightenment, and given enlightenment, there will be sincerity.

Ch. 22. Only those who are absolutely sincere can fully develop their nature. If they can fully develop their nature, they can then fully develop the nature of others. If they can fully develop the nature of others, they can then fully develop the nature of things. If they can fully develop the nature of things, they can then assist in the transforming and nourishing process of Heaven and Earth. If they can assist in the transforming and nourishing process of Heaven and Earth, they can thus form a trinity with Heaven and Earth.

Ch. 24. It is characteristic of absolute sincerity to be able to foreknow. When a nation or family is about to flourish, there are sure to be lucky omens. When a nation or family is about to perish, there are sure to be unlucky omens. These omens are revealed in divination and in the movements of the four limbs. When calamity or blessing is about to come, it can surely know beforehand if it is good, and it can also surely know beforehand if it is evil. Therefore he who has absolute sincerity is like a spirit.

Ch. 25. Sincerity means the completion of the self, and the Way is self-directing. Sincerity is the beginning and end of things. Without sincerity there would be nothing. Therefore the superior man values sincerity. Sincerity is not only the completion of one's own self; it is that by which all things are completed. The completion of the self means humanity. The completion of all things means wisdom. These are the character of the nature, and they are the Way in which the internal[72] and the external are united. Therefore whenever it is employed, everything done is right.

Ch. 26. Therefore absolute sincerity is ceaseless. Being ceaseless, it is lasting. Being lasting, it is evident. Being evident, it is infinite, it is extensive and deep. Being extensive and deep, it is high and brilliant. It is because it is extensive and deep that it contains all things. It is because it is high and brilliant that it overshadows all things. It is because it is infinite and lasting that it can complete all things. In being extensive and deep, it is a counterpart of Earth. In being high and brilliant, it is a counterpart of Heaven. In being infinite and lasting, it is unlimited. Such being its nature, it becomes prominent without any display, produces changes without motion, and accomplishes its ends without action . . . .[73]

Ch. 29. If he who attains to the sovereignty of the world has three important things (ceremonies, regulations, and the form and pronunciation of characters), he will make few mistakes. However excellent may have been the regulations of former times, there is no evidence for them. Without evidence, they cannot command credence, and not being credited, the people would not follow them. However excellent might be the regulations made by one in a low position, his position is not an honored one. The position not being honored does not command credence, and not being credited, the people would not follow them. Therefore the Way of the true ruler is rooted in his own personal life and has its evidence (in the following) of the common people. It is tested by the experience of the Three Kings[74] and found without error, applied before Heaven and Earth and found to be without contradiction in their operation, laid before spiritual beings without question or fear, and can wait a hundred generations for a sage [to confirm it] without a doubt. Since it can be laid before spiritual beings without question or fear, it shows that he knows [the Principle of] Heaven. Since it can wait for a hundred generations for a sage without a doubt, it shows that he knows [the principles of] man. Therefore every move he makes becomes the way of the world, every act of his becomes the model of the world, and every word he utters becomes the pattern of the world. Those who are far away look longingly for him, and those who are near do not get weary of him. The *Book of Odes* says, "There they do not dislike him, here they do not get tired of him. Thus from day to day and night to night, they will perpetuate their praise."[75] There has never been a ruler who did not answer this description and yet could obtain early renown through the world.

D. HSÜN TZU

□ Two significant contributions by Hsün Tzu (313–238 B.C.?)[76] to Chinese religious thought deserve our attention. One is that he carried the naturalist tendency of Confucianism with regard to Heaven to the extreme. The tendency was already noticeable in Confucius in his statement that Heaven does not speak but the four seasons rotate.[77] To Hsün Tzu, Heaven (*T'ien*) is simple Nature, which has nothing to do with man's goodness or evil nor with reward and punishment for his deeds. He makes a clear distinction between Nature and man, a distinction that culminated in the traditional doctrine of the "division of Heaven and man," which finds an emphatic restatement in ch. 13, A, 2. Man's duty is to cultivate a moral life and control Nature by adapting to it, and thus he will enjoy a good and long life.

The other contribution concerns the meaning of rites. It is difficult to tell whether Hsün Tzu drew from the *Book of Rites* (ch. 12, B.) or vice versa or both drew from a common source. But no one in the history of Chinese religious thought has emphasized more strongly than Hsün Tzu that rites are for the purpose of social control and their deepest meaning is the expression of human emotions. In the case of ancestral sacrifice, for example, Confucius' teaching on serving parents in the same way whether they are living or dead remains the central purpose. In Hsün Tzu, however, the new emphasis is on one's thinking of and remembering one's ancestors. Feelings need expressions in rites as "adornments," but the main thing is how one feels. He went as far as to suggest that whether there is really any spiritual being to come to enjoy the sacrifice is irrelevant, for it is one's psychological state that "completes" the rites. Hsün Tzu's naturalism is certainly not materialism; he does not deny the existence of spiritual beings outright. But to him it is man that counts.

The following selections are from his work, the *Hsün Tzu.*[78]

1. "On Nature" (Ch. 17)

□ Nature (Heaven) operates with constant regularity. It does not exist for the sake of (sage-emperor) Yao[79] nor does it cease to exist because of (wicked king) Chieh.[80] Respond to it with peace and order, and good fortune will result. Respond to it with disorder, and disaster will follow. If the foundations of living (agriculture and sericulture) are strengthened and are economically used, then Nature cannot bring impoverishment. If people's nourishment is sufficient and their labor in keeping with the seasons, then Nature cannot inflict sickness. If the Way is cultivated without deviation, then Nature cannot cause misfortune. Therefore flood and drought cannot cause a famine, extreme cold or heat cannot cause illness, and evil spiritual beings cannot cause misfortune. But if the foundations of living are neglected or used extravagantly, then Nature cannot make the country rich. If there is meager nourishment and little work, then Nature cannot enable the people to be preserved. If people violate the Way and act foolishly, then Nature cannot give them good fortune. There will be famine before flood or drought approaches, there will be sickness before the thrust of extreme cold or heat, and there will be misfortune before the approach of evil spirits. When what the (people in these circumstances) receive from the season (natural factors) is the same as people receive in a period of peace and order, and yet the calamities are different from what prevails in the period of peace and order, this cannot be blamed on Heaven; this is how the Way works. Therefore one who understands the distinctive functions of Heaven and man may be called a perfect man.

To accomplish without any action and to obtain without effort[81] is what is meant by the office of Heaven. This being the case, although the Way of Heaven is deep, the perfect man does not deliberate over it. Although it is great, he does not devote any effort to it. And although it is refined, he does not scrutinize it. This what is meant by not competing with Heaven. Heaven has its seasons, earth has its wealth, and man has his government. This is how they are able to form a triad. To neglect (human activities) which constitute man's part in the triad and put one's hope in those with which he forms a triad is indeed a mistake.

The fixed stars rotate in succession, the sun and moon shine alternately, the four seasons follow one another, yin (passive cosmic force) and yang (active cosmic force) effect their great transformations, and the wind and rain spread over all things. Each of the ten thousand things attains its harmony, and thus grows. Each obtains its nourishment, and thus achieves full development. We do not see their activities but we do see their results. This is what is called spirit. We all know how they attain their full development but none knows that such a process is invisible. This is called Heaven. The sage, however, does not seek to know Heaven. When the office of Heaven is established and the work of Heaven is done, the body will be provided for, the spirit born, and the feelings of like, dislike, pleasure, anger, sorrow, and joy embodied. These are called the natural feelings. The ear, the eye, the nose, the mouth, and the body are, each in its own way, able to respond to external things, and cannot be interchanged. These are called natural organs. The heart (mind) occupies the cavity in the center to control the five organs. This is called the natural ruler. To plan and use what is not of one's kind to nourish one's kind—this is called natural nourishment. To act in accord with (the principle and nature of) one's own kind means happiness, and to act contrary to (the principle and nature of) one's own kind means calamity. This is called natural government. To darken one's natural ruler, to confuse the natural organs, or abandon natural nourishment, to act contrary to the natural government, and to violate the natural feelings so as to destroy the work of Nature—this is called great misfortune. The sage purifies his natural ruler, rectifies his natural organs, sufficiently provides for his natural nourishment, follows the natural government, and nourishes his natural feelings so as to bring to completion the work of Nature. In this way he knows what to do and what not to do. Thus he rules heaven and earth and directs the ten thousand things. His actions are all well regulated, his nourishment all well adapted, and his life is not injured—this is called knowing Nature. . . .

2. "A Treatise on Rites" (Ch. 19)

What is the origin of rites? I say: Man is born with desires. If he does not get what he desires, he can but seek for it. If there are no degrees or limits to his seeking, he can but contend with others. Contention leads to disorder and disorder leads to exhaustion. As ancient kings hated such disorder, they established rites and moral principles to bring about the proper shares in order to nourish men's desires and meet their demands. They made it possible that men's desires did not exhaust the material supplies and the material supplies did not suppress the desires. Both desires and material supplies support each other and thus grew. This is how rites originated. . . .

Rites have three bases. Heaven and Earth are the basis of life, the ancestors are the basis of the species, and rulers and teachers are the basis of order. If there were no Heaven and Earth, how could there be life? If there were no ancestors, how could (the species) come into existence? If there were no rulers and teachers, how could there be order? If one of the three were missing, there would not be any man at peace. Therefore rites serve Heaven above and Earth below, honor the ancestors, and exalt rulers and teachers. There are the three bases of rites.

Therefore the king honors the oldest ancestor of the clan as a counterpart of Heaven, the feudal lords dare not destroy the temples of their forefathers, and officers and great officers maintain regular sacrifices in the clan uninterrupted for a hundred generations. This is the way to distinguish the honoring of one's beginning, and honoring one's beginning is the basis of virtue. . . .

All rites begin in simplicity, are brought to completion in ornament and end in joy. Hence when rites are performed in perfection, both the emotions and the ornaments are fully expressed. The next best is when either the emotions or the ornaments surpass the other. At the lowest level, one reverts to emotion in an attempt to return to one's origin.

[Through rites] Heaven and earth are united, the sun and moon shine, the four seasons rotate in order, the stars and planets move, the rivers flow, all things flourish, likes and dislikes are regulated, and joy and anger are made appropriate. When rites govern those below, they will be obedient. When rites govern those above, they will be enlightened. (Because of them) all things do not become disorderly, and anything departing from them will be destroyed. Are rites not excellent! . . .

Rites are strict in their ordering of birth and death. Birth is the beginning of man and death is his end. When both beginning and end are good, the way of man is complete. Therefore the superior man is reverent about beginning and careful about the end, treating them in the same way. This is the way of the superior man and the ornament of rites and moral principles. To be generous in serving the living but stingy in serving the dead is to be reverent to one who is conscious but contemptuous to one who is not. This is the way of a wicked man and indicates the will to rebel. The superior man would be ashamed to treat even a slave or a child with the will to rebel; how much more ashamed to serve those he exalts (the ruler) and loves (parents) in such a way! The way of serving the dead operates only once and never again. This is the occasion for the full expression of the minister's seriousness toward his sovereign and the son's seriousness toward his parents. Therefore to serve the living without devotion and generosity and without reverence for ornament would be rustic, and to send off the dead without devotion and generosity and without reverence for ornament would be miserly. . . .

Funeral rites are meant to adorn the dead with what applies to the living, and to send off the dead by greatly simulating his life. Therefore the dead is treated as the living and the departed as the existent, for beginning and end are the same . . . .

Sacrificial rites are expressions of one's will and emotions of longing. It is inevitable that at times there comes the feeling that there is something strange or that one's emotions are suppressed. Therefore when one is enjoying himself or is in harmony with others, if he is a loyal minister or a filial son, he will find that the feeling of strangeness has come upon him [for his deceased ruler or parent is not sharing his joy or harmony]. When this feeling has come upon him, he will be greatly moved. But if the emotions are allowed to be exhausted in emptiness (without expression in sacrificial rites), his best intentions will be frustrated and unfulfilled, and ritual expressions will be missing. For this reason, the ancient kings instituted certain ornaments (rites). The meaning of honoring the superior and showing affection to parents is thereby complete. . . .

"Serve the dead as they are served while alive, and serve the departed as they are served while still existent."[82] It seems there is no appearance or shadow (of spiritual beings) and yet in thus performing the rites the ornament is completed.

NOTES

1. His family name was K'ung, private name Ch'iu, and courtesy name Chung-ni. He was honored as the "Grand Master K'ung" or *K'ung Fu Tzu* and hence Confucius. A self-educated man, he became a magistrate at fifty and minister of justice perhaps in the same year. He traveled for almost thirteen years to try to influence the rulers of various states but did not

succeed. He taught throughout his life and, according to tradition, had three thousand pupils

2. For English translations, see Arthur Waley, tr., *The Analects of Confucius*; James Legge, tr., *Analects*; and Wing-tsit Chan, *A Source Book in Chinese Philosophy*, ch. 2.
3. Confucius' pupil, whose private name was Jo (538–c. 457 B.C.), thirteen years (some say thirty years) Confucius' junior.
4. Confucius' pupil, whose private name was Shang (507–420 B.C.). He was noted for literary abilities. This and other sayings of Confucian pupils undoubtedly reflect their Master's ideas.
5. Tseng Ts'an (505–c. 436 B.C.), pupil of Confucius, noted for filial piety, to whom are ascribed the *Great Learning* and the *Classic of Filial Piety*.
6. A young noble, also styled Meng-sun, who once studied ceremonies with Confucius.
7. Confucius' pupil, whose family name was Fan, private name Hsü, and courtesy name Tzu-ch'ih (b. 515 B.C.).
8. These various interpretations have been offered by different commentators.
9. A native of Lu, Confucius' native state. Most probably not a pupil of Confucius.
10. Great officer and commander-in-chief in the state of Wei.
11. Dedicated to the Duke of Chou (d. 1094 B.C.), whom Confucius praised as the builder of the culture of the Chou dynasty.
12. According to tradition, Confucius' father was an officer here.
13. Confucius' pupil, whose family name was Tuan-mu, private name Tz'u, and courtesy name Tzu-kung (520–c. 450 B.C.). He was noted for eloquence and was thirty-one years younger than the Master.
14. Hate here means dislike, without any connotation of ill will.
15. The term *wen-chang* can also mean literary heritage or simply the ancient Classics.
16. For him, see ch. 10. C, 3.
17. Po-niu's family name was Jan and private name Keng. He probably had leprosy and therefore Confucius did not enter the house. Others say that Po-niu had moved to near the window so his superiors could see him facing south, according to the etiquette.
18. This episode took place when Confucius was 57.
19. Legendary sage-emperors of the third millennium B.C.
20. A military officer in the state of Sung who attempted to kill Confucius by felling a tree. Confucius was then 59 years of age.
21. The people of K'uang, mistaking Confucius for Yang Hu, their enemy whom Confucius resembled in appearance, surrounded him. This happened when Confucius was 56.
22. Founder of the Chou dynasty (r. 1171–1122 B.C.).
23. The term *chiang-sheng* is also understood to mean a great sage, or almost a sage.
24. It was believed that when a sage received the mandate from Heaven to become a king, one of these things would appear as an indication.
25. Confucius' favorite and most virtuous pupil, whose family name was Yen and private name Hui (521–490 B.C.). He died at 32.
26. Name of Confucius' pupil, whose family name was Chung and private name Yu (542–480 B.C.). He was only nine years younger than Confucius and was noted for courage.
27. The term *k'o* has also been interpreted to mean "to control."
28. An old saying. Other interpretations: (1) To be able to return to propriety by oneself; (2) To discipline oneself and to act according to propriety.
29. Other interpretations: (1) Ascribe humanity to him; (2) Will follow him.
30. Confucius' pupil, whose family name was Jan, private name Yung, and courtesy name Chung-kung. He was noted for excellent character.
31. Paraphrasing two ancient sayings.
32. Confucius' pupil, whose family name was Hsiung.
33. Meaning that his brother Huan T'ui (see earlier passage, 7:22) was not worthy to be a brother.
34. Ordinarily meaning China, there is no doubt that here it means the entire world.
35. Some say that the last sentence is Tzu-hsia's utterance.

36. There is a general agreement that the higher level refers to matters of Heaven such as Heaven's mandate and the Principle of Nature (Heaven), and that the lower level refers to mundane matters.
37. Confucius' pupil.
38. Head of the Chi family in the state of Lu.
39. A great officer of Lu.
40. Courtesy name of Confucius' pupil, Chuan-sun Shih (503–c. 450 B.C.).
41. Specifically units of 25 families and 125 families.
42. Variously interpreted as sages or rulers. It is more likely a Platonic philosopher-king, for in the Confucian system, the sage should be a ruler and the ruler should be a sage.
43. Confucius' pupil, whose private name was Yu (520–481 B.C.).
44. Confucius' pupil, whose family name was Yen (b. 506 B.C.).
45. His family name was Meng and private name K'o. Like Confucius, he traveled extensively trying to influence the feudal lords, but he did not succeed any more than did Confucius. He has been honored as the second sage in China.
46. *Meng Tzu* in Chinese, this book consists of seven chapters each in two parts. For English translations, see James Legge, tr., *The Works of Mencius*, and Wing-tsit Chan, tr., *A Source Book in Chinese Philosophy*, ch. 3.
47. Kung-sun Ch'ou was Mencius' pupil. In opposition to Mencius, Kao Tzu held that human nature was neutral. See the *Book of Mencius*, 6A:1–6.
48. The word *ch'i* means breath, matter-energy, material force, power, etc.
49. Another interpretation: I understand the principle of things as expressed in words.
50. *Cheng* ("to expect") is also read as *chih* ("to stop").
51. It is possible to punctuate after "the mind" so that it reads "stop the mind." However, nothing is gained by this change.
52. The passage up to this point also appears with slight variation in the *Doctrine of the Mean*, ch. 20.
53. According to tradition, Hsi Shih was the most beautiful woman in ancient China.
54. Another interpretation: An evil man.
55. Mencius' pupil.
56. Legendary sage-emperor Yao and his successor Shun of the third millennium B.C.
57. *Book of History*, "Declaration of Ch'in."
58. Yü was Shun's minister who directed the flood waters to the sea.
59. On the northern slope of Mount Sung in present Honan Province.
60. Part of Mount Sung.
61. Some say that *yung-chü* is not a name but means an ulcer doctor.
62. He was a favorite minister of Duke Ling of Wei.
63. Confucius' pupil, Chung Yu (542–480 B.C.).
64. A similar saying is found in the *Book of Mencius*, 7B:33.
65. Hao-sheng was a man of Ch'i and Yo-cheng was an official of Lu.
66. King T'ang (r. 1751–1739 B.C.?) was the founder of the Shang dynasty and King Wu (r. 1121–1116 B.C.) was that of the Chou dynasty.
67. *Chung-yung* (The mean and the universal) in Chinese, this small classic in 33 chapters has been ascribed by tradition to Confucius' grandson Tzu-ssu (492–431 B.C.), an attribution rejected by many modern scholars. In these selections, Chu Hsi's arrangement of the chapters is followed.
68. Interpretation according to Cheng Hsüan, (127–200) *Chung-yung chu* (Commentary on the *Doctrine of the Mean*).
69. A similar saying is found in the *Analects*, 14:37.
70. This is Chu Hsi's (1130–1200) interpretation of *t'i-wu* in his *Chung-yung chang-ch'ü* (Commentary on the *Doctrine of the Mean*).
71. Ode no. 256.
72. It is not clear whether this refers to sincerity, the character of the nature, or the Way.

73. Perhaps this is a step further than described in *The Mean*, ch. 23, and the translation should be "becomes prominent without any display, can change others without moving them, and complete [the self and all things, as in the *Doctrine of the Mean*, ch. 25] without any action."
74. Founders of the Hsia (2183–1752 B.C.?), Shang (1751–1112 B.C.), and Chou (1111–249 B.C.) dynasties.
75. Ode no. 278.
76. His family name was Hsün and private name K'uang. He was also called Hsün Ch'ing. He was a most prominent scholar of his time. Three times he was honored as the officer for the sacrificial wine offering in one state and a magistrate in another.
77. *Analects*, 17:19.
78. For English translations, see H. H. Dubs, tr., *The Works of Hsüntze*, Burton Watson, tr., *The Basic Works of Hsün Tzu*, and Wing-tsit Chan, *A Source Book in Chinese Philosophy*, ch. 6.
79. See n. 56.
80. Chieh (r. 1802–1752 B.C.?) was the last ruler of the Hsia dynasty. Chinese historians have blamed his wickedness for the fall of Shang.
81. A similar saying appears in the *Lao Tzu*, ch. 47.
82. *Doctrine of the Mean*, ch. 19.

CHAPTER 12

Confucian Institutional Developments

□ With the establishment of the Han dynasty (206 B.C.–A.D. 220), China became "one family" as well as a united empire. The Chinese sense of a social order and a universal order now became sharpened. This was the time of organization on a vast scale. Both Taoism and Buddhism developed and flourished as formal religions. Confucianism was not institutionalized as an organized cult, but its basic beliefs were now formulated and regulated so that classical ideas became in fact institutionalized traditions. These concern chiefly social and religious rites, the meaning of sacrifice, and the teaching of filial piety. To illustrate these developments, the following selections have been made from the *Classic of Filial Piety*, the *Book of Rites*, and the *Comprehensive Discussions in the White Tower Hall.* □

A. THE *CLASSIC OF FILIAL PIETY*[1]

□ This little classic has been ascribed by tradition to Confucius. Eleventh-century Neo-Confucianists thought it was by the Confucian pupil, Tseng Tzu,[2] but modern scholars consider it a later compilation. At any rate, it was lost and did not reappear until the second century B.C. For all purposes it is a Han document.

Characteristic of Han thought, it declares that filial piety is rooted in the natural principles of Heaven and Earth. It is because of this universal relation that continuity in time, that is, continuing the family, assumes the utmost importance. So far as the need for remembering one's departed parents and the sincerity of this feeling are concerned, the Classic has no new ideas to offer. But in concentrating on the doctrine of filial piety and in stressing the expression of it in religious rites, it has made filial piety itself a religion. Twentieth-century rebels against Confucianism have attacked it as such. However, for some two thousand years, the doctrine has been the foundation of ancestral rites. The formalized aspects of it have been declining rapidly, but its essential merit has not been questioned, even by the rebels. □

Ch. 9. Tseng Tzu said, "May I ask if in virtue of the sage there is nothing that surpasses filial piety?" Confucius replied, "In terms of the nature bestowed by Heaven and Earth, man is the noblest among things. In man's conduct, nothing is greater than filial piety. In the performance of filial piety, nothing is greater than honoring one's father. And in honoring one's father, there is nothing greater than making him a counterpart of Heaven. The Duke of Chou (d. 1094 B.C.) was such a man.

"Formerly the Duke of Chou sacrificed to the god of agriculture as a counterpart of Heaven. He sacrificed to his ancestor, King Wen,[3] in the Hall of Light, as a counterpart of the Lord on High. Therefore all within the four seas[4] came to help him in the sacrifice, each performing his function. In the virtue of the sage, how can there be anything surpassing filial piety? Because parents' affection for the child grows during his childhood, (as he grows older), his desire to support his parents becomes stronger every day. The sage teaches reverence on the basis of (his own) strong desire and teaches love on the basis of (his own) affection. The teaching of the sage succeeds without his being stern, and his government is in order without his being severe, because what he has centered on is the foundation (filial piety).

"The relation between father and son is rooted in the nature of Heaven and is the principle of the relation between the ruler and the minister. Parents give birth to the child and there is nothing more important than to continue the line. (They) descend on him as rulers and parents, and the depth of their kindness cannot be greater. Therefore not to love one's parents but to love others is to violate virtue, and not to revere parents but to revere others is to violate propriety. If (the ruler) violates what should be followed, there will be no law or principle for his people to observe. If one does not abide by the good but abides entirely by evil, even if one may achieve success, the superior man does not value it. For the superior man is different. In his speech he thinks of what should be said. In his actions he thinks of what is enjoyable. His virtue and moral principles are honorable. His activities are exemplary. His deportment is worth seeing. And his advance or withdrawal can be taken as measure. He descends on his people with all those, and therefore his people regard him with awe and love, and emulate him. Thus he can bring his moral teachings into completion and put his governmental measures and orders into operation. The *Book of Odes* says:

> The virtuous man, the gentleman,
> Is faultless in his deportment.[5]"

Ch. 10. Confucius said, "In serving his parents a filial son shows utmost reverence while at home, achieves utmost joy in supporting them, worries to the highest degree when they are sick, grieves to the utmost at their death, and shows utmost gravity when sacrificing to them. Only when these five are complete will he be able to serve his parents. To serve one's parents means not to be proud in high position, not to be disorderly in low position, and not to be contentious among the masses. To be proud in high position will result in ruin, to be disorderly in low position will result in punishment, and to be contentious among the masses will result in violence. If these three things are not eliminated, even though he nourishes his parents with three kinds of meat,[6] he still cannot be regarded as filial."

Ch. 16. Confucius said, "In ancient times enlightened kings served their parents with filial piety and therefore they served Heaven and Earth clearly and penetratingly. The elders and the young were in concord and therefore both those above and below were in order. As Heaven and Earth become clear and penetrating, spiritual beings manifest themselves brilliantly. Therefore even the Son of Heaven must have someone to honor. This means his father. He must have someone to be his senior. This means his elder brother. To show utmost reverence in ancestral temples is not to forget one's parents, and to cultivate oneself and be careful in one's conduct is to fear that one might disgrace one's ancestors. When the utmost reverence is shown in ancestral temples, spiritual beings will (come to enjoy the sincere offerings) and manifest themselves. Perfect filial piety and brotherly respect penetrate spiritual beings. They illuminate the four seas, penetrating everywhere. The *Book of Odes* says:

> From west, from east
> From south, from north—
> There were none who did not submit.[7]"

Ch. 18. Confucius said, "When a filial son mourns his parents, he weeps without wailing; he performs the rites without caring for his appearance; he speaks without embellishment; he feels uncomfortable in fine clothing; he feels no joy in hearing music; and he does not enjoy delicious food—all these are his feeling of grief. After three days he breaks his fast to show the people that one should not hurt one's life because of the dead and not disfigure oneself through grief to the point of destroying his life. This is the governmental measure of the sage. The period of mourning does not exceed three years, thus showing the people that all things come to an end. Provide a coffin and grave clothes and put the body in. Array the square and round vessels with grief and sorrow. Beating the breast and stamping the feet, the mourner escorts the coffin away with grief. Select a burial place by divination and lay the body to rest. Build a temple and make offerings in the manner of offering to a spiritual being. Perform sacrifices in the spring and autumn in order to think of the dead from time to time. When one serves one's parents with love and reverence while they are alive and serves them with grief and sorrow when they are dead, the fundamental duty of man is fulfilled, the meaning of life and death is totally realized, and the service of the filial son to his parents is completed."

B. THE *BOOK OF RITES*[8]

□ As one of the Five Classics[9] the *Book of Rites* is supposed to have been transmitted from early times but modern scholars believe that it was compiled during the second century B.C. from various sources. It continues the theme that rites and ceremonies are based on the principles governing the universe. Man coexists with spiritual beings, standing by each other, and participates in the creative process of Heaven and Earth, thus forming a trinity with them. Political and social institutions are parts of the universal scheme. Through correct performance of rites man gets into correct relationship with his fellows, with his ancestors, with spiritual beings, and with the universe. From the political standpoint, rites are an instrument for political order. From the religious standpoint, they are the means by which man attains harmony with Heaven and Earth. Because the tendency of ceremonies is to be conservative, care must be taken not to be too restrictive, and because the tendency of music is to be expansive, care must be taken not to go too far. The main point is to achieve the mean that is a key to harmony.

The Classic details how to feel, how to fast, how to prepare for and how to act during religious sacrifice. If these seem too formal, it should not be forgotten that the goal was none other than purity of purpose, sincerity of feeling, and the need, through feelings and action for one to remember one's origin and to put oneself in the proper context of the social and universal order. The following are selections from only two chapters that deal with religious rite more directly. □

1. "Evolution of Rites" (Ch. 9)

Confucius said, "Rites are the means by which the ancient kings sought to carry on the way of Heaven and to regulate the feelings of men. Those who have neglected them will die and those who attain them will live. *The Book of Odes* says:

See even the mouse has a body (*t'i*)
And a human being is without rites (*li*)!
If a man is without rites,
Why does he not quickly die?"[10]

Rites are necessarily based on Heaven, patterned after Earth, spread before spiritual beings, and are extended to the rites and ceremonies of funerals, sacrifices, archery, carriage driving, capping,[11] marriage, court audience, and diplomatic receptions. Therefore the sage shows people the rites so the family, the state, and the world may be in order. . . .

Rites are a great instrument of the ruler. They are the means to distinguish the doubtful (from the true), bring to light what is subtle (the right or wrong), treat spiritual beings as guests, examine systems and institutions, and differentiate the proper use of humanity and righteousness. They are the means by which the government is rightly ordered and the ruler becomes secured. Therefore if the government is not correct, the ruler's position is in danger. When the ruler's position is in danger, great ministers revolt and small ministers usurp power. Punishments will then be severe and mores will degenerate. Laws will be irregular. As laws become irregular, rites will no longer be spread (before spiritual beings). When rites are not spread, officers will not perform their duties. When punishments are severe and more degenerated, the people will not turn to (be loyal to) (their ruler). This is called a sickly state. . . .

Therefore the sage assists Heaven and Earth and stands side by side with spiritual beings in order to put his government in order. By abiding by (the principles of) the existence of Heaven, Earth, and (spiritual beings), he brings about the order of rites, and by appreciating what (Heaven, Earth, and spiritual beings) enjoy and (extending it to the people), he brings about order among the people. Heaven produces the seasons and Earth produces wealth. Man is begotten by his father and taught by his teacher. The ruler uses these four agencies correctly and therefore he is in the position where there is nothing wrong. . . .

What are the feelings of man? They are joy, anger, sorrow, fear, love, hatred, and desire. We can experience these seven without having to learn them. What are moral principles for men? Affection in the father, filial piety in the son, goodness in the elder brother, respect in the younger brother, righteousness in the husband, obedience in the wife, kindness in the elders, willingness to follow in the juniors, benevolence in the ruler, and loyalty in the minister. These ten are called moral principles for men. The advocacy of faithfulness and cultivation of peace are called benefits for men, and quarrels, robbery, and murder are called calamities for men. Therefore, in order for the sage to regulate the seven feelings of men, cultivate the ten moral principles, advocate faithfulness and cultivate peace, exalt deference and compliance, and eliminate quarrels and robbery, how can he manage without rites? The great desires of mankind lie in food, drink, and sex, and the great hates of mankind lie in death, extinction, poverty, and suffering. Therefore desires and hatred are the fundamental elements of the human mind. Men, however, conceal their minds and they cannot be fathomed, for the good and the bad of them are all in the mind and are not revealed in outward appearance. If one wants to investigate them to the utmost by one (principle), how can one do so without rites? . . .

Rites are surely based on the Great One, which was divided to become Heaven and Earth, transformed into yin (negative cosmic force) and yang (positive cosmic force), changed to become the four seasons, and are arrayed to be spiritual beings. What it bestows on men is destiny (or fate) and its controlling authority is Heaven. . . .

2. "The Meaning of Sacrifice" (Ch. 24)

Sacrifices should not be frequently repeated, for repetition leads to importunity, and importunity leads to the lack of reverence. Sacrifices should not be far apart either, for being far apart leads to negligence and negligence leads to forgetting them altogether. Therefore the superior man, in harmony with the way of Heaven, offers the sacrifices of spring and autumn.[12] When frost and dew have descended (in the autumn), as the superior man treads on them (in performing sacrifices), he will surely have a feeling of sadness, but it is not due to the cold.[13] In the spring when the ground is already wet with rain and dew, as the superior man treads on it, he will surely have the feeling of being startled, as if he were seeing (departed persons). We meet the approach of them with joy (in the spring) and escort them away (in the autumn) with sorrow. Hence at the spring sacrifice there is music but none in the autumn.

The strictest fast is to be maintained internally and a looser fast is to be maintained externally. During the days of fasting, think of (the departed parents') places of abode, think of their smiles and speech, think of their will and intentions, think of what they enjoyed, and think of what they liked. After three days of fast, the type of person who fasts will be seen. . . .

When the filial son is about to sacrifice, he is anxious that all preparations are made. When the time arrives, all things should be ready, and none should be incomplete. Then he manages the affair with a mind totally devoted to it. The temple and its rooms having been repaired, the walls and roofs having been put in order, and all things being ready, husband and wife, having fasted and bathed wearing full dress, respectfully carry the offerings, go forward and offer them, solemn and reverent, as if they were not sufficiently able for the task and as if they were about to lose them. Their feeling of filial piety and reverence are perfect indeed! He presents the food and their stands. He puts the ceremonies and music in order, fully provides for the various officers, respectfully carries the offerings, goes forward, and offers them. Thereupon his will and intentions are expressed (in an invocation). In his hazy and indistinct frame of mind, he seems to be in communion with the spiritual beings, feeling that perhaps they will accept his offerings. Such is the intention of the filial son.

In sacrificing, the filial son is sincere to the highest degree, faithful to the highest degree, reverent to the highest degree, and performs the rite to the highest degree without making any mistake. Whether he advances or withdraws, he is always reverent, as if he were personally obeying the order (of his parents) or as if they were perhaps directing him. . . .

A filial son with deep love for his parents is sure to have a peaceful disposition. One who has a peaceful disposition will surely have a happy expression. And one who has a happy expression will surely have a pleasant countenance. A filial son (in conducting sacrifice) will move as if he was carrying a piece of jade or bearing a full vessel, solemn and reverent, as if he was not sufficiently able for the task and as if he was about to lose them. To be grave and austere is not proper to the service to parents; it is the way of a full-grown person (rather than a young son). . . .

(The ancients) sacrificed to the sun on the altar, and to the moon in the pit in order to distinguish the dark (represented by the night and the shaded pit) and the bright (represented by the day and the exposed altar) and to regulate the high and the low. They sacrificed to the sun in the east and the moon in the west in order to distinguish the outer (represented by the east from which things emerge), and the inner (represented by the west to which things return), and to make their positions correct. The sun rises in the east and the moon shines forth in the west. The yin (winter) and yang (summer), the long and short (days or nights in the summer or winter), and beginning and end rotate, thus attaining to the highest degree the harmony in the world.

Rites in the world are meant to achieve the return (of the mind) to one's beginning, (the honoring of) spiritual beings, the peace (among the people) and the utility (of all resources), and righteousness and compliance. To attain to the highest degree the return to one's beginning is to attach great importance to one's origin. To attain to the highest degree (the honoring of) spiritual beings is to honor the superior. To attain to the highest degree peace and utility is to establish regulations and principles for the people. When righteousness is attained to the highest degree, the high and the low will not be in opposition or conflict. And to attain compliance to the highest degree is to eliminate quarrels. When all these five rites for governing the world are combined, though there may be some perverse and wicked people who are not kept in order, they will be few.

Tsai Wo[14] said, "I have heard the term *kuei* and *shen* (spiritual beings) but I do not know what they mean." Confucius said, "The vital force (whose spirit is expressed in man's intelligence and power of breathing) is *shen* in its full measure and *p'o* (the spirit of man's physical nature expressed in bodily movements) is *kuei* in its full measure. The union of *kuei* (which returns to earth) and *shen* (which returns to heaven) (through sacrifices to them together) constitutes the best of doctrines.

"All the living must die. When they die, they will return to earth. This is called *kuei*. Bones and flesh deteriorate below. They are hidden in the dark and become the earth of the fields. But the vital force issues forth and extends above, clear and intelligent. The vapor and order that arise give people a feeling of sadness. This is the essence of all things and the manifestation of *shen*. . . ."

Music acts in one's internal life and ceremonies act in one's external life. Music results in perfect harmony and ceremonies result in concord. When one's inner life is harmonious and external life in concord, the people will behold his countenance and will not quarrel with him. The multitudes look to his demeanor and no feeling of rudeness or flippancy will rise in them. Therefore when (the ruler's) virtue shines and is active internally, people without exception will accept and listen to him, and when order is developed internally, the multitudes without exception will accept and obey him. Hence it is said, apply the principles of music and ceremonies to the utmost until the whole world is filled with them, and nothing will be difficult to undertake or apply.

Music acts in one's internal life and ceremonies act in one's external life. Therefore ceremonies emphasize (expressing our nature and feelings) less and less, while music emphasizes giving full expression. Since ceremonies emphasize expressing less and less, it is civilized to go ahead (to compensate for the restraining effect of ceremonies), and since music emphasizes full expression, it is civilized to turn back (in order to attain the correct expression). As ceremonies tend to emphasize less and less expression, if one does not go forward, one's feelings will be dissipated, and as music tends to give full expression, if one does not turn back, one's feelings will be out of control. Therefore in ceremonies there should be their compensation and in music there should be turning back. When ceremonies are compensated (so one does not express too little), there will be joy, and when music has its turning back (so one does not express too much), there will be peace. The meaning of compensation in ceremonies and the turning back in music is the same.[15]

Tseng Tzu[16] said, "There are three grades of filial piety. The highest is the honoring of one's parents, the next is not to disgrace them, and the lowest is being able to support them." Kung-ming I[17] asked Tseng Tzu, "Can you, sir, be considered a filial son?" Tseng Tzu said, "What are you talking about? What are you talking about? What the superior man means by filial piety is first to anticipate the parents' wishes and take into consideration their will, and help direct them toward the Way. I merely support them. How can I be regarded as filial?"

Tseng Tzu said, "The body is that which has been transmitted to us by our parents. In employing the transmitted body, dare one not be reverent? If in one's abode one is not grave, he is not filial. If he is not loyal in serving his ruler, he is not filial. If he is not serious in attending to his office, he is not filial. If he is not faithful toward his friends, he is not filial. And if he is not courageous in battle, he is not filial. If he fails in these five things, calamity will reach his parents. Dare he not be reverent? To prepare and cook fragrant flesh and grain, taste them, and present them to one's parents is not to be filial; it is merely to support them. . . ."

Yüeh-cheng Tzu Ch'un[18] hurt his foot in descending from the hall. For several months he did not go out and still appeared sad. One of his pupils said, "Master, your foot has been healed. Why do you not go out for several months and still appear sad?" Yüeh-cheng Tzu Ch'un said, "You have asked a good question indeed! You have asked a good question indeed! I have heard from Master Tseng what he had heard from the Grand Master (Confucius) say, 'Of all that Heaven has produced and Earth has nourished, none is as great as man. His parents give birth to his person all complete. When the son returns to them complete, he may be called filial.' When no part of his body is lost and his person is not disgraced, he may be called filial. Therefore the superior man does not take half a step and forget filial piety. But now I have forgotten the way of filial piety. Hence I appear sad. (A son) should not forget his parents whenever he lifts his foot or says a word. Since he dares not forget his parents whenever he lifts his foot, he will walk on the (safe) highway and will not take to (dangerous) bypaths. He will take a boat instead of swimming across a river. He does not dare take to any danger with the body transmitted to him by his parents. Since he dares not forget his parents whenever he says a word, no evil word will come out of his mouth and no angry word will come back to him. Not to disgrace his person and not to cause shame to his parents may be called filial piety. . . ."

C. THE *COMPREHENSIVE DISCUSSIONS IN THE WHITE TIGER HALL*[19]

□ The *Comprehensive Discussions* contains the digested records of a council of Confucian scholars compiled by the famous historian, Pan Ku (39–92), by imperial command. The council was held in 79 A.D. to discuss the various interpretations of the Five Classics[20] and to adopt an official view. Although the council had no final authority, the weight of official power had the effect of codifying ancient Confucian teachings on everything—from titles to dresses, from government to agriculture, and many others. The relationship between man and Heaven is reaffirmed, and the double standard in social relations sets the patterns for many centuries. One point to note is that there is no clear distinction between the religious and the secular—there had never been and there was not to be. The following are selections on only a few pertinent subjects. □

1. "The Five Deities" (Ch. 2, Sec. 1)

What are the Five Deities? They are the outer door, the inner door, the well, the hearth, and the center of the room. Why are they worshiped? Because they are the places where men live, where they go in and out, and where they drink and eat. For this reason they are worshiped as spiritual beings. How do we know that the Five Deities mean the outer door, the inner door, the well, the hearth, and the center of the room? The "Monthly Order" says, "(In the spring) they sacrifice to the inner door."[21] It also says, "(In the summer) they sacrifice to the hearth."[22] (In the middle of the year) "they sacrifice to the center of the room."[23] (In the autumn) "they sacrifice to the outer door,"[24] and (in the winter) "They sacrifice to the well."[25]

Why may only great officers and higher perform the sacrifice to them? An ordinary officer has a lowly position and a meager emolument. He sacrifices only to his ancestors. The *Book of Rites* says, "The Son of Heaven sacrifices to Heaven and Earth, the feudal lords sacrifice to the spirits of mountains and rivers, ministers and great officers sacrifice to the Five Deities, and officers sacrifice to their ancestors."[26] The "Summary of Ceremonies" says "(The Son of Heaven) sacrifices to Heaven and Earth, to the spirits of Four Cardinal Points, to the spirits of mountains and rivers, and to the Five Deities, all in the course of the year. The feudal lords sacrifice to the spirits in the various corners of their states, to the spirits of mountains and rivers, and to the Five Deities, all in the course of the year. The ministers and great officers sacrifice to the Five Deities, and the officers sacrifice to their ancestors."[27] To sacrifice to a deity to which one should not sacrifice means excessive sacrifice. An excessive sacrifice brings no blessing. . . .

2. "Ceremonies and Music" (Ch. 2, Sec. 3)

Why does the king exalt ceremonies and music? It is to regulate and adorn man's joy and anger. Music takes Heaven as its symbol, and ceremonies take Earth as their model. All men embody in them the material force of Heaven and Earth and the nature of the Five Constant Virtues.[28] Music is intended to arouse man to turn back from wickedness and evil, and ceremonies are intended to guard against lewdness and indolence and to check wasteful extravagance. Therefore the *Classic of Filial Piety* says, "For giving security to the ruler and order to the people, there are nothing better than ceremonies, and for changing the mores and improving the customs, there is nothing better than music."[29] Confucius said, "When, in the ancestral temple, the ruler and ministers and the high and the low listen to music together, none will not be in harmony and not be reverent. When, in the midst of clan elders and village communities, old and young listen together to it, none will not be in harmony and obliging concord. The instruments should be attuned to each other to embellish the measures, and the measures and melody should be harmonized to complete the adornment. This is in order to unite father and son, and ruler and minister in harmony, and enable all the people to be close and dear to one another. This was the purpose for which ancient kings established musical institutions. When one listens to the melodies of the (moderate, correct, and peaceful) *ya* and *sung* song,[30] one's will and thought are broadened. When one holds the shield and axe and practices looking up and down, and contracting and expanding, one's appearance becomes grave. When one goes to a dance stage in the center of the assembly and dances in harmony with the musical measures and melodies, the movements and formations will be correct, and the advancing and retreating will be uniform. So music is the (lesson) ordered by Heaven and Earth, the bond of equilibrium and harmony, and something that the nature of man cannot do without. Music is that with which the ancient kings adorned their joy, and army's arrows and battle axes were those with which (the ancient kings) adorned their anger. Therefore the joy and the anger of the ancient kings both had their accompaniments. When they were joyful, all under heaven followed them in harmony, and when they were angry, the violent and the disorderly feared them. In the way of ancient kings, ceremonies and music may be said to be glorious indeed."[31]

None who hears the note *mi* does not feel compassionate and kind; none who hears the note *fa* does not enjoy nourishing (the poor) and practicing charity. None who hears the note of *re* does not become strong, decided, and accomplishing. None who hears the note *so* does not think deeply and deliberate thoroughly. None who hears the note *do* does not become warm, mild, liberal, and peaceful.

What is the purpose of the ceremony of bowing complaisantly? It is to honor others and to humble oneself. It prevents contention. The *Analects* says, "(The superior man) bows complaisantly to (his opponents in archery contest) when he ascends and descends from the hall and when he joins the drinking bout. His way of contest is that of the superior man."[32] Therefore "The ruler employs his ministers according to ceremony and the ministers serve the ruler with loyalty."[33] "The superior man who adds humility to humility may with advantage cross a great river."[34] "By humbling himself from noble station to deal with people in low stations, he gains the strong support of the people."[35] It is the mind of the superior man to humble himself and revere others. Therefore Confucius said, "When one performs ceremonies without reverence, how should I regard such a thing?" . . .[36]

NOTES

1. *Hsiao ching* (Classic of filial piety) in 18 chapters. For English translation, see Mary Leslia Marka, tr., *The Hsiao Ching*.
2. Tseng Ts'an (505–*c.* 436 B.C.), noted for filial piety.
3. King Wen (r. 1171–1122 B.C.), founder of the Chou dynasty (1111–249 B.C.).
4. Meaning China.
5. *Book of Odes*, ode no. 152.
6. Beef, pork, and mutton.
7. Ode no. 244.
8. The *Li chi* (Record of rites) consists of 49 chapters dealing with general principles and specific details about social relations, religious ceremonies, etc. For English translation, see James Legge, tr., *The Li Ki*.
9. The *Book of History*, the *Book of Odes*, the *Book of Changes*, the *Book of Rites*, and the *Spring and Autumn Annals*.
10. *Book of Odes*, ode no. 52.
11. Putting a cap on a boy to signify his maturity.
12. The name of summer sacrifice is given in the text instead of spring sacrifice probably by mistake. Spring and autumn are the four seasons for short.

13. The feeling of sadness arises because the autumn and winter are the time to send the departed away.
14. Tsai Wo (520–481 B.C.) was Confucius' pupil.
15. The preceding two paragraphs also appear in the *Li chi*, ch. 19, "Records of Music."
16. Tseng Ts'an, Confucius' pupil. See n. 2.
17. Tseng Tzu's pupil.
18. Also Tseng Tzu's pupil.
19. *Po-hu-t'ung* (Comprehensive [discussions] in the White Tiger [Hall]) in Chinese, it is in ten chapters divided into 43 sections. For English translation, see Tjan Tjoe Som, tr., *Po Hu T'ung, the Comprehensive Discussions in the White Tiger Hall.*
20. See n. 9.
21. *Book of Rites*, ch. 6, "Monthly Order," § 1 and 23.
22. *Ibid.*, §§ 3, 35, 42, and 57.
23. *Ibid.*, § 62.
24. *Ibid.*, §§ 63, 69, and 83.
25. *Ibid.*, §§ 9 and 111.
26. *Ibid.*, ch. 5, "Royal Regulations," § 31.
27. *Ibid.*, ch. 2, "Summary of Ceremonies," pt. 2, § 20.
28. Humanity, righteousness, propriety, wisdom, and faithfulness.
29. Ch. 12.
30. Songs in pts. 2–4 of the *Book of Odes.*
31. *Book of Rites*, ch. 19, "Record of Music," pt. 3, §§ 28–30.
32. *Analects*, 3:7.
33. *Ibid.*, 3:19.
34. *Book of Changes*, hexagram no. 15, *ch'ien* (humility), commentary.
35. *Ibid.*, hexagram no. 3, *chun* (difficulty), commentary.
36. *Analects*, 3:26.

CHAPTER 13

Neo-Confucianism

☐ Neo-Confucianism has often been described as rationalistic and naturalistic. To some, it is devoid of a religious nature. Of course, it should not be characterized in simple terms, inasmuch as it involves hundreds of thinkers of a variety of opinions over several hundred years. By and large, however, it is safe to say that Neo-Confucianism is essentially religious in the best sense of the term. In fact, the system is called *Hsing-li hsüeh*, that is, the learning of nature and principle. The main subjects for discussion, therefore, are the nature of man and things and the principle underlying them. It is its major premise that nature is that which is endowed by Heaven and that *ming* (destiny, fate, that which is decreed or ordained by Heaven) is its full realization. The whole tenet of Neo-Confucianism may be summed up in its most often cited dictum, namely, "investigating principle to the utmost, complete realization of nature, and fulfilling one's destiny." This is also the substance of the religion of the enlightened Chinese.

Students of Chinese religion should sharply distinguish the religion of the masses and that of the intellectuals. The former worship all kinds of gods and spiritual beings, engage in divination and similar practices, and believe in superstition of many sorts whereas the enlightened shun all of these. There is no statement that sets forth the religion of the enlightened,[1] but the following selections embody its basic ideas concerning (1) Heaven, (2) the nature of the universe, of man and his destiny, and of spiritual beings, and (3) the unity of man and Heaven. They are represented by several ninth-century essays, sayings by Chu Hsi, and an inscription by Chang Tsai. ☐

A. DISCUSSIONS ON HEAVEN

☐ The separate discussions on Heaven between Liu Tsung-yüan (773–819)[2] and both Han Yü (768–824) and Liu Yü-hsi (772–842), started in 814, were the most exciting since Hsün Tzu's radical utterances on Heaven.[3] The debates are not so much on the nature of Heaven as on its relation to man. The term *t'ien* is used variously to mean Nature, Heaven as the supreme power, and physical heaven, but the fundamental issue is clear: whether man's actions are controlled and rewarded or punished by Heaven. The typical Neo-Confucian answer is that man's actions bring their own reward and punishment, and that there is a clear division between the function of man and that of Heaven. It seems that this clear distinction may prevent or hinder their unity, but Neo-Confucianists believe that unity comes only through harmony, and harmony is attainable only through a clear recognition of the division of functions. The earlier philosophy of the mutual correspondence and mutual influence of Heaven and man, taught in the *Book of Changes*, advocated by the Yin Yang and Five Agents Schools,[4] developed by Tung Chung-shu (176–104 B.C.),[5] and fully utilized in the Taoist religion (see ch. 15, A), a philosophy that had degenerated into fatalism and much superstition, is now entirely rejected.

The three thinkers were not Neo-Confucianists but forerunners of Neo-Confucianism. As such their ideas may be said to belong to the Neo-Confucian current of thought. □

1. "An Explanation of Heaven" by Liu Tsung-yüan

Han Yü said to Master Liu, "Do you know the explanation of Heaven? Let me explain it to you. Suppose someone is now seriously ill, tired, humiliated, and suffering greatly from hunger and cold, and because of these he looks up to heaven and cries out, 'Those who oppress people become prosperous while those who protect people meet with misfortune!' Again he looks up and cries out, 'Why have things been permitted to become so perverse?'

"Such a person does not know Heaven at all. When fruits and berries become rotten or food spoiled, worms grow in them. When man's blood and vital force deteriorate, go the wrong way, or are obstructed, they become ulcers, tumors, and piles, and worms grow in them. When a tree decays, grubs bore into it, and when grasses rot, fire flies fly from them. Aren't all these produced by deterioration? When things are spoiled, worms grow as a result. Man lives because the original material force and yin (negative cosmic element) and yang (positive cosmic element) are spoiled. As worms grow, the things are spoiled to a higher degree. They eat and gnaw them, and attack and create holes in them. The harm that worms do to things is very great indeed. Anyone who can eliminate them will render a service to things. One who multiplies and reproduces them is an enemy of things. The harm that man has done to the original material force and yin and yang is also very great indeed. Men open up barren lands, cut down mountain forests, dig wells for spring water to drink, make empty holes for graves to bury the dead, and in addition dig ditches for drainage, build walls and cities and pavilions and kiosks and places for visits and pleasure. They dredge and scatter bodies of water to be rivers, ditches, and artificial ponds. They create friction on wood to burn, take away metal to smelt, and mould and cut and grind, sadly causing the thousand things in the world to be out of accord with their nature. Taking chances and rushing about, they attack, destroy, ruin, and disturb without cease. Isn't the harm they do to the original material force and yin and yang greater than what the worms have done? My idea is that if someone can cripple this (crying) person so that he becomes thinner and weaker every day and can do very little harm to the original material force and yin and yang, he is rendering a service to Heaven and Earth. To multiply and reproduce (such a man) is to be an enemy of Heaven and Earth. Now, this man does not know Heaven at all and therefore cries out and complains like this. My idea is that when Heaven hears his cry and complaint, those who have rendered a service will surely receive great reward and those who do harm will receive heavy punishment. What do you think of what I have said?"[6]

Master Liu said, "Is it true that you said so because you have been aroused by something? You have surely argued well. However, I shall draw the conclusion. That which is dark above is what the world calls heaven, and that which is yellow below is what the world calls earth. That which is undifferentiated and dwells in their midst is what the world calls the original material force. The succession of winter and summer is what the world calls the operation of yin and yang. Although heaven, earth, yin, and yang are vast, they are not different from fruits and berries, ulcers and piles, or grass and trees. Suppose there is someone who can remove whatever attacks them or creates holes in them. Can these things reward him? If he multiplies and reproduces (that which does the harm), can they be angry at him? Heaven and earth are fruits and berries in a large scale. The original material force is ulcers and piles in a large scale. And yin and yang are grass and trees in a large scale. How can they reward for the service and punish for the harm? The one who renders service does so himself and the one who does harm also does so himself. It will be greatly mistaken to hope that (Heaven) will reward or punish them. For one who does harm to cry out and complain, and to hope that (Heaven) pities him and be kind to him is to be even more greatly mistaken. If you believe in your principle and live in this mundane world, you live and will die; that is all. How can you relate life and death, or gain and loss, to fruits and berries, ulcers and piles, or grass and trees?" (*Liu Ho-tung ch'üan-chi* [Complete works of Liu Tsung-yüan], 16:1a–2b)

2. "A Treatise on Heaven" by Liu Yü-hsi

Pt. I. There are two theories about Heaven today. Those who are bound by what is obvious say that Heaven and man really influence each other. Calamities will surely descend on us because of our sins, and blessings will surely come when induced by good deeds. If we are in distress and cry out, we will be heard, and if we keep our suffering to ourselves and pray, we will be answered. There seems to be definitely someone who rules them. Hence the theory of silent recompense wins.

On the other hand, those who are bigoted about what is hidden say that Heaven and man are really different. Lightning hits animals and trees without anyone committing any sin, and the spring nourishes flowering bushes without selecting any good deeds to reward. (Notorious robbers) Chih and Chao[7] enjoyed success but Confucius and (his most virtuous pupil) Yen[8] were in peril.[9] It seems there is no one who rules us. Hence naturalism wins.

My friend from Chieh of Ho-tung,[10] Liu Tzu-hou, wrote "An Explanation of Heaven" to demolish Han T'ui-chih's theory. His essay is very good indeed. He said what he said because he was aroused by something but it does not thoroughly explain the dividing line between Heaven and man. Therefore I have written "A Treatise on Heaven" to bring the argument to its final conclusion.

For everything that is included in the realm of physical forms and concrete objects, there are things it can do and things it cannot do. Heaven is the largest of things with physical form and man is the best among living things. What Heaven can do, man cannot, and what man can do, there is some that Heaven cannot do. Therefore I say that Heaven and man mutually overcome each other.

The explanation is this: The way of Heaven lies in producing and reproducing, and its function is expressed in strength and weakness, whereas the way of man lies in laws and regulations and his function is expressed in right and wrong. With yang, things flourish abundantly, whereas with yin, things are severely destroyed. Water and fire can harm things. Wood is firm and metal is sharp. (When a person) is full grown, he is strong and vigorous but when he gets old, his eyesight becomes dim. If his vital power is strong, he becomes an assistant to the ruler, and when his physical strength is strong, he becomes an assistant to an elder. This is the ability of Heaven. At the time of yang (spring), man plants trees, and at the time of yin (autumn) he harvests and stores. To prevent (meat) from spoiling, he boils it, and to prevent fire, he provides light. He cuts down lumber and makes holes in solid bodies. He smelts metals and sharpens edges. He formulates moral principles to control (such things as) oppression and accusation. He institutes ceremonies to distinguish old and young. He honors the worthy and exalts merits. He establishes standards and prevents depravity. This is the ability of man.

Law is the thing that helps man overcome Heaven. When law operates universally, what is right is right for all and what is wrong is wrong for all. All people under heaven will be rewarded if they follow the Way and will be punished if they violate it. . . .

When the enforcement of law is slightly slackened, right and wrong will both be contradicted. What is rewarded is not necessarily all good and what is punished is not necessarily all bad. . . .

When the enforcement of law is greatly slackened, right and wrong will be reversed. Rewards will then always be given to the deceitful and punishment will always be imposed on the upright. . . .

When the law operates extensively, people say, "What has Heaven to do with man? We follow the Way, that is all."

When enforcement of law is greatly slackened, people say, "What is the Way doing after all? People do as they like." When the enforcement of law is slightly slackened, both the theory of Heaven and the theory of man are contradicted. Now, to wish to inquire whether there is Heaven or not on the basis of one's own success or failure, is erroneous indeed.

I say, "Heaven always holds on to what it can do to people below, but it does not mean that Heaven has anything to do with the order or disorders of society. Man always holds on to what he can look up to Heaven for, but it does not mean that he has anything to do with heat or cold. When people live in the time of order, the way of man is made clear, and all know the cause and source of things. Therefore they do not attribute any kindness or unkindness to Heaven. When people live in the time of disorder, the way of man is obscured and they do not know (the cause and source of things). Therefore what is caused by man is all attributed to Heaven. It is not that Heaven has anything to do with man."

Pt. 2. *Someone says*, "Your theory that Heaven and man mutually overcome each other is subtle in principle. How can the ordinary people understand it? Why not give some examples?"

Master Liu says, "Do you know anything about travel? When a group go to a great wilderness, they seek rest under luxuriant trees and drink from springs. The strong and powerful surely get there first. Without power or strength, even the sage and the worthy cannot compete. Isn't this a case of Heaven winning? When the group halt in a city or suburbs (places of culture), they seek shelter under ornamental rafters and a full meal with the meat of a sacrificial ox. The sage and the worthy are surely the first to enjoy. If one is not a sage or a worthy, even if he is powerful and strong, he cannot compete. Isn't this a case of man winning? If the way is that of Yü and Jui (where King Wen exerted moral influence),[11] even a wilderness will be like cities and suburbs. If the way is that of K'uang and Sung (where Confucius was in peril),[12] even cities and suburbs will be like wilderness. Thus in a day's journey, Heaven and man mutually overcome each other. I therefore say that where the distinction between right and wrong exists, even in the wilderness the principle of man wins. Where the distinction of right and wrong disappears, even in the state the principle of Heaven wins. This is so not because Heaven insists on overcoming man. Why? In a situation of misfortune, man reverts to Heaven. Man, however, truly wants to overcome Heaven. Why? Heaven is not selfish and man therefore can undertake to overcome it. I can clarify the ways of Heaven and man by using the illustration of a day's travel because I use the example of something near at hand. . . ."

The questioner says, "I have seen boats crossing a river together. The conditions of wind and water were the same, and yet some sank and others did not. Who was in charge of that if not Heaven?"

Answer: "Water and the boat are two different things. When two things are combined, there is bound to be the natural course in the combination. With the existence of the natural course, there will be the force of circumstance. One boat sinks and the other succeeds in crossing. Both happen to be in a particular course and going along with the tendency, that is all. The tendency grows along with the thing itself very much like a shadow and an echo. . . ." (*Liu Meng-te wen-chi* [Collection of literary works by Liu Yü-hsi], 12:6a–9b)

3. "A Letter in Reply to Liu Hsi-yü's 'A Treatise on Heaven'" by Liu Tsung-yüan

. . . Isn't what you thought as different from me the fact that you praise Heaven as being able to produce? It has been a long time since Heaven could produce. This fact needs no praise to be prominent. Furthermore, is what you consider as Heaven's producing for the sake of Heaven, of man, or of production's own sake? If it is for man, I understand even less. If it is for the sake of production itself, well, things are produced and exist for themselves. How are they different from fruits and berries, ulcers and piles, and grass and plants existing for themselves? It is clear that they do not exist for the sake of worms, just as Heaven does not make plans for man. Since it does not make plans for me, why should I insist on overcoming it? What you mean by mutually overcoming each other seems to be that Heaven always does evil and man always does good, and that when man overcomes Heaven, good always prevails. This is to ascribe too much good to man and too much sin to Heaven. You also say that what Heaven can do is to produce and reproduce and what man does is to institute laws and regulations. This is to divide these into four things. But I say that production and reproduction, and floods and droughts, are all due to Heaven and laws and regulations, and violations and rebellions, are all due to man. There are but these two. Each does its own work without interfering with the other, and yet a plentiful year or famine, order or disorder, occur. This is perfectly clear.

In your discussion, the details are very good but you have not gone into the foundation directly to achieve success. In addition, your analogy of travel indicates nothing but man. Why do you say that in one case Heaven wins and in the other, man wins? Those who are the first in the wilderness win by strength and those first in the city and suburbs win by wisdom. What happened in Yü and Jui occurred because physical strength came to an end and what happened in K'uang and Sung occurred because wisdom came to an end. There is nothing to show that right and wrong, or rise and fall, can be an analogy of what Heaven does. . . . (Liu Tsung-yüan, *op. cit.*, 31:4a–5b)

B. CHU HSI

□ Master Chu (1130–1200) was the greatest Confucianist since Mencius. Not only did he synthesize the philosophies of Northern Sung (960–1126) Neo-Confucianists, notably, Chou Tun-i (1017–1073), Ch'eng Hao (1032–1085), his younger brother Ch'eng I (1033–1107) and Chang Tsai (1020–1077) into a harmonious whole,[13] he also had original ideas of his own, thus raising Neo-Confucianism to a new level. He was perhaps the most religious among the Sung Neo-Confucianists and has been compared with Thomas Aquinas.[14] Inasmuch as no Neo-Confucianist has formulated a code of belief or has written a systematic statement on religion, the best thing to do is to select passages from Master Chu's *Complete Works*, which is itself a selection from his 140-chapter *Classified Conversations* and 160-chapter *Collection of Literary Works*.[15] These passages cover the subjects of principle (*li*), material force (*ch'i*), the Great Ultimate, yin (negative cosmic force), yang (positive cosmic force), Heaven and Earth, man's nature and destiny, retribution, abnormal phenomena, spiritual beings, gods, ancestors, and religious sacrifice. Of special importance is the radical Neo-Confucian doctrine of *kuei* and *shen*, which they interpreted as earthly and heavenly spiritual forces instead of earthly and heavenly spiritual beings as traditionally understood. The ultimate religious goal of the Neo-Confucianists, namely, the investigation of things, the complete realization of one's nature, and the fulfillment of destiny, finds a rational basis and practical application in his philosophy. Inasmuch as Chu Hsi's brand of Neo-Confucianism has been the dominant philosophy in China in the last 700-odd years and has been followed by most Chinese intellectuals, his words may be taken as representative of the enlightened Confucianists in matters of religion. □

The Complete Works of Chu Hsi

a. PRINCIPLE, MATERIAL FORCE, AND THE GREAT ULTIMATE

1. In the universe there has never been any material force without principle or principle without material force. (49:1a)

2. Fundamentally principle and material force cannot be spoken of as prior or posterior. But if we must trace their origin, we are obliged to say that principle is prior. However, principle is not a separate entity. It exists right in material force. Without material force, principle would have nothing to adhere to. As material force, there are the Agents or Elements of Metal, Wood, Water, and Fire. As principle there are humanity, righteousness, propriety, and wisdom. (49:1b)

3. When questioned about the relation between principle and material force, Chu Hsi said, "I-ch'uan (Ch'eng I) expressed it very well when he said that principle is one but its manifestations are many.[16] When heaven, earth, and the myriad things are spoken of together, there is only one principle. As applied to man, however, there is in each individual a particular principle." (49:1b)

4. *Question*: "The Lord on High has conferred even on the inferior people a moral sense."[17] "When Heaven is about to confer a great responsibility on any man. . . ."[18] "Heaven, to protect the common people, made for them rulers."[19] "Heaven, in the production of things, is sure to be bountiful to them, according to their natural capacity."[20] "On the good-doer, the Lord on High sends down all blessings, and on the evil-doer, he sends down all miseries."[21] "When Heaven is about to send calamities to the world, it will always first produce abnormal people as a measure of their magnitude."[22] In passages like these, does it mean that Heaven has no personal consciousness and the passages are merely deductions from principle?

Answer: These passages have the same meaning. It is simply that principle operates this way. (49:4a)

5. When material force concentrates, it becomes physical form. As principle and the material force combine, there is consciousness. It is like when the lighting material gets oil, there will be fire and many flames. (49:5a)

6. Throughout the universe there are both principle and material force. Principle refers to the Way, which exists before physical form and is the course from which all things are produced. Material force refers to material objects, which exist after physical form; it is the instrument by which all things are produced. Therefore in the production of man and things, they must be endowed with principle before they have their nature, and they must be endowed with material force before they have physical form. (49:5b)

7. Principle of course cannot be spoken of as being one-sided or balanced, and penetrating or obstructed. But since people's endowment of material force are different, those whose material force is one-sided will get one-sided principle, and those whose material force is obstructed will naturally be obstructed from principle. Thus principle cannot be without being one-sided or obstructed in man. Hung-ch'ü (Chang Tsai) said "(Water's) reflection of light may be much or little, dark or bright, but in receiving the light, it is the same in all cases."[23] His theory is perfect. (49:7b)

8. The Great Ultimate is principle, and activity and tranquillity are material force. As material force operates, principle also operates. The two always depend on each other and are never separated. In the beginning there was nothing but this principle. As there is this principle, through activity the Great Ultimate generates yang and through tranquillity it generates yin. When tranquillity reaches its limit, activity begins again. And when activity reaches its limit, tranquillity begins again.[24] They go in cycles and circulate and move around. Their concrete principle is infinite, and the material force is also infinite along with it. (49:9b–10a)

9. The Great Ultimate embodies the principles of activity and tranquillity, but we should not divide activity and tranquillity into substance and function, for tranquillity is the substance of the Great Ultimate and activity is the function of the Great Ultimate. Take the fan, for example. There is only one fan. When it is waved, it is function, and when it is laid down, it is substance. When it is laid down, it is this one principle, and when it is waved, it is also this principle. (49:12b)

10. The Great Ultimate is like a tree. It grows into branches and further into leaves and flowers. It grows and grows indefinitely. When it bears fruits, there is again the principle to grow and grow (or to produce and reproduce) in them. This perpetually keeps going on and is an unlimited Great Ultimate. It does not stop. Only when fruits are born does the process rest a little, but it does not mean that when the process of growth reaches this point, it stops. (49:15a)

b. Heaven and Earth

11. In the beginning of the universe there was only material force consisting of yin and yang. This force moved and circulated, turning this way and that. As this movement gained speed, a mass of sediment was compressed, and since there was no outlet for it, it consolidated to form the earth in the center of the universe. The clear part of material force formed the sky, the sun, the moon, the stars, and planets. It is only on the outside that the encircling movement perpetually goes on. The earth exists motionless in the center of the system, not at the bottom. (49:19a)

12. When the undifferentiated had not yet become clearly defined, the material forces of yin and yang were mixed and obscure. When they were divided, a bright and extensive condition was opened up in them, and only then the two modes (yin and yang) were established. Shao K'ang-chieh (Shao Yung) called the period of 129,600 years one cycle.[25] Thus 129,600 years before that, there was another great opening and closing. It was the same further back. It simply means that "activity and tranquillity have no beginning and yin and yang have no starting point."[26] The small is the shadow of the great. You can see this in the rotation of the day and the night. As Wu-fung (Hu Hung, 1105–1155) has said, "As the one material force breathed greatly, there was unlimited shaking and agitation. The whole world changed. Mountains turned upside down and rivers sank and disappeared. Men and things were all destroyed, and all traces of the past were obliterated. This is called the primeval age of chaos."[27] Once I saw shells of snails and oysters in high mountains. Some of them were embedded in rocks. The rocks are as the earth of long ago and the snails and oysters were living things in water. What was low has changed into what is high and what was weak into what is strong. When we think this matter over deeply, we can find evidence for it. (49:20a–b)

13. *Question*: Is the mind of Heaven and Earth intelligent or is it merely indifferent and takes no action?

Answer: We cannot say that the mind of Heaven and Earth is not intelligent, but it does not think or deliberate like that of men. I-ch'uan said, "Heaven and Earth create and transform without having any mind of their own. The sage has a mind of his own but does not take any (unnatural) action."[28] (49:22b)

14. When questioned about the theory that Heaven and Earth have no mind. Chu Hsi said, "Humanity (*jen*, love) is the mind of Heaven and Earth. If they have a mind (as ordinarily understood), they must have thoughts and deliberations, plans, and activities. But when have Heaven and Earth any thoughts or deliberations? The reason why the four seasons rotate and the myriad things grow is that if it should be this way, then it is this way. It does not depend on any thinking. This is why the Way of Heaven and Earth is what it is."

"If so, how about the saying in the *Book of Changes*, 'In (things) returning (to their origin) we see the mind of Heaven and Earth.'[29] and 'In correctness and greatness the nature of Heaven and Earth can be seen?'"[30]

"They mean what they say. They merely explain how they have no (deliberate) mind. If they really have no mind at all, then cows would produce horses and peach trees would produce plum flowers. But these things are all self-determined. Master Ch'eng (Ch'eng I) said, '(Heaven) is spoken of as the Lord with respect to its being master . . . and *ch'ien* (Heaven, male, strong) with respect to its nature and feelings.'[31] These appellations are self-determined. The mind is that by which Heaven becomes the Lord. This is why it is said, 'The mind of Heaven and Earth is to produce things.'"[32] (49:23a–b)

15. The Lord is principle acting as master. (49:25a)

16. What is dark blue is called the sky. It is that which rotates and circulates around without cease. Now, of course, it won't do if we say that there is someone in heaven to pass judgment on sins. But it won't do either to say that there is completely no master. In such matters one must see (for himself). (49:25a)

17. Someone asked about I-ch'uan's saying that (heaven) is called the Lord

when spoken of in its aspect of being the master. "Who is the master (of heaven)?"

Answer: It has its own master, for heaven is a thing exceedingly strong and possessing yang in the highest degree. Naturally it rotates and moves unceasingly like this. For it to be like this, there must be that which is its master. In a thing like this, one must see for himself. It cannot be fully explained in words. (49:27b)

c. Yin, Yang, and the Five Agents (Elements)

18. Heaven and earth are completely a great system of yin and yang. Each year and each month have their own system of yin and yang. It is the same for a day or an hour. (49:28b)

19. There is only one system of yin and yang in the world. Therefore Master Ch'eng (Ch'eng I) said, "There is only one system of action and response. What we call yin and yang are everywhere. Take, for example, the front and rear. The front is yang and the rear is yin. Or take the two sides. The left is yang and the right is yin. Or again take the above and below. The above is yang and the below is yin."[33] (49:29b–30a)

20. *Question*: The two material forces and the Five Agents create and transform the myriad things. In their closing and opening, all the changes are produced. Is the material force of the Five Agents the same as the movement of thunder, wind, water, and fire? And are they the same as the variation, differentiation, and dispersion of the two material forces? Former scholars said that all things are sufficient. In that case, can we say that if a man is too heavy in his material endowment, he is sufficient? Others say that although all things are self-sufficient, some get more of the Five Agents and some get less. When I think about these, I feel especially vague and do not understand.

Answer: The material forces of the Five Agents are like warmth, coolness, cold, heat, dryness, wetness, strength, weakness, and so on. They are what fills the universe. Mention anything and it contains the Five Agents, except that they vary in amount. (49:43a–b)

d. Man's Nature and Destiny

21. *Question*: About the distinction between Heaven (Nature), destiny (*ming*, fate), nature, and principle. Heaven refers to what is self-existent; destiny refers to that which operates and is endowed in all things; nature refers to the total substance and that by which all things attain their being; and principle refers to the laws underlying all things and events. Taken together, Heaven is principle, destiny is nature, and nature is principle. Is this correct?

Answer: Yes. Nowadays, it is maintained that Heaven does not refer to the blue sky. In my view it cannot be left out of account. (42:1a–b)

22. Principle is the substance of Heaven, while destiny is the function of principle. One's nature is what is endowed in man. And one's feelings are the function of one's nature. (42:1b)

23. On being asked about (Chang Tsai's) section on moral character failing to overcome material force,[34] (Chu Hsi) said: Master Chang Tsai merely said that both man's nature and material force flow down from above. If my moral character is not adequate to overcome material force, then there is nothing to do but to submit to material force as endowed by Heaven. If my moral character is adequate to overcome material force, however, then what I receive from the endowment is all moral character. Therefore if I investigate principle to the utmost and fully develop my nature, then what I have received is wholly Heaven's moral character, and what Heaven has endowed in me is wholly Heaven's principle. The cases in which material force cannot be altered are life, death, longevity and brevity of life, for these, and poverty and wealth, and honor and humble station, all depend on material force. On the other hand, the practice of righteousness between the ruler and his ministers and the exercise of humanity between father and son, are what we call matters of fate. "But there is also man's nature. The superior man does not say they are matters of fate."[35] They must proceed from myself, not from fate. (42:3a–b)

24. *Question*: Destiny is what Heaven

endows in man and things and nature is what they receive from Heaven. But nature and destiny each has two aspects. From the point of view of their principle, the principle that is destined in man and things by Heaven is called destiny, and the principle received by them from Heaven is called their nature. From the point of view of material force, the material force that is destined in man and things by Heaven is also called destiny and the material force received by them from Heaven is also called their nature. Is this correct?

Answer: Material force cannot be called the nature or destiny. They exist because of it, that is all. When the nature and Heaven and Earth are spoken of, it refers to principle only; when the physical nature is spoken of, it refers to principle and material force combined. Material force is not to be referred to as nature or destiny. (42:4b)

e. THUNDER AND RAIN

25. *Question*: About thunder and lightning, Master Ch'eng (Ch'eng I) said that they are but material forces crushing each other in friction.[36] Is it correct?

Answer: Yes.

"Some people think there are spiritual beings in them."

"There must be the concentration of the material force. But after a moment it is dispersed. Things like lightning striking something are also produced by a concentration of the material force." (50:47a)

26. When questioned about the theory that a dragon moves and thus produces rain, Chu Hsi said, "The dragon is a living creature in water. It comes out and its vapor and the steam of the yang material force interact and therefore rain is produced. But ordinary rain is definitely produced by the repression of the yin material force and the rising in steam of the yang material force. It is certainly not made by the dragon. When there is a thick cloud and it still does not rain, this is because (the forces) can still go away, for only the material force below rises up and therefore there cannot be rain. Only when the rising force is blocked and curbed with no way of giving vent to it can there be rain." (50:48b)

f. *Kuei shen* AND SPIRITUAL BEINGS

27. When the subject of spiritual beings happened to be discussed, Chu Hsi said, "The matter of spiritual beings is of course of secondary importance. They are without form or shadow and difficult to understand, and we need not try to understand them. Let us devote our efforts to the important things in daily life. Confucius said, 'If we are not yet able to serve man, how can we serve spiritual beings? If we do not yet know about life, how can we know about death?'[37] This says all there is to say. This is something we should understand. As we understand it, at the end we shall be able to understand spiritual beings. But if we do not understand what should be understood and attempt to understand the unimportant, at the end we won't understand at all." (51:1a–b)

28. *Shen* (positive spiritual force) means to expand (*shen*)[38] and *kuei* (negative spiritual force) means to contract. When wind, rain, thunder, and lightning first arise, they are *shen*. When they stop or are over, they are *kuei*. (51:2b)

29. *Kuei* and *shen* are but the growth and decline of yin and yang. They are exemplified in things assuming physical form, in their attaining nature, in their transformation, and in their growth, in wind and rain, in gloomy weather—in all of these. In man his essence is *p'o* (earthly component of the soul). "*P'o* is *kuei* in its fullest measure." Man's vital force is *hun* (heavenly component of the soul).[39] "*Hun* is *shen* in its fullest measure."[40] Essence and vital force are combined to become things. What thing can be without *kuei* and *shen*? "The wandering away of the spirit (*hun*) becomes change."[41] Since *hun* wanders, we know that *p'o* descends (to the ground). (51:2b)

30. *Kuei* and *shen* are but force. What expands or contracts, comes or goes, is force. In the universe there is nothing which is not force. Man's force and the force of the universe are always in contact without interruption. Men themselves do not see it. As soon as one's mind acts, it affects the force (of the universe), and immediately there is the mutual influence between it and

that which expands or contracts, and comes and goes. In matters like divination, in all cases one already has the matter in his mind. He only talks about the matter in his mind and as soon as his mind acts, there is surely to be response. (51:2b–3a)

31. The principle of *kuei* and *shen* and life and death is definitely different from what the Buddhists say (the soul in transmigration) or what the popular masses understand (like spirits of the dead). But sometimes there are unmistakable facts which cannot be reasoned on the basis of principle. In matters like these, let us not try to understand. (51:3b)

32. When he happened to be discussing spiritual beings and strange phenomena, Chu Hsi said, "If man's mind remains at ease, everything will be all right. If it is fooled around with, spiritual beings and strange phenomena will appear." (51:4a)

33. When the matter of Hsüeh Shih-lung's[42] seeing a spiritual being in his house happened to be discussed, Chu Hsi said, "Those in the world who believe in spiritual beings all say that they really exist in the world. Those who do not believe in them are decidedly sure that there are no spiritual beings. But then some have actually seen them. Cheng Ching-weng[43] therefore regarded what Mr. Hsüeh saw as in accordance with concrete principle. These people do not realize that what they see are but something like rainbows." (51:4b–5a)

34. In such things as the wind arising, the rain forming, the thunder roaring, the lightning flashing, and flowers blooming and bearing seeds, if there is no spirit, what is there? People have simply not examined the matter. As soon as they hear other people talk about affairs of spiritual beings, they consider that strange. According to principle there should be such things in the world. We should not say that there is none, but they are not the correct things in the process of creation. They are cases where the material forces of yin and yang are not balanced. We need not be surprised or deceived by them. Therefore "Confucius never discussed strange phenomena,"[44] for he was quite clear that there were such things but he did not want to discuss them. (51:5a)

35. In terms of the two material forces, *kuei* is the spirit of yin while *shen* is the spirit of yang. In terms of one material force, that which comes and expands is *shen* and that which goes backward and returns is *kuei.* The one material force is the material force of yin and yang in circulation. It means that when part of it comes, all will come, and when part of it goes, all will go. The two material forces mean yin and yang in opposition to each of which certain things belong. For example, the inhaling and exhaling of breath is *hun.* *Hun* is *shen* and belongs to yang. The ear, eye, nose, mouth, and so on, are *p'o. P'o* is *kuei* and belongs to yin. "Essence and material force become things."[45] This means that essence and material force are combined to produce things. "The wandering away of spirit becomes change."[46] This means that the material force disperses and comes to an end. *P'o* then descends (to the ground). (51:5b)

36. Is expansion *shen* (positive spiritual force) and contraction *kuei* (negative spiritual force)?

The Teacher drew a circle on the desk with his hand and pointed to its center and said, "Principle is like a circle. Within it there is differentiation like this. All cases of material force which is coming forth belong to yang and are *shen.* All cases of material force which is returning to its origin belong to yin and are *kuei.* In the day, forenoon is the positive spiritual force, afternoon is the negative spiritual force. In the month from the third day onward is the positive spiritual force; after the sixteenth day, it is the negative spiritual force."

T'ung Po-yü[47] asked, "Is it correct when speaking of the sun and moon as opposites, to say that the sun is the positive spiritual force and the moon is the negative spiritual force?"

Chu Hsi answered, "Yes, it is. Plants growing are the positive spiritual force, plants deteriorating are the negative spiritual force. A person from childhood to maturity is the positive spiritual force, while a man in his declining years and old age is the negative spiritual force. In breathing, breath going out is the positive spiritual force, breath coming in is the negative spiritual force." (51:6b)

37. *Question*: When sages talked about *kuei* and *shen*, they always spoke of them in terms of the principle of expansion and contraction. When they talked about spiritual beings, blessings and calamities, and fortune and misfortune, they also spoke purely in terms of principle, for men, spiritual beings, and Heaven and Earth follow the same principle, and principle is always good. If man can follow principle, he will have good fortune, but if he violates principle, he will have misfortune. The same is true of blessings and calamities. Did they mean that Heaven and Earth and spiritual beings descend on people individually? The saying in the *Book of History*, "According to the Way of Heaven, blessing will come to the good doer and calamities to the evildoer."[48] and the saying in the *Book of Changes*, "Spiritual beings harm the full and bless the humble,"[49] mean nothing but this. . . .

Answer: From what you have discussed, it means there are no spiritual beings. Of course *kuei* and *shen* should be spoken of in terms of principle, but it cannot be said that no material force is involved. Therefore ancient kings offered roast meat or fragrant wine, for these have a certain odor (akin to the material force) and were therefore used to attract the spiritual beings. As to the matters of blessings and calamities, and good and evil fortune, what you said is correct. (51:9a–b)

38. Question about the principle of life and death and spiritual beings. (*Question*: Although we know that spiritual beings and life and death are governed by one and the same principle, we do not understand the exact point. *Answer*: "Essence and material force are combined to become things. The wandering away of the spirit becomes change."[50] This is the principle of life and death. The questioner did not understand. *Further remark*: Essence and material force consolidate to become man, and as they disintegrate, they become a spiritual being.

Further question: When essence and material force consolidate, is this a case of principle being attached to material force?)[51]

Answer: As the Way of Heaven operates, the myriad things develop and grow. There is [logically] principle first and then material force. Although they coexist at the same time, in the final analysis principle is basic. Man receives it and thus possesses life. (But material force may be clear or turbid.) The clear part of material force becomes his vital force, while the turbid part becomes his physical nature. (The clear part belongs to yang while the turbid part belongs to yin.) Consciousness and movement are due to yang, while physical form and body (bones and flesh, skin and hair) are due to yin. The vital force belongs to the heavenly component of the soul (*hun*) and the body is governed by the earthly component of the soul (*p'o*). In his commentary on the *Huainan Tzu*, Kao Yu (fl. 205) said, "*Hun* is the spirit of yang and *p'o* is the spirit of yin."[52] By spirit is meant the master of the body and the vital force. Man is born as a result of the integration of essence and material force. He possesses the material force only in a certain amount, which in time necessarily becomes exhausted. (This is what is meant by physicians when they say that yin or yang no longer rises or falls.) When exhaustion takes place, the heavenly component of the soul and the vital force return to Heaven, and the earthly component of the soul and the body return to earth, and the man dies. When a man is about to die, the warm material force leaves him and rises. This is called the *hun* rising. The lower part of his body gradually becomes cold. This is called the *p'o* falling. Thus as there is life, there is necessarily death, and as there is beginning, there must be an end. What integrates and disintegrates is material force. As to principle, it merely attaches itself to material force, but from the beginning it does not consolidate into a separate thing by itself. However, whatever is correct in one's functioning is principle. It need not be spoken of in terms of integration and disintegration. When a man dies, his material force necessarily disintegrates. However, it does not disintegrate completely at once. Therefore in religious sacrifices we have the principle of spiritual influence and response. Whether the material force (or vital force) of ancestors of many generations ago is still there or not cannot be known. Nevertheless, since those who perform the sacrificial rites are their descendants, the material force between them is after all the same. Hence there is the principle by which they can penetrate and respond. But the material force that has disintegrated cannot again be integrated. And yet the Buddhists say that man after death becomes a spiritual being and the spiritual being again becomes a man. If so, then in the universe there would be always the same number of people coming and going, with no need of the creative process of production and reproduction. This is decidedly absurd. . . .

Question: I-ch'uan said that *kuei* and *shen* are traces of creation. Are [spiritual beings terrifying people] also a trace of creation?

Answer: They all are. If we talk about correct principle, they are like trees suddenly producing blooms and leaves. They are traces of creation. Or take the wind, rain, thunder, or lightning suddenly happening in the sky. They all are. Only because people are accustomed to see these, they do not regard them as strange. When they suddenly hear a ghost hissing or see a will-o'-the-wisp and things like that, they consider them strange right away, without realizing that they are also traces of creation. These things do not follow the correct principle and therefore they are strange. (51:18b–20a)

39. Yung-chih[53] said, "When one prayed to Heaven and Earth, and the spirits of mountains and rivers, it is to influence what is in them with what is in oneself. When descendants sacrifice to ancestors, it is to use what is in the descendants to influence what does not exist in the ancestors."

Chu Hsi said, "The material force of gods (of Heaven and Earth, mountains and rivers) is always expanding without cease. The material force of spiritual beings (the deceased), however, will dissipate and disperse without anything left. The dissipation and dispersion may be rapid or may take a long time. Some people did not accept their death. Therefore although they have died, their material force has not dispersed and they have become apparitions. In cases of people who die violently or in cases of Taoist and Buddhist priests, their material force usually does not disperse [quickly]. (Original note: The priests cultivate their spirit and therefore their material force consolidates and does not disperse.) But sages and worthies are content with their death. Is there any case of their material force not dispersing and their becoming spiritual beings or apparitions?" (51:21a)

40. *Question*: When a person dies, that means his consciousness is dissipated right away. Is that right?

Answer: Not dispersed but exhausted. When one's vital force is exhausted, the consciousness is also exhausted. (51:30b)

g. Gods, Ancestors, and Sacrifices

41. *Question*: We talk about spiritual beings in terms of sacrifices. Heaven, Earth, the spirits of rivers and mountains, and so on, are clearly one material force circulating and penetrating; [Thus sacrifice to them is based on the unity of their material force with that of ours], but it is also based on principle. In the case of ancestors, generally speaking, principle is fundamental, but the earthly component of their soul based on the material force is also involved. In the cases of ancient sages, is the sacrifice to them entirely based on principle?

Answer: Where there is principle, there is material force. They can not be spoken of separately. Everything is principle and everything is material force. What thing is not principle and what thing is not material force?

Question: What is called material force in the cases of ancient sages and worthies is nothing but the material force common to all things in the world. But is it true that "the spirit of ancestors" is "in the final analysis one's own spirit?"[54]

Answer: The material force of ancestors is merely the material force common to all things. Since one's person is in the world, it is where principle and material force consolidate. The Son of Heaven united in him Heaven and Earth. He was responsible for the affairs within Heaven and Earth. Since he was concerned with Heaven and Earth, his mind penetrates Heaven and Earth. One should not say that the material force (of Heaven and Earth) was empty and had nothing to do with him. It was improper for the feudal lords to sacrifice to Heaven and Earth. They had nothing to do with Heaven and Earth and could not communicate with them. The principles of sages and worthies prevail throughout the ten thousand generations. Their service has been rendered to ten thousand generations. As we practice the principles of sages and worthies and perpetuate their minds, we are carrying their burden, and thus our material force and theirs penetrate each other. Take the case of sacrifice. Many vessels with fruit and meat are arrayed and many ceremonies have been instituted. It won't do if there is no communication with the spirit to perform the sacrifice in order to deceive people. In the family, descendants carry on much of the heritage of their ancestors. This mind of carrying on penetrates the minds of their ancestors. In the "Meaning of Sacrifice," it is said, "Offer the sacrifices of spring and autumn."[55] This is because when the yang of spring comes, the spirits also come, and when the yang of autumn goes away, the spirits also go away. Therefore sacrifices were performed at those times. Originally the Sage instituted some simple ceremonies for us to express our sincerity. Later on the ceremonies became elaborate. (51:40b–41b)

42. Ch'en Hou-chih[56] said, "Ancestors are a unifying force in the world. It integrates or disintegrates in accordance with the sacrifice of their descendants."

Chu Hsi said, "This is what Shang-ts'ai meant by saying that, 'When we want them (spiritual beings), there will be, and when we do not want them, there will not be.'[57] In that case, all depends on man. Fundamentally speaking, there are spiritual beings. Ancestors share the same material force with us. But there must be a point of concentration. The persons of the descendants are here, and the force of ancestors are therefore right here. Between them there is a penetration of blood and veins. Therefore spiritual beings are not attracted by the offerings of people outside of their class and people do not sacrifice to spiritual beings outside of their clan,[58] for their forces are not related. In the cases of the Son of Heaven sacrificing to Heaven and Earth, the feudal lords sacrificing to the spirits of mountains and rivers, and great officers sacrificing to the Five Deities,[59] although these are not their ancestors, nevertheless the Son of Heaven is the host of all under heaven, the feudal lords are the hosts of the spirits of mountains and rivers, and great officers are hosts of the Five Deities. Since the Son of Heaven, and so on, are hosts of Heaven and Earth, and so on, respectively, the force of Heaven and Earth, and so on, is united in the person of the Son of Heaven, and so on, respectively. In this way, there is a relationship. (51:42a–b)

43. *Question*: When a person dies, do his heavenly and earthly components of the soul disperse readily?

Answer: Of course they do.

Further question: But in the descendants' sacrifice they are influenced to come. How is that?

Answer: At bottom descendants are the force of ancestors. Although their own force has dispersed, its root remains with the descendants. If they show their sincerity and reverence to the utmost, they can draw the force of their ancestors to consolidate in them. It is like waves. The water in the front is not the same as the water behind and the water behind is not the same as the water in the front, and yet water pervades them all. The same is true of the force of descendants and that of ancestors. The ancestors' force immediately dispersed (when they died), but its root remains here. Since its root remains here, it can attract and consolidate the force here. This matter is difficult to explain. One must see for himself. (51:42b–43a)

44. Tzu-shan[60] asked about spiritual beings and said, "Fan[61] interpreted the saying, 'When (Confucius) offered sacrifice (to his ancestors, he felt) as if (his ancestral spirits) were actually present,'[62] and said that 'If there is sincerity (in the descendants), there will be the spiritual beings, and if there is no sincerity, there will be no spiritual beings.' The material force fills the entire space, and the dead can no longer be sought after. When descendants show their sincerity and reverence to the

utmost, the ancestors immediately respond to their sincerity. Is it the force in space that responds to their sincerity or the force in the descendants themselves that responds?"

Answer: It is only their own force, but the force of their ancestors is continuous with it. (51:46b–47a)

45. *Question*: In sacrificing to Heaven, Earth, and the spirits of mountains and rivers with offerings of meat, silk, and wine, is it merely to express one's sincerity or is there actually some force that comes to receive the sacrifice?

Answer: If you say that nothing comes, then why sacrifice? What is it that is so solemn above that causes people to make offerings with awe and reverence? But if you say that there are really spiritual beings riding in high chariots and coming in a group, that is just wild talk. (51:50b)

46. Kuang[63] said, "Where the human mind is concentrated, there is spirit. Therefore when the ancients sacrificed to Heaven in the altar, the spirit of Heaven came, and when they sacrificed in the ancestral temple, the spirits of (deceased human beings) came. The principle is the same."

Chu Hsi said, "Of course it is. But the will of the ancients was correct and therefore the spirits (that came) were correct. The minds of the people of later generations are not correct to start with, and therefore their influence cannot be correct." Thereupon he said further, "When the ancients sacrificed to the spirits of mountains and rivers, they merely set up an altar to sacrifice to. At the time of the sacrifice, they were there. After the sacrifice, they were no longer there. Hence the spirits were not blasphemed. But later generations built temples for them. In this way the people's minds are deceived and disturbed so that they sought from the spirits what they don't deserve and there is no limit to what they would do."

Thereupon Kuang spoke about the absence of propriety in the existence of excessive temples and the ability of the Buddhists to pacify spiritual beings. Chu Hsi said, "If people's minds are correct, open, and unobstructed both internally and externally, and without the slightest selfish idea, they can 'Face the Lord on High.'[64] Then what spiritual beings will not be pacified?" (51:52b–53a)

C. UNITY OF HEAVEN AND MAN

□ The highest goal in Confucianism is *jen* (humanity, love, benevolence). In human relations it means fully realizing one's own nature and treating others as one treats himself.[65] On a higher plane, it means forming one body with Heaven and Earth. This is a theme running through Neo-Confucianism. The best statement for *jen* is the *Western Inscription*[66] by philosopher Chang Tsai of the eleventh century. Here the unity of Heaven and man, the relation between them as father and son, self-realization, universal love for all, filial piety, doing one's best, and "waiting for fate" are all simply but sincerely expressed. He inscribed it on the western window of his study as a daily reminder. It is highly personal and it is meant as a constant vigilance. □

The *Western Inscription*

Heaven is my father and Earth is my mother, and even such a small creature as I find an intimate place in their midst.

Therefore that which fills the universe I regard as my body and that which directs the universe I consider as my nature.

All people are my brothers and sisters, and all things are my companions.

The great ruler (the emperor) is the eldest son of my parents (Heaven and Earth), and the great ministers are his stewards. Respect the aged—this is the way to treat them as elders should be treated. Show deep love toward the orphaned and the weak—this is the way to treat them as the young should be treated. The sage identifies his character with that of Heaven and Earth, and the worthy is the most outstanding man. Even those who are tired, infirm, crippled, or sick, those who have no brothers or children, wives or husbands, are all my brothers who are in distress and have no one to turn to.[67]

When the time comes, to keep himself from harm—this is the care of a son. To rejoice in Heaven and to have no anxiety—this is filial piety at its purest.

He who disobeys [the Principle of Nature] violates virtue. He who destroys humanity is a robber. He who promotes evil lacks (moral) capacity. But he who puts his moral nature into practice and brings his physical existence into complete fulfillment can match (Heaven and Earth).

One who knows the principles of transformation will skillfully carry forward the undertakings (of Heaven and Earth), and one who penetrates spirit to the highest degree will skillfully carry out their will.[68]

Do nothing shameful in the recesses of your own house[69] and thus bring no dishonor to them. Preserve your mind and nourish your nature and thus (serve them) with untiring effort.

The Great Yü hated pleasant wine but attended to the protection and support of his parents.[70] Border Warden Ying brought up and educated the young and thus extended his love to his own kind.[71]

Shun's merit lay in delighting his parents with unceasing effort,[72] and Shen-sheng's reverence was demonstrated when he awaited punishment without making an attempt to escape.[73]

Tseng Ts'an received his body from his parents and reverently kept it intact throughout life,[74] while Po-ch'i vigorously obeyed his father's command.[75]

Wealth, honor, blessing, and benefits are meant for the enrichment of my life, while poverty, humble station, and sorrow are meant to help me to fulfillment.

In life I follow and serve (Heaven and Earth). In death I will be at peace. (*Chang Tzu ch'üani-shü* [Complete works of Master Chang], ch. 1)

NOTES

1. For a discussion on the religion of the Chinese masses and that of the Chinese intellectual, see Wing-tsit Chan, *Religious Trends in Modern China*, chs. 4 and 6.
2. Liu Tsung-yüan was an investigating censor and one of the most outstanding literary men in Chinese history. Han, whose courtesy name was T'ui-chi, was the most prominent Confucianist in the first millennium and also a celebrated literary figure. Liu Yü-hsi was a minister of rites and a famous poet.
3. See ch. 11, D, 1.
4. For this philosophy, see Wing-tsit Chan, *A Source Book in Chinese Philosophy*, ch. 11.
5. For his philosophy, see *ibid.*, ch. 14.
6. This essay is not found in the *Han Ch'ang-li ch'üan-chi* or Collected works of Han Yü.
7. Robbers at the time of the legendary Yellow Emperor of great antiquity. Chih was from the state of Lu and Chao from Ch'u.
8. Yen Tzu, whose private name was Hui. Also called Yen Yüan. He was Confucius' most virtuous pupil.
9. Confucius was in peril in K'uang in 497 B.C. when he was 56. The people of K'uang, mistaking him for Yang Hu, their enemy whom Confucius resembled in appearance, surrounded him. His pupil Yen Hui got lost for a couple of days. See the *Analects*, 9:9 and 11:22.
10. Present Chieh-yü County in Shansi Province.
11. The two states (in present Shansi and Shensi Provinces) used to fight for land to cultivate. When King Wen (r. 1171–1122 B.C.) was there, his moral influence was such that people in the two states offered their lands to each other.
12. For K'uang, see n. 9. When Confucius went to Sung, a high officer wanted to kill him. He had to disguise himself to get away. See the *Book of Mencius*, 5A:8.
13. His anthology of the four Neo-Confucianists has been translated into English by Wing-tsit Chan as *Reflections on Things at Hand; The Neo-Confucian Anthology*.
14. See Chu Hsi, *Djin-sï lu*, tr. into German by Olaf Graf, vol. 1.

15. The Chinese titles for these three works are *Chu Tzu ch'üan-shu* (Complete works of Master Chu), *Chu Tzu yü-lei* (Classified conversations of Master Chu), and *Chu Tzu wen-chi* (Collection of literary works by Master Chu). For translations from the *Complete Works*, see J. Percy Bruce, tr., *The Philosophy of Human Nature, by Chu Hsi*, and Wing-tsit Chan, tr., *A Source Book in Chinese Philosophy*, ch. 34.
16. *Ts'ui-yen* (Pure words), 1:24a, also in the *I chuan* (Commentary on the *Book of Changes*), both in the *Erh-Ch'eng ch'üan-shu* (Complete works of the two Ch'engs). For the teachings of Ch'eng I, see Wing-tsit Chan, *A Source Book in Chinese Philosophy*, ch. 32.
17. *Book of History*, "Announcement of T'ang."
18. *Book of Mencius*, 6B:15.
19. *Book of History*, "Great Oath."
20. *Doctrine of the Mean*, ch. 17.
21. *Book of History*, "Instructions of I."
22. Source not traced.
23. Chang Tsai, *Cheng-meng* (Correcting youthful ignorance), ch. 6, § 32. For the teachings of Chang Tsai, see Chan, *Source Book*, ch. 30.
24. Paraphrasing the same. For the teachings of Chou Tun-i, see Chan, *Source Book*, ch. 28.
25. Shao Yung, *Huang-chi ching-shih* (Supreme principles governing the world), ch. 1. For the teachings of Shao Yung, see Chan, *Source Book*, ch. 29.
26. Ch'eng I, *Ching-shuo* (Explanations of the Classics), 1:2a. In the *Erh-Ch'eng chüan-shu.*
27. Cf. Hu Hung, *Huang-wang ta-chi* (Great records of emperors and kings), ch. 1.
28. *Ching-shuo*, 1:2a.
29. Commentary on hexagram no. 24, *fu* (to return).
30. *Ibid.*, commentary on hexagram no. 34, *ta-chuang* (great strength).
31. Ch'eng I, *I chuan*, ch. 1, commentary on hexagram no. 1, *ch'ien* (Heaven, male, strength).
32. See the *I chuan*, 2:33a.
33. Ch'eng I, *I-shu* (Surviving works), 15:7b. In the *Erh-Ch'eng ch'üan-shu.*
34. *Cheng-meng*, ch. 1, § 43.
35. *Book of Mencius*, 7B:24.
36. *I-shu*, 2B:7b.
37. *Analects*, 11:11.
38. The two *shens* are represented by two different Chinese characters.
39. For *hun* and *p'o*, see ch. 10, n. 1.
40. These two passages are from the *Book of Rites*, ch. 24, "The Meaning of Sacrifice," § 24.
41. *Book of Changes*, "Appended Remarks," pt. 1, ch. 4.
42. Hsüeh Chi-hsüan (1125–1173).
43. Cheng Po-hsiung (1127–1179).
44. *Analects*, 7:20.
45. *Book of Changes*, "Appended Remarks," pt. 1, ch. 4.
46. *Ibid.*
47. A pupil of Chu Hsi's.
48. "Announcement of T'ang."
49. Commentary on hexagram no. 14, *ch'ien* (humility).
50. *Book of Changes*, "Appended Remarks," pt. 1, ch. 4.
51. Passages in parentheses in this section are added in the record by Chou Ming-tso, Chu Hsi's pupil, who recorded his conversations after 1192.
52. *Ssu-pu pei-yao* edition, 7:6a.
53. Chu Hsi's pupil, Liu Li (fl. 1199), whose courtesy name was Yung-chih.
54. Hsieh Liang-tso (1050–1103), whose courtesy name was Shang-ts'ai, in his *Shang-ts'ai yü-lu* (Recorded conversations of Hsieh Liang-tso), pt. 1, p. 15b.
55. *Book of Rites*, ch. 24, "Meaning of Sacrifice," § 1.
56. Ch'en I (fl. 1196).
57. Hsieh Liang-tso, *Shang-ts'ai yü-lu*, pt. 1, p. 15a.

58. *Tso chuan*, Duke Hsi, 31st year.
59. See ch. 12, C, 1.
60. His family name was P'an and courtesy name was Shih-chü (fl. 1193).
61. Fan Tsu-yü (1040–1098). His commentary on the *Analects* is lost.
62. *Analects*, 3:12.
63. Fu Kuang (fl. 1205), Chu Hsi's pupil.
64. *Book of Odes*, ode no. 266.
65. For an analysis of this term, see Chan, *Source Book*, pp. 788–89.
66. *Hsi-ming* in Chinese.
67. See *Book of Mencius*, 1A:7; 1B:5.
68. Cf. the *Doctrine of the Mean*, ch. 19.
69. *Book of Odes*, ode no. 256. The recess refers to the northwest corner, the darkest in the house.
70. Founder of the Hsia dynasty (r. 2183–2175 B.C.). The story refers to the *Book of Mencius*, 4B:20.
71. See the *Tso-chuan* (Tso's commentary on the *Spring and Autumn Annals*), Duke Yin, 1st year.
72. Legendary sage-emperor of the third millennium B.C. See the *Book of Mencius*, 4A:28.
73. Heir-apparent of Chin who committed suicide because he was falsely accused of attempting to poison his father, Duke Hsien (r. 676–651 B.C.).
74. Tseng Tzu (505–c. 436 B.C.), pupil of Confucius, was well known for his filial piety. See the *Classic of Filial Piety*, ch. 1, and ch. 12, B, 2 of this anthology.
75. Yin Po-ch'i was a ninth-century B.C. prince who obeyed his father's order to exile so his stepbrother could be the crown prince. See the *Ch'ien-Han shu* (History of the Former Han dynasty, 206 B.C.–A.D. 8), ch. 79.

CHAPTER 14

Taoist Philosophy: Lao Tzu and Chuang Tzu

A. LAO TZU

□ It is a great irony in history that the philosophy taught by Lao Tzu should become a part, or even the basis, of a popular religion radically different from it. Its naturalistic philosophy was turned into a mysticism of a supernatural order. The philosophy is essentially atheistic but the religion that bears the name Taoism is highly polytheistic with a deity for almost anything imaginable. Its admonition to treat life and death equally has been supplanted by the search for everlasting life on earth. And its doctrine of simplicity finds a sharp contrast in elaborate rituals and religious paraphernalia. In short, its basic teaching of *wu-wei* (nonaction, or rather taking no unnatural action) has been negated by a great deal of activity—idol worship, divination, geomancy, astrology, and what-not.

No one knows exactly how the Taoist religion originated or how it began to utilize Taoist philosophy. From the very early days, the Chinese had practiced divination, astrology, faith healing, witchcraft. By the fourth century B.C. there was already the belief in immortals. Meditation, breathing exercises, sex techniques, medicine, and others were practiced to achieve everlasting life. In the first century B.C. a cult emerged bearing the names of the mythical Yellow Emperor and Lao Tzu. By 167 A.D. they were worshiped together in the national capital. Perhaps Chang Ling (fl. 156), the so-called founder of the Taoist religion, made use of Lao Tzu's popularity and in turn put him on a pedestal in the fast-growing movement. Perhaps the Taoist philosophy, in many ways opposed to the official ideology of Confucianism, was particularly attractive and useful to rebels like Chang Ling. Perhaps Lao Tzu's attack on social institutions and government gave great encouragement to the minority who readily incorporated the philosophy into their minority religion. Or perhaps Lao Tzu's intriguing ideas of the "Mother" and the female provided the necessary solace and comfort in a society dominated by masculine Confucianism. But there are also enough suggestions in the *Lao Tzu* to capture the imagination of followers of the popular cult. References such as "the spirit of the valley never dies" (ch. 6), the "profound (or mysterious) female" (ch. 6), being "free from danger throughout his lifetime" (ch. 16), "dies but does not really perish" (ch. 33), "long life and everlasting existence" or everlasting life (ch. 59), immunity from fierce beasts and poisonous insects (ch. 55), and so on, could not help reinforcing a frame of mind that was already strong.

On a higher plane, of course, the philosophy of Lao Tzu had much more to offer. Its vast concept of the oneness of Heaven, Earth, and all things, its radically new idea of nonbeing not as something negative but as the source of being, its strange synthesis of naive naturalism and profound mysticism, its doctrine of returning to the root, its fascinating emphasis on weakness as the way to a good life, and other equally significant concepts made its Way (Tao) unique, so that while practically all ancient Chinese philosophical schools had their own *tao*, this system alone came to be identified with the name.

This Way has remained the second strongest philosophy for the Chinese, challenging, supplementing, correcting, and enriching Confucianism so deeply and extensively that just as every typical Chinese is a Confucianist, he is also a Taoist. But the Chinese have made a clear distinction between this Taoist philosophy, which is called Tao-chia (the Taoist School), and the religion that has appropriated its teachings, which is called Tao-chiao (the Taoist religion). It is unfortunate that both have been known in the West as Taoism so that the relationship between the two has been confused.

This is not the place to discuss the extremely controversial questions about the historicity and the date of Lao Tzu or the authenticity and the date of the *Lao Tzu*.[1] It is enough to say that the little classic of slightly more than 5000 words in eighty-one chapters, also called the *Tao-te ching* (Classic of the Way and its virtue), is the most influential book in Chinese history outside of the Confucian *Analects*. Almost a thousand commentaries have been written on it in China and Japan and there have been more than forty English translations,[2] making it the most translated among the Chinese classics. There is no question that Lao Tzu was a historical person in the sixth century B.C. whom Confucius visited. The book, however, was not written by him as tradition has it but is a long evolution from some of his basic ideas until it assumed book form probably in the fourth century B.C. But its ideas transcend space, time, and personality (of which it mentions none). As such it is after all a truly religious document. □

The *Lao Tzu* (*Tao-te ching*)

1. The Tao (Way) that can be told of is not the eternal Tao;
The name that can be named is not the eternal name.
The Nameless is the origin of Heaven and Earth;
The Name is the mother of all things.
Therefore let there always be nonbeing so we may see their subtlety,[3]
And let there always be being[4] so we may see their outcome.
The two are the same,
But after they are produced, they have different names.[5]
They both may be called deep and profound.[6]
Deeper and more profound,
The door of all subtleties!

2. When the people of the world all know beauty as beauty,
There arises the recognition of ugliness.
When they all know the good as good,
There arises the recognition of evil.
Therefore:
Being and nonbeing produce each other;
Difficult and easy complete each other;
Long and short contrast[7] each other;
High and low distinguish each other;
Sound and voice harmonize with each other;
Front and back follow each other.
Therefore the sage manages affairs without action
(*wu-wei*)
And spreads doctrines without words.
All things arise, and he does not turn away from them.
He produces them, but does not take possession of them.
He acts, but does not rely on his own ability.[8]
He accomplishes his task, but does not claim credit for it.
It is precisely because he does not claim credit that his accomplishment remains with him.

6. The spirit of the valley never dies.
It is called the subtle and profound female.
The gate of the subtle and profound female
Is the root of Heaven and Earth.
It is continuous, and seems to be always existing.
Use it and you will never wear it out.

7. Heaven is eternal and Earth everlasting.
They can be eternal and everlasting because they do not exist for themselves,
And for this reason can exist forever.
Therefore the sage places himself in the background, but finds himself in foreground.
He puts himself away, and yet he always remains.
Is it not because he has no personal interests?
This is the reason why his personal interests are fulfilled.

10. Can you keep the spirit and embrace the One without departing from them?
Can you concentrate your vital force (*ch'i*) and achieve the highest degree of weakness like an infant?
Can you clean and purify your profound insight so it will be spotless?
Can you love the people and govern the state without knowledge (cunning)?
Can you play the role of the female in the opening and closing of the gates of Heaven?
Can you understand all and penetrate all without taking any action?
To produce things and to rear them,
To produce, but not to take possession of them,
To act, but not to rely on one's own ability,
To lead them, but not to master them—
This is called profound and secret virtue.

14. We look at it and do not see it;
Its name is The Invisible.
We listen to it and do not hear it;
Its name is The Inaudible.
We touch it and do not find it;
Its name is The Subtle (formless).
These three cannot be further inquired into,
And hence merge into one.
Going up high, it is not bright, and coming down low, it is not dark.
Infinite and boundless, it cannot be given any name;
It reverts to nothingness.
This is called shape without shape,
Form (*hsiang*) without object.
It is The Vague and Elusive.
Meet it and you will not see its head.
Follow it and you will not see its back.
Hold on to the Tao of old in order to master the things of the present.
From this one may know the primeval beginning (of the universe).
This is called the bond[9] of Tao.

16. Attain complete vacuity,
Maintain steadfast quietude.
All things come into being,
And I see thereby their return.
All things flourish,
But each one returns to its root.
The return to its root means tranquillity.
It is called returning to its destiny.
To return to destiny is called the eternal (Tao).
To know the eternal is called enlightenment.
Not to know the eternal is to act blindly to result in disaster.
He who knows the eternal is all-embracing.
Being all-embracing, he is impartial.
Being impartial, he is kingly (universal).[10]
Being kingly, he is one with Nature.
Being one with Nature, he is in accord with Tao.
Being in accord with Tao, he is everlasting,
And is free from danger throughout his lifetime.

19. Abandon sageliness and discard wisdom;
Then the people will benefit a hundredfold.
Abandon humanity and discard righteousness;
Then the people will return to filial piety and deep love.[11]
Abandon skill and discard profit;
Then there will be no thieves or robbers.
However, these three things are ornament (*wen*) and not adequate.
Therefore let people hold on to these:
Manifest plainness,
Embrace simplicity,
Reduce selfishness,
Have few desires.

21. The all-embracing quality of the great virtue (*te*) follows alone from the Tao.
The thing that is called Tao is eluding and vague.
Vague and eluding, there is in it the form.
Eluding and vague, in it are things.
Deep and obscure, in it is the essence.[12]
The essence is very real; in it are evidences.
From the time of old until now, its name (manifestations) ever remains,
By which we may see the beginning of all things.
How do I know that the beginnings of all things are so?
Through this (Tao).

25. There was something undifferentiated and yet complete,
Which existed before heaven and earth.
Soundless and formless, it depends on nothing and does not change.
It operates everywhere and is free from danger.
It may be considered the mother of the universe.
I do not know its name; I call it Tao.
If forced to give it a name, I shall call it Great.
Now being great means functioning everywhere.
Functioning everywhere means far-reaching.
Being far-reaching means returning to the original point.
Therefore Tao is great.
Heaven is great.
Earth is great.
And the king[13] is also great.
There are four great things in the universe, and the king is one of them.
Man models himself after Earth.
Earth models itself after Heaven.
Heaven models itself after Tao.
And Tao models itself after Nature.

28. He who knows the male (active force) and keeps to the female (the passive force or receptive element)
Becomes the ravine of the world.
Being the ravine of the world,
He will never depart from eternal virtue,
But returns to the state of infancy.
He who knows the white (glory) and yet keeps to the black (humility),
Becomes the model for the world.
Being the model for the world,
He will never deviate from eternal virtue,
But returns to the state of the Ultimate of Nonbeing.
He who knows glory but keeps to humility,
Becomes the valley of the world.
Being the valley of the world,
He will be proficient in eternal virtue,
And returns to the state of simplicity (uncarved wood).
When the uncarved wood is broken up, it is turned into concrete things (as Tao is transformed into the myriad things).
But when the sage uses it, he becomes the leading official.
Therefore the great ruler does not cut up.

31. Fine weapons are instruments of evil.
They are hated by men.
Therefore those who possess Tao turn away from them.

The good ruler when at home honors the left (symbolic of good omens).
When at war he honors the right (symbolic of evil omens).
Weapons are instruments of evil, not the instruments of a good ruler.
When he uses them unavoidably, he regards calm restraint as the best principle.
Even when he is victorious, he does not regard it as praiseworthy,
For to praise victory is to delight in the slaughter of men.
He who delights in the slaughter of men will not succeed in the empire.
In unauspicious affairs, the right is honored.
The lieutenant-general stands on the left.
The senior general stands on the right.
That is to say that the arrangement follows that of funeral ceremonies.[14]
For the slaughter of the multitude, let us weep with sorrow and grief.
For a victory, let us observe the occasion with funeral ceremonies.

33. He who knows others is wise;
He who knows himself is enlightened.
He who conquers others has physical strength.
He who conquers himself is strong.
He who is contented is rich.
He who acts with vigor has will.
He who does not lose his place (with Tao) will endure.
He who dies but does not really perish enjoys long life.

34. The Great Tao flows everywhere.
It may go left or right.
All things depend on it for life, and it does not turn away from them.
It accomplishes its task, but does not claim credit for it.
It clothes and feeds all things but does not claim to be master over them.
Always without desires, it may be called The Small.
All things come to it and it does not master them; it may be called The Great.
Therefore (the sage) never strives himself for the great, and thereby the great is achieved.

40. Reversion is the action of Tao.
Weakness is the function of Tao.
All things in the world come from being.
And being comes from nonbeing.

42. Tao produced the One.
The One produced the two
The two produced the three.
And the three produced the ten thousand things.
The ten thousand things carry the yin (negative cosmic force) and embrace the yang (positive cosmic force), and through the blending of the material force (*ch'i*)[15] they achieve harmony.
People hate to be children without parents, lonely people without spouses, or men without food to eat,
And yet kings and lords call themselves by these names.
Therefore it is often the case that things gain by losing and lose by gaining.
What others have taught, I teach also:
"Violent and fierce people do not die a natural death."[16]
I shall make this the father (basis or starting point) of my teaching.

43. The softest things in the world overcome the hardest things in the world.
Nonbeing penetrates that in which there is no space.
Through this I know the advantage of taking no action.
Few in the world can understand teaching without words and the advantage of taking no action.

51. Tao produces them (the ten thousand things).
Virtue fosters them.
Matter gives them physical form.
The circumstances and tendencies complete them.

Therefore the ten thousand things esteem Tao and honor virtue.
Tao is esteemed and virtue is honored without anyone's order.
They always come spontaneously.
Therefore Tao produces them and virtue fosters them.
They rear them and develop them.
They give them security and give them peace.
They nurture them and protect them.
(Tao) produces them but does not take possession of them.
It acts, but does not rely on its own ability.
It leads them but does not master them.
This is called profound and secret virtue.

55. He who possesses virtue in abundance
May be compared to an infant.
Poisonous insects will not sting him.
Fierce beasts will not seize him.
Birds of prey will not strike him.
His bones are weak, his sinews tender, but his grasp is firm.
He does not yet know the union of male and female,
But his organ is aroused.
This means that his essence is at its height.
He may cry all day without becoming hoarse,
This means that his (natural) harmony is perfect.
To know harmony means to be in accord with the eternal.
To be in accord with the eternal means to be enlightened.
To force the growth of life means ill omen.
For the mind to employ the vital force without restraint means violence.
After things reach their prime, they begin to grow old,
Which means being contrary to Tao.
Whatever is contrary to Tao will soon perish.

57. Govern the state with correctness.
Operate the army with surprise tactics.
Administer the empire by engaging in no activity.
How do I know that this should be so?
Through this:
The more taboos and prohibitions there are in the world,
The poorer the people will be.
The more sharp weapons the people have,
The more troubled the state will be.
The more cunning and skill man possesses,
The more vicious things will appear.
The more laws and orders are made prominent,
The more thieves and robbers there will be.
Therefore the sage says:
I take no action and the people of themselves are transformed.
I love tranquillity and the people of themselves become correct.
I engage in no activity and the people of themselves become prosperous.
I have no desires and the people of themselves become simple.[17]

59. To rule people and to serve Heaven there is nothing better than to be frugal.
Only by being frugal can one recover quickly.
To recover quickly means to accumulate virtue heavily.
By heavy accumulation of virtue one can overcome everything.
If one can overcome everything, then he will acquire a capacity the limit of which is beyond anyone's knowledge.
When his capacity is beyond anyone's knowledge, he is fit to rule a state.
He who possesses the Mother (Tao)[18] of the state will last long.
This means that the roots are deep and the stalks are firm, which is the way of long life and everlasting existence.

73. He who is brave in daring will be killed.
He who is brave in not daring will live.

Of these two, one is advantageous and one is harmful.
Who knows why Heaven dislikes what it dislikes?
Even the sage considers it a difficult question.
The Way of Heaven does not compete, and yet it skillfully achieves victory.
It does not speak, and yet it skillfully responds to things.
It comes to you without your invitation.
It is not anxious about things and yet it plans well.
Heaven's net is indeed vast.
Though its meshes are wide, it misses nothing.

B. CHUANG TZU

□ Chuang Tzu (b. 369 B.C.?), like Lao Tzu, has been canonized in the Taoist religion but his name is not as prominent to the faithful as other historical or mythical figures. Nevertheless, not only did he advance the Taoist philosophy beyond Lao Tzu very much,[19] but also his teachings promoted and developed certain tendencies basic in the Taoist religion. Lao Tzu was chiefly concerned with government and the mundane world but Chuang Tzu took us beyond worldly society, thus opening up a new spiritual and therefore religious dimension. His main interest was "nourishing life," to be sure, but the way to do so, according to him, was to cultivate the spirit (ch. 3). We should "fast with the mind" (selection 2), he said, that is, not to listen with the ear but with the mind. Only in this way can man get away from all the restrictions and regimentations (selection 6) and become "a companion of Nature" (ch. 2). Following Nature also means accepting life and death, richness and poverty, success and failure, and so on (selection 3), to be "contented and at ease when the occasion (of life or death) comes, and to live in accord with the course of Nature" (selection 4). There is no question that the fatalism, which is very strong in the Taoist religion, has owed much to Chuang Tzu.

Chuang Tzu did not teach submission to Nature, however. What he wanted was harmony with nature. To achieve this was the only way to spiritual freedom. Time and again he talked about release from bondage (ch. 3 and selection 4). This is to be achieved by one's own spiritual effort and not by divine intervention. In fact, he questioned the existence of a True Lord (selection 1). In some places he spoke of a divine person living on dew and riding on wind (ch. 1) and many other fictitious and mythological figures, thus reinforcing the cult of immortals. But the belief in spiritual beings and the subjective interest in immortality in the Taoist religion are definitely out of accord with his philosophy. His primary goal was spiritual emancipation.

The following selections are made from the *Chuang Tzu*.[20] □

"The Fundamental of Nourishing Life" (Ch. 3)

Our life is limited but knowledge is unlimited. To use the limited to pursue what is unlimited is fatal. This being the case, to presume that we know is fatal indeed. In doing good, never be attracted to fame. In doing evil, never be drawn to punishment. Follow the middle course as the standard and you will be able to protect yourself, preserve your life complete, support your parents, and live out your span of life.

A cook was cutting up an ox for Lord Wen-hui.[21] At every touch of his hand, every heave of his shoulder, every tread of his foot, every thrust of his knee, skin and bones split apart, making a distinct noise. He swung his chopper and the whole ox fell apart. All was in perfect rhythm, harmonious with the music of the *Mulberry Grove* dance and coinciding with the rhythm of the *Ching-shou*.[22]

Lord Wen-hui said, "Ah, very good indeed! Has your skill reached such height?"

The cook laid down his chopper and replied, "What I, your servant, like is Tao, which surpasses skill. When I first began to cut up oxen, all I could see was the ox itself. After three years, I no longer saw the whole ox. Now I get at it with my spirit and do not see with my eye. My sense perception stops but my spirit works voluntarily. I follow the natural pattern, strike in the big joints, lead the chopper through the big cavities, and follow things as they are. I do not even touch the convolutions of muscle, much less the large bones. A good cook changes his chopper once a year because he cuts. An ordinary cook changes his chopper once a month because he hacks. Now I have had this chopper for nineteen years. I have cut up several thousand oxen with it, and yet its edge is as sharp as it had freshly come from the grindstone. There are minute spaces between the joints, but the edge of a chopper has no thickness to speak of. When that which has no thickness is inserted into what is space, there is plenty of room, more room than is required by the swinging chopper to move about. That is why after nineteen years it is still as sharp as it had freshly come from the grindstone.

"However, whenever I come to a place where tendons and bones are interlocked, I realize that it is a difficult task. I seem to be frightened and warn myself. I keep my eyes on my work and nothing else, work slowly, and move the chopper very gently. Then the ox falls to pieces, like earth crumbling to the ground. I lift my chopper and look around, feeling at ease and satisfied. Then I wipe my chopper and store it away."

Lord Hui-wen said, "Very good indeed! I have heard the words of the cook and have learned how to nourish life."

When Kung-wen Hsien saw the Right Department Official, he was horrified and said, "What kind of man is he? Why did he lose a leg? Was it Heaven (Nature) or was it man?"

The Official said, "It was Heaven, not man. When Heaven produced me, it made me one-legged. In physical appearance, a man has a pair of legs. From this I know that my case resulted from Heaven, not from man."

A pheasant of the marshes has to go ten steps for one peck and a hundred for a drink, but if unexpectedly it is kept in a cage, although its spirit [is at leisure] like that of a king, it is no good.

When Lao Tzu died, Ch'in I went to mourn him. After giving three cries, he went out.

A pupil asked, "Aren't you our master's friend?"

He said, "Yes."

"Then you think it is all right to mourn him like this?"

He said, "Yes. At first I thought he was a [perfect] man and now I know he was not. A little while ago when I came to mourn him, there were old people weeping for him as if they were weeping for their own sons, and young people weeping for him as if they were weeping for their own mothers. In his way of association with others, there must be a way in which he did not ask people to weep for him and yet they wept for him. This is to escape from Heaven, violate one's [natural] feelings, and forget one's natural endowment. This is what the ancients called the punishment for escaping from Heaven. When your master had just come, it was his time to come. When he had just gone, it was his following [the natural course of things]. If one is to be content with the time and live with what should be followed, neither joy nor sorrow can enter him. This is what the ancients called freedom from the bondage of the Lord."

The fingers may be worn out breaking branches for firewood, but the fire is transmitted and no one knows when it will end.

Additional Selections

1. Pleasure and anger, sorrow and joy, anxiety and regret, fickleness and fear, impulsiveness and extravagance, indulgence and lewdness come to us like music from the hollows or like mushrooms from damp. Day and night they alternate within us but we don't know where they come from. Alas! These are with us morning and evening. It's here where they are produced.[23] Without them (the feelings) there would not be I. And without me who will experience them? They are right near by. But we don't know who causes them. It seems there is a True Lord who knows, but there is no indication of his existence. (Ch. 2; *Nan-hua chen-ching* [True classic of Nan-hua], 1:22b–23a)

2. Confucius said [to his pupil Yen Hui],[24] "You must fast! I shall tell you. Do you think it is easy to do anything while you have a [deliberate] mind? If you alter your [original mind], you will not be in accord with Bright Heaven."

Yen Hui said, "My family is poor, and for several months we have not drunk any wine or eaten any meat. Is that not fasting?"

"This is a fast pertaining to religious sacrifice but not the fasting of the mind."

Hui said, "May I ask what the fasting of the mind is?"

Chung-ni (Confucius) said, "Concentrate your will. Don't listen with your ears but listen with your mind. No, don't listen with your mind but listen with your spirit. Listening stops with the ears, the mind stops with the image of things, but spirit is empty and waits for things [to come]. Tao gathers only in emptiness. Emptiness is the fasting of the mind."

Yen Hui said, "Before I heard this, I was sure that I was Hui. Now that I have heard it, I feel that there was no Hui to start with. Can this be called emptiness?"

Confucius said, "That is all [that the fasting of the mind] is about." (Ch. 4; *Nan-hua chen-ching*, 2:12b–13a)

3. Duke Ai[25] asked, "What do you mean by perfect ability?" Confucius said, "Life and death, existence and nonexistence, success and failure, poverty and wealth, worthiness and unworthiness, slander and praise, hunger and thirst, and heat and cold—these are [the natural] changes of things and the operation of fate. Day and night they succeed each other in front of us, and our knowledge is not sufficient to inquire into their source. Therefore they should not be allowed to disturb our harmony or enter into the home of the spirit. One should see to it that one is at peace and happy, in harmony with things without loss of joy, so that day and night without interruption one can share the atmosphere of spring with things. This is to create continuously the seasons in one's own mind. This is called perfect ability."

"What is meant by virtue without outward form?"

"Being level is the best state of water at rest. It can serve as a model. It is well preserved within and is not agitated without. Virtue is the cultivation that brings about harmony. Virtue has no outward form, and things will not be able to keep away from it." (Ch. 5; *Nan-hua chen-ching*, 2:39b–40a)

4. Soon after Tzu-yu[26] fell ill, Tzu-ssu went to see him. "Great is the Creator!" said the sick man. "See how he (or it) has made me crumbled up like this!" His back was hunched and his backbone was protruding. His internal organs were on the top of his body. His cheeks were level with his navel. His shoulders were higher than his head. The hair on top of his head pointed up toward the sky. The yin and yang (passive and active cosmic forces) in him were out of order, but his mind was at ease as though nothing had happened. He limped and walked quickly to the well and looked at his reflection, and said, "Alas! The Creator has made me crumbled up like this!"

"Do you dislike it?" asked Tzu-ssu.

"No," said Tzu-yu, "why should I dislike it? Suppose my left arm is transformed into a cock. With it I should herald the dawn. Suppose my right arm is transformed into a sling. With it I should look for a dove to roast. Suppose my buttocks were transformed into wheels and my spirit into a horse. I should mount them. What need do I have for a chariot? When we come, it is because it was the occasion to be born. When we go, it is to follow the natural course of things. Those who are contented and at ease when the occasion comes and live in accord with the course of Nature cannot be affected by sorrow or joy. This is what the ancients called release from bondage. Those who cannot release themselves are not able to do so because they are bound by material things. That material things cannot overcome Nature, however, has been a fact from time immemorial. Why, then, should I dislike it?"

Soon afterward Tzu-lai fell ill, was gasping for breath, and was about to die. His wife and children surrounded him and wept. Tzu-li went to see him. "Go away," he said, "Don't disturb the transformation that is about to take place." Then, leaning against the door, he continued, "Great is the Creator! What will he make of you now? Where will he take you? Will he make you into a rat's liver? Will he make you into an insect's leg?"

Tzu-lai said, "Wherever a parent tells a son to go, whether east, west, south, or north, he has to obey. The yin and yang are like man's parents. If they pressed me to die and I disobeyed, I would be obstinate. What fault is theirs? For the universe gave me the body so I may be carried, my life so I may toil, my old age so I may repose, and my death so I may rest. Therefore to regard life as good is the way to regard death as good.

"Suppose a master foundryman is casting his metal and the metal leaps up and says, 'I must be made into the best sword (called *mo-yeh*)!' The master foundryman would certainly consider the metal as evil. And if simply because I possess a body by chance, I were to say, 'Nothing but a man! Nothing but a man!' the Creator will certainly regard me as evil. If I regard the universe as a great furnace and creation as a master foundryman, why should anywhere I go not be all right? When the body is formed, we sleep. With it visibly there, we wake.[27] (Ch. 6; *Nan-hua chen-ching*, 3:15a–18a)

5. Those who are perfectly correct never lose the character of their nature and life. Therefore for them the united is not like joined toes, the separated is not like extra fingers, what is long is not considered as excessive, and what is short is not considered as deficient. Therefore although the duck's legs are short, to lengthen them would be to give it sorrow, and although the neck of the crane is long, to cut it off would be to bring it misery. Therefore what is by nature long must not be shortened, and what is by nature short must not be lengthened. Thus there should be no need to avoid sorrow. I believe humanity (*jen*) and righteousness [as taught in Confucianism] are not the true characteristics of man. How many worries the man of humanity has! Furthermore, if you divide one's joined toes, he will cry. If you cut off one's extra long finger, he will scream. In the one case there is too much and in the other, too little, but what is worried about is the same. Now the men of humanity of the present age worry about the troubles of the age with their eyes anxiously looking ahead, while men of inhumanity let the characteristics of nature and life run wild to grab wealth and honor. Therefore I believe humanity and righteousness are not the true characteristics of man. Yet from the time of the Three Dynasties[28] downward—what a commotion has been raised about them!

Moreover, those who rely upon the arc, the line, compasses, and the square to make things correct injure their nature. Those who rely on the binding cord and the sticking glue to make things firm interfere with their character. And those who manipulate ceremonies and music and pretend to be human and righteous in order to satisfy the mind of man lose sight of its unchanging nature. There is an unchanging nature in things. Things in their unchanging nature are curved without the help of the arc, straight without the lines, round without compasses, and square without the measuring square, joined without glue, and bound without cord. Therefore all things exist as if following a direction but do not know how they exist. They all get along together but do not know how they have come to do so. Whether in the past or at present, [the principle] is the same and [its truth] cannot be diminished a bit. Why then should the doctrines of humanity and righteousness persist without interruption like glue or cord and move around in the sphere of morality? They are but to deceive people. (Ch. 8; *Nan-hua chen-ching*, 4:4a–7b)

6. Kuang-ch'eng Tzu[29] was lying down with his head toward the south. The Yellow Emperor[30] approached from below upon his knees, bowed twice upon the ground, and asked, "I hear that you understand what perfect Tao is. May I ask how to order one's life so it may last long?"

Kuang-ch'eng Tzu jumped up and said, "A good question indeed! Come, and I shall tell you about perfect Tao. Perfect Tao in its refinement is very mysterious and dark and silent at its height. See nothing, hear nothing, embrace spirit with tranquillity, and your physical existence will be correct by itself. Always be tranquil and always be pure. Do not toil your body and do not disturb your vital essence, and you will live forever. If your eyes see nothing, your ears hear nothing, and your mind knows nothing, your spirit will stay with your body and the body will therefore live forever. Be careful about what is within and shut off that which is without, for much knowledge means trouble. Thus I help you reach the height of great enlightenment; that is, reach the plateau of perfect yang, and enter the door of mystery; that is, reach the plateau of perfect yin. Yin and yang have their reservoirs. Guard carefully your body, and things will become strong themselves. I adhere to the One (Tao) and abide in the two (yin and yang). Therefore I have been able to cultivate my life for twelve hundred years and my body has never deteriorated."

The Yellow Emperor bowed twice and said, "Kuang-ch'eng Tzu may be said to be Heaven!"

Kuang-ch'eng Tzu said, "Come, and I shall tell you. That thing (Tao) is limitless and yet all men think it has an end. That thing is immeasurable and yet all men think it is finite. Those who have attained my Tao are august emperors above and kings below. Those who have lost my Tao [may] see the light above but become earth below. Now all things, though flourishing, are born out of earth and will return to earth. Therefore I shall get you away [from them], enter the gate of the unlimited and travel in the field of infinity. I shine like the sun and moon, and I coexist with Heaven and Earth permanently. Before me, all is nebulous; behind me, all is dark. Men may all die, but I alone exist [forever]." (Ch. 11; *Nan-hua chen-ching*, 4:34a–36a)

7. In tranquillity he (the man of Tao) becomes a sage, and in activity he becomes a king. He takes no action and is honored. He is simple and plain and none in the world can compete with him in excellence. For such a one understands this virtue of Heaven and Earth. He is called the great foundation and the great source of all being and is in harmony with Heaven (Nature, *T'ien*). One who is in accord with the world is in harmony with me. To be in harmony with men means human happiness, and to be in harmony with Heaven means the happiness of Heaven.

Chuang Tzu said, "Ah! My master, my master! He tears all things to pieces but did not make up his mind to be just. His blessing reaches the ten thousand generations but he has no partial love for anyone. He is more ancient than the highest antiquity but is not old. He covers heaven and supports the earth, and fashions the shapes of all things and yet he is not purposely skillful. This is called the happiness of Heaven. Therefore it is said that one who knows the happiness of Heaven exists like the operation of Heaven (Nature) and when he dies, he joins the universal process of the transformations of things. When tranquil, he is identical in character with yin, and when active, he is identical in movement with yang. Therefore he who knows the happiness of Heaven does not complain about Heaven and does not criticize men. Things do not impede him. and spiritual beings do not punish him, Therefore it is said that when active, he is Heaven, and when tranquil, he is Earth. Once his mind is settled, he becomes the king of the world. Spiritual beings in his kingdom will not bring calamities, and souls will not be exhausted. Once his mind is settled, all people will submit to him. By virtue of their emptiness and tranquillity, his words will extend throughout heaven and earth and penetrate all things. This is called the happiness of Heaven. By the happiness of Heaven is meant the intentions of the sage to nourish the world." (Ch. 13; *Nan-hua chen-ching*, 5:23b–24b)

NOTES

1. For a lengthy discussion of these questions, see "Lao Tzu, the Man" and "*Lao Tzu*, the Book" in Wing-tsit Chan, tr., *The Way of Lao Tzu*, pp. 35–83, in which all arguments, pro and con, have been collected and appraised.

2. For English translations, see Arthur Waley, tr., *The Way and Its Power*, and Chan, *op. cit.* among others.
3. This translation of *miao* as "subtlety" rather than "mystery" is according to Wang Pi's (226–49) commentary. For more notes on the *Lao Tzu*, see Chan, *ibid.*
4. Traditional commentators have punctuated the sentences to mean "have desires" and "have no desires." This interrupts the thought of the chapter. Some scholars have therefore punctuated the two sentences after *wu* (no) and *yu* (to be), thus making them to mean, "There is always nonbeing" and "There is always being."
5. Ch'en Ching-yüan (1025–1094), in his *Tao-te ching chu* (Commentary), punctuates the sentence after *t'ung* (the same) instead of *t'ung-ch'u* (produced from the same). This punctuation preserves the ancient rhyme of the verse.
6. The word *hsüan* means profound and mysterious.
7. Some texts substitute the character *chiao* for *hsing*, both of which mean to contrast. The former does not rhyme, whereas the latter appears in the older text.
8. Ho-shang Kung's (fl. 179–159 B.C.) interpretation in his *Lao Tzu chang-chü* (Commentary on the *Lao Tzu*): He does not expect any reward.
9. *Chi*, literally a thread, denotes tradition, discipline, principle, order, essence, etc. Generally it means the system, principle, or continuity that binds things together.
10. Instead of *wang* (kingly), one version has *chou* (comprehensive).
11. In some texts, this sentence precedes the first.
12. The word *ching* (essence) also means intelligence, spirit, life-force.
13. One text has "man" instead. However, "king" is here understood as the representative of man.
14. Most commentators agree that these last five sentences are commentaries interpolated in the text by mistake. They interrupted the preceding and following passages. They contain the terms "lieutenant-general" and "senior general" which did not appear until the Han (206 B.C.–A.D. 220) times, and this is the only chapter in Wang Pi's text that contains no comments, indicating that these five sentences were commentaries, although his commentaries in other chapters are more philosophical and more plentiful. It should be noted that the mention of Han generals is the only anachronism in the *Lao Tzu.*
15. Variously translated as matter, matter-energy, vital force, breath, etc.
16. An ancient saying.
17. Compare this idea of *laissez-faire* government with the *Analects*, 15:4.
18. According to the earliest commentary on the *Lao Tzu*, *Han Fei Tzu*, ch. 20, "mother" means Tao.
19. See Wing-tsit Chan, *A Source Book in Chinese Philosophy*, ch. 8.
20. The *Chuang Tzu* contains 33 chapters. For partial English translations, see Chan, *ibid.*, ch. 8, and Burton Watson, tr., *The Complete Works of Chuang Tzu.*
21. King Hui (r. 371–320 B.C.).
22. Name of dance music at the time of King T'ang (r. 1751–1739 B.C.?).
23. Commentators do not agree on what this means. The tendency has been to interpret this to mean that the self is the source of these psychological conditions.
24. Yen Yüan (521–490 B.C.), Confucius' most virtuous pupil. Chuang Tzu loved to put his words in the mouths of Confucius and his followers, sometimes making fun of them.
25. Ruler (r. 494–465 B.C.) of Lu.
26. This person and those following are all fictitious.
27. These two sentences are rather obscure.
28. Hsia (2183–1752 B.C.?), Shang (1752–1112 B.C.), and Chou (1111–249 B.C.).
29. Fictitious.
30. Legendary emperor of antiquity.

CHAPTER 15

Taoist Occultism and Popular Beliefs

□ Aside from objectives common to most religions, the Taoist religion especially aimed at health, restored youth, and immortality on earth. In the first several centuries since the religion was founded in A.D. 143, there were two different developments. One, the Way of the Heavenly Teacher, specialized in the use of charms, summoning deities, sacrificing and offering feasts to the dead, "calling forth wind and rain," and other magic for the chief purpose of driving away evil spirits and healing the sick. This school contributed many gods, rituals, and charms of all kinds. Its great regulator of ceremonies was K'ou Ch'ien-chih (d. 432).

The other development emphasized not only physical and mental health, but also restored youth and everlasting life on earth. It was the cult of immortals. It stressed cultivation instead of magic. In internal alchemy, the aim was to achieve correctness in nature and destiny by refining one's essence, vital force, and spirit through pills, breathing exercise, and so on, whereas in external alchemy, fire was used to turn materials like mercury into gold. Many methods were employed, including concentration of thought, breathing exercise and control, physical exercise including extending the body, bathing, diet, use of medicine, massage, and even attempts at rising in the air, changing the bodily form, and disappearance. Wei Po-yang (fl. 147–167) and Ko Hung (284–363) were the leaders.

The search for immortality on earth terminated centuries ago, but the hope for health and longevity has persisted, both of which are considered chief rewards for a good moral life.

The following five short treatises have been selected to show these tenets, the first three for their philosophical basis and methods, the last two for general teaching on ethical cultivation. □

A. THE *THREE WAYS UNIFIED AND HARMONIZED*

□ The whole premise of this fantastic Taoist movement is based on the theory of correspondence and mutual influence of Nature and man. In the Yin Yang (negative and positive cosmic forces) philosophy and more so in the Five Agents or Elements (Water, Fire, Wood, Metal, and Earth) School, everything corresponds to yin or yang or one of the Five Agents, so that there are five directions, five colors, five organs of the body, five ancient emperors, the five human relations, the five cardinal virtues, etc., corresponding to the Five Agents.[1] By the first and second centuries, the Eight Trigrams (*ch'ien* or male, heaven, NW, etc.; *k'un* or female, earth, SW, etc.; *k'an* a pit, water, N, etc.; *li* or brightness and separation, fire, S, etc.)[2] were interlocked and coordinated with the Ten Heavenly Stems (A to J) and the Twelve

Earthly Branches, which themselves correspond to twelve animals, directions, two-hour periods of the day, and so on.[3] The structure is most elaborate and intricate, but the whole network is reduced to the operation of yang and yin or Heaven and Earth and further reduced to the sun and moon. The sun is symbolized by the trigram *li* because in its figure ☲ both the upper and lower lines are undivided (yang) whereas the middle line is divided (yin), and the moon is symbolized by the trigram *k'an* ☵ because both its upper and lower lines are divided (yin) while the middle line is not (yang). In these symbols the *li* or the sun embraces the *chi* stem, which is the ground for yin and the *k'an*, or the moon embraces the *wu* stem, which is the ground for yang. In other words, yin and yang embrace each other for natural harmony

Furthermore, the brightness and dimness of the moon throughout the month are correlated with the trigrams. The *ch'ien* ☰, which has three undivided lines as its figure, receives triple light (yang), which means the fifteenth day of the month, whereas the *k'un* as ☷, which has three divided lines its figure, receives triple dimness (yin). Thus the rise and fall of yin and yang, and therefore of all forces in the universe, can be seen from the revolution of the moon. The whole attempt is to coordinate all elements in the universe and in the person so the sun and the moon will be in their proper places and correct relationship. By knowing the movements and tendencies of all these elements one can develop, cultivate, and control one's essence (more specifically, semen), vital force (more specifically, breath), and spirit (soul) to achieve immortality on earth.

The Taoists employed all possible methods for this goal, but the most important are breathing (ch. 6), the drinking of the gold fluid (ch. 11), and sex (pt. 2, ch. 10). Inhaling and exhaling are ultimately equated with being and nonbeing in the Taoist philosophy. By directing the relative factors in the universe to reinforce one's breathing, one can concentrate all the excellences in one's body. Similarly, because gold is unchangeable, imperishable, and furthermore, supposedly contains the light of sun and moon, obviously it can directly prolong life, all the more so if its use and breathing support each other (ch. 6). As the sun and moon influence each other and water and fire condition each other, so the male and female should interact in such a way as to bring together all the harmonizing forces of the universe ìn the union. In short, man should observe the phenomena in heaven and the movements on earth and bring them into accord with human affairs. Man is a microcosm. By following Nature which is in him, he can mobilize the entire universe for his blesssing, namely, everlasting life. Some Taoists claim that this technique is not only meant for personal gain; it can also be applied for general moral cultivation, ordering of society, and government.

As the name of the book *Ts'an-t'ung-chi* (three-same-harmony) indicates, the attempt is to unify and harmonize the *Book of Changes* (in which the yin yang philosophy and the mutual influence of man and Nature is expounded), internal alchemy (or the Yellow Emperor-Lao Tzu philosophy, especially the cultivation of the mind), and external alchemy (particularly the effort to transmute mercury into gold). Inasmuch as the *Book of Changes* is a Confucian classic, although taken over by the Taoists, the present book may be said to represent a synthesis of Confucianism and Taoism. Traditionally it has been attributed to a towering figure in Taoist history, Wei Po-yang, but is more likely a compilation of the late second century after the Han specialists on the *Book of Changes* interpreted the philosophy of Change in similar terms in the middle of the second century. It became the basis of the *Lung-hu* (dragon and tiger) *Scripture* of unknown date, the *Huang-t'ing* (internal and external) *Scripture* (third century), and the *Yin-fu Scripture* (see C). However, the main ideas may have come from him.[4] □

Pt. 1, Ch. 2. "Heaven and earth have fixed their positions, and the system of Change operates in them."[5] Heaven and earth are the mode of *ch'ien* (Heaven, male, strength) and *k'un* (Earth, female, weakness). Establishing the position means providing the matching positions for yin and yang. Change refers to the *k'an* (pit, symbol for the moon) and *li* (brightness and separation, symbol for the sun) trigrams. They represent the function of *ch'ien* and *k'un*. As the two function, they occupy no fixed positions but move freely among the six lines of the hexagram. They are indefinite in their coming and going and are not constant in either their going up or coming down. Hiding deeply or disappearing, they change and transform in the midst (of Change). They embrace the ten thousand things and are the regulations and principles of Tao. They control being with nonbeing and provide emptiness as the utility for utensils.[6] Therefore they infer what is to happen and (the functions of) *k'an* and *li* themselves disappear. Statements are not made carelessly and a theory does not come out from nothing. Evidences are cited (in this book) and results are shown. The spiritual transformation (of yin and yang) and the light (of sun and moon) have been weighed and measured. By inference and generalization (from the *Book of Changes*) conclusions are drawn in words and proofs are provided from basic principles. The *k'an* trigram embodies the *wu* (fifth Celestial Stem, symbol of the yin element of Earth) and represents the essence of the moon, while *li* embodies *chi* (sixth Celestial Stem, symbol of the yang element of Earth) and represents the light of the sun. The sun and moon constitute Change with their respective elements of strength and weakness. Earth [being central] brings prosperity to the four seasons and connects beginning and end like a thread. Green, red, white, and black (corresponding to the Elements of Wood, Fire, Metal, and Water) each occupy one region (East, South, West, and North, respectively). They all draw from the Central Palace (Yellow and the Earth of *wu* and *chi*, center of the vital power) the functions of *wu* (yin, moon) and *chi* (yang, sun).

Ch. 5. The Eight Trigrams are distributed among the planets. In their movements they never deviate from the center (of heaven). Their original essence is subtle and difficult to see, but evidence for them can be obtained by inferring and measuring (the movements) and signs (of the planets). As we live, we should observe their forms and symbols, precisely ascertaining their positions and expressions. Then we should set up a measuring instrument as the standard to foretell the time (of occurrence of events) and determine the fortune and misfortune (resulting from them). Orders should be issued according to the seasons, and the opportunity offered by the activation of the symbols of the different lines of a trigram should not be missed. Look above to scrutinize the signs of the Milky Way, look down to coordinate the outlines of hills and the flow of rivers, and look in between to investigate into the human mind. These Three Powers (Heaven, Earth, and man) should be brought together and examined. One's activity should follow the changes of the trigrams, and inactivity should follow the instructions in the commentaries on the trigrams (in the *Book of Changes*). Only when *ch'ien* and *k'un* function universally will the world be in order. Should we not be careful? . . .

Ch. 6. Cultivate the inner life in order to nourish oneself through peace, tranquillity, vacuity, and nothingness. Go back to the foundation and conceal the light. Look inward to illuminate the body. "Close the mouth"[7] (openings above) and firmly fortify the divine plant (outlets below). [Thus holding the breath], direct the Three Lights (of sun, moon, and stars shining in the human body) so they penetrate deeply into the self, and nourish the breath with gentle warmth. This method cannot be seen even if you look for it, but is near at hand and can easily be found. When the pattern is gradually understood in the Yellow Center (Earth, symbol of the center), its richness will permeate the flesh and the skin. If the beginning is correct, the end will be achieved, and when the root is firm, the branches will hold. All is covered by the One, but none in the world knows it.

The man of superior virtue takes no (unnatural) action.[8] He does not seek [the way of nourishing the inner life] through intellectual examination. The man of inferior virtue takes action, and his use is inexhaustible. Closing the opening above means being, and shutting the outlets below means nonbeing. Nonbeing is used to serve that which is on top, where the virtue of the spirit abides. This is the method of two cavities, in which the gold and the vital power depend on each other.

Ch. 10. When gold is thrown into hot fire, it is not deprived of the brilliancy of its color. Since the universe began, the sun and moon have never diminished their brightness. Gold has never lost its weight, and the shapes of the sun and of the moon have always remained the same. Gold (bright light) is originally produced by the moon. At dawn on the first day of the month, the moon is influenced by the sun and tallies with it [thus beginning a new cycle toward brightness and fullness]. When the gold goes back to its mother [on the last day of the moon], the moon wanes and is enveloped by the sun. The gold conceals its outline and sinks into vast emptiness. Thus the gold recovers its original nature. When the moon becomes bright again, the brilliancy (of gold) becomes prominent once more.

Ch. 11. *Tzu* (first Earthly Branch, symbol of Fire, which counts two) and *wu* (seventh Earthly Branch, symbol of Water, which counts one) together number three and *wu* (fifth Celestial Stem) *chi* (sixth Clestial Stem) (symbols of Earth) number five. Three and five are harmonious and the total of eight (Water, Fire, and Earth) is in accord with regulations and principles. (In this situation) let inhaling and exhaling embrace and nourish each other. Concentrate in thought as the union of husband and wife. Yellow Earth is the father of gold, and mercury is the son of water. Earth is the controlling spirit of (can overcome) water. When earth presses on water, water cannot rise. The Red Bird (being native of the south) is the spirit of fire. It holds on to the level and harmonizes the winner and the loser. When water becomes very strong, fire will be extinguished. They both cease to exist and return to thick earth. The three natures are thus merged. In their original nature, they have the same ancestry (earth).

If even sesame can prolong life, (how much more) can gold fluid do if fed to the mouth! It is the nature of gold that it does not deteriorate. Therefore it is the greatest treasure of all things. When a man of the occult art drinks it, his life can be prolonged. Earth, travelling in the four seasons, affirms boundaries and fixes regulations (for the other elements to operate). When the gold dust reaches the five internal organs, (the spirit will be as clear) as the fog having dispersed and (as pleasant as the sudden arrival) of wind and rain. The fragrance and vapor permeate the four limbs. One's complexion becomes pleasant and radiant. White hair turns black, and new teeth come out where the old ones used to be. Old men become rejuvenated, and old women become young girls. Such transfiguration will make one immune from the peril (of death). Such a person is called the true man.

Pt. 2, Ch. 10. The *k'an* trigram symbolizes the male and also the moon [suggesting that in yang there is also yin], while the *li* trigram symbolizes the female and also the sun [suggesting that in yin there is also yang]. The sun gives power and the moon spreads light. Both the sun and the moon undergo changes, but their bodies are neither diminished nor hurt. If yang loses its harmony (with yin) or yin interferes with the brightness (of yang), within the period from the first moon to the last moon, yin and yang will encroach upon and wear out each other. They will overshadow and destroy each other. Yang will physically decline and yin will advance to create disaster. Man and woman need each other. They hold in the mouth or spit out, each nourishing the other. The male and the female are mixed up, each seeking according to its kind. Metal changes into water. It is the nature of water to flow everywhere. Fire changes into earth (which absorbs water), and thus water cannot run wild. Therefore the male is active outside and gives while the female is tranquil inside and stores. If the male exceeds the proper measure and goes beyond the proper degree, he will be restrained by the female. *P'o* (the heavenly component of the soul) is there to restrict *hun* (the earthly component of the soul) so it will not go to excess. Not too cold or too warm, they go forward and backward at the right time. Each attains its harmony and both spit out the evidence.

B. THE *PAO-P'U TZU*

□ Ko Hung (284–363), who called himself Pao-p'u Tzu (Master Who Embraces Simplicity), was perhaps the most outstanding Taoist philosopher in the last 2000 years. He made at least three important contributions to the Taoist religion. He put the search for immortality on a theoretical basis, arguing as well as he could for the belief in immortals. He provided an extensive discussion on internal and external alchemy and offered some specific formulas. And he grafted Confucian ethics onto the Taoist religion. Although he wrote at length on external alchemy, he would not confine himself to any one method. In the following selections, those of breath, exercise, and sex are included. He denounced magic, witchcraft, prayers, and the solicitation of help from spiritual beings. On top of all the methods he recommended, he stressed the accumulation of good deeds, for which he devised a merit system. Methods are secondary; man is the key. Therefore he advocated the Confucian virtues of humanity, righteousness, wisdom, loyalty, faithfulness, and the like.

The *Pao-p'u Tzu* is a lengthy work of fifty chapters divided into Inner and Outer Chapters. Almost all subjects concerning human living are included in the discussion.[9] □

1. On Immortals

Someone asked: Is it really possible that spiritual beings and immortals do not die?

Pao-p'u Tzu answered: Even if we had the greatest power of vision, we could not see all the things that have physical form. Even if we were endowed with the sharpest sense of hearing, we could not hear all the sounds there are. Even if we had the feet of (expert runners) Ta-chang and Hsü-hai, what we had already trod upon would not be so much as what we have not. And even if we had the knowledge of (the sages and worthies) Yü, I, and Ch'i-hsieh, what we know would not be so much as what we do not know. The myriad things flourish. What is there that could not exist? Why not the immortals, whose accounts fill the historical records? Why should there not be a way to immortality?

Thereupon the questioner laughed heartily and said: Whatever has a beginning necessarily has an end, and whatever lives must eventually die . . . . I have only heard that some plants dry up and wither before frost, or fade in color during the summer; that buds do not bloom but wither and are stripped of leaves before bearing fruit. But I have never heard of anyone who enjoys a life span of ten thousand years and an everlasting existence without end. Therefore people of antiquity did not seek to become immortals in their pursuit of knowledge, and did not talk of strange phenomena in their conversations. They cast aside perverse doctrines and adhered to what is natural. They reasoned that the tortoise and the crane (symbols of immortality) belong to a different species, and looked upon life and death as morning and evening . . . .

Pao-p'u Tzu answered: . . . Life and death, beginning and end, truly are the great laws of the universe. Yet the similarities and differences of things are not uniform. Some are this way and some are that. Tens of thousands of varieties are in constant change and transformation, strange and without any definite pattern. Whether things are this way or that, and whether they are regular or irregular in their essential and subsidiary features, cannot be reduced to uniformity. There are many who say that whatever has a beginning must have an end. It is not in accord with the principle (of existence) to muddle things together and try to make them all the same. People say that things are bound to grow in the summer, and yet the shepherd's-purse and the water chestnut wilt. People say that plants are bound to wither in the winter, and yet the bamboo and the cypress flourish. People say whatever has beginning will have an end, and yet Heaven and Earth are unending. People say whatever is born will die, and yet the tortoise and the crane live forever.

When the yang (positive cosmic force) is at its height, it should be hot, and yet the summer is not without cool days. When the yin (negative cosmic force) reaches its limits, it should be cold, and yet even a severe winter is not without brief warm periods. . . .

Among creatures none surpasses man in intelligence. As creatures of such superior nature, men should be equal and uniform. And yet they differ in being virtuous or stupid, in being perverse or upright, in being fair or ugly, tall or short, pure or impure, chaste or lewd, patient or impatient, slow or quick. What they pursue or avoid in their interests and what their eyes and ears desire are as different as heaven and earth, and as incompatible as ice and coals. Why should you only wonder at the fact that immortals are different and do not die like ordinary people? . . . But people with superficial knowledge are bound by what is common. They all say that immortals are not seen in the world, and therefore they say forthwith that there cannot be immortals. . . .

Immortals have different interests and follow different paths. They consider wealth and honor as a misfortune, glory as dirt, great enjoyment as dust, and fame as morning dew. They walk on violent flames without getting burned, and step on huge dark waves as if they were walking lightly. They spread their wings and fly up to the clear heaven. They drive with the wind as their horses and the cloud as their chariots. When they look up, they reach the limit of the blue sky. When they bow down, they rest on the (highest) K'un-lun Mountain.[10] How can we walking corpses see them? . . . (Inner Chapters, 2:1a–4b)

Among people some are virtuous and others stupid, but everyone knows that his own person possesses the heavenly component (*hun*) and the earthly component (*p'o*)[11] of the soul. When they are separated and partly gone, the man becomes sick. When they are entirely gone, he dies. Therefore when they are partly gone, occultists have ways to retain and restrict them, and when they are entirely gone, there are principles in rites and institutions to recall them. These components are very close to us, and yet although we are born with them and live with them throughout life, we never hear them. Should we say that they are nonexistent simply because we have not seen or heard them? (Inner Chapters, 2:12a)

The secret of searching for everlasting life and cultivating the perfect Tao lies in one's will and not in wealth or honor. If one is not the proper person, his high position and great wealth turn out to be a tremendous handicap. Why? The way to learn to be an immortal requires one to lead a happy and simple life, to clean up and remove impure desires, to introspect, and as if to listen to oneself. . . . It requires one to be tranquil and calm, to take no (unnatural) action, and to forget one's own physical body. . . . It requires one to extend his love to wriggling worms and not to injure anything that contains any breath. . . . It requires one to abstain from meat and fish, to stop eating grains and clean his stomach, and to live motionless, as it were, without a (deliberate) mind. . . . (Inner Chapters, 2:7b–8b)

Someone asked: Is it definitely true that he who cultivates the way (to become an immortal) should first establish achievements and virtue?

Pao-p'o Tzu answered: Yes, it is true. The middle section of the *Yü-ch'ien ching* (Classic of jade handle) says, "The best is to establish achievements. The next is the removal of faults. For him who cultivates the Way, the greatest achievement is to save people from danger so they may escape from calamity, and to preserve people from sickness so that they may not die unjustly."[12] Those who seek to be immortals should regard royalty, filial piety, harmony, obedience, love, and faithfulness as their essential principles of conduct. . . . (Inner Chapters 3:7b–8a)

2. Alchemy and the Permeation of the Vital Force

Among the creatures of Nature, none is more intelligent than man. Therefore those who understand [creation] slightly can employ the myriad things, and those who get to its depth can enjoy "long life and everlasting existence."[13] As we know that the best medicine can prolong life, let us take it to obtain immortality, and as we know that the tortoise and the crane have longevity, let us imitate their ways to increase our span of life. . . . Those who have obtained Tao are able to lift themselves into the clouds and the heavens above and to dive and swim in the rivers and seas below. (Inner Chapters, 3:1a, 5a)

Pao-p'o Tzu said: I have investigated and read books on the nourishment of human nature and collected formulas for everlasting existence. Those I have perused number thousands of volumes. They all consider reconverted cinnabar (turned into mercury) and gold fluid to be the most important. Thus these two things represent the acme of the way to immortality. . . . The transformations of the two substances are the more wonderful the more they are heated. Yellow gold does not disintegrate even after having been smelted a hundred times in fire, and does not rot even if buried in the ground until the end of the world. If these two medicines are eaten, they will refine our bodies and therefore enable us neither to grow old nor to die. This is of course seeking assistance from external substances to strengthen ourselves. It is like feeding fat to the lamp so it will not die out. If we smear copper on our feet, it will not deteriorate even if it remains in water. This is to borrow the strength of the copper to protect our flesh. Gold fluid and reconverted cinnabar, however, upon entering our body, permeate our whole system of blood and energy and are not like copper which helps only on the outside. (Inner Chapters, 4:1a–3a)

Pao-p'o Tzu said: Although eating medicine is a fundamental of everlasting life, if one can direct one's vital force to permeate the body (through breathing, and so on) also, its benefit will be very quickly achieved. If one is unable to obtain the medicine but can achieve only the permeation of the vital force and completely follow its principle, one can also live for several hundred years. But one should also know the technique of sexual intercourse. If one does not know the technique of yin (female) and yang (male), one will be tired and lose energy again and again, but if one achieves (the permeation of the vital force), it will not be difficult to get a great deal of benefit. Man lives in the midst of the vital force and the vital force is in man at the same time. From heaven and earth to the myriad things, none can live without the need of the vital force. One who is skillful in achieving the permeation of the vital force can nourish his life internally and drive away evil externally. But ordinary people use it daily without realizing it. The states of Wu and Yüeh have ways to stop curses because there are people who know how to exert a tremendous amount of vital force. Whoever knows how to achieve the permeation of the vital force can go to the midst of a plague and sleep with a sick person without getting contaminated. He can also go with a group of tens of peoples and free them from fear. All these are cases where the permeation of the vital force can avert natural calamities. Perhaps there are demons and human-headed animal spirits who invade people's houses, throw rocks at people, or set houses on fire. They may reveal their shapes and walk to and fro or perhaps one can only hear their voices and conversations. One who is skillful in stopping them can do so with the permeation of the vital force and they will all disappear immediately. These are cases where the permeation of the vital force can stop spiritual beings. . . . (Inner Chapters, 5:6a–b)

3. The Merit System

To those who do great evil, the Arbiter of Human Destiny will take away three hundred days from their life. To those who do small evil, he will take away three days.[14] Because the offense may be heavy or light, the period to be taken away varies. When a man is given his life and receives a life span, these are in definite number of years. If the number is great, it will be difficult to exhaust his life through the deductions and he will die late. But if his endowment is small and his offenses are many, the deductions will quickly accumulate and he will die early.

(*Pao-p'u Tzu*) *also said:* Those who aspire to be terrestrial immortals should accomplish three hundred good deeds and those who aspire to be celestial immortals should accomplish 1,200. If the 1,999th good deed is followed by an evil one, they will lose all their accumulation and he will have to start all over. It does not matter whether the good deeds are great or the evil deed is small. Even if they do no evil but talk about their good deeds and demand for their charities, they will nullify the goodness of those deeds although the other good deeds are not affected.

(Pao-p'u Tzu) further said: If good deeds are not sufficiently accumulated, taking the elixir of immortality will be of no help. (Inner Chapters, 3:10a–b)

4. Moral Cultivation

It is hoped that those who nourish life will learn extensively and comprehend the essential, gather whatever there is to see and choose the best. It is not sufficient to depend on cultivating only one thing. It is also dangerous for people who love life to rely on their own specialty. Those who know the techniques of the *Classic of the Mysterious Lady* and the *Classic of the Plain Lady* (books on sexual regimen no longer extant) will say that only the "art of chamber" will lead to salvation. Those who understand the method of breathing exercises will say that only the permeation of the vital force can prolong life. Those who know the method of stretching and bending will say that only physical exercise can delay old age. And those who know the formulas of herbs will say that only medicine will make life eternal. They fail in their pursuit of Tao because they are so one-sided and bigoted. People of superficial knowledge think they have enough when they happen to know of only one way and do not realize that the true seeker will search unceasingly even after he has acquired some good formulas. (Inner Chapters, 6:4a)

Being is produced by nonbeing, and physical form needs spirit to get established. Being is the shelter of nonbeing and physical form is the house for spirit. They may be compared to a dam. When the dam collapses, the water will no longer stay. Or compare them to the candle. When the candle is destroyed, the fire will not remain. When the body is worn out, the spirit will dissipate, and when the breath is exhausted, one's life comes to an end. When the root is finished and the branches become too many, the green color will disappear from the tree. When one's vital force gets worn out and desires dominate, one's spirit and intelligence will leave him. What is gone will never return, and what has decayed will never live again. This is something about which scholars who understand Tao really feel sad. Is there no reason why [the far-sighted] take jade (symbol of official position) lightly and value obscurity highly? Therefore those who cultivate their nature in mountain forests and those who leave popular society behind to accomplish their purpose equate high honor with a tumor and regard the myriad things as light (unimportant) as the cicada's wings. Do they carelessly brag and despise world affairs? The truth is that they see those things clearly and therefore reject them as if they have already forgotten them. Therefore they stay in faraway places and retreat to quiet spots. They conceal their brilliance and cover up their elegance. They close their eyes that wish to see and leave behind the colors that hurt their sight. They shut their ears that desire for sound and stay far away from the sounds that disturb their hearing. They "clean and purify their profound insight," "keep to the female" (the passive force or receptive element), "embrace the One," "concentrate their vital force and achieve the highest degree of weakness,"[15] and guard them with tranquillity and simplicity. They avoid the evils of joy or sorrow and leave alone the glory and humiliation of loss and gain. They cut off the extreme poison of high living and shut their mouths when they are at a turning point. They listen as if listening to themselves and consequently they listen penetratingly. They introspect and consequently they can see even without any omen. They nourish their virtue with the silent equalizer (Tao). They remove temptations in dealing with things. They cast aside superficial matters and control things with contentment and indifference. They act by taking no (unnatural) action in order to preserve the Principle of Nature (Heaven) complete. (Inner Chapters, 5:1b–2b)

Those who seek immortality must set their minds to the accumulation of good deeds and the accomplishment of merits. Their hearts must be kind to all things. They must treat others as they treat themselves, and extend their humanity (*jen*) even to insects. They must rejoice in the fortune of others and pity their suffering, give alms to the destitute, and save the poor. Their hands must never injure life, and their mouths must never encourage evil. They must consider the success and failure of others as their own. They must not regard themselves highly, nor praise themselves. They must not envy those superior to them, and must not flatter dangerous and evil-minded people. In this way they become virtuous and blessed by Heaven. They must be successful in whatever they do, and may hope to become immortals.[16] (Inner Chapters, 6:6a)

Pao-p'u Tzu said: One who compares with heaven in covering things and the earth in sustaining things, who displays the brilliance of sun and moon to bring things to light, who possesses elegant ornament and perfect substance, and who clarifies his peculiar insight to the point of entering into spirit is a sage. One who is endowed with a high degree of purity, who raises a high standard and who looks down upon the worldly, who keeps his intelligent mind open and empty as if he is stupid, who never repeats a mistake to flatter people of impurity is a worthy. One who lives in quiet solitude in which he does not take any (unnatural) action and walks on the long and straight but holds to the level road is a man of Tao. He who fulfills his duty in service to the living and sacrifices to the dead, and preserves his body complete in order to bring glory to his parents is a man of filial piety. He who shows compassion to all living creatures, and in dealing with others treats them as he treats himself is a man of humanity. He who is correct in his life and destiny in sacrificing himself for his country and maintains his integrity under dangerous conditions is a man of loyalty. He who sees subtle principles that are difficult to discern and predicts how blessings and calamities will interact in the future is a man of enlightenment. One who weighs order and disorder so as to expand or contract, and is careful in advancing or withdrawing is a man of wisdom. He who follows the penetrating or the obstructed with the same feeling and lets his nature and life take their own course without impeding them is a man of understanding. One who does not bend only one cubit in order to make eight cubits straight[17] and who does not lower himself to shame in order to preserve his life improperly is a man of elegance. One who controls his appearance and expressions before he moves or stops, and is always clear and thorough so that there will be no regret is a man of seriousness. One who embodies the purity and simplicity of ice and dew and is not contaminated by power or wealth is a man of purity. One who is serious about beginning and end at all times and has no doubt even when he is approaching danger or death is a man of righteousness. He who keeps every word of his no matter how far back it goes and does not change even at old age is a man of truthfulness .... (Outer Chapters, 22:1a–b)

5. Superstition

Common folks all say that (in case of illness) they are caused by supernatural beings. They deceive and make each other more fanatic as time goes on. They are, on the one hand, not able to practice the techniques that cure their illness, and on the other, not able to get away from their strong superstition. They do not seek salvation through medicine but devote themselves solely to the foolishness of offering sacrifices. They pray endlessly and are never tired of divination. Mean people, the witches and priests, falsely talk about calamities and curses from spiritual beings, illness, crises, and all kinds of things. When people hear these, they forthwith do more (of the sacrificing, and so on). They spend a tremendous amount of money. Rich people exhaust their savings and poor folks borrow money at high interest rates. Houses and land are closed up with nothing left, and chests and bureaus are turned upside down and emptied. If by chance (the diviner's) prediction proves to be wrong, they say that is the blessing of gods, but if death occurs, people say that it is the punishment from spiritual beings. If they are lucky and live in contradiction to (what has been prophesied), they will become bankrupt and finally die of cold and starvation. Others become bandits or thieves. Thus they lose their lives at the tip of sharp (execution) knives or throw themselves into the suffering of other shameful punishments. All of this is because of superstition. (Inner Chapters, 9:3b–4a)

C. THE *SECRET ACCORD SCRIPTURE*

□ The two key words in this most interesting treatise are *activation* (*chi*) and *stealing*. The word *chi* means the moment or critical point where an incipient force is about to act or an action is about to spring. At this point one should seize the initiative and activate the situation or the event. In this sense one "steals" the secret of Nature. It seems that this approach is diametrically opposed to the basic Taoist teaching of nonaction, but nonaction really means taking no unnatural action. The technique here advocated is not unnatural but is in accordance with the way of Nature. One is taught to wait quietly for the proper time, to act and to follow the course of Nature. This is why there is a silent or secret accord. The appeal to militarists, strategists, and Ch'an (Zen) Buddhists is clear. In fact, the term *yin-fu* (secret accord) is also a military term.

The treatise, called *Yin-chih wen* in Chinese, is attributed to the mythical Yellow Emperor of great antiquity. In the bibliographical section of the *History of the Sui Dynasty* (581–618), there are two works bearing the title *yin-fu*. Li Ch'üan (fl. 1750) wrote a commentary on this treatise. It is generally believed that he forged the text. Because his understanding of the text is very poor, the probability is that the text was written sometime between him and the Sui dynasty. □

If one observes the Way of Heaven (*T'ien*, Nature) and gets hold of its operations, that is all that needs to be done. Heaven has the Five Robbers (fate, things, the proper time, one's merit, and spirit).[18] One who understands them will be prosperous. If one (starts with) the Five Robbers in his mind and puts them in operation in Heaven (Nature), the whole universe will be in his hands and the transformation of all things will originate from his person. The nature of Heaven is (also) that of man, and the nature of man is an activating power. When the way of Heaven is established, the (way of) man is thereby determined. If Heaven activates its power to destroy, dragons and snakes will rise from the ground. When man activates his power to destroy, heaven and earth will turn upside down. When Heaven and man become identical in character, the foundation of all transformations will be firmly established.

By nature man may be clever or stupid, but he can conceal these qualities [as the occasion may require]. The evil of the nine openings of the human body lies in the Three Essentials,[19] but they may be made active or inactive. When fire is produced from wood, the evil, once started, will surely end in the overcoming of the wood by fire. When treachery arises in the state, the tendency, once it becomes active, will surely end in the destruction of the state. One who knows how to cultivate (his nature) is called a sage.

It is the principle of Tao for Heaven to produce and also to destroy. Heaven and Earth are the thieves of the myriad things [stealing their activating power without their knowing it]. The myriad things are the thieves of man, and man is the thief of the myriad things. When the three thieves operate properly, all the Three Powers (Heaven, Earth, and man) will be at peace. Therefore it is said that when one eats at the proper time, his whole body will be in order, and that if the proper activating power is set in motion, all transformations will be at peace. Men know that spiritual beings can perform mysterious acts of the spirit but do not know how (man), who is not a spiritual being, can also perform mysterious acts of the spirit.

The sun and moon have their definite courses. The great and the small each have their definite (function). [When these are followed,] the service of the sage arises, and the spiritual intelligence reveals itself. None under heaven sees the stealing of the activation power, and none knows it. When the superior man gets it, he is willing to remain obscure. When the inferior man gets it, he will be [reckless to the point of] taking his life lightly.

The deaf are skillful in hearing and the blind in seeing. If one can derive all the benefits from one source, one can command a multitude ten times as big as otherwise, and if one can repeat [the skillful hearing and seeing] three times day and night, one can command a multitude ten thousand times as big.

(The activities of the) mind are produced from (its contact with) things and cease to exist with (the termination of contact with) things. The activating power is in the eyes. Heaven has no (special feeling of) kindness and thereby its great kindness is produced. At a sudden clap of thunder or the sweeping of a violent wind, (all things) come to life.

In perfect joy, one's nature is in the state of happiness. In perfect tranquillity, it is in the state of purity. Even the greatest impartiality of Heaven, when applied, will be absolutely impartial. The key to the control (of things) lies in the vital power. Life is the root of death and death is the root of life. Kindness comes from harm and harm from kindness. The stupid man becomes a sage by observing the patterns of heaven and earth, but I become a wise man by observing the patterns of things and their timely occurrence. People become stupid through anxious thinking, but I become a sage through having no anxious thoughts. Other people become sages through expecting to be so, but I become a sage through not expecting to be. Therefore is is said that if one sinks into water or plunges into fire, one is seeking extinction himself.

The way of Nature is tranquil, and hence Heaven, Earth, and all things flourish. The way of Heaven and Earth is gradual, and hence yin and yang excel. As yin and yang alternate and push each other forward, all changes and transformations are in accord. Therefore the sage knows that the way of Nature cannot be violated, and accordingly he controls it. The way of perfect tranquillity cannot be understood through numerical calculation. Therefore there is the wonderful instrument (theft of the activating power to control Nature) which produces all the phenomena of heaven, the Eight Trigrams, the sexagenary cycles, the activating power of heavenly spiritual beings, the secrets of earthly spiritual beings, and the method by which yin and yang excel over each other—an instrument clearly surpassing all possible phenomena.[20]

D. THE *TREATISE OF THE MOST EXALTED ONE ON INFLUENCE AND RESPONSE*

□ This and the following short treatises are among the most popular religious tracts in China. It is an act of devotion to distribute them, and millions and millions of copies have found their way to rural homes, small shops, and country schools. They have been fully as influential on the masses as any other book. They contain Confucian and Taoist ethical teachings, expressed, however, in the Taoist context. The main theme is that the good and evil doers bring their own rewards and punishments. To make things vivid and definite for the common people, however, there is in this treatise a dramatization involving gods, a point system, and bookkeeping; and to give divine authority to the teachings, there is in the following treatise the attribution of authorship to a god. Scholars have looked down upon these efforts as vulgarization, but they have generally approved the practical moral teachings that have done tremendous good.

No one knows when the tract, called *T'ai-shang kan-ying p'ien* in Chinese, was written. Inasmuch as it is mentioned in the biographical section of the *History of the Sung Dynasty* (960–1279), it cannot be later than the thirteenth century. A considerable portion comes from the *Pao-p'u tzu*[21] by Ko Hung (284–363), from which it has probably been derived. The Most Exalted One has been variously identified with "emperor," "the man of highest virtue," and the legendary emperors of great antiquity. In any case, the tract represents to a high degree what the Taoist religion means, ultimately speaking, to the masses. □

The Most Exalted One said, "Calamities and blessings do not come through any (fixed) gate; it is man himself that invites them."[22] The reward of good and evil is like the shadow accompanying the body. Accordingly there are in heaven and earth spiritual beings who record a man's evil deeds and, depending upon the lightness or gravity of his transgressions, reduce his term of life by units of three days.[23] As units are taken away, his health becomes poor, and his spirit becomes wasted. He will often meet with sorrow and misery, and all other men will hate him. Punishments and calamities will pursue him; good luck and joy will shun him; evil stars will harm him. When the allotted units are exhausted, he will die.

Furthermore, there are the Three Ministers of the Northern Constellation residing above man's head. They register his crimes and sins and take away from his term of life periods of three hundred or three days. There are also the Three Worm-Spirits residing inside man's body. Whenever the fifty-seventh day (of the sixty-day cycle, the day characterized by severity and change) comes around, they ascend to the court of Heaven and report man's sins and transgressions. On the last day of the month, the Kitchen God does the same. When a man's transgressions are great, three hundred days are taken away from his term of life. When they are small, three days are taken away. Great and small transgressions number in the hundreds. Those who seek everlasting life on earth must first of all avoid them.

Go forward if your deed follows the Way (Tao) but withdraw it if violates it. Do not tread evil paths. Do nothing shameful even in the recesses of your own house. Accumulate virtue and amass merits. Have a compassionate heart toward all creatures. Be loyal to your sovereign, filial to your parents, friendly to your younger brothers, and brotherly to your older brothers. Rectify yourself and so transform others. Be compassionate to orphans and sympathetic to widows. Respect the old and cherish the young. Even insects, grass, and trees you must not hurt. You should grieve at the misfortune of others and rejoice in their good fortune. Assist those in need and save those in danger. Regard others' gain as your own gain and their loss as your own loss. Do not publicize their shortcomings nor boast of your own superiorities. Stop evil and promote good. Yield much but take little. Accept humiliation without complaint and favor with a sense of apprehension. Bestow kindness and seek no recompense. Give without regret.

He who is good is respected by all men. The way of Heaven helps him, happiness and wealth follow him, all evil things shun him, and spiritual beings protect him. Whatever he does will succeed. He may even hope to become a god or an immortal.

He who seeks to become an immortal of heaven should perform 1,200 good deeds. He who seeks to become an immortal of earth should perform 300.

But if he acts contrary to righteousness or behaves in violation of moral principles; if he regards evil as ability; if he cruelly destroys others; if he secretly injures good people or secretly insults his ruler or parents; if he treats his seniors with contempt or rebels against their superiors; if he deceives the uninformed or slanders his fellow-students; if he makes false accusations, cheats, or is a hypocrite; if he attacks or exposes the faults of his relatives; if he is obstinate and inhumane; if he is vicious and self-willed; if he confuses right with wrong; if his inclinations or disinclinations are contrary to what is proper; if he oppresses his subordinates and appropriates their merits or flatters his superiors hoping for favor; if he is not grateful for kindness received or remembers forever any harm done him; if he despises the people of great virtue or disturbs the policies and measures of the state; if he rewards the unrighteous and punishes the innocent; if he murders others for their property or overthrows others for their position; if he executes those who have surrendered or kills those who have submitted; if he discredits the upright or is against the worthy; if he maltreats orphans or oppresses widows; if he disregards the law or accepts bribes; if he regards the straight as crooked or vice versa; if he reports a light (offense) as heavy or adds his anger when witnessing an execution; if he knows his mistake but does not correct it or knows what is good but does not do it; if he involves others in his own guilt; if he obstructs the practice of the occult scientists; if he backbites sages and worthies or violates moral principles; if he shoots birds in flight or chases after running animals; if he exposes the hibernating or surprises the nestlings; if he closes up entrance holes or upsets nests; if he injures the pregnant or breaks the egg; if he hopes for others to fail or disparages others' success; if he places others in danger for his own safety or impoverishes others for his own gain; if he exchanges the poor for the good or sacrifices public interests for his selfish ends; if he steals the skill of others or conceals their good deeds; if he portrays the ugly affairs of others or gossips about others' private affairs; if he wastes money or causes division in others' families; if he takes away what others love or helps others to do wrong; if he aggressively gets his own way and shows power or seeks success by humiliating others; if he destroys others' crops or wrecks their marriages; if he has improperly become rich and is proud or tries to escape punishment without shame; if he claims favor and disclaims mistakes, or maliciously brings evil upon others or puts the blame on them; if he sells and buys vainglory or harbors and keeps a dangerous heart; if he destroys that in which others excel or defends his own shortcomings; if he takes advantage of power to intimidate others or lets his cruelty run wild and kills and hurts others; if for no reason he cuts plants or kills animals and cooks their meat in violation of the rules of propriety; if he scatters and abandons the five grains or troubles and disturbs the multitude; if he breaks into others' houses to take away property and treasures or breaches dikes and sets fire to destroy people's homes; if he upsets others' plans to prevent their success or spoils others' utensils to diminish their efficiency; if seeing others enjoying glory and honor, he wishes them exiled, or, seeing others wealthy, wishes them bankrupt; if he sees beauty and thinks of seduction or is in debt and wishes his debtor dead; if when he is refused his requests he forthwith begins to curse and hates or when he sees others at a disadvantage he forthwith says that that is their fault; if he laughs at others when he sees their deformities or suppresses them when he sees their abilities worthy of praise; if he uses charms to oppress others or employs drugs to kill trees; if he gets angry at his teachers or contradicts his seniors; if he makes forcible demands and seizures or loves to encroach on others and grab things; if he kidnaps or plunders to get rich or seeks promotion through tricks and treachery; if he is unfair in reward and punishment or goes to excess in comforts and enjoyments; if he is harsh toward his subordinates or threatens others; if he complains about Heaven and blames others or shouts at the wind and rails at the rain; if he forms chance associations and then gets into dispute and litigation or foolishly joins factious associations; if he relies on the words of his wife or concubine or violates the instructions of his parents; if he forgets the old when he gets the new or does not mean what he says; if he is greedy for wealth; if he cheats or deceives his superiors; if he invents evil stories to slander faultless people; if he defames others and claims to be just or curses spiritual beings and claims to be upright; if he casts aside those who obey but imitates those who rebel or turns his back to his relatives and tends towards people of distant relations; if he points to heaven and earth (to swear) in order to prove his mean thoughts or induce spiritual beings to witness his improper deeds; if he regrets his charity or does not return what he had borrowed; if he seeks more than his share of plots and plans beyond his means; if his lusty desires exceed all measure; if he has a poisonous heart behind his compassionate face; if he feeds others with filthy food or deceives others with heterodoxical doctrines; if he shortens the foot rule, narrows the measure, lightens the scale, or reduces the peck; if he mixes the simulated with the genuine or takes illegitimate profit; if he forces good people to be mean and lowly or through deception controls the simple-minded; if he is insatiably covetous and greedy or takes oaths and swears to seek vindication; if he loves liquor and becomes rude and disorderly or is angry and quarrelsome with his relatives; if as a husband he is not faithful and good, or as a wife she is not gentle and obedient; if the husband is not in harmony with his wife; if the wife is not respectful to her husband; if he is always fond of boasting and bragging; if she constantly acts out her jealousy and envy; if he behaves immorally toward his wife and children; if she behaves improperly toward her parents-in-law; if he treats with slight and disrespect the spirits of his ancestors and disobeys the commands of his superiors; if he occupies himself with what is not beneficial to others or cherishes a disloyal heart; if he curses himself and others or is partial in his love and hatred; if he steps over the well or hearth (which should be taken seriously because water and fire are indispensable to life) or leaps over food (served on the floor) or a person (lying on a floor mat); if he kills babies or brings about abortion or does many actions of secret depravity; if he sings or dances on the last day of the month or year (when the end should be sent off with sorrow) or bawls out or gets angry on the first day of the year or the month (when the beginning should be welcomed with joy); if he weeps, spits, or urinates when facing north (the direction of the emperor) or chants and laughs facing the hearth (which should be treated solemnly because the family depends on it for food); and, moreover, if he lights incense with hearth fire (a sign of disrespect) or uses dirty fuel to cook food; if he shows his naked body when rising at night or executes punishment on the eight festivals of the year; if he spits at a shooting star or points at a rainbow; if he suddenly points to the Three Luminaries[24] or gazes long at the sun and moon; if in the spring months (when things are growing) he burns the thickets in hunting or angrily reviles others when he faces north; if without reason he kills tortoises or snakes (which are honored along with the Northern Constellation), if he commits these or similar crimes, the Arbiter of Human Destiny will, according to their lightness or gravity, take away from the culprit's term of life periods of three hundred or three days. When these units are exhausted, he will die. If at death there remains guilt unpunished, the evil luck will be transferred to his posterity.

Moreover, if one wrongly seizes another's property, his wife, children, and other members of his family are to be held responsible, the expiation to be proportionate up to punishment by death. If they do not die, there will be disasters from water, fire, thieves, loss of property, illness, quarrels, and the like to compensate for the wrong seizure.

Further, he who kills men unjustly puts a weapon into the hands of others who will turn on him and kill him. He who seizes property unrighteously is like one who relieves hunger with spoiled food or overcomes thirst with poisoned wine. He will be full for the time being, but death will inevitably follow.

E. THE *SILENT WAY OF RECOMPENSE*[25]

□ Like the preceding treatise, this one sets forth Confucian-Taoist moral teachings dealing with all aspects of life, but it includes Buddhist precepts also and thus reflects the general tendency in Chinese history to harmonize the three systems. Because of the Buddhist influence, compassion to both men and animals is more strongly emphasized. There is no intervention by gods, but the treatise has been attributed to the Taoist deity Wen-ch'ang (glory of literature), who ranks high enough in the Taoist hierarchy to be called the Lord Sovereign. He is supposed to have lived in beginning of the Chou dynasty (1111–249 B.C.) and after seventy-three incarnations appeared as Chang Ya in the early years of the fourth century. All of this is, of course, a myth. The treatise is certainly a much later product, probably later than the preceding tract which it greatly resembles. □

The Lord says: For seventeen generations I have been incarnated as a high official, and I have never oppressed the people or my subordinates. I have saved people from misfortune, helped people in need, shown pity to orphans, and forgiven people's mistakes. I have extensively practiced the Silent Way of Recompense and have penetrated Heaven above. If you can set your minds on things as I have set mine, Heaven will surely bestow blessings upon you. Therefore, I pronounce these instructions to mankind saying:

Whoever wants to expand his field of happiness, let him rely on his moral nature.

Do good work at all times, and practice in secret meritorious deeds of all kinds.

Benefit living creatures and human beings. Cultivate goodness and happiness.

Be honest and straight, and, on behalf of Heaven, promote moral reform.

Be compassionate and merciful and, for the sake of the country, save the people.

Be loyal to your ruler and filial to your parents.

Be respectful towards elders and truthful to friends.

Obey the purity (of Taoism) and worship the Northern Constellation; or revere the scriptures and recite the holy name of the Buddha.

Repay the four kindnesses (done to us by Heaven, earth, the sovereign, and parents). Extensively practice the three religions.

Help people in distress as you would help a fish in a dried-up rut. Free people from danger as you would free a sparrow from a fine net.

Be compassionate to orphans and kind to widows. Respect the ages and have pity on the poor.

Collect food and clothing and relieve those who are hungry and cold along the road. Give away coffins lest the dead of the poor be exposed.

If your family is well provided for, extend a helping hand to your relatives. If the harvest fails, relieve and help your neighbors and friends.

Let measures and scales be accurate, and do not give less in selling or take more in buying. Treat your servants with generosity and consideration; why should you be severe in condemnation and harsh in your demands?

Write and publish holy scriptures and tracts. Build and repair temples and shrines.

Distribute medicine to alleviate the suffering of the sick. Offer tea and water to relieve the distress of the thirsty.

Buy captive creatures and set them free, or hold fast to vegetarianism and abstain from taking life.

Whenever taking a step, always watch for ants and insects. Prohibit the building of fires outside (lest insects be killed) and do not set mountain woods or forests ablaze.

Light lanterns at night to illuminate where people walk. Build river boats to ferry people across.

Do not go into the mountain to catch birds in nests, nor to the water to poison fish and shrimps.

Do not butcher the ox that plows the field. Do not throw away paper with writing on it.

Do not scheme for others' property. Do not envy others' skill or ability.

Do not violate people's wives or daughters. Do not stir up litigation among others.

Do not injure others' reputation or interest. Do not destroy people's marriages.

Do not, on account of personal enmity, create disharmony between brothers. Do not, because of a small profit, cause father and son to quarrel.

Do not misuse your power to disgrace the good and the law-abiding. Do not presume upon your wealth or oppress the poor and needy.

Be close to and friendly with the good, this will improve your moral character in body and mind. Keep at a distance from the wicked; this will prevent imminent danger.

Always conceal people's vices but proclaim their virtue. Do not say "yes" with your mouth and "no" in your heart.

Cut brambles and thorns that obstruct the road. Remove bricks and stones that lie in the path.

Put in good condition roads that have

been rough for several hundred years. Build bridges over which thousands and tens of thousands of people may travel.

Leave behind your moral instructions to correct people's faults. Donate money to bring to completion the good deeds of others.

Follow the principle of Heaven in your work. Obey the dictates of the human heart in your words.

(Admire the ancient sages so much that you) see them while eating soup or looking at the wall. (Be so clear in conscience that) when you sleep alone, you are not ashamed before your bedding, and when you walk alone, you are not ashamed before your own shadow.

Refrain from doing any evil, but earnestly do all good deeds.

Then there will never be any influence or evil stars upon you, but you will always be protected by good and auspicious spirits.

Immediate rewards will come to your own person, and later rewards will reach your posterity.

A hundred blessings will come as if drawn by horses, and a thousand fortunes will gather about you like clouds.

Do not all these things come through the Silent Way of Recompense?

NOTES

1. Some of the correspondences are

Water	*Fire*	*Wood*	*Metal*	*Earth*
rain	air	wind	thunder	cloud
North	South	East	West	Center
black	red	green	white	yellow
six	seven	eight	nine	five
so	*fa*	*mi*	*re*	*do*
salty	bitter	sour	acrid	sweet
pig	fowl	sheep	dog	ox
millet	beans	wheat	hemp	panicled millet
kidney	lungs	spleen	liver	heart
hearing	vision	smell	taste	touch
Mercury	Mars	Jupiter	Venus	Saturn
wisdom	propriety	humanity	righteousness	faithfulness

2. The Eight Trigrams are

☰	☷	☳	☴	☵	☲	☶	☱
ch'ien	*k'un*	*chen*	*sun*	*k'an*	*li*	*ken*	*tui*
"male"	"female"	"arouse"	"yielding"	"pit"	"brightness, separation"	"stop"	"pleasure"
heaven	earth	thunder	wind	water	fire	mountain	collection of water
NW	SW	E	SE	N	S	NE	W
horse	ox	dragon	fowl	pig	pheasant	dog	sheep
head	belly	feet	thighs	ears	eyes	hands	mouth

3. The Ten Heavenly Stems are *chia*, *i*, *ping*, *ting*, *wu*, *chi*, *keng*, *hsin*, *jen*, *kuei*, corresponding to A to J or 1 to 10. The Twelve Earthly Branches are

tzu	*ch'ou*	*yin*	*mao*	*ch'en*	*ssu*	*wu*	*wei*	*shen*	*yu*	*hsü*	*hai*
rat	ox	tiger	hare	dragon	snake	horse	sheep	monkey	cock	dog	boar
N	NNE	ENE	E	ESE	SSE	S	SSW	WSW	W	WNW	NNW
11 pm to 1 am	1–3	3–5	5–7	7–9	9–11	11 am to 1 pm	1–3	3–5	5–7	7–9	9–11

4. The *Ts'an-t'ung-chi* has 35 chapters. For an English translation, see "An Ancient Chinese Treatise on Alchemy Entitled *Ts'an T'ung Ch'i*," tr. by L. C. Wu, with an introduction by T L. Davis, *Isis*, 18 (Oct. 1932), 231–89.

5. *Book of Changes*, "Appended Remarks," pt. 1, ch. 7.
6. Paraphrasing the *Lao Tzu*, ch. 1.
7. *Ibid.*, ch. 52.
8 *Ibid.*, ch. 38
9. For a translation of the *Pao-p'u Tzu*, see James R. Ware, tr., *Alchemy, Medicine, and Religion in the China of A.D. 320, the Nei P'ien of Ko Hung* (*Pao-p'u tzu*). For translations of selected chapters or passages, see Teeney L. Davis and Ch'en Kuo-fu, tr., "The Inner Chapters of *Pao-p'u-tzu*," *Procedings of the American Academy of Arts and Sciences*, 74 (1941), 297–325, and Eugene Feifel, tr., "*Pao-p'u-tzu* Nei-p'ien," *Monumenta Serica*, 6 (1941), 113–213; 9 (1944), 1–33; and 11 (1946), 1–32.
10. The K'un-lun Mountain in Tibet, the highest mountain to the Chinese.
11. For the *hun* and *p'o*, see ch. 10, n. 1.
12. This book is lost.
13. *Lao Tzu*, ch. 59.
14. Another interpretation: 12 years and 100 days, respectively. For the Arbiter of Human Destiny, see ch. 15, D.
15. *Lao Tzu*, chs. 10 and 28.
16. Here follows a long list of prohibitions on evil deeds that is substantially the same as that in ch. 15, D.
17. Quoting the *Book of Mencius*, 3B:1. The meaning is that one expects much by doing little.
18. Other interpretations: The five tastes; the Five Elements or Agents of Water, Fire, Wood, Metal, and Earth, etc.
19. Variously understood as the ears, the eyes, and the mouth; the mind, spirit, and the will; or activating power, nature, and feelings.
20. This paragraph, like some preceding it, is very obscure.
21. See n. 16.
22. *Tso chuan* (Tso's commentary on the *Spring and Autumn Annals*), Duke Hsiang, 23rd year.
23. There are different theories concerning the length of the units of time used here and in the following.
24. The sun, moon, and stars.
25. *Yin-chih wen* in Chinese.

CHAPTER 16

Chinese Response to Early Buddhist Teachings

A. THE *SCRIPTURE IN FORTY-TWO CHAPTERS*

□ Buddhism was known in China at least as early as 2 B.C. when a student at the national university received instructions from a foreign envoy on Buddhist scriptures. At first it was a handmaid to the Yellow Emperor-Lao Tzu cult.[1] From the middle of the first century A.D. on, for at least 150 years the Buddha and Lao Tzu were worshiped together. As in the Yellow Emperor-Lao Tzu cult, the Buddhist emphases were on medicine and religious sacrifice. Most probably Buddhism was considered a new version of the prevalent folk religion. In other words, Buddhism did not come in as an invader, but as a helper and supporter of the native religion. This had a tremendous significance for its future developments in China, for it explains its ready adaptation to things Chinese and the Chinese attitude of acceptance. It was under an atmosphere of harmony that the *Scripture in Forty-two Chapters* appeared.

The scripture is exceedingly important in the history of Chinese Buddhism not only because it is the first Buddhist scripture in China but also because of the teachings it embodies. Most scholars are satisfied that it was compiled from Buddhist scriptures in the second century A.D., for it was quoted in a document in 166,[2] although certain Ch'an (Zen) Buddhist terms crept in after the ninth century, like "having no thoughts" (ch. 2), "to think without thinking" (18), and "Perfect Wisdom" (*bodhi*) (19). But these are embellishments that do not alter the basic ideas of the scripture, which are very much Taoistic and consonant with the practical and mundane ethics of the Confucianists. Its fundamental tenets are purity and tranquillity (34), taking no action (2, 27), and having no impure desires (13, 21, 25, 27). There is a particular stress on the latter, and the reader is reminded again and again of the evil of sex (4, 22, 23, 29). Avoiding evil spirits must have had a special appeal to the Taoists, and a touch of moderation (34) could not fail to please the Confucianists. The whole tone of the ethical teaching admirably suited the Chinese temper, especially Taoist doctrines at the time. The very word *tao* is used to describe the Buddhist Path, and familiar Chinese phrases and metaphors are employed, such as "echoes and sounds" (7) and "an infinitesimal mistake" (18). There are, of course, the inevitable Buddhist teachings on nonego (20) and leaving home life (23), but these are meant only for the monk. There is not yet the later Buddhist idea of rebirth in Paradise. Strangely enough, the concept of the soul is implied but not clearly presented, and there is very little trace of asceticism. There is no doubt that the *Scripture in Forty-two Chapters*, or more correctly, through the teachings therein, Buddhism made a happy entry into China.[3] □

Ch. 2. *The Buddha said:* The monk (*śramana*)[4] who has left home life cuts off his selfish desires and gets rid of his wants. He knows the source of his own mind. He understands the profound principle of the Buddha and understands the uncreated elements of existence (*dharma*).[5] Internally he clings to nothing, and externally he seeks for nothing. His mind is not bound by the Way (Tao), nor is it wrapped up by action-influences (*karma*).[6] He has no [erroneous] thoughts and takes no [deliberate] action. He neither practices (the Way) nor realizes it [consciously]. He does not go through the various stages but naturally reaches the highest level. This is called the Way.

Ch. 4. *The Buddha said:* Sentient beings consider ten things to be good and also ten things to be evil. What are the ten evils? Three pertain to the body, four to the mouth, and three to the mind. The three pertaining to the body are killing, stealing, and unchastity. The four pertaining to the mouth are double talk, evil speech, lying, and perverse speech. The three pertaining to the mind are jealousy, anger, and delusion. These ten things are contrary to the holy Way and are called the ten devil deeds. When these are stopped, they are called the ten good deeds.

Ch. 5. *The Buddha said:* If one makes many mistakes and does not regret them quickly and stop his intention to make the mistakes, sin will come to his person like water returning to the sea, gradually becoming deeper and wider. If one makes mistakes, realizes it, and knows that he is wrong, changes his evil ways, and does good, sin will naturally disappear. It is like perspiration coming to a sick person. His illness will gradually be reduced and cured.

Ch. 6. *The Buddha said:* When an evil person hears about some good (in you) and purposely comes to create trouble, you should stop him but should not glare at him with anger. He who comes to do evil will merely do evil to himself.

Ch. 7. *The Buddha said:* Someone heard that I hold on the Way and practice great benevolence and compassion. He went as far as to scold the Buddha. The Buddha kept silent and did not reply. When he finished scolding, the Buddha asked him, "Suppose you treat another person with propriety and he refuses to accept it. Will that propriety return to you?" He answered, "It will return to me". The Buddha said, "Now you scold at me and I do not accept. You hold on to the evil yourself; it has returned to your person. It is like echo following sound and shadow following physical form. At the end there will be no escape. Be careful and do no evil."

Ch. 9. *The Buddha said:* If one merely hears extensively about and loves the Way, he will surely find it difficult to understand it, but if one adheres to one's intention and follows the Way, it will prove to be very great.

Ch. 10. *The Buddha said:* When you see people bestow benefits of the Way on others and you help them and make them happy, you will obtain a vast amount of blessing.

The monk said: Will these blessings be exhausted?

The Buddha said: They are like the fire of a torch. Hundreds and thousands of people each lights his own torch from it to cook his meals or illuminate the dark, but the torch remains the same. Blessings are like the torch.

Ch. 12. *The Buddha said*: There are twenty things which are difficult for the human being. It is difficult to practice charity when poor. It is difficult to study the Way when one is powerful and in a high position. It is difficult to give up one's life and accept sure death. It is difficult to have an opportunity to read the scriptures spoken by the Buddha. It is difficult to be born in the age in which the Buddha lived. It is difficult to suppress sex and other desires. It is difficult to see something attractive without seeking for it. It is difficult to be humiliated without showing an angry eye. It is difficult to possess power and not apply it to others. It is difficult to come in contact with things without a preconceived mind. It is difficult to study extensively and to investigate everything thoroughly. It is difficult to eliminate self-conceit. It is difficult to despise those who have not studied. It is difficult for the mind to exercise nondiscrimination and non-differentiation. It is difficult not to gossip about who is right or who is wrong. It is difficult to meet good friends (who can lead one to the Way). It is difficult to see one's nature and study the Way. It is difficult to save others according to their needs of the transforming influence of moral doctrines. It is difficult to see the different spheres (of color for the eye, and so on) without being moved. And it is difficult to understand how to use convenient means (to help others to salvation).

Ch. 13. *The monk asked the Buddha:* What primary and subsidiary causes will lead one to know his previous lives (which condition his present life) so he can understand the perfect Way?

The Buddha said: If he purifies his mind and holds his will firm, he will understand the perfect Way. It is like wiping the mirror. When the dirt is removed, its brightness remains. By cutting off desires and asking for nothing, one should understand his previous lives.

Ch. 14. *The monk asked the Buddha:* What is goodness and what is greatness?

The Buddha said: To practice the Way and to adhere to truth is good. When one's intention is identical with the Way, there is greatness.

Ch. 15. *The monk asked the Buddha:* What is great power and what is utmost enlightenment?

The Buddha said: To be able to bear humiliation means great power. If one does not harbor evil intentions, one's peace and strength will be doubled. One who bears (humiliation) has no evil and will surely be honored by others. To eliminate afflictions in the mind completely so it will be pure without any defect or filth means utmost enlightenment. When from the time before heaven and earth existed until today, and when in the ten cardinal directions,[7] nothing has not been seen, known, or heard, and when knowledge of all that exists has been attained, that may be called enlightenment.

Ch. 18. *The Buddha said:* According to my doctrine one should think without thinking, act without acting, speak without speaking, and practice without practicing. Those who understand my doctrine will find it near at hand, but those who are deluded will find it far away. Words fail to describe it, and it is not confined by things. If you make an infinitesimal mistake about it, it will be lost in a moment.

Ch. 19. *The Buddha said:* Examine heaven and earth and remember that they are impermanent. Examine the world and remember that it is impermanent. Examine and see one's own clear consciousness. That is Perfect Wisdom. With such knowledge, one will attain the Way quickly.

Ch. 20. *The Buddha said*: One should think about the fact that each of the Four Elements constituting the body (Earth, Water, Fire, Wind) has its own name but none has a self. Since none of them has a self, it (the body, the ego) is like a mirage.

Ch. 21. *The Buddha said:* There are people who, following their desires, seek fame, but by the time their fame becomes great, they are already dead. To covet worldly fame and not to study the Way is to waste effort and toil the body. It is like burning incense. By the time others smell the fragrance, the incense is already burned up. The fire that endangers the body comes afterwards.

Ch. 22. *The Buddha said:* People are not willing to relinquish wealth and sex. These are comparable to a knife with honey on its edge. The honey is not good enough for a meal. If a child licks it, he will be in danger of cutting his tongue.

Ch. 23. *The Buddha said:* People are bound by their wives, children, and home more than by a prison. One will sooner or later get out of prison, but people (naturally) have no thought of separating far away from their wives and children. The feeling of love (comes from) sex. Do people get tired of devoting themselves to it? Even if there is the danger of being eaten by a tiger, they will willingly submit to it. These people simply throw themsleves into the ditch and drown themselves. Therefore they are called ordinary people. If one understands this process thoroughly, one will be free from dust (afflictions) and become an *arhat* (a saint who enters Nirvāṇa).[8]

Ch. 27. *The Buddha said:* Those who

Kansas School of Religion
At the University of Kansas
Smith Hall, Rm. 109, Library
Lawrence, Kansas 66045-2164

practice the Way are like a piece of wood in the water. It seeks out the current to go without touching either bank. It is not picked up by men or impeded by the gods. It is not stayed by adverse currents nor does it rot. I can guarantee that this piece of wood will surely enter the sea. If he who studies the Way is not deluded by sensuous desires and not disturbed by all kinds of evil spirits, I can guarantee that he will attain the Way (be saved).

Ch. 29. *The Buddha said:* Take care not to look at beautiful women and do not talk with them. If you talk with them, think with a correct mind that you are a devotee to the Way and that living in a dirty world you should be like a lotus flower which is not defiled by mud. Think of older women as your mother, those older than you as your elder sisters, those younger as your younger sisters, and little girls as your children. Engender the mind to seek salvation and to stop and eliminate all evil thoughts.

Ch. 33. *The Buddha said:* He who practices the Way is like one fighting with ten thousand people. As he puts on his armor and goes out, his will may be timid. Perhaps after having gone halfway he turns back. Perhaps he may fight and die. Or he may return triumphant. The monk who studies the Way should hold his mind firm, make a serious effort, be courageous and valiant, fearing nothing in front of him, destroy all demons, and obtain the fruits of the Way.

Ch. 34. One night, a monk was reciting the *Scripture of the Teachings Bequeathed by Kāśyapa Buddha.*[9] His voice was sorrowful and tense. He began to regret [studying the Way] and wanted to withdraw. The Buddha asked him, "Before you left your home, what did you do?"

Answer: "I loved to play the lute."

The Buddha said: "When you loosened the strings, what happened?"

Answer: "There would be no more sound."

"How about pulling them tight?"

Answer: "The sound will stop."

"How about the medium between being loose and tight?"

Answer: "All the sounds will be realized."

The Buddha said, "The same is true of a monk learning the Way. If his mind is well adjusted, the Way will be obtained. If he forces his way, he will be tired, and if he is tired, his will will be troubled. When his will is troubled, his actions will retrogress. As his actions have retrogressed, his sin will accumulate. Only with purity and peace will the Way not be lost." (*Taishō daizōkyō,* [Taishō edition of the Buddhist canon], 17:722–24).

B. MOU TZU's SETTLING OF DOUBTS

□ As Buddhism spread in China and as more and more Buddhist literature came in, Buddhism gradually detached itself from the native religion and showed more independence as well as sophistication. Naturally its differences from the Chinese tradition began to appear. Questioning and criticism were bound to arise. Mou Tzu, or Master Mou, took it upon himself to remove the doubts. He became the first Chinese intellectual to be converted to the Indian religion and the first to defend it.

Mou Tzu lived in South China, in modern Kwangsi, in the second century.[10] Well versed in Confucianism and Taoism, he addressed himself to his fellow intellectuals. This indicates that by his time, Buddhism had already spread to South China from the East and Central North, and had reached the Chinese educated class. He took great pain to compare Buddhism with such Taoist doctrines as taking no (unnatural) action (*wu-wei*) (ch. 3), simplicity (18, 22), and nourishing life (19, 30), and stressed their similarity. He also translated *nirvāṇa* by the Taoist term *wu-wei* (3, 16). The greater issues he faced, however, were those that concerned the Confucian tradition the most, for the Han Dynasty was, after all, a Confucian state. He had to defend why China could learn from Buddhism in addition to what its own sages had provided (7); why the monk shaved his head, avoided marriage, and left home life, thus violating the Confucian teachings of preserving the body intact, supporting parents, and continuing the family line (9, 10); why money should be given to strangers rather than relatives (15); why human desires should be supressed (19); why human affairs should be neglected in favor of serving spiritual beings (13), and so on. There was also the criticism that Buddhism was a foreign religion (14), but that issue was quite secondary. Whether he succeeded in settling the doubts or not, we have not been told. But by answering an imaginary questioner in the way he did, he started the confrontation between Buddhism and Chinese intellectuals, paved the way for the Chinese tendency to see religious similarities rather than differences, and inaugurated the trend to interpret Buddhist ideas in Chinese, more especially Taoist, terms. □

§4. *Question:* Confucius' doctrines are contained in the Five Classics.[11] His teachings may be recited or put into practice. But the Way you talk about is inconcrete and elusive. Its ideas are not clear and supporting evidence for it is not specified. Why is it so different from the words of the Sage?

Mou Tzu said: Please do not consider what you are used to as important and what you are not used to as unimportant, and do not be deluded about outside things or lose your balanced judgment. Nothing can be accomplished without Tao and its virtue, just as no strings can be adjusted without notes.[12] The way of Heaven is modeled after the four seasons, while the Way of man is modeled after the Five Constant Virtues.[13] Lao Tzu said, "There was something undifferentiated and yet complete, which existed before heaven and earth. . . . It may be considered the mother of the universe. I do not know its name; perforce I call it Tao."[14] The thing that is Tao can be used to serve one's parents when one is at home, and to govern the people when one rules the state. By itself, it can be used to order one's own life. When put into practice, it fills the universe. When neglected it is not used up; when dispersed it does not leave you. You do not understand this. Where is it different? . . .

§7. *Question:* If the Way of the Buddha is supreme and is the greatest, why did Yao, Shun, the Duke of Chou,[15] and Confucius not practice it? His words are not found in the Seven Classics.[16] Since you are already fond of the *Book of Odes* and the *Book of History* and enjoy the *Book of Rites* and the *Book of Music*, why do you love the Way of the Buddha and why are you delighted in heterodoxical arts? Can they surpass the Classics and their commentaries and beautify the accomplishments of the sages? I dare say that it is not worthy of you.

Mou Tzu said: For books one does not have to read Confucius and for medicine one does not have to follow the formula of Pien-ch'üeh.[17] Whatever accords with moral principles should be followed and whatever can heal the sick should be good and effective. The superior man extensively takes in all kinds of good to assist himself. Tzu-kung said,[18] "When did our Master (Confucius) have a regular teacher?"[19] Yao served Yin Shou,[20] Shun served Wu-ch'eng,[21] Tan (Duke of Chou) learned from Lü Wang,[22] and Ch'iu (Confucius) learned from Lao Tzu.[23] None of these facts appears in the Seven Classics. Although these four teachers were sages, compared to the Buddha they are like the white deer is to the unicorn[24] or the sparrow to the phoenix.[25] Even Yao, Shun, the Duke of Chou, and Confucius followed these teachers. How much less should we reject and refuse to learn from the Buddha whose distinguishing marks are excellent and whose spiritual power of transformation is not spatially restricted? Some ideas and events are perhaps missing from the Five Classics. Why should the mere fact that the Buddha is not included in the records be enough to arouse puzzlement or doubt? . . .

§9. *Question:* The *Classic of Filial Piety* says, "We receive our body, including hair and skin, from our parents and we dare not injure them."[26] When Tseng Tzu[27] was about to die, he said, "Uncover my feet, uncover my hand"[28] (to show he had kept them from harm). But now monks shave their heads. Why do they violate the sayings of the Sage and remain out of accord with the way of the filial son like this? You, my friend, always like to discuss what is right or wrong, or what is crooked or straight. But now why do you praise them instead?

Mou Tzu said: It is inhumane to slander sages and worthies, and it is unwise not to arrive at the middle point in balancing anything. Without humanity or wisdom, how can one build up his virtue? If he does not build up his virtue, he is an obstinate and stupid fellow. Will it be easy for him to discuss things? Formerly a man of Ch'i was crossing a river in a boat. His father fell into the water. The son bared his arms, seized his father's head, and turned him upside down so that the water drained from his mouth. As a result his father's life was saved. Now, nothing is more unfilial than to seize one's father's head and turn him upside down. But that saved the father's life. If one folds his arms and performs the usual act of the filial son, the father's life will be lost to the water. Confucius said, "There are people with whom we may pursue the Way together but with whom we may not be able to weigh together its application under special circumstances."[29] Furthermore, the *Classic of Filial Piety* says, "Ancient kings possessed perfect virtue and essential principles,"[30] and yet T'ai-po[31] cut his hair short and tattooed his body, voluntarily following the custom of the states of Wu and Yüeh, thus violating the principle of [not hurting] the body, including its hair and skin. And yet Confucius praised him, saying, "His may be said to be perfect virtue."[32] Chung Ni (Confucius) did not discredit him because he cut his hair short. From this point of view, if one possesses great virtue, he is not to be restricted in small matters. Monks give up their property and wealth, forsake their wives and children, do not listen to music, and do not look at beautiful women. They may be regarded complaisant in the highest degree. Wherein have they violated the teaching of the Sage or are not in accord with filial piety? . . .

§10. *Question:* No blessing is greater than carrying on the family line, and no unfilial act is greater than leaving no posterity. Monks forsake their wives and children, give up their property and wealth, or perhaps do not marry all their lives. How opposed to the blessing and filial piety is such conduct! These people bring suffering upon themselves without feeling anything strange about it, and [try to] save themselves without feeling anything unusual about it.

Mou Tzu said: To make the left long it is necessary to make the right short, and to make the front wide it is necessary to make the rear narrow. Meng Kung-cho' was more than competent as an elder in (the families of) Chao and Wei but was not qualified to be a great officer in (the states of) T'eng and Hsüeh.[33] Wives, children, property, and wealth are luxuries in the world, but to maintain purity in oneself and to take no (unnatural) action are the excellence of Tao. Lao Tzu said, "Which does one love more, fame or one's own life? Which is more valuable, one's own life or wealth?"[34] He also said, "Let people observe the traditional customs of the Three Dynasties,[35] read about the principles and methods of Confucianists and Moists, read the *Book of Odes* and the *Book of History* and practice ceremonies and etiquette, honor humanity and righteousness, and pay attention to purity. People in their communities will preserve and continue their accomplishments, and their fame will spread everywhere. This is the mediocre scholar's way of doing things but is not cared for by one who is simple and at peace. Therefore when a tiger saw the pearl of Sui in the front, it ran away and dared not take it. Why? It puts life above any benefit."[36] Hsü Yu lived in a nest on a tree.[37] Po-i and Shu-ch'i starved in Shou-yang Mountain.[38] The Sage praised their virtue, saying, "They sought humanity (*jen*) and found it,"[39] and I have never heard that (Confucius) ever ridiculed them for having no prosperity or wealth. Monks cultivate a life of the Way and virtue in exchange for the pleasure of enjoying life, and return to pure virtue in exchange for the joy of wives and children. If this is not strange, what else is it? And if this is not unusual, what else is it? . . .

§12. *Question:* According to the Way of Buddhism, it is said that after a man dies, he will be reborn. I do not believe these words.

Mou Tzu said: At the point of a man's

death, his relatives go to the roof and call him. If he is already dead, whom is there to call?

Someone said: To call his *hun* (heavenly component of the soul) and *p'o* (earthly component of the soul).[40]

Mou Tzu said: If the spirit returns, the person lives again. If the spirit does not return, where does it go?

Answer: It becomes a spiritual being.

Mou Tzu said: Correct. The spirit, of course, does not perish; only the body itself decays. The body is like the roots and leaves of the five grains, while the spirit is like their seeds and kernels. Roots and leaves live but will die, but do the seeds and kernels come to an end and perish? Only the body of one who has achieved the Way perishes. Lao Tzu said, "The reason why I have great trouble is that I have a body. If I have no body, what trouble could I have?"[41] He also said, "Withdraw as soon as your work is done. Such is Heaven's Way."[42]

Someone said: One dies if one practices the Way and also dies if one does not practice the Way. What is the difference?

Mou Tzu said: This is what is meant by demanding fame for the whole lifetime without a day of goodness. Although one who has achieved the Way dies, his spirit returns to the Home of Blessing. If one does evil, when he dies, his spirit will suffer calamities. A stupid person is obscured by what has taken place but the virtuous and the wise prepare for things before there is any omen. The difference between possessing the Way or not is like that between gold and grass, and the difference between good and evil is like that between black and white. How can we say they are different if they are not?

§13. *Question:* Confucius said, "If we are not yet able to serve man, how can we serve spiritual beings? If we do not yet know about life, how can we know about death?"[43] This is the principle of the Sage. Now, Buddhists talk without hesitation about the matter of life and death and things concerning spiritual beings. This, I am afraid, is not the thing the Sage and wise people talk about. He who practices the Way should be empty, simple, and tranquil, and should direct his will back to the substantial and unadorned. Why say anything about life and death to disturb the will and talk about the unnecessary matter of spiritual beings?

Mou Tzu said: What you say is what is called understanding the outer learning but not knowing the inner learning. Confucius was sick. Tzu-lu[44] did not ask about what is of fundamental importance and what is of secondary importance. Therefore Confucius said so to check him. The *Classic of Filial Piety* says, "Build a temple and make offering in the manner of offering to a spiritual being. Perform sacrifices in the spring and autumn in order to think of the dead from time to time."[45] It also says, "Serve parents with love and reverence when they are alive and serve them with grief and sorrow when they are dead."[46] Does this not teach people to serve spiritual beings and to know about life and death? The Duke of Chou requested the order for King Wu [to punish the wicked king of Shang] and said, "I have many abilities and skills and can serve spiritual beings."[47] Why did he say that? Is the objective of the discussions in Buddhist scriptures about spiritual beings not similar to this? Lao Tzu said, "He who has understood the son and still keeps to its mother will be free from danger throughout his lifetime."[48] "Use the light. Revert to enlightenment, and thereby avoid danger to one's life."[49] This tells the objectives of life and death and where fortune and misfortune lie. Of the essentials of the perfect Way, silence is truly valued. Do Buddhists like to talk? We cannot help answering the questions you have to ask. Do bells and drums make noise by themselves? They sound only when something strikes them.

§14. *Question:* Confucius said, "The barbarians with a ruler are not as good as the Chinese without one."[50] Mencius ridiculed Ch'en Hsiang for shifting from his own learning to the ways of Hsü Hsing (a teacher from a neighboring state advocating a strange doctrine of economics) who said, "I have heard of using what is Chinese to change what is barbarian, but I have never heard of being changed by the barbarians."[51] You, my friend, a young man of twenty, have learned the way of

Yao, Shun, the Duke of Chou, and Confucius, and now you discard it, and instead study the arts of barbarians. Aren't you deluded?

Mou Tzu said: What I learned were unnecessary words when I had not understood the great Way. As to you, I may say you see the flower of social institutions but are obscured about the kernel of morality, and peep at the light of a candle but do not see the sun in the sky. What Confucius said was a way to correct the world, and what Mencius said was to show the defect of one-sidedness. Of old, when Confucius wanted to live among the nine barbarian tribes of the East, he said, "If a superior man lives there, what rudeness would there be?"[52]. . . . The land of China is not necessarily under the center of heaven. . . .

§15. *Question:* It is not charity to give one's father's property to a stranger, and it is not humaneness to kill oneself as a substitute for another. Now Buddhist scriptures say that Prince Sudāna[53] gave his father's property to people far away, gave precious elephants of the state to the enemy, and got rid of his wife and son and gave them to others. Not to respect one's parents but to respect others is called a violation of propriety. Not to love one's parents but to love others is called a violation of virtue. Sudāna was neither filial nor humane, and yet Buddhists honor him. Isn't that strange?

Mou Tzu said: The principle of the Five Classics is to designate the oldest son as the legal son to continue the family line. But when T'ai Wang saw the [laudable] will of Ch'ang (the future King Wen), he appointed (his second son and Ch'ang's father) Chi as the legal son instead. Consequently the great undertaking of the Chou dynasty was accomplished and peace established.[54] The principle of marrying a wife is (first) to inform one's parents (of one's intention). But Shun got married without informing his parents and thus a great human relation was established.[55] . . . Sudāna realized that the world is transitory and that wealth and property are not one's own treasures. Therefore he gave alms without restraint and thus realized the great Way. Both his father and his country received his benefits and the enemy could not come in. He reached the point of becoming a Buddha. His parents and brothers were all saved. If this is not filial or humane, what else is? (*Hung-ming chi* [Essays spreading and elucidating the doctrine], 1:2b–6b).

C. ISSUE OF THE MONKS' PROSTRATING BEFORE THE EMPEROR

☐ As translations of Buddhist scriptures proceeded rapidly, Buddhist thought started to develop in China. By the first quarter of the third century, there had been two Buddhist movements of thought: one, that of *dhyāna* (concentration), aiming at achieving calmness of the mind and removal of delusions through meditation; and the other, that of *prajñā* (wisdom), aiming at the enlightenment that things had no self-nature. These attracted the Chinese literati, especially the Neo-Taoists who were developing a new philosophy and methodology on top of those of Lao Tzu and Chuang Tzu.[56] The Buddhists started a movement of "matching concepts" of Buddhism and Taoism; that is, to interpret Buddhist ideas in Taoist terms, such as using the Neo-Taoist term, "original nonbeing" (*pen-wu*) for *tathatā* (thusness). In 316 the capital of China, Ch'ang-an, fell to the foreign invaders from the North, and subsequently, there was a great exodus of government officials, wealthy people, and the literati to the South. The refugee capital was established at Chien-k'ang near Nanking. For the next three hundred years Chinese culture was continued and developed in the South while the North was occupied by foreigners. Monks joined the exodus.

While in the South, Buddhists monks enjoyed the patronage of rulers and the fellowship of Confucianists and Taoists. Contact with the Chinese intellectual tradition, on the one hand, and intermingling with the government, on the other, went hand in hand. As to be expected, interaction produced friction. Certain sharp issues came to the surface, of which that of the monk's prostrating before the emperor was the most critical. In this Hui-yüan (334–417) was a central figure.

Hui-yüan was one of the most renowned Chinese monk-scholars in Chinese history. He was an authority on Lao Tzu, Chuang Tzu, and the *Book of Changes*. On the famous mountain, Lu-shan, in southeast China, where he lived for thirty years, he freely conversed with Confucian and Taoist scholars and exchanged poems with them. In 340 the issue of the monk's obligation to "pay respect" to the emperor, that is, to prostrate before him, as all laymen did, arose. The matter subsided but revived decades later and resulted in a great debate, "an important matter of a whole generation."[57] After much friendly but spirited discussion on the question,[58] the grand marshal, Huan Hsüan (369–404), who had usurped the power of the Chin emperor, asked Hui-yüan in 402 to submit his opinion. Evidently he did it convincingly and successfully, for as a result of his statement, the government decreed that monks were to be exempt from the obligation. The "Treatise on the Monks Not Paying Respect to the Sovereign" in five sections, is an elaboration of that statement.

With this encounter, the question of the separation of the different spheres of life between those living in "worldly society" and those in the "other-worldly society" was forever settled, and in a more narrow sense, the separation between religion and state. It is not that Chinese governments had not continued to support, utilize or persecute the Buddhist religion or that the Buddhist religion had not continued to serve or try to subvert the government, although such things happened in Chinese history far less often than in others. But by and large, the separation had been honored by both sides. □

A Monk Does Not Pay Respect to the Sovereign

§1. "Retaining Home Life"

Basically speaking, among the doctrines propagated by Buddhism, leaving home life is generally considered strange. There are four tasks assumed by those who have left home life. In spreading the doctrine and in bringing out the accord of things, their contribution matches that of emperors and kings and their influence duplicates that of the way of government. As to affecting mores and awaking the times, no age has been without them. It is only because circumstances may require them to engage in public life or to conceal themselves that they become prominent or hidden as the faith declines or prospers. In this matter there is room for discussion, and I beg to speak briefly.

Those who receive and serve the Law at home are people who follow the natural course of transformation (of production and reproduction and life and death leading to cycles of rebirth). In their feelings they have not changed from the worldly and the trace of their activities is the same as those in worldly society. Therefore there is love among natural kinship and the proprieties of serving the ruler. There is a foundation for propriety and reverence. Therefore instructions have been established on the basis of them. The merits of the foundation on which they are based, however, come from the past. Therefore love is taught on the basis of affection so that people may know that there is natural kindness, and reverence is taught on the basis of strictness so that people may know that there are things naturally important. The two things (propriety of serving the ruler and love for parents) have come about really because of some silent response. Since this response is not to be found in the present, we must look for its source. Therefore (the Buddhist religion) metes out punishment in accordance with the sin so people become fearful and consequently careful, and it offers Heaven as a reward so people may be delighted and thus do good. There are the retributions that follow like shadows and echoes, which have been made clear in the doctrine. This is to use the basis (of propriety and reverence) and the following (of the natural course of transformation) to (make life operate and) prevail without altering its natural aspects.

What is the explanation of this? Those who value their bodies highly and preserve their lives will become stagnated because they have limitations. Their roots of impediment are deep and firm, and they never for a moment forget self-preservation. As a result, they will treat their feelings and desires as parks and gardens (areas of enjoyment) and music and sex as places to linger. They will sink themselves in worldly pleasure and be unable to rise above it with their own effort. Therefore we teach them the restraints and let them consider this as the limit, for there is no need to explain to them what lies outside (worldly society). As what lies outside has not been made clear to them, they should achieve a great harmony in following the natural course of transformation. Therefore they should not accept (the ruler's) favors and violate the propriety (of serving him), or enjoy the kindness (of parents) and neglect the reverence for them. Therefore those who are delighted with the way of life taught by Śākyamuni[59] will forthwith serve their parents and revere the ruler first of all, and those who want to change from worldly life and resign from official posts (to become a monk) will wait for (their) commands and act accordingly. If the ruler or parents have doubts, they will withdraw and inquire of their wishes until all of them understand. This is how Buddhism takes seriously the process of life-giving (from parents to children) and assists the king's course of transformation in the way of government. Since there seems to be a superficial agreement among those who express their basic ideas, I want to make clear, on the basis of the distinction between worldly society and other-worldly society, the (Buddhists') intention to honor the ruler, parents, and the teacher. I shall briefly state the ideas in the scriptures and express what is harbored in my mind.

§2. "Leaving Home Life"

Those who have left home life are guests from an other-worldly society. Their traces of activity are completely different from those of other people. It is their doctrine to enable people to understand that one's troubles and impediments are caused by the possession of a body (which handicaps one's entrance to Nirvāṇa) and that by not preserving it one can end all troubles, and to realize that production and reproduction are caused by transformations due to endowment and that one should seek the source without following the natural cause of transformation. Since following the natural course of transformation is not the way to seek the source (Thusness, cessations of the cycle of life and death), no importance is attached to any help (the ruler's way of) making life operate and prevail everywhere may have to offer, and since preserving the body is not the way to end troubles, no value is given to any benefit that enriches (worldly) living. This is where principle and physical form are not in accord and where the Way is opposed to worldly life. People like these start their vows with throwing away their hairpins and demonstrate their determination by changing their garb. Therefore all those who have left their home life escape from the world in order to achieve their ideal and alter their worldly customs in order to attain their Way. Since they have altered their worldly customs, their garb cannot be in accord with the propriety of worldly standards, and since they have escaped from the world, the traces of their activities should be lofty and high-minded. This being the case, they can therefore save the sinking world from the currents engulfing them, pull up the hidden roots that have been bringing them repeated calamities, widely open up the fords to the Three Vehicles,[60] and broadly open up the road to reach the state of the man who has attained the Way. If one man is enabled to attain perfect virtue, the Way will penetrate through the Six Relations[61] and the benefit will flow out to the whole world. Although they are not in the position of kings and dukes, they will have been in full harmony with the supreme principles of government and and have enabled living beings to live spontaneously. Therefore, although internally out of accord with the importance of natural relationship, they have not violated filial piety, and although externally lacking the respect of serving the ruler, they have not lost reverence for him. From this point of view, we know that if we seek the source by going beyond the limit of natural transformation, we shall find that the principle is deep and its meaning real, but if people talk about the (Confucian doctrine of) humanity (*jen*) by clearly heaving a sigh, their contribution will be secondary and benefit thin. If so, although (we) may be facing the Ming Mountain,[62] we may turn back or even be ashamed of hearing about it. How much less would we embrace the filial piety and reverence of those people who follow the natural course of transformation and those gentlemen who get their emolument by sitting idly?

§3. "SEEKING THE SOURCE WITHOUT FOLLOWING THE NATURAL COURSE OF TRANSFORMATION"

Question: Lao Tzu's idea, as we inquire into and understand it, is that Heaven and Earth become great by attaining the One and that kings and dukes become honorable by personally following (the natural course of transformation).[63] (Heaven and Earth) have attained the One and therefore have become the source of transformations of the myriad things, and (kings and dukes) personally follow (the natural course of transformations) and therefore have the merit of (enabling life to) operate and prevail. Thus understanding the source necessarily rests in personally embodying the ultimate, and personally embodying the ultimate necessarily depends on following the natural course of transformation. Therefore worthies of the past often talked about this as an excellent idea and common opinions have all agreed with it. What differs from common agreement does not make sense, and yet you say that one should not follow the natural course of transformation. Why?

Answer: All things existing in the realm of being receive their endowment and life from the Great Transformation (process of Universal Creation). Although their varieties are many and refined ones and coarse ones do not form the same system, ultimately speaking, there are only those with souls[64] and those without. Those with a soul have a feeling for transformation (to be reborn), while those without a soul have no such feeling. When there is no such feeling, one's life (in the cycle of birth and rebirth) ends when the process of transformation is finished. When life has not come from feeling, as the body decays, all transformations cease. Those with a feeling for transformation, however, become active under the influence of material things. Since activity necessarily depends on feeling, one's life does not end. Since one's life does not end, its transformation becomes more and more far-reaching, its physical form piles up more and more, the feelings are more and more obstructed, and impediments become greater and greater. How can these troubles be fully described? Therefore the scriptures say that Nirvāṇa is changeless, with cessation of transformation as its home, and that the Three Worlds[65] are in constant flux, with sin and suffering as its stage, that when transformation ends, all causes and conditions (for birth and rebirth) will forever cease, while with constant flux, suffering will never end.

How do we understand that this is the case? Life is fettered by physical form and life depends on transformation. When there is transformation and one reacts with his feelings, his spirit will be stagnated at its source and his intelligence will be darkened from its illumination. Thus firmly limited, what is preserved is nothing but the self, and what is gone through is nothing but the flux. Consequently, the bridle of the soul loses its driver and the road to rebirth will be reopened everyday. Following one's desires, one will float in an unending stream. Will there be only one effect (rebirth) and no more? Therefore he who returns to the source to seek the fundamental does not impede his spirit with life, and one who has overcome worldly ignorance and delusions does not impede his life with feelings. If one does not impede his life with feelings, then life (birth and rebirth) can be wiped out, and if one does not impede his spirit with life, then his spirit (soul) can be obliterated. When spirit is obliterated and spheres of objects are eliminated, that is called Nirvāṇa. Is the name Nirvāṇa an empty appellation?

Let me extend and substantiate this discussion. Although Heaven and Earth are great in producing and reproducing things, they cannot prevent living things from dying, and although kings and dukes have the merit of preserving things, they cannot prevent what they have preserved from trouble. That is why I said above, "Understand that one's troubles and impediments are caused by the possession of a body and that by not preserving it one can end all troubles and realize that production and reproduction are caused by transformation due to endowment and that one should seek the source without following the natural course of transformation." Such is the meaning of what I said. As such is the meaning, the monk therefore refuses to perform ceremonies before the Son of Heaven, but in a lofty spirit attends to his own affairs and enjoys his kindness although without the rank of a king or a duke.[66] (*Hung-ming chi*, 5:5b–8a).

D. ISSUE OF THE DESTRUCTIBILITY OF THE SOUL

□ Because in the Chinese folk religion there has been a widespread belief in spiritual beings and therefore the soul, the Chinese Buddhists had taken the Buddhist concept of the ego, which, as spirit, rises and falls and is thus illusory, to mean transmigration. They, including even learned monks, held on firmly to the belief in the soul. This ran straightly against the Taoist scholars, who denied it outright, and the Confucianists, to whom the belief in the soul, as the popular masses and the Buddhists had it, would lead to superstition, undermine the ethical significance of religious sacrifice, and shift moral responsibility from man to spiritual beings. There was considerable discussion in the fourth and fifth centuries. Fa Chen (fl. 502), who was a prefect, wrote the *Shen-mieh lun* (Treatise on the destruction of the soul) in 507 in which he answered thirty-one imaginary questions and created a stir. The emperor called for refutation and sixty-two people responded.[67] Although most opposed Fan, no one really won the argument. But the treatise served to affirm and solidify once and for all the traditional belief of Chinese intellectuals that the belief in the soul is both philosophically false and ethically dangerous. Immortality consists not in perpetual existence but in the eternal reality of one's virtue, good works, and wisdom.

While Hui-yüan paid chief attention to retribution, Fan Chen concentrated on the philosophical side of the question. However, his basic motivation was still ethical, for he directed his attack on the corrupting effects of Buddhism on social economy, the family structure, national defense, government operation, and the economic nonproductiveness of monks (sec. 31). The essay is one of the most celebrated in Chinese history.[68] □

On the Destruction of the Spirit

§1. *Question:* You said that the spirit can be destroyed. How do you know that it can be destroyed?

Answer: The spirit is the same as the body and the body is the same as the spirit. Therefore when the body exists, the spirit exists, and when the body declines, the spirit is destroyed.

§2. *Question:* "Body" is the name for the conscious and "spirit" is the name for the unconscious. The conscious and the unconscious are in fact different and the spirit and the body are by principle not the same. I have never heard that the body and spirit are identified as one.

Answer: The body is concrete stuff of the spirit and the spirit is the function of the body. Thus the body refers to the concrete stuff and the spirit refers to the function. The body and the spirit cannot be different.

§3. *Question:* (You say that) the spirit is surely not concrete stuff and the body surely not function and yet they cannot be different. How do you explain it?

Answer: They are the same in substance but different in name.

§4. *Question:* If their names are different, how can their substance be the same?

Answer: The spirit to the concrete stuff is like sharpness is to the knife, and the body to the function is like the knife to the sharpness. The name of sharpness is not knife and the name of the knife is not sharpness. However, without sharpness, there will be no knife, and without knife, there will be no sharpness. I have never heard that when the knife is removed sharpness remains. How can it be possible that the body perishes while the spirit exists?

§5. *Question:* The relation between the knife and sharpness may be as you have said, but the relation between the body and the spirit is different. Why? The concrete stuff of wood has no consciousness whereas the concrete stuff of man has. Since man has a concrete stuff like wood and also a consciousness absent in wood, isn't it true that there is only one thing in the wood but there are two in man?

Answer: What strange things you have said! If man possesses a concrete stuff like wood to constitute his body and also the consciousness different from wood to constitute his spirit, what you have said may be all right. But the concrete stuff of man is not that of wood and the concrete stuff of wood is not that of man. Wherein has man the concrete stuff like wood and at the same time a consciousness different from wood?

§6. *Question:* The concrete stuff of man is different from that of wood because man has consciousness. If man has no consciousness, how different is he from wood?

Answer: Man has no concrete stuff which is not conscious. Similarly, wood has no body which is conscious.

§7. *Question:* Isn't the corpse of the dead concrete stuff without consciousness?

Answer: Yes, it is concrete stuff without consciousness.

§8. *Question:* If so, man indeed has a concrete stuff like wood and a consciousness different from wood.

Answer: The dead has concrete stuff like wood but not the consciousness different from wood, while the living has a consciousness different from wood but no concrete stuff like wood.

§28. *Question:* I have heard your explanation that the body and the spirit are not two. Of course it is correct that according to principles, as the body deteriorates, the spirit perishes. But may I ask what does it mean when the classic says, "Build a temple and make offering in the manner of offering to a spiritual being." [69]

Answer: It is the teaching of the Sage (Confucius). It was intended to satisfy the desire of the filial son and to arouse those who lack a sense of gratitude. This is what is meant by the saying, "Understanding by way of the spirit." [70]

§29. *Question:* (The ghost) Po-yu carried weapons (to frighten people) and P'eng-sheng appeared as a pig.[71] These facts have been conspicuous in the records. Are they only stories told to teach a lesson?

Answer: Apparitions are vague; they perhaps exist and perhaps not. Many people die a violent death (as did Po-yu) but not all become ghosts. How can P'eng-sheng and Po-yu be exceptions? Suddenly a person and suddenly a pig, but they were not necessarily the son (P'eng-sheng) of the Lord Ch'i and the son (Po-yu) of the Lord of Cheng.

§30. *Question:* The *Book of Changes* says, "Thus we know the situation of spiritual beings," "Resembling Heaven and Earth but not opposing them," and "Carry a cart-full of spiritual beings."[72] What does it mean?

Answer: There are birds and there are animals. They differ as the flying species and the running species. There are human beings and there are spiritual beings. They differ in being hidden or manifest. But I do not know if a man dies and becomes a spiritual being or a ghost dies and becomes a man.

§31. *Question:* If we know that the spirit perishes, what benefits will there be?

Answer: The Buddha harms government; monks injure customs. Like the wind startling people and the fog rising, the harm spreads rapidly and recklessly without stop. I grieve over its evil and want to save people from sinking. Why do people exhaust their treasures to please monks and go bankrupt to rush to offer to the Buddha but do not care for their relatives or pity the poor? It is certainly because of their strong feeling to regard themselves highly and their weak intention to help others. Therefore they will extract even an ounce from a poor friend, showing their stingy feeling in their countenance, and will give away thousands of pounds to wealthy monks[73] with a joyful feeling overflowing their faces and hairs. Isn't it because there will be a time when the monks will have an abundance of grains whereas the friends may not be able to return a mere stalk of rice? In their efforts at charity, they have no concern with giving at all, but in claiming merits, they insist on doing so for themselves. Furthermore, they are deluded with vague words and are frightened by the suffering in the lowest hell. They are induced by false and wild talks and are delighted by the pleasure in heaven. Therefore they give up the robe of the literati and wear a transverse dress. They abolish traditional sacrificial vessels and array flower vases and alms bowls. Every family abandons their beloved and dear ones, and every one terminates the family line. It reaches the point when soldiers are defeated in battle, government offices are emptied of officials, food is eaten up by the lazy and the idle (monks), and wealth is exhausted in constructing (temples). Consequently, crimes have become innumerable and yet praises are heaped upon them. These are the only reasons. The spread of their harm has no end and their evil is unlimited. If we know that man is produced from endowment by nature, and that the myriad things all go through transformations themselves, and that suddenly they exist by themselves and vaguely they seem not to, we shall not resist whatever comes or chase after whatever goes away. Let the inferior man be satisfied with his farm and the superior man preserve tranquillity and simplicity. Let us farm for food, and our food will never be exhausted. Let us cultivate sericulture for clothing, and our clothing will know no end. Let those below serve people above with their surplus, and let those above treat those below with non-action by leaving them alone. When this way is followed, we can preserve our lives, support our parents, help ourselves, aid others, assist our country, and make our ruler a feudal chief. (*Hung-ming chi*, 9 :30a–8a; *Liang shu* [History of the Liang dynasty], 502–57; 48:7a–13a).

NOTES

1. The Yellow Emperor was a mythical figure of high antiquity. For The Yellow Emperor-Lao Tzu Cult, see introduction to ch. 14.
2. In a memorial to the emperor. See the *Hou-Han shu* (History of the Later Han dynasty, 25–220 A.D.), 60B:23b.
3. For an English translation, see Chu Ch'an, tr., *The Sutra of* 42 *Sections*.
4. One who has left home and gotten rid of passions.
5. *Dharma*, "that which is held to," connoting all things, with or without form, real or imaginary, the material or principle of an entity, something that holds on to its nature as a particular thing. The uncreated is that which is not caused by anything.
6. *Karma*, the influence of one's action in past lives upon the present and that of the present upon the future.
7. That is, the four directions, their four corners, above, and below.
8. *Arhat* or *arhan*, the worthy or saint, who is no longer bound in the cycle of life and death or incarnation. See ch. 7, §4.
9. One of the seven Buddhas of the Past, that is, before the time of Gautama Śākyamuni, the historical Buddha of the sixth century B.C.
10. The treatise, entitled *Li-huo lun* (Treatise to settle doubts) in 38 sections (not numbered in the text), has been attributed in the last several centuries to Mou Jung, who was grand marshal during the reign of Chang-ti (r. 76–88) but earlier works made no such attribution. Besides, in his preface, Master Mou made clear that he was not interested in government service. He also referred to a contemporary, a prefect by the name of Chu, who lived in 178 A.D. (See his biography in the *Hou Han shu*, ch. 101). Some scholars dismissed the treatise as a forgery on insufficient evidence. See T'ang Yung-t'ung, *Han-Wei Liang-Chin Nan-Pei-ch'ao fo-chiao shih* (History of Buddhism from 206 B.C. to A.D. 589), pp. 73–78. But we do not know Mou's

name. Because of the mistaken attribution to the prefect Mou Jung, he has also been erroneously described as a prefect of Wu-chou in Kwangsi.

For French translation, see P. Pelliot, tr., "Meou Tse ou les Doutes Levés," *T'oung Pao*, 19 (1920), 255–433.

11. The Five Classics are *The Book of Odes, The Book of History, The Book of Changes, The Book of Propriety*, and *The Spring and Autumn Annals*.
12. Probably paraphrasing the *Scripture in Forty-Two Chapters*, ch. 34.
13. The Five Constant Virtues are humanity (*jen*), righteousness, propriety, wisdom, and faithfulness.
14. *Lao Tzu*, ch. 25.
15. Yao and Shun were legendary sage-emperor of the third millennium B.C. The Duke of Chou (d. 1094 B.C.) was son of King Wen and brother of King Wu, founders of the Chou dynasty. Confucius praised him as the builder of Chinese culture.
16. The Five Classics plus *The Book of Music* and the *Analects*. There have been other sets.
17. Ancient famous physician.
18. Confucius' pupil, Tuan-mu Tz'u (520–c.450 B.C.).
19. *Analects*, 19:22.
20. He loved the *Lao Tzu* and taught Yao the Way of not taking any action, according to tradition.
21. Called Wu-ch'eng Tzu. Nothing more is known of him. Probably fictitious.
22. He was Lü Hsiang, also known as Lü Tzu-ya. His original family name was Chiang, and in Chinese folklore he is called Grand Old Man Chiang. It is said that he was a fisherman. When King Wen met him by the Wei River, he invited him to become his teacher.
23. Confucius once went to the capital of Chou to interview Lao Tzu, who was then custodian of the archive, on ceremonies.
24. A mythical animal, the *ch'i-lin*, which looked like one-horned. Its appearance would signal the coming of a sage.
25. A mysterious bird whose appearance also indicated the coming of a sage.
26. Ch. 1.
27. Confucius' pupil, Tseng Ts-an (505–c.436 B.C.), noted for filial piety.
28. *Analects*, 8:3.
29. *Ibid.*, 9:30.
30. Ch. 1.
31. When King Wen was a child, his grandfather, T'ai Wang, seeing his good qualities, decided to designate his father Chi-li as the legal successor of the family line, instead of his uncle, T'ai-po, who, being the eldest son, should have been designated. In deference to Chi-li, T'ai-po withdrew to a southern barbarian country.
32. *Analects*, 8:1.
33. *Analects*, 14:1a. Kung-ch'o was the head of the Mang family in the state of Chin which was controlled by the families of Chao, Wei, and Han.
34. *Lao Tzu*, ch. 44.
35. Hsia (2183–1752 B.C.?), Shang (1751–1112 B.C.), and Western Chou (1111–770 B.C.).
36. The passage is not found in the *Lao Tzu*.
37. According to legend, Yao offered the throne to Ch'ao-fu (old man who dwelt on trees) and Hsü Hsing. Both declined. See the *Chuang Tzu*, ch. 28 (*Nan-hua chen-ching*, 9:18a).
38. *Analects*. 16:12. The brothers, being loyal to the Shang dynasty, refused to live under the Chou conquerors and eat their food.
39. *Ibid.*, 7:14.
40. For *hun* and *p'o*, see ch. 10, n. 1.
41. *Lao Tzu*, ch. 13.
42. *Ibid.*, ch. 9.
43. *Analects*, 11:11.
44. Confucius' pupil, Chung Yu (542–482 B.C.).
45. Ch. 18.

46. *Ibid.*
47. *Book of History*, "Golden knot."
48. *Lao Tzu*, ch. 52.
49. *Ibid.*
50. *Analects*, 3:9.
51. *Book of Mencius*, 3A:4.
52. *Analects*, 9:14.
53. Gautama Śākyamuni, the historical Buddha, as a prince in a former life.
54. See n. 31.
55. *Book of Mencius*, 5A:2.
56. See Wing-tsit Chan, *A Source Book in Chinese Philosophy*, ch. 20.
57. *Hung-ming chi*, 12:9b.
58. *Ibid.*, 9:6a–18a.
59. The historical Buddha, Gautama Śākyamuni, who lived in India in the sixth century B.C.
60. Those who attain their own salvation by personally hearing the Buddha's preaching, those who attain their salvation by their own exertions in an age in which there was no Buddha, and the vehicle of the bodhisattva, who delays his Buddhahood in order to help others to salvation.
61. Father, son, elder brother, younger brother, husband, and wife.
62. Refers to the mountain in the *Chuang Tzu*, ch. 14.
63. *Lao Tzu*, ch. 39.
64. *Ling* in Chinese, which variously means the soul, intelligence, light, etc.
65. The World of Sensuous Desire (heavens of desires, its human world, and hells), the World of Matter (various heavens that are free from desire), and the World of Pure Spirit (the highest level where the mind dwells in pure and nuptial meditation).
66. Quoting the *Book of Charges*, commentary on hexagram no. 18, *ku* (troubles).
67. See the *Hung-ming chi*, chs. 9 and 10.
68. For German translation, see Stefan Balázs, "Der Philosophy Fan Tschan und sein Traktat gegen den Buddhismus," *Sinica*, 7 (1932), 220–34.
69. *Classic of Filial Piety*, ch. 18.
70. *Book of Changes*, "Appended Remarks," pt. 1, ch. 12.
71. Po-yu died a violent death and became a ghost, and in 535 B.C. went around to frighten people. The story is told in the *Tso chuan*, Duke Chao, 7th year. For P'eng-sheng, see *ibid.*, Duke Chiang, 8th year.
72. *Book of Changes*, "Appended Remarks," p. 1, ch. 4, and commentary on hexagram no. 38, *ku-ei* (to part).
73. Literally, a 1,000 *chung*. A *chung* was 40,000 pecks (*tou*). Each *tou* was about 316 cubic inches.

CHAPTER 17

The Mahāyāna Ideal

□ The most important development of Buddhism in China has been the growth from the Small Vehicle (Hīnayāna)[1] to the Great Vehicle (Mahāyāna). In the former the ideal is the arhat and individual salvation, or to become, through one's own effort, a saint who is no longer subject to the cycle of life and death. In the latter, the ideal is universal salvation, that is, for all to become Buddhas through the compassion of the Buddha and the bodhisattva who defers his own Buddhahood to seek salvation for others. The Mahāyāna ideal has been expressed in the last 1,900 years in endless temples and pagodas, sculptures and paintings, and, most of all, in scriptures and treatises. The Buddhist Canon contains 3,053 titles, and its Supplement contains thousands more. The vast majority of them are Mahāyāna literature. It is true that each of the Buddhist schools has its own basic scriptures and treatises, but these are not considered either as final or as exclusive. Most well-known scriptures are read in many schools. So far as Buddhist followers are concerned, they are just the words of the Buddha, transcending school preference and individual interpretations. The following three are among the most common, the most important, and the most popular. They are common because they are read in many schools, important because they contain the most fundamental ideas, and popular because they have been recited, copied, offered in temples, and preserved in homes by the millions and millions over hundreds of years. □

A. THE PROMISE OF THE PURE LAND

□Of all the contributions Buddhism has made in China, and they have been innumerable, the one that has made the strongest impact and produced the greatest effect is the belief in rebirth in the Pure Land. Both Confucianism and Taoism had confined their vision to the mundane world. Even Taoist immortals were earthbound. Here is the gospel opening up an infinite vista of the future, giving the Chinese people a new perspective, a new direction, a new hope, and a new confidence. No wonder to this day the Pure Land School (Ching-t'u in China and Jōdo in Japan) is the most popular Buddhist sect in East Asia. But the belief is not limited to one school, even though it is the largest. Most Buddhists live by it.

The ideas contained in the following scripture are very simple. Here is Amitābha (nonmeasurable-light), also called Amitāyus (nonmeasurable-life), the Buddha who is Infinite Life and Infinite Light, proclaiming his gospel, and there are many other Buddhas in numerous Buddha-lands joining the chorus, cherishing and meditating on all sentient beings and promising all of them rebirth in the most precious, most beautiful Happy Land (Sukhāvatī).[2] One should recite the name of the Buddha, *A mi-t'o-fo* (*A-mi-tā-bha*), as an indication of devotion, but in addition, he should cultivate virtue, discipline the mind, recite the scripture, and achieve wisdom.

However, the promise is clear and definite. It would be most unfair and unkind to look upon this belief as selfishness or escape from the world. Indifference to others and shirking social responsibility can hardly be called virtue.

The scripture is technically one of the three basic scriptures of the Pure Land School[3] founded by T'an-luan (476–542). Broadly speaking, however, it represents an extensive movement going back at least 150 years earlier. (Hui-yüan, 334–417,[4] was a great devotee.) The literature it has inspired in the form of treatises and commentaries, has been tremendous, but the prominent note is the same, namely, rebirth in the Pure Land. □

The *Amitābha Scripture Spoken by the Buddha*

§1. Thus have I[5] heard:

Once the Buddha was in the Anāthapiṃḍada Garden of Jetavana Grove in the state of Śravastī[6] in a large company of 1,250 monks. They were all great arhats (saints)[7] as everyone knew, such as Śāriputra the elder, Mahāmāudgalyāyana, Mahākāśyapa, Mahākātyāyana, Mahākāuṣṭhila, Revata, Śuddhipanthaka, Nanda, Ānanda, Rāhula, Gavāṃpati, Piṇḍola-Bharadvāja, Kālodayin, Mahākapphiṇa, Vakkula, Aniruddha, and many other great disciples[8]; and many bodhisattva-mahāsattvas (those just behind the Buddha in enlightenment), such as Mañjusrī, Prince of the Lord of Law, Bodhisattva Ajita, Bodhisattva Gandhahastin, Bodhisattva Nityodyukta, and other great Bodhisattvas[9]; and innumerable heavenly beings (gods) such as Śakrodevānām-Indra.

§2. At that time the Buddha told Śāriputra[10] the Elder: Beyond a trillion Buddha-lands west of here there is a world called Most Happy Land. In that place there is a Buddha, Amitāyus (immeasurable life) by name, now preaching the Law. Śāriputra, why is that land called Most Happy Land? Sentient beings in that land have no pain of any kind but enjoy all kinds of pleasure only. Hence it is called Most Happy Land.

§3. Furthermore, Śāriputra, in Most Happy Land there are seven rows of balustrades, seven rows of (ornamental) nets, and seven rows of trees. They are all of four kinds of gems and surround the land. Therefore that land is called Most Happy Land.

§4. Furthermore, Śāriputra, in Most Happy Land there are lakes of seven gems filled with water, which is of eight merits.[11] The bottoms of the ponds are completely covered with gold dust, and the paths and steps on the four sides are made of gold, silver, beryl, and crystal. Above the ponds are towers, also elaborately adorned with gold, silver, beryl, crystal, white coral, red pearls, and agates. In the lakes lotus flowers are as big as chariot wheels. The green flowers had green brilliance; yellow flowers, yellow brilliance; red flowers, red brilliance; and white flowers, white brilliance. They are subtle, wonderful, fragrant, and pure. Śāriputra, such is the splendor in Most Happy Land achieved by the merits [of Buddha Amitāyus]!

§5. Furthermore, Śāriputra, in that Buddha-land heavenly music always goes on. The ground is made of yellow gold. In six periods every day and night, it showers mystical flowers from heaven. In that land sentient beings always hold many wonderful blossoms with their robes in the clear morning and make offerings to the trillion Buddhas in other regions. Precisely at the meal time they return to their own land to take their meal and stroll restfully here and there. Śāriputra, such is the splendor in Most Happy Land achieved by the merits [of Buddha Amitāyus]!

§6. And, again, Śāriputra, in that land there are always all kinds of wonderful birds of mixed colors—swans, peacock, parrot, parakeet, sparrow, and double-headed pheasant. In six periods every day and night, these birds utter harmonious and elegant sounds. Their tunes joyously broadcast such doctrines as the Five Virtues,[12] the Five Powers[13] the Seven Paths to Perfect Wisdom,[14] and the Eightfold Noble Path.[15] When sentient beings in that land have heard these tunes, they all contemplate on the Buddha, the Law, and the Order.[16] Śāriputra, don't you say that these birds were really born as punishment for their sins. Why? Because in that Buddha-land the Three Evil Realms[17] do not exist. Śāriputra, there is not even the name "Three Evil Realms" in that Buddha-land. How much less their reality! All those birds have been through transformation created by Buddha Amitāyus for the purpose of spreading the voice of the Law. Śāriputra, in the Buddha-land, as a gentle breeze blows and moves the several rows of precious trees and precious nets, they utter a subtle sound, like a hundred thousand kinds of music arising at the same time. Those who hear this music all naturally arouse in themselves the mind to contemplate on the Buddha, the Law, and the Order. Śāriputra, such is the splendor in the Buddha-land achieved by the merits [of Buddha Amitāyus]!

§7. Śāriputra, what do you think? Why is that Buddha called Amitābha (immeasurable light)? Śāriputra, the light of that Buddha is infinite, shining on all the lands in the ten cardinal directions[18] without impediment. Therefore he is called Amitābha. Furthermore, Śāriputra, the life of that Buddha and that of his people is infinite and unlimited in the number of aeons. Therefore he is called Amitāyus. Śāriputra, it has been ten aeons since Buddha Amitāyus attained Buddhahood. Furthermore, Śāriputra, that Buddha has an infinite and unlimited number of disciples who (attain their own salvation by) personally hearing (his teachings). They are all arhats and their number cannot be known by calculation. The same is true of the many bodhisattvas. Śāriputra, such is the splendor in that Buddha-land achieved by the merits [of Buddha Amitāyus]!

§8. Furthermore, Śāriputra, sentient beings born in Most Happy Land are those who will never turn back from bodhisattvahood. There are many among them who are to be born only once more before Buddhahood. Their number is very great and cannot be known by calculation, but can only be spoken of in terms of an infinite and unlimited number. Śāriputra, all sentient beings who hear about this should take a vow to be born in that land. Why? In order to be able to be in company with these people of highest good. Śāriputra! it is impossible to be born in that land by means of a small number of good qualities.

§9. Śāriputra, if there is a good man or a good woman,[19] who, upon hearing of Buddha Amitāyus, recites the Buddha's name for one, two, three, four, five, six, or seven days with a single and undisturbed mind, when he or she approaches death, Buddha Amitāyus and the many other holy beings will appear before him, and when death comes, he, with his mind not at all upset, will be immediately born into Buddha Amitāyus's Most Happy Land. Śāriputra, I have said this because I have seen how this works effectively. If any of the myriad beings hears this message, he should take the vow to be born in that land.

§10. Śāriputra, as I now praise the inconceivable merits of Buddha Amitāyus, there are also in the eastern region, Buddha Akṣobhya, Buddha Merudhvaja, Buddha Mahāmeru, Buddha Meruprabhāsa, Buddha Manjughoṣa, and other Buddhas as many as the sands in the Ganges River, each in his own land extending his long tongue complete to cover the world system of 1,000 million worlds, and speaking these truthful words: All you sentient beings should believe in this scripture which glorifies the inconceivable merits (of Buddha Amitāyus) and is protected by and contemplated on by all Buddhas.

§11–15. Śāriputra, there are in the southern region . . . western region . . . northern region . . . lower region . . . upper region . . . (repeated with the names of different Buddhas).

§16. Śāriputra, what do you think? Why is it called the scripture protected by and contemplated on by all Buddhas? Śāriputra, if a good man or a good woman hears the names (of Buddha Amitāyus) and the name of the scripture cited by these many Buddhas, it means that all good men and all good women are protected and contemplated on by all Buddhas together, and are all able to avoid turning back from having achieved the Highest Perfect Wisdom. Therefore, Śāriputra, all of you should believe in and accept my words and what all the Buddhas say.

§17. Śāriputra, if there are people who have made a vow, are now making a vow, or will make a vow to wish to be born in the Buddha-land of Amitāyus, all of them will be able to avoid turning back from having achieved the Highest Perfect Wisdom, as if they have been, or are now being, or shall be, born in that land. Śāriputra, those good men and good women who have the faith should make a vow to be born in that land.

§18. Śāriputra, as I am now praising the inconceivable merits of the many Buddhas, they are also speaking of my inconceivable merits and say thus: Śākyamuni Buddha was able to do things that were extremely difficult to do. He was able to attain the Highest Perfect Wisdom in a world in which imperfect beings endure suffering and in the period of Five Impurities, namely, impurity of degeneration of time, impurity of subjective viewpoints, impurity of afflictions, impurity of sentient beings (with inferior bodies), and impurity of the (the transitoriness of) life. He is now preaching to all sentient beings the Law that the world finds difficult to believe. Śāriputra, you should know that it is very difficult for me to do these very difficult things, to achieve the Highest Perfect Wisdom, and to preach to all the world the Law which it finds difficult to believe. These are considered very difficult things.

After the Buddha finished preaching this scripture, Śāriputra and the many disciples, heavenly beings, men, demons, and so on, having heard the Buddha's preaching, believed and accepted with joy, made sign of reverence, and left (*Taishō daizōkyō* [Taishō edition of the Buddhist Canon], 12:346–48).

B. UNIVERSAL SALVATION BY FAITH

☐ The *Lotus Scripture*, to which this section is devoted, is the most important Buddhist scripture in East Asia. It is so because it is used by virtually all Buddhist schools, because it was the first to preach revolutionary Mahāyāna doctrines and is as yet the most comprehensive statement of them, because it has been the main inspiration of Buddhist literature and art, and, most of all, because it has warmed the hearts of millions and millions of East Asians in the last 1,500 years. It is no exaggeration to say that it is the most representative and most meaningful among the several hundred Mahāyāna scriptures. No wonder that when Chang Jung, an ardent advocate of the harmony of Confucianism, Taoism, and Buddhism, died in A.D. 497, he held in his left hand a copy of the *Classic of Filial Piety* and the *Lao Tzu* and in his right hand the *Lotus*.[20]

The scripture is a cosmic drama on the greatest scale ever conceived by man. Its stage is many Buddha-worlds. Its time is eternity. And its actors are the Lord Buddha Śākyamuni and innumerable superhuman and human beings. The entire universe is shaking and flowers rain all over and perfume sweetens all space. Now Śākyamuni preaches. He is no longer just an historical being, but Tathāgata,[21] the eternal and perfect being, neither one Buddha nor many, the father of all Buddhas to whom all beings are Buddha-sons. All possess the Buddha-nature and all will be saved and become Buddhas. No misfortune, ignorance, or even sin will bar them, and no woman, child, the sick, the poor, or anyone will be excluded. He teaches the One Vehicle instead of the Three Vehicles,[22] the successive stages through which men arrive at Buddhahood, which are but convenient means of the One Vehicle. In this vehicle, Nirvāṇa is not extinction of existence as taught in Hīnayāna, but extinction of ignorance, that is, Enlightenment. Anyone who expresses his faith in the Tathāgata by reciting his name, charity, endurance, building a temple, or even drawing a picture of a pagoda in sand when a child is at play, will be saved. There are a great many bodhisattvas who defer their Buddhahood and dedicate themselves to the salvation of all. They will use any convenient means, assume any form, go anywhere, and run any risk to help people to salvation. So long as a person has the slightest devotion or faith, the Buddha's great compassion, personified in the bodhisattva, will deliver him from suffering. This magnificent idea of compassion and its dramatization in the dedication and sacrifice of the bodhisattva is perhaps the most potent force in the universal appeal and enduring vitality of the Buddhist religion in China.

Among the most adored of all bodhisattvas is Kuan-yin (see the world's sound [of suffering]).[23] He is the most complete embodiment of the Buddha's mercy and compassion. He has four, eight, eighteen, or a thousand hands, to save beings in all possible ways with all possible weapons and under all possible circumstances. Often he is presented in feminine form, perhaps to satisfy the Chinese love of sensuous beauty, perhaps to represent more appropriately the virtue of compassion—especially as a protector of women and bestower of children, or perhaps to give Buddhism a loving Mother, the tenderness and warmth which Confucianism and Taoism, in their teachings of moderation and simplicity, had not provided the Chinese. In the Taoist religion Kuan-yin has become a most popular deity, often called Goddess of Mercy in the West. The twenty-fifth section of the *Lotus Scripture* is devoted entirely to him and has been singled out as a separate scripture. It is an act of devotion to study, recite, copy, distribute, or offer it in temples, an act committed day after day by thousands and thousands.

The *Lotus Scripture*[24] was probably compiled in Khotan in Central Asia or in North India some time before A.D. 250 and came into China by way of Khotan. It was already highly regarded in China in the third century. Chinese translations were made of it in 286, 335, 355 (or 356), 406, and 601. The 406 version by Kumārajīva (344–413) is the most authentic and most popular. It is the basic text of the T'ien-t'ai (heavenly terrace) School. The founder of the school, Chih-i (538–597), lectured extensively on its terminology and phrases, its profound meanings, and the methods of concentration and insight that it teaches, lectures that were recorded and became known as the "Three Great Works". However, it is also basic to all Mahāyāna Buddhists.[25] □

The *Lotus Scripture of the Wonderful Law*

In the ten cardinal directions[26] of the
Buddha-land,
There is only the One Vehicle
There are neither two nor three,
Except the convenient means of the
Buddha,
Where he employs temporary means,
To lead living beings.
For the sake of explaining the Buddha
wisdom,
Many Buddhas have appeared in the
world,
Only for this One Reality,
Both the Śrāvaka Vehicle and the
Pratyeka-buddha Vehicle are not real.
For never by the Small Vehicle
Would the Buddhas save all beings.
The Buddha himself abides in the Great
Vehicle,
And in accordance with the Law he has
attained,
By meditation and wisdom and the effort
and ornament of virtue,
He saves all beings.
I have realized the Supreme Way,
The Law of the Great Vehicle applies to
all beings.
If I converted by the Small Vehicle
Even one single human being,
I should fall into stinginess and greed.
Such a thing cannot be done.
If men turn in faith to the Buddha,
The Tathāgata will not deceive him.
Nor will he have greed or envious desires.
He will cut off all evil among the
dharmas.[27]
Therefore in the ten cardinal directions,
The Buddha is afraid of nothing.
With a body of distinguishing marks and
splendor,
I shed light to shine on the world.
Honored by the infinite multitude,
I explain to them the seal of reality.[28]
Śāriputra,[29] you should know that
From the very start I made a vow
With the desire to enable all beings
To be the same as we are.
As what I wanted before,
Now my desire is satisfied:
To convert all living beings,
To enable them all to enter the Path of
the Buddha.

. . .

Although I preach Nirvāṇa,
It is not real extinction.

All dharmas from the beginning
Are always tranquil in themselves and are devoid of appearance.
When the Buddha-son fulfills his course,
He becomes a Buddha in his next life,
Because of my ability to use every convenient means,
I reveal the Law of Three Vehicles.
All the World Honored Ones
Preach the path of the One Vehicle.
Now all the multitudes
Should remove doubts and delusions.
There is no difference in what the Buddhas preach;
It is only the One Vehicle and not two.
In the innumerable long periods of the past,
There have been an infinite number of Buddhas saving people.
There have been hundreds of trillion kinds,
Whose number cannot be calculated.
All these World Honored Ones
Used all kinds of examples and parables under various conditions,
And their unlimited ability to employ the convenient means
To demonstrate and preach the characteristics of dharmas.
All these World Honored Ones
Preached the Law of One Vehicle.
They converted an infinite number of living beings
And enabled them to enter the Path of the Buddha.
There also have been many great holy lords (Buddhas)
Who knew that in the world at large
There were heavenly beings, men, and various species of living beings,
Who had desires deep in their hearts.
They employed different kinds of convenient means
To assist in making clear the Highest Truth.
Those among the living beings,
Who have come into contact with former Buddhas,
And have learned the Law and practiced charity,
Or have held on to discipline and endured forbearance and humiliation,
Or have made serious efforts at concentration and understanding,
Or have cultivated various kinds of blessing and wisdom—
All such beings as these
Have already achieved Buddhahood.
If, after the Nirvāṇa of the Buddhas,
Men who possess a tender heart,
All such beings as these,
Have already achieved Buddhahood.
After the Nirvāṇa of the Buddhas,
Those who have offered relics,
Or have built hundreds of millions of pagodas
And with gold, silver, crystal,
With white coral and agate,
And with jasper and beryl,
Clearly and splendidly displayed
Have adorned these pagodas;
Or have built temples of stone,
Of sandalwood or garu-wood,
Of fragrant wood or other material,
Of bricks, tiles, or earth and the like;
Or have heaped earth in the wilderness
To make Buddha temples;
Or even boys at play,
Who have accumulated sand to become Buddha pagodas—
All such beings as these,
Have already achieved Buddhahood.
Those people who, for the sake of the Buddha,
Have installed images of various shapes,
Or have had them carved in different forms,
All have already achieved Buddhahood.
Those who have made with the seven gems,[30]
Or brass, copper, bronze, lead, tin, pewter,
Iron, wood, earth, or lacquer-coated cloth,
Buddha figures with elaborate ornamentation—
All such beings as these
Have already achieved Buddhahood.
Those who have had pictures of the Buddha embroidered,
Expressing the great splendor
Which he achieved from a hundred merits and blessings,
Whether embroidered by himself or by others,
Have all achieved Buddhahood.
Even boys at play

Who have painted Buddha figures
With straws, wooden sticks, brushes, or finger nails—
All people such as these,
By gradual accumulation of merits
And with an adequate sense of compassion,
Have already achieved Buddhahood.
The bodhisattvas who have been converting people
Have delivered an infinite number of beings.
Those who have offered incense or canopies
To pagodas or temples, or carved or painted figures,
And served with a reverent mind;
Those who have asked people to play music,
To strike drums or blow conches,
To play horizontal or vertical flutes,
Different kinds of lutes, and the guitar,
To strike cymbals and bells, and make similar wonderful music,
And to serve the Buddha with all of these;
Or who with a happy frame of mind
Have sung the glory of the Buddha,
Even with a small sound,
All have already achieved Buddhahood.
Those who have gotten rid of their disturbed minds,
And make offerings to painted figures of the Buddha,
Even with a single flower,
Will gradually see an infinite number of Buddhas.
Those who have worshiped,
By merely folding their hands,
Or even by raising one hand,
Or merely slightly nodding their heads,
And made offerings to images of the Buddha,
Will gradually see an infinite number of Buddhas.
They will reach the highest level
And deliver an infinite number of beings
To enter Nirvāṇa which leaves nothing (elements that make up the self)[31] behind,
Like the fire wood with all flames extinguished.
Those who have gotten rid of their disturbed minds
And enter a pagoda or a temple
And have uttered a single "Namo" (Praised be . . .).
All have already achieved Buddhahood.
About the Buddhas of the past—
After they passed away from this world,
They heard the Law,
And all have already achieved Buddhahood.
As to the Buddhas of the future,
Their number will be infinite.
All these Tathāgatas
Will also preach the Law by convenient means.
All these Tathāgatas, with an infinite number of convenient means,
Will save all living beings
And enable them to enter into the pure wisdom of the Buddha.
Among those who have heard the Law,
None will fail to achieve Buddhahood.
All Buddhas from the very start have taken the vow:
"The Buddha-way which I walk,
I desire to enable all living beings
To attain the same way with me."
Although Buddhas in future ages
Preach hundred of trillions
Of methods, beyond number,
In reality there is only the One Vehicle.
(§2; *Taishō daizōkyō*, 9:8–9)

At that time Bodhisattva Aksayamati[32] rose from his seat, bore his right shoulder, folded his hands, faced the Buddha, and said, "World Honored One, for what reason is Bodhisattva Kuan-yin so called?"

The Buddha told Bodhisattva Aksayamati: Good man, if there are an infinite number, or a hundred trillion living beings who are suffering, when they hear about Bodhisattva Kuan-yin, praise his name wholeheartedly, Bodhisattva Kuan-yin will at once see their sound and they will all be saved.

If people hold on to the name of Bodhisattva Kuan-yin, they will not burn if they enter into a big fire, because of the majestic spiritual power of the bodhisattva. If they drift in a great river and praise his name, they will immediately get to a shallow spot. If a hundred trillion living beings, in search of gold, silver, beryl, agate, coral, amber, pearl, and so on, enter the sea and their boats, blown by a black storm, drift and sink into the country of malignant spirits, and if only one of them praises the name of Bodhisattva Kuan-yin, all of them will be saved from the calamities brought by the malignant spirits. For this reason the bodhisattva is called Kuan-yin.

Again, if a person is about to be murdered and praises the name of Bodhisattva Kuan-yin, the knife or staff held by the attacker will fall to pieces, and the person will be saved. If in the system of 3,000 million countries violent demons and malignant spirits want to annoy them in the darkness of the night, and if they are heard to praise the name of Bodhisattva Kuan-yin, the demons and spirits cannot even look at them with an evil eye. How much less can they harm them? If people, whether guilty or innocent, are fettered and locked, with their bodies tied, praise the name of Bodhisattva Kuan-yin, the locks and so on will all be broken and destroyed, and they will immediately be saved. If in the system of 3,000 million countries full of dangerous robbers a group of merchants, led by a head merchant, are carrying great treasures and traveling on a dangerous road, and if one of them call out thus: "All of you, good men, don't be afraid. You should wholeheartedly praise the name of Bodhisattva Kuan-yin. This bodhisattva can extend his fearlessness to all living beings. If you praise his name, you will be saved from these dangerous robbers," and if when the merchants hear these words, all will say out loud, "Namo! Bodhisattva Kuan-yin," they will immediately be saved. Aksayamati, the majestic spiritual power of Bodhisattva Kuan-yin, the great spiritual hero, is august like this!

If living beings with impure desires always think of and revere Bodhisattva Kuan-yin, they will forthwith be free from these desires. If people who are often angry always think of and revere Bodhisattva Kuan-yin, they will forthwith be free from anger. If they have many delusions but always think of and revere Bodhisattva Kuan-yin, they will be free from delusions. Aksayamati, Bodhisattva Kuan-yin has great and majestic spiritual power like this and confers much benefit on people. Therefore living beings should always think of him.

If a woman wants a son, worships and pays homage to Bodhisattva Kuan-yin, she will bear a blessed, virtuous, and wise son, or if she wants a daughter, she will bear a good and beautiful girl, who, rooted in virtue to start with, will be loved and respected by all. Aksayamati, Bodhisattva Kuan-yin possesses such power, if living beings revere and worship him, their blessing will not be wasted . . . (§25; *Taishō daizōkyō*, 9:56–57)

C. THE PERFECT WISDOM

□ Whereas the two preceding scriptures belong to devotion literature, the *Diamond Scripture*[33] belongs to the huge body of writing called wisdom literature, that of diamond wisdom which overcomes all illusory knowledge. It is metaphysical in nature. A few but fundamental concepts of Māhāyana Buddhism are here asserted and repeated again and again. There is no elaboration, much less analysis. These must be sought elsewhere, and there are hundreds of scriptures and treatises for such purpose. The goal of the short scripture seems to be reaffirmation of convictions, and it is for this reason that it has deep meaning for the majority of Chinese Buddhists to whom the scripture is a constant companion.

Here the Tathāgata[34] is presented as without marks. Marks, signs, appearances, characters, and so on do not reveal the true reality, and often falsify it. Real matter is therefore no-matter, and true dharma (elements of existence)[35] is no-dharma. Ultimate reality is beyond any words, conception, or description of any sort. The self or anything else is but a sign, a name, a temporary or dependent entity. One should not attach to anything and thus allow his pure mind to grow. One should perform charity, accumulate merits, attain the highest wisdom, and so on, but should do so without thinking of them as charity, merit, and so on. Even the Tathāgata is no-Tathāgata. If this sounds negative or other-worldly, let us not forget that the primary aim is still good work, profound wisdom, and merits. Fruits and rewards are not ignored, but there should be no attachment to them. This is the diamond cutter, or perfection of wisdom. □

The *Diamond Scripture*

§5. "Subhūti,[36] what do you think? Can the Tathāgata be seen by the possession of his marks?"

"No, World Honored One. The Tathāgata cannot be seen by the possession of his marks (signs). Why? The possession of marks spoken by the Tathāgata is indeed a no-possession of no-marks."

The Buddha told Subhūti, "All marks are false. If one has seen that all marks are no-marks, he will forthwith see the Tathāgata."

§9. "Subhūti, what do you think? Does One Who Has Entered the Stream (first stage of sainthood) think thus: I have obtained the fruit of One Who Has Entered the Stream?"

Subhūti said, "No, World Honored One. Why? Because although the name 'stream-enterer' means entering the stream, actually he has not entered into (obtained) anything. He has not obtained any dharma of form, sound, smell, taste, touch, or mental objects. Therefore he is called One Who Has Entered the Stream."

"Subhūti, what do you think? Does a Once-Returner think thus: I have obtained the fruit of a Once-Returner?"

Subhūti said, "No, World Honored One. Why? Because although the name Once-Returner means that one will come back and go once more, actually there is neither coming (to the world) nor going. Therefore he is called a Once-Returner."

"Subhūti, what do you think? Does a Never-Returner think thus: I have obtained the fruit of a Never-Returned?"

Subhūti said, "No, World Honored One. Why? Because although the name Never-Returner means never to return, actually there is no no-returning. Therefore he is called a Never-Returner."

"Subhūti, what do you think? Does an arhat (saint)[37] think thus: I have obtained arhatship?"

Subhūti said, "No, World Honored One. Why? Because there is no dharma called 'arhat'. World Honored One, if an arhat thinks thus: I have obtained arhatship, it means that he is attached to a self (an ego distinct from a combination of elements), a being (a separate individual identical with himself), living beings (souls), or a person (a permanent being migrating from rebirth to rebirth). World Honored One, the Buddha has said that I have obtained the contemplation in which there is no longer a distinction of self and others, and am the foremost among men, and am the first arhat free from worldly desires. World Honored One, if I thought thus: I am an arhat free from worldly desires, the World Honored One would not say that Subhūti is one who dwells in peace and virtue, for Subhūti actually does not dwell anywhere, and that is why Subhūti is called one who dwells in peace and virtue."

§10. The Buddha told Subhūti, "What do you think? Did the Tathāgata learn anything about dharma from the (former Buddha) Dīpaṅkara?"[38]

"No, World Honored One. When the Tathāgata was with Dīpaṅkara, he really did not learn anything about dharma."

"Subhūti, what do you think? Does a bodhisattva[39] adorn a Buddha land?"

"No, World Honored One. Why? Because to adorn a Buddha-land is indeed no-adornment. Therefore it is called adornment."

"Therefore, Subhūti, the bodhisattvas should in this way let their minds of purity grow, should not let their minds grow by abiding in matter,[40] should not let their minds grow by abiding in sound, smell, taste, touch, and mental objects, and should not be abiding in anything and in this way let their minds grow. Subhūti, suppose there is a man with a body like Sumeru, king of mountains. What do you think? Is this body (personal existence) considered great?"

Subhūti said, "Very great, World Honored One, Why? Because the Buddha has taught the nonexistence of personal existence. Therefore it is called great personal existence."

§14. At that time, Subhūti, having heard the scripture spoken, deeply understood its meanings, shed copious tears, and said to the Buddha, "It is wonderful, World Honored One. How profound a scripture like this has been preached by the Buddha! With all the knowledge acquired in the past, I have never been able to hear such a scripture. World Honored One, if there are also people who, upon hearing this scripture, believe it with a pure mind, they will receive a true perception (which is nothing but a sign). We will then know that they have accomplished extremely wonderful merits of the highest order. World Honored One, the true perception is no-perception. Therefore the Tathāgata taught that its name is 'true perception.' World Honored One, now I have heard this scripture. It is not difficult to believe, understand, accept, and hold on to it. But if beings in the last 500 years of the future period (when the Law declines)[41] hear this scripture, believe, understand, accept, and hold on to it, they will be wonderful indeed. Why? These people will have no perception of the self, no perception of being, no perception of living beings, and no perception of a person. Why? Because the perception of the self is no perception, and the perceptions of a being, living beings, and a person are no perception. Why? Those free from all perceptions are called Buddhas."

The Buddha told Subhūti, "So it is, so it is. If there are also people who hear this scripture and are not alarmed, terrified, or frightened, we will then know that they are very wonderful. Why? Subhūti, the highest perfection spoken of by the Tathāgata is indeed no highest perfection. Therefore it is called the highest perfection. Subhūti, the perfection of endurance spoken of by the Buddha is no perfection of endurance. Therefore it is called the perfection of endurance. Why? Subhūti, when the king of Kalinga cut off my limbs, I had no perception of the self, a being, living beings, or a person. Why? If at the time when my limbs were falling off I had a perception of the self, a being, living beings, or a person, hatred would arise in me. Subhūti, I also remember the past 500 births when I was a spiritual perception of endurance. At that time also I had no perception of the self, a being, living beings, or a person. Therefore, Subhūti, a bodhisattva should be free from all perceptions, produce in him the mind of the highest perfect wisdom, should not let his mind grow by abiding in matter, and should not let his mind grow by abiding in sound, smell, taste, touch or mental objects. He should let the mind that is abiding in nothing grow. If the mind abides in anything, it is indeed no-abiding. Therefore the Buddha has taught that a bodhisattva should not give alms with his mind abiding in form. Because the bodhisattva is dedicated to benefiting all beings, he should not give alms in this way. All those perceptions spoken of by the Tathāgata are indeed no-perceptions, and all those beings spoken of by him are indeed no-beings. Subhūti, The Tathāgata is one who speaks the truth, speaks what is in accord with reality, speaks of what is, and does not speak untruth or falsehood. Subhūti, the dharmas obtained by the Tathāgata have neither truth nor falsehood. Subhūti, if a bodhisattva practices alms with a mind abiding in dharmas, it is like a person with eyes, and, with sunshine shining brilliantly, seeing all kinds of colors. Subhūti, if in the future period there are good men and good women who can accept, hold onto, recite and study this scripture, they will be seen and known by the Tathāgata with his Buddha wisdom, and will all attain an unlimited amount of merits."

§16. "Again, Subhūti, if good men and good women accept, hold onto, recite, and study these scriptures, and if they are humiliated, these people, the action-influence[42] of whose sins in former lives should cause them to fall into the evil stage of existence (suffering), will have the action-influence of their sins of former lives wiped out because of the humiliation by people of this generation, and will attain the highest perfect widsom. Subhūti, I remember that in the past aeons before the time of Dīpaṅkara, there were 84,000 million Buddhas following after him. I have made offerings to them and served all of them without missing any. If there will also be people in the last period of the last age (when the Law declines) who will accept, hold on to, recite, and study these scriptures, compared to the merits they attain, my merits attained from serving the many Buddhas will not approach one hundredth part, not one thousandth part, not a one hundred thousandth part, not a ten millionth part, nor a one hundred millionth part, or a 100,000 millionth part, and so on beyond any calculation or illustration. Subhūti, if there are good men and good women in the last period of the last age who will accept, hold on to, recite, and study these scriptures, the merits they attain will be as what I have already said. Perhaps when people hear this, their minds will forthwith be disturbed and they will become skeptical. Subhūti, they should know that the meanings of the scriptures are inconceivable, and their fruits and rewards are also inconceivable."

§17. At that time Subhūti said to the Buddha, "World Honored One, how should a good man or a good woman make up his or her mind to obtain the highest perfect wisdom, in what should one abide, and how should one control one's mind?"

The Buddha told Subhūti, "Good men and good women who make up their minds to obtain the highest perfect wisdom should produce a mind like this: 'I must lead all being to Nirvāṇa; and yet, after beings have been delivered, no being at all has been delivered.' And why? Subhūti, if a bodhisattva has a perception of the self, a being, living beings, or a person, he is indeed no-bodhisattva. Why? Subhūti, because there is really no dharma called 'making up the mind to obtain the highest perfect wisdom.' Subhūti, what do you think? When he was with Dīpaṅkara, did the Tathāgata have the dharma by which to obtain the highest perfect wisdom?

"No, World Honored One. As I understood the meaning of what the Buddha said, when he was with Dīpaṅkara, he had no dharma by which to obtain the highest perfect wisdom."

The Buddha said, "So it is, so it is, Subhūti, there is really no dharma by which the Tathāgata could obtain the highest perfect wisdom. Subhūti, if there were a dharma by which the Tathāgata could obtain the highest perfect wisdom, Dīpaṅkara would not have prophesied for me, saying, 'You will be the Buddha in the future, called Śākyamuni.' Because there was really no dharma by which one could obtain the highest perfect wisdom, therefore Dīpaṅkara prophesied for me, saying, 'You will become the Buddha in future, called Śākyamuni.' Why? The name Tathāgata means the thusness of all dharmas. If someone says that the Tathāgata has obtained the highest perfect wisdom, why, Subhūti, there is really no dharma by which the Buddha could obtain the highest perfect wisdom. Subhūti, the highest perfect wisdom obtained by the Tathāgata is neither true nor false. Therefore all the dharmas spoken by the Tathāgata are Buddha-dharmas. Subhūti, what are spoken of as all dharmas are indeed no-dharmas. Therefore they are called 'all dharmas.' Subhūti, suppose a man has a large body."

Subhūti said, "World Honored One, the large human body spoken of by the Tathāgata is indeed not a large body. Therefore it is called a large body."

"Subhūti, it is the same with a bodhisattva. If he said, 'I must lead an infinite number of beings to Nirvāṇa,' he would not be called a bodhisattva. Why? Subhūti, because there is really no dharma by which one is called a bodhisattva. Therefore the Buddha says that all dharmas have no perception of the self, a being, living beings, or a person. Subhūti, if a bodhisattva said, 'I must adorn the Buddha-land,' he would not be called a bodhisattva. Why? Because the adornment of the Buddha-land spoken of by the Tathāgata is indeed no-adornment. Therefore it is called adornment. Subhūti, if a bodhisattva penetratingly understands that things have no self, he will be called a bodhisattva by the Tathāgata."

§29. "Subhūti, if someone says the Tathāgata goes or comes, sits or lies down, he does not understand the meaning of my teaching. Why? The Tathāgata means one who comes from nowhere and goes nowhere. Therefore he is called 'Tathāgata.'" (*Taishō daizōkyō*, 8:748–52)

NOTES

1. People in the so-called Hīnayāna Buddhist countries in South and Southeast Asia naturally resent the appellation. They insist that there is nothing small about their Buddhism, which has been handed down to them by the elder pupils of Gautama Buddha. The proper name is therefore Theravāda, "system of the elders."
2. According to Mahāyāna Buddhism, there are many world systems in the universe going through an infinite number of long periods. Sukhāvatī is in the present period.
3. The three scriptures are the *Wu-liang-shou ching* (Buddha Amitāyus scripture) (*The Larger Sukhāvatī-vyūha*, tr. by Max Müller in the Sacred Books of the East, vol. 49, pt. 2, 1–75), in which Amitābha, as the bodhisattva Dharmākara, took 48 vows to welcome all to the Pure Land; the *Kuan wu-liang-shou ching* or Meditation on the Buddha Amitāyus scripture (*The Amitāyur-Dhyāna-sūtra*, tr. by J. Takakusu, *ibid.*, pp. 161–201), which describes the merits leading to rebirth in the Pure Land; and the present scripture, the *Fo-shuo a-mi-t'o ching* or Amitābha scripture spoken by the Buddha (*Buddhabhāsita Amitātyuḥ sūtra*, the smaller *Sukhāvatī-vyūha*). the shortest of all. There have been a number of English translations of it. We do not know the author or date of the scripture. Scholars have assigned it to the second century A.D. Of the three Chinese translations from the fifth to the eighth century, the version by Kumārajīva (344–413) has been prevalent and has been used in the present translation. Section numbers have been added.
4. See ch. 16, C.
5. Ānanda, Gautama's favorite disciple.
6. Capital of Kośala in Northern India, near Nepal.
7. See ch. 16, n. 8.
8. Śrāvakas, those who have attained to their salvation by personally hearing the preaching of the Buddha.
9. An "enlightened being" who is destined to become a Buddha but postpones his Buddhahood in order to remain in the world of suffering to work for the salvation of others as well as himself. See ch. 7, §5.
10. "Son of Sari," one among the 80 chief disciples of the historical Buddha, Śākyamuni.
11. Purity, refreshing coolness, sweetness, lightness and softness, richness, peace, power to remove hunger, thirst, etc., and productiveness.
12. Faith, serious effort, meditation, calmness, and wisdom.
13. Powers acquired by the Five Virtues.
14. Discrimination, serious effort, joy, ease, calmness, meditation, and freedom from evil.
15. Right view, right mindedness, right speech, right action, right livelihood, right effort, right meditation, and right concentration.
16. These are the Three Treasures of Buddhism.
17. Those of hell, hungry ghosts, and animals.
18. The four directions, their four corners, above, and below.
19. Originally "family son" or "family daughter," who has good spiritual qualities or good social position, or both.
20. *Nan-Ch'i shu* (History of the Southern Ch'i dynasty, 479–502), 41:11a.
21. Literally "thus come" or "thus go," one of the ten titles of the Buddha. It means that the Buddha comes as all things come, that is, through causation, but he achieves perfect wisdom and attains Buddhahood in spite of it. It also means that he has come by the way of "thus come" to preach and save all sentient beings.
22. Those of the Śrāvakas who attain their salvation by personally hearing the Buddha's teachings, the Pratyeka-buddhas who attain their personal enlightenment by their own efforts, and the bodhisattvas who postpone their own Buddhahood for the sake of helping all beings to be saved.
23. Avalokiteśvara (*Avalokita-Īśvara*) means "seen-lord," that is "the Lord who is seen," or "the Lord who sees." Hsüan-tsang (596–664) correctly rendered it as *kuan tzu-tsai* (or "see-lord,"

that is, the Lord who sees. The earlier translations of *kuan-yin* (see-sound) or *kuan-shih-yin* (see-world-sound) probably comes from Avalokita-svara (see-sound), which may have been the original. The text has *kuan-shih-yin* throughout but the common appellation Kuan-yin is used in the translation instead.

24. The *Miao-fa lien-hua-ching* (*Saddharma-puṇḍarīka sūtra*, Lotus of the Wonderful Law scripture) is in 28 sections. For English translations, see W. Soothill, tr., *The Lotus of the Wonderful Law, or The Lotus Gospel* or H. Kern, *The Saddharma-puṇḍarīka or the Lotus of the True Law*.
25. The substance of this introduction has been taken from my essay, "The Lotus Sūtra," published in Wm. Theodore de Bary, ed., *Approaches to Oriental Classics*, pp. 153–165.
26. The four directions, the four corners, above, and below.
27. See ch. 16, n. 5.
28. The seal of the true nature of dharmas, Ultimate Reality, which is passed from Buddha to Buddha.
29. See n. 10.
30. Gold, silver, beryl, crystal, white coral, red pearls, and agates.
31. When Gautama obtained Enlightenment under the bodhi tree, he attained Nirvāṇa but still retained the Five Aggregates (form or matter, sensation, thought, disposition, and consciousness), elements that make up the empirical ego. In the Nirvāṇa Without Remainder, even these are left behind so that there is nothing but Nirvāṇa. Gautama attained this at death.
32. A disciple known for his exposition of dharmas.
33. The *Chin-kang ching* or the *Diamond Cutter Scripture* (*Vajracchedikā sūtra*) is in 32 sections. There were six Chinese translations from the fifth to the eighth century. The one by Kumārājiva about 400 is the most popular and is translated here. Section numbers have been added. For English translations, see Edward Conze, *Buddhist Wisdom Books*, pp. 21–71, and Shao Chang Lee, *Popular Buddhism in China*, pp. 27–52, followed by Chinese text.
34. See n. 21.
35. See ch. 16, n. 5.
36. One of the ten chief disciples of Śākyamuni, the historical Buddha; said to be the best exponent of the void.
37. One who is no longer bound by the cycle of life and death or reincarnation.
38. Twenty-fourth predecessor of the historical Buddha.
39. The saint who has postponed his Buddhahood to save others.
40. *Rūpa* in Sanskrit and *se* in Chinese, meaning matter, form, color, appearance, phenomena, thing, etc.
41. Buddhists believe that after the Buddha's Nirvāṇa, the Law declines in successive periods of 500 years.
42. Karma, action that influences one's life in the future.

CHAPTER 18

The Culmination of Chinese Buddhism

□ Chinese Buddhist philosophical ideas and religious practices are more variant than those in Confucianism or Taoism, but these different ways are but different roads to the same destination. A common saying in Chinese Buddhism is "Hua-yen and T'ien-t'ai for doctrines and Ch'an (Zen) and Pure Land for practice." The idea of Buddha-nature in all had been prevalent for a long time, and one of the chief practices, meditation, had been age-old. However, the former portion of the saying needed a solid philosophical foundation and the latter required further development to reach its climax. These took place in the Hua-yen and Ch'an Schools. □

A. THE HUA-YEN PHILOSOPHY OF UNIVERSAL BUDDHAHOOD

□ Philosophically, the Hua-yen (flowery splendor, Avataṁsaka) School arrived at the peak of development through extensive discussions and analyses by Fa-tsang (643–712), its founder, and Ch'eng-kuan (c.760–838). The *Hua-yen ching* (Flowery splendor scripture)[1] is a very lengthy work, and their writings are enormous. The literature of the school is often compared to a great sea. There are Indian roots, of course, but the development is essentially Chinese, for no such school existed in India.

The Hua-yen philosophy culminates in the idea of one-in-all and all-in-one. This is neatly summarized in Fa-tsang's *Treatise on the Golden Lion*,[2] which expounds the idea that every part of the lion involves the whole lion and vice versa, and every part and the whole of the gold involves every part and the whole of the lion and vice versa. Confucianism had taught that the individual and society are harmonious and indispensable to each other, and Taoism had taught that Tao is in everything, big or small. But Hua-yen Buddhism carried the idea to a higher point of mutual penetration and mutual identification of the individual and the universal. This is the philosophical justification for the doctrine that the Buddha is in all and all are basically Buddhas. Inasmuch as both Confucianism and Taoism had insisted that all men could become sages, the Buddhist conclusion was inevitable.

The conclusion in the following short treatise may be found in the statements that all sentients possess the Buddha-nature, which suggests that all is in one, and that every speck of dust contains all the Buddhist scriptures, which implies that one is in all.

The treatise is neither a basic scripture nor well known to many followers. It not only applies the philosophical conclusions to religious life but, more important, it is a synthesis of the doctrines of various Buddhist schools and Confucianism and Taoism as well. In this last respect it reflects the long Chinese tradition of the harmony of the three religions, although it still claims Buddhism to be the best. But the emphasis is not here, but rather on a totality in which all schools form a part, though some are more highly developed than others.

The author of the treatise, Tsung-mi (780–841), was Ch'eng-kuan's pupil and the fifth patriarch of the school. He was one of the most highly honored Buddhist patriarchs and a leading Buddhist scholar whose scholarship covers other Mahāyāna texts like the *Diamond Scripture* as well as Hua-yen works.[3] □

An Inquiry on Man

§3. "DIRECTLY MANIFESTING THE TRUE SOURCE"

The Doctrine of the Manifestation of Dharma-nature in the One Vehicle (of the T'ien-t'ai and Hua-yen Schools)[4] preaches that all sentient beings possess the true mind of natural enlightenment, which from time immemorial has always been there, clear and pure, shining and not obscured, understanding and always knowing. It is also called Buddha-nature and Tathāgatagarbha (Store of the Thus-come).[5] From the beginning of time, it has been obscured by erroneous ideas without knowing its own (Buddha-nature), but only recognizing its ordinary nature, loving it and being attached to it, accumulating action-influence, and suffering from the pain of life and death. The Buddha pitied these sentient beings. He preached to them that all things are empty. He also revealed to them that the true mind of spiritual enlightenment, being clear and pure, is completely identical with that of the Buddhas. Therefore the *Flower Splendor Scripture* says, "Among the Buddhas-sons (all sentient beings), none is without the wisdom of the Tathāgata complete in him. Only because of their erroneous ideas and clinging have they not realized it. If they are freed from erroneous ideas, the knowledge of all that exists, the knowledge naturally present from the beginning, and the knowledge without obstacle will immediately[6] come to the fore."[7] The scripture forthwith gives the analogy of one speck of dust containing a great scripture whose quantity is equivalent to the world system of 1,000 million worlds, equating the dust to the sentient beings and the great scripture to the Buddha-wisdom. Following this, it also says, "At that time the Tathāgata surveyed all sentient beings in the realm of dharmas[8] and said these words: How strange! How strange! Why are the sentient beings deceived and deluded and do not see the wisdom of the Tathāgata complete in them? I must teach them the Holy Path to enable them to be free forever from erroneous thoughts and see the great and vast Tathāgata-wisdom in their own persons, making them the same as the Buddha."

Comment: For many aeons we have not encountered the True Doctrine. We have not learned how to reflect on our own bodies, but have merely clung to false characters and willingly admit that we are ordinary or inferior—perhaps we are animals or perhaps we are men. Only now that we make the inquiry in accordance with the perfect doctrine do we realize that we are originally Buddhas. Therefore our deeds must be in accordance with those of the Buddha, and our minds must be harmonious with the mind of the Buddha. We must revert to the foundation and return to the source, and cut off the habits of an ordinary man. "Decrease and further decrease until one reaches the point of taking no action."[9] One will then naturally respond and function in as many ways as the number of sand grains in the Ganges River, and will be called a Buddha. We should know that both the deluded and the awakened share the same true mind. Great is this wonderful gate. This is the point to which our inquiry on man has come. (*Taishō daizōkyō* [Taishō edition of the Buddhist Canon], 45:710)

§4. "SYNTHESIZING AND INTERPENETRATING THE FUNDAMENTAL AND THE SECONDARY. (SYNTHESIZING THE DOCTRINES THAT HAVE BEEN STAMPED OUT SO THEY ALL RETURN TO THE TRUE SOURCE AND ALL THUS BECOME CORRECT PRINCIPLES.)"

Although the true nature[10] is the source of the body, there must be a cause for its emergence. It should not be the case that the characters of the body suddenly appear for no reason. Only because holders of the preceding doctrines have not finally understood the matter that we have stamped them out in one section after another. Now we shall synthesize and interpenetrate the fundamental and secondary doctrines, including Confucianism and Taoism. (The first paragraph deals only with the fifth doctrine [that of the Demolition of Dharma-nature in the Great Vehicle]. Thereafter each doctrine will be synthesized with it, as noted).

We mean to say that the only true spiritual nature neither comes into nor goes out of existence, is neither augmented nor diminished, and neither transforms nor changes. From time immemorial, sentient beings have been deluded and asleep without their realizing or knowing it. Because the true nature is hidden or covered, it is called the Store of the Thus-come. Because of this Store of the Thus-come, there are the characters of the mind's coming into and going out of existence. (Hereafter comes the synthesis with the fourth doctrine [that of the Demolition of Dharma-character in the Great Vehicle]. Together with it we also demolish the characters of coming into and going out of existence, etc., in the more elementary doctrines.)

What is called the true mind which neither comes into nor goes out of existence combines with the false ideas of coming into and going out of existence. They are neither the same nor different, and are called the storehouse consciousness.[11] This consciousness has two meanings: enlightenment [because of the true mind which neither comes into nor goes out of existence] and absence of enlightenment [because of the erroneous consciousness of coming into and going out of existence]. (Hereafter comes the synthesis with the third doctrine, that of Dharma-character in the Great Vehicle, which agrees with what we are going to say.)

Because of the absence of enlightenment, ideas are activated in the very beginning. This is the character of action-influence.[12] Furthermore, because there is not the realization that these ideas are originally nothing, they evolve and become the seeing consciousness and the seen objective spheres manifesting each other. There is also not the realization that these spheres are only false manifestations from the mind but are clung to as definitely existent. This is called clinging to dharmas. (Hereafter comes [the synthesis with] the second doctrine, that of the Small Vehicles, which agrees with what we are going to say.)

Because of our clinging to these dharmas, there arises the distinction between the self and the other. This becomes the clinging to the self. Because of this clinging to the character of the self, we desire those objective spheres that agree with our feelings, with the desire to enrich the self, and scorn those objective spheres that disagree with the feelings for fear that they might cause loss or trouble. These ignorant and deluded feelings turn on and on and augment each other. (Hereafter comes [the synthesis with] the first doctrine, that of the Sphere of Man and Heavens, which agrees with what we are going to say.)

Therefore the mind and spirit of the killer, robber, and so on, by virtue of the evil action-influences, are born in hells, among hungry ghosts, beasts, and so on.[13] Then some of them who are afraid of the suffering or perhaps whose nature is good, practice charity, discipline, and so on. By virtue of these good action-influences, their mind and spirit will move around in the intermediate stage which is after the previous death but before the next birth, and enter the womb of a mother. (Hereafter comes the [synthesis with] Confucianism and Taoism which agree with what we are going to say.)

[Man is] endowed with material force and receives the concrete stuff (this is synthesizing their doctrine that material force is the source). The material force possesses all at once the Four Elements [of Earth, Water, Fire, and Wind] and gradually becomes the various organs. The mind, on the other hand, possesses all at once the Four Aggregates [of sensation, thought, disposition, and consciousness] and gradually becomes the various consciousnesses. After ten full months, birth takes place and what is born is called a person. This is our present body and mind. Thus we know that body and mind each has its source. Only when the two different things are combined is there a person. It is generally true of the stages of deities, demons, and so on.

Although we have received this body because of the general and collective action-influences, it is also because of specific and individual action-influences that there are [the specific rewards of] noble or humble stations, poverty or wealth, longevity or premature death, sickness or health, prosperity or decline, suffering or joy. This means that if respect or disrespect in previous life is the cause, the effect now will be the fruits of noble or humble station, and so on, like longevity to the humane, premature death to the killer, wealth to the charitable, poverty to the stingy, and all kinds of specific rewards which cannot all be mentioned.

Consequently in this life there are cases where calamity comes by itself without one's doing any evil or blessing comes by itself without one's doing any good, longevity without one's being humane, premature death without one's having killed anything, and so on. All these are determined by the sufficient action-influence in previous life. In this life they naturally happen not because of any of one's actions. Students of outer learning [Confucianism and Taoism] do not know about previous lives. They only base on what they can see with their eyes and only cling to Nature. (This synthesizes their [the Taoist] theory that Nature is the source.)

Again, there are cases where in a previous life one performed good deeds when young but did evil when old, or did evil when young but did good when old. Therefore in this life he is wealthy, honorable, and happy when young, but poor, humble, and suffering when old, or poor and suffering when young but wealthy and honorable when old. People of outer learning merely hold that fortune and misfortune are due to luck. (This synthesizes their [the Confucian] theory that all depend on Heaven's decree.)

However, about the material force with which we are endowed, if we turn the matter in our mind and investigate further and further to its source, we will find that it is nothing but the undifferentiated and one original material force, and about the mind that arises, if we turn the matter in our mind and inquire its source to the utmost, we will find that it is nothing but the true and one intelligent mind. In the final analysis, outside of the mind there is certainly no other dharma. The original material force is also a transformation of the mind. It belongs to the objective sphere manifested by the preceding transforming consciousness and is evolved from the objective portion of the storehouse consciousness. From the character of action-influence of the instant of thought in the beginning, it is divided into the mind and its objective spheres.

As the mind turns on and on falsely to imagine things from the refined to the coarse[14] until it creates action-influence, so the objective spheres also turn on and on to transform and arise, from the subtle to the obvious, until heaven and earth are formed. (This is the same as in the outer schools which teach that in the beginning there is the Great Change [before the emergence of material force or form], which through five stages of evolution [from Great Change to Great Beginning when material force appears, to Great Beginning when form appears, to Great Simplicity when physical shape transforms and concrete stuff appears] and finally to the Great Ultimate [in which material force and concrete stuff are complete]. The Great Ultimate produced the Two Modes [yin, the cosmic negative force, and yang, the positive cosmic force]. What they call Nature or the Great Tao is similar to what we call True Nature. In reality, it is nothing but the one instant of thought which can transform into the seeing portion, which is what we call the one instant of thought becoming active in the beginning. In reality this is nothing but the character of the objective sphere.) As the action-influence ripens, the two material forces [yin and yang] are endowed from father and mother and combined with the consciousness formed by action-influence to become a human body. Accordingly, the objective sphere transformed by the storehouse consciousness is divided into two portions, one combining with the storehouse consciousness to become man; the other, without combining with the storehouse consciousness, becomes heaven, earth, mountains, rivers, and countries and cities. Among the Three Powers [Heaven, Earth, man], the most intelligent is man, because he is a combination of the mind and spirit. When the Buddha said that the Four Elements of the inner school, [Earth, Water, Fire, and Wind, which constitute such things as man's body, blood, heat, motion, and combine with the storehouse consciousness] and the [same] Four Elements of outer school [which do not combine with the storehouse consciousness] are different,[15] he meant precisely this.

Alas! How profuse and confused are scanty learning and heretical prejudices! Pass the word to all fellow travelers in the Way. Those who want to become Buddhas must clearly understand the refined and the coarse, and the fundamental and secondary, before they can abandon the secondary and return to the fundamental, introspect and illuminate the source of the mind, remove all the refined and coarse characters, brilliantly manifest the spiritual nature, and understand all dharmas without exception. This is called the Law-body and Reward-body. Naturally one can respond to all things and manifest in many ways without end. This is called the Transformation-body.[16] (*Ibid.*)

B. THE CH'AN DOCTRINE OF SUDDEN ENLIGHTENMENT

□ As the name of the school indicates, the chief objective of the Ch'an (Japanese, Zen) is meditation (*dhyāna*). But it is meditation in a revolutionary sense. The practice of meditation goes back to ancient times. Lao Tzu taught "Maintaining steadfast quietude."[17] Chuang Tzu urged "Fasting of the mind."[18] Meditation was a common practice in the Yellow Emperor-Lao Tzu cult. And it was a major method in the Taoist religion for the search for everlasting life. When Buddhism came into China, the Chinese either ignored or misunderstood the Indian conception of meditation, and instead of aiming at transcendental wisdom by ignoring external environment and suppressing the senses, the Chinese used Buddhist meditation for the traditional purpose of conserving vital energy, breathing, reducing desires, preserving nature, and nourishing life. As Buddhism reasserted itself, meditation was widely practiced either as devotion to Buddha Amitābha[19] or for Perfect Wisdom. The latter was the exclusive concern of the Ch'an School. But eventually it degenerated into sheer mechanical and formal sitting in meditation, devoid of the original high purpose or genuine feeling. By the seventh century, it was time for revolt.

Tradition says that the rebel was Hui-neng (638–713), an illiterate from Hsin-chou near Canton in South China, who went to the Fifth Patriarch of the school, Hung-jen (601–674), in Central China. In a poetic contest with the Head Monk Shen-hsiu (605?–706), Hui-neng won out and started the new doctrine of sudden enlightenment, which in the course of several decades, chiefly through his pupil Shen-hui (670–762), swept over China and has dominated China ever since. The Head Monk's poem was:

The body is the tree of Perfect Wisdom (*bodhi*).
The Mind is the stand of a bright mirror.
At all times diligently wipe it.
Do not allow it to become dusty.

Challenging the Head Monk, Hui-neng said:

Fundamentally Perfect Wisdom has no tree.
Nor has the bright mirror any stand.
Buddha-nature is forever clear and pure.
Where is there any dust?

Again,

The mind is the tree of Perfect Wisdom.
The body is the stand of a bright mirror.
The bright mirror is originally clear and pure.
Where has it been defiled by any dust?

There is of course much dramatization in the story which has many embellishments. The fact that an illiterate could compose poems is intriguing enough. For authority and prestige, the transmission of the patriarchy is traced back to Bodhidharma (fl. 460–534) who was declared the first patriarch. Some scholars have doubted the historicity of this Indian missionary but recent research by Chinese and Japanese scholars has conclusively shown that he was in China from about 520 to 534. It is not at all unreasonable to believe that a foreigner, coming through and having lived in the city of Canton, a frontier city far away from traditional authority and stereotype of thinking, did have some radical message to offer. (See §34 following.) There is also the possibility that it was Shen-hui who advocated the radical doctrine and ascribed it to his teacher out of respect. The probability is that the new thinking took some time to evolve and that Hui-neng and Shen-hui definitely played the leading role. At any rate, the new idea overthrew all traditional practices of reciting the Buddha's name, reading scriptures, temple worship, building pagodas, and, most of all, sitting in meditation, as a handicap and a waste of time. The human mind is originally clear and pure, according to the new gospel, because it is the Buddha-nature. Ignorance is comparable to the cloud that obscures the sun. If one only looks into his own mind, he will find his Buddha-nature, achieve Enlightenment, and become a Buddha immediately. Not only was the method of the "gradual enlightenment" in the so-called Northern School of Shen-hsiu rejected; the whole practice of traditional Buddhism was cast aside. Later followers of the "Southern School" of Ch'an, as Hui-neng's and Shen-hui's movement has been called, developed most unconventional techniques from the eighth to the tenth century, notably the methods of travel, "never telling plainly," the *kōan*[20] which usually consists of a searching question and an enigmatic answer, and shouting and beating, all calculated to stimulate, shock, and sharpen the mind so it can see the Buddha-nature inherent in man instantly. The impact of this new approach on Chinese and Japanese poetry, art, and philosophy has been terrific. The quick vision and the keen insight have brought forth new objectives and developed new techniques whereby one discovers and becomes identified with Ultimate Reality instantly. The new method is dramatically present in the following scripture. No wonder it is the only Chinese work that has been honored as a scripture in Buddhism.[21] □

The *Platform Scripture Preached by the Sixth Patriarch*

§13. Good and learned friends, calmness and wisdom are the foundations of my method. First of all, do not be deceived into thinking that the two are different. They are one substance and not two. Calmness is the substance of wisdom and wisdom is the function of calmness. Whenever wisdom is at work, calmness is within it. Whenever calmness is at work, wisdom is within it. Good and learned friends, the meaning here is that [calmness and] wisdom are identified. Seekers of the Way, arouse your minds. Do not say that wisdom follows calmness or vice versa, or that the two are different. To hold such a view would imply that that the dharmas[22] possess two different characters. In the case of those whose words are good but whose hearts are not good, wisdom and calmness are not identified. But in the case of those whose hearts and words are both good and in whom the internal and the external are one, calmness and wisdom are identified. Self-enlightenment and practice do not consist in argument. If one is concerned about which comes first, he is a [deluded] person. If he is not freed from the consideration of victory or defeat, he will produce the dharmas and the self. He cannot become free from the Four Characters[23].

§16. Good and learned friends, in method there is no distinction between sudden enlightenment and gradual enlightenment. Among men, however, some are intelligent and others are stupid. Those who are deluded understand gradually, while the enlightened achieve understanding suddenly. But when they know their own minds, then they see their own nature, and there is no difference in their enlightenment. Without enlightenment, they remain forever bound in transmigration.

§17. Good and learned friends, in this method of mine, from the very beginning, whether in the sudden enlightenment or gradual enlightenment tradition, absence-of-thought has been instituted as the main doctrine, absence-of characters[24] as the substance, and nonattachment as the foundation. What is meant by absence-of-characters? Absence-of-characters means to be free from characters while in the midst of them. Absence-of-thought means not to be carried away by thought in the process of thought. Nonattachment is man's orginal nature. Thought after thought goes on without remaining. Past, present, and future thought continue without termination. But if we cut off and terminate thought for one instant, the Law-body[25] is freed from the physical body. At no time should a single instant of thought be attached to any dharma. If one single instant of thought is attached to anything, then every thought will be attached. This is bondage. But if in regard to dharmas no thought is attached to anything, that is freedom. This is the meaning of having nonattachment as the foundation.

Good and learned friends, to be free from all characters means the absence of characters. Only if we can be free from characters will the substance of our nature be pure. That is the meaning of taking absence-of-character as the substance. Absence-of-thought means not to be defiled by external objects. It is to free our thoughts from external objects and not to have thoughts arise over dharmas. But do not stop thinking about everything and eliminate all thought. As soon as thought stops, one dies and is reborn elsewhere. Take heed of this, followers of the Way. If one does not think over the meaning of the Law and becomes mistaken himself, that is excusable. How much worse is it to encourage others to be mistaken! Deluded, he does not realize that he is so, and he even blasphemes the scripture and the Law! That is the reason why absence-of-thought is instituted as the doctrine. Because people who are deluded have thoughts about external objects, perverse views arise in them, and all sorts of afflictions resulting from passions and erroneous thoughts are produced.

However, this school has instituted absence-of-thought as the doctrine. When people of the world are free from erroneous views, no thoughts will arise. If there are no thoughts, there will not even be an absence-of-thought. Absence means absence of what? Thought means thought of what? Absence-of-thought means freedom from the character of the duality [existence or nonexistence of characters] and from all afflictions resulting from passions. [Thought means thought of the true nature of True Thusness.] True Thusness[26] is the substance of thought and thought is the function of True Thusness. It is the self-nature that gives rise to thought. Therefore in spite of the functioning of seeing, hearing, sensing, and knowing, self-nature is not defiled by the many spheres of objects and always remains free and at ease. As the *Scripture Spoken by Vimalakīrti* says, "Externally it skillfully differentiates the various dharma-characters while internally it abides immovably in the First Principle."[27]

§18. Good and learned friends, according to this method, sitting in meditation is at bottom neither looking at the mind nor looking at purity. Nor do we say that there should be imperturbability. Suppose we say to look at the mind. The mind is at bottom false. Since being false is the same as being illusory, there is nothing to look at. Suppose we say to look at purity. Man's nature is originally pure. It is by false thoughts that True Thusness is obscured. Our original nature is pure as long as it is free from false thoughts. If one does not realize that his own nature is originally pure and makes up his mind to look at purity, he is creating a false purity. Such purity has no objective existence. Hence we know that what is looked at is false. Purity has neither physical form nor character, but some people set up characters of purity and say that this is the object of our task. People who take this view hinder their original nature and become bound by purity. If those who cultivate imperturbability would ignore people's mistakes and defects, their nature would not be perturbed. Deluded people may not be perturbed physically themselves, but whenever they speak, they criticize others and thus violate the Way.

Thus looking at the mind or at purity causes a hindrance to the Way.

§19. Now, this being the case, in this method, what is meant by sitting in meditation? In this method, to sit means to be free from all obstacles, and externally not to allow thoughts to rise from the mind over any sphere of objects. To meditate means to realize the imperturbability of one's original nature. What is meant by meditation and calmness? Meditation means to be free from all characters externally; calmness means to be unperturbed internally. If there are characters outside and the inner mind is not disturbed, one's original nature is naturally pure and calm. It is only because of the spheres of objects that there is contact, and contact leads to perturbation. There is calmness when one is free from characters and is not perturbed. There is meditation when one is externally free from characters, and there is calmness when one is internally undisturbed. Meditation and calmness mean that external meditation is attained and internal calmness is achieved. The *Scripture Spoken by Vimalakīrti* says, "Immediately we become completely clear and recover our original mind."[28] The *P'u-sa-chieh ching* (Scripture of disciplines for bodhisattvahood) says, "We are originally pure in our self-nature."[29] Good and learned friends, realize that your self-nature is naturally pure. Cultivate and achieve for yourselves the Law-body of your self-nature. Follow the Way of the Buddha yourselves. Act and achieve Buddhahood for yourselves.

§30. All scriptures and writings, both the Great Vehicle and the Small Vehicle, and the twelve sections of the scriptures are provided for men. It is because man possesses the nature of wisdom that these were instituted. If there were no men in the world, there would naturally not be any dharmas. We know, therefore, that dharmas exist because of man and that there are all these scriptures because there are people to preach them.

The reason is that among men some are wise and others are stupid. The stupid are inferior, whereas the wise are superior. The deluded consult the wise and the wise explain the Law to the stupid and enable them to understand and to open up their minds. When deluded people understand and open up their minds, they are no longer different from the superior and the wise. Hence we know that without enlightenment, a Buddha is no different from other living beings. With enlightenment, even in a single instant of thought, all living beings become the same as a Buddha. Hence we know that all dharmas are immanent in one's mind and person. Why not seek in one's own mind the sudden realization of the original nature of True Thusness? The *Scripture of Disciplines for Bodhisattvahood* says, "We are originally pure in our self-nature. If we understand our minds and see our nature, we shall achieve Buddhahood ourselves."[30] (*The Scripture Spoken by Vimalakīrti* says), "Immediately we become completely clear and recover our original mind."[31]

§34. The imperial delegate paid reverence to the Master and said, "The Law Your Holiness has expounded is really wonderful. Your disciple has, however, some doubts and wishes to consult Your Holiness. I beg Your Holiness, with your great compassion, for further explanation."

The Great Master said, "If you have any doubts, please ask. Why hesitate?"

The imperial delegate asked, "Is not the Law the fundamental doctrine of the First Patriarch from the West, Bodhidharma?"

The Great Master said, "Yes."

The imperial delegate asked, "I have heard that when the Great Master Bodhidharma tried to convert Emperor Wu (r. 502–549), the emperor asked him, 'During my entire life I have built temples, given alms, and made offerings. Is there any merit (achievement and virtue) for these deeds?' Bodhidharma answered and said, 'No merit at all.' The emperor was disappointed and thereupon sent Bodhidharma out of his state. I do not understand Bodhidharmas's words. I beg Your Holiness to explain."

The Sixth Patriarch said, "There is really no merit. Imperial Delegate, please do not doubt the words of Great Master Bodhidharma. Emperor Wu was attached to perverse ways and did not understand the correct doctrine."

The imperial delegate asked, "Why is there no merit?"

The priest said, "Building temples, giving alms, and making offerings are only cultivating blessings. Blessings should not be considered as merit. Merit lies in the law-body, not in the field of blessings. There is merit in one's own dharma-nature. Not to make any differentiation but to be straightforward is virtue. [Internally see] the Buddha-nature, and externally practice respect and reverence. If one looks down on others and does not get rid of the idea of the self, he will have no merit. If his self-nature is unreal and imaginary, his law-body will have no merit. One should practice virtue at every moment, entertain no differentiation and be straightforward in the mind; then his virtue will not be slight. Always practice reverence. To cultivate one's personal life is achievement, and to cultivate one's own mind is virtue. Merit is the product of one's own mind. Blessings are different from merit. Emperor Wu did not know the correct principle. The Great Patriarch was not mistaken."

§35. The imperial delegate paid reverence and asked again, "I observe that monks, disciples who have renounced their families, and lay folk always recite the name of Amitābha with the hope of going to and being reborn in the Western Region (Pure Land, Paradise).[32] Will Your Holiness explain whether it is possible to be born there or not? Please remove my doubts."

The Great Master said, "Imperial Delegate, please listen, I will explain it to you. According to the scripture spoken by the World Honored One in Śrāvastī[33] about leading people to the Western Region, it is quite clear that it is not far from here. It is said to be far away for the benefit of people of low intelligence, but it is said to be near for the benefit of people of high intelligence. People are of two kinds, but the Law is only one. Because men differ according as they are deluded or enlightened, some understand the Law quicker than others. Deluded people recite the name of the Buddha hoping to be born in the Pure Land, but the enlightened purifies his own mind, for, as the Buddha said, 'As a result of purity of mind, the Buddha Land becomes pure.'[34] Imperial Delegate, if people of the Eastern Region are pure in heart, they will be free from sin, and if people of the Western Region are not pure in heart, they are sinful. Deluded people want to be born in the Western Region, but the locations of the two regions do not differ. If the mind is absolutely pure, the Western Region is not far away. But if one's mind is not pure, it will be difficult to go and be born there through reciting the name of the Buddha. If one has removed the Ten Evils,[35] he will have traveled a hundred thousand miles, and if one is free from the Eight Perversions,[36] he will have traveled 8,000 miles. One has only to be straightforward in his actions and he will reach the Pure Land in a moment. All Your Honor should do is to practice the Ten Good Deeds.[37] What is the need for wanting to go and be born there? If one does not get rid of the Ten Evils from his mind, what Buddha will come to welcome him? If one understands the doctrine of sudden enlightenment leading to the ending of the cycle of birth and death, it takes only an instant to see the Western Region. If one does not understand the Great Vehicle doctrine of sudden enlightenment, the way to go and be born there through reciting the name of the Buddha is very far. How can one ever get there?"

The Sixth Patriarch further said, "Suppose Your Honor and I move to the Western Region. In an instant it will appear before our eyes. Do you wish to see it?"

The imperial delegate paid reverence and said, "If it can be seen here, what is the need of going to be born there? Will Your Holiness be compassionate and reveal the Western Region here? It will be perfect."

The Great Patriarch said, "No doubt you see the Western Region in the passage way."[38] It immediately disappeared. The congregation were astonished, not knowing what was what.[39]

The Great Master said, "Will all of you please be alert and listen. Our own physical body is a city. Our eyes, ears, nose, tongue, and body are the gates. There are five external gates. Inside there is the gate of the mind. The mind is the ground and the nature is the king. With the nature, there is king. Without the nature, there is no king. When the nature remains, our body and mind exist. When the nature is gone, our body and mind are destroyed. The Buddha is the product of one's own nature. Do not seek it outside of your body. If the self-nature is deluded, even a Buddha becomes an ordinary human being. If their self-nature is enlightened, all living beings are Buddhas. Compassion is the same as Avalokiteśvara.[40] Happiness in alms-giving is the same as Mahāsthāma.[41] The ability to be pure is the same as Śākyamuni.[42] And not to make differentiation but to be straightforward is the same as Maitreya.[43] The view that the self exists is the same as Mount Meru.[44] A perverse mind is the same as a great ocean. Afflictions are the same as waves. A malicious mind is the same as an evil dragon. Afflictions are the same as fish and turtles. Falsehood and erroneous thoughts are the same as spiritual beings. The Three Poisons[45] are the same as hell. Ignorance and delusions are the same as beasts. And the Ten Good Deeds are the same as Heaven. When there is no view of the self, Mount Meru will crumble of itself. When the perverse mind is eliminated, the waters of the ocean will be exhausted. When there are no afflictions, waves will be annihilated. And when poisonous harms are removed, fish and turtles will be extinct. The Tathāgata[46] of Enlightenment within the domain of our mind extends the light of His wisdom through the Six Gates[47] and purifies them. It shines and pierces its way through the Six Heavens of Desire.[48] When the self-nature shines within, and when the Three Poisons are removed, hell disappears at once. When one is enlightened both within and without, his position is no different from that of the Western Region. If one does not practice this way, how can he reach there?"

When the congregation heard this, the sound of praise penetrated the heavens. No wonder deluded people understand thoroughly and immediately. The imperial delegate paid reverence and praised him, saying, "Excellent,! Excellent! May all beings in the realm of dharmas hear this and understand at once."

§36. The Great Master said, "Good and learned friends, if you wish to practice, you can do so at home, not necessarily in a monastery. Those in a monastery who do not practice are like people of the Western Region who are evil at heart. If one practices at home, he is like a person of the Eastern Region who practices the good. So long as one is willing to cultivate purity, that is the Western Region for him." . . .

NOTES

1. The *Avataṁsaka sūtra*. There are three Chinese translations—a 60-section version by Buddhabhadra (359–429) during 418–420, which is the standard; a 80-section version by Śikshānanda (652–710) in 699; and a 40-section (date unknown) version by Prajñā in 798, the last-mentioned being a portion of the whole scripture.
2. For translation of this, see Wing-tsit Chan, *A Source Book in Chinese Philosophy*, ch. 25.
3. The treatise is called *Yüan-jen lun* in Chinese. For a German translation, see H. Doumoulin, S.J., tr. "Tsung-mi's Traktat vom Urspring des Menschen," *Monumenta Nipponica*, 1 (1938), 178–221. The word *yüan* means to investigate. It also means "source" or "origin." In this case the investigation happens to be on man's origin.
4. All notes in parentheses in these selections (but not the brackets) are the treatise author's own. Notes that are extraneous comments have been omitted.
5. For the Tathāgata, see ch. 17, n. 21. The Store is the source of all things.
6. The first is initial enlightenment, the second, original enlightenment, and the third, the first two combined.
7. The 80-chapter section version of the *Hua-yen ching* (*Avataṁsaka sūtra* or the Flower splendor scripture), §51 (*Taishō daizōkyō*, 10:272).
8. For dharma, see ch. 16, n. 5.

9. *Lao Tzu*, ch. 48.
10. The character (*lakshaṇa*) of dharmas refers to their appearance, form, features, etc., in contrast to the nature (*svabhāva*) of dharmas, which has a substance of its own.
11. Paraphrasing the *Ta-ch'eng ch'i-hsin lun* or Treatise on the awakening of faith in the Mahāyāna, pt. 1 (*Taishō daizōkyō*, 32:576).
12. Karma, deeds in a previous life affecting the present or in the present affecting the future life.
13. Referring to the Six Stages of deities, human beings, hells, hungry ghosts, beasts, and demons.
14. There are the Three Refined Characters, namely, the character of action-influence, the character of transformation, and the character of manifestation, and the Six Coarse Characters, namely, those of wisdom, continuity, clinging, conjectures of names and words, initiating action-influence, and suffering tied to action-influence.
15. Quoting the *Pao-chi Scripture* or Scripture of the collection of jewels.
16. Buddhism conceives a Buddha to have a threefold body, namely, the Law-body or spiritual body (*Dharmakāya*), the Reward or Enjoyment-body (*Sambhogakāya*), and the Transformation-body or body of incarnation (*Nirmāṇakāya*). The Law-body is the Buddha-body in its self-nature, the body of the Dharma or truth, the body of reality, the body of principle. The "body" has no bodily existence. It is identical with truth. In various schools it is identical with the Realm of Dharma (*Dharmadhātu*), Buddha-nature, or the Storehouse of the "Thus-come" (*Tathāgatagarbha*). The Reward-body is the person embodied with real insight, enjoying his own enlightenment or that of others. The Transformation-body is a body variously appearing to save people. The three bodies are three in one, are possessed of all Buddhas, and are potential to all men.
17. *Lao Tzu*, ch. 16.
18. *Chuang Tzu*, ch. 4 (*Nan-hua chen-ching*, 2:12b–13a).
19. The Buddha of the Western Paradise. See ch. 17, A.
20. Japanese pronunciation of the Chinese *kung-an*, meaning an official document on the desk, connoting a sense of important decision and the final determination of truth and falsehood.
21. Most scholars believe that the scripture, the *Liu-tsu t'an-ching* (Platform scripture of the Sixth Patriarch), is a product of the eighth century with some of the basic ideas traceable to Hui-neng. The manuscript was discovered in 1900 in a Tun-huang cave in Northwest China. It is the oldest and shortest (57 short sections) of the six extant versions of the *Platform Scripture*. The version of 1291 included in the Ming Canon of 1440 is the most popular and the most elaborate. But all the important ideas came from the Tun-huang version, although it is a much corrupted text and needs many emendations. For my complete translation and for further discussion of the points mentioned in this introduction, see Hui-neng, *The Platform Scripture, the Basic Classic of Zen Buddhism.*
22. For *dharma*, see ch. 16, n. 5.
23. The Four Characters are coming into existence, remaining in the same state, changing, and going out of existence.
24. See n. 10.
25. See n. 16.
26. True Thusness or Suchness (*tathatā* in Sanskrit and *chen-ju* in Chinese) means truth and it-is-so. As truth, it is antithesis to illusion and falsehood, and "being so" it is eternal, unchangeable, indestructible, without specific character or nature, and is not produced by causes. It is the Absolute, the Storehouse of the Thus-come, the Realm of Dharmas, Dharma-nature, and Perfect Reality.
27. The *Wei-mo chieh* (*so-shuo*) *ching* (*Vimalakīrti nirdeśa sūtra*), §1 (*Taishō daizōkyō*, 41:537).
28. *Ibid.*, §3 (14:541).
29. This is part of §10 of the *Brahmajāla sūtra* (*Fan-wang ching* or Brahma-net scripture). (*Taishō daizōkyō*, 24:1003).
30. *Ibid.*
31. §3 (14:541).
32. See ch. 17, A.

33. In Central India. The World Honored One is the Buddha. The scripture referred to is the *Kuan-wu-liang-shou ching* (*Amitāyur-dhyāna sūtra*, Meditation on the Buddha Amitāyus).
34. *Vimalakīrti nirdeśa sūtra*, §1 (14:538).
35. For the Ten Evil Deeds, see ch. 16, A, ch. 4.
36. The perversion of the Noble Eightfold Path, namely, perverse views, perverse intention, perverse speech, perverse action, perverse livelihood, perverse effort, perverse mindfulness, and perverse concentration.
37. The opposite of the Ten Evils.
38. The word *t'ang* is here used in a most unusual meaning, the passage way.
39. Did the Sixth Patriarch create an illusion by some shocking gesture? Or did he merely shock the congregation by this needling statement? Or did he perform a miracle?
40. See introduction to ch. 17, B.
41. Avalokiteśvara, Mahāsthāma, and Amitābha are the Three Holy Ones of the Pure Land. See the following note.
42. Name of the historical Buddha. The Ming Canon version has Amitābha instead, obviously influenced by the concept of the Pure Land triad of Amitābha, Avalokiteśvara, and Māhasthāma. But here Maitreya is paired with Śākyamuni as Māhasthāma is paired with Avalokiteśvara. The coupling is neat and correct.
43. The next Buddha, the Buddhist Messiah who in time will follow Śākyamuni as the savior of the world.
44. The king of mountains, situated in the center of the universe.
45. The Three Poisons are greed, anger, and delusion.
46. See ch. 17, n. 21.
47. The Six Gates are the five sense organs and the mind.
48. The first is described as half way up level of Mount Sumeru, the center of the world, the second on its summit, and so on higher and higher with an increasing freedom from desires, but even at in the highest heaven, desires are not completely gone.

CHAPTER 19

The Harmony of Religions

☐ The most unique feature of Chinese religions is their syncretic character. Aside from less than ten per cent of the Chinese population who follow Islam or Christianity or who are Buddhist monks and nuns, the vast majority of the rest adheres to no particular religion exclusively but follows Confucianism, Buddhism, and Taoism at the same time. The common sayings are "The three religions are harmonious" and "The three systems are one." They have built many "temples of the three sages." The average Chinese wears a Confucian crown, so to speak, a Taoist robe, and Buddhist sandals.

There was much intellectual preparation for this mode of life. The Confucianists had taught that "Different courses are pursued without conflict"[1] and that "In the world there are many different roads but the destination is the same. There are a hundred deliberations but the result is one."[2] Likewise, the Taoists had taught that "Tao produces the one, the two, and the three" but "the sage embraces the one."[3] and that the man of Tao "follows two courses at the same time."[4] It was natural that when Buddhism was first known in China, Buddha and Lao Tzu were worshiped together and that Buddhist ideas were equated with Taoist concepts (see, ch. 16, A). As we have seen, with the Buddhist expansion and its coming into conflict with indigenous religions, its defenders sought to harmonize with them rather than oppose them. We have also seen how Mou Tzu pointed out the common features among the three religions (ch. 16, B). At about the same time, the belief grew that Lao Tzu went to India to convert the barbarians and became the Buddha. Evidently the belief was widespread. In 166 Hsiang Kai referred to it in his memorial to the emperor.[5] Later, Wang Fu (of the Western Chin dynasty, 265–316), wrote the *Hua-hu ching* (Scripture on the conversion of barbarians), which provided a record of the growing tradition. However silly this story may be, its real meaning is that the Chinese attempted to embrace Buddhism rather than fight it. When K'an Tse (fl. 241) was asked by the emperor of the state of Wu to compare the three religions, he said Confucianism and Taoism were superior but that all three obeyed the laws of Heaven, thus strengthening the view that they had important things in common.[6] It is significant that even during the bitter controversy between the Buddhists and the Taoists from the third to the fifth century, influential and decisive opinions followed the same line. To Sun Ch'o (320–377), the teachings of the Duke of Chou[7] and Confucius and that of the Buddha were no different, and the term *chiao* (awakening) in Buddhism and in Mencius[8] were synonymous.[9] Ku Huan (420–483), the Taoist priest, was definitely partial to Taoism, in his "Treatise on the Barbarians and the Chinese," as his biographer pointed out.[10] He stressed the differences between the two religions saying that while they are both good, one is Chinese and the other barbarian and they can be no more interchangeable than the cart and the boat. But he concluded just the same that the two are the same in reality although different in name, and similar in wisdom although different in empirical application.[11] Such utterances cemented and fortified the tradition. Taoist Ko Hung's synthesis of the Taoist religion and Confucian ethics (ch. 15, B, 4), Buddhist Hui-yüan's harmonization of the "worldly life" and the "other-worldly life" (ch. 16, C), and Confucianist Chang Jung's clinging to the three religions at his last moment (ch. 17, B, introduction) are examples of that tradition at work. Most educated Chinese are familiar with the story of the "three laughing gentlemen," that although Hui-yüan had never seen his visitors beyond a certain stream, one day he and two friends, one a Confucianist and the other a Taoist, were so absorbed in conversation that they crossed the stream without knowing it and only when a tiger roared did they realize it and broke into hearty laughter.

The syncretic tradition did not prevent the infamous persecutions of Buddhism, however. The Buddhists often referred to the "Three Wus and One Tsung," meaning the persecution of 446 under Emperor Wu of Northern Wei, of 574 under Emperor Wu of Northern Chou, of 845 under Emperor Wu of T'ang, and of 955 under Emperor Shih-tsung of Later Chou. The one in 845 was particularly severe. Some 4,600 temples and 40,000 shrines and monasteries were destroyed throughout the empire, 260,500 monks and nuns were forced back to lay life, and millions of acres of land were confiscated.[12] Undoubtedly the Taoist leader, K'ou Ch'ien-chih (d. 432), was a chief architect of the 446 affair, and the memorial (819) of the greatest Confucianist of the time, Han Yü (768–824), in urging the emperor not to welcome a relic bone of the Buddha into the palace, must have contributed to the event of 845. But significantly the issues in the most serious persecution were more political and economic than religious. Some temples and monks were allowed to continue, and images of clay, stone, and wood were left intact. Han Yü himself was a good friend of Taoist priests and Buddhist monks.

Similarly, the Neo-Confucianists from the eleventh to the fifteenth century persisted in criticizing the "heterodoxical schools" but they were personally on good terms with their opponents. They criticized both Buddhism and Taoism in the same breath. They strongly contrasted the Confucian doctrine of action and the idea of concrete being with the Taoist doctrines of inaction and nonbeing, rejecting them as unhealthy and dangerous. As to Buddhism, they attacked the Buddhists for regarding the world as illusory, for looking upon everything as the mind, for failing to understand the nature of life and death and trying to undermine them, for their inability to handle human affairs, for escaping from the world and public responsibility, for failing to fulfill human relations, for deserting parents, for leaving family life and thus eventually terminating the human race, for being lazy and selfish and aiming only at rebirth in the Pure Land, and for frightening people with transmigration.[13] In their criticism the Neo-Confucianists were much prejudiced and uninformed, but they were friendly. They visited Buddhist temples and gave lectures there. Their own philosophy was deeply influenced by heterodoxy. Their theory that principles and facts are interdependent and interpenetrated came from the Hua-yen philosophy, and their dual methods of exercising seriousness and investigating things are likely borrowings from the Ch'an formula of calmness and wisdom. Many of them were called Buddhists in disguise. In spite of their criticisms, few but bigots would say that the three religions are not "different roads to the same destination."

Among the masses, the syncretic spirit has always been even stronger. They seldom ask whether Kuan-yin (ch. 17, B, §25) is a Buddhist or a Taoist diety, and they would engage the service of Buddhist monks and Taoist priests at the same time. This spirit of harmony or unity is well expressed in the following selections. The I-kuan Tao (Way of Pervading Unity), to which the treatises belonged, came into existence soon after the Revolution of 1911 and has probably disappeared after the Communists came to power. It was one of the many offshoots of the White Lotus

Society that goes back to the eleventh century, if not earlier. These religious societies have always been syncretic in character. They have come and gone, but there is no reason to believe that the I-kua Tao was the last. □

A. QUESTIONS AND ANSWERS ON THE WAY OF PERVADING UNITY

Friend asked: It has not been very long since I joined the Way (Tao). I am ignorant about everything. Please enlighten me as to what the Way really is.

I answered: Our Way is called the Way of Pervading Unity. If you ask about its whats and whys, their answers are many. Let me select and comment on the most essential as an introduction for you.

The Way is the general name for all goodness; all charitable work may be called the Way. It is also the ultimate principle; whatever conforms to the principle conforms to the Way. It is also the correct principle, such as parental love for the father, filial piety for the son, righteousness for the husband, obedience for the wife; loyalty, obedience, love, and virtue are all the Way. It is also the natural principle. There is the principle of Heaven in Heaven, the principle of earth in earth, the principle of human nature in human beings. We also say that the nature is the embodiment of the Way. What is inborn in us is born of heavenly nature. The nature of man is originally derived from the Principle of Heaven. If we cultivate our nature with the Principle of Heaven as our guide, we will fulfill the Way. . . .

I have heard my teacher say that Yao and Shun[14] were born at high noon. Our epoch is at the transition from the high noon (of history) to the next period (1:00 to 3:00 P.M. of history). When noon reaches its height, sunshine is full and complete. Hence the possibility of universal salvation in three stages and the reclarification of the Way of Pervading Unity. By the three stages is meant that Fu-hsi drew the Eight Trigrams[15] and inaugurated culture and civilization, thus constituting the first stage. Confucius edited the Classics, formulated rites, developed moral principles, and established social standards, thus constituting the second stage. At present there are many religious societies both at home and abroad, each rectifying man's nature and destiny and probing into the nature and the principle, thus constituting the third stage. Since you, Sir, live in this generation, it means that circumstances bring you and the Buddha together. You should cultivate the Way with special effort, for happy circumstances should not be passed over. The nature is derived from the principle of Heaven; it is shared by all men. Who is he who cannot achieve a good and virtuous life? When one practices the Way, even if he cannot become an immortal or a sage, he still can avoid bringing shame to his ancestors or causing trouble to his descendants, and become a perfect man. There are now many religious tracts available. If you want the best, search extensively.

Friend said: I have heard you say that Confucianism is a religion. How about Buddhism and Taoism? Are they orthodox or heterodox systems? Kindly tell me.

I said: The Way is in essence the Ultimate of Nonbeing and the One Principle. The one is divided into three, as a man's person is divided into essence, vital force, and spirit. At first the one is divided into three, and now the three are united as one, which is the sign of perfect culmination.

However, among the three religions, the Law of the Buddha is the highest. For this reason, at all times past and present, the great leaders of religion have been Buddhists. The *Hsien-chieh ching* (Scripture of the worthy aeon)[16] says, "When the universe was formed out of chaos, it was decided that there would be ten Buddhas ruling the universe and there have already been seven." This can be proved by the fact that there are seven Buddhas in the Ta-hsiang Temple in the Fen-yang district of Shansi and also the Temple of Seven Buddhas in Ying village of Ma-chuang in the Hsiao-i- district of Shansi. In early times there was no written language and therefore their names are difficult to find out. The remaining three Buddhas are the

Dīpaṅkara Buddha, Tathāgata Buddha, and Maitreya Buddha. Dīpaṅkara ruled for 1,500 years and Tathāgata Buddha ruled for 3,000 years. The accounts of Maitreya need not be told here. He has already assumed the rule in his hands. . . .

The Tathāgata Buddha was born on the eighth day, the fourth month, in the year 1027 B.C. His father's name was Ch'a-li (Shuddhodana), meaning pure rice, and his mother's name was Lady Maya. He left home at the age of nineteen. Having received instructions from Dīpaṅkara, he preached for forty-nine years and wrote scriptures and left them for the salvation of the world throughout 10,000 years. His way is to point directly to one's nature and to become a Buddha, to explore directly to the source, to wipe out (the phenomenal characteristics of) sound and color, and to remove the distinction of the self and the other. Later generations call him the Founder of Buddhism. The *School Sayings of Confucius*[17] says, "There is a sage in the west whose name is Buddha. Without uttering a word, he speaks the truth. He transcends both chaos and order, for his is the way of nonaction." He also left these words: "My way runs in cycles of 3,000 years—1,000 years of Correct Law, 1,000 years of Semblance of Law, and 1,000 years of Decay of Law. After the period of Decay of Law, the period of Correct Law will begin again." This is the same as the principle of jointly observing the three religions today.

Lao Tzu's surname was Li, his name was Erh, his style-name was Po-yang, and his posthumous name Tan. He was born in the Ch'en district in the state of Ch'u in 604 B.C. He was once King Yu's custodian of documents. His father's surname was Han, private name K'un, and style-name Yüan-pi. His mother's name was Ching-fu. She was pregnant for eighty years before he was born under a plum (*li*) tree. For this reason he changed his surname from Han to Li. After Confucius interviewed him about rites, because of the stupidity of King Yu, he mounted a buffalo and rode through Pan-ku Pass to the west where he converted the barbarian king Yin-hsi. His way is to nourish the mind through simplicity. Its method is to draw water to supplement fire [to balance the passive and active forces of yin-yang]. When fire and water are harmonized, then one proceeds to refine gold fluid and reconvert cinnabar [after it has been turned into mercury which, in Taoist alchemy, represents the acme of the way to immortality]. He left the *Tao-te ching*, the *Scripture of Purity*, the *Treatise of the Most Exalted One on Influence and Response*, and the *Silent Way of Recompense*,[18] which now circulate throughout the world. As to Confucius, his work covers both government and religion and need not be recounted here.

The fundamental ways of the three religions are all directed at the nature and the principle. Their ethical standards and moral principles all flow out of the heavenly nature. When the substance of the nature is understood, moral principles will be correctly comprehended even without study. As is often said, when the substance is understood, the function is comprehended, and when the root is firm, the branches flourish. This is only natural.

Unfortunately, Buddhism has lost its wonderful truth and Taoism has lost its practice of alchemy and magic formulas. Their followers merely recite scriptures and chant vows and beg food from people. Confucianism has lost its central principles of the nature and the principle. Even world-renowned writers do nothing more than search for paragraphs and pick up sentences. If you ask them about the practice of knowing where to rest, unperturbedness, tranquility, and self-introspection, or the method for the investigation of things, or complete development and nourishment and fulfillment of human nature, few can answer. The result is that the three religions have almost completely disappeared.

In our Way all three religions are observed. We practice the social rites and moral principles of Confucianism, utilize the methods of the founder of Taoism, and follow the rules of Grand Old Buddha. When these are applied on a small scale, one's years will be increased and life prolonged. When applied on a large scale, one will be enlightened in the Way and become a true being (a saint). This is the work of reclarifying the principles of Pervading Unity.

Friend said: Since there is Pervading Unity in the three religions, do all of them require vegetarianism?

I said: Abstinence. There are the Five Precepts[19] in Buddhism, and not to kill is the first. Man exists for only a few scores of years and should not become an enemy of animals. The main thing is of course universal salvation. There are, I am afraid, cases where a person is not free [to abstain] and because of his vegetarianism his cultivation of the Way is sometimes hampered. Therefore while the discipline is there, its application must be flexible. Nevertheless, people who are cultivating the Way must hold compassion as fundamental. An insect or a bird shares with us the same heavenly nature. It is only because they differed in merits and demerits in their previous lives that they have changed in this life. If we kill and eat them, we are obstructing the principle of Heaven. (The Immortal) Lü Tsu[20] wrote a poem which says:

> My flesh is the same as the flesh of all creatures;
> Its shape is different but its principle is not.
> Do not let Yama (Ruller of Hell) judge you.
> Ask yourself what you should do.

If you, Sir, are willing to give up some enjoyment of the mouth, please burn incense in front of the altar and take vows (not to eat meat). I shall report to the Hall of Lao Tzu where your meritorious deed will be recorded. . . .

Friend said: If one wants to go ahead, what should be the first step?

I said: Build up a firm faith. Faith is the mother of the Way and the source of meritorious deeds. If a man has no faith, even divination will not be effective for him. It must be realized that all people are sufficiently endowed with the nature of Heaven, and Taoist immortals and Buddhas are identical in reality. It is due to various degrees of ignorance or enlightenment that we have become different. The round head and square feet of man resemble heaven and earth. His inhaling and exhaling are symbolic of yin and yang. His two eyes are comparable to the sun and the moon, and his five internal organs correspond to the Five Elements (Water, Fire, Wood, Metal, Earth). His pleasure, anger, sorrow, and joy are no different from wind, clouds, thunder, and rain, and his (four moral virtues of) humanity, righteousness, propriety, and wisdom[21] are basically the (four aspects of) origination, development, adaptation, and correctness (of the universe).[22] Babies at birth are of the same reality as Heaven and Earth, and the sages Yao, Shun, Confucius, and Mencius are no different from the common man. Those who understand the principle will become immortals and Buddhas, while those who violate it will become earthly spirits and wandering souls. Follow it and cultivate it—this is the Way. It is the unalterable principle. Do you believe in it?

Friend said: According to your theory, all scriptures are useless.

I said: Scriptures are a means. The great Way must be cultivated and intuited by oneself. A Buddha can show us the direction but cannot do the cultivation for us. The recitation of scriptures is merely a means whereby we may intuit the Law, that is all. If reciting the scriptures can always lead to an understanding of the Way, then what scriptures did the Buddhas of old have to recite? We should not avoid reading, but should not rely on it. Therefore it is said that reading scriptures is not so good as preaching them, and preaching them is not so good as acting according to them.

Friend said: The Deity we worship is called, on the one hand, the Twice Shining Lord on High, and, on the other, the Infinite Mother. Please tell me whether the Deity is male or female.

I said: By Twice Shining is meant that the Deity has shone and yet shines again. By being infinite is meant having no limit. It is called Mother because it is its nature to create. Heaven, Earth, and man above and below, immortals and Buddhas, heavenly and earthly spiritual beings, and all things with intelligence are creatures of the one Mother. Hence modern scholars speak of the 400,000,000 people as uterine brothers, and in Kuan-ti's[23] altar instructions there is the saying: "Your nature is originally my nature; you and I are essentially no different . . ."

Friend said: In past years when there was no kerosene in this country, our sesame oil and hemp-seed oil were very cheap. When opium poppy was grown everywhere, the price of rice was very low. At that time the cash was the unit and there was much money in circulation. Now that we light our lamps with kerosene, the opium poppy has disappeared, and a copper is worth ten cash, things should be much cheaper. How is it that money is scarce and droughts and floods are unduly severe?

I said: Gold and silver are the spirit of the universe. A person's spirit declines when he gets old. It is the same with the universe, and for the same reason the times are bad. Droughts and floods are determined by the state of the people's mind. Among the Five Elements[24], water is produced by Heaven. When rain fails to fall or when it falls at the wrong time, it is all because the people's minds are perverted and no longer in harmony with the mind of Heaven. There is only one way to restore normal conditions: it is goodness or moral character. Heaven can send down calamity, but can also bestow blessings. Just as water can overcome fire, so goodness can deliver us from suffering. Goodness in the person can protect the person. Goodness in the family can protect the family. If everyone is good, the world will be peaceful before sundown. Chu Hsi (1130–1200) said, "Our mind is one with the mind of the universe."[25] If man's mind is good, the mind of the universe is also good. The universe and all things form one body with me. As to things being expensive when they should be cheap—well, it does not matter. People who cultivate the Way only think of good and evil, and therefore what they enjoy is quite free from the price of things. All of us must be good in order to restore normal conditions. (*I-kuan tao li wen-ta* [Questions and answers on the principles of Pervading Unity], pp. 1–20.)

How should male and female friends of the Way practice meritorious deeds?

In practicing such deeds, male and female friends should divide the burden but work together, the total membership being mobilized. Some may take up the responsibility of Heaven, Earth, and man and write letters to propagate the principles of moral reform. Others may lecture on the teachings of the scriptures and propagate the gospel. Those with money may contribute according to their capacity to print holy scriptures and books of instruction. Those with energy may go in all directions to persuade and lead their good relatives and friends to join the Way as soon as possible. Some may donate money to build Buddha Halls to help a great number of people to practice meritorious deeds. Others may uphold with all their heart the Law of the Buddha so that the work of the Way will expand and grow daily. Some may be determined to practice earnestly and to abide reverently by the orders of the teacher. Some may cultivate the Way all their lives, thus setting an example for others. All these methods should be followed by male and female friends of the Way in their own ways to attain the fruits of goodness. . . .

What are internal meritorious deeds?

Cultivating the person, perfecting the self, seeing to it that all one's conduct conforms to the principle, making one's mind pure and desires few, and "seeking the lost mind"[26]—all these are internal meritorious deeds.

What is the way to seek the lost mind? Can you tell me the method?

The method of seeking the lost mind is simply the way of controlling the mind. Of course, the most important way to control the mind is quiet sitting. For wisdom is born of the spirit, and the spirit is born of peace and quiet. To refine one's essence in order to transform it into energy, to refine energy in order to transform it into spirit, and to refine spirit so that it may return to vacuity, there is no other way than quiet sitting.

To practice quiet sitting, sit cross-legged and erect, both in the morning and in the evening, with eyes closed in order to nourish the spirit, and with the tongue touching the roof of the mouth. Let the mind be calm and breathing be quiet. Get rid of all impure thoughts and erroneous ideas. Think neither of good nor of evil. Neither move nor shake, breathe neither in nor out. When sitting reaches the point that not a single thought arises and all anxieties have ceased, then there will be profound peace and purity and nothing inside or outside (the mind) . . .

What are external meritorious deeds?

Exhort others to do good and bring them to perfection. Enable all living creatures to be saved and everyone to turn toward the good. Do the work of assisting people and benefiting living beings. Harbor the thought of helping others in misfortune and saving the world. First rectify oneself and then rectify others. Deeds like these are external meritorious deeds.

What is the proper way of practicing an external meritorious deed?

In practicing an external meritorious deed, one must not have any intention of seeking for fame, and, what is more, one must not say any unkind word or show any angry expression. If one does a deed for the sake of fame, there is no merit in it to speak of. If one tries to exhort others with a bad temper or an angry expression, one is no longer a practitioner of the Way. In short, doing a meritorious deed, one must obey the holy teachings of the three religions and make the best real effort. Copying religious tracts, building Buddha Halls, propagating the doctrines of the Way so as to enlighten people—all these are meritorious deeds of the first order. We must realize that to transform a person so that he achieves the Way (and becomes a saint) is to make it possible for his ancestors of nine generations to ascend to Heaven, and to copy a sentence from a religious tract is better than to utter 10,000 words. Even the sages of the three religions did not go beyond this. As to the worldly work of rendering assistance in emergencies, helping people in their misfortunes, relieving others and removing danger, donate money to do it yourself if the need is small, and raise money and work with others if the need is great. Other meritorious deeds that require no money should be practiced whenever and wherever the occasion arises. (Kuo T'ing-tung, *et al.*, *I-kuan Tao i-wen chieh-ta* [Answers to questions on the Way of Pervading Unity], pp. 8a–9b.)

NOTES

1. *Doctrine of the Mean*, ch. 30.
2. *Book of Changes*, "Appended Remarks," pt. 2, ch. 5.
3. *Lao Tzu*, chs. 42 and 22, respectively.
4. *Chuang Tzu*, ch. 2 (*Nan-hua chen-ching*, 1:37a).
5. *Hou-Han shu* (History of the Later Han dynasty, 25–220), 30:31a.
6. *Kuang hung-ming chi* (Enlarged collection of essays spreading and elucidating the doctrine), 1:5b.
7. The Duke of Chou (d. 1094 B.C.) was a Confucian sage.
8. *Book of Mencius*, 5A:7, 5B:1.
9. *Hung-ming chi* (Essays spreading and elucidating the doctrine), 3:10a.
10. *Nan shih* (History of the Southern Dynasties, 420–589), 75:18b–20b.
11. *Ibid.*
12. *T'ang shu* (History of the T'ang dynasty, 618–907), 18A:11.
13. For these criticisms, see Wing-tsit Chan, *A Source Book in Chinese Philosophy*, pp. 496, 522, 547, 575, 593; Chu Hsi and Lü Tsu-ch'ien, comp., *Reflections on Things at Hand*, the *Neo-Confucian Anthology*, tr. by Wing-tsit Chan, ch. 13; and Wang Yang-ming, *Instructions for Practical Living and other Neo-Confucian Writings by Wang Yang-ming*, tr. by Wing-tsit Chan, §49, 236, 269, and 270.
14. Legendary sage-emperors of the third millennium B.C.
15. A mythical emperor. For the Eight Trigrams, see ch. 15, n. 2.
16. *Bhadra-kalpika sūtra.*

17. Actually this comes from the *Lieh Tzu*, 4:2a. The Buddha is not mentioned in the original.
18. See ch. 15, D and E.
19. Not to kill, not to steal, not to commit adultery, not to say false words, not to be intoxicated, and not to eat meat.
20. One of the Taoist deities.
21. Taught by Mencius. See *Book of Mencius*, 2A:6.
22. See the *Book of Changes*, text of the first hexagram, *ch'ien* (Heaven, male).
23. Kuan Yü (160–219), who fought heroically but failed to save the Shu-Han dynasty (221–263), was deified in the Taoist religion. Often wrongly called God of War in the West, he is one of the most popular Taoist deities.
24. The Five Elements or Agents are Water, Fire, Wood, Metal, and Earth.
25. Actually this is Ch'eng I's (1033–1107) saying, in the *I-shu* (Surviving works), 2A:1a (in the *Erh-Ch'eng ch'üan-shu* or Complete works of the two Ch'engs), *Ssu-pu pei-yao* (Essentials of the Four Libraries) edition.
26. *Book of Mencius*, 6A:11.

PART THREE

Religions of Japan

Joseph M. Kitagawa

CHAPTER 20

Myths and Legends

☐ The official chronicles of Japan are characterized by a smooth transition from the mythical past to the historic period, with the enthronement of the first legendary emperor in the seventh century B.C. Modern scholars, however, agree that the historic period of Japan started about 1,700 years ago. Of course, even before the historic period, the inhabitants of the Japanese islands had some kind of religion but the origins of the ancient Japanese religion are unknown. The early Japanese were an admixture of various ethnic groups who had migrated to Japan from the Asian continent, and their religion betrays both northern and southern Asian influences.

The early Japanese worldview, like its counterparts in other sections of the world, was based on mythic modes of apprehension of the origin and nature of man, kami (deities),[1] world, and cosmos. These myths, believed to be based on a sacred history of primordial time, tell how cosmos came out of chaos, how kami were born, and how the ancestors of the Japanese people came into existence. To the early Japanese the mythical world and the natural world interpenetrated one another to the extent that human activities are explained and sanctioned in terms of what kami, ancestors, and heroes did in the sacred past. Chief among them is the myth of the solar ancestry of the imperial family, which provided foundation for political theories in the subsequent periods.[2]

The life of the early Japanese was controlled by numerous spirits, benevolent and malevolent. To them, the important religious rites were fertility cults with special emphasis on purification. There were three kinds of persons who performed religious rites: (1) the heads of families or clans, (2) shamanic diviners who were specialists in divination, sorcery, and lustration, and (3) hereditary lines of priests. Significantly, it was the duty of the emperor, being the head of the imperial clan and also the sovereign, to take charge of religious rites and political administration, which were regarded as inseparable. ☐

A. MYTHS REGARDING THE PLAIN OF HIGH HEAVEN

1. Birth of Kami

At the beginning of heaven and earth, there came into existence in the Plain of High Heaven the Heavenly Center Lord Kami, next, the Kami of High Generative Force, and then the Kami of Divine Generative Force.

Next, when the earth was young, not yet solid, there developed something like reed-shoots from which the Male Kami of Excellent Reed Shoots and then Heavenly Eternal Standing Kami emerged.

The above five kami are the heavenly kami of special standing. (*Kojiki* [Records of ancient matters], ch. 1)

Then, there came into existence Earth Eternal Standing Kami, Kami of Abundant Clouds Field, male and female Kami of Clay, male and female Kami of Post, male and female Kami of Great Door, Kami of Complete Surface and his spouse, Kami of Awesomeness, Izanagi (kami-who-invites) and his spouse, Izanami (kami-who-is-invited). (*Ibid.*, ch. 2)

2. Solidification of the Land and the Divine Marriage

The heavenly kami at this time gave the heavenly jeweled spear to Izanagi and Izanami and instructed them to complete and solidify the land. Thus, the two kami, standing on the floating bridge in Heaven, lowered the spear and stirred around, and as they lifted up the spear, the brine dripping from the tip of the spear piled up and formed an island. This was the island of Onogoro.[3] (*Ibid.*, ch. 3)

Descending from heaven to this island, Izanagi asked his spouse Izanami as to how her body was formed. She replied, "My body is formed in such a way that one spot is not filled." Then Izanagi said, "My body is formed in such a way that there is one spot which is filled in excess. How would it be if I insert the portion of my body which is formed to excess into that portion of your body which is not filled and give birth to the land?" Izanami replied, "That would be excellent." Then Izanagi said, "Let us then walk around the heavenly pillar and meet and have conjugal intercourse." (*Ibid.*, ch. 4)

3. Birth of Other Kami

After giving birth to the land, they proceeded to bear kami [such as the kami of the wind, of the tree, of the mountain, and of the plains]. But Izanami died after giving birth to the kami of fire. (*Ibid.*, ch. 7)

Izanagi, hoping to meet again with his spouse, went after her to the land of Hades.[4] When Izanami came out to greet him, Izanagi said, "Oh my beloved, the land which you and I have been making has not yet been completed. Therefore, you must return with me." To which Izanami replied, "I greatly regret that you did not come here sooner, for I have already partaken of the hearth of the land of hades. But let me discuss with the kami of hades about my desire to return. You must, however, not look at me." As she was gone so long, Izanagi, being impatient, entered the hall to look for her and found maggots squirming around the body of Izanami. (*Ibid.*, ch. 9)

Izanagi, seeing this, was afraid and ran away, saying, "Since I have been to an extremely horrible and unclean land, I must purify myself." Thus, arriving at [a river], he purified and exorcised himself. When he washed his left eye, there came into existence the Sun Goddess, or Heavenly Illuminating Great Kami (Amaterasu), and when he washed his right eye, there emerged the Moon Kami (Tsukiyomi). Finally, as he washed his nose there came into existence Valiant Male Kami (Susanoo). (*Ibid.*, chs. 10,11)

Greatly rejoiced over this, Izanagi removed his necklace, and giving it to the the Sun Goddess, he gave her the mission to rule the Plain of High Heaven. Next he entrusted to the Moon Kami the rule of the realms of the night. Finally, he gave Valiant Male Kami the mission to rule the ocean. (*Ibid.*, ch. 12)

4. Withdrawal of the Sun Goddess

[At one time] the Sun Goddess [shocked by the misdeeds of her brother, Valiant Male Kami], opened the heavenly rock-cave door and concealed herself inside. Then the Plain of High Heaven became completely dark, and all manner of calamities arose.

Then the 800 myriads of kami gathered in a divine assembly, and summoned Kami of the Little Roof in Heaven and Kami of Grand Bead to perform a divination. They hung long strings of myriad curved beads on the upper branches of a sacred tree, and hung a large-dimensioned mirror on its middle branches. They also suspended in the lower branches white and blue cloth. These objects were held by Kami of Grand Bead as solemn offerings, while Kami of the Little Roof in Heaven intoned liturgical prayers (*norito*)[5]. Meanwhile, Kami of Heavenly Strength hid himself behind the entrance of the rock-cave, and Kami of Heavenly Headgear bound her sleeves with a cord of vine, and stamped on an overturned bucket which was placed before the rock-cave. Then she became kami-possessed, exposed her breasts and genitals. Thereupon, the 800 myriads of kami laughed so hard that the Plain of High Heaven shook with their laughter.

The Sun Goddess, intrigued by all this, opened the rock-cave door slightly, wondering why it was that the 800 myriads of kami were laughing. Then Kami of Heavenly Headgear said, "There is a kami nobler than you, and that is why we are happy and dancing." While she was speaking thus, Kami of the Little Roof and Kami of Grand Bead showed the mirror to the Sun Goddess. Thereupon, the Sun Goddess, thinking this ever more strange, gradually came out of the cave, and the hidden Kami of Grand Bead took her hand and pulled her out. Then as the Sun Goddess reappeared, the Plain of High Heaven was naturally illuminated. (*Ibid.*, ch. 17)

5. Pacification of the Izumo Region[6]

□ According to the *Kojiki* myth, the Sun Goddess dispatched two divine messengers to pacify the Central Land of the Reed Plains[7], which was ruled by Great Land Ruler Kami. The two kami persuaded the sons of Great Land Ruler Kami to surrender, and then approached the ruler himself. □

"Your sons have promised not to disobey the commands of the heavenly kami. What is your sentiment on the matter?" To this question he replied, "In keeping with the words of my sons, I too will not disobey and present this Central Land of the Reed Plains in accordance with your commands. However, I would like to have my dwelling place built modelled after the heavenly dwelling with the posts firmly embedded in the bed-rock below and the cross-beams raised high reaching the Plain of High Heaven. Then, I will retire there, and my children the 180 kami will serve the heavenly kami." As he said these words, he hid himself, and a heavenly temple palace was established for him in the land of Izumo. The grandson of the Kami of the Sea Straights served the food and pronounced the words of blessing. (*Ibid.* ch. 37)

6. Descent of Ninigi, Grandson of the Sun Goddess

□ As the pacification of the Japanese islands was duly reported, Ninigi, the grandson of the Sun Goddess, was sent to rule the land with the following instruction. □

"This Land of the Plentiful Reed Plains and of the Fresh Rice-ears[8] has been entrusted to you as the land to be governed by you. Therefore, you must descend from heaven in accordance with the divine command." (*Ibid.*, ch. 38)

Then Ninigi, accompanied by Kami of the Little Roof in Heaven, Kami of Grand Bead, Kami of Heavenly Headgear, Kami of Stone Cutter, and Jewel Ancestor Kami, descended from heaven. The Sun Goddess gave Ninigi the myriad curved beads, the mirror, and the "grass-mower" sword,[9] and also commissioned Thought Collecting Golden Kami of the Eternal World and two other kami to accompany Ninigi. She said, "Take this mirror as my spirit, and venerate it as you would venerate my own presence. Also, let Thought Collecting Golden Kami of the Eternal World take charge of affairs which come before you, and let him carry on the government matters."

Thus, Ninigi, now leaving the heavenly rock seat, pushed through the myriad layers of heavenly clouds and descended on the peak of Mount Takachiho.[10] (*Ibid.*, ch. 39)

B. LEGENDARY HEROES

1. Emperor Jimmu (first legendary emperor)[11]

[Jimmu], living with his brother Lord of Five Rapids in the palace of Takachiho, asked one day, "Where will be the most strategic place for us to live in order to govern the country peacefully? I am inclined to go eastward for that purpose." (*Ibid.*, ch. 47)

As Jimmu thus travelled [eastward] and came to the village of Kumano,[12] he saw a large bear move around and disappear. Suddenly Jimmu as well as his entire army felt faint and lay down. At this time a certain man called Takakuraji appeared with a sword, and as he presented the sword to him, Jimmu suddenly awoke and said, "I must have slept a long time." At the moment when he received that sword, all the unruly kami in the Kumano mountains were slain instantaneously. (*Ibid.*, ch. 49)

Jimmu, after pacifying the unruly kami and the unsubmissive people, dwelled in the palace of Kashiwara at Unebi[13] and ruled the kingdom. (*Ibid.*, ch. 52)

2. Prince Yamatotakeru[14]

When he received the imperial command and started off, he went to the Shrine of the Great Kami (the Sun Goddess) of Ise and worshiped at the kami's court. At that time the prince told his aunt, Princess Yamato,[15] "It must surely be that the emperor wishes me to die soon; otherwise why would he have dispatched me again without any troops to subdue the evil people of the twelve regions of the East so soon after sending me to fight against the evil people of the West! Indeed, he must wish me to die soon." As he departed, lamenting and crying thus, Princess Yamato presented him with the "grass-mower" sword and a bag, saying, "Open the bag if there should be an emergency." (*Ibid.*, ch. 82)

As he reached the district of Sagamu,[16] the ruler of the district lied to Prince Yamatotakeru, saying, "There is a great lagoon in this plain, and an unruly kami resides in it." And, as Prince Yamatotakeru entered the plain to see that kami, the ruler set fire to the plain. Realizing that he had been deceived, he opened the bag given to him by his aunt and found in it a fire-striking instrument. Then, after moving away the grass with his sword, he lit a fire with the fire-striking instrument and started a counter-fire to keep the fire away. After that, he killed the ruler of the district and destroyed all his clan. (*Ibid.*, ch. 83)

From there he proceeded to cross the sea of Hashirimizu.[17] It so happened that the kami of the crossing raised the waves, so that the boat could not go forward. Then, the consort[18] of the prince said, "I will enter the sea instead of the prince, because he has to complete the mission." Saying thus, she laid many layers of carpets on top of the waves and went down onto them. At this time the violent waves calmed down at once, and the boat was able to go forward. (*Ibid.*, ch. 84)

[When Prince Yamatotakeru went to Mount Ibuki], he said, "I will overcome the kami of this mountain empty-handed." As he ascended the mountain he encountered a white boar, whereupon the prince said, "This must be a messenger of the kami. I will not kill it now, but will do so when I return." The kami of the mountain caused a heavy hail storm and perplexed the prince. Actually, the white boar was not a messenger but the kami himself, and because the prince dared to speak to the kami directly, he was thus perplexed. At any rate, when he descended from the mountain, he reached a fresh spring and rested his body and mind for a while.

When he departed there and came to the plain of Tagi, he said, "My heart always wanted to fly through the sky, but my legs now refuse to walk." Nevertheless, he proceeded a little further with the help of a staff. Then his sickness became critical. He sang, "I placed a sword at the maiden's bedside. Ah! That sword." When he finished singing, he passed away. . . . The Prince was transformed into an eight-furlong white bird, and flew away towards the beach. (*Ibid.*, chs. 86–88)

3. Empress Jingū (or Jingō)[19]

The empress became kami-possessed when the emperor was about to attack the Kumaso tribes.[20] The emperor played a harp,[21] while the Great Minister named Takeshiuchi-no-sukune sat by their side to seek the will of the kami. The empress in the state of kami-possession uttered these words of divine instruction, "In the West, there is a land (Korea) full of gold and silver as well as other dazzling precious treasures. I will now give this land to you." The emperor, however, replied, "Even if I ascend a high place and look towards the West I could not see any land because there is only the ocean." The emperor, thus thinking this was a deceiving kami, pushed aside the harp and sat silently without playing it. Whereupon the kami, greatly angered, told the emperor, "This kingdom is not to be ruled by you. As far as you are concerned, you should go straight in one direction."[22] The Great Minister, Takeshiuchi, said, "I am greatly alarmed, Your Majesty; please continue playing the harp." Reluctantly the emperor drew his harp and started to play again, but almost immediately the sound of the harp became inaudible. When the lights were brought, they saw that the emperor was already dead. (*Ibid.*, ch. 92)

The Great Minister was astonished and awed, and moved the emperor's body to a mortuary place. He ordered a great exorcism of the entire country for the purification from such defilements as skinning alive, skinning backwards, breaking down ridges, covering up ditches, evacuating excrements and urine, incest, and sexual intercourse with animals and fowls.[23] Then the Great Minister sat in the ceremonial ground and once again sought the divine will.[24] The instructions given were exactly the same as those given before, except that the land in question was now said to be ruled by the unborn child in the womb of the empress and that the child was to be a boy. The Great Minister inquired as to the name of the great kaṃi who gave those instructions, and the answer given was, "This is the will of the Sun Goddess. And, if you truly seek that land [of Korea], you should present offerings to all the heavenly and earthly kami, as well as to all the kami of the mountains and of the rivers and seas. Enshrine our spirit on top of the vessel, put wood ashes into a gourd, make a large quantity of chopsticks and plates, and cast all of these on the waves of the ocean. Then, you may cross the ocean." (*Ibid.*, ch. 93)

Following these instructions, the army was properly equipped and the vessels were prepared. Then with the help of a favorable wind the ships proceeded upon the waves and came to the shore of Silla.[25] The king of Silla, greatly awed by this, petitioned, saying, "We will obey the will of the divine sovereign from now on. Let us take care of your horses and vessels each year." Thus, the land of Silla was made the imperial stable-groom, whereas the land of Paekche[26] was declared to be the overseas imperial granary.

Then the empress placed her staff on the gate of the king of Silla and worshiped the rough spirit of the great kami of Sumi-no-ye[27] whom she made the guardian kami of the land [of Korea]. Then she crossed the ocean back to Japan. [Incidentally], as the child was ready to be born before she completed her mission, she kept a stone around her waist in order to restrain the womb. Only after she returned [to Japan] was the child born.[28] (*Ibid.*, ch. 94–95)

C. FROM LEGENDS TO HISTORY

1. Cultural Contact with Asian Continent

[During the reign of the 15th emperor, Ōjin, son of Empress Jingū] some immigrants crossed over from Silla. Also, the king of Paekche presented as tribute one stallion and one mare which were sent together with Master Achiki [who became the ancestor of the clan of scribes]. He also presented as tribute a sword and a large mirror. Then, the emperor commanded the land of Paekche to send a wise man as tribute, whereupon a man called Master Waniki was presented together with the Confucian *Analects* in ten volumes and the *Thousand-Character Classic* in one volume, totaling eleven volumes. Paekche also presented two artisans, a Korean smith and a Chinese weaver. Then there came over the ancestor of the chieftains of the Hata[29] clan, the ancestor of the chieftains of the Aya[30] clan, a man who knew the art of distilling liquor, whose name was Niho,[31] also known as Susukori, and others. This man, Susukori, distilled some liquor and offered it to the emperor, who greatly enjoyed it. (*Ibid.*, ch. 104)

2. A Sage-Emperor[32]

[During the reign of the 16th emperor, Nintoku (r. 311–399)], people of the Hata clan were put to work for the construction of the embankment and the granaries at Mamuta as well as the ponds of Wani and Yosami. Also, the Naniwa channel was dug and it was connected to the sea. (*Ibid.*, ch. 109)

At this time the emperor, ascending a high mountain and looking around over the land, said, "I do not see smoke rising throughout the land. The entire land must be poverty-stricken. Therefore all taxes and conscriptions will be remitted for three years." Therefore, the imperial palace became dilapidated, and although the roof leaked, no repairs were made. The leaking rain was caught in vessels, and [those who lived in the palace] moved around to spots where it did not leak.

Later, the emperor looked over the land and found smoke rising from everywhere. Realizing that the people were well off, he reinstated taxes and conscriptions. In this manner the common people prospered, and did not suffer from conscriptions. Thus in praise of his reign, it was called the reign of a sage-emperor. (*Ibid.*, ch. 110)

NOTES

1. Often translated as god, kami is spirit or anything that commands the awe and reverence of man. The term refers to both the "sacred" nature in general and the specific objects of worship in Shintō.
2. One of the best sources for ancient Japanese myths and legends is the *Kojiki*, compiled in 712. It is entirely Chinese in style and diction but Japanese in content. The following are abridged translations from the *Kojiki*. I have consulted Basil Hall Chamberlain's translation of "'Ko-ji-ki' (Records of Ancient Matters)," *Transactions of Asiatic Society of Japan*, vol. 10 (1882), Supplement, and Donald L. Philippi's unpublished translation of *Kojiki*.
3. An island believed to be situated near the present Ōsaka bay.
4. Literally, land of yellow spring inhabited by the dead.
5. See ch. 23, B.
6. The present Shimane Prefecture in western Honshu.
7. Ashihara no nakatsu-kuni, a designation of Japan.
8. Toyo-ashihara no mizuho no kuni, another designation of Japan.
9. The myriad curved beads, the mirror (the one that had been used to lure the Sun Goddess out of the cave), and the "grass-mower" sword are the three sacred regalia of the imperial authority.
10. Believed to be situated in the island of Kyūshū.
11. He was then called Kamu Yamato Iwarebiko no Mikoto. His reign is traditionally dated 660–585 B.C.
12. Situated in the present Wakayama Prefecture; not far from Ōsaka.
13. In the present Nara Prefecture.
14. One of the most popular legendary heroes recorded in the *Kojiki* is Prince Yamatotakeru (Brave man of Yamato), son of the 12th legendary emperor, Keikō (r. 71–130). This prince was dispatched by his father to pacify the unruly kami and the unsubmissive people of the west. Again, he was commanded to pacify the twelve regions of the eastern part of Japan.
15. She was the High Priestess of the Ise Shrine.
16. An area not far from present Tōkyō.
17. Literally, "running water."
18. The *Kojiki* uses the title, *kisaki*, which is usually translated as the empress or the chief consort of the emperor.
19. Among all the shamanic-diviners mentioned in the *Kojiki*, the most prominent is Empress Jingū, the consort of the 14th legendary emperor, Chūai (r. 192–200).
20. Unsubmissive people living in Kyūshū.
21. In order to summon down kami.
22. Meaning death.
23. See ch. 23, B.
24. Through the kami-possession of the empress.
25. A kingdom in modern southeastern Korea.
26. A kingdom in modern southwestern Korea.

27. Inlet of Sumi, near present Ōsaka.
28. He became the 15th legendary Emperor Ōjin (r. 270–310).
29. Ch'in in Chinese.
30. Han in Chinese.
31. Jen-fan in Chinese.
32. Note the influence of the Chinese concept of the sage-emperor on this account of Nintoku.

CHAPTER 21

Early Japan: Shintō

□ With the ascendancy of the imperial clan in the third or fourth century A.D., a stratification of Japanese society that had been going on gradually for centuries became accentuated, as evidenced by elaborate cemeteries constructed for aristocrats. The construction of great tombs must have required a considerable labor force, which implies the existence of serfs or peasants. Also, judging from the items discovered in burial chambers, there must have been professional artisans who produced shoes, tailored clothes, silver and gold jewelry, bows, arrowheads, armor, horseback riding equipment, eating utensils, and agricultural tools. Equally interesting is a series of clay figures, discovered in and around the great tombs, which portray warriors with swords and shields, musicians, dancers, female diviners, ordinary housewives, and children. However, our knowledge of the life of the early Japanese is very fragmentary. We can only conjecture, based on scattered references in the Chinese and Korean sources and by piecing together some accounts of later Japanese sources, that the Japanese kingdom, which was in effect a confederation of powerful and autonomous clans, was gradually consolidated by the religious authority and military power of the imperial clan, and that the political influence of Japan reached even to the southern tip of Korea by the fourth century.

The historic situation in the fourth and fifth centuries A.D. brought about a series of social, cultural, political, and religious changes in Japan under the influence of Sino-Korean civilization and of Buddhism. Japan, which previously had no written language, adopted the Chinese script. Japanese society, based on primitive communal rules and authorities, accepted Confucian ethical principles and political theories. Also, after an initial period of resistance on the part of Shintō priestly families and conservative aristocrats, Buddhism gradually captured the Japanese. Many scholars, priests, nuns, and ecclesiastical artists were welcomed from Korea and China. Although the majority of the people did not understand the lofty Buddhist doctrine, they were dazzled by the arts, ceremonies, and architecture of Buddhism. The relatively rapid expansion of Buddhism in Japan during the seventh and eighth centuries resulted in large part from the support it received from the imperial court which, however, maintained strict political control over Buddhist as well as Shintō clergy and institutions. □

A. EARLY JAPANESE VIEWS AND ATTITUDES[1]

1. Seasons

"Spring" (8:1444)

In the meadow full of yellow roses,
violets have blossomed forth with spring
rain.

(*Manyōshū* [Collection of a myriad leaves], vol. 2, pp. 288–89)

"New Year" (17:3925)

This year promises to be a fruitful one
because of the deep snow that fell on
New Year's day.
(*Ibid.*, vol. 4, pp. 186–87)

"Autumn" (2:209)

As I see the messenger walking on the fallen
leaves,
I think of the time when I first met my
beloved.
(*Ibid.*, vol. 1, pp. 116–17)

2. Mountains

"Mount Fuji" (3:319–21)

Between the provinces of Kai and Suruga
Stands the lofty peak of Fuji.
Heavenly clouds would not dare cross it;
Even birds dare not fly above it.
The fire of volcano is extinguished by snow,
and yet snow is consumed by fire.
It is hard to describe;
It is impossible to name it.
One only senses
the presence of a mysterious kami.

. . .

In the land of Yamato,
the land of the rising sun,
The lofty Mount Fuji is its treasure
and its tutelary kami. . . .
One is never tired of
gazing at its peak in the province of
Suruga.
(*Ibid.*, vol. 1, pp. 168–71)

3. Prayer

"Prayer of a Soldier" (20:4372)

Ascending the mountain-road of Ashigara
without looking back homewards;
Then as I come to the Pass of Fuwa
where even the brave men fear to cross,
I stop my horse for a moment and pray
for the safety of my family until my return.
(*Ibid.*, vol. 4, pp. 426–27)

4. Life After Death

"Nether World" (5:905)

O messenger from the nether world
here is some money for you;
Please carry on your back my son
who is so young and does not know the
way.
(*Ibid.*, vol. 2, pp. 120–21)

"On the Uncertainty of Life" (1:4160)

It has been told from the beginning of the
world
that life on earth is transitory. . . .
Indeed we see even in the sky
the moon waxes and wanes. . . .
In the spring
flowers decorate mountain-trees,
But in the autumn with dew and frost
leaves turn colors and fall on the
ground. . . .
So it is with human life:
Rosy cheek and black hair turn their
color;
The morning smile disappears in the
evening
like the wind which blows away.
Changes continue in life like the water
passing away,
And my tears do not stop over the uncertainty of life.
(*Ibid.*, vol. 4, pp. 326–27)

B. DEVELOPMENT OF EARLY SHINTŌ

☐ The term Shintō,[2] which means literally "the way of the kami or gods," was adopted in the sixth century A.D. in order to differentiate it from the newly introduced Buddhism. Early Shintō was a loosely organized, indigenous religious cult, embodying within it many contradictory features. With the ascendancy of the imperial clan roughly around the third or fourth century, much of the local religious beliefs and practices came under the influence of the religious tradition of the imperial clan.[3] ☐

1. Enshrinement of the Sun Goddess and the Kami of Yamato

During the reign of the 10th legendary emperor, Sujin,[4] there were many people who wandered away from their homes, and there were also some rebellions. The situation was such that the imperial virtue alone could not control the nation. Therefore, the emperor was penitent from morning till night, asking for divine punishment of the kami of heaven and earth upon himself. Prior to that time the two kami, the Sun Goddess and the Kami of Yamato were worshiped together within the imperial palace. The emperor, however, was afraid of their potencies and did not feel at ease living with them. Therefore, he entrusted Princess Toyosukiiri to worship the Sun Goddess at the village of Kasanui in Yamato,[5] where a sacred shrine was established. Also he commissioned Princess Nunakiiri to worship the Kami of Yamato. (*Nihongi* [Chronicles of Japan], bk. 5, 6th year)

[Then] the emperor stated, "I did not realize that numerous calamities would take place during our reign. It may be that the lack of good rule might have incurred the wrath of the kami of heaven and earth. It might be well to inquire the cause of the calamities by means of divination." The emperor therefore assembled the eighty myriads of kami and inquired about this matter by means of divination. At that time the kami spoke through the kami-possession of Princess Yamatototohimomoso, "Why is the emperor worried over the disorder of the nation? Doesn't he know that the order of the nation would be restored if he properly venerated me?" The emperor asked which kami was thus giving such an instruction, and the answer was: "I am the kami who resides within the province of Yamato, and my name is Ōmononushi-no-kami." Following the divine instruction, the emperor worshiped the kami, but the expected result did not follow. Thus the emperor cleansed himself and fasted as well as purifying the palace, and addressed himself to the kami in prayer, asking, "Is not our worship sufficient? Why is our worship not accepted? May we be further instructed in a dream as the fulfillment of your divine favor toward us."

That night a noble man who called himself Ōmononushi-no-kami appeared and spoke to the emperor in his dream, "The emperor has no more cause to worry over the unsettled state of the nation. It is my divine wish to be worshiped by my child, Ōtataneko, and then the nation will be pacified immediately." Upon learning the meaning of the dream, the emperor was greatly delighted and issued a proclamation throughout the country to look for Ōtataneko, who was subsequently found in the district of Chinu and was presented to the court. Whereupon the emperor asked Ōtataneko as to whose child he was, and the answer was: "My father's name is the Great Kami Ōmononushi. My mother's name is Princess Ikutamayori." The emperor then said, "Now prosperity will come to us." Thus, Ōtataneko was made the chief priest in charge of the worship of the Great Kami Ōmononushi. After that the emperor consulted divination as to the desirability of worshiping other kami, and found it desirable to do so. Accordingly he paid homage to the eighty myriads of kami. Thereupon the pestilence ceased and peace was restored in the nation, and good crops of the five kinds of grain made the peasantry prosperous. (*Ibid.*, 7th year)

2. The Enshrinement of the Sun Goddess at Ise

(The eleventh legendary emperor, Suinin,)[6] proclaimed, "Our predecessor (Emperor Sujin), had complete oversight of the government and venerated the heavenly and earthly kami. Moreover, he disciplined himself and lived reverently each day. Therefore, people enjoyed prosperity and the nation was peaceful. And now, during our reign, how can we be negligent of the worship of the heavenly and earthly kami?"

Accordingly, the Sun Goddess, who had been cared for by Princess Toyosukiiri, was now entrusted to Princess Yamato. Thereupon Princess Yamato visited various places, looking for the permanent settling place of the Sun Goddess, and finally reached the province of Ise.[7] At this time, the Sun Goddess instructed Princess Yamato, saying, "The province of Ise, whose divine wind blows, is washed by successive waves from the Eternal Land. It is a secluded and beautiful place, and I wish to dwell here." Thus, in compliance with the divine instruction, a shrine [which became the most important Shintō shrine] was erected in honor of the Sun Goddess in the province of Ise, and at the same time an Abstinence Palace was established along the river Isuzu[8] where the Sun Goddess originally descended from heaven. (*Ibid.*, bk. 6, 25th year)

3. Prince Shōtoku's Proclamation for the Worship of Kami

[In 607 during the reign of Empress Suiko, r. 592–628] the following edict was issued [by the Prince Regent Shōtoku, 573–621]: "We are told that our imperial ancestors, in governing the nation, bent humbly under heaven and walked softly on earth. They venerated the kami of heaven and earth, and established shrines on the mountains and by the rivers, whereby they were in constant touch with the power of nature. Hence the winter, (yin, negative cosmic force) and summer (yang, positive cosmic force) elements were kept in harmony, and their creative powers blended together. And now during our reign, it would be unthinkable to neglect the veneration of the kami of heaven and earth. May all the ministers from the bottom of their hearts pay homage to the kami of heaven and earth." (*Ibid.*, bk. 12, 15th year)

4. The Reform of Taika (645–650 A.D.)[9]

[In 645, Emperor Kōtoku, r. 645–654] together with the empress dowager and the crown prince summoned all the ministers to gather together under a great planera tree, and commanded them to take the following oath: "We solemnly declare to the kami of heaven and earth that heaven covers us and earth upholds us, and that there is only one imperial way. In recent years, however, the principle which regulates the relationship between throne and subjects was violated, so that the guilty subjects had to be eliminated by us with assistance from heaven. Now all of us realize the truth in our hearts to the effect that from this time onward there shall be no administration other than that of the emperor, and that the subjects shall not act contrary to the will of the sovereign. Should we violate this oath, we would invite the heavenly and earthly curse, and would be slain by demons." (*Ibid.*, bk. 25, Taika, 1st year)

[Two years later, the following edict was issued:] "According to the way of the kami[10] the Sun Goddess commanded her divine descendants to rule the nation. Accordingly, this nation from its inception has been governed by the sovereigns. Indeed from the time of the first august emperor this nation under heaven maintained order and no one questioned it. In recent years, however, the names of the kami and the emperors came to be distorted and are claimed by the clan chieftains and local barons. No wonder the minds of the people lost coherence, and it became difficult to govern the nation. Therefore at this time when we are destined to rule according to the way of the kami, we must first compel the people to realize these things in order to govern properly the nation and the people. Then, we shall issue a series of edicts, one today and another tomorrow." (*Ibid.*, Taika, 3rd year)

[In the year 650] the governor of the province of Anato presented a white pheasant to the emperor. Whereupon Great Minister Kose offered the following words of salutation: "We, the ministers and functionaries of the government offer our congratulations to Your Majesty. The appearance of a white pheasant in the western province is a sure sign that Your Majesty is ruling the nation with serene virtue. May Your Majesty continue to provide peaceful rule of the four corners [of Japan] for a thousand autumns and ten thousand years. In turn, it is our humble wish to serve Your Majesty with utmost fidelity." Having completed the salutation, the Great Minister made repeated obeisances. Then the emperor declared, "We know that heaven gives good omens as a response to the good rule of the sage king. Not only such birds and animals as the phoenix, unicorn, white pheasant, and white crow but also herbs and trees have been chosen by Heaven and Earth as instruments of good omens. One can understand why sage kings have received such favorable omens, but why should we, the unworthy one, merit it? This is due, we are certain, to the work of those who assist us, the ministers, clan chieftains, government officials, and provincial governors, who meticulously abide by the rules and regulations with utmost fidelity. This being so, we trust that all of you, from the ministers down to the functionaries of various offices, venerate the kami of heaven and earth with pure hearts, and endeavor to bring about the prosperity of the nation in response to the good omen." (*Ibid.*, Hakuchi, 1st year)

5. Drought and the Great Purification Rite[11]

[In the year 676, during the reign of Emperor Temmu, r. 673–686,] a great drought took place. Thus, the imperial emissaries were dispatched in various directions to make offerings and pray to all the kami, and even the Buddhist priests were solicited to pray to the [Buddhas]. But there was still no rain, and the five grains did not grow; thereby the peasantry was starving. The emperor also propitiated the Wind Kami of Tatsuta Shrine and the Great Kami of Abstinence of Hirose Shrine.

Meanwhile a star of seven or eight feet in length appeared in the eastern sky. Then the emperor proclaimed, "Let a great purification rite be held in every section of the land. In each province its governor should provide one horse and one piece of cloth to be used for the ritual. Also the official of each district should supply one sword, one deerskin, one mattock, one small sword, one sickle, one set of arrows, and one sheaf of rice in the ear, whereas each household must offer a bundle of hemp for this purpose." It was further decreed that "all sentences of death, confiscation, and banishment shall be mitigated one degree. Other sentences of minor degree, such as banishing the guilty from one area to another within the same province, whether or not they have been arrested, except those who have already been banished, shall be pardoned." On this day the emperor also commanded that living animals and birds be turned loose. (*Ibid.*, bk. 29, 5th year)

6. Rituals in Connection with the Erection of a New Capital

[In the year 691, during the reign of Empress Jitō, r. 687–697,] imperial messengers were dispatched to perform a service praying for the peace of the newly constructed capital. In this connection, the festival of the first-fruits[12] was also celebrated. The chieftain of the Nakatomi clan, minister of the Department of Shintō Affairs, invoked the blessing of the heavenly kami. (*Ibid.*, bk. 30, 5th year)

The empress then proclaimed her intention of visiting Ise [ostensibly to report the establishment of the new capital to the Sun Goddess], and appointed Prince Hirose [and others] to take charge of state affairs during her absence. Thereupon Takechimaro, the chieftain of the Miwa clan, leading advisor to the throne, took off his cap of rank and repeatedly admonished the empress that her chariot should not travel during the farming season because it might interfere with agricultural activities. But the empress, refusing to abide by his remonstrance, proceeded to Ise.

Upon her return from Ise, the empress dispatched Prince Niniwa and others to perform a service praying on her behalf for the peace of the site of the capital at Fujiwara.[13] Emissaries were also sent to make offerings to the kami of the shrines of Ise, Ōyamato, Suminoye, and Kii, reporting to them the erection of the new capital. (*Ibid.*, 6th year)

7. Empress Gemmyō's Edict upon Her Enthronement[14]

"We, the living kami, the ruler of the Great Land of Eight Islands and the empress of Yamato, proclaim to all the imperial princes, nobles, officials of the one hundred departments of the government and all the subjects of the realm: [In the year 697 the celebrated Empress Jitō,] who ruled the nation at the capital of Fujiwara, commissioned our august child (Emperor Mommu) and us, who are now on the throne, together to rule the nation. Last year our august child, the emperor, fatigued by ailment, wished to rest and recuperate, and asked us to assume the throne. But we, knowing that the task of the imperial rule was unbearable, did not accept his wish, even though he repeatedly expressed his desire to abdicate.

However, in the sixth month of this year [because of the death of the emperor] we, obeying his wish, assumed the throne, reverently relying on the guidance of the will of Heaven and Earth. We think that it is possible for us to rule this nation peacefully with the assistance of the imperial princes, nobles, officials of the one hundred departments of the government who would serve faithfully with pure and bright hearts. We are determined to preserve the eternal law of the realm, which is as old as the beginning of heaven and earth, without any deflection or change." (*Shoku Nihongi* [Chronicles of Japan continued], bk. 4, Keinen, 4th year)

C. LOCAL LEGENDS

□ In the course of its development, Shintō added to its pantheon numerous kinds of kami, who were venerated in various provinces of Japan. Many of them remained solely as local kami, whereas some of them came to be considered as descendants of the kami who are recorded in Shintō myths.[15] □

1. The Snake Kami of the Hitachi Province

[In the early sixth century during the reign of the 26th Emperor Keitai, r. 506–531,] a certain man named Matachi cultivated new rice fields in the district of Namekata of the Hitachi province.[16] His work was greatly hindered by a large number of snakes. People in that district called them the snake kami, for they have the bodies of snakes and horns on their heads. When one tries to run from them and happens to turn around and look at these snakes, his family is believed to be doomed to die out. Matachi became angry over the interference by the snakes. Thereupon he put on armor and chased the snakes towards the mountain, killing as many of them as he could in the meantime. As he came to the trench at the foot of the mountain he placed a stick as a mark of dividing line, and he addressed the snake kami, saying, "The territory above this mark is to be the property of the kami, but the land below the dividing line is to become man's rice fields. From now I shall serve as the priest and venerate the kami, and I beseech you to bring no curse on us." In so stating he erected a shrine and offered the first service to the snake kami. Then, he came down and cultivated rice fields. We are told that Matachi's descendants have continued to venerate the snake kami to this day. (*Hitachi-no-kuni fudoki* [Records of customs and land of Hitachi Province], section on Namekata County)

2. The Great Kami of Kashima

Before the separation of heaven and earth, the heavenly ancestors of the imperial family addressed the 800 myriad kami at the Plain of High Heaven, saying, "The land [of Japan] is destined to be ruled by our august descendants." At that time there were many unruly kami in the land [of Japan]. Thus, in order to pacify and prepare the land for the descendants of the heavenly kami, the Heavenly Great Kami of Kashima[17] was dispatched to Japan.

According to a legend [transmitted in the Hitachi Province], during the reign of the 10th legendary emperor (Sujin) a certain kami, clad in a white robe and carrying a white halberd, appeared at the peak of Mount Ōsaka and declared to the emperor saying, "If you should venerate us properly, you would be able to rule the country peacefully." The emperor, not knowing the name of the kami, inquired of the chieftains of various leading clans. The chieftain of [the hereditary Shintō priestly family of] Ōnakatomi identified the kami as the Great Kami of Kashima, who had been sent by the heavenly kami to pacify Japan. Upon learning this, the emperor was greatly awed, and presented to the Great Kami of Kashima [ten swords, two halberds, two iron-bows, two iron arrows, as well as one horse, one saddle, two mirrors and one set of five colored silk, as the offerings]. (*Ibid.*)

3. The Kami of One Word[18]

In the year 460 (?), Emperor [Yūryaku, r. 457–479] went to Mount Katsuragi[19] for hunting. There he suddenly encountered a very tall man who stood facing the valley. In his physical appearance this man resembled the emperor. Although the emperor was aware that he was a kami, he nevertheless inquired, "Of what place are you the lord?" The tall man replied, "You are speaking to a kami in human form. Tell me your noble name, and then I will identify myself." The emperor said that his own name was Wakatake no Mikoto, and the tall man identified himself as the Kami of One Word. Then, both of them enjoyed the hunting, offering to each other to shoot first at a deer, galloping side by side, and speaking politely like holy men to each other. When the evening came and the hunt ended, the kami escorted the emperor to the Kume River. Seeing this, the people said in unison, "What a virtuous emperor he must be!" (*Nihongi*, bk. 14, 4th year)

4. The Thunder Kami

[In the year 618] the chieftain of the Kawabe clan was dispatched to the province of Aki[20] with the commission to build ships. There he went to the mountain, looking for appropriate timber for the construction of ships. It so happened that he found good timber and was ready to cut it. But a certain man told him that it was known as the tree of thunder and should not be cut. But the chieftain of the Kawabe declared, "Should even the Thunder Kami dare disobey the imperial command?" Thus, he propitiated the kami with many offerings, and sent workmen to cut the tree. But they were confronted by heavy rainfall, thunder and lightning. Seeing this, the chieftain of the Kawabe drew his sword and declared, "O Thunder Kami, if you should harm anyone, harm me and not these workmen." In so saying he looked upward and waited, but he was not harmed even by the ten-odd thunders. Instead, the Thunder Kami became transformed into a small fish and was caught by the branches of the tree. The chieftain of the Kawabe picked up the fish and burnt it. After this, he was able to construct the ship. (*Ibid.*, bk. 22, 26th year)

5. The Kami of the Eternal Land

[In the year 644,] a certain man called Ōube-no-ōshi, who lived by the River Fuji in eastern Japan, advocated the worship of an insect by asserting that it was the Kami of the Eternal Land and that those who worship this kami will be rewarded by prosperity and longevity. Soothsayers, falsely claiming the divine message, told people that by worshiping the Kami of the Eternal Land the poor would become rich and the aged would be rejuvenated. Thus, the people were persuaded to discard the family treasures, placing wine, vegetables, domestic animals by the road side, and shout that new wealth has come to them. Seeing how people have been deceived by the soothsayers and have lost their treasures, Kawakatsu, the governor of the province, punished Ōube-no-ōshi. Whereupon the soothsayers became afraid and ceased to urge people to worship the insect. (*Ibid.*, bk. 24, 3rd year)

D. SHINTŌ PRIESTHOOD

□ In the early period of Japan there were several hereditary Shintō priestly families who claimed to be descendants of heavenly kami, such as the Nakatomi clan, the Imbe clan, the Sarume clan, and so on.[21]

The author of the *Gleanings from Ancient Sources*, Imbe no Hironari, holds that the Imbe and the Nakatomi were two equally important hereditary Shintō priestly families, tracing their ancestries to the kami of the Plain of High Heaven. He laments the fact that the Nakatomi had become all too powerful, overshadowing the Imbe family. In order to substantiate his view, Hironari cites many examples of how the traditional priesthood functioned in early Shintō. □

We are told that in old days there was no writing in Japan, whereby everybody, noble and humble, old and young, memorized ancient traditions and transmitted them orally from one generation to the next. Since the introduction of the art of writing from China, however, people have become frivolous and do not seem to like to discuss ancient matters. Meanwhile, with the passage of time traditional accounts have undergone certain changes, and very few nowadays seem to be aware of the original accounts. Fortunately, by the imperial command I have been given this opportunity to write down for the benefit of the throne some of the ancient traditions which have been handed down in my family. (*Kogo shūi* [Gleanings from ancient sources], 1:545)

[In the days of the first legendary emperor Jimmu,] after the imperial forces conquered their foes throughout the nation, the imperial palace was established at Kashiwara in the province of Yamato. At that time, Prince Ame no Tomi ("heavenly wealth") was commissioned to build the palace, securing timber from the mountains, grounding the palace pillars into the nethermost rock-bottom and raising the palace beams to reach the Plain of High Heaven. Prince Ame no Tomi was also commissioned, with the assistance of the various branches of the Imbe clan, to produce such sacred treasures as mirrors, jewels, spears, shields, cotton and hemp clothes. (*Ibid.*, 1:550)

Then, in accordance with the commandment of the two heavenly ancestral kami, [the Kami of High Generative Force and the Sun Goddess,] a sacred site[22] was established inside the palace compound for the worship of [various] kami. Prince Hi no Omi, chieftain of the Kume clan, was placed in charge of the palace gates, while Prince Nigihayahi with the members of the Mononobe clan were placed in charge of swords and shields. When all the preparations were done, Prince Ame no Tomi, with the assistance of the members of the Imbe clan, placed the sacred mirror and sacred sword, which are the imperial regalia, in the main hall of the palace, and, after hanging the jewels and presenting offerings, recited the liturgy for bringing good fortune to the imperial palace. It was followed by the solemn service for the guardian kami of the palace gates. (*Ibid.*, 1:551)

In those days the distinction between the emperor and the kami was not so sharply made, so that it was taken for granted that they dwell together in the same palace. Also, the properties of the kami and those of the emperor were not differentiated, and both were kept in the sacred treasure house which was kept under the supervision of the Imbe clan. It was by the imperial command that Prince Ame no Tomi and other families under his rule were to make great offerings to the kami, and Prince Ame no Taneko, [the chieftain of the Nakatomi clan,] was to conduct the ceremony to cleanse both the heavenly and earthly sins and defilements. Accordingly, a sacred enclosure was built on Mount Tomi,[23] where Prince Ame no Tomi presented offerings and recited sacred liturgy (*norito*) to thank the heavenly kami for the blessings bestowed on the emperor. From that time onward, it became the hereditary duties of the Nakatomi and the Imbe clans to be in charge of the divine worship, while the Sarume clan was charged with the sacred dance and pantomime. Other clans were also given respective duties in the court. (*Ibid.*, 1:551)

During the reign of the [tenth legendary emperor, Sujin, r. 97–33 B.C.], the sovereign, who was awed by the potency of the kami, did not feel right to dwell with them in the same palace. Thus, he commissioned the Imbe clan to produce the mirror and the sword for his own protection. It is to be noted that the mirror and the sword thus made have been used as the symbol of imperial dignity at the time of the enthronement ever since. At any rate, Emperor Sujin established the sacred site at the village of Kasanui in the province of Yamato in honor of the Sun Goddess and the sacred sword and appointed his daughter, Princess Toyo-suki-iri, to be the chief priestess there. The emperor also established "heavenly" and "earthly" shrines and set aside lands and houses in order to maintain worship of the 800 myriads of kami. The practice of offering portions of what is secured in hunting by men as well as the practice of offering handicraft by women were initiated at this time. This explains why we still use the skins of bear and deer, stags' horns and clothes as offerings in the worship of the kami of heaven and earth. (*Ibid.*, 1:551–52)

In the days of the [eleventh legendary emperor, Suinin, r. 29 B.C.–A.D. 70], his daughter, Princess Yamato, was appointed to serve as the high priestess of the Sun Goddess. A shrine was established for the Sun Goddess, following her wish, in the province of Ise, and an "abstinence palace"[24] was also built [there] for the dwelling of the imperial high priestess. (*Ibid.*, 1:552)

In the days of Emperor [Kōtoku, r. 645–654],[25] the chieftain of the Imbe, named

Sakashi, was made the chief official governing Shintō priests, and he was put in charge of the census registration of imperial princes and princesses, court rituals, marriage of high government officials, divinations for the throne and the government. Under his supervision, the summer and winter ceremonies of divination were established in the court. Unfortunately, his descendants were not capable of carrying on the competent leadership exercised by Sakashi, and thus the prestige of the Imbe family has declined to this day. (*Ibid.*, 1:553)

During the reign of Emperor [Temmu, r. 673–686], the hereditary family titles were reclassified into eight ranks, based on the services rendered by those families to the government during his reign, but not based on the services rendered by their ancestors at the time when the grandson of the Sun Goddess descended from heaven. Accordingly, the Nakatomi was given the second highest rank and the sword which signifies this rank, while the Imbe was given only the third rank and a smaller sword which signifies this rank. (*Ibid.*, 1:553)

It was in the [early eighth century][26] that the first record of the kami was established, but it was far from being complete. Besides, ceremonials for the worship of the kami were not very well regulated. Only [in the middle of the eighth century][27] was a more complete record of the kami compiled. By that time, however, the Nakatomi took advantage of their influence and registered arbitrarily even the remote shrines if they had connections with the Nakatomi, whereas they excluded some of the greater shrines which had no connections with them. Furthermore, let me write down some of the items which also have been overlooked by the authorities. They are as follows:

It is well known that the sacred sword called the "grass mowing sword" is one of the heavenly symbols of the imperial dignity, and that it has supernatural potency. And yet the Atsuta Shrine[28] which is the dwelling place of this sacred sword has not as yet been honored properly by receiving annual offerings from the court.

Veneration of ancestors is supremely important in our proprieties. For this reason the emperor at the occasion of enthronement pays homage to the kami of heaven, mountains, rivers, as well as other kami. Chief among the kami is the Sun Goddess, the ancestress of the imperial clan, whose supremacy over other kami cannot be questioned. It is a regrettable matter that now the offerings of the Ministry of Shintō Affairs are first offered to other kami before they are presented to the shrine of the Sun Goddess at Ise.

The third matter which must be mentioned is the fact that from the time of the Plain of High Heaven the ancestors of the Nakatomi and the Imbe clans served the Sun Goddess and that the ancestress of the Sarume clan also propitiated the Sun Goddess [when the latter hid herself in the heavenly rock-cave]. In other words, the duties of the three clans—the Nakatomi, the Imbe, and the Sarume—are inseparable. And yet, today the priestly offices of the Ise Shrine are entrusted only to the Nakatomi clan, excluding the Imbe and the Sarume clans. (*Ibid.*, 1:553)

Similarly, the ceremony for quieting the emperor's spirit was originally performed by the [ancestress of the Sarume clan], and this function should have been inherited by the members of this clan. Nowadays, however, the members of other clans are assigned to perform this rite, which is contrary to time-honored custom.

In accordance with the tradition from the age of kami, the staff of the Ministry of Shintō Affairs ought to include the members of the Nakatomi, the Imbe, the Sarume, the Kagami-tsukuri (mirror makers), the Tama-tsukuri (jewel makers), the Tate-nui (shield makers), the Kan-hatori (makers of divine clothes), and other clans. However, today the staff of the ministry include only the members of two or three clans, such as the Nakatomi and the Imbe, while members of other qualified clans are excluded. It is lamentable to see that the descendants of the kami decrease and are doomed to disappear. (*Ibid.*, 1:554)

NOTES

1. The collection of the *Manyōshū* is an anthology of poems compiled in the latter half of the eighth century. It is an important source for the study of the beliefs and attitudes of the early Japanese. There are several translations of this work into Western languages. Original texts are found in *Nihon koten bungaku taikei* (Great series of Japanese classical literature), *Manyōshū*. 4 vols., Tōkyō, 1957–1962. I have consulted the Iwanami edition of *The Manyōshū: One Thousand Poems*, Tōkyō, 1940, pp. 43, 92, 163, 211, 215–16, 240, and 254. In its "Introduction" (p. xxxviii) we read: "The Manyō man lived in a world peopled by multitudes of gods and spirits, genii and fairies. And it is noteworthy that despite the wide acceptance of Confucianism and Buddhism, almost all the gods whom he sang, or who fed the well-spring of his lyric inspiration, were purely Japanese."
2. For more details on Shintō, see Joseph M. Kitagawa, "Shintō," *Encyclopaedia Britannica* (1967), vol. 20, pp. 390–93, and "Japan: Religion," *Ibid.*, vol. 12, pp. 882–86.
3. The following accounts concerning the development of early Shintō are abridged translations of the *Nihongi* or *Nihonshoki*, which was compiled in 720 A.D., and represents the viewpoint of the imperial clan. I have consulted W. G. Aston's translation, the *Nihongi: Chronicles of Japan from the Earliest Times to* A.D. *697*.
4. C. third century A.D. (However, according to the *Nihongi*, he reigned from 97 to 33 B.C.) It is interesting to note that both the first legendary Emperor Jimmu and Emperor Sujin are called the "Emperor, the August Founder of the Nation." The similarities of their accounts in the *Chronicles of Japan* has caused many scholars to believe that they refer to the career of the same person.
5. Present Nara Prefecture.
6. The son of Emperor Sujin (r. c. third or fourth century A.D.).
7. Not far from Nagoya.
8. Near Ise.
9. For more details on the Taika reforms, see Ryūsaku Tsunoda *et al.* (comps.), *Sources of Japanese Tradition*, pp. 70–87.
10. *Kannagara* or *kamu-nagara* in Japanese. The terms imply to follow exactly the way of the kami as it was in ancient times, or to hold the way of the kami within one's heart. See ch. 25, C and D, the works of Motoori Norinaga and Hirata Atsutane.
11. A ceremony to cast off the sins and defilements of the entire populace is regularly performed on the last day of the sixth and twelfth months but can be performed in times of disasters. See ch. 23, B, the section on Shintō ritual prayers.
12. Usually celebrated when the new emperor or empress begins his or her reign. On this occasion, the first-fruits are offered to the Sun Goddess as well as to other kami.
13. Situated in the central part of the present Nara Prefecture.
14. The following is an abridged translation from bk. 4 of the *Shoku Nihongi* (Chronicles of Japan, continued, from 597–791), compiled in 797. I have consulted J. B. Snellen's translation of "Shoku Nihongi," *Transactions of Asiatic Society of Japan*, 2nd ser., vol. 14 (1937), 211–13. According to this document, in the year 706 Emperor Mommu, son of Empress Gemmyō, became ill and wished his mother to ascend the throne, but she declined. However, when Mommu died in 707, his mother went to the Eastern Tower of the Palace and addressed herself to the eight ministers and five military commanders, proclaiming that she now assumed the imperial rule. Shortly afterward, she ascended the throne at the Ceremonial Hall of the palace and issued the edict.
15. The following accounts of the "snake kami" and the "kami of Yashima" are summary translations selected from the *Fudoki* (Records of customs and land), compiled in the eighth and ninth centuries. I have consulted Kono Shōzō's article, "The Hitachi-Fudoki or Records of Customs and Lands of Hitachi," tr. by Sakai Atsuharu, *Cultural Nippon*, 8, no. 2 (1940), 145–81.
16. Present Ibaraki Prefecture, north of Tōkyō.

17. In the eastern section of present Ibaraki Prefecture.
18. The following three accounts, abridged translations selected from the *Chronicles of Japan*, show that the imperial court had to recognize the existence of local kami of various kinds.
19. This is the mountain (situated in the western part of present Nara Prefecture) where the legendary magician, En no Kimi Otsunu (or Shōkaku), the spiritual father of the shamanic Buddhists and the Order of Mountain Ascetics, lived. See ch. 22, E.
20. The present Yamaguchi Prefecture (western end of Honshū).
21. One of the important source materials for the development of early Shintō priesthood is the *Kogo shūi*, compiled in 807 by Imbe no Hironari. Although this document contains some of the same materials as the *Kojiki*, it also records many legends transmitted in the Imbe clan but ignored by the *Kojiki*. The following are abbreviated translations of portions of the *Kogo shūi*. I have consulted *The Kogoshūi: Gleanings from Ancient Stories*, tr. and annot. by Genchi Katō and H. Hoshino, pp. 16–19, 31–32, 34–38, 43–50.
22. Called *himorogi*, a very early form of Shintō shrine. It consists of a sacred ground surrounded by evergreens.
23. In the central part of present Nara Prefecture.
24. See ch. 23, A, 5, for the interpretation of the "abstinence palace."
25. According to the *Nihongi*, Kōtoku honored Buddhism and despised Shintō.
26. I.e., the Taihō period (701–704).
27. Known as the Tempyō period (728–748).
28. In the present city of Nagoya.

CHAPTER 22

Early Japan: Buddhism

□ One of the most significant events in the religious history of Japan was the introduction of Buddhism to the Japanese court during the reign of the 29th emperor, Kimmei (r. 540–571). Buddhism by that time had already a long history in India, Central Asia, and China. It had developed and articulated its doctrines, scriptures, systems of meditation, monastic orders, and disciplines for the laity. No less important was the adoption of images of Buddhas and bodhisattvas[1] as objects of worship. While Buddhist influence was beginning to wane in India around the sixth century, Buddhism was then busily establishing itself in China. The voluminous scriptures were translated into Chinese, indigenous sects arose, and monastic as well as lay disciplines were adjusted to give meaning to human existence in the phenomenal world.

The historical situation in the sixth, seventh, and eighth centuries in Japan brought about a series of social, cultural, political, and religious changes under the influence of Chinese civilization, and of Buddhism. At first the Japanese considered the Buddhas as foreign counterparts of the native kami. But, soon they learned the intricacies of Buddhist art, architecture, and ritual with the encouragement of the court. The main characteristics of Japanese Buddhism might be succinctly stated as (1) preoccupation with the particular rather than the universal dimension of religion, (2) accommodation of indigenous religious beliefs and practices, and (3) alliance with local cultural, social, and political structures.[2] □

A. INTRODUCTION OF BUDDHISM

[In the year 552,] the kingdoms in Korea, Kudara,[3] Kara, and Ara[4] sent [envoys] to the Japanese court, stating that the two other kingdoms, Koguryŏ[5] and Silla,[6] were joining forces in order to destroy Paekche as well as Mimana [Imna].[7] They requested the Japanese government to send forces to help them, so that they could first attack Koguryŏ and Silla unawares. Emperor [Kimmei], hearing the request, commanded Paekche, Kara, and Ara to cooperate wholeheartedly with the Japanese forces in Imna. [A few months later,] the king of Paekche through his envoys presented to the Japanese court a golden copper image of the Buddha Śākyamuni,[8] sacred ornaments, and several volumes of Buddhist scriptures. He also wrote a special note praising the merits of the worship of the Buddha, stating, "This Law is superior to all other teachings. It is difficult to understand and to comprehend, and even the wise Duke of Chou[9] and Confucius had no knowledge of it. However, this Law will bring about boundless rewards and blessings, and enable men to attain supreme enlightenment. To have this wonderful Law is like having a treasure which would bring about everything one asks for according to his wish, because everything one asks the Buddha in prayer will be fulfilled without fail. Therefore, from India in the distant west to Korea in the east everyone upon receiving the Law pays utmost respect to it. For this reason, thy servant Mei,[10] King of Paekche, is entrusting his subject,

Nurishichikei, to transmit the Law to Your Majesty's country in accordance with the commandment of the Lord Buddha who said, 'My Law should be spread to the East.'"

On that day the emperor, having heard this, could hardly keep his joy, and commented to the Korean envoy, saying, "We have never before heard of such a wonderful Law. However, we cannot decide alone." Thus, he repeatedly consulted his ministers, saying, "We have never seen such a dignified face as that of the Buddha which has been presented to us by [Paekche]. Should we worship [the Buddha]?" The Great Minister, Soga no Iname, stated, "How can [Japan] refuse to worship the Buddha, since all the nations in the west without exception are devoted to Him?" However, the two ministers, Mononobe no Okoshi and Nakatomi no Kamako, petitioned the throne, saying, "It has been the established custom of the emperors of our nation to worship the 180 kami of heaven and earth in spring, summer, autumn, and winter. Should a foreign kami be worshiped instead, it might incur the wrath of the kami of our nation." Therefore, the emperor decided to give the image of the Buddha to anyone who wished, and allowed Soga no Iname to worship it as an experiment.

Soga no Iname, overjoyed, received the image of the Buddha by kneeling down. He enshrined it in his house at Owarida, where he pursued the discipline of "leaving the world," following the Buddhist teaching. He also cleansed his house at Mukuhara and converted it into a Buddhist temple. Shortly afterward, a pestilence prevailed in the land and there was no way of stopping it. Thereupon, Mononobe no Okoshi and Nakatomi no Kamako simultaneously petitioned the throne, saying, "Our previous advice to the throne was not followed. Consequently, sickness and death resulted. Now the situation has not yet gone too far, if we return to our old way, happiness would return to the nation. May Your Majesty order the throwing away of the image of the Buddha for the sake of securing happiness in the future." The emperor agreed to follow this advice, whereupon the image of the Buddha was thrown away by the officials into the canal of Naniwa. The temple was also burnt until nothing was left. In consequence, there was no rain-cloud in the sky and a sudden fire swept away the Great Hall of the imperial palace. Also in this year Paekche abandoned the cities of Han-syöng[11] and Phyöng-yang,[12] whereby Silla forces occupied Han-syöng. (*Nihon-shoki* [Chronicle of Japan], bk. 19, 13th year)

[In the year 553] it was reported to the court from the province of Kawachi[13] that a voice of Buddhist chants, loud as thunder, was heard coming from the sea and that a light, brilliant as the sunshine, was observed. Intrigued by this report, the emperor sent a certain Mizobe no Atai to [inquire about this matter]. He entered the sea and found a piece of shining camphor wood floating on the water, and he took it and presented it to the court. The emperor ordered an artist to make two images of Buddha out of this piece of wood. These shining camphor-wood images of Buddha have been preserved at the Temple of Yoshino.[14] (*Ibid.*, 14th year)

B. DEVOTION OF THE SOGA CLAN

[In the year 577,][15] Prince Ōwake and Okuro no Kishi were sent as Japanese envoys to Paekche. When they were returning to Japan, the king of Paekche sent along with them a number of Buddhist scriptures as well as an expert on Buddhist discipline, an expert on Buddhist meditation, a nun, an expert on Buddhist magical spells, a maker of Buddhist images, and a temple architect, six persons in all, to the Japanese court. They were housed in Prince Ōwake's temple in Naniwa.[16] (*Ibid.*, bk. 20, 6th year)

[In the year 584,] the chieftain of the Kafuka clan brought from Paekche a stone image of Maitreya (the Buddha yet to come), while the chieftain of the Sayeki clan brought an image of Buddha. The Great Minister, Soga no Umako,[17] asked for these images, and sent Shiba Tattō and Ikebe no Hita to various parts of the country to look for persons who practiced Buddhism. They only discovered in the province of Harima[18] a certain Koma no Ebin, a layman who had once been in the priesthood. The great minister appointed him as the teacher of the Buddhist Law, under whose tutelage the daughter of Shiba Tattō, Shima [then eleven years of age], entered the religious life and was given the name Nun Zenshin. Also two other maidens, Toyome, the daughter of Ayahito Yao, and Ishime, the daughter of Nishigori no Tsubu, entered religious life and were given the names Nun Zenzō and Nun Ezen, respectively. Now, Soga no Umako, devout as he was to the Law of Buddha, paid utmost respect to the three nuns and entrusted them to be clothed and housed by Ikebe no Hita and Shiba Tattō. Also, having placed the stone image of Maitreya Buddha in the temple built on the east side of his mansion, Umako invited the three nuns to a great Buddhist "maigre entertainment"[19] performed in their honor. On this occasion, Shiba Tattō presented a Buddhist relic to Soga no Umako. Then, Soga no Umako, in order to test the efficacy of the relic, placed it on a block of iron and beat it with an iron sledge hammer. The iron block and the sledge hammer were crushed to pieces, but the relic remained intact. Next, the relic was thrown into water, but it floated and sank as one desired. Seeing this, Soga no Umako, Ikebe no Hita, and Shiba Tattō accepted firmly the Law of Buddha and followed it diligently. Soga no Umako built another temple in his mansion at Ishikawa.[20] This marked the establishment of the Buddhist Law in Japan. (*Ibid.*, 13th year)

[In the year 585,] the Great Minister, Soga no Umako, having built a pagoda on the hill of Ōno, held a great Buddhist "maigre entertainment," and at this occasion placed the Buddhist relic [presumably Buddha Śākyamuni's ashes] obtained by Shiba Tattō on top of the central pillar of the pagoda. [A few days later,] Soga no Umako became ill. Upon inquiry with the diviner, he was told that his illness was caused by the curse of the kami (Buddha) venerated in his father's time. Soga no Umako duly reported this matter to the emperor, who in turn commanded him to venerate the kami (Buddha) venerated by Soga no Umako's father (Soga no Iname). Whereupon Soga no Umako paid homage to the stone image of the Buddha and offered prayers asking that his life be prolonged. However, it so happened that at this time a pestilence arose and caused many deaths among the people. [In this situation,] the two ministers, Mononobe no Moriya and Nakatomi no Katsumino, urged the emperor to forbid the worship of Buddha. Indeed, Mononobe no Moriya himself went to the Buddhist temple and set fire to the pagoda, the image of Buddha, and the temple. [Shortly afterward,] the emperor and Mononobe no Moriya suffered from the sores which also caused much suffering and deaths in various parts of the country. Privately, both the old and the young whispered to one another, saying, "This disease might have been caused as the punishment for the burning of the image of Buddha." [Meanwhile,] Soga no Umako addressed himself to the throne, saying, "My sickness, which has not been cured as yet, can only be healed by the help of the Three Treasures."[21] The emperor told Soga no Umako that he alone could practice the Buddhist faith, so long as he did not involve others, and returned the three nuns to him. Soga no Umako, rejoicing, paid homage to the nuns and received them in the new temple which he had built. (*Ibid.*, bk. 20, 14th year)

[In the year 587,] the nun Zenshin and others asked the Great Minister, Soga no Umako, to let them go to Paekche to receive instructions in the Buddhist disciplines because the life of the religious is based on the Discipline (*Vinaya*).[22]

In the seventh month of that year, the Great Minister, Soga no Umako, tried to persuade the imperial princes and the ministers to join him in a plot to destroy Mononobe no Moriya. The Great Minister himself was in command of the young members of his clan and its army. But, the forces of the imperial princes and the ministers were afraid [of the troops of Mononobe no Moriya], and fell back three times. At this time the imperial prince, Umayado,[23] with his hair tied around the temples, [following the custom of that time,] was following in the rear of the army. He cut the lacquer tree and made images of the four heavenly guardian kings and then vowed, "If you enable use to be victorious over our enemy, I solemnly pledge to build a temple in honor of the Four Heavenly Guardian Kings."[24] The Great Minister also made a similar vow. When the armed conflict was over [in favor of the Soga clan and the imperial princes], the Temple of the Four Heavenly Guardian Kings was established [by Prince Shōtoku] in the province of Settsu.[25] Also, in accordance with the vow made by the great minister of Soga, a temple called Hōkōji was built in Asuka.[26] (*Ibid.*, bk. 21, Yōmei, 2nd year)

In the year 588, the Land of Paekche sent envoys and along with them some Buddhist priests as well as Buddhist relics. Soga no Umako invited the Paekche priests and inquired about the principles of the Buddhist Discipline. He also entrusted the nun Zenshin and others to the envoys of Paekche, sending them to Korea for the purpose of receiving Buddhist training. [Two years later,] Zenshin and other nuns returned from Paekche and settled down in the temple at Sakurai.[27] There Zentoku, daughter of Ōtomo no Sadehiko, and others entered the religious life. Also, Tasuna, son of Shiba Tattō, renounced the world and was given the priestly name, Tokusai. (*Ibid.*, Sushun, 1st and 3rd years)

C. PRINCE REGENT SHŌTOKU'S PROMOTION OF BUDDHISM

[In the year 593,] the imperial prince, Umayado [better known as Shōtoku, 573–621] was appointed prince regent and was entrusted with the administration of the government. He was the second son of Emperor Yōmei (r. 586–587). He studied the "inner teaching" (Buddhism) and the "outer teaching" (Confucianism) and attained profound understanding in both.[28] (*Ibid.*, bk. 22, 1st year)

[In the year 594, Empress Suiko (r. 592–628)] instructed Prince Regent Shōtoku and the Great Minister, Soga no Umako, to promote the cause of the Three Treasures. At this time, many of the ministers and clan chieftains built great halls for the Buddha, namely, temples, for the repose of the souls of their lords and parents. [In the following year,] a priest from Koma (Koguryŏ) called Eji (Hye-cha) settled in Japan, and was appointed by the prince regent as his instructor. In the same year another priest from Paekche called Esō (Hye-chhong) also settled in Japan. These two Korean priests did much in spreading Buddhism and came to be considered as the pillars of the Three Treasures. [In 596] the construction of the Hōkōji was completed, and Zetoko, son of the great minister, was made the chief official of the temple, whereas the two Korean priests, Eji and Esō, were made the resident-priests there. [In 602,] a priest from Paekche called Kanroku (Kwal-leuk) arrived, bringing with him as a tribute some books on the calendar, astronomy, geography, and magic. Thereupon three or four students were chosen to take instruction from Kanroku in these arts. [Shortly afterward] two priests from Koguryŏ, named Shōryū (Seung-nyung) and Unsō (Un-chhonh), also migrated to Japan. (*Ibid.*, 2nd, 3rd, 4th, and 10th years)

[In 604,] the prince regent personally drew up the following seventeen articles as the first constitution of the land:

1. You should uphold the precious virtue of harmony and avoid conflict and opposition. All men belong to certain groups, and there are only a few who have intelligence to transcend their own groups. This accounts for their disobedience to their lords and parents or for their conflicts with people of the neighboring villages. Only when people in the upper and lower strata attain harmony and friendship in their dealings can they achieve the principle of reason and together accomplish anything.

2. You should sincerely venerate the Three Treasures, namely, the Buddha, Buddha's Law, and the Buddhist Order, which are the final refuge of [all creatures] and have indeed been venerated by everyone at every age. There are only a few in this world who are by nature bad, and even they can be corrected if they be properly taught about the Three Treasures.

3. You should endeavor to obey the imperial commands, realizing that the lord is Heaven while the subject is Earth. When heaven covers and earth upholds the seasons

will be regulated and all force will circulate. Should the earth try to overspread heaven, the order will be ruined. Similarly, when the lord speaks, the subject should listen, and when the superior acts, the inferior should obey. . . .

4. The ministers and officials should abide by propriety, which is the principle of governing the people. If the superior lacks propriety, the inferior disrupts the order, and the lack of propriety on the part of the inferior inevitably results in offences. Only when the ministers abide by propriety, the hierarchical ranks will not be disrupted, and when the people abide by propriety, the nation will be governed peacefully by its own accord.

5. The ministers should endeavor to attend to the law suits impartially, rather than indulging in gluttony and their own personal desires. Considering the fact that there are about a thousand suits submitted by the people each day, how many more suits there must be over the years? Nowadays those who listen to the complaints take their own personal gains for granted, so that their decisions are influenced by bribes given by rich men, whereas the cases of the poor men are ignored. No wonder the poor people do not know whom they can trust.

6. From the ancient time it has been accepted as the just law to punish the evil and honor the good. Therefore, endeavor to make known the honorable deeds and correct the wrong doings of men. Those who flatter their superiors, and those who inform their superiors about the faults of their inferiors and criticize their superiors in the presence of their inferiors, lack fidelity to their lord and compassion for the people.

7. Every official ought to discharge his duty in an orderly manner. Wise officials bring about praise from people, while unprincipled officials bring much confusion and disaster. While very few have innate intelligence, it is possible for men to attain wisdom by serious reflection. When such right men are available, all things, great or small, can be managed. . . .

8. All the ministers and officials should attend the court early in the morning and retire late, because the demand of public duty is such that even a whole day does not provide enough time to attend to it adequately.

9. Faithfulness, which is the basis of righteousness, should be upheld in everything, for the good or bad results and success or failure is determined by faithfulness or lack of it. If the ministers lack faithfulness, everything is bound to fail. . . .

10. One must attempt to be free from anger, inwardly and outwardly, and try not to resent others who hold different views. All men have minds and their own inclinations, so that others may be wrong when one is right and vice versa. Just as one is not necessarily a sage, others are not complete fools, because we are all ordinary human beings.

11. Merit and demerit should be clearly evaluated and proper reward and punishment should be given accordingly. . . .

12. Provincial officials and governors should not on their own accord levy taxes on the people. Because there are not two lords in this country, people do not have two masters. The emperor is the master of all people including the officials who are appointed by him.

13. All the officials should acquaint themselves with their duties equally well. When one is sick or is on special mission elsewhere, one might neglect his function, but one should reacquaint himself with his work upon his return to the office. Public affairs must not be neglected because of one's ignorance.

14. Ministers and officials should not be jealous of others. If we envy others, others may envy us, and there is no end to the anxiety caused by envy and jealousy. . . .

15. The way of the emperor's [minister] is to turn his attention to the public duty, forgetting his private interest. Those who are motivated by selfish interests inevitably resent others and thus cannot work with others. The lack of harmony in turn prevents the execution of public interests due to selfishness.

16. As according to the good rule established in ancient times, we have to know the right seasons to utilize the labor of the people. It is better to put people to work in

the winter months, because they have more leisure, but it is better not to use their labor from spring to autumn because people are engaged in agriculture and sericulture. . . .

17. Important decisions should not be reached by one person alone, but rather they should be discussed thoroughly with many others, whereas minor decisions of less consequence do not have to involve many persons. . . . (*Ibid.*, 12th year)

[In the year 606,] the empress asked the prince regent to give expositions on the *Shōman Scripture*[29] (Scripture of Lady Malyaśrū) which he completed in three days. He also lectured on the *Hokke Scripture* (Scripture of the lotus of Law)[30] at the palace. . . . (*Ibid.*, 14th year)

[In the year 610,] the king of Koma (Koguryŏ) sent to the Japanese court the two priests, Donchō (Tam-chi) and Hōtei (Pŏp-chŏng). Donchō not only was well versed in the Five Classics,[31] but also knew the art of making colors, paper, and ink for painting as well as mills . . . (*Ibid.*, 18th year)

[In the year 613,] the prince regent on his journey to a place called Kataoka found a starving man lying on the roadside. He asked for his name, but the man did not answer. Whereupon the prince gave him food and drink as well as his own cloth. Later the prince sent a messenger to look into the starving man. The messenger reported that the man had died. Greatly saddened, the prince had the man buried in a mound which was then sealed tightly. Several days later, the prince told his attendants that the man who was starving on the roadside was not an ordinary man and that he must have been a holy man. He sent another messenger to the place where the man was buried. The messenger upon his return reported that the tomb was empty and that the garment was folded on the coffin. The prince sent the messenger to fetch the garment, and he wore it as before. Seeing this, the people said, "It is true that only a holy man recognizes another holy man."

[In the year 614,] the great minister, (Soga no Umako), became ill, whereat a thousand persons, including men and women, entered religious life, forsaking the world. (*Ibid.*, 22nd year)

[In the year 621,] the prince regent died at the palace of Ikaruga. Not only all the imperial princes and ministers but all the people, especially the old, felt as though they had lost a dear child and lost appetite, while the young, feeling as though they had lost dear parents, wept loudly on the streets. The farmers who were ploughing and the pounding women stopped their work, and they all said that the sun and moon lost their brightness and that heaven and earth have begun to crumble, leaving no one for us to depend on. The body of the prince was buried in the cemetary at Shinaga. At this time, Eji (Hey-cha), a Buddhist priest in Koma, upon hearing the death of the prince regent in Japan, performed a ceremony with other priests and expounded on the scriptures. He also made a vow, saying, "The prince of Japan, who was endowed with the virtues of the holy man, knew the principles of heaven, earth, and man, and revered the Three Treasures to save people from their sufferings. He indeed was a holy man, but alas he is now dead. Although I belong to another country, I was united to him in spirit. Now that he is dead, what good will there be even if I alone survived? Thus, I shall die on the fifth day of the second month of next year, so that I will be able to meet the prince in the Pure Land[32] and together we will work toward the redemption of all creatures." On the appointed day the priest died, and the people said that not only the prince regent in Japan but the priest Hey-cha must be a holy man. (*Ibid.*, 29th year)

D. BUDDHISM DURING THE REFORM ERA (645–704)

[In the year 645, Emperor Kōtoku (r. 645–654)] sent his emissary to the great temple (Kudara-dera) where the following imperial proclamation was given to the assembled priests and nuns: "In the thirteenth year of the reign of Emperor Kimmei (552) the king of Kudara (Paekche) transmitted Buddhism to Japan. At that time, most ministers did not welcome the introduction of Buddhism with the exception of Soga no Iname who received it. During the reign of Empress Suiko, Soga no Umako exalted Buddhism, and venerated the priests and nuns. Now it is our determination to exalt anew the true teaching of the Buddha and propagate it for the enlightenment of the people. Accordingly, the ten priests, namely, Fukuryō, E-un, Jōan, Ryōun, Eshi, Min, Dōtō, Erin, Emyō, and E-on, are designated as the Ten Masters, while Emyō is also to serve as the chief priest of the Kudara Temple. These Ten Masters are to teach and guide other priests regarding the practice and doctrine of the Buddha. We will render assistance when such is needed in the maintenance or repairment of temples which had been built either by the emperors or the local magnates. We will also let temple commissioners and chief priests survey all the temples in order to find out the exact conditions of the priests and nuns as well as one of the slaves and the farm lands which belong to the temples." Following this proclamation, Kume no Omi, Miwa no Shikofu, and Nukatabe no Muraji were appointed the officials of Buddhist affairs. (*Ibid.*, bk. 25, Taika, 1st year)

[In the year 658,] by the order of Empress Saimei (r. 655–661), the Buddhist priests Chitsū and Chitatsu went to China on board a Silla boat in order to study under Master Genjō (Hsüan-tsang, 596–664) on the doctrine regarding the enlightenment of all creatures. [In the following year] the empress, in her decree sent to the ministers, ordered that the *Urabon Scripture*[33] be expounded in all the temples of the capital for the repose of the souls of ancestors of seven generations. [In the year 660] the ministers were ordered by the empress to prepare one hundred ceremonial seats and one hundred priestly robes for the purpose of holding the ritual of the benevolent king.[34] (*Ibid.* bk. 26, 4th, 5th, and 6th years)

[In the year 673,] the governor of the province of Bingo caught a white pheasant and offered it to the court. Accordingly Emperor Temmu (r. 673–686) not only remitted the forced labor in that district but also granted an amnesty throughout the nation. Also, Emperor Temmu assembled the scribes and ordered them to copy, for the first time [in Japan], the Buddhist scriptures at the Kawara Temple. [In the year 679,] the emperor established rules governing the style and colors of clothing for the priests and nuns, as well as the horses and attendants used by them when they go into towns. He further decreed, stating, "All the priests and nuns should stay within their own temples and attend to the Three Treasures. However, the very old or sick, especially those who are confined to bed for a long period of time, might find their movement very difficult in the temple, and also they might contaminate the sacred compounds. Therefore, henceforth they should ask their relatives or faithfuls to build cottages in vacant places where the aged and sick monks and nuns can be cared for." [In the following year] by the imperial order the twenty-four temples of the capital city were given the gifts of coarse silk, floss silk, raw silk, and cloth. Also by the imperial order the *Scripture of the Golden Light*[35] was expounded in the palace and in the various temples. It so happened that the empress became ill [that year], whereby the emperor made a vow on her behalf to construct a temple for Yakushi[36] for the first time [in Japan], and he ordered one hundred persons to enter the religious life. Owing to these meritorious deeds performed on her behalf, the empress regained her health. [In the year 685,] the emperor decreed that every household throughout the nation ought to establish a Buddhist altar with an image of the Buddha and scriptures for the purpose of regular worship. The priests and nuns were invited for the first time to hold a retreat in the palace. The emperor himself went to the Asuka Temple where he presented precious objects and worshiped Buddha. [In 686] the imperial command was conveyed by Prince Ise and other officials to the assembled priests at Asuka Temple, stating, "We, who have not been well of late, wish to regain our health by relying on the potent power of the Three Treasures, and thus ask the hierarchy and all the priests to perform rituals on our behalf." Then, the government officials were sent to the Kawara Temple where offerings of the lighted lanterns were made to the Buddha, while later one hundred priests were asked to recite the *Scripture of the Golden Light* in the palace. Furthermore, seventy adherents of Buddhism were chosen to enter the religious life. Images of Kannon[37] were made by the imperial princes and ministers, the *Scripture of Kanzeon* (Kannon) was recited in the Great Temple of the government, and eighty men took priestly vows—all for the sake of the emperor. (*Ibid.*, bk. 29, Temmu, 2nd, 8th, 9th, and 14th years and Shuchō, 1st year)

[In the year 688,] the drought was so severe that Empress Jitō (r. 687–697) ordered the Paekche priest, Dōzō, to recite prayers for rain, which resulted in abundant rainfall throughout the nation. [In the year 694] the empress sent one hundred copies of the *Scripture of the Golden Light* to various provinces with the provision that the scripture should be recited annually in the first month when the moon was in its first quarter, and that the offering should be paid out of the public treasury. (*Ibid.*, bk. 30, 2nd, and 8th years)

E. JAPANESE BUDDHISM DURING THE EIGHTH CENTURY

□ The eighth century is usually referred to as the Nara period, because the capital of Japan was situated at Nara from 710 to 784. During this period Buddhism prospered with the active support of the court, overshadowing Shintō and Confucianism. The six orthodox Buddhist schools established at Nara were (1) the Kusha (Abhidharmakośa), (2) the Jōjitsu (Satyasiddhi), (3) the Sanron (Mādhyamika), (4) the Hossō (Yogācāra), (5) the Kegon (Avataṁsaka), and (6) the Ritsu (Vinaya) schools.[38] In the main, Buddhism, as much as Confucianism, penetrated only the upper strata of Japanese society at this time. The lofty doctrines and elaborate rituals were appreciated to be sure by monastics, but the laity for the most part adhered to Buddhism in order to gain this-worldly benefits and assurances of the life to come. As far as the illiterate masses were concerned, they continued to live close to the rhythm of nature. Their kami were unpredictable, and they depended on shamanic diviners, healers, and magicians to intercede on their behalf. It is significant to note that these rustic "spiritual leaders" of the masses came under the nominal influence of Buddhism and came to be called *ubasoku* (*upāsaka*) or "lay ascetics." These shamanic Buddhists advocated a simple path of salvation among the masses, disregarding the doctrines and disciplines of orthodox Buddhist schools.[39] The tradition of the *ubasoku*, which combined Buddhist, Shintō, and folk religious elements, prepared the ground for the subsequent developments of the Order of Mountain Ascetics (Shugen-dō) as well as the Shintō-Buddhist coexistence (*Ryōbu Shintō*) pattern.[40] □

In [the year of 699 or] the third year of the reign of Emperor Mommu (r. 698–707), En no Kimi Otsunu (or Shōkaku) was banished by the order of the court to the island of Izu. He had lived earlier on Mount Katsuragi and had been called an expert on magical arts. A certain Karakuni no Muraji Hirotari, who at one time studied magical arts under him, later became jealous of his ability and slandered him for leading people astray. Consequently, En no Kimi Otsunu was sent away to a distant place. According to tradition, En no Kimi Otsunu was able to control demons and made them draw water or gather firewood for him. Those who did not obey his orders were bound by his magic as punishment. (*Shoku Nihongi*, bk. 1, 3rd year)

[In the year 700,] the priest Dōshō (629–700) died. Emperor Mommu, greatly grieved, sent a messenger to convey his condolences. This priest observed the Buddhist disciplines faultlessly and endured hardships. It was in 653 that Dōshō accompanied the Japanese envoy to China, where he encountered Master Genjō (Hsüan-tsang) and studied under him. By the special favor of Hsüan-tsang, Dōshō shared his master's chamber. Once the master told Dōshō, "The profound meanings of the scriptures and their commentaries are such that it is difficult for you to master them. Rather, I urge you to master meditation and transmit it to Japan." Accordingly

Dōshō received instruction regarding meditation. Later, when he was getting ready to leave for Japan, Hsüan-tsang gave him the holy relics, scriptures and commentaries, [urging him to spread Buddhism in Japan]. Upon his return to Japan, Dōshō established a meditation hall at the southeastern corner of the Gangōji, where many students came to take instruction regarding meditation from him. In later years Dōshō traveled widely, digging wells, building ferry boats and bridges in various parts of Japan. After ten years of traveling, he was asked by the imperial order to return to the meditation hall. He concentrated on meditation as before. He only rose once in three days or once in seven days. One day a fragrance suddenly came out of his room, and when his disciples went in to see him, they found him in a sitting position but not breathing. He was then seventy-two years old. His disciples, following his instruction, cremated him. This was the beginning of the practice of cremation in Japan. (*Ibid.*, 4th year)

[In the year 705,] Emperor Mommu issued the following edict: "We, despite our unworthiness, have been placed above all princes and nobles. But, because our virtue is not sufficient to influence Heaven and our benevolence is not sufficient to reach the people, the order of yin (negative cosmic force) and yang (positive cosmic force) has become disrupted, so that rain and drought do not follow their seasons. The failure of crops cause the people to look thin and pale. Deeply grieved as we are with this situation, we decree that the *Scripture of the Golden Light* be recited at the five great temples for the alleviation of the sufferings of the people." (*Ibid.*, bk. 3, Keiun, 2nd year)

[In the year 749,] Emperor Shōmu (r. 724–749) visited the Tōdaiji where he took up his position facing north towards the statue of Lochana Buddha,[41] while the empress, the imperial princes, and ranking government officials were seated behind him. Then, the Minister of the Left, Tachibana no Moroye, stepped forward to read the following imperial edict: "We, the emperor and the slave of the Three Treasures, would like to address the statue of Lochana. From the beginning of heaven and earth, no one thought that gold existed in Japan, although it has been presented to this country from abroad. Now, however, the governor of the eastern province of Mutsu (or Michinoku)[42] has reported that gold was found in his domain. This report has brought happy surprise, and we gratefully accept the gold as the benevolent gift of Lochana Buddha. In order to offer our veneration and thanksgiving, we come to the presence of the precious Three Treasures, accompanied by the government officials." Then, [another official,] Isonokami no Otomaro, turning to the people, read the following edict: "Hear the word of the Manifest Kami, the Ruler of the World and the Emperor of Japan, addressed to all the imperial princes, nobles, ministers, and the people of the realm. It has been reported to us that gold was found in the eastern province of Mutsu. Now, among all the laws, the teachings of Buddha are most efficacious for the safeguarding of the nation. Therefore it is our wish to distribute copies of the *Scripture of the Most Excellent King*[43] to all the provinces under heaven and also to construct a statue of Lochana Buddha. While we have endeavoured, by praying to all the kami in heaven and earth as well as the august imperial ancestors, to guide the nation so that evil might be transformed into good and peril into peace, there was doubt in the mind of the people as to whether this was possible. Indeed, we too have had some anxieties because of the shortage of gold. However, now the sign has been given, revealing the most excellent will of the Three Treasures, according to the benevolence of the kami of heaven and earth as well as the imperial ancestors. Realizing this, we have joyfully and reverently received the gift of gold. On the other hand, we are haunted by the question day and night that why such a gift, which should be given to the reign of a sovereign who rules the nation with great compassion, has been given during the reign of us, who are unworthy to receive it. Indeed, thinking about it makes us feel very grateful and also humble. How, then, can we alone receive such a great and important sign? It is only right for us to share the joy of receiving it with everybody under heaven." (*Ibid.*, bk. 17, Tempyō Shōro, 1st year)

F. THE *LAW GOVERNING MONKS AND NUNS*

☐ The *Law Governing Monks and Nuns* (*Sōni ryō*), promulgated by the imperial court during the seventh century, was modeled after the Chinese *Tao-seng ko* (Law governing Taoist and Buddhist priests) of the Yung-hui period (640–655) with some modifications to meet the Japanese religious situation. It was revised in 701, and was further revised in 718.[44] ☐

1. Monks and nuns who predict disasters based on observations of natural phenomena, discuss politics, mislead peasants, read military books, commit murder and robbery, or claim falsely to have attained sainthood, shall be punished by the government officials.

2. Monks and nuns who indulge in sorcery or magic for the treatment of the sick shall be returned to lay life. However, those who heal the sick by the magical power following the Buddhist Law are exempted from this law.

3. Regarding the monks and nuns who return to lay life on their own accord, their ecclesiastical superiors must report it to government officials.

4. If the monks and nuns should use ecclesiastical property as gifts to government officials, or form a party, or cause disorder among the people, or abuse ecclesiastical superiors, or slander their elders, they shall be punished by hard labor of one hundred days.

5. Monks and nuns who establish their own training centers, which are not temples, for the purpose of gathering people and preaching to them false doctrines of sins and happiness or those who assault their elders shall be returned to lay life. Those who beg food must secure their ecclesiastical superiors' seals which in turn should be approved by the civil officials upon verifying that such begging is done for ascetic training. Begging by presenting a bowl should be done only in the morning, and only food can be received.

6. A monk is permitted to take a pious boy from his relations or home town as an attendant, with the understanding that the boy shall be returned to his home on reaching the age of seventeen. A nun is permitted to take a young girl [with similar conditions].

7. Monks and nuns who indulge in drinking wine, eating flesh, or using the five pungent seasonings,[45] shall be put to thirty days hard labor. Should these things be needed for medicinal purposes, they should be secured from their superiors each day. Those who get drunk or brawl shall be returned to lay life.

8. Monks and nuns who present petitions directly to the government or disturb the homes of the officials regarding their own controversial matters shall be put to fifty days hard labor and if the offence is repeated to one hundred days hard labor.

9. Monks and nuns who play music or gamble shall be put to one hundred days hard labor. However, the harp and chess[46] are excluded from this rule.

10. Monks and nuns can only wear robes of brown, green, black, yellow, or dust color, but not robes of other colors or of embroidered materials.

11. No woman is allowed to stay in a monks' quarters, and no man is allowed to stay in a nuns' quarters.

12. Except on special occasions, such as death, sickness, religious services or instructions, which responsible ecclesiastical superiors supervise, no monk may enter a nunnery and no nun may enter a monastery.

13. Those monks and nuns who wish to retreat to a mountain, away from the world, in order to practice meditation and discipline shall inform the proper government officials with their ecclesiastical superiors' seal, so that the officials will know the whereabouts of such ascetics.

14. It is essential that those who head the monastery should be persons endowed with virtue and leadership, respected both by clergy and laity, and with ability to manage ecclesiastical affairs. Recommendations of such persons can be with joint seals of the monastics to the proper government office. Once appointed, the head of the monastery cannot be removed unless he commits an

offence or for reasons of sickness and old age.

15. Those monks and nuns who are condemned to hard labor should be assigned to works of meritorious nature, such as straightening and cleaning the Buddha halls, and so on.

16. If monks and nuns should transfer their registered names for illicit purposes, they should be returned to lay life and they as well as the other party to the fraud shall be punished according to law.

17. When monks and nuns are engaged in law suits concerning nonecclesiastical personal matters, they should appear in their lay robes before the civil authorities.

18. Monks and nuns are not permitted to secure private properties, such as land, houses, and other forms of wealth, nor are they permitted to engage in profit-making enterprises.

19. Should monks and nuns meet a person of the third rank or higher on the road they should conceal themselves. If the person is of the fifth rank or higher, monks and nuns should halt their horses and salute him until he passes by; if they were on foot, they should conceal themselves from him.

20. The ecclesiastical superiors should present monthly reports regarding the deaths of monks and nuns to provincial officials, who in turn should report them annually to the central government.

21. If monks and nuns should be found guilty of civil crimes, the terms of their punishments should be based on the regulations of penal laws minus one year by virtue of their ordained status, even though they should automatically be returned to lay life. The offences of monks and nuns to which penal codes do not apply shall be judged by their ecclesiastical superiors according to Buddhist Law.

22. Should persons who pretend to be clerics or those who had been clerics but were returned to lay life be found wearing clerical robes they shall be punished in accordance with law.

23. If monks and nuns should entrust the scriptures or images of Buddha to lay persons and let them visit the houses of the faithful for the purpose of solicitation, they shall be punished by one hundred days hard labor, and the lay persons in question shall be punished according to law.

24. If former slaves or servants who had become monks or nuns should return or be forced by law to return to lay life, they shall have no choice but to return to their former status.

25. Monks and nuns who had been punished by hard labor of one hundred days for three times shall be banished to temples in distant places away from provinces adjacent to the capital.

26. Slaves, male or female, domestic animals, and military weapons shall not be used as offerings on Buddhist festivals nor should they be accepted privately by monks and nuns.

27. Monks and nuns shall not mutilate their bodies or take their own lives, and those who assist monks and nuns in such offences shall be punished in accordance with law. (*Ryō no shūge* [Collection of laws], pp. 207–55)

NOTES

1. Saints who postpone their own Buddhahood to work for the salvation of others.
2. The following accounts of the introduction and development of Buddhism in early Japan are abridged translations of pertinent passages from the *Chronicles of Japan* (*Nihonshoki* or *Nihongi*).
3. Paekche in southwestern Korea.
4. Both in the southern tip of the Korean peninsula.
5. In northern Korea.
6. In southwest Korea.
7. Which was the Japanese foothold in the Korean peninsula.
8. The wise man of the Śākya clan; Gautama, the founder of Buddhism.

9. The Duke of Chou (d. 1094 B.C.) was a sage and founder of the culture of the Chou dynasty (1111–249 B.C.)
10. Pronounced Myöng in Korean.
11. The leading city in Paekche.
12. In northern Korea.
13. Near present Ōsaka.
14. Near Nara.
15. During the reign of Emperor Bidatsu (572–585).
16. Present Ōsaka.
17. Son of Soga no Iname.
18. Near present Kobe.
19. A vegetarian feast given to the Buddhist monks and nuns.
20. In southwestern Nara Prefecture.
21. The Buddha, Buddha's Law, and the Buddhist Order.
22. The Buddhist moral code for monks (250 articles) and nuns (348 articles).
23. Prince Shōtoku.
24. The Four Heavenly Guardian Kings are guardians of the four quarters of the world and of temples.
25. Present Ōsaka.
26. Not far from Nara.
27. South of Nara.
28. According to *Nihongi*, Prince Shōtoku's intelligence was such that he was able to listen to the suits of ten men simultaneously.
29. The *Shrīmālādevī-siṃhanāda* scripture spoken by Princess Śrīmālā at an assembly.
30. *The Saddharma-puṇḍarīka sūtra*, commonly referred to as the *Lotus Scripture*.
31. The *Book of History*, the *Book of Odes*, the *Book of Rites*, the *Book of Changes*, and the *Spring and Autumn Annals*.
32. Western Paradise.
33. *The Ulambana sūtra* or the *Avalambana sūtra*, the scripture on the offering of food to the monks and nuns for the benefit of hungry ghosts.
34. A ritual based on the *Ninnō Scripture* (Scripture of the benevolent king) which explains how benevolent kings may protect their countries. For details on this ritual, see M. W. de Visser, *Ancient Buddhism in Japan*, I, 116–89. The ritual is performed to bring peace and prosperity to the nation.
35. The *Suvarṇa-prabhāsa sūtra*, called *Konkōmyōkyō* in Japanese. It contains a Buddhist doctrine of kingship based on merit. For more information concerning this scripture, see Tsunoda *et al.*, *Sources of Japanese Tradition*, pp. 99–101.
36. Bhaiṣajyaguru, the Healing Bodhisattva. He is usually portrayed with a medicine bowl. Incidentally, the temple for Yakushi was not constructed during Emperor Temmu's lifetime.
37. Avalokiteśvara is the embodiment of mercy and compassion. He appears in various forms. The feminine form of Avalokiteśvara is very popular in Japan. See ch. 17, no. 23.
38. On these schools, see Junjirō Takakusu, *The Essentials of Buddhist Philosophy*, chs. 4, 5, 6, 7, 8, and 14.
39. For the significance of the *ubasoku*, see J. M. Kitagawa, *Religion in Japanese History*, pp. 38-45.
40. The following are abridged translations of passages from the *Shoku Nihongi* (Chronicles of Japan, continued, from 697 to 791).
41. The Buddha revealed in the *Wreath* scriptures.
42. Present Iwate Prefecture, north of Sendai.
43. The *Suvarṇa-prabhāsottama-rāja sūtra*, called the *Konkōmyō-saishōō kyō* in Japanese, generally abbreviated into *Saishōō kyō*.

44. The texts of the different editions of the *Sōni ryō* are slightly, though very slightly, different. The following are abridged translations of the 718 text, known as the *Yōrō sōni ryō* (Law governing monks and nuns issued during the Yōrō era, 714–724). Its original text is found in the *Ryō no shūge* (Collection of laws), which is included in Kuroita Katsumi, ed., *Shintei zōho kokushi taikei*, 23:207–55.
45. Garlic, scallions, ginger, onion, and mustard.
46. *Koto* and *go*, respectively.

CHAPTER 23

Medieval Japan: Shintō and Esoteric Buddhism

□ Following the Nara period (710–781), which was marked by strong influences of Buddhism and Chinese culture, the Heian period (794–1191) fostered the gradual assimilation of Buddhist and Chinese influences into the Japanese religious and cultural framework. Then, the Kamakura period (1192–1333) witnessed the development of indigenous forms of Buddhism.[1]

During the early Heian period, the imperial court controlled the affairs of the nation by means of minutely defined laws and regulations, which were compiled in 927 in the form of the *Engi shiki* (Institutes of the Engi period). Its sections dealing with Shintō matters provide important data regarding the state of Shintō during the Heian period. As for Buddhism, two new schools—Tendai (Chinese, T'ien-t'ai) and Shingon (Chinese, Chen-yen)—were introduced from China in 805 and 806, respectively, and they overshadowed the six schools of Nara Buddhism.[2] Both the Tendai and Shingon schools upheld the cause of the "Shintō-Buddhist coexistence," known as Ryōbu Shintō, and also patronized the Order of Mountain Ascetics, which was the spiritual heir of the shamanic Buddhists of the Nara period.

The prosperity of the Tendai and Shingon schools, however, resulted in their spiritual bankruptcy during the later Heian period. Then, the serious seekers came to be attracted by the simple faith in Amida[3] or by the vigorous spiritual disciplines of Zen Buddhism, both of which brought about the golden days of Japanese Buddhism during the Kamakura period, as evidenced by the establishment of the Pure Land School, the True Pure Land School, the Nichiren School, as well as the Rinzai and Sōtō schools of Zen Buddhism. In sharp contrast to the Heian period, which was dominated by the courtiers, the Kamakura period, ruled as it was by the warrior-statesman, exhibited a new ethos characterized by a nostalgia for the ancient way on the one hand and a determination to build a new society on the other. □

A. *ENGI SHIKI* (INSTITUTES OF THE ENGI PERIOD)

□ The *Engi shiki* is the *kyaku shiki* (supplementary rules to previously promulgated edicts and ceremonial rules) compiled during the Engi period (901–922), but completed in 927. It was put into effect in 967. It consists of fifty sections, of which ten are devoted to Shintō matters. The following is a brief abridged outline of some sections of the *Engi shiki*.[4] □

§1 and 2. [Festivals are classified into three grades.]

The great food festival celebrated upon an emperor's succession is regarded as the high grade festival. The middle grade festivals include those of the early spring festival, the monthly service of thanksgiving, the divine testing of the new crop, the harvest festival, and the festival of the kami enshrined at Kamo. [All others, such as] the great abstaining, the service to the kami of the wind, the prayers for freedom from sickness, the festival of the Isakawa Shrine of the Yamato Province, and so on, are regarded as the low grade festivals.

[A list of the regular festivals:][5]

The 2nd month: Early spring festival: Prayers for harvest are offered to 3,132 kami, among whom 737 kami are worshiped by the officials of the Ministry of Shintō, while 2,395 kami are worshiped by provincial officials.

Festival of the thunder kami.

Festival of the four kami enshrined at Kasuga at Nara.

The festival of the four kami enshrined at Ōharano.

The 3rd month: Prayers for freedom from sickness [addressed to the kami of the Ōmiwa Shrine and the kami of the Sai Shrine].

The 4th month: Festival of the three kami of the Isakawa Shrine [of the Yamato province].

The great abstaining festival of [the female kami of food of] the Hirose Shrine.

The festival of the two wind kami of the Tatsuta Shrine [praying for protection of crops from storm].

The 6th month: Prayers for the health of the emperor [offered daily during the first eight days of the sixth month].

Service of divination.

The festival of the gate of the imperial palace.

The great exorcism of the last day of the sixth month.[6]

Fire pacifying festival [to prevent fire in the palace].

Service to the kami of the crossroads [outside the capital].

The 9th month: The divine tasting of the new crop at the grand shrine of Ise. Veneration of the kami by the high priestess (or female diviner) [at the shrine of the Shintō Ministry]. Veneration of the kami by the priestess [who prays for the protection] of the imperial gates.

The 11th month: The festival of the new crop [in which the emperor, together with seventy-one kami enshrined at various places, takes wine and food made from rice].

Soul-pacifying festival.

The harvest festival.

The 12th month: Service for the (emperor's) soul-pacifying. (*Engi shiki*, pp. 9–47)

§3a. [A list of the occasional festivals, such as:]

Ceremony to pacify the water kami.

Festival of the kitchen range.

Festival of the well.

The ceremony of the luck-wishing of the Great Palace.

Ceremony to ward off the kami of the epidemic at the four corners of the imperial palace.

Ceremony to ask for rain—(addressed to) eighty-five specified great kami.

Ceremony before dispatching an envoy to (China).

The ceremony to send the envoy [from China] to the port of Sakai.

b. [A list of fifty-seven general regulations,[7] such as:]

That the high priest must be chosen from among those who have familiarity with the activities of the diviners, and that the diviners should be chosen from the most talented—five from the Izu Province, five from the island of Iki, and ten from the island of Tsushima.

That [all the officials] must observe the abstinence of thirty days after a death occurs in the family, seven days after a childbirth, five days after the death of a domestic animal, three days after the birth of a domestic animal.

That no one should enter the imperial palace who is in mourning, or has visited the sick or the cemetery, or attended Buddhist memorial services, no matter how undefiled he himself may be.

That on days immediately before and after the [regular] festivals, as well as on those days of partial abstinence,[8] those who are in the Buddhist order are forbidden to enter the imperial palace.

That court ladies, should they become pregnant, should leave the imperial palace the day before the partial abstinence takes place, and that those who are menstruating should retire to their residences the day before the festival takes place; they should leave the palace before the purification ceremonies of the third and the ninth month.

That within the compound of a Shintō shrine no tree should be cut and no corpse should be buried. (*Ibid.*, pp. 49–73).

§4. This section [deals with the administration and ceremonial rules regarding] the Grand Shrine of Ise, [including] the regulation that the shrine buildings should be rebuilt every twenty years.[9] Persons with a rank of *ō* (one rank below the imperial prince) or below are not permitted to present offerings to the Great Kami (the Sun Goddess). The imperial consort and the crown prince, should they wish to make offerings to the Great Kami, are required to secure the imperial permission to do so. A diviner is appointed to serve under the head priest of the Grand Shrine of Ise, and he is to perform divination regarding all the affairs that take place throughout the year. Those who are armed are not permitted to enter the sacred compounds of Ise. (*Ibid.*, pp. 75–97)

§5. [This section deals with] the abstinence hall,[10] [which is a small palace for Itsuki no miko ("an abstinence princess"), an imperial princess who serves as the ceremonial high priestess at the Grand Shrine of Ise]. The abstinence princess is chosen from the unmarried imperial princesses (or the ladies of the next rank) by divination immediately after the succession of the emperor to the throne. [From the moment of her choice, her activities are minutely prescribed—how she must purify herself at the temporary abstinence hall within the imperial palace, how she must cleanse herself in the river outside the imperial palace, and continue to observe abstinence in the country palace before she enters the abstinence hall at Ise.] Inside the abstinence hall certain words, such as those referring to the Buddha, scripture, priest, and nun as well as those referring to death, sickness, blood, and cemetery, are forbidden.[11] [What the abstinence princess and her attendants are expected to do at various ceremonials, and the kinds of offerings they must present as well as taxes to underwrite all these expenses, are specified.] (*Ibid.*, pp. 99–130)

§6. [This section deals with the regulations concerning] the abstinence princess who serves the Great Kami of Kamo [in Kyōto].[12] [Regulations governing this abstinence princess are similar to those governing the abstinence princess of Ise, but are simpler]. (*Ibid.*, pp. 131–41)

§7. [This section provides ceremonial rubrics and regulations concerning] the great food festival celebrated upon an emperor's succession. [All the preparatory ceremonials are minutely described, including the requirements of] one month of complete abstinence during which time officials cannot participate in Buddhist ceremonials and are forbidden to use certain words referring to death, sickness, blood, and cemetery. In connection with the food festival, crops must be collected from various provinces by the government representatives consisting of one priest and three diviners. [Other regulations cover the materials, styles, and shapes of the vestments for all the participants, the processes of manufacturing the utensils to be used for the ceremony, and the method of making the rice wine, which involves veneration of the kami of the well, the kami of the cooking stove, and the kami of the rice wine. The construction of the Great Food Festival Palace is also minutely prescribed. The last section of this part is devoted to the description of the ritual itself.] (*Ibid.*, pp. 143–57)

§9 and 10. These present a comprehensive list of the kami, 3,132 in number, and the names and locations of their shrines. (*Ibid.*, pp. 179–320)

B. SHINTŌ RITUAL PRAYERS

□ Although Shintō has no rigid system of doctrines, it has developed a rich variety of rituals. There are twenty-seven ancient official ritual prayers (*norito*) included in section 8 of the *Engi shiki*. The following is a translation of the prayer for "great exorcism celebrated on the last day of the sixth month." On this occasion, prayers are offered for the general purification of the nation, whereby defilements of the nobles and officials are transferred to "defilement bearers"—narrow pieces of wood and sedge reeds—which are then thrown into the river.[13] □

He says [referring to the sovereign, in whose behalf a priest of the Nakatomi clan or a diviner of the Urabe clan recites]:

Hear all of you assembled—imperial and royal princes, nobles and officials.

Hear all of you assembled that on the occasion of the great exorcism of the sixth month of the current year, various offences and defilements incurred by the functionaries of the government offices, including those attendants who wear the scarf, the sash, the quiver and the sword, as well as those attendants of the attendants, will be cleansed and purified. Thus He speaks.

Hear all of you assembled that the ancestral kami of the sovereign dwelling in the Plain of High Heaven commanded the gathering of the 800 myriads of kami for consultation, and then declared, "Our august grandchild is commissioned to rule and pacify the country of the Plentiful Reed Plains of the Fresh Ears of Grain (Japan)." Following this commission, the unruly kami [of the land of Japan] were either pacified or expelled, and even the rocks, trees, and leaves which had formerly spoken were silenced, and thus enabling the august grandchild (Ninigi) to descend from the heavenly rock-seat, dividing the myriad layers of heavenly clouds, and reach the entrusted lands.

Thus pacified, the land became the Great Yamato or the country of the Sun-seen-on-high, where the palace pillars were deeply grounded in the rock below and the palace beams were built to reach the Plain of High Heaven for the dwelling of the august grandchild, who, living in the shadow of heaven and sun, ruled the peaceful nation. With the increase of the descendants of the heavenly kami, however, various offences were committed by them. Among them, the offences of destroying the divisions of the rice fields, covering up the irrigation ditches, opening the irrigation sluices, sowing the seeds over the seeds planted by others, planting pointed rods in the rice fields, flaying living animals or flaying them backwards, emptying excrements in improper areas, and the like, are called the "offences to heaven," whereas the offences of cutting the living or the dead skin, suffering from white leprosy or skin excrescences, violating one's own mother or daughter, step-daughter or mother-in-law, cohabiting with animals, allowing the defilements by creeping insects, the thunder or the birds, killing the animals of others, invoking evils on others by means of witchcraft, and the like, are called the "offences to earth," and are differentiated from the "offences to heaven."[14]

When these offences are committed, the chief of the Nakatomi priestly clan is commanded, in accordance with the ritual performed in the heavenly palace [of the Sun Goddess], to cut off the bottom and the ends of a sacred tree and place them in abundance as offerings on divine seats, and also to cut off the bottom and ends of sacred sedge reeds and slice them into thin pieces, and then to recite the potent words of the heavenly ritual prayers.[15] When this ritual is performed properly, the heavenly kami will hear the words of petition by opening up the heavenly rock door and by dividing the myriad layers of heavenly clouds, while [at the same time] the earthly kami will hear the words of petition by climbing up to the peaks of high and low mountains and by pushing aside the mists of the high and the low mountains.

When the heavenly and the earthly kami thus hear the ritual prayers, all the offences will be gone from the court of the august grandchild as well as from the four quarters of the land under the heaven, just as the winds of morning and evening blow away the morning and evening mists, as the anchored large ship is untied and is pushed out into the ocean, or as the dense bushes are cut off at the bottom by sharp sickles. Indeed, all offences and defilements will be purified and will be carried to the ocean from the peaks of the high and low mountains by the princess whose name is "Descent into the Current," the kami dwelling in the currents of the rapid stream which surges down the hillside.

When the offences are thus taken to the ocean, the princess named "Swift Opening," the kami who lives in the meeting place of eight hundred currents of the brine, will swallow them up.

When the offences are thus swallowed up, the kami who dwells at the breath-blowing-gate called the "Lord Breath-blowing-gate" will blow them away into the netherworld.

When the offences are thus blown away, the princess named "Swift Wanderer," the kami who dwells in the netherworld, will wander away with them and lose them.

And when the offences are thus lost, it is announced that from this day onward there is no offence remaining among the officials of the sovereign's court and in the four quarters of the land under heaven, while the horses with their ears turned toward the Plain of High Heaven stand listening.

Hear all of you assembled that all the offences have been cleansed and purified on the great exorcism celebrated in the dusk on the last day of the sixth month of the current year.

Oh, you diviners of the four provinces, leave here carrying the offences to the great rivers, and cast them away by the rite of purification. Thus he speaks. (*Ibid.*, pp. 169–70)

C. ESOTERIC BUDDHISM

□ During the early Heian period two new schools of Buddhism were established. (1) The first was the Tendai (Chinese, T'ien-t'ai) School, introduced from China in 805 by a Japanese monk Saicho, better known by his posthumous title Dengyō Daishi (767–822). While he was a devotee of the T'ien-t'ai doctrine based on the *Lotus Scripture*, Saicho intended to incorporate within his system esoteric Buddhism, Zen (Chinese, Ch'an) meditation, and Ritsu (Vinaya) practices. Shortly after his time, however, the Tendai School stressed the esoteric elements, so that it came to be known as the Taimitsu (esoteric Buddhism of the Tendai tradition). (2) The second was the Shingon (Chinese, Chen-yen) School, introduced from China in 806 by Saicho's younger contemporary, Kūkai, also known as Kōbō Daishi (774–835). The Shingon School considered itself as the only esoteric school and classified all other schools of Buddhism as exoteric. It came to be known as the Tōmitsu (esoteric Buddhism of Tō-ji, the main temple of the school in Kyōto). These two esoteric schools of Buddhism, Taimitsu and Tōmitsu, exerted decisive influences on the religious and cultural life of the nation during much of the Heian period. □

1. The Tendai School[16]

□ Saicho, who took monastic training and was ordained in Nara, where he was introduced to the three great works of Chih-i (also pronounced Chih-k'ai, 538–597), the systematizer of the T'ien-t'ai School in China.[17] He was disillusioned by the moral decadence of the clergy in Nara, and thus built a small temple on top of Mt. Hiei where he endeavored to lead a disciplined spiritual life based on the teachings of the *Lotus Scripture*. The following is an abridged translation of his Vow, written by him when he was about twenty years of age. □

a. The Vow

The phenomenal world, from remote past to distant future, is full of sufferings, and there is no room for peacefulness. The lives of all beings, tangled as they are with difficulties and complications, present only sorrows and no happiness. The sunlight of the Buddha Śākyamuni[18] has been hidden in the distant cloud, and we have not as yet seen the glimpse of the moonlight of the merciful future Buddha (Maitreya). No wonder we are approaching the Three Disasters[19] and are doomed to various kinds of impurities. Human life, like wind, is not easily preserved, and the body is destined to vanish like a dewdrop. Both the old and young vainly look for security in the grass-roofed dwelling place, but the souls of noble as well as humble persons will soon have to find a resting place in narrow and dark graves. This principle becomes unmistakably clear as we observe and reflect on our own life and that of others.

Having found no medicine of immortality

we cannot hold the departing soul, and we cannot understand when death comes to our life. If we should fail to do good works while we live, we would certainly end up as firewood in hell. Life, though precious, is so transitory, and a virtuous heart is difficult to achieve, and easy to forego. Therefore, Śākyamuni likened the difficulty of fulfilling one's life to the task of locating a needle at the bottom of the ocean or of trying from the top of Mt. Sumeru[20] to put a thread in the hole of a needle at the bottom of the mountain. The ancient virtuous man, King Yü[21], considered a short time or even a moment to be precious, and admonished that one should not waste his whole life. Since there is no result without a cause, it would not be possible to avoid suffering without doing good. However, as I look back on my own life, I have received the benefit of four things (clothing, food, bed, and medicine) without any merit. Also, because of my stupidity, I might cause others' enmity in the future.

We read in a certain scripture that those who are charitable to others will be born in heaven, while those who receive charity from others will find themselves in hell. Thus, Dinna who had served four things [to others was reborn as the consort of the king], Queen Mallikā, and received benefit, while the five ascetics who coveted her charity were reborn as barren women and had to carry [Queen Mallikā's] chariot . . .

How clear is the law of cause and effect concerning good and evil! Anyone who has any amount of intelligence should be able to recognize the truth of the teaching of the scriptures on this point. We are also reminded by the Buddha that one who, knowing the cause of suffering, fails to realize its consequences is a man who lacks propensity toward goodness, and that one who, having received the opportunity to live, fails to do good deeds might be likened to a person who enters the treasure mountain and comes out empty-handed.

Thus, I, Saicho, the greatest among all fools, and the least worthy among men, having violated the teachings of the Buddhas and the laws of the sovereign, and having failed in filial piety and propriety, herewith pledge myself to the following five vows in order to realize the ultimate principle [of Enlightenment]: . . .

First, I will not engage in an act of charity until I attain the state of purity[22] comparable to [that of Buddha].

Second, I will not be concerned with my talents and accomplishments so long as my mind is not enlightened by the truth.

Third, I will not participate in religious services sponsored by lay patrons until I am able to fulfill the precepts of purity.

Fourth, I will not be involved in worldly interhuman activities so long as I have not acquired the mind of transcendental wisdom (*prajñā*).

Fifth, I will not monopolize the merit which we receive in this life, but rather distribute it to all men so that they would be able to realize the supreme enlightenment (*bodhi*).

I pray that I will not drink the sweet taste of deliverance all by myself, but share it with all other creatures so that we will together be able to attain ultimate buddhahood and the supreme enlightenment. If by the strength of the vow I should be able to attain the state of purity and Five Occult Powers,[23] I am determined not to seek my own enlightenment alone. May I be led by the Four Great Vows[24] to dispense merits to all others in the Six Realms,[25] to transform this world into the Buddha Land, to assist the deliverance of all creatures, and to participate in the Buddha's enterprise always. (*Nihon Bukkyō shisō shiryōshū* [Collection of source materials on the history of Japanese Buddhist thought], pp. 3–4)

b. "Introduction" to the Regulations for Monastic Students at Mt. Hiei[26]

What is the nation's treasure? The treasure is nothing but the heart of supreme enlightenment, and the one who has acquired it is called the nation's treasure. It was well said by the ancients that the ten pearls (i.e., owned by a famous emperor) are not the nation's treasure, but that the person who brings light even to a remote corner of the land can truly be called the nation's treasure. According to an ancient philosopher, the nation's teacher is the one who excels in speech but not in deed, while the nation's servant is the one who excels in deed but not in speech; but the nation's treasure is the one who excels in both. Furthermore, the one who has no aptitude either for speech or deed may be called the nation's traitor.

There are Buddhists who have acquired the heart of *bodhi*, called the bodhisattva,[27] in India and a superior man in China, who search within themselves in case of bad things but give good things to others. They forget themselves and benefit others, and are compassionate to the extreme. Among the two kinds of monks of Buddhism, namely those of Hīnayāna (Small Vehicle) and of Mahāyāna (Great Vehicle), the latter possess the heart of *bodhi*. But in Japan there has been only the discipline of the Small Vehicle tradition, but not that of the Great Vehicle. Since the path of the Great Vehicle has not been spread, men of the Great Path[28] have not arisen. I thus pray, following the august wish of the late sovereign (Emperor Kammu), that all those who are annually initiated into the Tendai School will be trained in the Mahāyāna disciplines and become monks of the bodhisattvahood. This is the best way to increase the altruistic paths of the bodhisattva.[29] [The heart of *bodhi*] is as deep as the ocean, and it will benefit not only those who now live but also those in the future. (*Ibid.*, p. 5)

2. The Shingon School[30]

□ Kūkai originally aspired to enter the government service and took Confucian training at the government college. His brilliant and promising career, however, was suddenly terminated by his conversion to Buddhism. He therefore left the college and became a hermit. He was ordained to the priesthood at Nara, where he came across the *Dainichi kyō* (*Mahāvairocana sūtra* [Great sun scripture]), the supreme scripture of esoteric Buddhism.[31] The following is an abridged translation of the introduction of *Sangō shiki* (Arriving at the fundamentals of the Three Teachings, namely, Buddhism, Confucianism, and Taoism), one of Kūkai's earliest writings. □

a. "Introduction" to the *Sangō shiki*[32]

. . . I began to study when I was fifteen under the tutelage of my maternal uncle, Ato Ōtari. At eighteen I entered the college and pursued further study. At that time a certain Buddhist monk introduced me to the *Kokuzōgumonji-hō*[33] (Rules [spoken by the Buddha] for seeking to hear [and keep the *dhāraṇī*[34] of the most excellent heart], by means of which the bodhisattva Ākāśagarbha [womb of ether, meaning full of blessings of inexhaustible space] is able to fulfill all wishes). In this scripture I read that if one recites the *mantra*[35] one million times in the proper manner, one can memorize all the scriptures. Following this statement as the true admonition of the Buddha, I undertook austere discipline with great diligence without wasting a single moment. Thus I climbed Mt. Ōtaki in the Awa province, and meditated at the point of Murodo in the Tosa Province.[36] As I might have expected, the valley echoed, the planet Venus appeared, [and other miracles took place].

From that time, I lost interest in worldly fame and great wealth. Rather I was eager to lead a life close to nature away from human habitation. I was overcome by a sense of sorrow as I watched people's luxurious living with dainty clothes, fat horses, and fast chariots, knowing that these things were short-lived and would soon vanish. I was also taken by the sense of pity when I encountered the maimed and the poor, wondering about the karma[37] which produced such miseries. Observing such things led me to decide to renounce the world.

But my relatives objected to my renouncing the world on the ground that by so doing I could not fulfill my obligations to society, my loyalty to the sovereign, and filial piety to my parents. However, I reasoned, "As some creatures such as birds fly in the sky and others such as fishes swim in the water, there are different kinds among men. Buddhism, Taoism, and Confucianism, different though they may be in their depth, are all teachings of sages to guide human beings. Choosing one of these teachings (Buddhism) could not be considered a violation of one's loyalty and filial piety."

Another thing I must mention is that I have a nephew who has a perverse disposition. He leads a wretched life day and night, spending his time in hunting, drinking, lusts, and gambling. Undoubtedly, his habits have been influenced by his environment.

My concerns with these two matters[38] motivated me to write the present book. The design of the book is to let one Kimō (tortoise hair) represent Confucianism. The host named Tokaku (hare's horn) also invites a certain Kyobu-shi (adept on nothingness) who preaches Taoism, and one Kameiji (man with temporary name), a Buddhist mendicant. These men are to carry on discussions in order to admonish the unruly Shitsuga (leech's tusk). The book, three volumes in all, is entitled the *Sangō shiki*. I was compelled to write this book as the expression of my feelings, and not for the edification of others. (*Sangō, shīki*, pp. 84–86)

b. "INTRODUCTION" TO THE *Hizō hōyaku* (PRECIOUS KEY TO THE ESOTERIC STORE)[39]

Boundless, boundless, it is infinitely boundless,
There're millions of scrolls about Buddhism and other teachings.
Deep, dark and abysmal,
There are multitudes and multitudes of ways.
And yet, who can comprehend the teachings
If letters and words should be lost?
I do not claim to understand however hard I concentrate,
Not even the sages of old would have comprehended.
The god of fertility grieved over the sick
And the Duke of Chou[40] led Yüeh-ch'ang [who had presented a white pheasant to the court] not to go astray on his way home.
Lunatics of the triple world[41] do not realize their own insanity;
The blind creatures fail to see their blindness.
O birth, which begins darkness!
O death, which is dark even at its very end!
Does not overcome darkness even at its end!

Imagination, though vain, dazzles our sight; and illusion, though devoid of existence, deceives our mind. Man, thus intoxicated with the thought of self, clings to it as if it were real. He, like a thirsty deer or a wild horse, loses direction and rushes around in the world of senses; then, like a mad elephant, he is driven to commit the ten evils day and night. Since his ears are closed, the Six *Pāramitās* (perfections required for bodhisattvahood)[42] cannot enter his heart. Condemning mankind as well as the Dharma (the Buddhist Law) and burning the seed of Buddhahood, he indulges in drinking and lust, not realizing the retribution that awaits him. While the ruler of hell[43] and his subordinates prepare the dungeon where they would destroy the sinners, and the departed spirits and beasts with flames in their mouths drag along heavy carts, man transmigrates within the triple world and goes through the cycle of Four Beings.[44]

Having seen such a state of affairs (beastly existence), how could the Great Enlightened One, being the Compassionate Father, rest in silence? He was therefore moved to provide various medicines to redeem creatures from their illusions. It was his intention to teach as follows: That the observance of the Three Human Relations,[45] and Five Cardinal [Confucian] Virtues[46] would establish proper order between the ruler and the minister and between the father and the son, thereby eliminating discord among them. That by the observance of the Six Ascetic Practices (fasting, enduring the cold, withstanding the heat, squatting on the ground, refraining from speaking, and imitating the ways of cows and dogs as advocated in Brahmanism) and Four Meditations (on the heavens of Brahmas, light, purity, and final limit of desire), one is led to despise that which belongs to the world and to seek pleasure in heaven. That by negating the self which is unreal [i.e., the Kusha or Abhidharmakośa School and the Jōjitsu or Satyasiddhi School of Hīnayāna Buddhism], one comes to realize the Eight Means of spiritual liberation (to free the mind from the cause of greed, to strengthen the perception of the object world, to concentrate on the state of nonaffliction, to concentrate on the state of boundless space, to concentrate on the state of boundless consciousness, to concentrate on the state of nothingness, to concentrate on the state of neither perception nor nonperception and to enter the state of annihilation trance) and Six Occult Powers of the Buddha (to see anything, to hear anything, to know the moral law of cause and effect regarding oneself and others, to comprehend whatever is in other persons' minds, to be at any desired place, and to do away with all illusions). That by the observance of the Twelve-fold Chain of becoming and extinction (ignorance, motive to live, subconscious mind, name-form, six senses, contact, perception, desire, cleaving, existence, birth, and old age and death), the wisdom of *Śūnyatā* (Void) will pluck out the seed of ignorance. That with all-embracing compassion together with the insight of the ideation-only [i.e., the Hossō or Yogācāra School of Buddhism], one can conquer the two hindrances [i.e., his own cravings and the objective conditions which prevent enlightenment] and transform the mind into the Four Wisdoms (all-reflecting knowledge, all-equal knowledge, supreme perception, and magical power). That by realization of the nature of the original state of mind through the principle of no-origination [i.e., the Sanron or Mādhayamika School of Buddhism] which leads one to the truth of *Śūnyatā*, the mind can reach the state of tranquility without hindrances of clinging to the state of differentiation. That the meditation on the original purity of the One Vehicle [i.e., the one vehicle leading to Buddhahood as taught in the Tendai School] would cause Avalokiteśvara (Kannon in Japanese; the embodiment of mercy and compassion)[47] to smile with joy. That addressing the first invocation to *dharma-dhātu* [i.e., element of the elements or the realm of ultimate truth as taught in the Kegon or Avataṃsaka School] would cause Samantabhadra (the bodhisattva symbolizing the *dharma-dhātu*) to smile.

The dusts of the world having thus been removed, the grandeur of the world of the *maṇḍalas* (the graphic representations of the cosmos) now unfolds itself. The wisdom eyes bring to naught the dark night of ignorance, and the wisdom light[48] reveals Vajrasattva (the bodhisattva of wisdom). The Five Buddhas [i.e., those revealed in the *Vajrasekhara Scripture* (Diamond head scripture), namely the Buddha of the center (the Great Sun Buddha), the Buddhas of the east, west, south, and north] making the gesture of wisdom-seal dominate the scene. The Realm of Principle is permeated by the splendor of the Four *Maṇḍalas.*[49] The wind of karma wanes beneath the withering glance of Acala (the immovable god), and the waves of ignorance subside under the three blasts of Trailokyavijaya.[50] The Eight Heavenly Maidens (of flower, light, ornaments, joy, necklace, song, incense, and dance) with their precious offerings fly through the sea of clouds, and the Four Princesses (of gold, treasure, the Buddha's Law, and the moral law of cause and effect] of Pāramitā (perfections) receive the bliss of the Dharma. The grandeur of the esoteric realm is such that even those who have ascended the traditional Ten Stages of Bodhisattvahood (joy, purity, illumination, insight, invincibility, mental presence, expediency, immovability, wisdom, and "ideal cloud") and those who have mastered the Three Divisions (morality, meditation, and wisdom) cannot conceive it, for it is the secret and enlightenment *par excellence.*

The trouble with men is that they do not know their own treasure, conceiving delusion as if it were the truth. This is nothing but stupidity. The heart of Mahāvairocana[51] is full of compassion. Without his teaching men cannot be saved. Here are the medicines offered by him, but unless men consume them there is no cure for them. He will indeed reproach men if all they do is to discuss the Dharma and recite chants without serious intention. While the nine spiritual medicines[52] can clean off the outer dust and cast away the illusions, only in the Palace of Vajra[53] does the inner repository exist from which the esoteric treasure is freely given. Whether or not to take and enjoy them must be decided by men themselves. Enlightenment cannot be acquired through one's father or mother, it must be acquired by one's own realization; those who seek the truth of Buddhism must be able to differentiate a jewel from stone or the milk of the cow from the milk of the ass. That which is profound (esoteric Buddhism) and that which is shallow (other teachings), which have been clearly stated in the scripture and their commentaries, are described in the present volume. (*Hizō hōyaku*, §2, pp. 1–14)

NOTES

1. For more detailed accounts of the Heian and the Kamakura periods, see G. B. Sansom, *Japan: A Short Cultural History*, pp. 185–347; Tsunoda *et al.*, *Sources of Japanese Tradition*, pp. 111–282; Masaharu Anésaki, *History of Japanese Religion*, pp. 107–214; and Joseph M. Kitagawa, *Religion in Japanese History*, pp. 46–130.
2. See ch. 22, n. 38.
3. Amitābha, the Buddha of infinite light, and also Amitāyus, the Buddha of infinite life. See ch. 17, A.
4. For the interpretation of the *Engi shiki*, I depended on Miyagi Eishō, *Engishiki no kenkyū* (Study of the lustitutes of the Engi period).
5. A brief description of these rituals is given by Ernest Satow in "Ancient Japanese Rituals, I," *Transactions of Asiatic Society of Japan*, vol. 8, pt. 2 (1879), 97–113.
6. The text of the ritual prayer for this service is given in B.
7. These regulations are more thorough than the earlier *Jingi ryō* (Law concerning Shintō affairs). For a brief outline of the *Jingi ryō*, see G. B. Sansom, "Early Japanese Law and Administration," pt. 2, *Transactions of Asiatic Society of Japan*, vol. 11, 2nd ser. (1934), 122–27.
8. In contrast to the days of complete abstinence, normal official business of the government is carried on during the days of partial abstinence.
9. In the earlier period many Shintō shrine buildings were rebuilt every year in order to gain new blessings from the kami. With the appearance of more elaborate shrine buildings, the practice of "removing the kami to a new shrine building" came to be carried out less frequently. The Grand Shrine of Ise is rebuilt every twenty years, while the Kasuga Shrine of Nara is rebuilt every thirty years.
10. According to the *Chronicles of Japan*, the first abstinence hall was built at Ise during the reign of the 11th legendary Emperor, Suinin.
11. Instead, the Buddha is referred to as "middle child," scripture as "stained papers" priest as "long hair," which implies the opposite of the shaved head, and nun as "long haired woman," etc.
12. The first abstinence priestess for the Kamo Shrine was appointed in 810. This institution was terminated in 814 but restored in 824.
13. For a detailed description of the ritual itself, see Karl Florenz, "Ancient Japanese Rituals," *Transactions of the Asiatic Society of Japan*, vol. 27, pt. 4 (1899), 1–112. For the translation of the text, I have consulted the rendering of Florenz, *ibid.*, 59–63, as well as a new translation, *Norito* (Ritual prayers), by Donald L. Philippi.
14. According to early Shintō, the "offences to heaven" were initially committed by Susanoo, the brother of the Sun Goddess, in the Plain of High Heaven. Other offences and defilements were believed to be caused by the evil kami (Magatsuhi) who came to this world from the nether world at the time when Izanagi, father of the Sun Goddess and Susanoo, returned from there. The purpose of the purification ceremonies is to eliminate the effects of the evil kami. This view of evil was later advocated by Motoori Norinaga. See ch. 25, C.
15. The Shintō ritual prayers are based on the belief that spiritual power dwells in the word. Accordingly, it was believed that beautifully phrased words pronounced correctly bring about good effects, while the poorly phrased or incorrectly pronounced words bring about bad results.
16. On the Tendai School, see Charles Eliot, *Japanese Buddhism*, pp. 321–35, and Junjirō Takakusu, *The Essentials of Buddhist Philosophy*, pp. 126–41.

17. On the Chinese background of the T'ien-t'ai School, see Fung Yu-lan, *A History of Chinese Philosophy*, tr. by Derk Bodde, vol. 2, pp. 360–84, and Kenneth Ch'en, *Buddhism in China: A Historical Survey*, pp. 303–13.
18. Gautama, the founder of Buddhism.
19. According to Buddhism, there are two sets of three disasters. One set consists of the disasters that are caused by fire, water, and storm, whereas the second consists of the disasters that are caused by war, epidemic, and famine.
20. A mythological mountain believed to exist at the center of the universe.
21. King Yü (r. 2183–2175 B.C.?) was the founder of the Hsia dynasty.
22. It refers to the state of purity of eyes, ears, nose, tongue, body, and will.
23. Power (1) to see anything, (2) to hear anything, (3) to know the moral law of cause and effect regarding oneself and others, (4) to comprehend whatever is in other persons' minds, and (5) to be at any desired place.
24. To save all creatures, to cut off all worldly lusts, to learn all the truth, and to attain Buddhahood.
25. The realms of hell, of beasts, of fighting spirits (*asura*), of departed spirits, of human beings, and of heavenly beings.
26. This was written in the form of a petition presented to the Emperor Saga in 818 by Saicho.
27. One who has postponed his Buddhahood to work for the salvation of others.
28. I.e., monks of the Mahāyāna tradition.
29. The altruistic paths of the bodhisattva refer to the last three of the five vehicles, i.e., those of (1) man, (2) heavenly beings, (3) one who attains sainthood by listening to the Buddha's words, (4) self-awakened saint, and (5) one who vows to save all beings.
30. On the Chinese background of the Shingon School, see Ch'en, *Buddhism in China*, pp. 325–37. On the Japanese Shingon School, consult Eliot, *Japanese Buddhism*, pp. 336–59, and Takakusu, *The Essentials of Buddhist Philosophy*, pp. 142–52.
31. On the life of Kūkai, see Joseph M. Kitagawa, "Master and Saviour," *Studies of Esoteric Buddhism and Tantrism*, pp. 1–26.
32. The main outline of the text of the *Sangō shīki* is given in Y. S. Hakeda, "The Religious Novel of Kūkai," *Monumenta Nipponica*, vol. 20, nos. 3–4 (1965), 283–97.
33. *Nanjiō Catalogue*, No. 501. Kokuzō (womb of ether) was believed to be the counterpart of Jizō or Kshitigarbha (womb of the earth). See M. W. de Visser, *The Bodhisattva Ākāśagarbha (Kokuzō) in China and Japan*, pp. 6–8.
34. I.e., magic formula.
35. Sacred syllable used in the esoteric tradition.
36. Awa is present Tokushima Prefecture and Tosa is present Kōchi Prefecture, both in Shikoku.
37. Action that brings about inevitable consequences or the law of cause and effect.
38. Referring to the reaction of Kūkai's relatives to his religious vocation, and his nephew's frivolous habits.
39. This work was compiled by Kūkai around 830. In translating this section, I have consulted the unpublished doctoral thesis on *The Treasure Key to the Esoteric Store* by Minoru Kiyota, presented to Tōkyō University (1962).
40. The Duke of Chou (d. 1094 B.C.) was a Confucian sage.
41. The worlds of sense desire, of form, and of pure spirit.
42. (1) Almsgiving, (2) moral precepts, (3) fortitude, (4) diligence, (5) meditation, and (6) perfect wisdom.
43. Emma in Japanese; Yama or Yamarāja in Sanskrit.
44. Creatures born from the womb, eggs, moisture, and self-created ones.
45. Between the ruler and minister, between father and son, and between husband and wife.
46. Humanity, righteousness, propriety, wisdom and faithfulness.
47. See ch. 17, n. 23.
48. The wisdom light refers to the light of the moon and the sun, which are symbols of the virtue of wisdom and the virtue of meditation, respectively.

49. The Four Maṇḍalas represent the body, thought, speech, and the work of the Buddha, respectively.
50. The god who overcomes desire, rage, and ignorance.
51. Literally, the Great Sun Buddha, who is the supreme Buddha of esoteric Buddhism.
52. The nine spiritual medicines refer to Brahmanism, Taoism, and various schools of Buddhism except the esoteric school.
53. The uppermost stage according to the *Vajrasekhara sūtra*.

CHAPTER 24

Medieval Japan: Amida Pietism, Nichiren, and Zen

A. AMIDA PIETISM[1]

□ By the middle of the Heian period the two esoteric schools of Buddhism, namely, the Tendai and the Shingon, lost their spiritual vitality, even though they enjoyed worldly prestige, wealth, and prosperity. Meanwhile some of the serious seekers at the Tendai monastic center at Mt. Hiei began to be attracted by Amida (Amitābha)[2] pietism. The popularity of the faith in Amida was greatly stimulated by the Buddhist eschatological notion called *mappō* (latter end of the Law), based on the legend that divides world history into three periods: the first thousand years after the Buddha's death being the period of Perfect Law (*shōbō*), the second thousand being the period of Copied Law (*zōbō*) in which piety continues but true faith declines, and the last thousand being the period of the Latter End of Law (*mappō*) in which the Buddha's teaching declines and the world is overwhelmed by vice and strife.[3] In the age of the Latter End of Law, so it was widely believed, man can be saved only by the mercy of Buddha Amida. The pioneers of Amida pietism during the Heian period were Kōya or Kūya (903–972), Ryōgen (912–985), and Genshin (942–1017). □

1. The Essentials of Salvation (Ōjō yōshū) by Genshin.[4]

a. "Preface"

I am persuaded that in the age of the Latter End of Law of this contaminated world the doctrine and practice concerning birth in Paradise are as essential to us as are eyes and feet. This is the teaching which must be adhered to both by monks and laymen, by men of noble birth as much as by men of humble origin. It must be mentioned in this connection that Buddhism, here including both the esoteric and exoteric schools, has more than one doctrine and various methods of meditation regarding the phenomenal and the absolute realms. This fact may not present difficulties to those who are endowed with aptitude, intelligence, and diligence, but for me, being stupid, it is difficult to comprehend. Therefore I have turned to the gate of *nembutsu* (recitation of the holy name of Amida in order to gain salvation), and have collected essential passages relating to it from various scriptures and commentaries. The practice of *nembutsu* with the help of these passages will, I trust, result in easier understanding and better practice of the subject matter.

My work has three parts in ten chapters. They are as follows:

Ch. 1, concerning the importance of detesting and leaving this unclean world.

Ch. 2, concerning the earnest seeking of the Pure Land (the abode of Amida).

Ch. 3, scriptural evidences regarding Paradise.

Ch. 4, concerning the proper practice of *nembutsu*.

Ch. 5, concerning the means to help *nembutsu*.

Ch. 6, concerning *nembutsu* to be practiced at certain designated times.

Ch. 7, concerning the benefits to be received from the practice of *nembutsu.*

Ch. 8, concerning evidences which would promote *nembutsu.*

Ch. 9, concerning various practices, besides *nembutsu,* which would lead to birth in Paradise.

Ch. 10, questions and answers dealing with comparative inquiries.

These, I hope, to be my constant reminders.

By Shamon Genshin.

b. Sub-headings of Ch. 1, Concerning the Importance of Detesting and Leaving this Unclean World.

§ 1, the realm of Hell.

(1) The hell of repetition of misery.

(2) The hell of black rope.

(3) The hell of the multitudes.

(4) The hell of wailing and lamentations.

(5) The hell of greater wailing and lamentations.

(6) The hell of scorching heat.

(7) The hell of greater scorching heat.

(8) The hell of constant torment.

§ 2, the realm of the hungry ghosts.

§ 3, the realm of beasts.

§ 4, the realm of *asura* or fighting spirits.

§ 5, the realm of human beings.

(1) The reality of impurity.

(2) The reality of suffering.

(3) The reality of transitoriness.

§ 6, the realm of heavenly beings. [The realms of (1) hell, (2) hungry ghosts, (3) beasts, (4) fighting spirits, (5) human beings, and (6) heavenly beings, are called the Six Realms of Desire in Buddhism.]

§ 7, conclusions regarding the state of detesting the unclean world.

c. Main Outlines of §7 of Ch. 1

In conclusion, it must be reiterated that in this life there are only sufferings, such as those of birth, old age, death, and decrepitude, and no pleasure. But many persons, blinded by greed and the feeling of attachment, are enslaved to the desires of the five senses, without realizing that what appears to be constant and pleasurable is transitory and devoid of true pleasure. Since the mountain of swords and the agony in boiling water (sufferings in hell) are approaching before one's eyes, how can one not detest [the false pleasure of this world]? Indeed, as the verse in the *Shōbōnen gyō* (*Saddharma smrityupasthana sūtra* [Scripture for invoking the Law's aid]) says, "The wise worries as if he were in prison, while the fool seeks pleasure as if he were in paradise." [Another scripture reminds us], "One might consider it a pleasure to accumulate wealth, even by questionable means, and to provide for his wife and children. However, they cannot help him from the approaching pain at the moment of death. In the horrible realms of hell, of the hungry ghosts, and of beasts, one cannot see his family or friends. While one's earthly possessions pass on to the hands of others, no one else will share his suffering. Not even his parents, brothers, wife, children, friends, and servants, to say nothing of his earthly treasures, can accompany him to death, only the consequence of his bad deeds follow him. Then the ruler of hell would tell the sinner that one's evil deeds, according to the law of karma,[5] have resulted in his coming to hell, and that neither his parents nor his wife and children can save him from the consequences of his misdeeds. Therefore, one should [while on earth] follow the principle of renouncing [the world] by casting away the deeds of lust and the way of the world, and by seeking true peace and comfort."[6]

[In another scripture[7] we read] that "The bones of a person in his many births during one world period, if they should be preserved, would be piled up like Mt. Vipula."[8] If this were true of one world period, how many more bones might one accumulate through innumerable world periods! It is really lamentable that we have spent many world periods in vain, because we did not follow the path of the Buddha. And unless we should diligently practice [the path of the Buddha] now, our future will also be the same. We have to remind ourselves in the first place that it is not an easy thing to be born as a human being in the chain of birth and rebirth. Birth as a human being does not always mean that one is born in perfect physical condition. Even if one were born in perfect physical condition, it is not easy to be exposed to the teaching of Buddhism. And, even if one might be exposed to Buddhism, it is difficult for him to [acquire] a pious heart.

As for us, who have had the rare opportunity [to learn the Buddha's Law], we have to remind ourselves that the opportunity to leave this world of suffering and to be born in the Pure Land is given to us only in the present life. However, our mind, even at old age, is still contaminated by the dust of the world, and we are not freed from physical and materialistic desires even though the end of our life is approaching. Then, leaving this world and going to the bottom of the nether world, we will invoke heaven and earth to rescue us from the scorching fire, but it will be too late. Therefore, I urge all the seekers to learn to depart from the world of suffering, which means to renounce this world. Otherwise, they will be like those who go to the treasure mountain and go away empty handed.

Question: On what grounds may one gain the heart to detest (the unclean world)?

Answer: In order to have a comprehensive observation, one must understand the law of cause and effect operating in the Six Realms of Desire, as presented in previous chapters, and the state of impurity as well as the problem of sufferings.

Question: It is not difficult to comprehend the doctrines of impurity, suffering, and transitoriness; one can even see (their consequences) with one's own eyes. And yet, you interpret them as emptiness or void. Why?

Answer: Because they are in reality what the scripture calls "dream, vision, or temporary phenomena." When one is not yet awakened from the dream of illusion, one takes the emptiness or the thing which does not exist as though it were real. Therefore the *Vijñapti-mātratā-siddhi* (Completion of mere ideation) tells us that those who have not reached the state of true enlightenment are living in a dream, and that the Buddha used the expression of the long night of life and death for this reason.

Question: Is not the path to acquire enlightenment, based on the observation of transitoriness, suffering, and emptiness, (similar to) the path of self-practice and self-deliverance as taught by the Small Vehicle?

Answer: This observation is applicable not only to the Small Vehicle but also to the Great Vehicle. Thus, the *Lotus Scripture* [ch. 2] exhorts us to dwell in the room of compassion, to wear the cloth of meekness and humility, to sit on the emptiness of all elements of existence, and to expound the Buddha's Law therefrom. In other words, the view of emptiness of all elements of existence does not contradict the heart of great compassion. Furthermore, the ideas of suffering, transitoriness, and so forth, facilitate the vow of the Mahāyāna bodhisattvas[9] to save all creatures. Also, the idea of purity is considered as an essential feature for the path of the bodhisattva.

Question: What benefits does one gain by the realization of transitoriness, suffering, and emptiness?

Answer: By constantly keeping one's mind under control with the realization of transitoriness, suffering, and emptiness, the desires of the five senses wither away, and one can maintain the righteous and calm mind at the hour of death, and thereby prevent himself from falling into the realm of hell. (Shinsho Hanayama, annot., *Ōjō yōshū*, pp. 1–66)

2. The *Tales of Long Ago*

□ The *Konjaku monogatari* (Tales of long ago), compiled in the latter half of the eleventh century, contains many stories based on Buddhist motifs. The following is an abbreviated, free translation of the thirty-ninth story in Ch. 15, "The Death of the Mother of the Vicar-general Genshin." □

Long ago, there was a vicar-general of Yokawa called Genshin, who was a native of the County of Katsuraki-no-shimo in the Province of Yamato. As a young boy he entered the Tendai monastic center at Mt. Hiei, and after many years of study he became a renowned Master of Learning. Once he was invited by the consort of Emperor Sanjō to lecture on the *Lotus Scripture* and received many precious gifts from her. The vicar-general sent a part of the gifts to his mother with a note stating that he had the honor of lecturing to the empress. His mother, [although appreciative of her son's thoughtfulness,] wrote to him, saying, "You did not become a priest in order to associate with the nobility. I sent you to Mt. Hiei in order to make you a learned and virtuous holy man so that you will be able to help the poor as well as to bring about salvation to me in my future life." The vicar-general, [greatly touched by his mother's letter,] vowed to remain at Mt. Hiei and endeavor to become a holy man. He promised his mother that he would not leave the mountain until he was sent for by her. His mother, then, wrote another letter admonishing him not to become a slave to worldy fame.

Six years passed, and [the vicar-general, anxious to know the welfare of his mother,] inquired whether he could come to see her. But she wrote, "While I am, of course, eager to see you, my seeing you would not help to diminish the sins of my previous births. The greatest consolation to me is the knowledge that my own son is devoting his life to the Buddha's Law. Therefore I urge you not to leave Mt. Hiei until I send for you."

Nine years passed. One day the vicar-general felt an unusually strong longing to see his mother. Feeling that it might be a premonition of the approaching death of his mother, he decided to descend from Mt. Hiei and set out on a journey toward home. As he approached the border of Yamato Province, he met a messenger who was carrying a note to him from his mother, stating that she was critically ill and that she wanted to ask him to come at once to see her. He reached home late that day and found that his mother was not expected to live much longer. She was particularly happy to see him once more in this life. The vicar-general asked his mother whether she was practising *nembutsu*. She said that she had neither the physical strength to recite nor a spiritual instructor who would explain the meaning of *nembutsu*. The vicar-general immediately expounded on the compassion of Buddha Amida and urged her to recite His name following the formula [of "Namu Amida Butsu," (Adoration to the Buddha Amida)]. His mother, whose heart was now awakened to the deep meaning of the Buddha's teaching, followed her son's instruction. After reciting the formula of "Namu Amida Butsu" nearly 200 times, the light of her life went out like the vanishing of the morning star.

The vicar-general in tears said to himself, "Had I not come, the end of my mother's life would not have been so peaceful. Fortunately, I was able to be with her at the end of her life. Since her heart was awakened to the path of salvation, and since she died reciting *nembutsu*, there is no question that my mother will be born in the Pure Land of Amida. Her happiness in the future life was caused by the fact that she had urged me, her son, to follow the path of the holy man. In this manner, the mother in helping her son's salvation in turn received her son's help in her own salvation." (*Konjaku monogatari*, 2:304–09)

3. *Exhortation about mountain climbing* by Hōnen

□ Hōnen (1133–1212), the founder of the Pure Land School (Jōdo) of Buddhism, is often characterized as the "Luther of Japan."[10] The following is an abbreviated translation of his *Tozanjō* (Exhortation about mountain climbing), dictated by him around 1206 when he and his disciples were being persecuted by the clergy of the old schools of Nara and the Tendai School at Mt. Hiei.[11] This work was compiled by his disciple, Shōkaku (1167–1235).

In this work, Hōnen affirms that the Buddha's teaching includes many doctrines which may seem contradictory and irreconcilable, but that any one of these doctrines would ultimately lead men to the same goal. On the other hand, he makes it clear that for most people the path of sanctification and enlightenment by means of precepts, meditation, and knowledge is practically impossible. He thus defends the path of salvation based on faith in Amida as the only option to attain rebirth in the Pure Land. At the same time, he cautions his followers not to slander other schools of Buddhism. □

I wonder at what corner of the Three Worlds[12] I was wandering and thus failed to encounter Buddha Śākyamuni[13] during his life-time. Which phase of the chain of transmigration I was going through and thus failed to hear him preaching the Law? Could it be that I was like those who lived at the town of Śrāvastī where the Buddha lived and yet had no knowledge of him? Or, I might have been dwelling at the bottom of the scorching hell! Wherever I was, and however I think, I am struck by a sense of shame and sorrow.

But now, after many births I was born as a human being, and had the good fortune of encountering the teaching of the Buddha. While I still lament the fact that I failed to live at the time when the Buddha lived, I rejoice that I was born in the age when the Buddha's Law is spreading, whereby we are all able to learn about the path of deliverance. Wouldn't it be regrettable, then, if we wasted our days and nights instead of taking advantage of our good fortune and pursue the spiritual life? There are some who become slaves to the affection of their families and relatives, while others become slaves to hatred which keeps the torch of anger burning in their hearts. In so doing, they simply pile up karma day and night as they walk, as they stand, as they sit, and as they sleep. Indeed, as the scripture reminds us, a man's action in every second of the day produces karma to lead him to hell. In this manner, our yesterdays were wasted, and our todays too are passing away. How long do we keep on living this way? Is it not the truth that the glory of the morning flower vanishes by the evening breeze, and the life of the dew which develops at night is melted by the morning sunshine? But the people, not realizing this truth, think of the temporary glory and life in this world as permanent realities. And yet, the dew of our life is bound to disappear by the onslaught of the wind of transitoriness, and our corpses are thrown into the wilderness or sent to distant mountains. Our corpses, then, remain under the moss, and our souls are destined to wander alone in the journey of after-life. No one, not even the members of the family, can accompany our lonely souls, and no amount of wealth can help us; only the sense of regret follows us. Eventually, we come to the seat of the ruler of hell who evaluates the weight of our sins and karma. And, when the ruler of hell asks why we, living in the age when Buddha's Law was widely spread, failed to follow its teaching and return to hell, what kind of answer can we present to him? In order to avoid such an eventuality, you should seek the path of deliverance while you are here on earth.

It is to be noted in this connection that the doctrines preached by the Buddha included both the exoteric and esoteric teachings as well as the Great Vehicle and the Small Vehicle. Subsequently different schools of interpretation developed, so that some of them teach the emptiness of all phenomena, while others teach the existence of reality in the heart. Also, according to some schools there are five distinct natures,[14] whereas according to others all existences share the same Buddahood. All these teachings, different though they may appear to be, were based on the scriptures or their commentaries, and as such they can be traced to the golden words of the Buddha himself, who gave different teachings to different people depending on the circumstances. If we follow any one of these doctrines and endeavor to practice it, we will be able to attain the same enlightenment. Take, for example, the difference between the two gates of the Holy Path and of the Pure Land, as taught by Dōshaku (Tao-ch'o in Chinese; 562–645). The former is the path for a person to seek enlightenment by eliminating worldly passions while he is on this earth, whereas the latter is the path for a person to be born in the Pure Land where he eliminates passions and attains enlightenment.

As far as the gate of the Pure Land is concerned, there are various kinds of methods of attaining salvation. The important thing is for a person to adopt any one of the methods, to which he is attracted, and put it into practice with diligence, and he will be able to attain salvation. He should never have any doubt on this point. As for me, my attempt to follow the thirteen meditative disciplines (meditations on the sun, the water, the land, the treasure trees, the treasure lakes, the treasure halls, the lotus stands, the images of the Buddha, Amida, Kannon,[15] the bodhisattva Seishi, the stage of his own development, and all the foregoing considered together) only results in my mind being driven to various objects of the six senses,[16] while my attempt to practice the [nonmeditative] good deeds lures me to the Ten Evil Deeds.[17] Fortunately I find that the scripture teaches that even if a person has committed the Ten Evil Deeds and the Five Great Sins,[18] if at the hour of death he should have the benefit of a spiritual instructor and recite the holy name of Amida once or ten times, he will attain salvation in the Pure Land. This certainly is the very method of salvation for me!

I am told that there are some learned monks of various sects who argue that the spread of the practice of reciting Amida's name might cause the decline of Buddhism, and that some people have given up the practice of *nembutsu* for that reason. This I find difficult to comprehend.

It must be stated emphatically that those who practice *nembutsu* should not slander other Buddhist practices. Conversely, those who follow other practices should not speak disparagingly of *nembutsu*. Such behavior is against the spirit of Amida's vow.

It is clear that for ordinary mortals living in this contaminated world there is no way to reach the Pure Land except by depending on the saving power of Amida. To be sure, all the Buddhas of the ten regions[19] teach on the one hand the enlightenment of this world for those who live here, and on the other, the enlightenment of the Pure Land for those who live there. Only Amida, unlike other Buddhas, pledged simultaneously to teach the enlightenment of the Pure Land and to save those who live in this world. Understandably, ordinary mortals who have not eliminated their illusions cannot be expected to be born in the Pure Land which is a realm set aside for superior bodhisattvas as the reward for their good deeds in this world. However, Amida's Pure Land was created by his compassion to save those who have committed evil deeds, those who have failed to keep the precepts, and those who, otherwise, because of their lack of saving knowledge, are destined to be caught endlessly in the illusory chain of transmigration. With great compassion, Amida reflected on the principle of cause and effect for as long as the five aeons, and devised a means to bring the unworthy creatures, who could not possibly attain salvation by their own meritorious deeds, to this Pure Land. He resolved, therefore, that he himself would undergo many years of disciplines, engage in numerous good deeds, and practice bodhisattvahood, whereby all his accumulated merit would be represented by his name which can be recited by all creatures. It is the power of this vow which enables those who recite his name in faith to attain salvation. Indeed, according to the eighteenth article of Amida's [48] vows [vows to save all beings, made by Amida when he was still a bodhisattva called Dharmakara], if any one should fail to attain salvation after reciting his name at least ten times, Amida himself would not accept the gift of enlightenment.

Therefore, I beseech all of you, practitioners of *nembutsu*: If you have not lost the treasure of Amida's original vow, safeguard it in the depth of your believing hearts. There is no Buddha except Amida who has vowed to save all creatures by means of *nembutsu*. And it is no other than us who are given the promise of attaining birth in Amida's Pure Land by reciting the six-syllable formula.[20] Just think for whose benefits did Amida undergo many years of disciplines? He did so in order to pass on his merits to all future creatures. Also think why did he make such a vow? He did so for the benefit of us who live in the age of the Latter End of Law. If we should fail to attain salvation, how could Amida accept enlightenment? And, if he should not accept enlightenment, how could we attain salvation? Ultimately, our salvation depends on Amida's enlightenment, while Amida's enlightenment depends on our attainment of salvation. The intent of his vow, as expressed in such phrases as "if they should fail to attain salvation" and "I would not accept the gift of enlightenment," is based on such [reciprocal conditions]. (Ishi Kyōdōi, ed., *Hōnen-shōnin zenshū* [Complete works of Priest Hōnen], pp. 416–32)

4. *Notes Lamenting Differences* by Shinran

□ Shinran (1173–1262),[21] the founder of the True Pure Land School (Jōdo Shin Shū), was a disciple of Hōnen. The following passages are selected from the *Tanni shō* (Notes lamenting differences),[22] a collection of Shinran's sayings, compiled thirty years after his death by one of his disciples in order to correct the heretical views that arose among the followers of the True Pure Land School. The compiler quotes Shinran's statements which show the subtle danger that one's faith can degenerate into "faith in one's own faith," so that faith in the "other power" (Amida) is not so easy a way as it may seem. □

At the moment when one's mind is moved to recite the holy name of Amida with the firm faith in salvation[23] by the help of Amida's vow, that person is already embraced by Amida's saving light from which he will not be forsaken.

Amida's original vow, be it noted, did not differentiate persons on the basis of their being old or young, or being good or evil, so long as they had faith, which is the only qualification needed, because his vow was made ostensibly to help those creatures who cannot otherwise be saved because of the weight of their sins and their uncontrollable passions. Thus, one does not need to do any other good deeds in order to believe in Amida's vow, because nothing is as good as the act of reciting Amida's holy name. It follows, then, that one should not be afraid of the power of evil, because there is no evil which can obliterate Amida's original vow. (*Tanni shō*, ch. 1)

As for me, Shinran, I have no other recourse except to believe in the salvation by Amida by reciting his holy name, which is the teaching I received from my master, Hōnen. I have no way of knowing whether the *nembutsu* has the seed of our birth in the Pure Land or the karma of our going to hell. Nevertheless, I would have no regret even if it turned out that I have been misled by Hōnen and find myself going to hell on account of reciting Amida's name. I might have regret for being misled and having descended to hell by reciting Amida's name if I could have attained Buddhahood by following other paths. However, not being able to master any other path, hell would have been my lot anyway even if I tried to follow paths other than that of *nembutsu*. However, I am persuaded that, assuming Amida's original vow were true, the words of Buddha Śākyamuni could not be false, and that in turn assuming Buddha's words were true, the exposition of Zendō (Shan-tao in Chinese, d. 681)[24] could not be false. It follows then, that assuming Zendō's expositions were true, Hōnen's teachings could not be false, and that assuming Hōnen's teachings were true, what I, Shinran, hold cannot be false. This is how I reflect, and this is what I, an ignorant person, affirm as my faith. (*Ibid.*, ch. 2)

I, Shinran, have not recited, not even once, Amida's name as an act of filial piety toward my own parents, because I consider all sentient beings as my parents and brothers in one incarnation or another. Upon my attaining Buddhahood in the next life, I would hope to help all sentient beings without any discrimination. The potency of the *nembutsu* would have helped one's parents, if the *nembutsu* were like a good deed to be achieved by one's own power, but it is not. Therefore, surrender one's own power in order to attain enlightenment, whereby, with the occult power and expedient means thus gained, one could save all beings whether they are wandering in any part of the Six Lower Stages or the Four Higher Phases[25] of the transmigratory chain, starting with one's closest relations. (*Ibid.*, ch. 5)

According to the teaching [of our Master, Shinran], the *nembutsu* is based on the principle of nondiscrimination, because it cannot be mentioned, spoken of, or conceived. (*Ibid.*, ch. 10)

In those days when our Master was alive, those who came to [Kyōto] from distant places were united in their longing for salvation in the Pure Land, and they received the same teachings directly from the Master himself. I am told, however, that nowadays certain heretical views, which are against the Master's teachings, are circulated by the *nembutsu* practitioners, both old and young, who are the followers of the immediate followers of Shinran. Let me list some of the views and behaviors which are contrary to the Master's teachings, [such as]: (*Ibid.*, "Special Preface")

Frightening illiterate people, who are practicing the *nembutsu*, by raising the question as to whether they believe in the incomprehensibility of Amida's vow or the incomprehensibility of his holy name. In raising such a question without even explaining the distinction between the two kinds of incomprehensibility they only cause bewilderment in the minds of the people (*Ibid.*, ch. 11)

Advocating the view that those who have not read and studied the scriptures and their commentaries cannot be assured of salvation. Such a view is completely unworthy. To accuse the simple-minded people who practice *nembutsu* in responding to Amida's original vow for their lack of learning is to be a hindrance to the Dharma and an enemy of the Buddha. (*Ibid.*, ch. 12)

Asserting the view that those who are not afraid of evil, based on the principle of incomprehensibility of Amida's original vow, cannot attain salvation. To hold such a view is in effect to question the merit of Amida's original vow and to ignore the principle of cause and effect regarding good and evil. After all, one's past karma causes all sins, even those sins one commits by his overdependence on the Amida's vow. To believe in the Other-Power (Amida), means to leave our good and evil deeds to the dictates of karma with a sense of utter reliance on Amida's original vow. (*Ibid.*, ch. 13)

Advocating the necessity of believing that by reciting once the *nembutsu* one's grave sins, committed during the eight billion world-periods, can be erased. Is salvation not possible without erasing one's sins? Such a view represents the mind of depending on one's self-power, as usually expressed in the prayer to acquire the right view at the hour of death, and shows the faithlessness in the Other-Power. (*Ibid.*, ch. 14)

Affirming the attainability of enlightenment in this life even with the physical body which is ridden by evil passions. The True Pure Land School holds, in accordance with the teachings of the late Master, Shinran, that our faith in Amida's original vow during our present life enables us to attain salvation in his Pure Land. (*Ibid.*, ch. 15)

The matters just cited, I suppose, have resulted from the lack of unity in the faith among our fellow believers.... It would be a sad thing if in spite of the good fortune of practicing the *nembutsu* one should, because of the lack of true faith, fail to be born directly in the Pure Land but remain in its border realm. With tears in my eyes I have jotted down these things in order to avoid differences in the faith among the believers of the same teaching. This is to be called "*Notes Lamenting Differences*," and is not meant to be read by outsiders. (*Ibid.*, "Conclusion.")

B. THE NICHIREN SCHOOL

□ Nichiren (1222–1282), the founder of the unique Buddhist school bearing his name, was a Buddhist prophet as much as a patriot.[26] His militant and exclusivistic teaching on righteousness was ironically based on the *Lotus Scripture* which advocates the doctrine of universal salvation. The following is a summary translation of his *Risshō ankoku ron* (The establishment of righteousness and the security of the nation), written in 1260.[27] □

A visitor came and lamented, saying, "In recent years there have been strange phenomena in heaven, while famines and plagues have occurred all over the earth, so that it is not uncommon to find not only dead animals but also human corpses on the streets. I rather fancy that death has claimed over half of our population, and every family without exception has been in grief. In this situation, people have been prompted to seek various forms of superhuman help, such as uttering the holy name of the Buddha of the Western Pure Land [Amida], or offering the incantations of esoteric Buddhism to avoid calamities, or practicing Zen meditation to attain liberation from worldy cares, or worshiping the Shintō kami of heaven and earth at various places to avoid pestilence. The rulers, too, are concerned with the plight of peasants and people, and they have remitted taxes. In spite of such kindness to the people, the famine and the plague are more oppressing, there are beggars everywhere, the dead can be seen everywhere, and more corpses are piled up each day. The sun, moon, and five stars follow their proper courses, Buddhism is respected, and the influence of the ruler is still great, and yet the life has gone out of the world, and religion too is losing its [spiritual] vitality. What is the cause of all this, I wonder?"

The Master of the house said, "I too have been anxious about these things and feel very indignant. Now that we share the same concerns, let us exchange our views on the subject. As far as I can ascertain, on the basis of my reflections and reading of the scriptures, all kinds of calamities have descended on us because the people have violated righteousness and turned to evil. That is why good kami have left the land, and sages have not returned, and thus demons and evil spirits have come."

The visitor said, "I have learned for the first time from you [that our troubles were caused by the departure of good kami and holy men and by the arrival of demons and evil spirits]. I would like to know the scriptural evidences for your view, though."

The Master replied, "Scriptural passages and their evidences are extensive. Among them, let me mention the *Scripture of the Golden Light* (*Konkōmyō kyō*), *Mahāsannipāta sūtra* (*Daishū kyō* or Scripture of great assembly), the *Scripture of the Divine Healer* (*Yakushi kyō*), and the *Scripture of the Benevolent Kings* (*Ninnō kyō*).[28] The contents of these four scriptures are so clear that no one can question their meaning. However, those whose eyes have been blinded and those whose minds have been misguided would rather believe in the false teaching, not realizing the true doctrine. This accounts for the fact that people are discarding the Buddhas and scriptures instead of protecting them. And, since good kami and sages have left this country, evil spirits and heretical teachings are causing various kinds of troubles and calamities."

The visitor, who was now angered by the foregoing answer, stated, "Emperor Ming (r. 58–75) of the Eastern Han dynasty (25–220) was guided by a dream of a golden image and opened the door for the introduction of Buddhism to China. . . . [In our own country, since the time of the noble Prince Shōtoku, 573–621] . . . the sovereign as well as all his subjects have venerated Buddhist statues and scriptures. Our country is dotted with great temples, and scriptures are found in every corner of the land. Seeing all this, on what ground do you say that Buddhism is being neglected and discarded in our country?"

The Master explained to the guest, saying, "You are right in stating that there are many temples, many store-houses for scriptures, and many monks, and that Buddhism has for a long time been venerated and is still venerated. However, the monks are so degraded and lead people astray with flattery, whereas the sovereign as well as his subjects cannot tell good from evil because of their ignorance. . . . [Our present tragic situation is exactly like what was prophesied in the *Scripture of Benevolent Kings*, the *Nirvāṇa Scripture*, and the *Lotus Scripture*.] In this situation, righteousness cannot be restored unless we first remonstrate and correct the evil monks."

The guest, now angrier than ever, asked, "Isn't it the duty of the monarch to influence the nation according to the [great way of] heaven and earth, while the sages bring order by distinguishing right and wrong? Now, the monks of the world are highly respected by the people, [and that implies that these monks are not evil]. Otherwise, why does the wise monarch trust them? Why do you speak so disparagingly of the venerable clergy? Tell me, for instance, who is an evil monk?"

The Master replied, "I shall tell you. During the reign of Emperor Go-Toba (r. 1184–1198) there was a certain monk called Hōnen who wrote a book entitled "Collection of passages" [on the original vow of Amida in which the *nembutsu* is chosen above all ways of achieving rebirth].

In this "Collection," following the false interpretations by Donran (Tan-luan in Chinese, 476–542), Dōshaku (Tao-ch'o, d. 645), and Zendō (Shen-tao, d. 681), which divided Buddhism into the Gate of the Holy Path or the Path of Difficult Practice and the Gate of Pure Land or the Path of Easy Practice, [Hōnen classified all teachings except that of Pure Land into the former category.] Thus, he urged people to give up, close, discard, or destroy 637 scriptures, 2,883 sections in all, including those of the Lotus, the esoteric, and all the Mahāyāna teachings taught during the life of the Buddha, all other Buddhas and bodhisattvas and heavenly beings. . . . Hōnen's teaching is counter to the [original] vow of Amida, who pledged to save all beings except those who commit the Five Great Sins[29] and those who falsely accuse the True Law, as clearly stated in the three Pure Land scriptures from which Hōnen presumably derived his own views. However, in this period of Latter End of Law there is no holy man; rather, [many clergy] have forgotten the right path and lead others to distorted faith instead of helping them to see things clearly. [Under the influence of Hōnen's writing, people] venerate only Amida, the Buddha of the Western Pure Land, forgetting even the supreme Buddha Śākyamuni. No wonder temples other than those of Amida are neglected, and offerings are given only to the priests of the *nembutsu* sect. Since the main traditions of Buddhism, such as the most comprehensive and central vehicle of the Lotus (the Tendai School), are neglected in favor of the Pure Land teaching, which lies at the border of historic Buddhism, it is understandable that the good kami are angry and evil spirits take advantage of the situation. Thus, the foremost task before us is not to offer various kinds of prayers to ward off famine and pestilence, but to forbid the very evil which is the cause of all these troubles."

The visitor, now looking a little more pleasant, said, "I now realize [Hōnen's mistakes in renouncing all other scriptures, and you have explained how Hōnen's writing has been the cause of all our troubles]. Now, everyone, from the sovereign to all his subjects, are concerned with the peace of the land. If the nation declines and the people vanish, who will be left to venerate Buddha and his Law? Thus, I feel that we must first pray for the security of the nation before thinking about Buddhism, and would like to know the means of eliminating the troubles which are now confronting the nation."

The Master replied, "Being stupid by nature, I cannot offer any clever solution of my own. However, based on the scriptures, I am convinced that the nation will attain peace and prosperity if those who slander the True Law are rejected and those who preach the true doctrine are given important positions. Concretely, if we want the security of the nation, we must first eliminate the false teaching [of Hōnen]. All the scriptures consider the act of slandering the Law a grave sin. Is it not foolish for one to be caught by the net of this grave sin and eventually descend into the flame of hell? Let me exhort you to be converted straightway to the true teaching of the Lotus, and when people follow the teaching of the Lotus, the Three Worlds and the ten regions will be transformed into the Buddha Land, and be it noted that the Buddha Land will never be destroyed by any calamity or trouble. When the nation thus attains security, we will all attain the safety of the body and peace of mind. You should believe and respect this statement." (*Nihon Bukkyō shisō shiryōshū* [Collection of source materials on the history of Japanese Buddhist thought], pp. 537–52)

C. THE ZEN SCHOOL

□ Meditation (*dhyāna* or the concentration of mind) has been an important component of Buddhism from its inception. But the Meditation School (Ch'an in Chinese, Zen in Japanese) was the product of Chinese Buddhism. The following four schools of Zen were established in Japan: (1) the Rinzai School, introduced by Eisai (1141–1215) in 1191, (2) the Sōtō School, introduced by Dōgen (1200–1253) in 1227, (3) the Fuke School founded by Kakushin

(1207–1298) in 1255, and (4) the Ōbaku School introduced by the Chinese priest, Ingen (Yin-yüan, in Chinese, 1592–1654) in 1654. Zen Buddhism exerted profound influence on various aspects of Japanese culture during the Muromachi period (1338–1573).[30]

The following are abbreviated translations of passages from the *Shōbōgenzō zuimonki* (Eye and treasure of the True Law recorded by his pupils), a collection of teachings of Dōgen recorded by his disciple, Ejō. Being an independent and thoroughgoing seeker of truth, Dōgen throughout his life followed his own line of thought based on his own religious experience. Unlike Hōnen, Shinran, and Nichiren, who felt that they were living in the Period of the Latter End of Law, Dōgen never questioned that a true seeker was not separated from the Period of Perfect Law (*shōbō*). Thus, he rejected the necessity of depending on the mercy of Amida or anyone else. Instead, he urged his disciples to "sit and meditate," just as Śākyamuni did at the time of his own enlightenment. □

A certain man [came to Dōgen and] said, "Because my health is poor and my aptitude is not good, I do not think I will be able to undergo the learning and practice of Buddhism, What I would like to do, therefore, is to find out the most essential features of the Law, and to lead a solitary life, while taking care of my weak health." To which Dōgen replied, "You must bear in mind that not all those who had attained enlightenment in the past were endowed with a strong constitution or superior aptitude. As I reflect about the time of the Buddha, and be it understood that it has not been such a long time since his death, not everyone of his followers was intelligent. Also, some of them were good men, but others were not. Even among the monks, there were some who had committed unusually evil deeds, and there were some who had the worst kind of potentialities. Nevertheless, they did not let their sense of unworthiness stand in the way of seeking enlightenment; they did not let their poor intellectual quality interfere with their determination to study Buddhism. If one neglects the learning and practice of Buddhism during his lifetime, in what phase of the chain of birth and rebirth can he expect to be born with high aptitude and good health? Indeed, the most essential feature [of the path of Buddhism] is awakening one's mind to the goal of enlightenment and undergoing the disciplines without worrying about one's life and health." (Vol. 1, ch. 2)

Once Dōgen taught, "One must remember how quickly the wind of transitoriness blows our life away, and how important are life and death. If one wishes to do and study something worthwhile during his short life, he ought to practice Buddhist disciplines and study the Law. It goes without saying that one should discard literary composition and writing poems inasmuch as they are of no value. One should not attempt to cover too many subjects even in his study and practice of Buddhism. Moreover, one should have nothing to do with those schools of Buddhism such as all the exoteric and esoteric sects, which unlike Zen build their doctrines based on scriptures and commentaries. Even the Buddha's own sayings should not be studied indiscriminately. Most people with limited abilities can hardly concentrate even on one thing. It is not desirable, therefore, for them to indulge in many things simultaneously, for in so doing their minds will lose control. (Vol. 2, ch. 8)

Once, Ejō inquired, "What is the one thing in the Buddhist Law which we should practice." The Master said, "What you should practice depends on your own abilities. However, the one practice which has been handed down in the tradition of Bodhidharma[31] is *zazen* (meditation).[32] This practice is suited for all people, regardless of differences of innate ability. When I learned this principle under the tutelage of the late master (Ju-ching, 1163–1268) of the T'ien-t'ung Monastery [in China], I started practicing *zazen* day and night and continued it even when some other monks gave it up in the extremely hot and cold days. I then said to myself, 'I should practice *zazen* even if I should become ill or die on account of it. What good would it do if I, who am not sick, failed to do so! If

I should die in following the practice of *zazen* before attaining enlightenment, I might at least create a cause to be born in future life as a follower of the Buddha. After all, it is useless simply to live long without undergoing Buddhist disciplines. Even if I take great care of my health, I might drown or encounter unexpected death, and then I will surely have cause to regret.' I, therefore, urge all of you to practice *zazen* most intensely. All of you without exception will find the true path. Such was the teaching of my late master [Juching]." (Vol. 2, ch. 11)

During one of the evening conversations Ejō asked, "What shall we do to repay our indebtedness to our parents?" Dōgen replied, "One should observe filial piety, of course. However, there is a difference between the filial piety of the monk and that of the layman. In the case of the layman, he should, as taught in the *Classic of Filial Piety*,[33] serve his parents during their lifetime and engage in acts of repaying gratitude to them after their death. On the other hand, the monk who has entered the Buddhist life—which is characterized by inactivity, [by forsaking the indebtedness toward his parents]—should not try to repay gratitude only toward his physical parents. His sense of indebtedness toward all living beings must be considered as deep as his sense of indebtedness toward his parents of this lifetime, so that the latter should not be singled out as special objects of filial piety. This attitude is in keeping with the Buddhist principle of inactivity.[34] To follow the path of the Buddha in one's daily disciplines and in one's study of the Law is the true filial piety. Holding a memorial service on the memorial days of the parents or doing charitable deeds for the repose of the parents during the forty-nine days following their death are examples of the way of the laity, [and not the way of the monks]. (Vol. 3, ch. 16)

Once Dōgen taught, "When a certain man is said to have a dull nature, it simply means that his determination has not gone far enough. As a man falls from a horse's back, many thoughts come to him before he hits the ground. This shows that when one encounters the possibility of injury to his body or an event in which he might lose his life, resourcefulness and senses readily come to him. On such an occasion, men of keen senses and those of a dull nature think alike and they are bound to be concerned with the meaning of life. Thus, if one should strive with firm determination, thinking as if he might die the following day or that night or as if he might encounter a very serious event, there is no likelihood that he would not attain enlightenment. A man with a dull nature but with firm determination is able to attain enlightenment more quickly than the one who is sagacious in worldly knowledge. During the lifetime of the Buddha, [one of his direct disciples] Cūḍapanthaka was not capable of reciting even one verse, but succeeded in attaining enlightenment in one summer[35] because of the earnestness of his nature. Our life exists only now. If one should study the Law of the Buddha with the earnest thought of attaining enlightenment before one dies, everyone without exception will not fail to attain his goal. (*Ibid.*, ch. 17)

Once a certain nun said, "Considering the fact that some housewives are learning the Law of Buddha, it seems to me that a nun (who has renounced the world) cannot fail to follow the Law of the Buddha even if some of her conduct may not be altogether what it ought to be. What do you think?"

Dōgen said, "Your statement is not correct. While it is possible for a woman in her state of a householder to learn and gain some insights into the Law of Buddha, it would not be possible for a monastic to acquire the Law of the Buddha unless a monastic thinks like a monastic. It is not that the Law of the Buddha chooses [certain persons to stay in the life of the householder and others to renounce the world]; it is up to men and women either to enter or not to enter the Law of the Buddha. There must be differences in the thinking of a monastic and that of a householder. If a householder should have the mind of a monastic, he should renounce the world. On the other hand, it would be a double mistake if a monastic should have the mind of a householder. In principle it is not difficult to do anything, but it is very difficult to do anything well. Everyone seems to be concerned with the path of renouncing the world and acquiring the Law of the Buddha, but many find it difficult to do it well in practice. But, life and death is a serious matter, and transiency comes quickly [and does not wait for us]. Thus, one's mind should never be inattentive. If one renounces the world, one must really and truly renounce the world, without any concern with the temporary designations [such as the householder or the monastic]." (Vol. 4, ch. 2)

During one of the evening conversations Dōgen said, "As I look at the people of the world (the householders), those who are blessed with good fortune [which according to Buddhism is the result of one's good deeds in the past] and who cause the advancement of their families are invariably honest and do good deeds to others. That is why their families are well maintained and their descendants do not die out. Those whose minds are not straight and who are not good to others may appear at times to be fortunate with prosperous families, but their lot is doomed in the long run. Even if they may enjoy good fortune during their own lifetime, their descendants will not be so lucky. Also, the fact that one does a good deed to another person with the desire to make that person think well of and be grateful to oneself is certainly better than doing evil to another person, but since such a good deed is motivated by the concern with one's own well being, it cannot be called a truly good deed to another person. A truly good deed to others must be done for the benefit of others, even when those who received the benefits may not know, or for the future welfare of the people without any consideration as to who might be the beneficiary. The Zen monk must have the mind which is superior to that of the householder. When he thinks of other human beings, he must not discriminate between those who are close and those who are distant; he must think of saving everyone equally. He must not think of this-worldly or other-worldly benefit to himself, without any thought of being known or being appreciated by others. In his heart he must think only of the benefit of others, and yet even the fact that he thinks thus must not be known by others. The secret key [for attaining such a state of mind] is for the Zen monk to renounce the world and himself first of all. If one truly renounces himself, there will be no mind (i.e., thought) to be well thought of by others. On the other hand, it would be against the will of the Buddha to do evil or licentious deeds just because one is not bothered by how he is thought of by others. The first condition for renouncing himself is to do good deeds for others with the concern for their well being, without any thought of acquiring a good name for himself as a reward or receiving any benefit, but solely for the welfare of the future life. In order to acquire such a mind, one has to think constantly of the transiency of life and the world. Our lifetime is like a dream, and time moves on quickly. Our life resembles the dew which disappears before the morning light. Thus, while in this life one must think of the welfare of others concerning even a trivial matter in obedience to the will of the Buddha. (*Ibid.*, ch. 3)

Once a certain monk said, "I have an aged mother, and I am her only child. She makes a living solely with the allowance which I send her. Her affection towards me is deep, and my sense of filial piety toward her is also deep. For this reason, following partially the way of the world and of man I manage, thanks to the kindness of others, to receive clothing and food for my mother. Should I really leave the world and isolate myself, she cannot continue to live even for one day. Thus, I have been living in the world [even though I am a monk]. On the other hand, it is unsettling for me not to enter the path of the Buddha completely. Please show me if there is any reason for me to enter the path [of the Buddha completely], even forsaking my own mother."

Dōgen said, "This indeed is a difficult matter, and others cannot dictate what you should do. If only you, after careful consideration, should have the will and determination to do so, you could enter the path of the Buddha, by making careful preparations and by devising a means to assure your mother's livelihood. Then, it will be good both for your mother and yourself.

. . . [We are told that] the Sixth Patriarch[36] took care of his mother by selling firewood [in his youth]. One day in the market he heard a customer reciting the *Diamond Scripture* and experienced a religious awakening. Thus he took his leave from his mother and went to Huang-mei[37] [where he became a disciple of the Fifth Patriarch, Hung-jên (601–674)]. It is said that he received thirty silver pieces for the wood which he left for the clothing and food of his mother. This must have been a gift from heaven because of his earnest desire [to enter the path of the Buddha]. . . . It would seem to be orderly and ideal if one waits for the end of his mother's lifetime and then enters the path of the Buddha without any drawback. But, no one can be certain that the aged will die before the young. And, if by chance the order is reversed whereby one should die while his aged mother remains, one would have cause to regret not having entered the path of the Buddha and his mother would commit the sin of not allowing [her son's pursuing the spiritual life]. In that event, both would be guilty and gain no benefit. . . . (*Ibid.*, ch. 10)

Once Dōgen taught, "It has often been said by many persons, 'I aspire to study Buddhism, but we are living in the Period of the Latter End of Law of the Buddha whereby man's inborn capacity has declined; my own nature is certainly inferior. Thus I will not be able to undergo the Buddhist discipline properly. Therefore, I should find an easier path, so that I could at least enter into a relationship [following the principle of cause and effect] which would enable me to attain enlightenment in one of my future existences.' This kind of statement misses the point. The formulation of the theories of the Three World Periods,[38] was simply a means based on expediency at one time, and has nothing to do with the true teaching of the Buddha. Any person at any time can attain enlightenment by following the path of the Buddha. Not every monk during the lifetime of the Buddha was endowed with superior nature. On the contrary, there were some whose natures were surprisingly despicable and inferior. The Buddha thus established various kinds of disciplines to meet the needs of those whose inborn capacities were inferior. Actually, every person has the potentiality to be affected by the Law of the Buddha. No one should think that he is not endowed with such a capacity. One should only follow the path of the Buddha in order to attain his spiritual goal. So long as one has the mind, he can differentiate between good and evil. So long as one has hands and legs, he can clasp his hands in veneration of the Buddha and walk. In following the Law of the Buddha, there is no difference in the kinds of men. Every being in the realm of man is endowed with the capacity to follow the Law of the Buddha, which is not the case with animals. Those who are learning the Law of the Buddha, however, must not expect anything from tomorrow. They should follow the Buddha as though they have only today and the present hour. (Vol. 5, ch. 8)

Once Dōgen taught, "Those who are learning the path of the Buddha should not rejoice upon receiving alms from the laity, but they should not refuse it. According to the late (Rinzai) Zen Master, Yōsai (also called Eisai, 1141–1215), 'to rejoice over the alms presented by the laity is against the rule established by the Buddha, whereas not to rejoice over the alms goes against the sentiment of the benefactor.' The secret key in dealing with this question is to consider the alms not as something presented to the monk himself but rather as the offerings given to the Buddha. Therefore, in reply to the benefactor, one should state, 'I am sure that the Buddha will accept this alms; I will humbly transmit it [from the benefactor to the Buddha].'" (Vol. 6, ch. 6)

One day Dōgen taught, "In order to study the way of the Buddha, one must forsake one's own self. Even if one has studied one thousand scriptures and ten thousand commentaries, one would fall into the devil's cave [from which one cannot escape] unless one can be liberated from the attachment to one's own self. An ancient said, 'Without [surrendering one's] body and mind to the Law of the Buddha, how can one expect to become a Buddha or a pioneer [in spiritual life]?' To be liberated from one's own self means to forsake one's body and mind, so that one studies the Law of the Buddha not for himself but for the sake of the way of the Buddha. When one throws his body and mind into the Law of the Buddha, one has to follow the disciplines of the Law of the Buddha. If one thinks that going out (as a mendicant) begging might appear unrespectable to others, one cannot enter the Law of the Buddha. One has to forget the views of the world and study the path of the Buddha solely following the truth. To evaluate oneself, and to think that he might not have the capacity to live up to the Law of the Buddha, shows that one still has attachment to one's own self, because worrying over the views of the world and being inhibited by the human sentiment are the very sources of one's attachment to himself. Concentrate solely on acquiring the Law of the Buddha, and do not follow the trends of the world. (*Ibid.*, ch. 10)

Once Dōgen said, "The Zen monk should not give any thought ahead of time what he might wear or what he might eat. To think where he might beg food, or to whom he might go asking for contributions, just in case he finds himself without anything to eat or cook whatsoever, amounts to the same thing as accumulating properties or eating improper food. Only those who like the cloud have no permanent living quarters and who like water flow constantly without being attached to any spot may be called Zen monks. So long as one gives thought to even one patron or one relative, thinking of the possibility that one might someday have no possessions outside of the cloth and food given to him, he is binding himself to others and existing on improper food. And, when one's body and mind are nurtured with such improper meals and so on, it would be impossible to acquire the pure and great Law of various Buddhas. Just as a piece of cloth becomes blue when dyed in blue and becomes yellow when dyed in yellow, one's self becomes [contaminated] when his body and mind are nurtured by an improper way of living. To expect to acquire the Law of the Buddha with such a body and mind resembles the vain effort of trying to secure oil from sand. The Zen monk must deal with each moment in accordance with the truth without prior thought, which goes against this principle. One should reflect carefully on this principle." (*Ibid.*, ch. 22)

Dōgen taught, "*Zazen* is the most supremely important matter in Buddhism. Many persons in China attained enlightenment by practicing *zazen*. Even the illiterate, unintelligent, or mentally slow persons, if they devote themselves to *zazen*, will achieve more than the intelligent persons who spend years on sheer learning. Indeed, the path of the Buddha is nothing but *zazen*. Nothing should interfere with its practice."

I, Ejō, then asked, "In comparing the *zazen* and the *kōan*,[39] I have a feeling that I might at least comprehend one among a hundred or a thousand *kōan*, whereas I do not have that much confidence in the way of *zazen*. Even then, should I practice *zazen*?"

To which the Master said, "Although you might have a feeling that you understand the *kōan*, it causes you to depart from the way of the Buddha. Devote yourself to *zazen* without any desire to receive either reward or enlightenment—that is the path of the Buddha. Although both *kōan* and *zazen* were taught by the masters of the past, the latter was considered as more important." (*Ibid.*, ch. 24)

NOTES

1. On Amida pietism in China, see Ch'en, *Buddhism in China*, pp. 338–50; for brief descriptions of general characteristics of Amida pietism in Japan, see Eliot, *Japanese Buddhism*, pp. 360–95, and Takakusu, *The Essentials of Buddhist Philosophy*, pp. 166–75.
2. The Buddha of Infinite Light, or Amitāyus, the Buddha of Infinite Life, who resides in the Pure Land. See ch. 17, A.
3. A famous Tendai prelate, Jien (1155–1225), wrote a history of Japan from a Buddhist point of view, utilizing the formula of the three periods. His work, *Gukanshō* (Miscellany of a

personal view of an ignorant fool), was partially translated by J. Rahder, *Acta Orientalia*, 15 (1936), 173–230.

4. In this abridged translation, I have consulted the translation of the Ōjōyōshū, "Collected Essays on Birth into Paradise," by A. K. Reischauer, *Transactions of Asiatic Society of Japan*, 7, 2nd ser. (1930), 16–97.
5. The influence of one's action upon life in the future.
6. This is a quotation from the *Hōshaku kyō*, or more fully the *Dai hōshaku kyō* (*Mahāratnakūta sūtra* or Great treasure accumulation scripture, which is the 11th translation, attributed to Bodhiruci in 713 A.D., of the large *Sukhāvatīvyūha* Amitābha scripture spoken by the Buddha), ch. 6.
7. *Daishū kyō* (*Mahāsannipāta sūtra*), ch. 1.
8. One of the mountains situated at Magadha, not far from Calcutta.
9. Those who have postponed their Buddahood to work for the salvation of others.
10. The most comprehensive work in English on Hōnen is the *Hōnen the Buddhist Saint* by Harper H. Coates and Ryūgaku Ishizuka.
11. I have consulted *ibid.*, pp. 563–88 in this abridged translation.
12. The Worlds of Sensuous Desires, the World of Form, and the World of Pure Spirit.
13. Gautama, the historical Buddha.
14. Those who are desired to be born as (1) the Buddha's direct disciples, (2) the self-awakened saint, (3) the bodhisattvas, (4) those whose salvation is uncertain, and (5) those who can never attain salvation.
15. See Avalokiteśvara, ch. 17, n. 23. Seishi (Mahāthāmprata) is bodhisattva of wisdom.
16. Eye, ear, nose, tongue, body, and mind.
17. Killing, stealing, unchastity, double talk, evil speech, lying, perverse speech, jealousy, anger and delusion. See ch. 16, A, ch. 4.
18. Patricide, matricide, killing of saints, causing disorder to the Buddhist community, and injuring the Buddha's body.
19. The four cardinal directions, the four corners, above, and below.
20. *Na-mu-A-mi-da-Butsu* (Praised be Amida Buddha).
21. There are many works in English on the life and teaching of Shinran. Among them are Arthur Lloyd, *Shinran and His Work*, Gesshō Sasaki, *A Study of Shin Buddhism*, Takeichi Takahashi and Junjō Izumida, *Shinranism in Mahāyāna Buddhism and the Modern World*, Kōshō Yamamoto, *The Private Letters of Shinran Shōnin*, Kōshō Yamamoto, tr. and annot., *The Kyōgyō shinshō or The Teaching, Practice, Faith, and Attainment*, Gendō Nakai, *Shinran and His Religion of Pure Faith*, D. T. Suzuki, *A Miscellany of the Shin Teaching of Buddhism*, and Daien Fugen, tr., *The Shōshin Ge: The Gatha of True Faith in the Nembutsu.*
22. In this abridged translation, I have consulted Ryōsetsu Fujiwara, tr. and annot., *The Tanni shō: Notes Lamenting Differences.*
23. "Salvation" means in this context birth in Amida's Pure Land.
24. A prominent Chinese teacher of the Pure Land School.
25. Births in the womb, in the egg, in water, and by sudden transformation. The Six Lower States or the six transmigatory spheres are the realms of hells, hungry ghosts, animals, demons, human beings, and heavenly beings.
26. On his life, see Masaharu Anesaki, *Nichiren, the Buddhist Saint*. See also Eliot, *Japanese Buddhism*, pp. 416–31.
27. The following is an abridged translation. A more informal translation of this work is included in Arthur Lloyd, *The Creed of Half Japan*, pp. 307–28.
28. All these scriptures contain prophecies regarding the coming of grave calamities as the result of the people's negligence of true Buddhism.
29. See n. 18.
30. For the historical development of Zen, see Heinrich Dumoulin, *A History of Zen Buddhism*, tr. by Paul Peachey. See also Eliot, *Japanese Buddhism*, pp. 396–415, and Takakusu, *The Essentials of Buddhist Philosophy*, pp. 153–65.

31. A famous Indian monk who settled in China early in the sixth century A.D.; regarded as the founder of the Ch'an School of Buddhism.
32. Meditation in a special sitting posture practiced in Zen Buddhism.
33. *The Hsiao ching* (*Classic of Filial Piety*), one of the Confucian works, written during the Han period (206 B.C.–A.D. 220) of China, which stresses that filial piety is the basis of all virtues. This book was enormously influential in Japan as it was in China.
34. "Inactivity" is more than the state of doing nothing; it implies opposition to artificiality. It is an attitude to transcend the realm of differentiation (phenomenal world) and reach the realm of the Absolute (Dharma).
35. Ninety days during the rainy season which was a period of retreat for the Buddhist monk.
36. Hui-neng (Enō in Japanese) (638–713). For him, see ch. 18, Introduction.
37. In present Hupeh Province.
38. See introduction to A, this ch.
39. *Kōan* (*kung-an* in Chinese), literally means a "public document." In Zen tradition, it refers to some statement made by a Zen master usually in baffling language, transcending logical reasoning, leading to ultimate truth.

CHAPTER 25

Resurgence of Shintō

□ It is to be recalled that from the eighth century Shintō came to be subordinated to Buddhism within the syncretistic system called the Ryōbu Shintō (Dual Shintō). From the fourteenth century onward, however, there developed a gradual, and checkered, movement to restore the glory of Shintō, which culminated in the excessive ethnocentricism of the nineteenth and twentieth centuries.

The pioneers of this movement were the leaders of the Ise Shintō[1] who developed their apologetics within the structure of the Shintō-Buddhist syncretism, because Buddhism was too deeply rooted to be rejected altogether. Similarly, Kitabatake Chikafusa (1293–1354)[2] accepted the values of Buddhism and Confucianism on the ground that they contained partial truths of Shintō. In the fifteenth century, Ichijō Kanera (1402–1481), a nobleman and philosopher, advocated Shintō without rejecting other teachings. Following the same motif, Yoshida Kanetomo (1435–1511)[3] advocated the "Unique Shintō," stressing the unity of Shintō, Buddhism, and Confucianism. He twisted the earlier Buddhist argument and suggested that Buddhas and bodhisattvas[4] were manifestations of the Shintō kami (deities).

Meanwhile, Zen Buddhism received the support of the feudal regime during the Ashikaga period (1338–1573) and exerted significant influence on various aspects of Japanese art and culture.[5] Ironically, many of the Zennists were attracted by the newly introduced Neo-Confucianism, especially the tradition of Chu Hsi (Shushi in Japanese 1130–1200). They accepted the unity of Zen and Confucian learning, with the former on top and the latter as subordinate components. Gradually, however, some of the Japanese Confucian scholars began to accept the superiority of Neo-Confucianism to Zen Buddhism to the extent that in the seventeenth century many Confucian scholars allied themselves with Shintō, rejecting Buddhism altogether. This sentiment was articulated by Yamazaki Ansai (1618–1682),[6] who based his theory of the "Suiga Shintō" (descent of divine blessing Shintō) on the *Chronicles of Japan* with some Confucian elements added. On the other hand, Yamaga Sokō (1622–1685)[7] and other Confucian scholars closely identified themselves with the "Way of the Warrior" (*bushidō*), which also had strong Shintō features.

The Tokugawa period (1600–1867)[8] also produced many scholars of "National Learning" (*koku-gaku*) and Shintō, such as Deguchi Nobuyoshi (d. 1690), Yoshikawa Koretaru (1616–1694), Kada Azumamaro (1706–1736), Kamo Mabuchi (1697–1769), Motoori Norinaga (1730–1801) and Hirata Atsutane (1776–1843). Among them, the most significant for our purpose are Motoori and Hirata. Incidentally, it was the combination of the Shintō-Confucian ideologies that championed the cause of the restoration of monarchical rule and the termination of the Tokugawa feudal regime in the mid-nineteenth century.

The nineteenth century was also marked by the growth of syncretistic, popular messianic cults among the lower strata of Japanese society. Many of them, with notable exceptions, had little connection with the main traditions of Shintō, Buddhism, and Confucianism. The Japanese government during the Meiji period (1867–1912) placed thirteen such popular religious cults under a misleading category of "sect Shintō denominations."[9] In a real sense they were the precursors of the so-called "new religions," which have mushroomed in Japan since the end of World War II.[10] □

A. MAIN OUTLINES OF THE *SHŌDAN JIYŌ* (PRINCIPLES OF GOOD RULE) BY ICHIJŌ KANERA[11]

[First] is the importance of venerating the kami. Our nation is a divine nation. After the separation of heaven and earth, the seven generations of the heavenly kami, followed by the five generations of earthly kami, initiated all the activities on earth. The sovereigns as well as their subjects, both noble and humble, are all descendants of the kami. The fact that the Ministry of Shintō Affairs was considered the first in importance among the one hundred offices of the government, and that the activities of the government begin each year with the repair of Shintō shrines and celebration of worship services, indicates the extent to which the kami are venerated. For instance, on the occasion of the New Year festival, which is celebrated on the fourth of the second month of each year, offerings are presented to the 3,132 kami in order to avoid calamities and to pray for good harvest for the year. There are other important festivals for which the imperial emissaries present offerings to the kami. These festivals are celebrated by the court, not for the benefit of the sovereigns themselves but for all their subjects. Since the kami do not accept unworthy worship, the emperor being the master of one hundred kami takes supreme charge of all the worship of the kami of the nation. There are, of course, some shrines for which provincial and local officials are in charge, and there are also certain kami who favor the worship offered by their descendants, such as the kami of Iwashimizu Hachiman who are worshiped by the members of the Minamoto family,[12] the kami of the Kasuga Shrine by the Fujiwara, and the kami of the Kitano Shrine by the Sugawara family. In addition, there are the eight shrines which enshrine the spirits of those who for political reasons or otherwise have died unnatural deaths. They were not the kami who descended from heaven, but in order to prevent them from haunting the people their descendants were given government ranks and have been entrusted with the worship of these shrines. As to the repair of the shrines, there should be no negligence. While the Grand Shrine of Ise alone has been designated to be rebuilt in every twenty-first year, other shrines should be repaired according to their needs from time to time. Unfortunately, for the past ten-odd years due to the disorder of the nation many shrines have become dilapidated and the worship of the kami has been neglected. [Under these circumstances,] it is useless for the officials to offer prayers privately. Rather, they should repair the shrines and diligently attend to the worship of the kami. If they do so with pure heart, the kami are bound to impart blessings.

[Second] is the importance of respecting the Law of the Buddha, because the law of the Buddha is nothing other than the law of the sovereign, and also the teaching of the Buddha is the same as the teaching of the Chinese classics. As far as Buddhism is concerned, it was originally the one teaching of the Buddha but came to be divided into the eight sects.[13] It must be noted that only in Japan these eight traditions of Buddhism have been preserved intact. Thus, [those who rule the nation] ought to be concerned with the preservation of all eight traditions. Which tradition is to be adhered to depends on the destiny and sentiment of different persons. More important than following the Buddhist discipline is for the emperor to be benevolent to the people and to restore the dignity of the imperial court, and for the shōgun (generalissimo, commanding general) to be concerned with the arts of the warrior and to eliminate the anxieties on the part of the people. It would be a mistake for the emperor and the shōgun to be excessively devout to Buddhism at the expense of their more important duties. It is well known that the merciful bodhisattva made a vow to accept the suffering of the people on their behalf. It would be difficult for the rulers of the nation—to do exactly what the bodhisattva vowed to do, but to be diligent day and night in governing the nation is just as significant as the bodhisattva's act of vowing to accept the sufferings of all creatures or as benevolent as the way of the ancient Chinese sage kings. Even if a ruler should build a temple and give a feast to the monks, if they should be motivated from impure desire and involve hardships of the populace, such acts might bring worldly fame but would not become the good seed for enlightenment. It is well to remember that a poor woman's offering of a single lantern is more meritorious than a millionaire's offering of one thousand lanterns. As to the priests, their desire to spread their own sect is understandable. But, should they persuade the ignorant men and women and develop partisanship, perform sorcery, and disturb the daily activities of the people, they should be considered devils in the eyes of the Law of the Buddha and enemies to the law of the sovereign, and thus should be reprimanded strictly according to the rule [of the shōgun]. One should never forget that the prosperity of various Buddhist sects today owes much to the hidden virtues of various prelates of old days, who considered it the blessing of Buddha as much as the sovereign to be permitted to renounce the world and enter the priesthood.

[Third] is the principle of integrity for the position of constable.[14] The position of constable was established [in 1185 by Minamoto Yoritomo, the founder of the Kamakura Shōgunate], as the military governor, which in effect was the deputy of the shōgunate in various provinces. From then till now there have been some constables who have abided by the law, never indulging in activities other than those which are their duties, loyal to their masters and benevolent to the people, and known for their integrity and virtues. Unfortunately, today it is a common practice for them to ignore the will of their superiors, fail to appreciate the wisdom of their subordinates, steal other people's territories by force, and accumulate wealth according to their selfish desires. In so doing, they invite the criticism and enmity of others. One can understand the constables' desire to have a large number of retainers, but they often pay inordinate amounts to persons [who in turn have no sense of integrity]. Such retainers stick to their master only so long as it is profitable for them to do so, but desert their master when he really needs them. Every person would like to have both fame and profit, but be it remembered that profit lasts only for a short period of time while fame is a matter to be counted for generations to come. A real warrior is willing to die to preserve his fame, whereas one who risks a bad name would consider riches more precious than his own life. We learn from the priest Jichin[15] that everything we do must be based on reasonableness.[16] Being ordinary mortals everyone fails to follow reasonableness at one time or another, but those who refuse to correct their mistakes and shortcomings are doomed to invite great misfortune for themselves.

[Fourth] is the principle of selecting just persons for the position of the magistrate.

[Fifth] is the principle of selecting the right personal attendants with such qualities as honesty, loyalty, selfishness, courage, learning, and willingness to risk their lives to remonstrate with their master over his mistakes.

[Last] is the principle of dignity and power needed for the ruler of the nation. [That is to say, a person with real dignity and power is sensitive to reasonableness and does not demonstrate his influence by force.] His influence should be felt naturally by people around him and eventually spread to distant places. A ruler with dignity and power should not neglect small things, otherwise he would not accomplish great things. Above all, he should follow the way of humaneness. (*Shinkō gunsho ruijū* [Classified collection of Japanese classics, newly edited edition], 21:36–45).

B. SELECTIONS FROM THE COLLECTION OF LETTERS BY KUMAZAWA BANZAN (1619–1691)[17]

Question: I think you are right in stating that it is senseless to criticize Buddhism, and that one should rather endeavor to [cultivate] one's own virtues. [If we should follow your principle,] there may not be any rivalry, but might it not result in the danger [or crime] of asserting the fundamental unity of the three teachings (Confucianism, Buddhism, and Shintō)?

Answer: I do not understand how one can talk falsely about the unity when there is no unity [among the three teachings]. Besides, unity is usually followed by disunity. Even within Buddhism there are quarrels based on different views. [On the other hand,] if each other's differences are kept so as to avoid quarrels, there will be no problem. [After all,] Buddhists are children of Heaven and Earth. We [Confucianists] are also children of Heaven and Earth. All persons are in this sense brothers, only divided according to their views and professions. If one stresses the view of Confucianism, the other would stress the view of Buddhism, and there will be debates [as to which one is right and which one is wrong]. However, if our association is based solely on our [basic] brotherly [love], there will be no room for quarrels. (*Shūgi washo* [Collected essays on private matters], ch. 1, §18)

Question: I understand that worship is to be performed by persons of appropriate status, [so that in China] the Son of Heaven offers worship to heaven and earth, the three lights (sun, moon, and stars), and famous mountains and great rivers of the empire, the feudal lords offer worship to famous mountains and great rivers of the state, and the descendants of the sages and worthies are entrusted with the worship of their ancestors. In other words, there are ranks of high officials, knights, and common people. Why, then, in Japan do people regardless of their differences in status and sex pay homage to the Sun Goddess, who should properly be worshiped only by the emperor and not even by the feudal lords. I fail to understand how people, noble [and humble] as well as old [and young], follow such improper practices.

Answer: As you rightly point out, in China only those who have acquired propriety offer worship; otherwise, worship might be polluted by selfish desires and also by evil magic. Furthermore, it is believed that it is senseless for people to offer prayers if they had sinned against Heaven.[18] Thus, the Chinese hold that one has to be emancipated from the illusion of serving parents [merely as human parents] and that one should consider parents as nothing but noble deities. It follows, then, that men being the children of the deities house the deities in their own bodies, and that they share the same spirit with heavenly deities. And, inasmuch as the virtues of heavenly deities are humanity, righteousness, propriety, and wisdom, they are expected to serve heaven with propriety in order to receive blessings. If they act against the way of heaven, they will have misfortunes.

Japan, on the other hand, is the nation of the kami. While ancient Japan might have not attained propriety, it was permeated by the influence and virtues of the kami, so that people did not do evil deeds because they felt as if the kami were present [in this world]. When they paid homage to the kami, their selfish desires disappeared [and they became free from] evil magic. In so doing, they acted according to the way of Heaven, being filial to parents and loyal to the lords. However, the difference between China and Japan is based on the differences of time and place. For example, nowadays the sovereign [cannot be approached directly by the lowly populace]. But Emperor Yao[19] provided a drum [in front of the palace] and declared that if farmers, artisans, or merchants wished to speak directly to him they should strike the drum and the emperor would come out to listen to them. Thus, people were made to feel as if they were speaking to their own parents. In the days when the Sun Goddess ruled, she being full of divine virtues treated the nation as her child, and like Yao and Shun she was close to the lowly populace. It is due to her legacy, which was intended to remain as an example to later generations, that her palace with thatched roof has been preserved [at the Grand Shrine of Ise]. Moreover, now that she has moved up to the divine status, [she is free to live among common people], so that anybody can approach her. In other words, the Sun Goddess, not only during the time of her direct reign but also [until ten thousand ages to come] continues to dispense bright virtues as the sun and moon illuminate the world. When one pays homage to her, or even when one recalls her like a saintly teacher, one receives divine assistance abundantly. (*Shūgi washo*, vol. 2, §38)

Question: According to an old saying, the law of the sovereign and the Law of the Buddha resemble the two wheels of the same chariot. If this were so, was Japan before the introduction of the Law of the Buddha like a one-wheeled chariot, only with the law of the sovereign?

Answer: What was known as the way of the kami during the divine age and what is called the way of the true king are one and the same in substance. Now, as to the analogy of the two wheels, it referred to the civil (literary) and military (defense) arts of the great way which is the principle of ruling the world. Before the wheel of the Law of the Buddha existed, in the age of the heavenly and earthly kami and in the age of the early human sovereigns, the great way was followed whereby people were blessed with good rule. After the expansion of the Law of the Buddha, the sovereign neglected the wheel of the military arts in favor of Buddhism, so that the way of the true king declined because of the loss of the virtues of wisdom, humaneness, and courage. And, since there cannot be true civil arts without the military arts, the imperial house lost the rule of the nation. Then, the military families, [which took over the rule of the nation,] neglected the wheel of the civil arts in favor of Buddhism. But, since the military without the civil arts is the way of a barbarian and not of the superior man, the rule by the military families was bound to be defective. Some say that the Law of Buddha, being the way of ascetics, transcends others. If it were so, it should stay above Shintō, the way of the kami, and [Confucianism], the way of man, instead of posing itself as one of the two wheels, [the other being either Shintō or Confucianism]. (*Shūgi gaisho* [Collected essays on public matters], ch. 1)

Question: I fail to understand why the Grand Shrine of Ise despises Buddhism and does not allow Buddhist monks to enter its sacred compound. The Sun Goddess, being the kami long before the establishment of Buddhism, had no reason to despise it.

Answer: You must be aware of the fact that the imperial court is called the "forbidden territory," which implies a place where persons of [questionable character] are not allowed to enter. The Grand Shrine of Ise, [being more strict than the imperial court,] should not allow not only Buddhist priests but all persons of [questionable character], as it was the case with the imperial court. Later, when some of the emperors became enamored with Buddhism, Buddhist clerics were allowed to enter the imperial court. However, the old rule has been preserved at Ise until the present time. In this connection, I might mention that according to the divine oracle given to Princess Yamato, the Sun Goddess made it very clear that she rejected Buddhism on the ground that it would harm the way of the kami and ruin the way of the true king. Upon learning his account, any one born in Japan, even if he happens to be lured into Buddhism through temporary delusion, ought to repent. On the other hand, we must recognize the fact that many persons have gone into the Buddhist priesthood for economic reasons. Thus, unless the great way is put into effect and rectifies [the present lamentable situation], even [those Buddhist priests] who are inwardly unhappy cannot do anything else. (*Ibid.*, ch. 2)

C. SUMMARY OF THE *TAMAKUSHIGE* (JEWELED COMB BOX) BY MOTOORI NORINAGA

□ Motoori, undoubtedly the greatest theoretician in the history of Shintō, devoted his life to the philological and theological study of the *Kojiki* (The records of ancient matters). In his view, the tradition of the divine age provided the best and universal principle for the human race, and he attempted to show the pristine quality of Shintō by rejecting the Buddhist and Chinese influences upon it. However, his attitude toward other religions was amazingly conciliatory in comparison with the attitude of Hirata Atsutane, who followed him.[20] □

In this world there is only one true way [for man to live], and as such it knows, in principle, no national boundaries. In reality, however, this true way has been correctly transmitted only in Japan whereas it has been lost since ancient times in foreign countries. To be sure, in other countries various ways have been advocated, each claiming to be the true way. But these are branch ways, so to speak, and not the main correct way. Such branch ways may here and there resemble the true way, [but they cannot be confused with the true way].

In order to consider the one true way, we must first understand the [underlying] principle of the total structure of this world. That is to say, everything in this cosmos as well as all the deities were produced by the creative spirit of the two kami, namely, the Kami of High Generative Force and the Kami of Divine Generative Force.[21] Without such divine creative spirit the development of the human race and the growth of other creatures would not have been possible. Needless to say, it was due to this divine creative spirit that Izanagi and Izanami were able to produce lands, animate, and inanimate beings and kami at the beginning of the divine age.[22] The operation of the creative spirit is so mysterious that it is beyond human comprehension. But, because the correct truth has not been transmitted there, people in some foreign countries have attempted to explain the principles of heaven and earth and myriad other things in terms of yin (negative cosmic force) and yang (positive cosmic force), the Eight Trigrams, and the Five Elements.[23] But such explanations are false views based on speculations of human knowledge, and as such are contrary to the correct principle. (*Motoori Norinaga zenshū* [Complete works of Motoori Norinaga], 546–47)

It is to be recalled that when Izanami died, Izanagi, greatly grieved, followed her to the nether world. And as he returned to this world, Izanagi cleansed himself. In order to purge himself of the defilements of the nether world. While he was thus purifying himself, the Sun Goddess was born, and it was by her father's divine order that she was made to rule permanently the Plain of High Heaven. The Sun Goddess is no other than the sun of heaven itself which illuminates the world now. Then, the Sun Goddess sent her grandson (Ninigi) to rule Japan with the divine commission that the throne which his descendants would occupy would prosper forever. This divine commission is the basic foundation of all the principles of this world. Therefore, those who are interested in the true way must first inquire what had taken place during the divine age, and then they would understand the principles [of the world]. It is to be noted that what took place during the divine age is found in ancient legends, which were not told by any one person but have been transmitted orally [from the divine age] and were subsequently recorded in the *Kojiki* and the *Nihongi* (The chronicles of Japan). While the accounts of these two books are so clear that there can be no room for doubt, many interpreters of these divine scriptures in later generations advanced false interpretations, presumably based on mysterious oral transmission [outside the scriptures]. Or, some scholars [of our country] have been influenced only by the foreign logic and failed to believe in the [sacred events] of the divine age. Some of them, not realizing that all the principles of the world had been already provided in the events of the divine age, cannot understand the legitimacy of the ancient legends of our country. Because of their sole dependence on the theories of foreign countries, they interpret falsely whatever does not agree with the views of foreign countries. Some of them would go so far as to say that the Plain of High Heaven refers to the capital on earth and has nothing to do with heaven, and that [the Sun Goddess], being the great ancestress of our imperial dynasty, was nothing but a sacred person living in this nation and thus is not the sun in heaven.

These interpretations are erroneous theories, derived from private opinions of some scholars who distorted and belittled the ancient legends of Japan in order to harmonize them by coercion to foreign logic. In so doing they lost the great fundamentals, and their views are contrary to the meaning of the divine scriptures. (*Ibid.*, 4:547–48)

We must bear in mind that there is no line which divides heaven and earth, and that the Plain of High Heaven is situated above all countries. And, since the Sun Goddess rules heaven and illuminates every corner of heaven and earth, thus without her blessing no country on earth can exist even for a single day or single hour. In short, she is the most precious kami in this world. Unfortunately, foreign countries, which have lost the ancient accounts of the divine age, have no way of knowing that the Sun Goddess is to be venerated, and they reduce, based on the speculation of human knowledge, the movements of sun and moon to the activities of yin and yang. In China, the Heavenly Deity is regarded as the most precious, supreme being, whereas in other countries some other deities are venerated. But such deities were concocted by mere speculations and given certain names, but what is known as the Heavenly Deity or the Way of Heaven has no reality. It is lamentable that foreign countries venerate such beings who are unreal, not knowing of the Sun Goddess, while we must be grateful to know the legacy of the Sun Goddess, thanks to the ancient legends of the divine age which have been correctly transmitted. Indeed, our country, being literally the homeland where the Sun Goddess was born, is destined to be the great center of all other nations. It is impossible to cite all the reasons why our nation is superior to foreign countries. However, we must first point out the unrivalled quality of rice crops, which are most important for the preservation of human life, produced in our country. This being the case, you might infer other reasons [for the supremacy of Japan]. Unfortunately, however, those who were born in this country have come to take it for granted, and fail to think of the blessing of imperial kami when they eat rice every morning and every evening. (*Ibid.*, 4:548–49)

More important is the heritage of the imperial family, which being the descendants of the Sun Goddess, is destined to survive undisrupted for generations until the end of the world as proclaimed in the divine commission [given by the Sun Goddess]. The fact that the divine commission [has been fulfilled in actuality] makes it evident that the ancient legends of the divine age are not false. Other countries may boast their own ways as though they alone were noble countries, but the fact that their respective imperial dynasties, which are the foundations of nations, have been broken frequently indicates clearly that their claims are not based on the truth. Yet, other countries consider Japan solely as a small island nation beyond the ocean and never seem to realize that the real true way has been preserved there. More tragic are those [Japanese scholars] who have been enamored with the deceptive theories of foreign countries, so that they too regard Japan only as a small nation, never dreaming that the true way has been transmitted in such a small nation. In reality, the value of anything cannot be judged by its size. For example, our country, though small in size, has a higher density than other countries, and judging by the numerical strength of people our country may be regarded as a large country, unequaled in its richness and bravery. (*Ibid.*, 4:549–50)

It goes without saying that every event in this world is willed by the kami. There are various kinds of kami, noble and humble, good and evil, and just and unjust. Among the events there are some which may be regarded as unreasonable or unjust; these are operated by evil kami, such as the events which cause troubles to the nation and harm to the people. The evil kami is the one who came out of the nether world with the great kami Izanagi when he [returned from there and] purified himself. Although the heavenly kami attempt to overcome the power of the evil kami, they cannot always restrain him.[24] There are certain reasons, established already during the divine age, why evil is mingled with good, as recorded in the *Kojiki* and *Nihongi*. I have elaborated on this point in my *Commentary on the Kojiki*.[25] (*Ibid.*, 4:552)

As to the nether world, I might mention one or two things such as that it is situated at the bottom of the earth, and that it is an unclean and undesirable place, to which all the dead are destined to go. Everyone in this world, both noble and humble, and good and bad, must go to the nether world when they die. This is a sad fact and is seemingly unreasonable. But, inasmuch as it has been preordained for mysterious reasons, according to the true legend of the divine age, we should not speculate on it with our limited human knowledge. We should accept the fact that when one dies, he has to part with his wife and children, wealth, and everything else which is dear to him, and once he goes to the unclean nether world he will never be able to return. This being the case, there is nothing sadder than death in this world. And yet, there are various teachings in the foreign countries which advocate that death is not lamentable and that there are various kinds of future life depending on one's goodness or badness or degrees of spiritual discipline while on earth. Under the influence of such [foreign] teachings, there are some people who pretend not to be sad when death occurs or those who write certain poems or passages to the effect that they have attained enlightenment before death. These teachings, however, are deceitful fabrications, contrary to the human sentiment and the true principle. Because death is a sad affair, even the great kami Izanagi cried like a child when his spouse passed away, and he followed her even to the nether world. This is an honest human sentiment, and everyone must feel that way. Our ancestors, before they came under the influence of foreign ideas, accepted the simple truth that all the dead are destined to go to the nether world, so that there was nothing else for them to do except to cry and mourn. Unfortunately, foreigners, not knowing that evil is caused by evil kami, attempted to find a rational explanation for seemingly unreasonable phases of life and invented such theories as the moral law of cause and effect[26] or destiny which has been preordained by Heaven.[27] (*Ibid.*, 4:552–54)

As stated previously, events of this world are caused alternately by good kami and evil kami. Thus, historically, there were periods in Japan when the power of the imperial family, who are direct descendants of the Sun Goddess, was usurped by such families as the Hōjō[28] and the Ashikaga.[29] Yet, in accordance with the divine commission, evil could not overcome good in the end, whereby the families of the traitors declined and the imperial family has remained unshaken. Nevertheless, before the decline of the Ashikaga feudal regime the social and political disintegration reached its lowest point. Only when the two generals, Oda Nobunaga[30] and Toyotomi Hideyoshi,[31] restored the dignity of the imperial court by subduing insurrectionists did the nation regain peaceful order. Moreover, credit goes to Azumateru Kamumioya no Mikoto[32] who, on the one hand, restored the rightful place of the imperial court from decline and, on the other hand, extended benevolent rule to the warriors and other people, and thus established an unprecedented prosperous age which certainly should be approved by the Sun Goddess and is to be guarded by all the kami of heaven and earth. This statement is not made to flatter the present feudal regime but is based on careful reflection of the state of affairs of our time. It must be said in this connection that fuedal regimes, such as those of the Hōjō and the Ashikaga, despite their efforts to befriend themselves to the warriors and to show compassion to the people, neglected the respect for the imperial court. As such, their policies were contrary to the true way. In foreign countries, it has been their custom that those who are capable of pacifying the people were to assume the kingship. On the other hand, in Japan only the direct descendants of the Sun Goddess have been commissioned to rule the country. Therefore, those who rebel against the will of the Sun Goddess cannot possibly survive. Of course, there are some who, based on the principles and evil customs of foreign countries, try to justify the rule of the rebellious Hōjō, but we should not lose sight of the fundamentals of the true way of all times. (*Ibid.*, 4:544–55)

The question whether or not the nation is ruled peacefully depends on whether or not the man of inferior status respects and obeys the man of superior status. If a superior person respects his superiors, his subordinates will respect him, and in this manner the whole nation can be ruled in an orderly manner. Now the rule of the nation has been entrusted to the Tokugawa feudal regime from the time of [Tokugawa Iyeyasu (1542–1616), the founder of the regime] by the imperial court, and in turn various feudal lords have been assigned by the feudal regime to rule their respective fiefs. This means that the people have been entrusted to the feudal regime by the Sun Goddess and that the regulations established by the feudal regime are in effect the regulations of the Sun Goddess herself. Both the feudal lords and the lower functionaries must bear in mind that they participate in the rule of the Sun Goddess and that the people under their rule belong to the Sun Goddess. Also, they must remember that inasmuch as there are good and evil kami who operate, it is impossible for us to improve this world over night. In this respect, Confucianism, for example, attempts to accomplish something which is impossible, namely, to clean up every corner of the world so that only good things will remain. Nevertheless, even during the days of the sages it was not possible to wipe out all the evil. Even the wisdom of the most intelligent person is limited, and in the end we have to abide by the operation of the kami. Conversely, we cannot leave everything as it is without making any effort, for human beings must endeavor to do everything they can, realizing, however, that there are things which cannot be accomplished by their efforts alone. (*Ibid.*, 4:556–57)

Generally speaking, worship of the kami is important both for the welfare of the nation and of the people. Not only good kami should be invoked to ask for blessing, but also malevolent kami should be pacified in order to ward off troubles, according to the ancient way. As to the rule of the nation, in ancient times our sovereigns reigned according to the way of the kami,[33] which meant a faithful preservation of the will of the Sun Goddess. In the old days, if the will of the kami was not clear, the emperors inquired the will of the kami by means of divination instead of following what might be considered their own wise opinions; this was the correct manner of [ruling the nation] according to the true way. Since in those days the minds of the emperor's ministers and of lowly people were straight and correct, they all abided by the will of the sovereigns. They respected the imperial court and followed the imperial edicts without asserting their own opinions. Thus there was harmony between the superiors and the inferiors, and the whole nation was peacefully ruled. However, since the way of China was appropriated, the Chinese ideas and customs have been transplanted to Japan, whereby people have come to assert what they regarded as wise opinions. In so doing, inferiors no longer abide by the will of superiors, so that it has become difficult to rule the nation. (*Ibid.*, 4:558–59)

As far as the people's behavior is concerned, we must bear in mind that men were born with [the knowledge], provided by the creative spirit of the great kami of creation as to what human beings should do in life, such as to serve faithfully one's master, to be filial to one's parents, to venerate ancestors, to be benevolent to wives, children, and servants, to be true in one's association with one's fellow men, and to work hard in one's occupation. For these, which are essential for any human being to follow, people certainly do not need foreign teachings. (*Ibid.*, 4:559)

D. MAIN OUTLINES OF THE *ZOKU-SHINTŌ TAII* (A SUMMARY OF PSEUDO-SHINTŌ) BY HIRATA ATSUTANE

□ Hirata Atsutane, a physician turned a militant advocate of Shintō revival,[34] wrote this work in order to combat Confucianism and Buddhism and also to purify Shintō. The term, pseudo-Shintō (*zoku-Shintō*), is used to contrast with the "ancient way" (*kodō*), which to him was the pure Shintō. His objective was to restore the glory of the ancient pure Shintō, rejecting the Buddhist influence, as is evident in the Buddhist-Shintō amalgamation, and the Confucian element, as is evident in the Confucian-Shintō amalgamation. In this sense, Hirata was the most thoroughgoing champion of the "restoration Shintō" (*fukko Shintō*) movement, which exerted tremendous influence on the political scene in mid-nineteenth century, climaxed by the dissolution of the feudal regime and the restoration of imperial rule under Emperor Meiji (r. 1867–1912). □

In this world, there are often different expressions referring to the same thing, while, on the other hand, the same designations are often used to refer to different things. Among the examples of the same designation referring to different things, the most conspicuous is the case of Shintō which might be minutely divided into twelve or thirteen traditions. Even if we classify Shintō on the basis of major differences, there are at least five traditions, which must be kept in mind by those who aspire to the true study. (*Hirata Atsutane zenshū* [Complete works of Hirata Atsutane], vol. 1, "Zoku-Shintō taii" [Summary of Pseudo-Shintō], p. 2)

Firstly, as I stated in my work, *The Summary of the Ancient Way* (*Kodō taii*),[35] true Shintō follows the tradition initiated by the two creator kami, the Kami of High Generative Force and the Kami of Divine Generative Force, which was inherited by the two kami, Izanagi and Izanami, whose union begot everything in this world as well as all kami including the Sun Goddess. When Ninigi, the grandson of the Sun Goddess, descended from heaven, he received the commission from the Sun Goddess to the effect that her descendants were to rule the world from generation to generation. Accordingly, the successive sovereigns, following the divine commission without asserting their own ideas, have ruled the nation which is to last as long as heaven and earth exist. It is this tradition which has been called Shintō, as evidenced by the edict (647) of Emperor Kōtoku, stating, "Our nation has always been ruled according to the will of the Sun Goddess who entrusted it to her divine descendants." In this edict the expression, *kannagara*, is used, and this expression is interpreted in the *Chronicles of Japan* to mean "to follow the way of the kami," or again "to possess the way of the kami." This indeed expresses clearly the intent of the ancient way, which is what we call Shintō. It must be pointed out that the way of the kami does not imply anything unusual. It simply means that the sovereigns are to abide by the divine commission faithfully, and that we too, inasmuch as we originally came out of the creative spirit of the kami, are endowed with the way of the kami. It implies therefore that we have the innate capacity to venerate the kami, the sovereign, and our parents, to show benevolence to our wives and children, and to carry out other obligations which are taught by Confucian scholars. To live according to these [kami-given virtues] without distorting them is nothing but to follow the way of the kami. Thus, the sovereign is to rule the nation, following this way, while it is the duty of all subjects to abide by the will of the sovereign. In this respect, no one, here including the scholars of Confucianism and Buddhist priests, can be exempted from the way of the kami. Those who are not satisfied with it had better not live in this country. (*Ibid.*, pp. 2–3)

[The second usage of the term,] *Shintō*, is mentioned in the *Chronicles of Japan* in describing Emperor Yōmei (r. 586–587) as having "believed in the Law of the Buddha and venerated the Way of the Kami." The [second] meaning of this term is the broad designation of the cultic activities regarding the kami, such as worship, prayer, and the rite of purification, which to be sure are ultimately rooted in Shintō, but this is greatly different from the first meaning of the term, namely, *kannagara*, just as the branches and leaves are different from their main trunk. The second meaning of the term, Shintō, is often confused with the first, even by many so-called Shintōists of later generations simply because [the *Chronicles of Japan*] mentioned this term side by side with the Law of the Buddha.

Thus, those who call themselves scholars of Shintō today, not knowing what the true Shintō is, equate Shintō only with such things as the rite of purification and prayer. (*Ibid.*, p. 3)

The third meaning of the term, *Shintō*, is found in [one of the Chinese classics] which uses it to refer to the way of heaven such as the principles of the four seasons and the growth of plants. In this sense, the Chinese character, *shen* (*shin* or *kami* in Japanese),[36] does not mean anything so specific as a kami who has real substance. It must be kept in mind that when the Chinese characters were introduced to Japan, many ancient Japanese concepts were matched to the written characters, some of which were appropriate whereas others were not. In the case of the kami of our nation for which the character *shen* was used, it was half correct and half wrong. In reality, the Chinese used the expression, *shen*, to refer to the mysterious way of heaven and nature. However, nowadays the ancient matters are interpreted through the literal meaning of the written characters, which is a great mistake and causes confusing ideas. For example, Dazai Yayemon[37] wrote that Shintō originally existed in the way of Chinese sages because the expression, the way of *shen*, was first used in [one of the Chinese classics]. For the most part, Japanese] Confucian scholars are very foolish. Particularly, this man Dazai has a twisted mind and is determined to slander our nation and thus advanced such a false theory. (*Ibid.*, pp. 3–5)

The fourth and fifth meanings of the term, *Shintō*, are used by "Dual or Two-sided Shintō" (Ryōbu Shintō) [which is the Buddhist dominated system of Buddhist-Shintō amalgamation], and the "Unique Shintō" (*Yuiitsu Shintō*) [which advocates the unity of Shintō, Buddhism, and Confucianism, even though it considers Shintō as basic], respectively.[38] The notion of *ryōbu* was never meant to refer to Shintō and Buddhism. It refers to the two realms of the universe, called the "Realm of Diamond Element" and the "Realm of Matrix Repository,"[39] in the Shingon Buddhism systematized by Kūkai (774–835). But the tradition of Dual Shintō modified this notion of the two realms and concocted the system of Buddhist-Shintō amalgamation by deceiving people with the theory that the kami are the manifestations of the Buddha [in Japan] and that the Buddha is the original nature of the kami. Dual Shintō claims to have synthesized all the good elements, and discarded the undesirable elements, of Shintō, Buddhism, and Confucianism. But [Motoori Norinaga] refuted this claim in his work, *The Jeweled Bamboo Basket* (*Tama katsuma*), and stated that Dual Shintō is predominantly Buddhist with certain features of Confucianism, but that it has not appropriated the intent of the way of the kami, and only mentions certain names of the kami. It is neither Buddhism nor Confucianism; it goes without saying that it is not the way of the kami. (*Ibid.*, pp. 5–6)

E. MAIN OUTLINES OF THE DOCTRINE OF TENRI-KYŌ[40]

□ Tenri-kyō (Religion of Divine Reason) was founded by a peasant woman, Nakayama Miki (1798–1887), in Nara Prefecture. Brought up as a devotee of the Buddha Amida, she married and lived as an ordinary housewife. When she was forty-one, she was possessed by the Divine Reason Kami. Miki's utopian teachings, based on oracles, shamanistic practices, and ecstatic dances attracted many followers. At first recognized as a branch of Shintō, this group changed its affiliation to Buddhism in 1880; finally, in 1908, Tenri-kyō was recognized as one of the thirteen "Sect Shintō" denominations, and appropriated Shintō elements into its rites and doctrines. Ironically, the cosmogonic myth of Tenri-kyō, contained in a sacred document entitled the *Doroumi koki* (Ancient accounts of the muddy ocean), does not agree with the official Shintō cosmogony. For this reason, this document was eliminated from the doctrinal system of Tenri-kyō in 1938 under pressure from nationalist groups. It was restored, however, after the end of World War II. The following are excerpts from the official doctrine of Tenri-kyō.[41] □

1. The Revelation of the Kami[42]

I, the foremost and true kami, have descended at this time from heaven to this house [of the Nakayama family] in order to save everyone of the world, and intend to dwell in the person of Miki as my living shrine. (*Tenri-kyō kyōten* [Doctrinal manual of Tenri-kyō], p. 3)

This world being based on reason, I am going to express my will through poetry. Since what I have spoken in the past might be forgotten, I have decided to reveal [my will] in the *Tip of the Writing Brush.*[43] (*Ibid.*, pp. 6–7)

Using the analogy of the road, I might say that beyond the mountain paths and thorny lanes along the cliff there is a narrow way. (*Ibid.*, p. 8)

In order to receive my assistance, you should not approach me with magical incantations and prayers, although it is permissible for you to inquire about my will. (*Ibid.*, p. 10)

My wish is like the concern of parents who try to help their children everyday. (*Ibid.*, p 12)

2. Salvation

I am going to perform something which is just as marvelous as the creation of the world by me. What I am going to initiate is a brand new type of a religious service. Should you wish to engage in a religious service, choose the service at the "sweet dew stand" [the central altar of Tenri-kyō]. I have placed the "sweet dew stand" [at the *jiba*, literally a "spot on earth," in Tenri City, Nara Prefecture] to indicate that I created human beings there. (*Ibid.*, pp. 16–17)

As for me, I can hardly wait for the next performance of "joyous service" [conducted around the "sweet dew stand"] which is nothing other than the service of sacred dance. (*Ibid.*, p. 18)

Performing this service is the way for mankind to be saved, whereby even the mute will begin to speak. Indeed, by diligently offering this service each day, you will avoid every kind of trouble. In fact, even the most serious sickness will be cured by performing the service diligently. (*Ibid.*, pp. 19–20)

Salvation, which to be sure depends on the sincerity of your heart, will not only enable you to prevent sickness but also death and decay. Indeed, if everyone united in mind should perform this service, all the problems of the world will be solved. Even the gravest sickness will be eliminated by the rhythmic breathing and hand gestures [of the sacred dance]. (*Ibid.*, pp. 20–22)

3. Cosmogony

In the beginning of the world there was only an ocean of muddy waters. The divine parents, known then as the Moon-Sun, bored with the state of chaos, decided to create man in order to enjoy himself by looking at man's joyous life. He found in the muddy water a merman and snake mixed with a bunch of loaches, and brought them home by promising them that they would be venerated as kami. He then brought a dolphin and a sea-tiger in order to make them as the materials for the male and female elements, and inserted them into the merman and the snake, respectively, which he intended to use as the prototypes of man and woman. The seed of the man's prototype was given the sacred name of Kami-who-invites (Izanagi), while the seed-plot or potentiality of the prototype of woman was given the name of Kami-who-is-invited (Izanami). Besides, the principles of the functions of human bodies were given such names as Moon Kami and Kami of the Nation's Spirit. Next he called the eel, flat-fish, black snake, and globe-fish, and ate them in order to test their mental flavor, according to which these creatures were used for appropriate instruments of creation, such as the eel for ingressing and egressing, and the flat-fish for breathing and speaking.

The divine parent then ate all the loaches and decided to use them as the material for human beings. Now, the moon element of the divine parent entered the body of Izanagi, while the sun element entered the body of Izanami, both teaching them the art of human procreation. Meanwhile, 999,999 seeds were inserted into the womb of Izanami during the period of three days and three nights, Izanami remained where she was for three years and three months, and it took seventy-five days for her to give birth to all these children.

The first group of offspring were all half an inch long at their birth, but grew half an inch at a time. After ninety-nine years they became about three inches long, and then all of them, as well as their father Izanagi, died. Then, Izanami, following the art of procreation which had been given her before, conceived the same number of seeds and delivered them after ten months. The offspring were again born half an inch long but grew to the height of three inches and a half after ninety-nine years, and then died. In her third attempt, the offspring were born half an inch long but grew to the height of four inches. Looking at them, Izanami smiled and said that they would eventually grow into human beings of five feet. She then died, and her offspring without exception followed her footsteps.

Subsequently, human beings went through 8,008 stages of rebirth, including those of the worm, birds, and animals, and eventually died out, leaving only one female monkey behind. From her womb, five men and five women were born. They were half an inch long at the time of birth but grew first to the height of eight inches and later to one foot and eight inches. About that time, by the operation of the divine parent, the muddy ocean began to be solidified, whereby ocean and mountains, heaven and earth, and sun and moon became differentiated. Meanwhile, many pairs of twins, each with male and female children, were born, and grew to the height of three feet. By that time, it became normal for one child at a time to be born from a mother's womb, and they also learned the art of speaking. When human beings reached the average height of five feet, they began to live on the ground.

[In retrospect, according to the scheme of the divine parent,] mankind lived the first period consisting of 990,000 years in water, and acquired intelligence during the second period consisting of 6,000 years. Finally, during the third period consisting of 3,999 years they learned the art of writing and reading letters. (*Ibid.*, pp. 25–29)

4. Some Characteristic Concepts

"*Divine guidance.*" Although [one and the same] divine parent is shared by all mankind, human beings, not knowing this truth, fail to understand that all others are equally brothers and sisters who are the children of the divine parent. Thus, motivated by the false notion that each one lives only for his own sake, they tend to live with self-centred thinking and selfish actions, which harm and cloud others' minds and disrupt the harmony of the world. Moreover, they are unaware that [such a way of living] harms and clouds their own minds. The divine parent, concerned with his children who go astray along the dangerous paths, pities them, and tries to teach them as to who is their true parent as well as the way of joyous life which he wishes them to lead. In order to correct the misguided notions of human beings. [the divine parent] shows concrete signs in their lives. Thus, every kind of sickness, misfortune, and complication [of human relations] is the expression of paternal concern [of the divine parent] whose compassionate divine guidance leads men to the true joyous life. (*Ibid.*, pp. 57–59)

"*Lending and borrowing things.*" Inasmuch as we borrowed our life from the divine parent, it is essential that we use it to follow his will. (*Ibid.*, p. 65) But, human beings, not realizing this principle, tend to think that they can do everything according to their selfish desire based on their limited human minds. Preoccupied by their own suffering, happiness, and profit, human beings often think contrary to the will of [the divine parent] who wishes the harmony and happiness of all mankind. The divine parent warns men against such selfish concern by using the analogy of dust [which can easily accumulate and clouds our minds]. (*Ibid.*, p. 67) He cautions us to reflect on the eight kinds of mental dust—vindictiveness, possessiveness, hatred, self-centeredness, enmity, anger, greed, and arrogance. (*Ibid.*, p. 68) The important thing is for all of us to realize that we have borrowed our life and that it is [the divine parent who had lent it to us], and do not neglect the daily dusting of our minds. (*Ibid.*, p. 62)

"*Daily offering of labor.*" When one realizes his indebtedness to his divine parent concerning whatever happens in daily life, his grateful joy is automatically expressed in his attitudes and actions, [more concretely] in daily offering of labor. (*Ibid.*, p. 76) It does not refer to any [particular] activity but to daily, continuous, and joyful activities. Such a joy cannot be kept to one's own self only but is bound to influence others. so that all like-minded people will join together and share their joyfulness. (*Ibid.*, p. 78)

"*Timber.*" One's joy of having received salvation leads him to engage in activities to help others. In so doing, he becomes the "timber" [i.e., instrument] of the divine parent's enterprise to bring joyful life [to mankind]. (*Ibid.*, p. 84) When the effort of the "timber" bears fruit, whereby the seekers of the way gradually gather together, [such a group thus formed] will be given the title of a church. The life of a church should deepen the joyous happiness of the people, by their mutual assistance, wherever they may be, and become a model for the joyous life which would foster the mental growth [of all human beings]. (*Ibid.*, pp. 90–91)

"*Joyous life.*" When one spends each day diligently helping others, his heart will be filled with bright joyfulness because he is warmly embraced by the divine parent and rests in the sense of peacefulness derived from the assurance that he is saved by the act of helping others. This is the state of joyous life. The divine parent, be it remembered, created human beings in order to enjoy happiness with them by watching their joyous life. The fulfillment of his divine wish is the meaning of life and the ultimate purpose of human existence.(*Ibid.*, p. 92)

NOTES

1. It was called the Ise Shintō, because its spokesmen were hereditary priests of the Watarai family who served at the Outer Shrine of Ise. They were instrumental in the compilation of the five-volume work, the *Shintō gobusho* (Shintō Pentateuch).
2. He was a leading royalist and the author of the *Jinnō shōtōki* (Record of the valid succession of divine sovereigns).
3. The Yoshida family belonged to the ancient Urabe (diviner) family and served as hereditary priests at the Yoshida and Hirano Shrines in Kyōto. Kanetomo's works reflect the strong influence of esoteric Buddhism. The full title of his school is Yuiitsu Sōgen (unique and fundamental) Shintō, but is also known as Yoshida Shintō and Urabe Shintō.
4. Saints who have postponed their Buddhahood to work for the salvation of others.
5. See Masaharu Anesaki, *History of Japanese Religion*, pp. 215–28, and George B. Sansom, *Japan: A Short Cultural History*, pp. 348–400.
6. He was venerated as a kami during his lifetime.
7. See Ryūsaku Tsunoda *et. al.*, *Sources of Japanese Tradition*, pp. 398–410.
8. For a general description of religious development during the Tokugawa period, see Joseph M. Kitagawa, *Religion in Japanese History*, pp. 131–76, and Robert N. Bellah, *Tokugawa Religion.*
9. See Kitagawa, *Religion in Japanese History*, pp. 177–261.
10. See *ibid.*, pp. 262–340.
11. Written in 1481. This work, together with another work entitled the *Bummei ittōki* (Unification of the nation during the Bummei period, 1469–1487) contains a series of advices addressed to the Ashikaga Shōgun, Yoshihisa. The present translation is abbreviated.
12. They founded the feudal regime in 1192 at Kamakura and ruled Japan for a period.
13. According to Ichijō Kanera, the eight sects are the Kegon, Sanron (which incorporated the Jōjitsu), Hossō (which incorporated the Kusha), Ritsu, Tendai, Shingon, Jōdo, and Zen.
14. *Shugo* in Japanese. George B. Sansom, in his *Japan: A Short Cultural History*, p. 278, translates the title of this office as "protector."
15. Jichin was the posthumous name given to the learned Tendai priest Jien (1145–1225) who

wrote a history of Japan from a Buddhist point of view. See Johannes Rahder, tr., "Miscellany of Personal Views of an Ignorant Fool (*Gukanshō*)," *Acta Orientalia*, 15 (1936), 173–230.

16. *Dōri* in Japanese. Joseph J. Spae in his *Itō Jinsai*, translates *dōri* as "*justice immanente des choses*."
17. Kumazawa Banzan was a disciple of Nakaye Tōju (1608–1648). Both belonged to the tradition of Wang Yang-ming (Ōyōmei in Japanese, 1472–1529), one of the three main branches of Japanese Confucianism. Kumazama, like Hayashi Razan (1583–1657) and Yamazaki Ansai of the tradition of Chu Hsi and Yamago Sokō of the tradition of Classical Learning (*ko-gaku*), stressed the close affinity between Confucianism and Shintō. He wrote many learned treatises on this subject as well as two sets of collections of letters entitled *Shūgi washo* (Collected essays on private matters) and *Shūgi gaisho* (Collected essays on public matters). The following translation is abbreviated.
18. Confucian *Analects*, 3:13.
19. Legendary emperor of the third millennium B.C. who transmitted his throne to Shun.
20. For Motoori's thought, see Tsunetsugu Muraoka, *Studies in Shintō Thought*, tr. by Delmer M. Brown and James T. Araki.
21. Both are important kami in the Japanese mythology. See ch. 20, A.
22. It might be translated as the age of the kami.
23. For these concepts, see Wing-tsit Chan, *A Source Book in Chinese Philosophy*, pp. 242–50, 262. The Eight Trigrams are those representing Heaven, Earth, Thunder, Wind, Water, Fire, Mountain, and Collection of Water. The Five Elements are Water, Fire, Wood, Metal, and Earth.
24. This is a characteristic Shintō view of evil. See Tsunetsugu Muraoka, *Studies in Shintō Thought*, pp. 30–32. For accounts of the *Kojiki* and the *Nihongi*, see ch. 20.
25. The *Kojiki den* (Commentary on the *Kojiki*) is still considered the most authoritative interpretation of Shintō orthodoxy.
26. I.e., karma, one of the central Buddhist theories.
27. Referring to a theory of Confucianism.
28. The *de facto* ruler during the Kamakura period (1192–1333).
29. The shōgun's family during the Muromachi (or Ashikaga) period.
30. See Ryūsaku Tsunoda *et al.*, *Sources of Japanese Tradition*, pp. 311–21.
31. See *ibid.*, pp. 321–30. For accounts in the *Kojiki* and *Nihongi*, see ch. 20.
32. This is a divine name of Tokugawa Iyeyasu, founder of the Tokugawa regime.
33. The expression mentioned in the *Chronicles of Japan*, referring to Shintō.
34. According to Masaharu Anesaki, *History of Japanese Religion*, p. 308, Hirata was a "man of great ability but a bigot of a doubtful character."
35. Portions of this work, as well as other works by him, are included in Ryūsaku Tsunoda *et al.*, *Sources of Japanese Tradition*, pp. 542–51.
36. See Wing-tsit Chan, *A Source Book in Chinese Philosophy*, pp. 789–90.
37. Also known as Shundai (1680–1747). In his *Bendō sho* (Definition of the Way).
38. Although Hirata attacks mainly the Ryōbu Shintō in this work, the same argument is implicitly applied to his evaluation of the movement to unite Shintō and Confucianism and the movement to unite Shintō, Buddhism, and Confucianism.
39. For an explanation of the "Realm of Diamond Element" and the "Realm of Matrix Repository," see Junjirō Takakusu, *The Essentials of Buddhist Philosophy*, pp. 150–51.
40. For the sociopolitical background of Tenri-kyō, see Hideo Kishimoto, com., *Japanese Religion in the Meiji Era*, tr. and adapted by John F. Howes, pp. 327–34. For the overall description of this religion, see H. van Straelen, *The Religion of Divine Wisdom*.
41. My abbreviated translation of the passages from the *Tenri-kyō kyōten* differs from the official translation of this work, entitled *The Doctrine of Tenrikyō*, 2nd edition.
42. His official name is Tenri-ō no Mikoto (Kami of Divine Reason), but is affectionately referred to as Oyasama (beloved parent), which is also used as the designation of the foundress.
43. *Ofudesaki* in Japanese, one of the sacred writings of Tenri-kyō.

PART FOUR

Islām

Isma'īl Rāgī al Fārūqī

Introduction

Islām is the youngest of the world religions. It is the only religion that related itself specifically to two other world religions, namely, Judaism and Christianity, and generally to all other religions of man. It is the only religion that contended and fought with most of the world religions on their own homeground, whether in the field of ideas or on the battlefields of history. Islām has been engaged in these wars —whether spiritual or political—even before it was born, before it became autonomous at home, even before it had completed its own system of ideas. And it is still vigorously fighting on all fronts. Moreover, Islām is the only religion that in its interreligious and international conflict with Judaism, Christianity, Hinduism, and Buddhism, succeeded significantly and in major scale in all the fights it undertook. Equally, it was the only religion that marshaled all its spiritual efforts to fight Western colonialism and imperialism throughout the world when its territory— indeed, its very heartland—was fragmented and practically all its adherents subjected to the colonialist yoke. Finally and yet more significantly, Islām is still winning today and growing by means of mission and conversion at a greater rate than any other religion. No wonder, then, that it is the religion with the greatest number of enemies and, hence, the religion most misunderstood.[1] For the fourteen centuries of its existence, non-Muslims have in the main studied it only to combat it. Where such ulterior motive was absent, Western study of Islām has been "scientific" and "empirical" to the point of missing the meanings of piety, ethicality, and sense of beauty that constitute the core of Islāmic religiosity. The unprejudiced study of the history of religious discipline, which normally aims at understanding this religiosity in its moments of action and expression, of growth and consummation, was never aimed at it. Not only have the historians of religions not been interested in such pursuit, but their discipline has as yet not developed the methodological tools requisite to the undertaking. The suspension of the scholar's religious and cultural categories, the more to lay all his facilities open to the determination by the religious data under examination,[2] which is the distinctive break-through of the phenomenological school of comparative study, cannot yet be said to have governed any works of lasting significance in the Islāmics field, though one must gladly admit, that the demand itself has in the West recently had eloquent spokesmen.[3]

WHAT IS THE ESSENCE OF THIS RELIGION?

First, Islām is rationalistic. Its very word for faith, namely, *īmān*, is contrasted severely with that state wherein man "submits," or "surrenders to," "accepts without question," or "believes without rational conviction," items of pseudo-knowledge on the basis of authority. In Islām, the highest state of religious certainty —*īmān*—is not merely the act of believing, an "act of faith," but a state in which religious knowledge produces an intuition of its certainty as a result of the consideration and weighing of all possible alternatives. Here, the subject is wholly determined by the data and his "will to believe" is nil. Nothing is allowed that overpowers his intellect, that demands its "yea" or "nay" before analysis and the most searching scrutiny of which that intellect is capable. "No coercion in religion," the Qur'ān (Koran) asserts, ruling out all forms of coercion, physical as well as mental, and explains, "Truth is now manifest and is clearly distinguishable from falsehood."[4] This rationalization has been institutionalized by Islām negatively, by its demanded absence of priesthood and of a church magistery. For though every Muslim is dutybound to teach every other Muslim and non-Muslim in the world and make known to him all the fruits of his research and endeavor, no Muslim is ever required to accept anything as true because some other Muslim or group of Muslims have found it so. Islām does not require him to believe except that which he himself, if capable of undertaking a fresh examination of it, will find convincing and worthy of acceptance, as rational, coherent, and corresponding to reality. The Muslim's own mind is his last and only resort in religious matters. Certainly Islām has its teachers and traditions which Muslims venerate; but none of these carry any authority which, in the eye of Islām, stands to any of its stages beyond question. Scripture itself, as well as the example of the Prophet, are not authoritative unless the subject has himself found them so on their own intrinsic merits. Any Muslim doing otherwise would have achieved *islām* but not *īmān*, whereas Islāmic excellence consists in an *islām* resulting from and following upon *īmān*. In the former case, *islām* is intellectually passive; in the latter, it is an active search for ways and means of actualizing the truths grasped in *īmān*.

The modern reader is tempted to observe that under the claim to rational, critical truth made by Islām the thesis of God's existence is untenable and thus the whole edifice of ideas would tumble down. This fear is misplaced. The Qur'ān has used rational arguments for the existence of God and His unity, which man found rationally convincing. If these arguments are said not to hold their philosophic ground today—which is by no means certain—the assumption on the basis of which they were made, namely, the finality of reason and the Islāmic call to rationality are not affected. Man is still obliged to consider the claim and bring all the light possible to this fundamental issue. The Muslim is not convinced of the counterclaim, made by some schools of modern thought, that a transcendent reality standing as a kind of entelechy to the cosmos does not or cannot exist. On the other hand, the establishment for thought of such a being and the elaboration of its relation to the cosmos, he regards as a permanent need of the human intellect, a need which Islām recognizes and whose satisfaction in every case and age it declares imperative.

Furthermore, Islām puts its trust in reason, the supreme faculty of knowledge with which man is endowed, as the only method possible for ever deciding the issue. The alternative to reason is irrationalism; and this, whatever its form—authority, gnosticism, esotericism, mysticism, surrealism—does not decide the issue at all because it either imposes its view imperiously without rational grounds or admits the contradictory theses without recognizing the need for solution. Once reason is admitted as judge, the Muslim is encouraged to appropriate the truths of his religion anew, and thus deepen his *īmān*, even if he must begin by denying them all and starting, as the great al Ghazzālī (d. 1111) did, to be followed by Descartes half a millennium later—with the simple factuality of his own doubt.[5] Such accommodation to the requirements of intellectual integrity is indeed unique to Islām among the world religions.

Second, Islām is transcendentalist. It repudiates all forms of immanentism. It holds that reality is of two generic kinds—transcendent and spatiotemporal, creator and creature, value and fact—which are metaphysically, ontologically unlike and different from each other. These two realms of being constitute different objects of two modes of human knowledge, namely, the a priori and the empirical. Consciousness of this duality of being is as old as man; but it has never been absolutely free of confusion, absolutely clear of itself, as in Islām. Ever since the fourth millennium B.C., when in the speculations of Theban and Memphite theologies[6] the two realms of being were so confused by man as to become one, the consciousness of transcendence, or of the duality of being, has been struggling to attain clarity. Although it was denied in the Indian religions which, while taking their stand on monism, have denied reality to the spatiotemporal and assigned it all to the transcendent, the consciousness of transcendence was confused by the anthropomorphic understanding of deity in Judaism and the incarnational theology of Christianity. Islām takes its distinguishing mark among the world religions precisely by insisting on an absolute metaphysical separation of transcendent from the spatiotemporal.[7]

The duality of being as such is, in Islām, an ultimate category. However, Islām does not deny that the two realms can be related; but it rules out any understanding of this relation as one of ontological fusion because such would be the end of transcendence and its denial. Moreover, such understanding would hopelessly confuse the two realms of being. Hence, Islām has sought a relation that would safeguard their mutual otherness and obvious difference. Obviously, the only relation capable of this is the ideational relation between knower and known, which obtains between man and God, the creature in space-time and the transcendent creator, and which Islām duly recognizes as the only basis for a theory of revelation as a theory of knowledge as well. Here too, the problem is not simple. The transcendent is by definition beyond the ken of human knowledge. What is therefore knowable in such relation is not the transcendent in actual existence, but a modality of it. Any human knowledge of it by whichever means it was obtained or established, must perforce be a knowledge of the transcendent in perception, never of the transcendent in itself. This distinction Islām learned as that between God and His will, recognizing that although no man can ever claim to know God in His divine essence, it is possible by the twin roads of reason and revelation to know his will. In this way, the Muslim characterized all that can be said of the transcendent status. The ubiquitous catch phrase of Muslim thinking, namely, ". . . and, surely God knows better!" is an index of his awareness of this limitation of his knowledge of things religious or divine. As from the standpoint of critical philosophy, one can neither assert that the knowing of an object affects its ontic nature, nor that man can know the transcendent in itself, so the Muslim, confronted with the claims for certainty presented by religious consciousness as well as by a sophisticated moral consciousness, looked upon God as the eternal "$= x$" of all and everything, that is, but of Whom he could and did not know the will, the command, or the morally imperative, which is neither God in Himself, nor not-God, but God as He is or ever will be known to man. Such has been the foundation of Islāmic criticality.

In Islām, transcendent reality, or the holy, comes into contact with empirical reality at one point only—the Qur'ān—and this, consistently enough, it holds to be a body of ideas absolutely devoid of any other being besides the ideational. To hold, then, that contact with the transcendent is possible only in the realm of the mind, by means of the activity of intellection, is to imply that nothing in the world and nothing in history is transcendent or touched by the holy, unless it be an idea communicated to or grasped by a human consciousness. Thus, Islām identifies the prophets and their revelations as moments of man's consciousness in which the transcendent in perception has become partially known through an activity of intellection called intuition or inspiration, but an act of the mind nonetheless.

Islām's limitation of the transcendent to its own transcendent realm, of the transcendent's contact with the world to a few flashes in consciousness and to a few moments in human history, was meant to save the autonomy of nature and the moral dignity of man.

Nature is not transcendent and constitutes an autonomous realm. There is no divinity either in its materials or in its forces. It is totally real, totally a creature, totally belonging to the realm of the actual, the objective. It contains no mystery. None of its phenomena may claim to be secret, none beyond man's searching eye or hand. It is all utterly profane, and nothing in it or of it is or can be sacred. It is utterly closed to any penetration of, fusion with, or contact by, the holy. Its relationship with the latter has always been, and will always be, that of a creature to its creator, of an artifact to its maker. Only such dissociation of nature from the transcendent can safeguard its autonomy. Otherwise, the processes of nature would be interfered with; their regularity and order broken or liable to be broken; their study, knowledge, and consequent public mastery would become impossible. Indeed, paganism would become inevitable; for, to be pagan consists in no more than regarding nature, or the forces of nature, as holy, numinous, or transcendent, and it is all one whether nature or any part thereof, devoid as it is of mind and intellection, is taken to be itself holy or that the holy did or has come to be present therein by any kind of incarnation or objectification. If some acts of unintelligent nature are or can be acts of the holy, its orderliness can never be trusted. A nature in which the transcendent can or does break into is not one in which laws are discernible and their applicability testable; for supernatural causation cannot be distinguished from natural causation on the realm of empirical knowledge. And in this case, if Peter may explain a natural phenomenon *A* as a supernatural event, there is no reason whatever why Paul may not explain the same phenomenon, or all other phenomena as supernatural events of a different transcendent authorship. And if any transcendent authorship is as valid as any other, then this new category for explaining natural phenomena has availed nothing. Science is here in the predicament of an 'Alī Bābā who, by letting in one thief, automatically lets in the remaining thirty-nine and thereby brings about his own ruin. The laws of a nature under such predicament may not be called laws at all, properly speaking; for they have here become occult. The knowledge of such nature is esoteric. Pursuit of mastery and use of it by man are nothing short of blasphemous rebellion. Men would have to be satisfied with magic or alchemy, a power to influence the flow of events possessed solely by a priest. Mankind and science made the greatest advance only when nature was desacralized; and they are at their lowest and most backward ebb when nature is still looked upon as carrying, embodying, or objectifying the holy. Judaism, Islām's predecessor in the history of Semitic consciousness, had elaborated and crystallized the point against paganism, or the identification of the transcendent realm with that of the actual, in this case, nature. At the advent of Islām little of this paganism remained and that remainder was given the *coup de grâce* by Islām. The pre-Islāmic Arabs had recognized the transcendent nature of God, but they added to His principality, to the transcendent realm of being, demigods which they addressed as intercessionaries with God on their behalf. Against this association (*shirk*), or association with the transcendent that which is not so, Islām poured the vials of its wrath and hardly a vestige of this paganism was left as Islām spread over Arabia.

As for man, his dignity is violated when some member or members of his species are declared incarnations of the transcendent; when their acts and thoughts are declared embodiments or expressions of the holy and hence, beyond critique; indeed, when they are declared to stand in a special relation to the transcendent from which all other men are excluded by birth. Just as natural law and order are possible only if all nature is profane, human dignity and moral responsibility are possible only when all men are human and none is transcendent. The human kind is a peculiar part of the realm of a space-time, distinguished from the other parts in a variety of ways. *Vis-à-vis* the transcendent realm, however, all men are one and alike—their only difference from it is identical in all. All men stand obliged by the ought of value, the command of the transcendent being. Some individual men possess sharper, clearer, or wider visions of the ought; but no man is ruled out from such vision and none possesses a monopoly of it. Whatever one does in fact possess is capable of being possessed by others, and is a public trust which any member of the human race may question. Otherwise, the critical spirit, the questioning and analysis of the assertions of men, and the exposure of their incoherence or lack of correspondence with reality, the demand for proofs and corroborative evidence—all fall to the ground. Rationalism and its persistent demands become nothing short of blasphemy and rebellion when the claimant—whether man, institution, or group—is wholly or partly divine and nonhuman; when his assertions are made, as the claim goes, under the influence and guidance of the transcendent and belong to a realm above human contention. That is why Islām pressed all its morals, social theory, and view of the world under the single concept of *tawḥīd*, or unity of the transcendent being. The transcendence of God, apparently, cannot be long maintained if the equality or humaneness of all men is broken in favor of any member, church, priesthood, or group. Hence, Islām eliminated the privileged and their privileges and declared religious truth to be public truth and the road to the deity to be always an open freeway to all. It was thus that the Qur'ān became a "best seller" before the age of printing, copied by every literate man and recited by the literate and illiterate alike. It was for this that the religious egalitarianism of Islām knows no bounds; that every adherent, whether learned or common, is a minister unto himself and a possible minister, not only to all other Muslims, but to mankind as well; that the Prophet Muḥammad, despite the strongest incentive on the part of his followers to raise him above mankind, remained a human like any other man—indeed, all too human![8]

Third, Islām is world-affirmative. The world, or space-time, is good. It was not created in vain, or in sport, but for a good purpose, namely, the fulfillment of divine will. Inasmuchas divine will is value, or the good, and because its fulfillment is its concretization or actualization in space-time, the final objective of Islām is not extrinsic to this world but in and of it. Islām does not regard the final realization of the absolute as something that will take place outside of space-time, after this world had come to a cataclysmic end. On the contrary, it regards that realization as taking place in this world. The so-called *al ākhirah*, or "end of the world," which does, in Islām, come suddenly and cataclysmically, is not a "kingdom of God," another space-time, however different from this one, but a "Day of Judgment," a category of the moral life by means of which the imbalance of virtue with happiness and reward, and of vice with suffering and punishment, is finally redressed. Paradise and hell are not, in Islām, places and/or regimes beyond space-time but moral principles whose reality is so vividly grasped by the Islāmic consciousness as to give them the appearance of a space-time beyond space-time. They do not constitute an alternative to space-time; nor do they have a content—human life with its great and little moments—other than that of men in space-time. Hence, the metaphysics of ethics of Islām is not a theory of salvation, of deliverance from a predicament. Unlike Christianity and the religions of India, Islām never regarded itself as a religion of redemption. Rather, its morality is one of active realization, of doing, and of works in space-time. There is no book claiming to present Islām which does not open with the definition, "*Al Islām īmān wa 'amal,*" i.e., "Islām is conviction and action." It is symptomatic of the whole religious view of Islām that its terminology has no word such as *save* or *salvation*, a concept in which the subject, God, is active and the object, man, is passive. Those Arabic terms which imply the nearest relation of God as subject, to man as object, to that implied by the term *saving*, refer to specific meanings, such as *forgiving*, *guiding*, *inspiring*, and so on, never to something general such as salvation. Here, the only term Islām knows is *falāh* (felicity) or the verb *aflaḥa* (to become felicitous), which is a thoroughly active concept. In its exercise, man is the sole subject of his own *falāḥ* and a passive form of the verb has never been used in scripture and is hardly known in religious literature. Obviously, then, there is for Islām something yet greater than the greatest good, that is, that very good realized in the world. Indeed, the ethic of Islām is so activistic that it often regarded the *summum bonum* an idle dream unless it was walking on the grounds of history. Salvation was never in Islām the cessation or end of this world, but its continuation and eternal yea. Instead of seeking to exit therefrom, man is supposed to transform this world into the divine pattern, to reknead and mold its materials, including man, the masterpiece of creation, into the likeness of the ought-to-be, of the content of divine will and command.

Thus, Islām is this-worldly inasmuch as, firstly, it teaches no escape and no deliverance from this world, not even on the Day of Judgment. Secondly, it is affirmative of this-world inasmuch as it seeks religious felicity in actions in this world, in actions that transform the human and other creatures of the world without altering their humanity, without loss to their this-worldliness, and with the continuation of the world as a general conditioning ethical desideratum.

But if this world is to continue and to be preserved though transformed, without loss of ontological identity, into something other than it presently is or was at creation, it must be good, and its goodness must be of its essence. Though imperfect and standing still to be perfected by man, God's "vicegerent" on earth, this world cannot be in itself evil. The world's imperfection is necessary but not evil. In the first place, imperfection is the presupposition of value-realizing, of perfecting, because any change of the perfect is undesirable by definition. In the second place, imperfection involves no moral guilt inasmuch as it is not a deed of man but a state of creation as a whole. In Islām, man is essentially guilt free. He always begins his career in the world innocent, as it were with a clean slate. Certainly, he may be already predetermined with all sorts of innate fixation, or come to acquire such fixations as a child through nurture that is not of his personal making, and which may determine his success or failure in the perception as well as the realization of value. That is indeed true; but none such fixation is moral and therefore none incurs for man any guilt. If such fixations are immoral it is, rather, the duty of others, of those who know better—God and men—to teach and guide him otherwise. Cosmic or divine government is not unjust, not whimsical; and there is no imputation of guilt without due warning, without the accused being proven to have wrought his deed against the dictates of a moral conscience that had become public, whether by revelation or rational research. Even the false religion—which is in Islām the highest moral consideration—is, according to a *ḥadīth* (transmitted text) of the Prophet, the work of man's parents. Morally speaking, against the Augustinian anthropology of sin, guilt, and damnation at birth, Islām declares man essentially wholesome and innocent, and judges him only with regard to his deliberate, conscious, free-willed and mature deeds. In contrast to Christianity and Indian religions, both men and this world receive from Islām credentials of innocence. Both exist and subsist on sufferance, not merely as of right, but as a highly moral, ethically-conditioning good.

That Islām is world-affirmative requires yet the establishment that the content of divine will, that into which this world is to be transformed, is *of* this world and not some antiworld ideal. It is quite possible that an ethic may demand the continuation of this world but seek to turn it into a realm of ghosts, or life- and world-denying saints. What is then the evidence that Islām's world-affirmation is a truthfulness to this very world? And how does such ethic avoid being merely a truthfulness to space-time as it is, and not as it ought to be?

These are indeed serious questions. The answer to them must be sought in the content of the moral imperatives of Islām. First, Islāmic morality is not anchored to a point outside of this-world determining it to have a final objective alien to it. To the general question of who are the saved, the felicitous, the men of final success, the Qur'ān repeatedly answers, "those who believed and did the good,"[9] so that doing the good things in the world is inseparable from the faith and is tantamount to it as well as to salvation. On the other hand, to the opposite question of who is the damned, the denier of religion, the rebellious, unjust, and evil, the Qur'ān answers: "It is he who violently repels the orphan, who does not urge the feeding of the deprived, who is oblivious to what he says in prayer; the pretender, who stands in the way of assistance to the needy."[10] The beliefs of such a man, his "religion" in the Western sense of the term, is not even mentioned in this connection. Indeed, it is even taken for granted that he is a Muslim. But even the Muslim, and all the more, the non-Muslim, is for Islām a "denier of religion" if and only if he flouts the call or need of his fellowmen. Islām then anchors its moral ideal not in faith in the transcendent, not in a realm outside of space-time, but on "doing the good" here and now, on realizing the demands of social justice here and now.

Secondly, the content of the moral imperatives of Islām is of this world because all that is of this world is declared the work of God designed and fashioned for man's service and enjoyment. God gave man of himself a spouse, woman, that he may find quiescence in her and ordained between them love and affection. He created the elements and ordered them into a stretched-out earth with mountains, rivers, fruits of all sorts and pairs of all creatures; into day wherein to see, and night wherein to find rest, and in both to reckon the months and years; into seas and oceans in which ships bring the world together for their mutual benefit, into cloud and rain that resurrect the earth after a scorching death; into an earth cultivable, producing food and grapes and dates of many a variety, grain and olives, gardens and orchards—all for man's enjoyment and benefit. He created all the creatures of the world that man may have therein his sustenance, pleasure and enjoyment, clothing and meal; cattle, that he may find therein his pleasure and utility; horses and beasts of burden, for his comfort. Indeed, God gave man the whole earth for inheritance, to live in and to enjoy. In the long run of history, He increases this enjoyment as the reward of virtue. Privation and denial of this bounty is the reward of evil, "the promise of Satan," as the Qur'ān calls it.[11] "Your women are fruits for you; take them and enjoy them whenever you wish," the Qur'ān asserts.[12] Indignantly, it asks, "Who dared to forbid man the enjoyment of his things of beauty, of the delicacies of food, of raiment and other good things of God's bounty?"[13] It commands the Prophet, "Teach that these things all belong to this earth to those who are faithful . . . Teach that God forbids only indecencies, such of them as are apparent and such as are hidden. He forbids sin and wrongful oppression."[14] It counsels man to pray, "O God, appoint for us in this world the good things of it." And it warns man, "To seek—not to forget or give up—his share of the good things of this world."[15] There can be little doubt that the import of all this is to orient man towards this world and to enable him to concentrate all his efforts into transforming it into the paradise of promise, and to enjoy in the process its sweet, beautiful, and pleasant things in good conscience.

Fourth, Islām is "societistic." Because the whole world, creation itself, is the object of the Muslim's will to transform and refashion, the society of Islām is the human race in its totality. Here, every man is a citizen and everyone counts. None is excluded by virtue of his progeny, religion, or culture. Man's humanness constitutes his full candidacy for membership. Even if he is not a Muslim, his entry into a contract of peaceful coexistence with the Muslims makes him a constituent member of the society of Islām. His entry into the faith, on the other hand, creates for him new privileges and obligations, but in an over-all world order of which he has already been a member. As to the governmental and other societal superstructures of the world, the Muslim is duty-bound to "islāmize" them. But this means no more than for such superstructures either to acknowledge the supremacy of the transcendent and the normativeness of its imperatives, or to safeguard the security of those who, by their eloquence, their teaching and argument, or by the example of their own conduct or living, peacefully seek such acknowledgment on the part of the individual citizens of the world. If there is an alternative at all to the rule of might and the play of the big stick in intersocietal relations, it must be that of ideation and intellection. The human mind or soul has no vision of a relation between man and his fellows greater or nobler than that of intellectual intercourse, and certainly no vision of a world other than that in which any man may influence, determine, or transform his fellowmen by argument and example. Thus the world Islām envisages may have one government or many national governments as it pleases. But these must be either themselves Islāmic or maintaining a free order in their societies in which ideas and men from within or without its national frontiers are free to move, to associate and dissociate, to compete and to win—in peace. "Pull down the barriers and let the best thought win!" is the first principle of world order Islām furnishes, confident that the truth, which is one as God and value are one, will emerge victorious. Naturally, its own government is the first to pull down its barriers. This is why Islām has never had a *varṇa* (color), a "color line," a "doctrine of election," or a "theory of the remnant." Its religious scale is that of an absolute justice wherein every man, blest or unblest, gets exactly what he deserves, whether sooner or later. The Qur'ān warns the Muslims unequivocally that if they fulfill the morally imperative, they will be granted power and affluence. If, on the other hand, they do not, they will be punished, nay liquidated and obliterated while God would bring forth another people to take their place and carry out the divine trust. The majestic sweep of this ethical universalism of Islām, of its final and absolute disposal of all divine and metaphysical favoritism and prejudice, of all ethical determinism, have hardly a parallel in the religious literature of the world.[16]

An islāmized society, however, is one in which man is constantly on the move to understand, to know, and to master creation. It is one where the fruits of each person, won in peace and justice, are his to own and to enjoy regardless of limits; where to be rich is, rather than a thing of shame, a matter for rightful pride. It is one where the destitute and the deprived are blameworthy if their poverty and misery is their own decision and work. But if their misery is not their own responsibility, it is their right and title to partake of the prosperity and wealth of others, as to give is the duty of the affluent. There has always been charity; and alms are as old as man. But only in Islām did charity become institutionalized and a matter of law. Islāmic society was the first ever to collect these charities publicly, according to given rules and a ratio proportionate to wealth, and by force were it necessary, in order to bring the benefits of this world to its deprived members, whether Muslims or others. The state to which Islām gave birth was the first social welfare state in history.

Furthermore, Islām is "societistic" in that it regards every man on earth, not as an instrument of the subject's search for his own salvation or felicity, but as an end in himself. Should there be a *jinni* (a spiritual being between angels and men) who, following the saintliest saint in the world, undoes everything the saint does when acting in saintly capacity, so as to make the man's whole life absolutely and utterly without effect in history—is such a saint saved? Can his life be said to have been truly felicitous? No, answers Islām. Whereas, according to most religions, such a man would have achieved a glorious salvation because real effects are religiously irrelevant, according to Islām he had fulfilled only the subjective condition of salvation, the negative requirment that man's deeds ought to be willed for their sake, or of God's but not for personal ulterior motives. In other words, such a saint would have put the house of his own self well in order. But he had failed to bring about any change in space-time, to invade and to affect the houses of other selves, to realize value elsewhere besides his own person. Had salvation consisted of nothing more, religion would be hopelessly egotistic and from the Islāmic viewpoint, of little moral worth. Therefore, Islām requires such "selfishness"—the realization in oneself of the personalist values of the good will—as a necessary condition of, a preparation for rather than consummation of, felicitous religious endeavor. Such a man would then be meritorious for having made but the first step in the direction of Islāmic felicity. It is not enough that he has acted. He ought to have acted as well as succeeded; that is, willed as well as made history and altered space-time for better. He must enter history and space, disturb the natural flow of events, take the business of history as it were into his hands and bring about the realization of the divine pattern. It is not enough to will that, nor to seek to realize it, without success. Pursuit of felicity, the Muslim argues, cannot therefore be a pursuit of the subject's own felicity as this would not earn him the felicity or salvation he seeks. His duty is simply to bring about the actual felicity of others; his salvation is the measure of success he achieves in the performance of this duty. Only under a scheme such as Islām provides can it be said that man is really regarded as an end in himself. No other altruism is free of egotism.

To invade the selves of others and to bring therein changes! This sounds less like ethical universalistic altruism and more like a totalitarianism in which men are inanimate materials rather than persons. Indeed, this is so, as long as we do not remember the nature of the change the Muslim seeks to bring in the persons of others. Had such changes been all of material nature, all pertaining to men's bodies, their health, food, raiment, housing, survival, security, comforts, and material pleasures, Islāmic societism would have been a call to the strongest totalitarianism and collectivism. The case of Islām, however, is otherwise.

Islām seeks to bring about the realization of all values. Of these, the highest are the moral. The moral are precisely those which cannot be enforced. When they are the result is not a realization of them but of something else. The genuinely moral values can be realized in man at all only by himself acting as subject of the realization. The deed in question must be his own, personal, individual deed. Above all it must be deliberate and free, his own decision and choice. Only then will it be moral. The divine trust which, as the Qur'ān reports,[17] God offered to the angels, to the heavens and mountains, was turned down by them because it required the exercise of moral freedom which they did not have. Man alone accepted it because only he is a free moral agent, capable of realizing moral value and hence, of fulfilling the general purpose of creation. What can the Muslim, or any other man, contribute to this extremely personal and free decision of the moral subject? Obviously, the Muslim's role can be only that of teaching, of causing the moral subject to perceive for himself, of exposing him to examples and situations of realization or violation of the various imperatives. Only such assistance to, or "invasion" of, the other man's person does not violate its holy territory. That is precisely the meaning of Islāmic altruism when all the preparatory conditions of ethical goodness are realized and the Muslim has carried his ethical and religious activism to its furthest limits. Man may be made to do; but his doing will not be moral. For it to be moral, it has to be his own free choice. In turn, this presupposes man's perception of the goodness and moral obligatoriness of that which is to be brought about by his deed; and here, no compulsion and no outside material causation can help, because for perception to be perception at all, it must be the subject's own perception. Here, man may be helped, but never coerced, to perceive. The processes in which such help takes place constitute education in its highest sense; and that is the final practical purpose of Islāmic societism. The society Islām envisages and seeks to establish is a school on the grandest scale possible, where every member is teacher and student seeking eternally to discover, express, and establish value, to the end that all men will give it, of their own free will, the real existence its very nature calls for from its depths.

The curriculum of such a world school has been institutionalized by Islām in the twin principles of self-exertion (*ijtihād*) and consensus (*ijmā'*). In the dialectical relation between them, Islām found its societism in knowing and perceiving. The former is the creative interpretation of the morally imperative, the fresh discovery of ever new spatiotemporal materials of value to be made actual, and of disvalues to be avoided or transformed. This is a duty incumbent upon every adult Muslim with the promise of a reward for its fulfillment even if the discovery should be erroneous and a double reward should it prove correct. Even so, every self-exertion is, for Islām, idle daydreaming and invalid unless its author takes it to the market place, to the rough and tumble of history, risks his reputation as a man of knowledge and wisdom on it, and convinces his fellowmen of its truth. When *ijmā'* or an approving consensus of his fellowmen is reached (his fellowmen are immediately those with whom he is usually in contact, and mediately all the Muslims of the world and then the whole of humanity), the *ijtihād* in question becomes Islāmic law. Apart from the Qur'ān or conceptualized statement of the general religious and ethical principles, and the *sunnah* (example, life, tradition) of the Prophet, or perceptualized exemplification of Islām, there is no source of knowledge and/or law except man's one self-exertion purged of its errors by the fire of a consensus of one's fellowmen freely asked and gratuitously given. The "consent of the governed" neither demands nor promises more than just this.

On the other hand, the societism of actualizing the good consists in the publicization of it so that it becomes the concern of everyone. The Muslim is under the duty to command the doing of the good and the prevention of evil; and such duty runs thoughout the Qur'ān like a constant refrain. In an Islāmic society, therefore, the doing of the good and prevention of evil are the credit of all the citizens and their opposites are the moral failure and bane of all.

In a pertinent tradition, the Prophet said, "If you see an evil being perpetrated or a good being avoided, seek to prevent the evil and to bring about the good with your own arm. If you cannot, then with your tongue; and if you cannot, then in your heart; but that is the least faith!" Islām desires such public and group action and ranks it far above all individualistic conduct, because the good itself stands to reveal more of its nature and to command its own realization the more other men are involved in the process of realization even when personal. The good has a strong moving appeal and its realization is universally contagious. Undoubtedly, no ideology that seeks an objective as wide as the universe and as manifold as mankind can afford to lose the advantages the "societism" of value-realization brings, to overlook how closer to the goal such "societism" brings it with every deed.

Such is the essence of the faith we are about to study in the following pages. This assertion itself is indeed a big claim. But it is made under the Islāmic proviso that is also crucial to every sound scholarship, namely, ". . . and God knows better!"

NOTES

1. For details of this unfortunate and long misunderstanding, see Norman Daniels, *Islam and the West: The Making of an Image*, and *Islam, Europe and Empire*.
2. Al Fārūqi, I. R., "History of Religions: Its Nature and Significance for Christian Education and the Muslim-Christian Dialogue," *Numen*, 12, Fasc. 1, 2; (1965), 35–95.
3. Notably, Wilfred Cantwell Smith.
4. Qur'ān, 2:256; 17:81.
5. See the intellectual autobiography of Al Ghazzālī, *Al Munqidh Min al Ḍalāl* (Deliverer from error), tr. by W. Montgomery Watt under the title, *The Faith Practice of Al Ghazzālī*.
6. On Immanentism verging on a monophysitic view of the universe as characteristic of ancient Egyptian religion, see John A. Wilson, *The Culture of Ancient Egypt*, pp. 224 ff.; John A. Wilson, "Egypt: The Values of Life," in H. Frankfort, *et al.*, *Before Philosophy: The Intellectual Adventure of Ancient Man*, pp. 103ff.
7. For further detail, see I. R. al Fārūqī, *On Arabism*, vol. I, '*Urūbah and Religion: A Study of the Fundamental Ideas of Arabism and of Islām as its Highest Moment of Consciousness*, pp. 11 ff., 86–87; al Fārūqī, *Christian Ethics*, pp. 22–23.
8. This did not come to pass without struggle. For, like some of the early Christians, the Muslims too—indeed, no less a person than 'Umar, the second caliphi!—were tempted to deify Muḥammad, to bring their will to eternity to satisfaction in some confusion of his person with the Holy. But their better sense triumphed in Abū Bakr's declaration to the Muslim congregation assembled to plan the Prophet's funeral. (See ch. 28, B, 3.) With this, the separation and dual otherness of the transcendent and the actual realms, the creator and the creature, was complete. True, some of the later generations of Muslims were to weave around the prophet's person many legends tending to confuse this clear separation. Surely, this was a lapse from the ethos and doctrine of the Qur'ān. Nonetheless, no Muslim has known of any Muḥammad who has not kept his feet firmly on earth, of whose humanity and distinction from the deity he was not absolutely convinced.
9. The instances in which this expression occurs in the Qur'ān are so many as to obviate any listing of them.
10. Qur'ān, 107:1–7.
11. *Ibid.*, 2:268.
12. *Ibid.*, 2:223.
13. *Ibid.*, 7:31.
14. *Ibid.*, 7:32–33.
15. *Ibid.*, 7:155; 28:77.
16. *Ibid.*, 5:57; 9:40; 47:38; 76:27–28.
17. *Ibid.*, 33:72.

CHAPTER 26

Knowledge

□ Islām bases itself upon claims which it regards as rationally certain and convincing. Whether the claims themselves are so is a matter for the philosopher and theologian to discuss. But that Islām avers all ignorance, conjecture, probability, irrationality, uncritical opinion, paradox, and demands that all claims pertaining to religion including its own ought to be subject to critical analysis and rational consideration, is unquestionable. In its eye, there is no substitute to true knowledge.

Just as Islām is prepared to lay its own claims and propositions on the table of public and critical dissection and analysis, it demands that all religious claims and propositions be treated in like manner. This implies that truth is, and that knowledge of the truth is possible for man through exercise of his gnoseological faculties. Skeptics may rejoin that this very assumption is an article of faith—which is certainly true, inasmuch as the Islāmic standpoint is not one of skepticism. But Islām holds that skepticism cannot be maintained by man without involving him sooner or later in self-contradiction. For to assert the thesis itself of skepticism and to contend on its behalf with Islām or any other movement or philosophy is to contradict the very content of the thesis being asserted. That would be the position of Epimenides, the Cretan, who asserted that "all Cretans are liars" and thus gave the lie to his own assertion in the very act of asserting it.

Islām, furthermore, holds certain knowledge to be the condition of moral responsibility. Were knowledge impossible, as thoroughgoing skepticism has to hold if it is to be consistent with itself, no action, no responsibility, and no imputation of merit or demerit would be possible. Action implies choice; and choice implies conviction that one alternative is better than another. Otherwise, what we call action—indeed inaction—would be merely a happening, an event, of which it makes no sense to call any man either guilty or worthy. Skepticism in knowledge is hence the other side of cynicism in ethics.

Finally, Islām regards revelation not as something necessary, without which man could not prosper. That would be tantamount to distrusting man's innate capacity to know. That is why Islām holds that all revelations from God made to any man or people were acts of mercy designed to complement and assist man's quest of the truth. Revelation therefore can never run counter to true knowledge, to the findings of the cognitive faculties of man. Certainly error is possible and ubiquitous; but that is the fault of the individual cognizing, not of man as such or of human cognition as such. Indeed, Islām asserts, revelation is God's gift to man as a safety-check against cognitive aberration. God being one, the truth is one; and the unity of truth demands that revelation and reason be identified with one another. Such identity of revealed truth with truth cognized or cognizable by man has been the running problem and theme of all Islāmic philosophy. □

A. SCRIPTURAL: NATURE OF RATIONAL KNOWLEDGE AND ITS RELATION TO MORALITY AND REVELATION

1. Rational Knowledge and the Alternatives to It

Do not follow that of which you have no certain knowledge. The hearing, the sight, and the heart—all these (as faculties of knowledge) are responsible. (Qur'ān or Koran, 17:36) God brought you out of the bosoms of your mothers knowing nothing, but gave you the faculties of hearing, sight, and perception. Would you not thank Him? (16:78) We have made them strong in that which, were We to make you strong, you too would have been convinced; for We have given them hearing, sights, and hearts. They disbelieved the truths of God and were engulfed by the reality which they had mocked. (46:27) Call men unto the path of your Lord through wise argument and fair preaching; and argue with nonbelievers with arguments yet more sound.... (16:125) Our messengers came to the nonbelievers with truths evident. Thereafter, those who still contend are excessively skeptical. (5:32) Most of them rely only on conjectures; but conjecture is no substitute for true knowledge. (10:36) Say: Is the man devoid of knowledge the equal of the man in the know? Do you not think? (6:50) He who is blind and he who is with clear sight are not equal; nor are darkness and light; nor are shade and sun! (35:19) Read . . . for your Lord is the more generous. He taught by the pen. He taught man that which he did not know. (96:3–6) *Al Raḥman* (the Merciful God) taught the Reading (the Qur'ān). He created man and taught him the art of letters, the science of clarification. (55:1–4) The worst of the lowly creatures are those men whose minds are utterly closed; for they do not hear a thing while they hear, and they do not reason. (8:21–22) Take the side of pardon, command what is plainly good, and avoid the ignorant. (7:199) Servants of the Merciful tread softly on this earth and, when the ignorant contend with them, say; Peace, (and gently pass). (25:63) O you who have believed, be always upright in justice, witnesses unto the truth even though it be against yourselves, or your parents and relatives, against rich or poor. . . . Therefore, do not pursue prejudice and capricious opinion, that you may do justly. For if you twist the truth or refrain from acknowledging it, God will know it. (4:135) Those who act unjustly are those who pursue their capricious opinions, without knowledge (30:29). O David, We have made you a *khalīfah* (vicegerent of God) in the world. Judge them by the truth and do not follow conjecture lest it guide you astray. (38:26)

2. Rational Knowledge and Morality

We have sent to mankind messengers proclaiming the truth and warning that men may henceforth have no excuse for ignorance. (4:165) No village has God condemned whose people had not been duly warned beforehand. (26:208) But every people condemned had denied the revelations of the prophets and thereby incurred their just punishment (38:14).

3. Rational Knowledge and Revelation

The word of your Lord is perfect in its truth-value and justice-value. . . . Those who follow whatever is doubtful are far from the truth. (6:115) We have sent the prophets with truths evident and arguments reasoned out that what was revealed may be clearly established, that men may think and consider. (16:44) In the prophet's stories lies a moral for those who have minds and use them. Past revelations were no haphazard talk, but confirmation of the present revelation, clarifying analyses of everything, guidance and mercy and conviction to those who will listen. (12:111) God gives the parables that men may reason and consider. (14:25) Those are the evident truths of a book of wisdom, (10:1) . . . of the clarifying book; (12:1) . . . and in every case We have informed you concerning the prophets, We did so but to strengthen your conviction of the truth. What has been revealed to you so far is the truth, a lesson and reminder addressed to mankind. (11:120) Those who deny the revelation do so insomuch as they are ignorant of its truths and have not learned to understand it. (10:39) But those Christians and Jews who are sound in knowledge will recognize that which was revealed to you (Muḥammad) and to your predecessors in prophethood. (4:162) This Qur'ān is a Book which We revealed to you that you may bring men out of the darkness of ignorance to the light of certain knowledge. (14:1) And We have sent no prophet but in the language of his own people, that he may rationally convince them. . . . (14:4)

B. CIVILIZATIONAL: FOR AND AGAINST MAN'S RATIONAL FACULTY

1. Against the Deprecators of Rational Knowledge

A group of people incapable of study and learning who made ignorance their capital, and inclined towards strainless contentment while leaving thinking to others, attacked those who examine the principles of religion and accused them of misguidance. They claimed that the study of such matters as motion and rest, substance and accident, color and constitution, part and whole, the divine attributes, are misguidance and innovation. They argued that if this were not the case, the Prophet—God's peace and blessing be upon him—his successors and companions would have had something to say thereon; that since the Prophet had before he died answered every religious question and defined every religious matter, leaving nothing unsaid which the Muslims need for obtaining God's grace and avoiding His wrath, and that since no tradition on any one of these subjects has ever been reported, indulgence in such matters is undesirable innovation. They argued, further, that there are only two alternatives: Either the Prophet and his companions knew about these matters but kept silent deliberately, or they were ignorant of them. In the former case, it behooves us to emulate them in their deliberate silence, for these matters could not be essential to religion. And in the latter, we too can ignore these questions since they could not have been essential to religion. On either count, therefore, to indulge in such discussion is to err. Such is the substance of their argument. . . .

The answer to this is threefold: The first consists in reverting the criticism to them. Since no tradition has ever been reported that the Prophet has condemned the exercise of one's reason in such matters as impious innovation, it must follow that they themselves are guilty of innovation and misguidance for diverging from him. They accuse men of that which the Prophet has never accused anyone. The second consists in exposing their erroneous assumption that the Prophet as well as his learned companions were ignorant and hence had nothing to say on these questions (of philosophy and theology) by showing that all these matters had been touched upon in the Qur'ān and in the *sunnah* (example, life, tradition). . . . Finally, the third consists in showing that the Prophet could not be expected to have spoken on all these matters in great or specific detail, because they had not been subjects of contention in his day but became so later. The case is not unlike that of the law of Islām (*sharī'ah*) whose general principles all come from the Qur'ān and the *sunnah* but whose specific details did not become subjects of specific discussions and elaborations until centuries after the Prophet. (Al Ash'arī [d. 942], *Risālat Istiḥsān al Khawḍ fī 'Ilm al Kalām* [Epistle on the advantages of indulging into theological science], pp. 3, 48–49)

2. Reason: Innate Faculty and Primary Foundation

Reason is the foundation of all virtues. Know that every imperative has a foundation and every virtue has a source; that the foundation of all imperatives and source of all virtues is reason. God made reason the first principle of religion, the support of the world. He commanded us to cultivate and perfect it, to submit the affairs of the world to its judgment. By it, He has brought men into harmonious relation with one another despite their different natures, needs, and objectives. He made His imperatives of two kinds: One is necessary by reason and the revealed law only confirmed it; the other is possible by reason and the revealed law commanded it. For both, therefore, reason is the base. The Prophet is reported to have said, "Man has no better gain than the cultivation of a reason to guide him to good and away from evil." Everything has a ground, and the ground of human action is reason. Man's worship of God is commensurate with his reason. Did you not hear the cry of the evil doers? "Alas," they said, "had we listened, had we reasoned, we would not have been consigned to hell!" (Qur'ān 35:6) 'Umar ibn al Khaṭṭāb (Second Caliph of the Muslim State in Madīnah, 634–644), said, "The first principle of man is his reason." Al Ḥasan al Baṣrī, early father of Islāmic thought, said, "God gives no reason to anyone but enables him to save himself thereby." The wise said, "Reason is the best desideratum, ignorance the worst enemy. . . . Know that by reason the truth is known, and by it good is separated from evil."

Reason is of two kinds: Natural and acquired. The former is the more significant. On it moral obligation depends, extending where it extends and stopping where it stops. It distinguishes man from the animals. Only when it is perfect, may man reach moral perfection. . . . Some said, "It is a spiritual substance, by which facts are sifted." Others disagreed on its locus. Some said it was in the brain because this is the locus of sensation. Others said it is in the heart because this is the organ of life and sensitivity. . . . Others said, "Natural reason is that which knows the realities of things." Though better than the first, this view is also false because knowledge belongs only to living persons, whereas reason is incapable of life by itself. Others said, "Reason is the sum of necessary truths." But these answers are all indefinite, and the indefinite constitutes no definition. . . .

The true definition of natural reason is that it is the knowledge of necessary truths. The latter are of two kinds: those which come through sense and those which issue in the mind. . . . If the person, as subject of knowledge, is capable of sense perception, presentation to sense constitutes necessary knowledge of that which is thus presented. Voluntary or involuntary suspension of his sensing faculties constitutes no proof against this argument which claims that, had he sensed, he would have known for certain that which he had sensed. On the other hand, those necessary truths which issue in the mind, such as the principles that things either or are not, that existents are either created or eternal, that one is less than two, etc., are impossible to separate from rational beings so long as they are alive and sane. . . . This reason was called by its name, *'aql*, by derivation from the binding (*'aql*) of the camel; for, just as the reins of the camel (*'iqāl*) bind it and prevent it from straying, so man's reason (*'aql*) binds him and prevents him from following his instincts and passions when they seek release.

As for the acquired reason, it is the product of natural reason. Its function is the completion of knowledge, the true guidance of conduct. . . . This reason has no boundary, for it grows under cultivation, and degenerates under neglect. It grows with experience and practice. . . . There is no ignorant man but that time instructs and educates him. . . . Enough honor for experience is the lessons it teaches; and for the passing of days, the counsels they give. . . . (Al Māwardi [d. 1059], *Adab al Duniā wa al Dīn* [Refinement of the world and of religion], pp. 3–4)

CHAPTER 27

Religion and Religions

□ Religions, from the Islāmic standpoint, are not all true in everything they teach. True religion is that which recognizes God as Lord and Creator and leads man to a life of moral value. It is natural, free, serious, and should constitute no hardship for man. Only such religion leads to bliss here and in the hereafter. Though true religion may be arrived at by natural reason alone (ch. 26), the merciful God did not leave a people to whom He has not revealed it by means of prophets, warners, and wise men. Men, however, forget and lapse, thus necessitating repetition. The core of such revelations was always one and the same; the laws of conduct developed with the times. Judaism and Christianity are particularly fitting illustrations. Both began as truly divine religions but continued to be so only among some of their adherents. The rest lapsed and altered their scripture to accommodate their invented theologies. *Judaism:* To the Jews God revealed a scripture, the *Torah.* He made a covenant with them that if they worshiped Him and acted morally, He would bless them with power and prosperity; otherwise He would punish them. Some of them did and prospered; others falsified the scriptures, anthropomorphized God, developed a chosen race complex, and earned His punishment. *Christianity:* To the Jews, God also sent Jesus, a prophet and messenger, born of Mary by divine command. He was given *al Injīl* (the *Evangel*), taught to relieve the hardships of Jewish legalism, and to exemplify the ethic of love, humility, and mercy. The Jews falsely accused Mary and claimed they killed her son. God, however, had raised Jesus from their midst. Some of his followers remained true to his teaching and are blessed. Others associated Jesus with God, invented trinitarianism and monkery, and falsified the *Evangel.* The concept of "People of the Book," though denotatively restricted to the Jews and Christians on account of their endowment with the *Torah* and the *Evangel,* has a connotation of divine religion, piety, and the pursuit of moral value. As long as the adherents of any religion bear out this connotation, they are brothers to the Muslims.

Muḥammad's prophethood was the last, because—inasmuch as the essential principles of the law were revealed once and for all in the imperishable Qur'ān (Koran), man is henceforth mature enough to elaborate the law and find its various applications to the human situations without external aid. □

A. SCRIPTURAL: MONISM AND UNIVERSALISM; MAN'S RELIGIOUS HISTORY AND ITS CULMINATION IN ISLĀM

1. Monism of Religion as Monism of Truth and Value

Avoid those who regard religion jestfully, who are bewitched by the lowly life. (Qur'ān, 6:70) The unjust took other than God as their Lord . . . who legislates for them their religion—a religion God never permitted. (42:9) Do the unbelievers seek a religion other than God's when to Him submit all that is in heaven and earth? (3:83) God's guidance alone is true guidance. (2:120) Orient your face to religion as a *ḥanīf* (believer in God and the moral law), that is the nature which God implanted in all men. His pattern is immutable. That is the true religion. (30:30) And whose religion is better than that of he who orients his face towards God and does the good? (4:125) Whoever of you abandons his religion and dies an unbeliever, his works will surely fail him in this world and the next. (2:217) Those who repent, do good, hold fast to God, and offer all their devotion sincerely to Him are on the side of the believers. . . . (4:126) Have the unbelievers not traveled in the world and seen the end to which their predecessors had come? (40:81) O children of Adam, whoever of you is pious and does the good shall have no reason to fear, nor to grieve. (7:35) There is no compulsion in religion. Right guidance is now clearly separate from erring and vice. (2:256) God did not mean religion to cause you difficulties. (22:78) He desires no hardship for you, but ease. (2:185)

2. Universality of True Religion

To every people, a guide. (13:7) There is no nation to whom a warner has not been sent. (35:24) We have sent prophets even unto the ancients. (15:10) . . . (all of whom) were human, eating food and walking in the market places. . . . (25:20) armed with indisputable evidence, delivering the Book and the Scale that men may fulfill the imperatives of justice. . . . (57:25) We sent no prophet before you (Muḥammad) but that We revealed to him that there is no God but Me. . . . (21:25) Those who . . . distinguish between God and His prophets, who accept some and reject others seeking thereby to differentiate between their revelations, are truly the unbelievers. . . . But those who believe in God and His prophets and who do not distinguish between their revelations shall have their just reward. . . . (4:150–52) To every people we sent a prophet to teach them to worship God and to avoid evil. Some of them were rightly guided; others erred and were rightly punished. Go unto the nations, and see to what end those who erred had come. (16:36) Those who repudiated resolutely the evident truths their prophets brought (14:9–10) . . . were misled by their own works and followed evil—to them belong the painful punishment. (16:63)

3. Man's Religious History: Two Illustrations

a. Judaism

God made a covenant with Banū Isrā'īl and sent unto them twelve judges. God said to them: I am with you. If you hold the supreme act of worship (*salāt*), pay the *zakāt* (sharing of wealth), believe in My prophets and honor them, if you live the life of virtue, I will forgive your misdeeds and enter you into gardens underneath which rivers flow. (5:12) We revealed the *Torah*, a light and a guidance. By its precepts, the prophets who submitted to God judged the Jews, as did the rabbis and the priests who learned the Book of God and were commissioned to witness thereunto. . . . (5:44) The Jews said: The Christians have no point. And the Christians say: The Jews have no point. And yet both recite the Book. . . . (2:113) Say: O People of the Book, neither of you has a point until you carry out the *Torah* and the *Evangel* and what God had revealed for your benefit. . . . (5:68) Those who believed, the Jews, Christians, and Sabaeans —whoever believes in God, in the Day of Judgment and lives the life of virtue—have their reward with their God. Neither do they fear nor do they have reason to grieve. (2:62) Some of the People of the Book truly believe in God, in that which has been revealed to you and to them. They are reverently pious and do not sell God's revelations for a mean price. Their reward is with God. (3:199)

We have tried them (the Jews) with favors and disfavors that they may repent. Some of them . . . singled out the favorable of its (the *Torah*'s) passages and bragged that God had forgiven them everything. Have they not covenanted with God never to claim anything on His behalf but the truth? (7:167–170) After contracting the covenant, some of them rejected it. (2:100) Hence, We divided them into separate groups and dispersed them. . . . (7:168) Moses was sent to you with evident signs; but you have taken the golden calf, in injustice. (2:92) Will you, whenever My prophets come to you with what you do not like, reject them in pride, belie some, and kill the others? (2:87) The Jews . . . said: We are the sons of God and His favorite people. Say: Why then do you commit evil and are punished by Him? You are only men, like all his other creatures. . . . (5:18)

b. CHRISTIANITY

The angels said: O Mary, God has singled you out among all the women of the world and purified you. Be obedient to your Lord, kneel and prostrate yourself with the worshipers. . . . He sends you glad tidings of a son whose name shall be the Messiah, Jesus, son of Mary. He shall be honored in this world and in the next. (3:42) Mary preserved her chastity. We breathed into her of Our spirit and made her and her son a lesson unto mankind. (21:92) God taught Jesus the scripture and wisdom, the *Torah*, and the *Evangel* and sent him a prophet of the children of Israel. Jesus said to them: I bring to you a sign from your lord . . . curing the blind and the leprous, resuscitating the dead by God's permission, . . . confirming the *Torah*, making legitimate some of that which was forbidden to you. . . . Fear God, therefore, and obey me. God is your Lord and my Lord, let us worship Him. That is the straight path. (3:48) The Jews . . . accused Mary falsely of a great crime, and claimed that they killed the Messiah, Jesus, son of Mary, the prophet of God. But they did not kill him, nor did they crucify him. It only seemed so to them. Those who contend in this matter are themselves in doubt regarding it. Having no certain knowledge of the matter, they only conjecture. None is certain they killed him. God, the Glorious and Wise, raised Jesus unto Him. (4:156–58) Surely the People of the Book are not all equal: The Christians are upright, recite the revelations of God during the night hours, and prostrate themselves in worship. They believe in God and in the Day of Judgment. They enjoin the good, forbid evil, and compete in the performance of good works. Those are certainly righteous. (3:113) And you will find among the People of the Book the closer to you those who said that they were Christians; for many of them are priests and ascetics and are humble. When they hear that which was revealed to the Prophet, their tears flow in emotion for they know it is true. (5:82) In their hearts We planted compassion and mercy, but We did not enjoin them to become monks. That was their invention. (57:27) The Byzantines (i.e., the Christians) were defeated on the nearer front. But after this defeat they shall be again victorious, in a few years. . . . Then will the believers celebrate God's victory. (30:2–5)

The Christians said: The Messiah is the son of God, thereby surpassing in unbelief the unbelievers of old. . . . They have taken their priests and monks for gods, as well as the Messiah, son of Mary, whereas they were commanded never to worship but one God, beside Whom there is none else, gloried be He above their associations. (9:30) O People of the Book! Do not go to extreme in your religion and never say anything on behalf of God except the truth. Jesus, the Messiah, the son of Mary, is only a prophet of God, a fulfillment of His command addressed to Mary, a spirit from God, given unto Mary. So believe in God and in His prophets and do not hold the trinitarian view. Listen to this, for it is better for you: God is the One God; may He be exalted above having a son. To him belongs everything in heaven and earth. (4:171)

Some of the People of the Book truly believe in God, in what was revealed to you and to them reverently, and do not violate the revelations of God for a mean advantage. Their reward is with God. . . . (3:199) Say: O People of the Book! Come now to a fair word common to both of us, that we shall not worship anyone except God, that we shall never associate aught with Him, and that we shall not take one another for Lord beside God. But if they turn away, then say: Remember, we do submit to

God. (3:64) Say: We believe in that which has been revealed to us and that which has been revealed to you (People of the Book), and our God and your God is One; it is to Him that we submit. (29:47) If the unbelievers repent, hold the supreme act of worship and pay the *zakāt*, then they are your brethren in religion. . . . But if they violate their solemn promises and attack your religion, then fight the leaders of unbelief for they are unworthy of their own covenants. Perhaps they will repent. (9:11–12)

4. The Imperishable Revelation: Final Establishment of True Religion

Muḥammad is the Prophet of God and last of the prophets. (33:40) The truth has now come; error and falsehood have been dissipated. The latter was ephemeral. (17:81) Henceforth, men shall have no excuse before God. . . . Right guidance is now clearly separated from misguidance. (2:150, 256) It is We Who revealed the Qur'ān; and We shall safeguard it. (15:9) Upon Us devolves the holding of the Qur'ān together as well as the establishment of its correct reading. Follow then Our reading of it. Upon us too devolves its elucidation. (75:17–18)

B. CIVILIZATIONAL: *RELIGIONSWISSENSCHAFT*, BIBLICAL CRITICISM, AND THE FINAL RETURN TO REASON

1. *Religionswissenschaft:* Ninth–Twelfth Centuries

As God had enabled me to learn the beliefs of mankind—those who belong to religions and sects as well as those who belong to various philosophies and schools—to master their sourcebooks and texts, to understand their popular and sophisticated views, I decided to collect this knowledge in a brief book for the stimulation of research and the guidance of the seeking student. . . . My purpose is to show the thought of the men of religion and the views of the others from Adam onwards, according to the clearest and most comprehensive plan, to confirm their sincere claim, to harmonize their dissonant views, and to bring together their divergences. . . .

Scholars divided mankind in many ways to suit their purposes. Some divided men according to regions and climates. . . . Others, according to the continents they inhabit. . . . Others according to the civilization to which they belong . . . etc. Others, divide men according to their religious views and that is what this book proposes to do. Primarily, men fall into two main groups: Religions and sects, such as the Majūs (Manichaeans, Zoroastrians, etc.), Jews, Christians, and Muslims; and philosophies and schools, such as the philosophers, the materialists. . . . Every group is subdivided into many subgroups. Unlike the philosophies and schools which are so varied that it is impossible to systematize them comprehensively, the religions and sects are so amenable because their tenets derive from given scriptures and traditions. However wide or narrow the differences that separate them, it is known that the Majūs divide into seventy sects, the Jews into seventy-one, the Christians into seventy-two, and the Muslims into seventy-three. Only one of all the beliefs and views held by these sects may claim to be true. For no two sects share a point and contradict each other thereon but that one must be right and the other wrong, or both wrong. To declare both judgments true would be to deny the unity of truth. Therefore, since truth is one, only that sect with acknowledges it and holds the beliefs which accord therewith may be said to be truly saved. (Al Shahrastānī [d. 1153], *Al Milal wa al Nilḥal* [Sects and religious factions], pp. 1–7)

Many authors have written on the religions of mankind and produced a great number of books. Some are long and detailed. Most of them have criticized so severely and condemned their subject-matter so harshly that the reader is diverted from understanding to judging without sufficient knowledge. They have summarized or suppressed, omitted or neglected much of the counter arguments of the religions discussed. Such authors are unfair to their own minds for depriving them of complete understanding and they are unfair to their opponents for not granting them the right to have their views fully aired. Furthermore, they are disrespectful to their readers because what they offer them is insufficient and has to be supplemented by other books. Only a very few refrained from using a complex form of presentation which is difficult to grasp. All of them interpreted so widely that one cannot tell whether he is reading them or the religions they are discussing. That is why their books are hardly understood by men of learning. They deserve no praise at the present and their works are doomed to oblivion in the future.

Having sought God's blessing for the project, I wrote this work with the express purpose of marshalling the evidence from given, observable facts, whether mediate or immediate. I based my analyses on materials which truly belong to the faith investigated, and never pulled any out of its proper context. Where I have done otherwise, I ask the reader to discount my words, for justice demands it. I have emphasized the commonsense meaning of the words of the texts and avoided obscurantism, hoping only for the reward of God. (Ibn Ḥazm [d. 1064], *Al Fiṣal fi al Milal wa al Ahwā'wa al Niḥal*, [Book of the branches in sects, schisms, and religious factions], vol. 1, pp. 2–3)

2. Higher Biblical Criticism: Ninth–Twelfth Centuries

a. Judaism

The Jews are divided into five sects. First, the Samaritans who claim that the holy city is not Jerusalem but Nablus, situated eighteen miles north of Jerusalem. Their *Torah* is different from that which is common to all other Jews, and they do not believe either in the prophets after Moses and Joshua or in the resurrection. They all live in al Shām, for they do not permit themselves to leave. Second, the Zadokites who refer themselves to Zadok and who, alone among all Jews, call Ezra the son of God. They live in Yemen. Third, the 'Anānīs, followers of 'Anān al Dāwūdī al Yahūdī, called by the Jews Al 'Urās and al Muss. They claim they observe the codes of the *Torah* and of the prophets but reject the sayings of the rabbis. They live in Iraq, al Shām, and Egypt, and some of them have settled in Toledo and Talibra. Fourth, the Rabbinic Jews, also called al Ash'anīs, who follow the sayings of the rabbis and constitute the majority. Fifth, the 'Īsawīs, followers of Abū 'Īsā al Iṣfahānī. . . . They accept the prophethood of Jesus as well as that of Muḥammad. . . . I have met a large number of Jews belonging to these sects and read, among other things, a history of them written by an ancient Aaronite Jew. . . . His name was Joseph, son of Aaron (Flavius Josephus); and in his book, he gave the whole history of the Jews, of their kings and wars, down to the execution of John, son of Zechariah (the Baptist). . . .

The *Torah* says (*Genesis*, 2:10–15) that a river springs in Eden which irrigates paradise and then divides into four streams. The first is the Nile which runs in the Zuwaylah country where there is pure gold, pearls, and crystals. The second is Jihon which runs in Abyssinia. The third is the Tigris which runs east of Mosul; and the fourth is the Euphrates. . . . Anyone with the least knowledge of geography . . . or has traveled between Egypt, al Shām, and Mosul knows that this is utterly false. . . .

The *Torah* says (*Genesis*, 5:18–32) that Methuselah, son of Enoch, grandson of Jared, lived 969 years; that Lamech, his son, was born when he was 187 years old; that Noah was born to Lamech when the latter was 182. At Noah's birth, then, Methuselah was 369 years old. At Methuselah's death, Noah must have reached the age of 600 years. Mind this well! The *Torah* goes on then to say (*Genesis*, 7, 8) that on the seventeenth day of the second month of the 600th year of Noah's age, the deluge came; and that on the twenty-seventh day of the second month of the 601st year, Noah left the ark with all who were with him. Evidently, Methuselah must have entered the ship and died thereon two months and three days before anyone disembarked. But the *Torah* tells (*ibid.*) us definitely that no man but Noah, his three sons, his wife and three daughters-in-law ever entered the ship, and that no man was saved from drowning except those who were in the ark!

Obviously, this *Torah* must have been tampered with by the scribes and forged. For, no rational being will claim divine or prophetic status for such ignorance in . . . elementary geography and simple arithmetic. This is incontestable evidence that the *Torah*, as it now reads, is the work of an ignorant scribe or blasphemous forger. (*Ibid.*, pp. 98–100, 117–19, 122–23)

b. CHRISTIANITY

We do not need to prove here, as we did in the case of the *Torah* and the books attributed to the prophets, that the *Evangels* and other Christian books are neither from the hand of God nor from that of Jesus Christ. . . . No Christian claims this. Rather, they all know that the *Evangels* were composed by four well-known men, in different periods of time. . . . Nor is there doubt that the early history of Christianity was full of secrecy and persecutions . . .; that in Jesus' time, no more than 120 persons believed in him . . .; that the Christians did not feel safe for some 300 years after Jesus. During this time, the *Evangel* which was revealed by God to Jesus was lost. Only a few parts thereof survived and it constitutes evidence against the forgeries of the later Christians. . . . Any religion with such tumultuous beginnings could not have preserved a continuous tradition. Many an alien element could have easily entered into that which could not be had except secretly, which could not be publicly safeguarded against attack or forgery. Thus Manichaeanism made deep inroads into Christianity in the early period. . . .

Our point is not to blame the scribes and reporters of tradition for the wrongs they wrote or reported. . . . Where evidence is produced against any tradition, it should be abandoned. . . . There is nothing to cavil at in the fact that such works contain mistakes; neither do we hold the Christians responsible for them. But we do blame the Christians for accepting the reporters' attribution of falsehoods to God or to His prophet, and their declaring such reportage infallible as a source of religious truth. They should have critically investigated the contradictory claims . . . as the Muslims had done in the case of the traditions of Muḥammad.

(For instance), in Chapter 5 of *Matthew*, it is told that Jesus said to his disciples, "Do not think that I have come to destroy the law and the books of the prophets, but to fulfill them. I say unto you that heaven and earth will pass before a jot or tittle of the law passes. . . ." This statement confirms the *Torah* and rejects the doctrine of abrogation (of one revelation by another). However, only a few lines further, we read, "It has been said to you that whoever repudiates his wife, let him write her a title of divorce; but I say unto you that whoever repudiates his wife except for adultery has caused her to commit adultery; whoever marries a divorced woman is an adulterous person. . . ." This is clearly an abrogation of the *Torah*. . . . The Christians also tell about Paul that he abrogated circumcision . . . and about Peter, that he relieved the Christians from the prohibition against pork. . . . The Christians, in fact, repudiate the whole *Torah*, including the sabbath . . . while at the same time agree that Jesus was apprehended while he himself was celebrating Easter according to the *Torah*. . . . How then do they not reject *Matthew's* attribution to Jesus of a falsehood which the latter never said? (*Ibid.*, pp. 2–5, 28, 21–22)

3. "People of the Book": A Category of Inter-religious Coexistence and Dialogue

(Commander) Muḥammad Kāsim (d. 93 A.H.; 711) admonished every man separately, and said, "Be happy in every respect, and have no anxiety, for you will not be blamed for anything. I do not take any agreement or bond from you. Whatever sum is fixed and we have settled you must pay. Moreover, care and leniency shall be shown you. And whatever may be your requests, they should be represented to me so that they may be heard, a proper reply to be given, and the wishes of each man be satisfied. . . .

The Brahmans did not receive the alms which were given to them according to the old custom, by the merchants, the infidels, and thākurs, who took delight in worshiping the idols. The attendants of the temples were likewise in distress. For fear of the army, the alms and bread were not regularly given to them, and therefore they were reduced to poverty. They came to the gate of his palace, and lifted up their hands in prayer. They said, "May you live long, oh just lord! We people obtain our livelihood and maintenance by keeping the temple of Budh. You showed mercy upon the merchants and the infidels, confirmed them in their property, and made them zimmīs (tolerated subjects). Hence we, your slaves relying upon your bounty, hope permission may be given for them to worship their gods, and repair the temple of Budh." Muḥammad Kāsim replied, "The seat of government is Alor, and all these other places are dependencies of it." The Hindus said, "The edifice (temple) of this city is under the Brahmans. They are our sages and physicians, and our nuptial and funeral ceremonies are performed by them. We have agreed to pay the taxes in the expectation that every one would be left to follow his own persuasion. This our temple of Budh is ruined, and we cannot worship our idols. If our just lord will permit us, we will repair it, and worship our gods. Our Brahmans will then receive the means of living from us. . . ."

Muḥammad Kāsim wrote to Hajjāj (c. 40–100 A.H.; c. 661–718), and after some days received a reply to the following effect: The letter of my dear nephew Muḥammad Kāsim has been received, and the facts understood. It appears that the chief inhabitants of Brahmanabad have petitioned to be allowed to repair the temple of Budh and pursue their religion. As they have made submission, and have agreed to pay taxes to the Khalīfa, (Muḥammad's heir), nothing more can be properly required from them. They have been taken under our protection, and we cannot in any way stretch out our hands upon their lives or property. Permission is given to them to worship their gods. Nobody must be forbidden or prevented from following his own religion. They may live in their houses in whatever manner they like. . . .

When the orders of Hajjāj reached Muḥammad Kāsim, he had left the city, and had gone on a march. He directed the nobles, the principal inhabitants, and the Brahmans to build their temple, traffic with the Muḥammadans, live without any fear, and strive to better themselves. He also enjoined them to maintain the indigent Brahmans with kindness and consideration, observe the rites and customs of their ancestors, and give oblations and alms to the Brahmans, according to former practice. They were to allot three dirams out of every hundred dirams capital, and to give them as much of this as should be necessary—the remainder was to be paid into the treasury and accounted for; it would be safe in the keeping of Government. They were also to settle allowances upon the officers and nobles. They all fully agreed to these conditions before Tamīn bin Zaidu-l-Kaisī and Hukm bin 'Awāna Kalbī. It was ordained that the Brahmans should, like beggars, take a copper basin in their hands, go to the doors of the house, and take whatever grain or other thing that might be offered to them, so that they might not remain unprovided for. This practice has got a peculiar name among the infidels. . . .

Muḥammad Kāsim granted the request which the people of Brahmanabad had made to him, and permitted them to retain their position like the Jews, the Christians, and fire worshipers of 'Irāk and Shām. He then dismissed them, and gave their head men the appellation of Rānā. (Al Kūfī [N.D.], tr. by Q. M. Elliott, in *The History of India as Told by Its Own Historians, Shāh-Nāmah*, vol. 1, pp. 184–87)

It is natural that the Islāmic state have some citizens—new or original inhabitants of the land within state territory—who do not belong to Islām, be they former friends of the Muslims or their previous enemies, but who entered into the covenant of the Islāmic polity by submitting to the state and paying the poll (*jizyah*) tax. The Qur'ān imposed no limitation whatever on such people's exercise of their personal, civil, social, economic, or religious rights. It emphasized their freedom and right to manage their personal status and community affairs according to their own laws.

. . . Indeed, verses 5:43–49 not only grant such right to the People of the Book but demand that the laws of the *Torah* and the *Evangel* must be honored and applied. The Jewish and Christian citizens of the Islāmic state are not free to discard their laws and the state is obliged not to allow this to happen. (Darwazah, *Al Dustūr al Qur'ānī fī Shu'ūn al Havāt* [The Qur'ānic constitution relative to the affairs of life], pp. 125–26, 169–70)

The first of the prophets was Adam, and the last of them, Muḥammad. The total number of prophets had better not be specified, since God had told about some and not about others. Otherwise, it is not impossible to include in their rank some who were not prophets and to exclude therefrom some who were. All of them were messengers from God, truthful and rightly guiding their people. The last and best of the prophets was Muḥammad. (Al Nasafī [d. 1310], '*Umdat 'Aqidat Ahl al Sunnah wa al Jamā'ah* [Basic conviction of the people of the *Sunnah* and the majority of the community] p. 4)

4. The Final Return to Reason and to True Religion

Many centuries passed and many nations rose and fell, progressed and decayed, differed and agreed, suffered and achieved happiness. Through all these changes, the bitter and the sweet, there developed a sensitivity more delicate than the five senses, something more akin to the empathy and compassion stirring within women's hearts and children's. Thus, a new religion (Christianity) arose which addressed itself primarily to these feelings and appealed to the intuitions of the heart. It laid down for its adherents the example of an ascetic ideal, seeking to liberate them from their gross concern with this world and to orient them towards the spiritual realm. It asked the man with a right to forgo his right though legitimate. It shut the gates of heaven in face of the rich, and proclaimed a number of other precepts for conduct. As for worship, it established a system well in tune with these objectives. Undoubtedly, the converts to the new faith did much to alleviate the ills of their communities and to redress their wrongs. However, only a few generations passed when the original enthusiasm motivating these moral efforts began to wane and men found themselves incapable of fulfilling its principles. This failure of moral nerve impressed upon the adherents that their ethic is really impossible for man, that it belongs to another kingdom and another order of being. Liberated from it by their own delusion, the men of religion (i.e., of Christianity) took to competing with the kings of the earth in the pursuit of power, and with the rich and aristocrats in the pursuit of well-being and luxury. The overwhelming majority of the adherents followed suit, and they looked for justification by interpreting the given scripture and adding thereto what they found lacking therein.

Such was the history of the disappearance of purity and sincerity in moral conduct. As for the history of doctrine, the adherents split into many sects each innovating in religion as it saw fit; but they all agreed on one point which they regarded as the essential principle of religious truth, namely, the unquestionable authority of the church or the prohibition of reason to look into the faith, into the deeper problems of the world . . . to penetrate the secrets of creation. . . . Therefore, they proclaimed that reason and religion are twain and never meet, that science is the enemy of religion, and they sought to bring about one another's conversion to these tenets by every means possible. So strong was the excessivism of this religion that it inflicted upon mankind some of its worst tragedies—the religious wars and persecutions. The result was the severance of relations between human groups, the abolition of peace, and isolation and enmity took the place of cooperation and good will. . . . This continued to be the case until the advent of Islām.

At that time, human association had brought man to an apex of development and the events of the past prepared him for a return to reason. . . . Thus, the prophethood which began with Adam came to an end with Muḥammad and divine revelation was complete with the revelation he brought. . . . That is just as the Qur'ān had declared, the *sunnaḥ* (example, life, tradition) corroborated and later history has proved. For, ever since Muḥammad, every claimant of prophecy failed and mankind felt secure in its understanding that there shall henceforth be no more prophets carrying messages from heaven. ('Abduh, [1849–1905], *Risālat al Tawḥīd* [Epistle on the unity of God], pp. 154–67)

CHAPTER 28

The Moment of Islām in the History of Revelation

□ Muḥammad, son of 'Abdullah, was of the Quraysh tribe of Makkah. He was illiterate and a man like other men. His character, however, was exemplary, and he was deeply religious. Chosen for prophethood by God, He received the revelations called *al Qur'ān* (Koran, literally, the Reading), through the agency of Gabriel, the angel who appeared and recited the revelations to him. The advent of the revelations did not give Muḥammad any supernatural power or knowledge, the miracle being the ideational content revealed rather than any transformation of its human recipient and carrier. Moreover, Muḥammad had no power to save or to condemn, not even to intercede for those whom he loved. He remained absolutely true to the absolute dictum that all power belongs to God. He preached religion, founded the *ummah*, or universal brotherhood under the moral law, and launched it on its world mission.

The Qur'ān is the work of God in His own words. It, as well as its predecessors—*Torah*, *Evangel*, and so on, which it had superseded inclusively but not exclusively—is the only holy communication revealed to man. It is all that man may know of God, of his will and pattern for man and creation. Its content is inseparable from its Arabic form, which acts as a rock-anchor for its ideational and linguistic meanings. It is the fountainhead of religion, ethics, and law, as well as their final authority. This authority is not mystical or irrational, but rational and critical. It does not coerce, but convinces the mindful reader.

The *sunnah* (example, life, tradition) consists of the sayings and deeds of the Prophet, or of the practices of his companions which he had initiated. Its role is that of an exemplification of the Qur'ān, of a clarifiant and specificative commentary thereon. Where it is certain, it is equally authoritative as the Qur'ān. □

A. SCRIPTURAL: MUḤAMMAD, THE QUR'ĀN, THE SUNNAH

1. Muḥammad, The Prophet

Say: O men, I am God's prophet sent to all of you by God, whose dominion is heaven and earth. . . . (Qur'ān, 7:158) Muḥammad is no relation to any of you; he is the Prophet of God and the last of the prophets . . . a witness, a missionary, and a warner, a caller unto God by his permission and a guiding light . . . a mercy to all mankind. (33:40, 45–46; 21:107) We have revealed to you (Muḥammad) the Book in truth, that you may judge among men by that which God has taught you. . . . (4:105) O Prophet, convey that which has come down to you from your Lord. Unless you have done so, you have not fulfilled your prophethood. . . . (5:67) Say: I am only a warner. . . . I have no transcendental knowledge such as they claim to have disputing among one another. (38:65)

2. Al Qur'ān: The Revelation

It (al Qur'ān) is a revelation from the Lord of the universe, brought down by the faithful spirit (Angel Gabriel) upon thy heart, that you may warn mankind. (26:192–211) Your man (i.e. Muḥammad) had neither erred nor gone astray. Neither is what he says mere conjecture, but a revelation revealed, taught him by one of extreme strength and power (the Angel) who stood poised between heaven and earth, who approached and came as near or nearer than two bows' length. Then God revealed to His servant what He did. The heart has not forged what it beheld. Would you contend with him as to what he actually saw? . . . His sight has not erred, nor deviated. He has only witnessed some of the great truths of His Lord. (53:2–18) And do not anticipate the revelation of the Qur'ān before it actually comes to you. Rather, say: O God, increase my knowledge. (20:114)

This is the Book . . . confirming the already-given revelations. (2:2, 97) For it is He who revealed the *Torah* and the *Evangel* in the past as guidance to the people who now revealed the Qur'ān to supersede them. (3:4) It is a Book whose verses are articulated in Arabic, for a people who reason. (41:3) We have brought down the revelation as an Arabic reading that you may consider . . .; as an Arabic judgment . . . absolutely flawless . . ., that they may become pious. (12:2; 13:37; 39:28) Upon Us devolves the collection of its verses, as well as the establishment of its reading. (75:17) This Book is doubtless. (2:2) It is a clear teaching for mankind, a guidance, and an exhortation to the pious. (3:138) Its truths are articulated by the All-wise and Omniscient. (11:1) It is a glorious Qur'ān, preserved (forever) on the tablet of heaven. . . . Had We brought this Qur'ān down upon a mountain, you would have seen it humbled and cleft asunder. . . . (85:21–22; 59:21) And if there is any doubt regarding what We have revealed to Our servant, try to bring about the like of one of its chapters. . . . But if you fail, then fear the fire. . . . Say: If all men and genii put themselves shoulder to shoulder and mobilize their resources for the invention of a Qur'ān such as this, they will not succeed. (2:23–24; 17:88) This Qur'ān guides to that which is more right and better. It reassures the believers who do the good that their reward will be great. (17:9) Those who hold fast to the Book of God . . . would certainly meet their recompense from God and receive more than His bounty. . . . (35:29–30) And when the Qur'ān is recited, listen carefully and hear, that you may become blessed. (7:204) Follow what has been revealed to you from your Lord and do not follow aught beside Him. (7:3)

3. Al Sunnah: Concretization and Exemplification of Islām

Whoever covenants with you (Muḥammad) has covenanted with God. (48:10) Whoever obeys the Prophet has obeyed God. . . . (4:80) Say: If you love God, then follow me; God will love you and forgive your misdeeds. . . . Say: Obey God and the Prophet. If they turn away, remember that God does not love the unbelievers. (3:31–32) We have sent no prophet but to be obeyed, with God's permission. (4:64) Whether man or woman, it is not for a believer to do as he pleases, once the matter in question has been decided by God and His Prophet. (33:36) Verily, the Prophet constitutes the model and his conduct the standard for you, if your hope is in God. (33:21)

B. CIVILIZATIONAL: MUḤAMMAD'S CHARACTER AND HUMANITY; NATURE OF THE QUR'ĀN; AUTHORITY OF THE SUNNAH

1. Muḥammad's Person: Among His Followers

Muḥammad, God's Peace and Blessing be upon him! This noble name has been on the lips of countless millions of men. For almost fourteen centuries millions of hearts have palpitated with deep emotion at the pronouncement of it. Many more millions of people, for a period as long as time, will pronounce it, and will be deeply moved thereby. Every day, as soon as the black thread becomes distinguishable from the white, the *mu'adhdhin* (one who calls for prayer) will call men to prayer. He will call them to the worship of God and the invocation of blessing upon His Prophet, a task the fulfillment of which is better for them than their sleep. Thousands and millions of men in every corner of the globe will undoubtedly respond to the *mu'adhdhin*'s call, springing to honor through their prayer God's mercy and bounty, freshly evidenced for them with the break of every new day. At high noon, the *mu'adhdhin* will call again for the noon prayer; then at mid-afternoon, at sunset, and after-sunset. On each of these daily occasions, Muslims remember Muḥammad, the servant of God and His Prophet, with awe, reverence, and piety. Even in between these prayers, the Muslims never hear the name of Muḥammad but they hasten to praise God and His chosen one. Thus they have been; and thus they will be, until God vindicates His true religion and completes His bounty to all. . . . "God and His angels bless the Prophet. O men who believe, invoke God's peace and blessing upon him." (Qur'ān, 33:56) Haykal, *Ḥayāt Muhammad* [Life of Muḥammad], p. 1)

2. Among His Contemporary Enemies and Friends

The Makkans (people of Mecca) said to Abū Ṭālib (the Prophet's paternal uncle), "O Abū Ṭālib, your nephew blasphemed our gods, repudiated our religion, ridiculed our ideals and hereticated our ancestors. Either you stop him or you renounce your guardianship of him, for you too agree with us to disagree with him. We can then dispose of him for you." Abū Ṭālib spoke to them gently and let them go appeased but not satisfied. Muḥammad however continued his preaching of the religion of God. As more people converted to the new faith, the situation became ever more serious and men began to cultivate hatred for one another . . ., the Makkans went once more to Abū Ṭālib and said, "O Abū Ṭālib, we acknowledge that you are an honorable elder of our clan and recognize the position of eminence you occupy among us. We have asked you to stop your nephew but you did not. We shall not allow his attacks upon our Gods, religion, ideals, and ancestors to go on. Either you stop him forthwith or we shall fight him, even if this brings about the destruction of our clan, your clan, or both." Abū Ṭālib called Muḥammad and said to him, "My nephew, your people had addressed to me such and such complaints against you. Would you not save yourself and myself and not impose upon our house what it cannot bear?" . . . The Prophet answered, "O my uncle! By God I swear, even if they should put the sun in my right hand and the moon in my left that I may adjure this religion, I shall never do so. Rather, I shall persist until God vindicates His religion or I perish in the process." (Ibn Hishām [d. 828], *Sīrat al Nabiyy* [Life of the Prophet], vol. 1, pp. 277–78)

The companions of the Prophet used to find in his conduct, his good example, and righteous leadership the moving inspiration and true guidance which are the cornerstones of education and discipline. Between a prophet and his disciples, a master and his pupils, a pastor and his pastorate, a leader and his followers, there can be no better relation than that of the learner to the good example. The search has never stopped and the demand has never ceased, on the part of education and moral teachers whether on the personal, national, or universal level, for those who could fill the post of the good example. Obviously all men are aware of the extreme importance of such a post in the building of personal and societal character. And yet, history has never known and will never know a good example as noble, as great, and as magnanimous as Muḥammad. For he was truly perfect in every human meaning as of the term and his moral character, his discipline, his gentlemanliness, his loyalty to principles and attention to detail, his truthfulness and exactitude—all these qualities of his have never known and will never know a parallel.

Indeed, his truthfulness and fidelity have been known to all long before he carried the burden of prophethood. His contemporaries used to call him "*al sādiq*" (the truthful) and "*al amīn*" (the faithful) and never question his report or judgment. It was precisely these qualities of the Prophet which helped convince his contemporaries of his mission. Even his direct enemies, not to speak of his followers and friends, could not but acknowledge them. Abū Sufyān ibn Ḥarb, leader of the Prophet's opponents, when questioned by the Byzantine emperor concerning the new religion being preached in Makkah, admitted that Muḥammad never told a lie before his prophethood and the emperor was deeply moved by this testimony of the Prophet's greatest enemy. . . . The Makkans constantly repeated to Muḥammad, "We do not belie *you*, but that which was given to you." (Al Zarqānī [d. 1710], *Manāhil al 'Irfān fī 'Ulūm al Qur'ān* [Sources of knowledge in the sciences of the Qur'ān], pp. 319–20)

One day when Muḥammad was praying alone in the temple and the Makkans were gathered in the Quraysh community house, 'Utbah, his uncle, said to them, "Would you not that I approach Muḥammad and offer him something on your behalf that he may be swayed from his path?" . . . 'Utbah said, "O my nephew, you know very well the love and respect that we all feel towards you, the place of honor in which we hold you, the noble descendance and reputation which we enable you to enjoy among us. You have wrought upon your people an ominous thing, destroying their unity, castigating their religion. . . . Would you not listen to me for I am about to offer you something which would surely satisfy you." The Prophet said, "Proceed, for I am listening to you." 'Utbah said, "If by bringing about this affair you sought to increase your wealth, we shall bring forth to you so much of all our wealth until you become by far the richest among us. If your objective was honor and position, we shall proclaim you our unquestionable leader and none shall have the right to disobey you. If it is a throne you seek, we shall call you king. If, moreover, you cannot get rid of these apparitions that seem to possess you, we shall seek for you all the medical service at all cost until you are completely cured." The Prophet then said, "Have you finished?" 'Utbah said, "Yes." Thereupon the Prophet said, "Listen now to me" and he recited to him *surah* (division) 41 of the Qur'ān while 'Utbah listened, his hands held together behind his back. . . . When the Prophet finished . . . and 'Utbah returned to the community house, his fellows said to one another, "Behold! 'Utbah has come back to you with a different face from that with which he left. . . ." When asked, he said, "By God, I have heard a recitation such as I have never heard before. It is neither poetry, nor magic, nor divination. O People of Quraysh, listen to me and obey. Leave this man alone . . ." (Ibn Hishām, *Sīrat al Nabiyy*, vol. 1, pp. 313–14)

3. Muḥammad: Man, Man, Man and not God

When the Prophet died, 'Umar ibn al Khaṭṭāb (second caliph, 634–644) arose in the mosque and said, "Some hypocrites are claiming that the Prophet of God is dead. But he is not dead. He merely went to join his God. Moses too went to join his God and was absent for forty days, but he returned; so would Muḥammad. Whoever repeats such a claim as that Muḥammad died, I shall cut off his arms and legs with this sword." Abū Bakr (third convert to Islām) having heard of the news of the Prophet . . ., visited the house of the Prophet and ascertained his death . . . arrived at the mosque and overheard 'Umar. He said, "Softly, 'Umar." But 'Umar kept on speaking and threatening. Abū Bakr then stood up and said, "O people! Whoever of you has been worshiping Muḥammad, let him know for certain that Muḥammad is dead. But whoever of you has been worshiping God, then let him know that God never dies. 'Muḥammad is but a prophet, like so many other prophets before him. Would you, in case he dies or is killed, abjure your faith and renounce your religion? Whoever apostatizes will not hurt God. Whoever is constant in his praise of God, him will God reward.'" (Qur'ān, 3:144) (*Ibid.*, vol. 4, pp. 334–35)

4. Al Qur'ān, the Fountainhead Uncreated and External

The Qur'ān is the totality of the law of Islām (*sharī'ah*), the pillar of the community, the fountainhead of wisdom, the evidence of prophecy, the light of mind and eye. There is no path to God except through it, no salvation without it and no holding to anything that diverges from it. . . . Whoever therefore seeks to understand the principles and purposes of the *sharī'ah* or to join those who make its pursuit supreme, must take the Qur'ān as a constant companion, friend, and instructor, both theoretically and practically and never pursue the one without the other. Such a seeker would achieve the high objective, win the final prize, and join those who are first in heaven. . . . He should therefore instruct himself in the Arabic tongue in order to train himself in the understanding of it. . . . He should learn the historical circumstances surrounding the revelation of each one of its verses. . . . He should learn the customs, sayings, conduct, history, and ethos of the Arabs before and during its revelation. (Al Shāṭibī [d. 1389], *Al Muwāfaqāt fī Uṣūl al Sharī'ah* [Agreements on the first principles of Islamic law], vol. 3, pp. 346–47, 351–52)

The Mu'tazilah [School] claimed that prior to this controversy (regarding the createdness or eternity of the Qur'ān), the Muslims generally agreed that the Qur'ān is the word of God, that it consists of chapters, of verses, or compositions of words and letters actually audible and legible, that it has a beginning and an end, that it is a miracle by God establishing Muḥammad's genuine prophethood. There is no miracle but that it is an act of God. . . . Etymologically, the word *Qur'ān* refers to collection and grouping . . . which apply only to the divisible. Now, all these descriptions are inapplicable to anything eternal. Furthermore, the *ummah* (the society of Islām) agrees that the words of God are here with us and that we read them with out tongues, touch them with our hands, behold them with our eyes, and hear them with our ears. The Qur'ān itself said: "And if any unbeliever asks for your protection, grant it to him so that he may hear the words of God," (9:6) and "Only the purified shall touch it." (56:79) How then could an eternal attribute of divinity be so described (if, as the Sunnīs (followers of the *sunnah*) claim, the Qur'ān is eternal)?

The Ash'ariyyah (theological school) retorted (to the Mu'tazilah), "You are the first to diverge from this consensus; by holding that the words of God are letters and words created in given circumstances, you imply that the Qur'ān is, like any creature, liable to destruction. That which we write with our hands is our creation, for which we are rewarded; that which we read with our tongues is our acquisition, for the violation of which we are punished. The Qur'ān which we have then is not the words of God but our own; and whatever is so cannot be the Qur'ān and constitutes therefore neither guidance nor miracle. What we do read and do hear is only a story—as it were—about the words of God. . . . It was such difficulty which drove Abū 'Alī al Jubbā'ī to assert that every hearer creates a second set of words for himself by which to apprehend what he reads or is read for him . . . whereas no rational being doubts that the letters and words he hears from a reader are those which the reader deliberately pronounces and not another set of words and letters which the hearer creates, so that every letter and every word and every verse of the Qur'ān, as of any other book, is really double. That is an absurd view. . . .

Rightly, however, we assert the following: It is undeniable that the Qur'ān is made up of verses, parts, and *surahs*, which are in turn made up of words and phrases, and that the whole has a beginning and an ending; that that which begins and ends is not eternal; that from this respect the Qur'ān is a (created) miracle granted to the Prophet. . . . The question, however, does not concern any one of these aspects, but only that which is read in these words and verses. Is that which is read in the Qurān eternal and not created? one and not many? Or is the Qur'ān merely the words and verses read rather than the meanings apprehended therein? We agree with our opponents that the words of God are not the sounds produced by the larynx, tongue, and lips but the meanings behind all these. Whereas we hold that such meaning is one and eternal, you believe that it is many and created. Thus, it was our opponents who diverged from the consensus . . .

The true solution to this dilemma is that the verses which Gabriel recited to the Prophet are the words of God just as the *persona*, or visible form, by which Gabriel appeared is called "Gabriel". The former is the speech of God as it appears, and the *persona* is Gabriel as he appears. When we say to someone, 'Your word is true,' we do not refer to the expression apart from the meaning but as expressing that meaning. . . . To honor the scripture, therefore, is to honor what is "scriptured," as to respect a house is to respect the human domiciled therein. (Al Shahrastānī [d. 1153] *Nihāyat al Iqdām fī 'Ilm al Kalām* [The ultimate in the science of theology], pp. 309–13)

5. The Qur'ānic Disciplines: An Example

The cause of revelation is that which constitutes the subject matter of a verse or a number of verses, or underlies the judgment therein contained, as its sufficient reason. It could be an event which took place in the lifetime of the Prophet; or a question that was addressed to him, thus occasioning the revelation of the verse or verses in question as judgment, comment, clarification, or solution. . . .

Some men claimed that there is no point to the study of the causes of revelation besides the purely historical one of knowing the situational circumstances in which some verses were revealed. But that is an erroneous judgment. Knowledge of the causes of revelation is advantageous from many respects. First, it enables us to know the wisdom underlying a specific revelation, which is beneficial to Muslim and non-Muslim alike. The Muslim would find his *īmān* (faith by conviction) strengthened by the new knowledge and would, as a result, seek a closer fulfillment of the divine imperative, of the realization of God's pattern. For the causes of revelation demonstrate the values and ethical grounds for the sake of which these commands were revealed. As for the non-Muslim, his apprehension of these first principles of wisdom, of the axiological grounds of revelation should convince him of the truth of the faith if he were but just and fair. Knowledge of these causes will teach him that the pattern of Islāmic life is founded on the welfare of man, not on extortion, tyranny, prejudice, or unreason. . . . (Al Zarqānī, *Manāhil al 'Irfān fī 'Ulūm al Qur'ān*, pp. 99–102)

6. Al Sunnah: Its Authority and Validity

The word *sunnah* applies to all that has been reported about the Prophet besides the text of the Qur'ān. . . . The word is also applied to the actions of the Prophet's companions—whether such were reported in the Qur'ān or in the Prophet's *sunnah*—because either such actions were concretizations of some *sunnah* of the Prophet which has not come down to us, or applications of a consensus achieved by them concerning the Prophet's *sunnah*. . . . The *sunnah* is secondary with respect to the Qur'ān, for several reasons. The first is that, whereas the Book is definite as well as final and authoritative as a whole and in its detail, the *sunnah* is not definite, nor final and authoritative but only as a whole. There are three possible relations of the *sunnah* to the Qur'ān. The first is where the *sunnah* agrees with the Qur'ān in all respects. In this case, the two corroborate and reinforce the given point. The second is where the *sunnah* explains and illustrates the Qur'ān. The third is where the *sunnah* legislates in a matter on which the Qur'ān is silent. No other possibilities exist. The *sunnah* cannot ever run counter to the Qur'ān. Even in the third alternative, whatever addition the *sunnah* makes to Qur'ānic law is not legislation anew, as it were, by the Prophet. Such laws are certainly obligatory for us; but this obligation cannot be construed as an addition to God's authority, but as falling under the Qur'ānic general commands and principles. (Ibn al Qayyim al Jawziyyah [d. 1292–1350), *I'lām al Muwaqqi'īn 'an Rabb al 'Ālamīn*

[Instruction of the convicted in the lessons of the Lord of the universe], vol. 2, pp. 288–89)

As for the relation of the Book and the *sunnah* to the religion of Islām, the Book is certainly the first source of all legislation and the comprehensive constitution of all the good of earth and heaven. The *sunnah* is the second source; for it explains the Qur'ān, detailing the general, particularizing the absolute, specifying the universal, clarifying the obscure, and unravelling that which is not obvious. . . . The *sunnah* rules over the Book, not vice versa. In elaborating this principle, al Suyūṭī (1445–1505) said, "By the Qur'ān's need for the *sunnah*, we mean that the *sunnah* clarifies and illuminates the Book, that it concretizes what is abstract and unknowable with certainty, that it does so by the mind and hand of Muḥammad, the first recipient of the revelation . . ." (Al Zarqānī, *Manāhil al 'Irfān fī 'Ulūm al Qur'ān*, pp. 292–93)

The *ahl al kolām* (rationalists jurists and theologians) have castigated the *ahl al ḥadīth* (traditionalist jurists and theologians) and ridiculed them, writing against them in their books and accusing them of contradicting one another's reports. Thus the differences and the sects multiplied and the Muslims have antagonized and hereticated one another. And yet, each part clings to its own collection of transmitted texts (*ḥadīths*). . . . Nonetheless, the *ahl al ḥadīth* have sought the facts and attempted to sort them out from masses of conjectures and fabrications, through critical investigation of the reported traditions. In this quest, they crossed the mountains and the seas, traveled east and west seeking a given tradition from its living fountainhead and then subjected the chain of reporters and the text of the tradition to the most critical scrutiny. The truth, which was hardly noticeable under the accumulated scum, . . . showed forth by means of their labors. Perhaps the great reproach ever addressed to them concerns their inclusion in their collections of *ḥadīths*, some that are weak or extraordinary. But this is founded on a misunderstanding of their purpose. They did not preserve the questionable *ḥadīths* for their own sake, but in order to keep for posterity all the materials of their research, to present the genuine transmitted texts as contradistinguished from the weak and the extraordinary. (Ibn Qutaybah al Dīnawarī [d. 889], *Ta'wīl Mukhtalaf al Ḥadīth fī al Radd 'Ala A'dā' Ahl al Ḥadīth* [Interpretation of the variants of traditions in answer to the enemies of traditionalists], pp. 2–3, 88–89)

CHAPTER 29

God

□ God is a being unlike all and everything known to man, whether material or other. For knowledge, God is the "wholly-other," and that is the meaning of His transcendence. He created out of nothing all that has being, and He continues to sustain creation and to create new being. His work is perfection; His will is law and His desire is the highest and final good. In nature, everything works according to a necessary and immutable pattern which God implanted therein. Man is dual. As a being in nature, he is subject to the same necessary and immutable laws. However, to him God is not only creator and sustainer, but guide as well as judge. Hence, God's desire, the highest and final good, is to man the law or divine command which he, as the only free being in creation, may and may not fulfill. God has communicated His desire to man through revelations to prophets, and He will judge man's obedience and fulfillment on a Final Day. God, then, is maker of the natural order and Lord of the moral. Without Him, neither order can stand; indeed, neither order is possible.

For the Muslim, God is one. He has no associates, and no partners. He exhausts the transcendent realm. Neither gods, nor natural forces, nor men are to be confused, diffused, or associated in any way with Him. That there is no God but God is the first principle of all Islamic theology. Unless God is one, both the natural and the moral orders will collapse. Indeed, none has the power even to intercede with Him.

Of God we know only that He exists as Creator, Designer, Sustainer, Lord of Creation, and that He has a will for nature and a desire for free man. The former is the object of the natural sciences, the latter that of the humanities. The revelation provides a shortcut to the latter; and the divine attributes constitute a summation of the highest good for man. These attributes are neither He, nor not-He. They are He insofar as He may be object of human knowledge and He has predicated them of Himself in the revelation. They are not-He insofar as no human knowledge may ever grasp Him and He is transcendent.

To know God in the sense of learning His will and desire in the revelation and of discovering that will and desire in the sciences and humanities is, in Islām, to worship Him. To fulfill the desire is to serve Him. To achieve conviction of the truth and to realize the good—that is the religiously, morally, and rationally imperative in Islām. □

A. SCRIPTURAL: DIVINE EXISTENCE; UNITY AND ATTRIBUTES; WORSHIP

1. God: His Transcendent Existence and Unity

It is God who created heaven and earth in truth; Who says "Be" to any creature and it is. . . . Dominion is His on the day the trumpets shall sound (the Day of Judgment), and knowledge is His of the orders of the real as of the transcendent. (Qur'ān or Koran, 6:73) Your God is one God; there is no God but He, the Merciful, the

Compassionate . . . the Living, the Self-subsisting. . . . He witnessed that there is no God but He, the Eternal and Just; and so did His angels and all men of knowledge. (2:163; 3:2,18) God will not forgive man's association of other gods with Him. But He will forgive lesser sins to whomsoever He pleases. For whoever associates other gods with God has wrought a grave sin. (4:48) Praise the name of your Lord on high, Who created and well-formed His creation; Who ordered and guided; Who caused the pasture to be, and then to dry up and discolor. (87:1–5) Which is better? Those whom they associate with God? Or God? Or He Who created the heavens and the earth and caused the rain to fall by which the beauteous gardens grow and without which there would be no cultivation? Another god with God? Surely, they go astray. Is it not God alone Who gave man the earth as a habitation, combed it with rivers, punctuated it with mountains, and separated the seas? Another god with God? Surely most of them are ignorant! Is it not God Who answers the man in need when he calls on Him? Who removes the evil? Who made you His vicegerents on earth? Another god with God? Little do they heed! Is it not God Who guides you in the darkness of land and sea? Who sends the winds heralding His bounty? Another god with God? Gloried be He above their associations! Is it not God who first creates, then recreates? Who sends you his bounty through sky and earth? Another god with God? Say: Bring forth your proofs if your claim is true. (27:59–65) God, to Whom be praise, cannot take anyone unto Him as a son. For were He to will anything, He says to it, Be, and it is. . . . This claim of theirs that God has a son is so monstrous that it would feign collapse the skies, break up the mountains, and cleave the earth. (19:35, 88–91) Whoever among the unbelievers claims divinity for himself, We shall punish with hellfire. . . . If there were other gods besides God, heaven and earth would dissolve in chaos. . . . As for those humans whom they call gods, do they raise the dead? . . . Say: Bring forth your proofs. (21:22, 29) The unbelievers have appointed intercessionaries beside God. Say: Do you do so despite the fact that these intercessionaries have neither power nor intelligence? Say: To God belongs all intercession; to Him belongs the dominion of heaven and earth. (39:43) No three men meet together but God is their fourth; nor five men but He is their sixth; nor of many more or less but that God is with them wherever they may be, knowing of everything they do and revealing it to them on the Day of Judgment. (58:7) Whithersoever you turn your face, there will be God's face. (2:116)

2. His Attributes

He is God, and there is no other God besides. He knows the present and the future. He is the Merciful, the most Compassionate . . . the Sovereign, the Holy, the Peace-maker, the Protector, the Supreme, the Omnipotent, the Tremendous, the Exalted . . . Lord . . . the Creator, the Giver, the Fashioner. His are the holy names. . . . He is the Wise, the Glorious. (59:22–24) He is the Forgiver, the Endearer, Lord of the glorious throne, Doer of all that He wishes. (85:14–16) The Most High, the Greatest (4:34). The Wise, the Omniscient. (34:1) . . . Who knows what they hide and what they proclaim. . . . No man knows anything of God's knowledge except such as He may reveal. (2:77, 255) It is He Who taught with the pen, taught man what he did not know. (97:4–5) God provides for you and for your children. (6:151) He gives of His bounty to whomsoever He wishes, without measure. (2:212) God cares for mankind . . . wills no injustice for them . . . loves the doers of good deeds. (3:30, 108, 134) He is self-sufficient, praiseworthy. (2:267) And who is truer of word than God? (4:122) God never fails the promise. (3:9) God has written upon Himself to be merciful. (6:2) Other than God, you have neither friend nor helper. (42:30) Say: O my people who have transgressed against themselves, do not despair of God's mercy. God forgives all your misdeeds. (39:53) Were they to come to you, to ask for God's forgiveness when they do injustice, and were you to pray for them, they would find God merciful and forgiving. (4:64) There is no change to the order God has laid down. (48:23) God is the judge after whose judgment there is no appeal. (13:41) No sight can see Him, but He sees all sights. He is the Gentle, the Knowing. (6:103) No man may hear the speech of God except through revelation. (42:51)

3. The Worship of Him

All praise belongs to God, Lord of the
Universe,
The Merciful, the Forgiving,
Lord of the Day of Judgment.
You alone we worship and You alone we
ask for help.
Guide us unto the straight path,
The path of those whom You have
blessed,
Not those who incurred Your wrath
Nor those who had gone astray.
Amen! (1:1–7)

The Messenger of God believes in what was revealed to him from his Lord; and so do the believers. All of them believe in God, His angels, His Books, His messengers and do not differentiate between any of His messengers. They say, "We hear and we obey; we ask Your forgiveness, O our Lord, for our return is to You alone." God does not burden a soul but within measure of its capacity and holds it deserving of what it earned and responsible for what it incurred. (They pray), "O our Lord! Overlook our forgetfulness and error, and do not hold us to grave account as You held those that went before us. O our Lord! Do not burden us with any more than we can bear. Pardon us and have mercy on us. Grant us Your grace, for You alone are our Master, and help us against those who do not believe in You." (2:286–87) No female conceives or gives birth except with His knowledge. Likewise, no man's age is lengthened or shortened except as set out in His record. (35:11) No animal on earth but God provides for it, knowing its place and settlement. (11:6) No injury or catastrophe befalls man or earth except as set out in God's book with His permission. (57:22) By the soul and He Who perfected it, Who inspired it with its piety and impiety. . . . (91:7)

B. CIVILIZATIONAL: HUMAN KNOWLEDGE OF GOD

1. God and the Human Knowledge of Him

God is the Creator of the world. He is the One and the Eternal, the Living, the Omnipotent, the Omniscient, Who hears, sees, and wills everything. He is neither a body, nor an essence, nor an accident; has neither a body, nor an essence, nor an accident; has neither form nor limit nor number; has no parts and is neither divisible, compound, nor finite; neither whatness nor howness are attributable to Him; He is neither in space nor in time. Nothing is like unto Him. Nothing escapes His knowledge and power. He has eternal attributes subsistent in Him which are neither He nor not-He; namely, knowledge, power, life, capability, hearing, sight, will (*irādah*), pattern of action (*mashī'ah*), action, creation, provision, and speech. He—Glory be to Him!—speaks with one speech which is an eternal attribute of His and which is unlike our letters and sounds, but which is not silent, nor subject to deficiency. By such speech God commands, forbids, and informs. The Qur'ān is God's speech, uncreated and yet written in our Qur'ān texts, memorized in our minds, acknowledged by our tongues, and heard by our ears without becoming infused therein. Creating the world and every part thereof in its time is an eternal attribute of God, unlike any creating on man's part. Equally, willing is an eternal attribute subsistent in Him. The seeing of God is possible rationally, necessary according to scripture which informs that the believers will see God in paradise. By then, He would be seen neither in a place, nor in a spatial relation such as being on the side or in the front of something, by reflection of light on Him, or at a distance from the beholder. God is the Creator of all actions of man, those of believing and obeying as well as those of disobeying. All human actions occur in accordance with God's pattern for creation, with His efficacy, judgment, ruling, and providence. (Alī, Nasafī '*Umdat 'Aqīdat Ahl al Sunnah wa al Jamā'ah*, pp.1–2)

The first principle of theology and true foundation of the faith is the witness that one believes in God, His angels, His books and prophets, in resurrection after death, in divine providence whether for good or ill, in the Day of Judgment, in the scale of justice, in paradise and hell—all of which are true. It is the conviction that God is One, not numerically but in the sense that He has no associate, that He has no progeny and no ancestry, and that nothing is His equal or partner; that nothing in creation is like unto Him, nor He like anything in creation; that He is and has always been, eternally, with His names, with His essential and actional attributes. The former are life, power, knowledge, speech, hearing, sight, and willing. The latter are those of creating, providing, generating, causing growth and composition, and other such attributes pertinent to acting and doing. Nothing ever happens to Him. He has always been knowing with His knowledge. (Abū Ḥanīfah [d. 767], *Al Fiqh al Akbar* [Great Islāmic knowledge], pp. 3–8)

If someone asks, what is the proof that creation is the work of a creator, we answer that man who now stands complete and perfect was once a sperm, then a clot, then a piece of tissue, then flesh and bone and blood. We know that man did not himself change himself from state to state. For we observe that even in his state of maturity, strength, and rationality, he is incapable of creating for himself a sense of hearing or sight or any other sense. In his state of imperfection and weakness, man would be even less capable of creating those states which he is incapable of creating when in a state of perfection. Thus, it is established that it is not man who moves himself from one state to another, and that he must have a mover to move him and bring him through to his present state.

If someone asks, why do you claim that the Creator is unlike His creatures, we answer that if He were like His creatures, He would stand to change in the same relation as His creatures do . . . whether in all respects or only in some. It would then be impossible for such moved being to be eternal.

And if someone asked, why did you claim that the Creator of things is One, we answer that two creators would not design their creation always in the same way, nor would they always observe the same schemata or principles. It is necessary that one of them (with regard to the other), or both, be deficient. For if one were to will to save a man and the other to let him perish, either the wish of the one or the other, or the wishes of both, or of neither must be realized. The last two alternatives are impossible . . . since frustration is contrary to divine nature. On the other hand, the realization of the one rather than the other is proof of the deficiency of the frustrated and hence, of his nondivine nature. Therefore the Creator of the world is One. God said, "If there were other gods beside God, heaven and earth would dissolve in chaos." (Qur'ān, 21:22)

If someone asks, what is the proof that God is knowing, we answer that a product fulfills its reason for existence only if it is made by a knowing maker. As it is not possible for a brocaded silk to be woven and its intricate designs to be executed by someone who has no foreknowledge of what he is about and who is incapable of producing a complete piece of work, so is man impossible to have been created by someone who is not knowing. For, we observe that man is so constituted that his various organs and parts stand to one another in well-ordered relations. The instilling of life and the provision of organs of hearing and seeing, of the digestive system—all of which play roles well adapted to the life of man, to man's will to complete, perfect, and realize himself; likewise, the ordering of the heavens and the courses of the sun, moon, planets, and stars running in their orbits—all these show that the Maker of the world could not have made it without knowledge of its plan, design, and pattern or purpose. . . .

If someone asks, why is it that God is not weak, deficient, and frustrated in the pursuit of this purpose when He did not cause His human creatures to be what He wanted them to be in the first place, we answer that God's purpose was rather that man's faith be arrived at freely and deliberately and thus become deserving of His reward. Had He made them faithful by necessity, their faith would not be deliberate and it would hence deserve no reward. Just as you would attribute weakness, deficiency, and frustration to Him for His not forcing men to fulfill His design, we should attribute weakness, deficiency, and frustration to Him for His causing men to fulfill His design necessarily, that is, in a way which He could not affect as He pleases. (Al Ash'arī [d. 942], *Kitāb al Luma' fī al Radd 'Alā Ahl al Zaygh wa al Bida'* [Book of insights in answer to sectarians, deviators, and innovators], pp. 6–8, 10, 27)

The Islāmic view of God is the most rational and the most religious. God is the unique Creator Who has neither beginning nor end, Who is omnipotent and omniscient and unto Whom there is no like. The world is created—and so by God—and returns to Him; and it will come to an end as it had come to be, by God's will. Put philosophically, there are two orders of being, the eternal and the temporal. It is impossible that the latter be a part of the former; that the temporal, if extended indefinitely at both its extremities, would become the eternal. Nor is it possible that the eternal order be lessened or reduced so as to become temporal. For no matter how much one deducts from or adds to the eternal, it remains one and the same. The two are twain; different in their core and essence and subject to different orders of knowledge. The eternal is an order devoid of motion or change; the temporal is inconceivable without both. If we are sure of the existence of any of the two orders, we are rationally certain of the existence of the eternal.

Only the eternal order is conceivable without logical difficulties. If we were to assume the impossibility of its existence, our very idea or precept would already have assumed the certain existence of a rational order which makes our very doubt possible. Equally, the same is assumed if we were to prove the limitation of the eternal in size, depth, or time. On the other hand, the notion of an eternal order existing by itself, devoid of beginning and end, of "how" or measure, is free of contradiction (and hence possible).

Thus the Muslim thinks of God's existence. . . . The Muslim knows that time is not eternal, that the eternal order is so much more perfect than the temporal and therefore utterly different therefrom. That is the transcendence which God imposes through Islām upon those who believe in Him. This disparity notwithstanding, the relationship between the two orders is not problematic. The eternal is absolutely perfect; and absolute perfection is impossible without capacity for and the actual doing of, the good; and the latter are impossible without creation. It is therefore nonsense to say that creation was a need (i.e., a satisfaction of a necessary privation) on the part of God; for that would contradict His absolute perfection. . . . Rather, creation was an effluence of God's perfection, of His capacity for and actual beneficence. . . . Every one of the divine attributes in the Qur'ān is one demanded by an absolute perfection such as God's. Absolute perfection is one, indivisible, and comprehensive of all values. . . . It is a great error to limit such attributes when they are by nature illimitable, or to compare them with aught besides which they are themselves the absolute standards. "There is nothing like unto God . . . He sees all sights and no sights see Him." (Qur'ān, 42:11; 6:103)

The most we can say regarding the eternal order is that it is absolutely perfect; that from this perfection, the creation of a less perfect order follows and that the two orders are not unrelated. The specificative how of these facts escapes us. But this should not surprise us; for many such hows of things in nature escape us too. . . . At any rate the opposites of our assertions are not the least bit more open to specificative observation and analysis. . . . All religions affirm a relation between creator and creature and they all differentiate between the natural or mechanical relation between cause and effect and the spiritual one between creatures and their creator. . . . The natural relation, however great it may be, provides no foundation for religion, for the certainty which religious conviction demands. . . . The world is undoubtedly great, but its greatness leaves man uncertain. Only conviction of the existence of a living will behind the world and all its casual efficacies gives man the certainty he seeks. That relation which religion affirms then is that of a conscious Creator, responsive to conscious creatures who call on, and pray to, Him. Here, the Qur'ān is clear and emphatic: "If My servants ask you concerning Me, tell them that I am near, that I respond to him who calls on Me. Let them call on Me, and believe in Me, that they may become the wiser." (2:186)

Equally, the Qur'ān is emphatic in exhorting all men to help themselves, to depend upon their own capacities and powers. It is not commendable for man to exaggerate either his own capacities, and thus fall under illusion concerning the reach of his efficacy, or his hope for divine action and assistance in dire need. It is far better to keep both confidence in oneself and hope in God in harmony and check. That is as far as religion can go in this matter. "O men who believe," says God, "help yourselves with patience and prayer. God is with the patient." (2:153) The Qur'ān then does not promise men that God will not frustrate them if they strive and help themselves, as well as that He will not deny them His superior power if they ask Him for it. No religion can survive which does not assure men of this hope. . . .

It is not oppugnant to reason to assert that spiritual factors can bring about real effects in this world. . . . Those who disagree, unjustly deny the effect of spirit upon spirit, of mind upon mind and their stand is ultimately based on a skepticism wherein the only evidence recognized is that which eye and hand can alone furnish. Their prejudice against things spiritual shows in that they do not demand that much even in the domain of science. . . . On the other hand, the efficacy of prayer does not contradict the orderliness of the cosmos, for those who pray are part of that cosmos and their prayer is part of its order and system. On the contrary, denial of efficacy to prayer implies denial of creation by the Creator who is at once Master of His creation. For such denial blots out the difference between creator, master of his creation, . . . and a mechanical first cause utterly indifferent and neutral *vis-à-vis* its creation.

The Qur'ān's emphasis on the unity of God is as important as its emphasis on His existence. Indeed, in the Islāmic creed, it is even stronger. For belief in the one God is more necessary than in His existence, as it is not impossible to have latter but in a form—polytheism or associationism—which vitiates the very understanding of divine existence and reality altogether, as well as of the morally and religiously imperative, of man's knowledge of man. The Qur'ān's arguments for unity—"If there were other gods beside God, heaven and earth would dissolve in chaos"; and "Say: If God had gods as associates, they would have sought his throne" (21:22; 17:42)—are final, though some philosophers claimed for them the status of oratorical appeal. The philosophers claimed that difference between two or more gods is not necessary and that their agreement is possible—a perverse and obviously false opinion. For the absolutely perfect cannot be two. Neither can the eternal. Any such two beings who agree perfectly from beginning to end, who agree perfectly in their doing of everything, in their conduct of every affair, and who therefore cannot ever be differentiated in any respect, are not really two beings but one. As for the many gods, if they obey God and do not stand beyond His power, they must be creatures rather than gods. Otherwise, they would compete with God and "seek his throne." (17:42) (Al 'Aqqād [d. 1963] *Al Falsafah al Qur'āniyyah* [Qur'ānic philsophy], pp. 125–38)

2. The Divine Names and Attributes: God in Perception

. . . The names of the Lord are divided into three kinds: First, those names which are indicative of Himself and His existence, the appellative names, properly speaking, of which we say that they are He (such as *Allah*—or God, *Rabb*—or Lord). Second, those of which we say that they are not-He, i.e., the descriptive-qualitative names connoting an eternal attribute such as knowing and capacity. Some men, identifying the name with the named, held that when we say "creator" we actually mean the Lord himself and not merely the creator as creating or the creating process as a name for the creator; and this rule they applied to all the divine names. What is approved with us is the method . . . whereby the names are regarded as attributes affirming something positive besides the selfness or existence of God, unless, of course, they are themselves negative. When we say God the Creator, we affirm something, namely creation, and thus mean to refer by that name to God as He Who creates, or as the creating One. In this understanding there is no implication that creator-ness is constitutive of the divine self. That is why our elders claimed that God may not be described as creator in His eternity. . . .

The other names are: the Merciful, the Always-merciful, the Sovereign, the Holy, the Source of Peace, the Protector, He Whose power is everywhere preponderant, the Strong, the Dominant, the Glorified, the Creator, the Originator, He Who gives everything its form, the Forgiver, the Irresistible, the Provider, the Giver, He Who gives victory, the Omniscient, He Who orders everything, the Source of all affluence, the Depriver, the Just Judge Whose verdict exalts or debases, strengthens or weakens, the Source of honor, the All-Hearing, the All-Seeing, the Judge, the Just, the Benevolent, the All-Aware, the Forbearing, the Magnanimous, the Most Forgiving, the Most Appreciating, the High, the Guardian, the Incomparably Great, the Reckoner, the Lord of Majesty, the Generous, the Watchful, He Who answers the prayers, the Bountiful, the All-Wise, the Affectionate, the Glorious, the Resurrector, He Who remains after all has passed away, the Witness, the Truth, He upon Whom everything depends, the Omnipotent, the Mighty, the Friend, the Always-praiseworthy, He Who counts everything, He Who makes everything come to be, He Who makes everything come again to be in the resurrection, the Life-giver, the Life-taker, the Living, the Always-rising, the Fortune-giver, He Who gives glory, the One, the Master, the Always-capable, the Source of all power, the Source of order, of felicity, of punishment, the First, the Last, the Manifest, the Mysterious, the Ruler, the Beneficent, the Compassionate, the Forgiver of all sins, the Equity-giver, the Light, the Creator out of nothing, the Righteous, the Guide, the Patient, the Speaker, the Healer, the Sufficient, the Unique, the Lord of Majesty and Nobility (Al Juwaynī [d. 1083], *Al Irshād* [The guidance], pp. 80–88).

CHAPTER 30

Man

□ In Islām, the world was not created in vain; and neither was man. The purpose for which man was created is the realization of a divine trust which neither heaven and earth nor the angels were capable of realizing. This trust is the realization in space and time of God's desire. God's will being realized in nature by necessity, through the workings of natural law, His desire awaited the arrival of man who can realize value morally, that is, freely. Because only man may do so under the open possibility of realizing as well as denying and violating the divine command a prequisite without which no realization of value would be moral—man is a cosmic bridge through whom the moral law, as God's eminent desire, may be fulfilled in space-time. The content of divine desire is the highest and final good. It is a pattern into which every part of creation—above all man's own self—ought to be molded. The moral order of the cosmos is precisely one where the man who realized the pattern is blessed and given his due reward, and he who fails is damned and awarded his due punishment. Salvation then is a man's own work. Any other kind of salvation must either deny man's moral freedom and responsibility or expose him to demonization or apotheosis. Man is built of body and soul, each of which is perfectly equipped for its task, the latter to discover the divine pattern and to will it, the former to be instrument, material carrier, and theater for its realization.

The Islāmic imperative is twofold: personal and societal; and it consists of duties to God and duties to man. This notwithstanding, every duty Islām has enjoined aims at the self as well as at the other selves, and it is aimed at once at the service of God as well as of man. None may be exclusively the one or the other.

The confession of faith (*shahādah*) (as solemn acknowledgment of the Islāmic imperative and commitment to its cause), the supreme act of worship (*salāt*) (as devotion to God and His will), sharing one's wealth with one's fellows (*zakāt*), fasting (*ṣawm*) (as self-discipline and commiseration), and, lastly, pilgrimage (*ḥajj*) (as self-identification with Islāmic history and personal and societal stock-taking) constitute "The Five Pillars" or the institutionalized minimum expected of the Muslim in his life on earth. If he is to do more, the Muslim is expected first, to realize the personal values in himself, then to enter into all the processes of history in space-time, whether in the persons of others or in the group life of human societies everywhere, and there to alter the course of every casual chain for the better to bring them to a realization of the divine pattern. His ideal is the felicitous life of the universal brotherhood under the moral law, to whose fate his fate is inextricably attached, not as a passive object of history but rather, as history's active subject, as the second master of creation. □

A. SCRIPTURAL: MAN'S PERFECTED NATURE AND COSMIC STATUS; THE ISLĀMIC IMPERATIVE

1. Man: God's Vicegerent on Earth

And when your Lord said to the angels, "I shall create a vicegerent for Myself on earth," they answered, "Will You plant therein a being who sheds blood and works evil, while we perennially worship You and praise You?" God answered, "I know better; and you do not." (Qur'ān or Koran, 2:30) We have offered Our trust to heaven and earth and mountain, but they feared and withdrew from undertaking it. Man, however, came forward and assumed it. (33:72) Say: It is God Who established you as His vicegerents on earth and raised some of you higher than others and of different ranks, that, with all that He had endowed you, you may excel one another in the deed. (6:166) O men who believe, if you turn back from your religion . . . if you will not go forth to fight in God's cause, to obey His command, to realize the divine pattern, He will inflict upon you a painful punishment and will choose in your stead a people other than you who will not be irresponsive like you, who will love Him and whom He will love . . . who will strive in His cause fearful of nothing. (5:55; 9:40) O God, You have not created all this in vain. (3:191) We have not created heaven and earth and all that is between in idle sport. . . . Rather, that truth and goodness may be hurled against falsehood and evil; that the latter may be crushed and disappear. (21:16) Teach and remind (man, O Muḥammad)—for teaching does benefit the believers—that I have not created man and *jinn* (spiritual beings between angels and men) except to serve Me. (51:55–56) God has covenanted away paradise to the believers for what they spend of their lives and property in His cause; . . . a true covenant proclaimed in the *Torah*, the *Evangel* and the Qur'ān. Who is truer to his covenant than God? Look forward therefore to the consummation of this covenant in which you have entered. (9:111) Every man, We have entrusted with his own destiny. On the Day of Judgment, We shall unroll for him the record of his own deeds and say, "Read it yourself! And you be the judge thereof." (17:13–14)

2. His Perfected Nature

We have created man out of a substance of clay. We then transformed him into a small organism, and this we have made into a clot, then into a tissue, and then into bones. We covered the bones with flesh. Then We caused him to become a new creature. Blessed is God, the best Creator . . . Who created everything at its best . . . Who well-formed man and breathed into him of His own spirit, Who gave man his hearing, his sight, and his faculties of knowledge. (23:12–14; 32:9) It is He Who creates you out of clay . . . brings you out as a child, causes you to grow to full maturity, then to grow old, some to die sooner, others to reach an appointed time, that you may consider. O men! Fear your Lord, Who created you all of one soul, Who created woman therefrom, as well as all the men and women that ever lived. (40:67; 4:1) It is He Who created you all out of one man, Who created out of him his female partner, that he may find rest in her. (7:189) O men! We have created you from male and female, constituted you into diverse peoples and nations that you may know and cooperate with one another. The best among you in the eye of God is the most pious, the most virtuous. (49:13) We have created man to strive and to struggle. . . . Have We not given him his eyes, his tongue and lips, and shown him the two ways of good and evil? (90:4–10) Man was created impatient; he panics at the fall of evil and proudly withdraws unto himself at the fall of good; except those who steadfastly pray, who recognize the right of the destitute and deprived, who believe in the Day of Judgment . . . who maintain their chastity . . . remain true to their trust and covenant and fulfill their testimony. (70:19–33)

3. His Cosmic Status

We commanded the angels to submit and to serve Ādam, and they complied except Iblīs (or Satan), who refused and took to pride. . . . We told Ādam and his spouse to live in Paradise, to eat happily of its fruits except that tree, which would make them unrighteous. Satan caused them to slip and drove them out of their state. We said, "Go forth, some of your enemies of others, and inhabit the earth for a limited time." Ādam then received a revelation in words from his Lord. He repented and was forgiven. God always listens to the repentant voice. (2:34–37)

God said to the angels, "I am about to create man . . . and when I complete his fashioning and breathe into him of My spirit, submit yourselves to him. All the angels did submit except Iblīs who refused . . . and incurred eternal damnation. (15:28–35) And having taught Ādam all the names (i.e., natures) of things, God asked the angels to tell the names. . . . They replied, "Glory to You! We have no knowledge other than what you taught us." . . . God then asked Ādam, and Ādam told the names. (2:31–33) We have favored the sons of man, provided transportation for them on land and sea, granted them the good things of the world and many significant privileges which We did not accord to many of Our other creatures. (17:70) Do you not realize that God has made what is in heaven and on earth subservient to you, and has accorded to you blessings hidden and apparent? . . . that He has made even the sun and the moon subservient to you? (31:20–29) God has made the sea subservient to you, that you may set sail through it and seek His bounty . . . everything in heaven and earth He made subservient to you. (45:12) He made the rivers subservient to you, the constantly rising and setting sun and moon, the alternating night and day and He granted to you everything which you have asked of Him. Were you to count His favors, you would find them innumerable. (14:32–34)

4. The Islāmic Imperative

a. The Five Pillars or the Institutionalized Minimum

(1) *Confession* (*shahādah*). God witnesses that there is no god but He; that He is righteous; that none is God but He, the Wise and Omnipotent; and so do the angels and men of knowledge. (3:18) God Himself witnesses to the veracity of what has been revealed to you, O Muḥammad. For that was revealed in His full knowledge. And so do the angels witness. (4:165) Say: We believe in God, in that which was revealed among us, in that which was revealed to Ibrahīm (Abraham), Isma'īl (Ishmael), Isḥaq (Isaac), Ya'qūb (Jacob), and his children, in what was revealed to Mūsā (Moses), 'Īsā (Jesus), and all the prophets. We make no difference between them. To God we submit ourselves. (2:136)

(2) *Prayer* (*ṣalāt*). Establish the prayers. . . . Command your people to hold the prayers. . . . Those truly believe in Our revelation who fall to the ground in worshipful prostration whenever the revelation is remembered to them, and humbly praise their Lord. (29:45; 20:132; 32:15) Proclaim good tidings . . . to those who establish the prayers . . . whenever We establish their authority in the world. Felicitous are the believers who hold the prayers and do so reverently. . . . Prayer forbids evil and debauchery. (22:34–41; 23:1–2; 29:45) O you who believe! When you ready yourselves for prayer, wash your faces and arms to the elbows, wipe your heads and your feet to the ankles. In case you are impure, then bathe yourselves; and if sick, on a journey, or you have answered a call of nature or touched women and you find no water, then take clean sand and wipe your hands and faces clean therewith. God does not wish to make things difficult for you but only to help you become clean and to complete His favor unto you. (5:7) Do not come to prayer while in a state of drunkenness, but refrain until you can clearly cognize what you recite. (4:43) Woe to those who are in a state of distraction while they pray, to those who feign piety. (107:4) Do not raise your voice in prayer, nor make it inaudible but follow a mean between the two ways. (17:110) And when you travel over the earth, or fear that the unbelievers may attack you by surprise, it is not blameworthy for you to shorten your prayers. (4:101) When the call to prayer is made on Friday, hurry thereto and put away your business. That is better for you. . . . But when the prayer is done, strike out into the world and seek God's bounty. (62:9–10) Righteousness does not consist

in turning your faces east or west (i.e., merely in prayer). Rather, it consists of faith in God, in the Day of Judgment, in His angels, Books, and prophets, in giving lovingly of one's wealth to relative and orphan, to the destitute, the deprived, and the wayfarer, in spending freely for ransoming the slave. It consists in the payment of *zakāt*, fulfillment of trusts and covenants made, in firmness through misfortune and adversity. . . . Such men as do these things are the righteous. (2:177)

(3) *Sharing of wealth* (*zakāt*). Establish the prayers and pay the *zakāt*. (2:43) My servants are those who . . . give of what We have provided them. (14:31) You will not achieve righteousness unless you give of that which you cherish. (3:92) Give to the relative, the destitute, and the wayfarer, to each his due. But do not squander your wealth away. Those who do are brothers of Satan. . . . Do not hold your hand so tight as to choke thereby, nor extend it all the way and thus become destitute yourself. (17:26–30) A kind speech and forgiveness are better than charity followed by harm. . . . Do not nullify your charity by showing off your generosity or by allowing injury to follow it. (2:263)

(4) *Fasting* (*ṣawm*). O you who believe! Fasting is ordained for you, as it was ordained for those who went before you, that you may become virtuous. Fasting is for a set number of days. However, those who are sick or on a journey should make up the days later on; or, if they can afford it, by feeding a destitute man. To volunteer in this however is better, and to fast is better still. . . . God wants your well-being, not your discomfort. . . . Go to your women . . . eat and drink until dawn, when the white thread is discernible from the black, then complete your fast until night. (2:183)

(5) *Pilgrimage* (*ḥajj*). And we have made the House of God a place of assembly and a place of safety for the people. Make then of the house Ibrahīm built a place of prayer for We entrusted it to Ibrahīm and to Isma'īl before you, to keep it pure and open for pilgrimage and prayer. (2:125) The first house to be built for man's worship of God is the blessed house in Bakkah (i.e., Makkah or Mecca), a guidance for mankind. It is man's duty to God to make the pilgrimage to the house if such is in his power. (3:96–97) Pilgrimage is during months well-known. Whoever undertakes it shall avoid all obscenity, all wickedness, and all wrangling. (2:197)

b. Moral Freedom and Responsibility

Whoever wills to believe, or to disbelieve, does so of his own accord. (18:29) God does not require of any person except that of which he is capable. (23:62) God does not change the situation of any group of men until they transform their own selves. (13:11) Do not ask anyone to bear the burden of another. (17:15) God commits no injustice to anyone. It is to themselves that men are unjust. Say: O men, the truth has come to you from your Lord. Whoever accepts this guidance does so to his own merit and whoever errs does so to his own demerit. . . . Teach the Qur'ān, that man may learn that it is by his own deeds that he delivers himself to ruin. . . . Whatever man has earned, he will certainly be given. (10:44; 6:70; 53:40)

c. Ethical Striving

God commands that justice be done, that man should act in charity and contribute to the welfare of the relative. He forbids adultery, wickedness, and rebellion. . . . Fulfill the covenant of God, now that you have entered therein, and do not repudiate your solemn promises of which you made God guarantor. . . . Do not take your oaths as means of deceiving one another. . . . Do not sell away God's covenant. That which is with God is better for you, if you only know. What you have is temporary; what God has is eternal. . . . Whether man or woman, whoever does the good in faith, We shall cause him or her to live a good life rewarding him or her with better rewards than he or she had deserved. (16:90–97) Your Lord commands . . . kindness to parents . . . Do not show them any sign of disrespect however small and do not speak harshly to them but kindly. Humble yourself to them in love and pray: May God have mercy on them as they nursed me when young. . . . Even if you have to avoid them on account of your fulfillment of God's call, give them a kind and compassionate explanation. . . . Do not kill any man—that is God's prohibition—except after due process of law. Whoever is killed unjustly, to his heir a right of revenge is established. But he may not kill wantonly, for his right shall be recognized. Do not touch the wealth of the orphan unless it be to increase it, until the orphan comes of age. Be true to your covenants, for to covenant is a serious and responsible affair. Fill the measure when you measure, and weigh with the true weight; that is better and more rewarding. Do not pursue that of which you have no knowledge; and remember that your hearing, sight, and heart, as cognitive faculties, were given to you for a responsible function. Do not walk around with impudence and false pride for you will never be a match either to earth or to mountain. (17:23–37) Those believers are felicitous who refrain from gossip . . . and guard their chastity except against their spouses. (23:1–6) The servants of the Merciful are those who tread softly on this earth who say "Peace" when the ignorant contend with them . . . who repent, believe, and do the good. God forgives their past misdeeds and counts their good deeds. . . . They are those who never give a false oath; who pass the gossip of men gently by, who do not fall blindly and overhastily over their Lord's revelations when these are brought to their mind. (25:63–74) Those who believe and rely on their Lord . . . are those who forgive the trespasses of others even in anger . . . and resist victoriously the temptations of evil and rebellion. Punishment for an injury is an equal injury but whoever forgives and reconciles has his merit with God. God does not love the unjust, and whoever avenges the injustice he suffered does so legitimately. Lawlessness is on the side of those who act unjustly, who inflict injuries on the people without right. Theirs will be a painful suffering in the hereafter. Nonetheless, those who bear patiently and forgive are truly endowed with greatness. (42:36–43) Tell My servants that they should always stand by the kindlier alternative. (17:53) Never will the good deed be the equivalent of an evil one. Respond, therefore, always with the better deed and you will find that your enemy immediately becomes your closest friend. Only the patient are capable of this, and they are of great fortune. (41:34–35) Let no people speak contemptuously of another people, or woman of another woman. . . . Do not tease one another with offensive nicknames and titles; that is unbecoming of you after you have entered the faith. . . . Avoid indulgence in doubt or suspicion, for even a little of it is a crime. Do not spy on one another. Do not speak ill of one another in the person's absence. (49:11–12) Do not turn the other cheek in abjection, and do not take to false pride. . . . Observe prayer, enjoin the good and forbid evil and endure with patience whatever may befall you. To do so belongs to great character. Let your walk be serious, and your voice be gentle. Remember the ugliest voice is that of the donkey because it is the loudest. (31:17–18) God will surely bring victory to those who . . . if established on earth will hold the prayers, pay the *zakāt*, enjoin the good and forbid evil. (22:39–41) Let there be of you a people who enjoin the good and forbid the doing of evil. Such people are the felicitous. (3:104)

B. CIVILIZATIONAL: ISLĀMIC VALUES, WORLDLINESS, AND OTHERWORLDLINESS; ISLĀMIC FELICITY

1. Morality as the Meaning of Human Existence

If man moves from contemplation of the beauty of the cosmos, expression of his gratitude for being placed therein, for his capacity to penetrate it with his mind and to enjoy it, to the consideration of his place as man in that cosmos, then will he be seized with the majesty of divine perfection and his will to moral perfection will begin to stir. While his tongue invokes and praises God, his heart will ponder, in fear and in hope, that "O God! Surely You have not created all this in vain. Glory be to you!" (Qur'ān, 3:191) Thus, those who combine thought with remembrance express their achievement of the two virtues, their synthesis of the two requisites, in the thought that God has not created all the heavenly and earthly bodies in vain, that He has not completed and perfected them all, as it were in sport. His transcendence and glory demand that we think of Him as standing above vanity and sport, as assigning to every creature its proper nature, role, and place in the cosmos. For He does not undo what He has done, and He Himself is eternal. As creatures in the cosmos, we too could not have been created in vain; nor could our presence in creation come finally to nought. Our bodies may disintegrate and our parts may dissolve after death. But that is merely the corruption of the corruptible in us. "Your holy face," we may say to God in praise and gratitude, "that which remains in us of Your eternal knowledge (that is, our human soul as subject of knowledge of the divine) will by Your power come back for another life, just as You have brought it the first time in this life on earth. Then will you divide men into those whose earthly life was one of true guidance and those whose life was one of error and misguidance; the former to enter paradise for their works and Your grace, the others to enter hell for their works and Your justice . . ."

That God has not created the cosmos in vain means that the greatness, perfection, and sublimity of everything therein could not have been meant merely to run their short course and pass into eternal oblivion. Man, who was endowed with a mind capable of perceiving this truth and appreciating this sublimity and whose predilection for this knows no bounds, could not have been created merely for this brief span between two eternal "nothings." Rather, man was so endowed and perfected that he may live an eternal life, a life in which each receives the reward of his deeds. (Muḥammad Rashīd Riḍā [d. 1935], *Tafsīr al Qur'ān al Karīm* [Exegesis of the Holy Qur'ān], vol. 4, pp. 299–301)

2. Man as Carrier, as Material, and as Theater of Value Realization

Know, that all men are instances of manliness . . . that manliness is synonymous with being naturally capable of ethical action . . . and, hence, with being God's vicegerent on earth. That is the element common to all humanity.

Know, O Brother, that man's imperfect soul has been attached to his imperfect body that the soul's virtues may be realized, that its potentialities of goodness and felicity may be fulfilled, just as the revelation of God's existence, mercy, grace, beneficence, providence, and wise government are impossible without His creation of this great, well-ordered cosmos and all that it contains.

What is the purpose of the instincts built into man's nature? It is to stir the person to seek what benefits his body and to avoid what injures it, to discover and to learn the deeds and habits which lead to its advantage and disadvantage.

Know . . . that since man is composed of the four elements (Earth, Water, Air, and Fire), and these give him his four temperaments (respectively, the hard, the cold, the humid, and the fiery), the wise and praiseworthy Creator made his activities and affairs to correspond to these innate elements, that he may be helped by them to achieve the objective of each. Thus we find that some of his deeds are innate; others are psychic and voluntary; others are of the nature and thought and intellect; and others are political and pertain to the law. Know . . . that nature is a servant to the animal soul and precedes it, that the animal soul is servant to reason and precedes it, that reason is servant of *al Nāmūs* (the Law) and precedes it. For, after nature has implanted a habit and ingrained it in a person, the soul deliberately stirs it into activity and enables it to achieve its objective. Here, reason comes with its deliberation and criticism to guide the soul and help it to realize itself through the satisfaction of these habits. Then the law, with its commandments, rectifies and redresses these pursuits so that when an instinct realizes itself as it ought, under the circumstances that it ought, and for the purpose that it ought, it would be good and otherwise evil; that when man allows and pursues such realization as he ought, under the circumstances that he ought and for the purpose that he ought, he would be virtuous and praiseworthy, and otherwise vicious and blameworthy; and that when man's choice and volition are the result of rational deliberation and critique, then he is wise, philosophic, and virtuous and otherwise ignorant, plebeian, and crude, and that when man's deeds, volition, choice, and thought are commanded by the law, and performed as they ought, then he would be rewarded and praised and otherwise punished and blamed.

Know . . . that in ordering the various souls of man (i.e., the elemental, vegetal, animal, rational, etc.), God linked them together so that the higher may assist the lower to realize itself as well as to rise to the higher rank. Thus, the vegetal soul stands in an order lower than the animal which it serves; the human, speaking soul stands in an order lower than the rational, wisdom-seeking soul which it serves; the rational soul in an order lower than the law-pursuing soul which it serves; and, finally, the law-pursuing soul stands under the Divine Essence Which it serves.

I considered, investigated, thought, and re-examined. Then I found the true meaning of Satan and of his numerous soldiers, of their enmity and evil inspiration to man. Satan and his host are nothing but internal forces, innate and hence "hidden" powers, built into mankind. They are the immoral pursuits, the blameful habits perpetuated since youth and enhanced by ignorance, by accumulated false opinions and repeated evil and shameless deeds. They are the commonplace passions gone berserk and excessive, usually attributed to the irascible animal soul. . . .

Furthermore, I found that all the virtuous deeds and moral acts are those which proceed from the rational, speaking soul on account of its true opinion and perfect convictions. But I found that such opinions, convictions, and all the habits which realize them proceed from an ethos of the soul acquired and developed by learning and thinking and such just temperaments as are innate to the rational nature of man. . . . Then I understood the saying of the Prophet on his victorious return from the battlefield, "Now we have returned from the lesser struggle to the greater one." [I.e., from the struggle against the external, conspicuous enemy to one internal to and hidden within man.]

. . . Thus I learned that if I sought my Lord's help, rolled up my sleeves, exerted myself, and opposed the passions of my irascible and animal soul and warred against all those enemies within which run counter to the purposes and principles of my rational soul, I would vanquish them with His power. Then, commanding them as my servants and slaves, I would put them to work at the service of my rational soul and enable her to perform her good deeds and moral acts, to proclaim its true knowledge and certain convictions and to fulfill its beauteous ethos.

But then . . . looking deep within myself, . . . I found my nature composed of various, mutually conflicting elements, of firebrand passions imbedded in sulphuric bodies . . . whose flames are inextinguishable—like the huge waves of the sea that sweep everything before them; hunger bestirs eternally to make me fall on its object like a starved wolf; the fire of my ambition and anger would fain consume the world, that of my pride regards myself as the best of all and mankind as my slaves and agents whose necessary and sole duty is to obey me. . . . Its desire to recreation makes of myself a mad, drunken god; its love of praise, the most virtuous and worthiest of all; its passion for vengeance weighs on it like a tremendous mountain. . . . Looking closer at this self of mine, I have found that it is all raging flames and inextinguishable fire, perpetual fighting and war between irreconcilable elements, incurable disease, unabatable anxiety, struggle incessant—except in death. (Ikhwān al Ṣafā wa Khillan al Wafā [The Brethren of Purity and Friends of Fidelity, anonymous encyclopaedists and philosophers of the eleventh and twelfth centuries], *Rasā'il Ikhwān al Ṣafā* [Epistles of Ikwān al Ṣafā], vol. 2, pp. 306, 318–20; vol. 3, pp. 364–69)

There is no man in the whole world, from its beginning to its end, who approves of anxiety and calls it good, and who does not seek to dissipate it. When I understood this general principle well, it appeared as if I had come by God's guidance upon a wonderful discovery. I then began to search for the way to banish anxiety, which is the objective of all men whether ignorant or refined, noble or ignoble. I found it only in the total orientation to God through works conducive to Paradise. (Ibn Ḥazm, *Kitāb al Akhlāq wa al Siyar fī Mudāwāt al Nufūs* [Book of ethics and conduct for the curing of souls], pp. 10–11)

Passion, or man's inclination by nature to that which accords with him, was created in man on account of its necessity for survival. Were it not for his passion for food, drink, and sex, man would have neither eaten, drunk, nor procreated himself. Passion moves him to seek that which he desires, just as antipathy moves him to remove that which he avers. By itself, therefore, neither passion nor its opposite is to be either commended or condemned. What is so is the excessive satisfaction of either. Most men, however, are excessivists in this regard. They pursue their passion or antipathy for objects of desire and aversion beyond the legitimate point of useful advantage for their persons as wholes. That is why passion is more often condemned than praised. . . . Only few men are so just in their natures as to use their passions appropriately. (Ibn al Qayyim al Jawziyyah, *Rawḍat al Muḥibbīn wa Nuzhat al Mushtāquīn* [Garden of the loving and recreation of the longing], pp. 463–479, 321)

3. Conditions and Props of Felicity

Confession (*shahādah*). I witness that there is no god but God and I witness that Muḥammad is the Apostle of God. (From the Muslim call to prayer)

Abū Ḥujrah reported from Ibn 'Abbās that some people from Rabī'ah tribe arrived in Madīnah to see the Prophet and that the Prophet welcomed them. They complained that it was not possible for all the members of their tribe to come to proclaim their Islām in front of the Prophet because of the presence of the pagan Muḍar tribe on the lands between them and Madīnah. They asked the Prophet to give them instructions which they might convey to their people to insure their proper Islāmization. . . . The Prophet commanded them to observe the pillars of Islām. Then they asked, "What is *īmān* (faith by conviction)?" The Prophet answered that it is the witnessing that there is no god but God and that Muḥammad is the Prophet of God. (*Al Muntakhab min al Sunnah* [Selections from the *Sunnah*] vol. 1, pp. 303–4)

Prayer (*ṣalāt*). The Prophet said, "No *jinn* and no man hears another man's call to prayer but he witnesses in favor of that man on the Day of Judgment." It was of such men that God said, "And who is greater than he who calls unto God and does the good works?" (Qur'ān, 41:32)

The Prophet said, "God imposes five prayers upon all men. Whoever performs them obtains from God a covenant that he shall enter Paradise. Whoever does not has no such covenant, and God may permit entrance or exclude him therefrom." The Prophet said, "The five prayers are like a wide stream of fresh, clean water right in front of every man's house. Should man plunge himself therein five times a day, what would be left of his dirt?" He also said, "The five prayers dissolve the evil deeds and they are an expiation for the grave sins committed in the hours separating them."

The Prophet said, "Nothing brings man closer to God than prostration in prayer. Piety and presence of mind are indispensable for it." God said, "Hold the prayer in remembrance of me." (Qur'ān, 20:14) Remembrance is impossible without presence of mind. The Prophet said, "If prayer does not induce man to avoid immorality and evil, it removes him further from God." Know that Friday is the day appointed by God for Islām and the Muslims. He forbade work and concern on that day, all that which deters from hurrying to the mosque when the call to prayer is made. The Muslim should prepare for it through will and emotion, by reciting invocations and remembrances of God from Thursday afternoon. In the morning, he should bathe himself. Bathing the whole body is a definite duty. He should beautify himself with good clothes, cleanliness, and perfume. (Al Ghazzāli [d. 1111], *Iḥyā' 'Ulūm al Dīn* [Vivification of the science of religion], vol. 1, pp. 80–91)

Sharing (*zakāt*). God made *zakāt* one of

the foundations of Islām. He joined it to prayer, thus assigning to both of them an equal rank. God said, "Those who hoard their gold and silver and do not spend it in the cause of God, announce to them that their punishment will be painful. (Qur'ān, 9:35) *Zakāt* is obligatory for every free Muslim, regardless whether he is adult or minor, sane or insane. . . . It applies to all wealth which is completely appropriated . . . cattle, cash, stocks in trade, mines and minerals, and food as in the case of *zakāt al fiṭr*. The latter prescribes that the Muslim shall give to the poor on '*Īd al fiṭr* (the feast falling at the end of the month of fasting) two and one third *rotols* (unit of weight approximating 3 kgs) of the very food he and his family eat on that day on behalf of every member of his family and every dependent under his legal protection. For *zakāt* to be proper, four principles ought to be observed: 1. The Muslim ought to solemnly declare to God his intention to disburse his *zakāt*, as well as his understanding of its assessment; 2. He must surrender the *zakāt* immediately before sunset on the date it falls due; 3. He is not free to convert his assessed *zakāt* from one commodity to another, but must give it in kind; 4. *Zakāt* may not be transferred from one locality to another, but must be distributed where it is levied. It must also be spent there in order that the needy of the locality may derive benefit first.

The Prophet said, "Save yourselves from the fire, even with a bushel of dates. And if you cannot find that much, then contribute to your salvation with a good word." 'Umar ibn al Khaṭṭāb (second caliph, 634–644) used to give sugar away to the poor and say, "God said, 'You will not attain to heaven until you have spent of that which you cherish' (Qur'ān, 3:92)—and He well knows that I love sweets." (*Ibid.*, pp. 100–108)

Fasting (*sawm*). Know that fasting is of three kinds: First, that of the many which is the restriction of hunger from achieving its end. Second, that of the few which is, in addition to the former, the restriction of hearing, sight, speech, hand, foot, and all other organs and faculties from doing evil. Third, that of the special few which is, in addition to the first two, the restriction of the heart from all lowly desires and ideas, from all things other than God. Here the fast is violated with every idea not of God, the Day of Judgment, or of His Will, but of the world instead—except an idea of the world desired for the sake of Islām.

Fasting has five conditions: 1. The fast should begin on the first day of Ramaḍān (fasting during the ninth month) upon beholding the new moon of that month, or upon the lapse of thirty days in the preceding month of *sha'bān* (the eighth). 2. The intention to fast the following day should be repeated anew, every night. 3. One should maintain total abstinence from anything that enters the body, whether through the mouth such as food and drink, or other. 4. One should totally abstain from sexual activity. 5. One should prevent anything from leaving the body, unless it be a call of healthy nature. These are the conditions without which fasting becomes invalid. On the other hand, fasting more than the month of Ramaḍān is voluntary and desirable but permanent fasting is excessive and many have given good reasons against it. (*Ibid.*, pp. 109–12)

Pilgrimage (*ḥajj*). The Prophet said that whoever performs the pilgrimage and, during its period, does not go unto his woman and commits no evil deed will return from the pilgrimage as innocent as he was on the day of his birth; a good pilgrimage deserves no less than paradise. . . . If standing on the Mount of 'Arafāt falls on a Friday, that day would be the best of all. For it was on such a day that the Prophet performed his last pilgrimage, delivered his last sermon and the following verse was revealed: "Today I have completed for you your religion and instituted for you Islām as the religion." (Qur'ān, 5:4) After Makkah (Mecca), there is no spot on earth better than Madīnah, the city of the Prophet. In its precincts, good works have a double merit. The next best place after the mosque areas of Makkah and Madīnah is al Aqṣā Mosque in Jerusalem. After these three places, all other places are equal in value except the frontier towns where holding the watch against the enemy is very meritorious. The conditions of pilgrimage are four:

Adulthood, Islām, freedom, and capacity. . . . The pilgrim should begin with repentance, with undoing the evils he had committed, settling his debts, making provisions for his dependents during his absence, returning the trusts in his keeping to their owners, and setting aside an appropriate sum for travel from his legitimately earned profits. (*Ibid.*, pp. 113–21)

4. The New Order

When we arrived in Abyssinia, we became the protected neighbors of the Negus. We felt secure in our faith and we worshiped God as we pleased, without let, hindrance, or attack from anyone. When the Makkans heard of this, they plotted against us by sending presents to the Negus . . . and then asking him to deliver us into their hands. . . . The Negus was told by 'Amr ibn al 'Āṣ (leader of Makkah) that a group of mean Makkans who abjured their religion and never entered into that of the Negus had invented a religion of their own, unknown to both Makkans and Abyssinians; and that the leaders of Makkah demanded their repatriation. . . . When the Negus asked the Muslims for an explanation. . . . Ja'far ibn Abū Ṭālib (first cousin of the Prophet) delivered the following speech: "O King! We were in a state of ignorance and immorality, worshiping idols, eating carrion, committing all sorts of iniquities. We honored no relative and assisted no neighbor. The strong among us exploited the weak. Then God sent us a prophet, one of our own people, whose descendence, truthfulness, loyalty, and purity are well known to us. He called us to worship God alone, and to repudiate all the stones and idols which we and our ancestors used to worship. He commanded us always to tell the truth, to remain true to trust and promise, to assist the relative, to be good neighbors, to abstain from blood and things forbidden, to avoid fornication, perjury, and false witness. He commanded us not to rob the wealth of the orphan, or falsely to accuse the married woman. He ordered us to worship God alone and associate nought with Him, to hold the prayers, to fast, and to pay the *zakāt*. . . . So we believed in him and followed him in that which he brought to us from God. We worshiped God alone and associated nought with Him. We forbade to ourselves all that God has forbidden, and we tolerated and encouraged all that He has declared legitimate. For this reason our people attacked and persecuted us, and inflicted upon us great suffering. . . . As they vanquished and treated us unjustly and made life intolerable for us in Makkah, we chose you and your country and came thither to live under your protection in justice and peace." . . . 'Amr pleaded again to the Negus saying, "They claim that Jesus is only a man." Whereupon the Negus asked the Muslims, "What do you think of Jesus?" Ja'far answered, "We think of Jesus exactly as the Qur'ān, the scripture revealed to our Prophet, told us about him; namely, that he is the servant of God and His Prophet, His spirit and command addressed to Mary, the virgin and pure. . . . He then read the *surah* (division) of Mary (Qur'ān, 19). The Negus then said, "What you have just recited and that which Jesus had brought to us must have issued from one and the same source. . . . What you say of Jesus is not different from the real Jesus by as much as this little straw. . . . Go your way in peace. I shall never betray you." ('Ibn Hishām, *Sīrat al Nabiyy*, vol. 1, pp. 357–60)

At his last pilgrimage to Makkah in the year 10 A.H. (632) the Apostle of God gave the following sermon: "O men, listen to my words, for I do not know whether I shall ever meet you again under the same circumstance. O men! Your blood and your properties are forbidden to you until you meet your Lord. They are as inviolate as this day and this month. You will certainly confront your Lord Who will ask you concerning your works. You have been warned. Whoever holds something in trust for another, let him return it to its owner. All interest is prohibited, and only your capitals are yours. Neither perpetrate nor suffer injustice. God has decreed that there shall be no interest. The interest due to 'Abbās ibn 'Abd al Muṭṭalib (the Prophet's uncle) shall all be relinquished, and so is every right of vengeance incurred in pre-Islām. The first such right that I hereby declare relinquished is that of Ibn Rabī'ah ibn al Ḥarth ibn 'Abd al Muṭṭalib, the adopted son of Banū Layth tribe, who was killed by the tribe of Hudhayl.

"O men, the devil has despaired of being worshiped in this land of yours but he hopes to be listened to in the lesser areas of your conduct. Beware of him, for your religion's sake. O men, intercalation is anathema. By means of it, the misguided who follow its practice alternately forbid that which God had allowed and allow that which He had forbidden. Time is a complete cycle, just as it was on the day God created heaven and earth and the months are twelve in number. Four of them are holy, of which three are consecutive; and the seventh month (*rajab*)—held holy by Muḍar (tribe)—standing between the sixth (*jumāda*) and the eighth (*sha'bān*).

"O men, your women have an obligation to you and you have an obligation to them. Their obligation is to allow no man other than you to lay down with them, and to commit no fornication. If they fail, then God permits you to separate yourselves from them at home, and to chastize them gently. If they fulfill their obligation, then to them belongs the right to be provided for and clothed in love and goodness. If you absent yourselves from your homes, cause food to be brought to your women in your absence. Provide for them after your death, for they are bound to you and helpless on their own. You have taken them over by God's trust, and you have enjoyed their bodies by God's command. Reason well what I say.

"I have delivered the message, and left with you that which, if you but adhere thereto, you will never go astray in any important matter—the Book of God and the *sunnah* (example, life, tradition) of His Prophet. Hear well my words and ponder them: Learn that every Muslim is a brother to the Muslim, that the Muslims constitute a single brotherhood, that no man may take from his brother except what that brother has willingly given him. Perpetrate no injustice against one another. O God! Have I conveyed the message?" He said to me that the people answered, "Yes." The Prophet then said, "O God, be my witness!" (*Ibid.*, pp. 275–76)

5. Otherworldliness: A Satanic Deception

Iblīs (Satan) has deceived many people into believing that *tawakkul* (trust in God) implies the giving up of earning and acquiring of wealth. I heard Muḥammad ibn Abū al Qāsim . . . say that (renowned Sufi theologian) Tustarī (c. 200–293 A.H.; 816–899) said, "Whoever condemns trust in God, condemns the faith and whoever condemns earning and acquiring of wealth condemns the *sunnah*. Some claim that earning and acquiring are for those who are incapable of the state of trust in God . . . and that if a young man is engaged in earning, he will not amount to anything. Such are the opinions of men who are ignorant of the meaning of trust in God. Trust is an action of the heart. It has nothing to do with the movement of organs and faculties. If by being a worker and an earner of livelihood man could not have trusted in God, then such were all the prophets. Ādam was a farmer, Nūḥ (Noah) and Zakariyyā (Zechariah) carpenters, Idrīs (Enoch) a tailor . . . Muḥammad a herdsman and trader . . . The companions were men of various professions. . . . 'Umar ibn al Khaṭṭāb said, "O poor men, raise your heads and compete in earning and acquiring the good things, for the road is now open before you. Do not be liabilities to one another. . . ." The Prophet said, "Consider the birds of the field; they go and come back in search of provision." God said commendingly, "Others strike out in the world seeking the bounties of your Lord." (Qur'ān, 73:20) . . . Trust in God is good for its own sake. However, in addition thereto, it is necessary to work and earn and provide for oneself and one's family. . . . Those who counsel differently want to dissolve the world. . . . Likewise, the seeking and application of medicines do not contradict trust in God and had been commanded by the Prophet. The Prophet said to Sa'd, "It is better that you leave behind your children rich than poor, provided for rather than begging others for their food. If poverty were preferable, the companions would have left no inheritance; but they did! . . .

It is not true that to save something for one's children or for the morrow is incompatible with trust in God. On the contrary, the Prophet saved for his family a whole year's provision. (Ibn al Jawzi [d. 1201], *Talbīs Iblīs aw Naqd al 'Ilm wa al al 'Ulamā'* [Deceit of Satan and criticism of the knowledge or religion and its men], pp. 271–78, 175–76)

6. "Better Than the Worship of Sixty Years"

The great among our ancestors preferred solitariness only, to use it in the pursuit of learning and worship. It did not cut them off from the community, nor from the Friday prayer, from visiting the sick and defending the right. Their isolation was really a separation from evil and its people, the do-nothings. But Iblīs deceived some Muslims about this so that they isolated themselves like monks in a remote dwelling. . . . However, any isolation is prohibited in Islām, which prevents a person's participation in learning and holy war (war in the cause of God). . . . When a companion consulted about the possibility of a monkish life of worship in a cave in the wilderness, the Prophet said, "That with which I was commissioned is neither Judaism nor Christianity, but temperate *Hanīfism* (belief in God and the moral law). A sortie in the cause of God is better than anything the world offers, and the taking of one's place in the march is better than the worship of sixty years. . . ." The principle, "There is no salvation in the other world save in the denial of this," is a deception of Iblīs, by which only the ignorant are taken. The world as such is never to be condemned. It is necessary for the survival of man, for his learning and worship. . . . Whoever takes to worship rather than learning, for instance, has given up the greater for the lesser gain. The good of worship is for the subject alone; that of learning is for the human kind. . . . Asceticism, or abstinence from the permissible, eating barley gruel, denial to oneself of fruits and cold water, wearing of rough garments, etc.—all these are deceptions of Iblīs. The Prophet used to eat meat, chicken, sweets, and drink cold drinks and he enjoyed them. . . . To impose upon the body hardships to which it is not used is evil. (*Ibid.*, pp. 278–80, 145–47)

7. The Great Muslim

The great Muslim is a man strong but pious in the exercise of his strength, resolute but gentle in carrying out his resolution, faithful but rationally convinced of his faith, skeptical but well-informed, knowing but critical in his knowledge, seeking but rich in what he already has. He is reverent in his worship, self-respectful in his poverty, patient in the face of hardship. He presses forth after the permission and is active and stirring, but he stands constantly under true guidance. He does the good but in fear of God. He ends his day still anxious to praise and to thank, and begins the morrow anxious to remember. When he retires, he is cautious lest he has omitted some duty; when he rises, he is joyous for the grace and mercy he has gained. If his soul rebels against the duties it does not like, he denies it the privileges which it does like. His greatest joy is always in the eternal, his asceticism is always towards that which perishes. Criticalness and knowledge are as strongly joined in him as professing and doing. His hope is the possible, his erring scarce, his heart reverent, his soul content, his food little, his problem easy, his religion fast, his passion dead, his anger subdued. The good is always expected of him, the evil never to come from him. . . . He forgives the perpetrator of an injustice against him, gives freely to whosoever had deprived him, and rejoins whosoever had separated himself from him. Fornication is at the farthest remove from him and adultery ever absent. His speech is gentle, his charity ever present; he is always well disposed to do the good deed, immune against the doing of evil.

In earthquake, he keeps his composure; in hardship, his patience. Grateful in prosperity and in want, he does no injustice, neither in condemning those whom he hates, nor in commending those whom he loves. He acknowledges the truth before he is officially required to do so. He carefully keeps what was entrusted to him, and remembers well that of which he is reminded.

He does not vie with others for titles, and is not troubled by the impositions of his neighbor. He feels no joy at the suffering of others and he neither enters into an evil deal nor exits from a fair one. When silent, he is not annoyed by his silence; when he laughs, he is hardly noticed. When done an injustice, he is patient until God acts for his revenge. His own self troubles him, but he is comfort and peace to all. He belabors himself for the Day of Judgment, and saves the people from belaboring themselves for him. When he keeps his distance, he does so out of detachment and restraint, not pride and self-glory; and when he draws himself near, he does so out of kindness and mercy, not ruse or ulterior motive. (*'Alī Ibn Abū Ṭālib's Nahj al Balāghah* [Path of eloquence], ed. by Ibn Abū al Ḥadīd and Muḥammad Abu al Faḍl Ibrahīm, vol. 10, pp. 24, 28, 30, 148–49)

CHAPTER 31

Society

□ Society, in Islām, is a threefold consensus. It is a consensus of minds insofar as its members share with one another their same perception and expression of reality. It is a consensus of hearts insofar as its members share the same ideals and values, the same attitudes and dispositions. It is a consensus of arms insofar as its members act in cooperation with one another in realizing the contents of their ideational and volitional consensus. Such society is, in Islām, the theater of ethical action. In it the Muslim enjoys the rights to which he has title as well as discharges the duties incumbent upon him. Without a society within which the Islāmic vision is established, and with the concurrence of which the vision is realized, the Muslim cannot be a Muslim. Society is one as God and truth are one, not because all its constituents are Muslims but because the world order requisite for its existence comprehends the universe, and every man, whether Muslim or non-Muslim, is either an equal member or an outlaw. The reason for existence of society is the realization of the divine pattern by man. This pattern consists not in denial of the world but in its affirmation, subject to the requirements of the ethically imperative.

In the social fabric, the family is elemental. God has instituted between its members the relationships of love and care, of respect and sympathy. Marriage is a civil contract, not a sacrament, and may be terminated by repudiation, provided fairness and equity are not violated. Man may marry more than one but on condition that the requirements of justice, equity, and loving care are met. Private property and the pursuit of wealth are inviolate and limitless, as long as these rights are exercised ethically and under the law. But whoever has, must give of what he has to the deprived. Here Islām saw an acid test of all religiosity, of all devotion and piety. The life of one's fellowman is inviolate, except by due process of law. Nothing may henceforth be decided by force or violence. Such recourse is legitimate only in self-defense and in the safeguarding of the security of missionaries. For the Muslim is dutybound to bring his faith to the knowledge of mankind with sound preaching and wise counsel, to convey the warning and command of his Lord. He cannot do more than teach and help his fellowmen see and decide for themselves. It is his right to demand a world order of peace and security, of freedom to speak and to listen. He trusts that, because the truth is manifest, it cannot but win in the end. That is the basis of his new order for society and the world. □

A. SCRIPTURAL: NECESSITY, UNITY, AND STRUCTURE OF THE UMMAH, OF THE FAMILY; NATURE OF SOCIAL JUSTICE AND WORLD ORDER

1. The Ummah (people and society of Islām) Its Necessity and Unity

We have sent Our prophets with manifest truths, brought down with them the Book and established the scale of justice that men may fulfill justice. We have also established iron (the symbol of political power) laden with power and advantage to the people, that it may become manifest who of them will act in fulfillment of God's Law and on the side of His prophets. (Qur'ān or Koran, 57:25) God promised those who believed among you and did the good deeds that He will cause them to be His vicegerents in the world, as He did to your ancestors, to strengthen their religion which He agreeably instituted for them, and to exchange their fears with peace and safety as long as they worship Him and do not associate aught with Him. (24:55) Let there be of you an *ummah* who call for the good, enjoin the good deed, and forbid evil. Those are the felicitous. (3:104) You have been the best *ummah* given to mankind, enjoying the good, forbidding evil, and believing in God. (3:110) Thus We have made you an *ummah* of the golden mean; that you may give witness to mankind, and that the Prophet may give witness to you. (2:143) O you who believe, if you cooperate with one another, let it be over some good deed or act of piety, not over some evil, aggression, or disobedience to the Prophet. (58:9) Hold fast together to the rope of God and do not separate. (3:103) O men of faith! Why do you knit your brows and grumble whenever you are asked to go forth in the cause of God? Have you preferred the lowly life of contentment to the pursuit of higher values? Did you forget that the life of contentment is short-lived? Unless you spring to your feet and go ever forward, God's punishment will be very painful. Indeed, God will exchange you for another people who will, and His cause will sustain no damage. God is omnipotent, and you are dispensable. Your failure to help the Prophet in this cause will not matter. Don't you know that God Himself has helped him . . . and made His word alone supreme? (9:39–40) O men who believe! If you ever turn your back to Islām, God will bring forth another people who will love and be loved by Him, who will be gentle towards the believers and hard towards the unbelievers, who will fight in the cause of God and fear not a thing thereby. (5:57) Obey God and His Prophet. Do not dispute with another and fail and be lost. (8:46) Those who give you (Muḥammad) fealty give their oath to God Whose hand is above their hand. Whoever therefore betrays this trust, does so against himself and whoever remains true to what he pledged to God will be given great reward. (48:10)

2. Its Constitution

a. Muslim Sovereignty

Obey God, the Prophet, and the men of authority among you. (4:59) Shameless and perverse are those who do not fight for God's cause when helpless Muslim men, women, and children in a tyrannous city cry out to God to relieve them of this tyranny and to send them a helper and a just ruler. (4:75) When, after death, the angels meet those who are unjust to themselves, ask them, "Wherefore were you miserable" and hear their answer, "We were weak in this earth!" the angels will rejoin, "Was not the earth large enough to accommodate you? Was there no other city to which you could have migrated rather than persist under the tyrant's yoke? Your abode shall be the fire!" Only the truly helpless men, women, and children shall escape this fate. (4:97) Those who believed, emigrated, fought, and spent of their wealth in the cause of God, and those who protected and helped them may be taken into one another's confidence. Those who believed but did not emigrate may not, unless they emigrate. . . . Do not take any of the hypocrites into your confidence until they emigrate. (8:72, 489) If a matter affecting their security should come to their notice, it would be better if they simply refer it to the Prophet and to the men in public office who would examine it and give it the attention it deserves. (4:83) The felicituous believers are those who respond to their Lord, uphold the prayers, carry out their public affairs in consultation with one another, and spend freely of what they gained of Our bounty. (42:38)

b. Consultation (Shūrā)

Consult your people in every matter. Then, if you resolve, trust in God and proceed. (3:159) Those are blessed who respond to Our call, hold the prayers, run their affairs in consultation with one another, and spend of Our bounty which We give them. (42:38) Together, hold fast to God's rope and do not separate. (3:103) Woe to those who, when good or evil befalls them which is of concern to all, dispose of it singlehandedly. They had better refer all such matters to the Prophet and their chiefs. . . . (4:83) Obey God and His Prophet, do not dispute with one another in vain and thus waste away your power. (8:46)

c. Equality and Universality

O Prophet! When the women believers came to give you their *bay'ah* (i.e., their oath of fealty) and promised never to associate aught with God, never to steal, to commit adultery, to kill their offspring, to do any misdeed, or to disobey you in anything good, accept their oath and pray God to forgive them. (60:12) Whoever does a good deed, whether man or woman, We shall give him or her a happy life and a reward surpassing his or her fondest expectations. (16:97) God will not forget to give all men and women their due, for their emigration, their suffering, expulsion, and persecution for My sake, for fighting and dying for Me. . . . (3:195) The male and female believers are guardians of one another; they shall enjoin the good, prohibit evil, uphold the prayers, give the *zakāt* (sharing of wealth) and obey God and His Prophet. (9:71)

O men! Fear your Lord Who created you all from one and the same soul. It is He Who created from the first soul a spouse for it, and from these, all men and women that populate the earth. (4:1) Say: O men! I am but the messenger of God to all of you . . . Believe in God and His illiterate Prophet. . . . and follow him. You will then be rightly guided. (7:158) We have sent you (Muḥammad) but a mercy unto mankind . . . a preacher and a warner unto all men. (21:107) I (Muḥammad) ask no reward for anything I convey or do. For it is all a lesson to mankind. (6:90) O men, We created you all from a single male and female. We constituted you into nations and tribes that you may cooperate one group with another. Remember that the noblest among you in God's eye is the most pious, the most virtuous. (49:14) It is God Who made you His vicegerents on earth and raised some of you above others. For it is His plan to challenge you in what He gave you. . . . It is He that divided among men their wealth, and gave some more than others. (6:165; 43:32) O men who believe! Do not ridicule or hold one another in contempt. . . . Do not boast, do not vie with one another for titles. . . . (To the aristocrats accustomed to a place of honor in the pilgrimage:) Walk in the same path as all men do. (49:11, 2:99)

d. Order and Discipline

If you dispute in any matter, take it to God and the Prophet for a verdict. (4:58) Verily, We revealed to you the Book that you may judge between men by that which God made manifest to you. (4:105) O men, accept whatever the Prophet brings to you. Avoid that which he forbids you. (59:7) Whenever called to God and His Prophet that the latter may judge between them, the believers say, "We have heard and we obey." Those are the felicitous. (24:51) Whoever disputes with the Prophet after the truth has become manifest, and follows other than the path of the believers, will be awarded the sad fate which he deserves—to burn in hell-fire. (4:115)

e. Commandery of the Good and Forbiddance of Evil

Men are surely to perish unless they believe, do the good deeds, and enjoin one another to do the right and to be patient in face of evil. (103:2–3) For every man there is a purpose which he sets up for his life and which he pursues. Let yours be the doing of all good deeds. (2:148) Let there be of you an *ummah* calling for the good. (3:104) O believers, kneel, prostrate yourselves, and worship your Lord. But above all, do the good, that you may be felicitous. (22:77) O believers! Do not take your parents and brothers as friends in case they preferred unbelief to Islām. Such is unjust and harmful. Are then your parents, sons, brothers, spouses, and relatives, wealth and business and households dearer to you than God, His Prophet, and fulfillment of His trust? (9:23–4) God does not command not to do good and not to act fairly towards those (unbelievers) who did not fight against your religion and did not expel you from your homes. God does love the just. Rather, He commands you only not to befriend those who fought against your religion, who expelled you from your homes and boasted thereof. It is unjust to take them as friends. (60:8–9)

f. Cooperation

The believers are surely brothers. Reconcile them one to another as your brothers and fear God, that you may receive His grace. (49:10) The believers, men and women, are guardians and friends to one another. (9:71) Cooperate with one another in everything that is good and do not cooperate in anything evil or in aggression. (5:2) O believers! If you confide with one another, let not your objective be one of aggression, of disobedience to the Prophet or of an evil deed, but one of beneficence and piety. (58:9) Munificence belongs to those who believe, who require one another always to do the good and assist one another therein with patience and mercy. (90:17–18) If they repent, uphold the prayers, and pay the *zakāt*, then they are your brethren in religion. (9:11)

g. This-Worldliness of the Healthy-Minded

Say: Come, let me list to you all that God had prohibited you to do. Do not associate aught with God. Hurt not, but do good, to, your parents. Do not kill your children out of fear of poverty, for We shall provide for you and them. Do not fornicate, either apparently or in secret. Do not kill any man except under due process of law. . . . Do not partake of the orphan's wealth, except to increase it, until he comes of age. Never fail to measure justly with a true scale and measure. Do not ask a person to do more than he can. Whenever you render judgment, never fail to do so justly even against the relative. Never fail to be true to your covenants. (6:151–52) Say: I find no dietary restriction in all that has been revealed to me except against the dead animal, the shed blood, and pork. These are either unclean or offered to other-than-God. However, if one is pressed by circumstance and does not will it in rebellion then God is forgiving and merciful. (6:145) Say: Who prohibited the beautiful things which God created for men to enjoy, and the delectable things of his providing? Say: All these are for the believers to enjoy in this world, and to enjoy purely in the hereafter. (7:32) Felicitous are those who follow the illiterate Prophet whose mission they find inscribed in their own Books—the *Torah* and the *Evangel*; who follow the Prophet when he commands them to do the good, when he forbids them the evil, makes legitimate for them the good things they were previously forbidden and forbids them only the evil things, thus liberating them from their previous restrictions and yoke. (7:157)

3. The Islāmic Family: Its Structure and Ethic

O men! Fear your Lord Who created you all of one soul and made of it its female partner and then multiplied you numerous men and women. (4:1) Of His signs is that He created from yourselves women; that you may find in them peace and rest; and has instituted between them and you love and tenderness. (30:21) To men belong what they have earned and to women what they have earned. . . . Whoever does the good, whether male or female, in faith, shall enter Paradise and will be done no injustice whatever. (4:32) The people of Paradise are happily engaged. Both the men and their wives are in the shade, reclining on cushions. (36:55) God will punish the male and female hypocrites, the male and female associationists, who think so ill of God. (48:6) Men have priority over women, by virtue of what God had endowed to them and by what they spend on women of their wealth. (4:34) What is due to women is like what is due from them, all in love and gentleness. (2:228) Your women are fruits for you. Present them to yourselves and enjoy them as you desire. But fear God knowing that you shall confront Him. (2:223) Enable your women to lead an affluent life, the rich according to his means and the poor according to his, all in love and kindness. That is a duty for men of good faith. (2:237) Give residence to your women in your own abodes, and do not press them in order to make life difficult for them. If they are pregnant, spend on them freely until they give birth, and if they nurse your children give them their due wages and talk to them kindly. . . . Let the affluent spend of his affluence on them, and man of limited income spend of his limited income, each according to his means. (65:6)

Those who cannot find anyone to marry, let them maintain their chastity until God gives them of His bounty. (24:33) Do not commit adultery; it is an evil deed. (17:32) Those of your women who commit adultery, let four witnesses testify against them. If they do, then hold such women in their houses until death comes or God finds a way for them. (4:15) If you believe in God and the Day of Judgment, punish the convicted adulterer and adulteress mercilessly with one hundred lashes and let many believers witness their chastisement. . . . Those who accuse married women of adultery and fail to bring forth four witnesses to this effect, punish with eighty lashes and never accept their testimony thereafter; for they are the evil doers, unless they repent later and make amends. God is merciful and forgiving. (24:2) Marry the unmarried women among you and the righteous among your people and servants. If these be poor, God will give them of His bounty. (24:32) Permitted unto you is marriage to the chaste freewomen, believers, or People of the Book, if you give them their dowries and go to them in chastity, not in license or promiscuity. (5:5) And if you cannot afford to marry from among the believing freewomen, then marry from your believing slaves and handmaidens . . . with the permission of their relatives and render unto them their dowries and wages in kindness without license or promiscuity. (4:25) And if you fear that you may not act justly to orphaned women, then marry whomsoever you desire, two, three, or four women. But if you fear to fail in justice, then marry only one, or take from your slaves. In this case, it is likelier that you will not be unjust. And give women their dowries. If they offer you some of their dowries freely, you may take thereof in good conscience and happily. (4:3) You cannot possibly keep perfect balance and justice between many wives however you may try. (4:128)

Those who forswear their women should wait four months. Perchance they may change their resolve. In this case, God is merciful and patient. But if they persist in wanting divorce, God is wise and all-hearing. Divorced women shall wait three periods, and should not keep secret what God has created in their wombs if they believe in God and the Day of Judgment. Their husbands are better entitled to take them back should they desire reconciliation. (2:226–28) Solemn repudiation of the wife and reconciliation to her may be repeated twice. Thereafter, it must be either a kindly retention or a kindly emancipation (divorce). It is not lawful for you to take back anything that you had given them during or before the marriage unless you fear that both spouses would thereby transgress God's law. But if you fear that they may so transgress, it is not blameworthy for them if she chooses to ransom herself by such arrangement. . . . A divorced woman, (i.e., a woman finally divorced after the third repudiation) may not be lawfully remarried to her previous husband unless she has married someone else in the meantime. If the divorced spouses fear they would transgress God's bonds after divorce, then it is legitimate for them to revoke their divorce. If you have divorced a woman and she has spent her term, then keep them in your houses only out of charity. Otherwise, set them free kindly, and do not keep them spitefully for aggressive purposes. Whoever does so has wronged himself. . . . In kindness, do not obstruct the marriage of such women if agreement is reached between them and their prospective husbands. That is purer and more becoming for you. (2:229) Mothers who want to complete the nursing of the children may do so for two full years. The father shall carry the burden of providing for the mother and child in kindness. However, no soul may be charged with more than it is capable to bear. (2:233) You are not blameworthy if you divorce your wives whom you have not yet touched, or, in other cases, if you assign for them a provision. (2:236)

4. Social Justice: The Sharing of Wealth (*Zakāt*)

Felicitous are the believers who are reverent in their prayer, who abstain from gossip and remit their *zakāt*. (23:1–4) Pay the *zakāt*. The good you do for your soul's sake, you will find with God. . . . Lend to God a fair loan. (2:110; 73:20) And give the relative his right, as well as the destitute and the wayfarer, to each his right. (17:26) The righteous ones are men who do not claim every portion of their wealth, but recognize that a portion thereof belongs by right to the poor and the deprived. (51:16, 19) Who is it that really rejects religion? Who rejects Islām? Surely, it is he who drives away the orphan, who does not urge the feeding of the destitute. Woe to those who worship without conscience, who put a semblance of faith but never give assistance to the needy. (107:1) Take of their wealth a share for the man in need and God's cause, by which to purify and justify them. (9:103)

5. The Rendering of Justice: The Absolute Scale, Forgiveness, and Charity

We have revealed to you the Book that you may judge between man by that which God had taught you. (4:105) Say: My Lord commands justice and equity. (7:29) O you who believe! Be upright in upholding God's law, and act as witnesses for justice. Anybody's hatred should not affect your rendering justice. To act justly is closer to piety . . . Be steadfast in justice, witnesses unto God, even if it be against yourselves, your parents, or relatives rich or poor; for it is more proper that God's standard be applied in every case. Do not follow your desires, that you may judge justly. If you charge your language so as to avoid justice, or evade the doing of justice, remember that God knows all that you do. (5:8; 4:135) O you who believe, when you lend or borrow for a definite term, write it down in an instrument for that purpose. Let a scribe write it down for you faithfully. No scribe shall refuse to write as God has taught him to. Let the borrowing party therefore dictate, while the scribe writes it down, and fearing God his Lord, let him not reduce the obligation due by one jot or tittle. If the borrowing party is a plebeian, weak, or unable to dictate, let his legal guardian or agent do it for him. Invite two witnesses from among you to witness the deed. . . . And do not forget to write it down, whether the matter in hand be great or insignificant, and to specify its definite term. That is more equitable with God. It makes testimony more definite and certain, and it reduces the chances of doubt. (2:282)

No believer may kill a believer, unless it happens by mistake. Whoever kills a believer by mistake shall bring about the emancipation of a believer-slave and pay the blood money to the next of kin unless these wish to forgive. If the killed is a believer but citizen of a country at war with you, then the setting free of a believer-slave is obligatory. But if the killed is a citizen of a country at covenant with you, then blood-money must be given to his relatives as well as a believer-slave shall be set free. If no believer-slaves are found, then the fasting of two consecutive months in repentance to God. . . . Whoever deliberately murders a believer shall dwell eternally in hell, accursed and condemned of God. (4:92–93) And the thief whether male or female, cut off his or her hand in punishment for what he or she earned of God's anger. (5:38–39) The punishment of those who fight God and the Prophet and seek to corrupt the world is to be killed, crucified, or have their arms and legs cut off or be banished. They are to be put to shame in this world while a great punishment is in store for them in the other; except those who repent before you conquer them. Remember that God is merciful and forgiving. (5:33–34) And those who violate the covenant of God after its enactment, repudiate that which God commanded to be enjoined, and spread corruption in the world, are accursed and shall have a grievous life. (13:25)

6. The World Order: The Universal Call to Reason and Felicity

We have sent to mankind a proclaimer of the truth, a warner to men to call them unto God, to be by His leave an illuminating light.... We have revealed to you (Muḥammmad) the Book, that you may lead mankind from darkness to light. (2:119; 3:45; 14:1) We have sent you but a mercy to the whole world.... Praised be God Who revealed the standard Book to His servant to enable him to warn mankind.... We have sent you to all men to proclaim and to warn ... Say: "This is my purpose and my way; I and my followers plainly and openly call men unto God. We praise Him and we repudiate all associationism." (21:107; 25:1; 34:28; 12:108) Call men unto the path of your Lord by good preaching and wise speech. Argue with them, always presenting the truer argument and the better consideration. Your Lord knows better who is on the right path and who is astray.... Proclaim that the truth has come from your Lord. Whoever wills, let him believe; whoever wills not, let him persist in disbelief. (16:125; 18:29) No coercion in religion. Truth and right guidance are now clearly distinct from error and misguidance.... Remind and warn. That is your commission. You have no imperial authority over any man. (2:257; 88:21–6) Had God willed it, all men on earth would have been believers. But he did not! Would you then compel men to believe?... Say: O men, the truth has been revealed by your Lord. Whoever accepts it does so for his own good, and whoever rejects it does so at his own peril. (10:99, 108) If the unbelievers argue with you, answer: I have opened myself to God's determination.... As to the People of the Book and the uninstructed, ask them whether they too have submitted to God.... If they did not, then your duty ends with your conveyance of the revelation. (3:20) Say: O people of the Book! Let us now resolve together to abide by a principle common to both of us, namely, that we shall worship none but God, that we shall not associate aught with Him, and that we shall not take one another as lords beside God. (3:64) Lesser than the beasts in the eye of God are the unbelievers for they have covenanted with you and violated their covenant shamelessly in every case. If you lay hold of them in war, make of them a lesson to the others. If you fear treachery from a group, disown them beforehand in justice.... The unbelievers who violated their covenant and ran away with it shall not last. Prepare for them all the military power you can muster, that you may dissipate them and all other enemies besides ... with fear. What you spend therein in the cause of God will be repaid to you by Him, and you will not be wronged. But if they incline toward peace, then incline yourself to it also and put your trust in God. (8:55–61) Fight those that fight you but do not commit aggression, for God loves not the aggressors. Kill them wherever you catch them and expel them from wherever they had expelled you. Subversion is a worse crime than murder. Do not fight in the Holy Mosque of Makkah (Mecca) unless they open hostilities against you there. In that case, fight them. Should they refrain and stop, God is forgiving and merciful. Fight them ... until religion is all God's and if they give up, remember that you are to fight only the unjust aggressors ... and pay them back in kind exactly what they had perpetrated against you. In all this, however, fear God and remember that He assists only those that fear Him. Give generously in His cause but do not expose yourselves to unnecessary dangers and always do good. God loves the good-doers. (2:190–95) Those believers who, for no physical incapacity, stay behind and do not go to war are not the equals of those who spend their fortunes and fight in God's cause. The latter stand higher in God's view, though He promised reward for both. (4:95) No prophet shall have or keep any slaves, or imperialize on earth. (8:67)

B. CIVILIZATIONAL: THE MODEL STATE AND RULER; ISLĀMIC DEMOCRACY AND LAW OF NATIONS

1. The Covenant of Madīnah: Constitution of the Universal State

The Prophet of God wrote out a covenant between the *muhājirūn* (Makkan Muslim emigrants to Madīnah) and the *anṣar* (helpers or native Muslims of Madīnah) in which he granted the Jews peace, safeguarded their property and religious establishment, and laid down upon them certain conditions. He wrote:

In the name of God, the Merciful, the Compassionate. This is a covenant from Muḥammad, the Prophet, between those who are convinced of their Islamic faith (*al Mu'minūn*, hereafter referred to as "believers") and Muslims of Quraysh, Yathrib, and their followers and affiliates who fight with them. All these constitute one *ummah*, separate from all people. In this *ummah*, the *muhājirūn* retain their present social order and mutual ties, and ransom their prisoner in love and goodness among the believers. The Banū 'Awf . . . and every other tribe do likewise. Whenever needed, the believers will spare nothing of value for the ransom of a prisoner or the fulfillment of a bond. . . .

No believer shall ally himself to the prisoner of a believer without that believer's consent. Pious believers will unite against whoever perpetrates an injustice or wrongly extorts the property of other believers or seeks to divide them. They will all act together in single formation against such a man even if he be one of theirs. No believer shall kill a believer for the sake of, or in retaliation for, an unbeliever. The bond of God being one and the believers being bonded in brotherhood to one another in contradistinction to other men, any protection given by the least of them shall be honored by all. To the Jews who follow us belong assistance and equal treatment from us without either injustice or discrimination. No alliance directed against them may be entered into by the believers. The believers' peace being one, no believer shall make peace in a war for the cause of God without the other believers, but all together in equality and justice. Every tribe which conquers with us shall be bound by this same bond. The believers shall avenge. in favor of one another their losses in life sustained in the cause of God. Pious believers follow the best and most righteous guidance. No wealth belonging to Quraysh shall be protected or safeguarded in favor of an unbeliever, and no unbeliever or client thereof shall be given protection or safety. No one may prevent a believer from attacking such wealth or persons. Whoever murders a believer without justifying cause shall be bound in responsibility until the heirs of the murdered are satisfied, while all believers shall rise in unity against the murderers. Only such unified action against him is permissible to them.

No believer who has entered into this covenant, believed in God and the Day of Judgment, shall rescue or lodge a criminal or violator, and whoever does so shall suffer under God's anger and curse on the Final Day, and shall be an outlaw in this world. No indemnity and no compensation is acceptable for such an offender. In whatever matter you may dispute, it shall be referred to God and to Muḥammad.

The Jews shall expend of their fortune along with the believers as long as they join them in battle against the unbelievers. The Jews of Banū 'Auf are an *ummah* with the believers; to them belongs their religion and to the Muslims theirs; and to each of them, their own clients and themselves. None shall be excepted but the criminal and the unjust—who destroys by his crime or injustice only himself and his own folks. To the Jews of Banū al Naggār belong the same rights and duties as those of Banū 'Auf, and likewise to the Jews of Banū al Ḥarth. . . .

No Jew among them shall make war but with the permission of Muḥammad. Any Jew may seek retaliation on his own for a wound he or any of his dependents have suffered. But if he should kill another man on his own, he and his family will have to bear responsibility therefor. Whoever acts in violation of this principle does so at his own and his family's peril, unless, of course, it be that an injustice had been committed against him. God will be the guarantor of this provision. The Jews and the believers shall assist one another against those who fight the people of this covenant or attack the city of Madīnah. They shall advise, guide, and warn against evil for each other's benefit, and each shall work for the good rather than the disadvantage of the other. No party may be said to be disadvantaged by its ally. Immediate assistance to the sufferer of injustice is imperative. The town of Yathrib (i.e., Madīnah) shall be inviolate to those who entered into this covenant, and every man shall treat the neighbor as himself and be protected against injury and crime. No privilege or right shall be violated except with the permission of its owner. Whatever disputes of consequence may arise between the people who are party to this covenant and concerning the provisions it contains, shall be referred to God and to Muḥammad, the Prophet of God. God inclines towards Muḥammad and keeps him under His protection, and He is guarantor of the most scrupulous fulfillment of the provisions of this covenant. Neither Quraysh nor her allies shall be befriended or protected by the parties to this covenant, but they shall together cooperate against any attack on Yathrib. If the parties to this covenant are called upon to enter into a peace treaty, they shall do so and honor it. In case the Jews are called upon to do so, the believers shall safeguard the Jews' interests except those of them who fight against Islām. . . . The Jews of al Aws and their clients are entitled to the same rights and duties as the parties to this covenant, together with good will and beneficence on the part of the latter. (Ibn Hishām, *Sīrat al Nabiyy*, vol. 2, pp. 119–223)

2. The Model Ruler

a. Abū Bakr (10–12 A.H.; 632–634)

After thanking God and praising Him in appropriate terms, Abū Bakr took the floor and said, "O men! Here I have been assigned the job of being a ruler over you while I am not the best among you. If I do well in my job, help me. If I do wrong, redress me. Truthfulness is fidelity, and lying is treason. The weak shall be strong in my eye until I restore to them their right, and the strong shall be weak in my eye until I have restored that right from them. No people give up fighting for the cause of God but God inflicts upon them abject subjection; and no people give themselves to lewdness but God envelops them with misery. Obey me as long as I obey God and His Prophet. But if I disobey God's command or His Prophet's, then no obedience is incumbent upon you . . ." (*Ibid.*, vol. 4, pp. 240–41)

b. 'Umar Ibn al Khaṭṭāb (12–22 A.H.; 634–644)

It is commonly said that upon his accession to the caliphate, 'Umar ibn al Khaṭṭāb delivered the following inaugural speech:

"The Arabs are like that proud camel which resists being yoked by anyone, and their leader is hence well advised to look where he is leading them. As for me, by the Lords of the Ka'bah I swear that I shall, if I have to, carry them on the road. . . . I am told that the people are fearful of my hardness, apprehensive of my severity. The markets hum with their bemoaning: 'Umar was too hard even when the Prophet was here with us, and he was harder while Abū Bakr, rather than he, was our chief. What is to be our lot now that all power is his?' Let me tell you plainly that such bemoaning is in place. . . .

"I was the companion of the Prophet, his servant and worker and I knew too well his compassion and love, his mercy and friendly love—qualities which God Himself had confirmed in him. But I was in his hands a drawn sword until he would see to put me back in the sheath or let me go forth. Nonetheless I remained with him all the time until his death, and he was pleased with me. May God be praised! For He made me thereby the happier. . . .

"Now I am your chief. Know, therefore, that my hardness and severity shall henceforth be doubled, but against the unjust, and the aggressors, Muslims or others. To those who seek peace, piety, and virtue I shall be kindlier than they can ever be even to themselves. Know that I shall not tolerate injustice. I shall fight the unjust and cause him to grovel in the dust until he acknowledges justice. But that I, the same chief, shall grovel in the dust in front of the pious, the virtuous, the just.

"Certainly I have duties of my own and it is your right to take me to account therefor: It is your right and my duty that I touch none of your incomes except that which God had ordained in the way He ordained; that whatever is collected from you be spent by me only according to law; that I cause your incomes to increase and your bounty to multiply; that I promise your towns to construct and your frontiers to guard; that I expose you to no danger and restrict your movements to no locality; that whenever you go out on an expedition, I become the father of your families until your return. Be therefore pious. Help me against yourselves by refraining from asking more than is your due. Help me against myself by constantly enjoining the good and forbidding evil, by offering me your counsel in everything pertinent to the government of your affairs. . . . The Prince of Believers should be a brother to the believers. Otherwise he is an enemy to them. . . . The man whom I shall appoint as governor of a province should be such that, when not a governor, he would seem to be the people's governor, and when actually a governor, he would seem to be only a commoner among the people." (Muḥammad Ḥusayn, Haykal, *Al Fārūq 'Umar* ['Umar the "just separator of justice from injustice"], pp. 95–96)

c. Hārūn al Rashīd (169–193 A.H.; 786–809)

The Prince of Believers, may God confirm him, asked me to write a comprehensive book for him to govern the collection of revenue (*kharāj*), tithes, charities, and poll taxes and other affairs which it is his duty to administer and to govern. His purpose in this is to lift whatever injustice may have befallen his people in this regard and to bring happiness to them. May God help the Prince of Believers to stand firm by what he has undertaken, to succeed therein, and to avoid what is undesirable and frightful. He asked me to show, analyze, and explain clearly what he intends, and is supposed to do. This I have done in this book.

O Prince of Believers! God, may He be praised, has entrusted to you a grave matter the desert of which, if well performed, is the greatest reward and, otherwise, the greatest punishment. By God's entrusting of the leadership of this *ummah* to you, you have become overnight the one to work for the welfare of numerous peoples whom God has put under your direction and protection and for whom He holds you responsible. No work lasts, however, which is not founded on piety; God will sooner or later shake its foundations and cause it to collapse over its architects and protagonists. Do not therefore waste away the trust of this *ummah* which God has laid in your hands. Act therefore, for strength is in the doing of this trust.

Do not postpone today's work for the morrow, or else you will lose it. The term of time for the doing of a deed always expires before one's hope for getting it done. Overtake the terms of your duties therefore with initiative and action. Action, after its right time, is futile. Pastors must render account to their Lord, just as any shepherd must to his lord. Establish justice therefore in that which God has entrusted to you if but for an hour a day, and remember that the happiest shepherd with God on the Day of Judgment is one whose pastorate brought happiness to his flock. Do not swerve and thus cause your flock to swerve. Never give an order based on desire and inclination or affected by anger. Whenever two alternatives face you, one worthy of the other world and the other worthy of this, always prefer the former. The other world is eternal; this one is transient. Let the fear of God put you constantly on the alert, and cause you to regard all men alike, whether they be near or distant. In doing and voicing God's will, fear not the slightest blame or criticism. Be always careful, not so much in the use of tongue as in the desires your heart entertains. Fear God; to fear Him is to take due precaution and care, and whoever fears God, him will God protect. Pursue the appointed term, the trodden path, the known way, the remembered deed, and the familiar recourse. Such just recourse, which is also the great moment for which the hearts fly with joy and all arguments are nullified, is precisely that at which the people stand humble in front of a ruler whose power has overwhelmed them, and await his verdict or punishment as a thing irrevocable. In such a moment, when the feet stumble and the faces change color, when expectation is long enduring, and rendering account is precise, repentance and bemoaning are futile for the man who knew but did not act. God, may He be gloried and praised, said, "A day with your Lord is like a thousand years of your reckoning"; "Today is the Day of Judgment; today We bring you together with the ancestors"; "The Day of Judgment is their appointed term"; "When they shall behold what was promised them, it would seem to them that their lives were but a single hour of the day"; "When they shall behold it, it will seem to them that their wait was only the time between evening and morning." (Qur'ān, 22:49; 77:38; 44:40; 44:34–35; 79:46) O what an unspeakable stumbling block, a futile regret, a mere shift of night and day had brought it all about, wearing out the novelty of every new thing, bringing close the distant and realizing the promised. God metes to every soul that which it has earned. Certainly, His judgment is swift.

O God! Life is short; the earth and all that is on it will perish; the danger is grave; and the other world is the final destination. Do not therefore have to confront God after following the path of transgressors. The Lord of the Day of Judgment will judge men by their deeds, not by the positions they held.

God has warned you. Keep His warning in mind. He has not created you in vain and your work will not be without effect. God will ask you to give account of your station, of every one of your public deeds. Consider what would be your answer. Know that no man may withdraw from God's presence before giving account. The prophet—may God's peace and blessing be upon him—said, "No man shall withdraw on the Day of Judgment until he answers four questions: First, concerning his knowledge, what did he do to further it? Second, concerning his years of life, how did he spend them? Third, concerning his wealth, how did he acquire it and how did he spend it? Fourth, concerning his body, what use did he make of it?" So, O Prince of Believers, prepare your own answers to these future queries. Whatever you do and approve of will have to be read out tomorrow. Remember that you will have to shed all appearances when you confront God and His hosts.

I therefore counsel you, O Prince of Believers, to guard what God has entrusted to you and care for those whom He put under your protection. And in doing so, have your vision fixed only on Him and for His sake. Otherwise, the ease of righteousness will become hard and rough for you, its boundaries and outlines will become confused and hardly visible, its freedom will become oppression, its self-evident truths will appear as falsehoods and its self-evident falsehoods as truths. Contend with yourself therefore, and do so with the severity of a person who seeks the welfare of righteousness, not of his own self. The shepherd is responsible for what is lost during his tenure precisely because he could have spared it from destruction and peril and is supposed to have guided it to the pasture of life and salvation. If he lost his flock, it is because he relinquished his duty and if destruction comes all the sooner and its effect is all the greater, it is because other cares than the pursuit of righteousness had occupied him. And yet, if he fulfilled his duty, he would be the happier and God would pay him his due many times. Beware then of losing your flock, for if you do, God will extract from you its price and mete to you the same punishment and ruin.

Before it falls down, a damaged or faulty building may yet be repaired. Only the service you do to those whom God has entrusted to you will count in your favor, and the disservice will be counted against you. Do not forget your trust, therefore, and you will not be forgotten. Do not omit the care of them, to bring about their good, and God will not omit to take care of you. Do not allow your enjoyment of this world in day or night, to stop your remembrance of God, your praise of Him, your blessing of His Prophet, the Prophet of mercy and the true guide.

It is by God's mercy and benevolence that He made the rulers vicegerents in His earth, that He established for them a beacon of light to dissolve the darkness of injustice and the ambiguities of their rights and duties. The light of such beacon is the upholding of the sanctions of the law of Islām (*Sharī'ah*), the giving of each man his due after careful examination. The promulgation of the practices established by the righteous predecessors is equally deserving. Their application is goodness imperishable and eternal. Tyranny first, and then the ruler's recourse to men devoid of wisdom or righteousness, always constitute the people's peril. Complete therefore, O Prince of Believers, the blessings which God has accorded to you by pursuing the virtues through gratitude. God, may He be praised and glorified, said, "If you are grateful, I will increase My bounty to you; if you are ungrateful, My punishment will be severe." (Qur'ān, 14:7) Nothing is more loved by God than good deeds. Nothing is more hateful to Him than evil doing and ingratitude. Few are those who, having declared their ingratitude by denying God's blessings and have not repented, have not been denied their glory and made to suffer the terror of their own enemies.

I pray God, O Prince of Believers, Who was good to you in that He blessed you with the knowledge of Him in that which is entrusted to you, that He never throw you upon yourself alone, but that He care for you as He cared for His friends and saints. It is He alone to whom such a prayer can be made.

I have written for you the book you commanded and explained it to you clearly. Study it, therefore, understand it and repeat its reading until you have really mastered it. I have exerted myself for your sake and spared no advice or counsel that is good for you or the Muslims, for the sake of God and in feat of His punishment. I do hope that, if you implement what is written therein, God will see to it that your state revenues will be collected without injustice to Muslim or *dhimmī* i.e., covenanter, whether Christian, Jew, etc.; that He will guide you to bring your own people to their own good, namely, to the observance of God's commandments, to the lifting of the oppressive injustice affecting their relations and transactions with one another. For your benefit I have recorded therein many sound affirming and denying transmitted texts (*ḥadiths*) concerning all that you inquired about and sought to follow in your government. May God give you success in all that incurs His blessing. May he make you the instrument of the people's felicity and happiness. (Abū Yūsuf Ya'qūb ibn Ibrahīm [d. 798], *Kitāb al Kharāj* [Book of revenue], Preface)

3. Islāmic Democracy

Islāmic democracy—the system under which man chooses his government in exercise of a positive right which is truly his own to enjoy rather than a means for avoiding evil or preventing civil wars, or for facilitating government of the ruled and securing their obedience and cooperation—is founded on four principles: 1. individual responsibility; 2. equality; 3. obligation of the people's leaders to advise the government; and 4. mutual security among all citizens. . . . The first is established in Islām in clear and comprehensive terms. "Do not transfer guilt from one person or deed to another," the Qur'ān said. (6:164; 17:15; 35:18; etc.) No man, hence, is responsible except for his own deeds; and no man is accountable for deeds perpetuated by his parents, relatives, or predecessors. Referring to a preceding nation, the Qur'ān says, "That was the case of a foregone nation. It got what it earned. What you will get will be what you will have earned. You will not be responsible for what they had done." (2:134, 141) Man is, however, responsible for people whom he has taken under his charge, for deeds which fall within normal discharge of his function. The Prophet said that each of you is a pastor responsible for his flock, the leader for those whom he leads, the father for his children, the mother for her household, the servant for the master's wealth entrusted to his care, and so on.

Equality is emphatically asserted in the

Qur'ān. "O men, We have created you all of a male and a female. We constituted you in various tribes and nations that you may cooperate with one another. The better among you is only because he is the more pious and virtuous." (49:13) Who every man is, carries no weight at all with God. "On the Day of Judgment, lineage will avail nothing." (23:102) "O men of Quraysh," the Prophet said, "earn your own salvation; for I cannot avail you on the Day of Judgment in any way. O House of 'Abd Manāf, (The Prophet's great, great grandfather), I shall not be then of any advantage to you. O 'Abbas (The Prophet's paternal grandfather), son of 'Abd al Muṭṭalib, that I am your nephew will avail you nothing in front of God. O Fāṭimah, my daughter, ask of me anything here and I will give it to you. But with God I shall be as nothing to you. I have my works and you have yours." The Prophet also said that there is no advantage to being an Arab over being a Persian, to being of Quraysh over being an Abyssinian—except in piety and virtue. No white is superior to a black unless it be in piety and virtuous deeds. Likewise, there has never been any mistaking that Muḥammad was sent "but unto all men" (34:28), not exclusively to any particular tribe, people, or race.

As for the obligation to seek the advice and consent of the governed, it is clearly laid down by the Qur'ān on the Prophet himself and, all the more, on all rulers. "Seek their advice and consult with them," it commands. "Thereafter, when you reach a decision, trust in God and proceed." (3:159)

Finally, since it is possible that a whole people may undesirably suffer consequences of the deeds of any one of its members, it is the right of the member to protect not only himself but his fellows as well. "Fear—and hence, seek to prevent—a misdeed which may not touch its perpetrator alone but others," the Qur'ān enjoins. (8:25) In this, every man is obliged to the extent of his ability. "God does not oblige any person beyond his capacity." (2:286; 65:7) It is possible that a member may be affected by the misdeed of another without his being held accountable therefor.

This Islāmic democracy and the rights which it enjoins are not established as a utilitarian need, nor in fear of social and political calamities. Islām presented this societal order without the weak asking for it; indeed, with the realization that the strong will fight it. Surely there have been revolutions by the weak before. But in these cases, the weak did not revolt out of principle, but in simple reaction to their oppression, very much as an animal would when beaten, restricted, or starved. When they dislodged the strong from their seats of power, they put themselves in their place and followed in their footsteps. Thus Roman law recognized as perfectly legitimate the right of the creditor, for instance, to subjugate his debtor, as did the custom laws of pre-Islāmic Makkah. Islām, however, taught a new order of society in which the person has dignity because he is a person, and nullified the right of power and capital to violate that dignity. (Al 'Aqqād [d. 1963], *Al Dīmuqrāṭīyyah fī al Islām* [Democracy in Islām], pp. 41–47)

4. The Islāmic State: Replica and Subordinate of the Cosmic State

The Muslim believes in a God capable of doing whatever He wills. The notion of an omnipotent God is often mistaken by others as implying that divine government stands under no law, and that any worldly government seeking to mold itself after that of the cosmos must hence be lawless and tyrannical. The truth, however, is that the Muslim who believes in an omnipotent godhead equally believes in immutable laws of nature and cosmos. This conviction of this is corroborated by the Qur'ān's repeated declarations, such as, "The law of God was applied in the case of the ancients For the law of God never changes." (48:23); and "Would they not consider their predecessors? The law of God is beyond change. There is no escape from its reach." (35:43) Cosmic government in the Islāmic view is constitutional and runs in strict compliance with unalterable laws. It is not chaotic or whimsical. It does not condemn anyone without due warning, without making its will absolutely clear through revelation. "We would not punish a people until an apostle came to them from Us." (17:15) "There is no people but We have sent them an apostle to warn them." (35:24) "Your Lord does not act unjustly to men." (41:46) Man, himself, in the Islāmic view, is one of the constituting elements of cosmic law. He is not an extra addition to it, but integral to the forces that operate within it. "God will not change the prosperous state of a people unless they first change their own hearts and selves." (8:54; 13:12) Nor is it sufficient that there be due notice, due warning, and immutable law which applies to all. It is yet necessary that man himself know the law, why and how and for what he is being held responsible.... If he does, convinced that the world is run by a divine government such as Islām teaches, he would naturally refrain from acknowledging or submitting himself to any authority greater than or even equal to that which belongs to God. He would by nature and deeply within his consciousness be opposed to tyranny before he opposes it in word and deed. Unless he deliberately perverts himself into something else, he would, as it were by nature, be a democrat.

The word *hukm* or government occurs many times in the Qur'ān. Its usage points to the fact that just government is essential to and constitutive of the Islāmic faith. It is not merely an ethical desideratum. There is no dispute but must have a just solution separating right from wrong; and there is no injustice but must have a just order overruling it. Injustice is never final. In the final stage, [and yet in this world and in history, not merely in an extra-space-time kingdom,] there is the government of God, the just and perfect government with jurisdiction over all. Just government is therefore inseparable from the business of life and history; it is a universal recourse in every case, big or small. Its verdict is a universal law of nature, applicable to all. Islām's emphasis upon this cosmic order was certainly meant to impress upon man's consciousness that the men and women of this world do have a protective immunity against the strong and the unjust which the latter had better heed.... The least man in Islām can afford even to smile in the face of the mightiest injustice, convinced as he is that above it, there is yet the other verdict of justice. (*Ibid.*, pp. 50–56)

5. The Caliph and His Office

Perhaps no Islāmic concept is as clearly betrayed by the Arabic word used to express it as the *imāmate*. Indeed, the etymological meaning of the word already includes, in general manner, the necessary qualifications of the *imām* or leader. The *imām* is the man who leads men in the upholding of the law. The qualifying requirement is the capacity to uphold the law; and any man capable of such leadership and upholding of the law qualifies for becoming the *imām* in Islām.

In Islām no person or institution has an exclusive monopoly over the nomination of the *imām*. That is why the jurist and wise judge, al Báqillānī (d. 1013), said that the *imāmate* is established when one of (those who bind and loosen) contracts to give it to a person satisfying the requisite qualifications. Nomination to the *imāmate* is to be followed by the entry of the public into a solemn contract with the nominee under which they agree to be governed and the nominee agrees to govern by the law of Islām. In case many are nominated, the first to receive nomination and the people's contract is considered prior, and the people are obliged to submit to and obey him.

Between the *imām* and the *ummah* there is hence a mutual covenant. The *imām* is responsible for the *ummah* because he is its pastor, and "every pastor is responsible for his pastorage." The *ummah* is responsible for its *imām* because it chooses him, contracts to turn over leadership to him, and as the Prophet said, "As you are in yourselves, so will your leaders be."

Obedience to the *imām* is a duty which may not be suspended except when he commands the performance of evil in violation of the law of Islām. Many traditions of the Prophet emphasized this point. The trustworthy report of Ibn 'Umar is that the Prophet said, "Regard and obedience to the ruler are obligatory on the Muslim as long as the thing commanded does not violate Islāmic law, regardless of whether it is pleasing or harming. Whenever the Muslim is commanded to violate the law, there shall be neither regard nor obedience." Another such tradition is that reported by 'Ibādah ibn al Ṣāmit (The Prophet's companion), which says, "We have contracted to accept the leadership of the Apostle of God, to obey in good and in ill, in the pleasant and the harmful, even against our preferences; that we shall not dispute the authority of our leaders and commanders. But our contract has also established that we shall always voice the truth, unafraid of anything but God"; or, according to another version, "that we shall not question the authority of our leaders unless we have evidence that they have flagrantly violated the law."

No harm should be inflicted upon the people and be borne by them obediently unless it be necessitated by war, whether foreign or civil. . . . Nonetheless, advising the *imām* is a universal duty. The Prophet said, "Advising the ruler and the ruled for the sake of God and His Prophet is of the essence of Islām"; and "The worthiest courage, self-exertion, or sacrifice is the voicing of a just counsel to a tyrannous ruler."

The requisite qualifications of the *imām* are understanding, justice, sufficiency, and capacity to maintain the security and prosperity of the *ummah* with armed might and wise government. A small number of jurists would add to these that the *imām* must be of the Quraysh tribe, following the Prophet's admonition that leadership belongs to Quraysh. But the majority of jurists do not regard this as essential, the other conditions being far more important. They invoke contrary traditions of the Prophet, such as, "Listen and obey the man appointed to be your leader even if he were an Abyssinian slave"; and of 'Umar, "Were Salim, the servant of Ḥudhayfah, alive, I would have appointed him your leader."

There is no disagreement at all among jurists that the *imām* may be discharged in case he violates the covenant of the *ummah* or suffers from an incurable incapacity. Their reason for this is again the prevention of civil war. In case there is no fear of such, none would disagree that the *imām* is impeachable and his appointment revokable. But if civil war does break out, the question is taken over by the powers that are; and the matter cannot be settled until the cessation of hostilities. Some among the Shī'ah sect hold that the *imāmate*, once properly contracted, cannot be revoked because it is a trust of the Prophet passed from one *imām* to another. This is certainly true of the Shī'ah; but it is only a description of what they regard as the ideal state of affairs. In actuality, the Shī'ah believed the *imām* to be hidden and his place taken by the so-called "apparent" *imām*. As for this latter who is in all actuality the real ruler, the Shī'ah do not differ from the Sunnīs sect regarding the *ummah* as the final source of authority, capable of contracting the *imāmate* with, and revoking it from, anyone.

The great awe in which the *imāmate* is held is universal among all Muslims. It is the institution upon which devolve the security and felicity of the state, as well as all the rights of the *ummah*. . . . To the *imām* belongs the greatest respect accorded to a human not because that man has a right of dominion over his subjects but because the rights and duties of men, their security and felicity devolve upon him for their free exercise and realization. (*Ibid.*, pp. 68–73)

6. Islāmic Breakthrough in the Law of Nations

Islām has been called unique in its theory of international order because such theory is allegedly built upon holy war. In truth, however, Islām furnishes the system best suited to the establishment of peace among men. This is evident in Islām's inclusion of all men in its threefold division of society and its regulation of their mutual relations.

According to Islām, mankind is divided into three main groups: the Muslims, the covenanters, and the enemies. It is not reasonable to have any more categories than these; and there are, in actual reality, none besides them recognized by any state.

The Muslim peoples, of *Dār al Islām* (The House of Islām) as the jurists call it, may consist of many countries and many governments. These may disagree, but they cannot legitimately recourse to war against one another. Islāmic law permits no war between them. Should any one Muslim people start hostile or warlike activities against another, Islāmic law requires all other Muslims to rise and stop the aggression and solve the dispute by peaceful means first, and by war in case this fails to restore peace and harmony. The Qur'ān says, "If two parties among the believers fight each other, reconcile them. If one of them persists in its hostility, then fight it until it returns to reason. When it does, seek to reconcile the two parties again in justice. Do justice and be fair. God loves the righteous." (49:9) The transmitted text says, "If two Muslims confront each other with drawn swords, both killer and killed shall be condemned to the fire. When it was objected that this fate belongs more to the killer than to the killed, the Prophet answered that the killed too sought to kill his fellow Muslim. . . ."

As for the covenanters, once they have entered into covenant with the Muslims, their rights and duties are identically those of the Muslims themselves. International covenanting is of many varieties. Even in modern times, international law has not developed this form of relation between nations with as great detail or vision as the Islāmic law had done. Throughout man's relations with other men, Islām demanded fidelity at all costs unless the covenant in question has been violated by the other party. "Fulfill the covenants in which you enter and be true to your oaths. Have you not made God your guarantor in both?" (16:91) Even covenants with the polytheists are not excluded from this command of loyalty and fidelity. The Muslims are duty bound to honor them "You shall fulfill with piety the terms of your covenants with the polytheists as long as they remain true to them. God loves the pious." (9:5)

Finally, those who belong neither to the category of Muslims nor to that of covenanters, shall be called to join the ranks of either. The methods and forms of such call are governed by the Qur'ānic principle, "Call unto the path of your Lord by wise argument and righteous preaching and contend with your audience presenting arguments yet more sound. Do not force the issue! Your Lord knows better than you who is astray and who is rightly guided." (16:125) Islām has no argument other than that which aims at personal, free conviction. The Qur'ān said, "There shall be no coercion in religion. Truth is now clearly distinguished from error. Whoever renounces the latter and believes in God has entered into the strongest—nay, unbreakable—bond of friendship with God. God knows best; and He responds best to all." (2:256; 31:22)

7. Holy War: Collapse of Peaceful Communication

Holy war (*jihād*) becomes necessary only when "the righteous, sounder argument" is met not by another argument, but by violence from the other side. In such a situation there is no place for reason either to convince, or to be convinced, in freedom. With security under threat and communication brought to a standstill, there is no escape from the deployment of force to meet force. The Muslim must seek security where his call to peace, friendship, and covenant regulating normal relations is rejected, but he must never open hostilities with those who are not hostile to him. "God does not command you to avoid exercising your good will, or pursuing your fair deeds in justice and equity towards those who are not hostile to you, who do not violently oppose your religion, who do not evict you from your homes. God loves the fair and equitable." (60:8)

. . . Islām is certainly blameworthy if it combats ideas with the sword, since ideas are all combatable with argument and evidence. But it is not blameworthy for it to combat with the sword the sword which stands between it and man, preventing Islām from conveying its call and men from listening to or receiving it. The sword cannot be removed except with the sword; there is no escape from using might to bring the mighty to reason who uses his might to stop the mouths and ears of men. . . . If he is fair at all, the historian will acknowledge that the Muslims have been victims of the sword before they deployed it against their enemies; that their "aggression" was not agression because it was intellectual, an appeal to the mind and soul; that they did not recourse to armed defense except when their plea for rational intercourse was violently stopped or impeded.

To condemn the recourse to force after the other party has rejected the call of the mind to intercourse and the invitation of the heart to a relation of peace is to condemn all and every call as nonsense. Such a position implies that no reformer shall ever seek to carry out his reform, whatever it may be. Without a doubt, Islām rejects such enslavement to the *status quo*. It regards the call to the good as a sacred duty incumbent upon all men and every group without distinction. . . . No emphasis in the Qur'ān is greater than that of the duty "to enjoin the good, to call for the good deeds, and to forbid the evil." (3:110; 9:72; etc.) Nobody's fate is more condemned than that of a people "who did not forbid one another the perpetration of evil." (5:82)

At any rate, Islām demands from its adherents the calling of men to the good. It is natural for it to be hostile to that political power which stands in the way of the Muslims' fulfillment of this duty, or violently impedes their missionary activity. Such a power is treated by Islām as if in a state of war, unless and until it enters into a treaty of peace. When it does so, Islām acknowledges to such a state the same rights and duties as belong to itself.

When holy war becomes necessary, the Muslim is obliged to restrict his fighting to the fighters on the opposite side. He is under strict law not to kill women, children, and old men; nor is he to molest the invalid, the blind, the armless, the insane, the priest, or the meditating recluse. The first caliph collected the commands of the Prophet on this matter and issued them to his soldiers, "Do not be treacherous and win by ruse. Do not disfigure the corpses of your victims. Never kill a child, an old man, a woman. Never damage a date tree or destroy a fruit tree. Never kill a goat, a cow, or a camel except for the purpose of food. Whenever you pass by men who devote themselves to worship and meditation in their cells, do not even disturb them. . . ."

Islām not only approved but created laws for the regulation and effective application of group and/or individual pacts for security of aliens (*amān*), for a temporary cessation of hostilities (*muhādanah*), for friendly intercourse (*muwāda'ah*) with the enemy across the front line. It commanded the Muslims strictly to observe the pacts in which they entered. There was to be no violation of these pacts except for protection against disaster, and only with incontestable evidence that the other party had marched to war against the Islāmic state.

Alien security is defined by the men of law as follows: It is "the suspension of all rights to attack either the person of the enemy alien or his property in the case of war against him, his people, or his state." *Isti'mān* is defined as "the application for and granting of alien security by an enemy alien for a period of time enabling him to achieve a specific objective within the Islāmic state." Armistice is defined as "the covenant of the Muslim with an alien-at-war to suspend hostilities for a period of time during which the alien is regarded as falling outside the pale of Islāmic law." Finally, friendly intercourse is defined by the jurists as "a pact for a given period, during which the Muslim and his enemy could enter into friendly relations. This pact is revokable at any time under the condition of giving due warning of such intention to the other party as well as to the central authorities fo that party's state." (*Ibid.*, pp. 125–31)

8. Islām: A Synthesis of Realism and Idealism

It would seem that such lofty ideals of society and social living are too idealistic to be followed and put into practice. The truth, however, is that these ideals did find men who believed in them and gave them real existence. The Muslims' realization of these ideals is unusual, indeed extraordinary. As soon as Islām was established on earth, men accepted these principles and followed them. The early period of Islāmic history was especially distinguished by an exemplary fulfillment of them. The ethical perfectionism of these early Muslims is a permanent source of inspiration. Such for instance was the regime of ‘Umar ibn al Khaṭṭāb who was entitled *Al Fārūq* ("the righteous judge"). No other period of Islāmic history knew as many cases of realization of Islāmic ideals as his. The justice rendered between Abū Sufyān, the "lord of Quraysh," and one of his plebeian neighbors; against Khālid ibn al Walīd, the "sword of Islām"; between a king and a tramp; between the greatest companions of the Prophet and the least bedouins, non-Arabs, and even non-Muslims—all these were so exemplary and perfectionist that they constitute part of the moral wonders of the whole world, not only of Arabia.

Light breaks through the pages of history and shines forth for all when these pages tell the story of Jabalah ibn al Ayham, King of Ghassān, and the miserable bedouin from Fazārah who inadverently stepped on the king's garment.

At that time the Empire of Byzantium was constantly urging the Princes of Ghassān under its protectorate to invade the Arabian Peninsula. The fledgling Islāmic state expected such invasion all the time and feared it. It then appeared to Jabalah ibn al Ayham, King of Ghassān, to seek his fortune with his own fellow countrymen, the Arabs, and to withdraw from his own throne, protected as it was by an empire whose star had set. He wrote to ‘Umar about his intent, and the caliph was extremely pleased and wrote back, "Come forth! Our own rights as well as duties shall be yours." Jabalah came forth, and he entered Madīnah wearing his crown which held the great diamond of his grandmother Mary. Five hundred knights on horseback wearing gold and silver brocaded apparel accompanied him. When the procession reached Madīnah, everybody went out to welcome and to wonder at the magnificent spectacle of which one had never seen such a parallel. The occasion was truly one of great promise for the cause of Islām.

Jabalah, now converted to Islām, went to pilgrimage in Makkah, and was circumambulating the Ka‘bah when a poor bedouin from Fazārah in the hustle and scuffle of the crowd, stepped on the hem of Jabalah's garment, causing it to be loosened. Furious with rage, Jabalah hit the bedouin in the face and broke his nose. The bedouin took his complaint against the king to the caliph. The caliph called Jabalah and asked, "What made you, O Jabalah, hit your brother and break his nose?" The king listened with surprise; for he thought he had shown great restraint and mercy. He replied that, had the event taken place outside the sacred area of the Ka‘bah, he would have taken off the poor man's head. ‘Umar said, "You have confessed. Now, either satisfy the man with something or I shall have the man avenge himself on your person." Bewildered, Jabalah said, "You let a plebeian avenge himself on me, the king?" ‘Umar answered, "Islām has made you and him equals." The king said, "I had thought I would be in Islām yet more respected than before." ‘Umar's only reply was, "That's it!" Jabalah then said, "Well, I shall go back to my Christianity." ‘Umar answered, "You will then make yourself guilty of apostasy." At this the king's tribesmen and those of Fazārah came almost to blows, but the king was given twenty-four hours in which to satisfy the bedouin. Such was the justice ‘Umar rendered against a king whose entry into Islām was a big concern of the state. Neither the nonentity of the plaintiff and the greatness of the king nor the momentousness of his conversion to Islām prevented the justice of Islām from taking its course.

In another case, a serviceman of the lowest rank complained that his general, Abū Mūsā al Ash‘arī, had not given him the full share to which he was entitled. When he insisted, his commanding general beat him and shaved off his hair. The serviceman took his case to ‘Umar and the latter wrote to the general, "If you have done it in public, you are commanded to sit in public while the serviceman avenges himself on you in the same manner. If you have done it in private, then let it be done unto you in private." When the plaintiff returned to the field with ‘Umar's letter in his pocket, his companions naturally tried to dissuade him from his course. The man, however, was adamant, and Abū Mūsā had no alternative but to sit motionless in front of him to receive his punishment. The spectacle of the great and mighty brought low by justice overwhelmed the man. He lifted his arms to heaven and cried, "O God! I have forgiven him!"

A third case involved the conqueror of Egypt and its first Muslim governor 'Amr ibn al 'Āṣ. Competing in a horse racing tournament, 'Amr's son was annoyed by an Egyptian commoner in the race and struck him saying, "Don't you know I am the son of the great man?" Moreover, the father imprisoned the Egyptian youth for a time, fearing that he might appeal to the caliph. When the youth was released, he went all the way to Madīnah and complained to 'Umar. The caliph recalled both the governor and his son, both of whom confessed and sat down awaiting their punishment. 'Umar ordered the Egyptian to beat both father and son, arguing that the son would not have dared to do what he did had the father not been governor. Turning to the governor, 'Umar made his great cry which history can never afford to, nor ever will forget, "By what right do you tyrannize over men? Have they not emerged from their mothers' wombs as free citizens?" Many tried to intercede, but the caliph would not change his mind. 'Amr was saved, but only when the Egyptian said, after beating the governor's son, "I struck him who struck me. I want no more than this." These and many such anecdotes of social justice seem nothing short of fantastic when compared with the tyrannies and social iniquities which ruled then and still rule over the world. Indeed, they are even more fantastic than dreams; more striking in their reality than the ideals themselves which they embody.

Here, one can feign hear the small, Philistine, indolent soul objecting, "These are but rare, isolated cases!" . . .

Before such justice as 'Umar's could become possible many presuppositions must have been fulfilled. Men must have known that complaining against injustice avails. They must have been certain that the undoing of a real injustice was a real possibility, no matter how great the perpetrator, how humble the victim. Men must have had a perfect trust in the administrators of justice. They must have felt absolutely secure that their seeking justice would bring to them no hidden retaliation, even though it might fail.

Before we say, "These are but rare, isolated cases!", we should ask how all these men, from Ḥijāz to Egypt and from Egypt to Irāq, the Muslims among them as well as the non-Muslims, the noblemen as well as the commoners, came to realize that justice was real and that the road leading to it was open and secure? How did they all come to feel that justice was easier in their own individual cases than patience and bearing? Had 'Umar's regime not been preceded by a period in which a radical transformation of men's faith in justice on earth took place, men would not have gone to the length they did in seeking it. They would not have exerted themselves in its pursuit across the wide deserts.

True, it is "rare" (indeed unheard of in our times as in any other time!) that the conqueror and governor of a country be ordered back to his capital across hundreds of miles because his son had raised his whip on the race course against a youth from among the vanquished people. It is equally "rare" that any plaintiff would cross these long hardshipladen miles in the certainty that justice would be rendered; that whatever the result, his own security was equally certain. And it is indeed "rare" that kings are made the equals of plebeians because of a blow struck in rage; that a serviceman be made the equal of his own commanding general, and enabled to mete blow for blow and humiliation for humiliation in front of the whole army.

All that is indeed rare and surprising. But far rarer and more surprising still should be men's trust and faith in justice, their refusal to bear injustice, whatever the cost. That is a trust, a faith, a conviction, of each and every good in the life of man.

Whence did this trust come?
From God indeed!
Didn't it? (*Ibid.*, pp. 138–44)

Bibliography

WORKS CITED

PART ONE: RELIGIONS OF INDIA

Abhidhānarājendra (Great king of names). Ratlam: Sri Jaina Prabhakara Printing Press, 1934.

Āchārya, Narayan Ram, ed., *see under Manusmṛti.*

Ādi Granth (Original book), tr. by Ernest Trumpp, *The Holy Scripture of the Sikhs.* London: Wm. H. Allen, 1877.

Apte, V. G., ed., *see under* Pātañjali.

Sri Aurobindo, (1872–1950), *The Divine Life.* New York: Sri Aurobindo Library, 1949.

Avalon, Arthur, tr., *see under Ṣāṭcakranirūpaṇa.*

Ayyangar, K. V. Srinivasa, ed., *see under Tyāgarāja hṛdayamu.*

Bādarāyaṇa (c. 4th century B.C.), *Brahma sūtras* (Aphorisms on the Brahman).

Bhagavadgītā (The Lord's song).

Bhāradwāja, tr., *see under* Sarasvati.

Bhāskaranandi (13th or 14th century), *Bhāskaranandi-bhāṣya* (Commentary by Bhāskaranandi), ed. by A. Shantiraja Sastri. Mysore: Government Branch Press, 1944.

Conze, Edward, *Buddhist Texts Through the Ages.* New York: Philosophical Library, 1954.

Frankfort, H. *et al., Before Philosophy.* Baltimore: Penguin Books, 1964.

Jain, Uggar, tr., *see under* Kunda Kunda Āchārya.

Kingsbury, F. and G. E. Phillip, tr., *Hymns of the Tamil Śaivaite Saints.* New York: Associated Press, 1921.

Krishnamurti, J., *Education and the Significance of Life.* New York: Harper, 1953.

Kunda Kunda Āchārya (1st century B.C.?), *Niyamasāra* (Essence of regulations), ed. and tr. by Uggar Jain. Lucknow: Central Jaina Publishing House, 1931.

Madhva (13th century A.D.), *Aṇubhāṣya* (Atomic commentary), ed. by Ananta Vasudeva Vidyabhushana. Dacca: Manamohan Press, n.d.

———, *Pūrnaprajña-darśana* (Philosophy of Madhva), tr. by S. Subbarao, *The Vedānta-sūtras with the Commentary of Śrī Madhvāchārya.* Madras: Thompson, 1904.

Mahābhārata (Great Bhārata people).

Mahāvagga (Great classification).

Manu dharma śāstra (Manu's ethical code).

Manusmṛti (Manu's ethical code), ed. by Narayan Ram Āchārya. Bombay: Nirnaya Sagar Press, 1946.

Nārada bhakti sūtras (Nārada's aphorisms on devotion) tr. by Swami Tyāgīsananda. Mylapore: Sri Ramakrishna Math, 1955.

Nikhilananda, Swami, *Ramakrishna: Prophet of New India.* New York: Harper, 1948.

Patañjali (4th century B.C.?), *Patañjalā-yoga sūtras* (Aphorisms of Patañjali's yoga), ed. by V. G. Apte. Poona: Anandarsrma Press, 1932.

Prajñākaramati (date unknown), *Bodhicaryāvatārapañjikā* (Exposition of the conduct of the awakened), ed. by Louis de la Vallée Poussin. Calcutta: Bibliothetica Indica, 1894.

Pūrnaprajña-darśana, see under Madhva.

Radhakrishnan, S., *An Idealist View of Life.* London: Allen and Unwin, 1932.

——— and J. H. Muirhead, ed., *Contemporary Indian Philosophy.* London: Allen and Unwin, 2nd ed., 1952.

Raju, P. T., *Idealistic Thought of India.* London: Allen and Unwin, 1953.

Rāmānuja (11th century), *Śri bhāṣya* (Rāmānuja's commentary).

Ramachandran, K., ed., *see under Tyāgarāja-kīrtana-hāramu.*

Ratnagotravibhāga (Division of the language of gems).

Rhys Davids, Mrs., *Kindred Sayings*, New York: Oxford University Press, vol. 2, 1920.

Saṁyutta-nikāya (Combined collection).

Śaṅkara (8th century), *Brahma sūtra Saṅkarabhāṣyam* (Śaṅkara's commentary on the *Brahma Scripture*).

Śaṅkara, attributed, *Saundaryalaharī* (Wave of beauty).

Sarasvati, Dayānanda (1824–83), *Satyārthaprakāśa, Light of Truth*, tr. by Chīrañjīva Bhāradwāja. Madras: The Ārya Samāj, 1932.

Sastri, A. Shantiraja, ed., *see under* Bhāskaranandi.

Śatapada Brāhmana (Ritual text of hundred feet).

Ṣāṭcakrānirūpaṇa, tr. by Arthur Avalon, *The Serpent Power*. Madras: Ganesh, 1924.

Subbarao, S., tr., *see under* Madhva.

Tagore, Devendranāth (1817–1905), *Autobiography*. Calcutta: S. K. Lahiri, 1909.

Tagore, Rabindranath (1857–1930), *The Religion of Man*. London: Allen and Unwin, 1953.

Trumpp, Ernest, tr., *see under Ādi Granth.*

Tyāgarāja (1767–1847), *Tyāgarāja hṛdayamu* (Heart of Tyāgarāja), ed. by K. V. Srinivasa Ayyangar. Madras: A. Adi, 1922.

———, *Tyāgarāja-kīrtana-hāramu* (Garland of Tyāgarāja's songs), ed. by K. Ramachandran. Madras: V. S. Sastrulu, 1956.

Tyāgīsananda, Swami, tr., *see under Nārada bhakti sūtras.*

Umāsvāmi (3rd century A.D.), *Tattvātha sūtra* (Aphorisms on the meaning of truth).

Vallée Poussin, Louis de la, ed., *see under* Prajnākaramati.

Venkataramanayya, *Rudra-Śiva* (On the gods Rudra and Śiva).

Vidyabhushaṇa, Ananta Vasudeva, ed., *see under* Madhva.

Viṣṇu purāṇa (Epic of Viṣṇu), tr. by H. H. Wilson, *The Viṣṇu Purāṇa*. Calcutta: Punthi Pustak, 1961.

Wilson, H. H., tr. *see under Viṣṇu purāṇa.*

PART TWO: RELIGIONS OF CHINA

Amitābha Scripture (Buddha of Immeasurable Light scripture), *see under Fo-shuo a-mi-t'o ching.*

Amitāyur-Dhyāna-sūtra, see under Kuan wu-liang-shou ching.

Analects, see under Confucius.

Avataṁsaka sūtra (Flowery splendor scripture).

Balázs, Stefan, "Der Philosoph Fan Tschan und sein Tratat gegen den Buddhismus," *Sinica*, 7 (1932), 220–34.

Bhadrā-kalpika sūtra, see under Hsien-chieh ching.

Book of Changes, see under I ching.

Book of History, see under Shu ching.

Book of Odes, see under Shih ching.

Book of Rites, see under Li chi.

Brahmajāla sūtra (Brahma-net scripture).

Bruce, J. Percy, tr., *see under* Chu Hsi.

Buddhabhasita Amitayuḥ sūtra, see under Fo shuo a-mi-t'o ching.

Chan, Wing-tsit, *Religious Trends in Modern China*. New York: Columbia University Press, 1953.

———, *A Source Book in Chinese Philosophy*. Princeton, N.J.,: Princeton University Press, 1963.

———, tr., *see under* Chu Hsi; Hui-neng; Lao Tzu; Wang Yang-ming.

Chang Tsai (1020–77), *Cheng-meng* (Correcting youthful ignorance), in the *Chang Tzu ch'üan-shu* (Complete works of Master Chang).

———, *Hsi-ming* (Western inscription), *ibid.*

Ch'en Ching-yüan (1025–94), *Tao-te ching chu* (Commentary on the *Classic of the Way and Its Virtue*).

Ch'en Kuo-fu, tr., *see under* Ko Hung.

Cheng Hsüan (127–200), *Chung-yung chu* (Commentary on the *Doctrine of the Mean*).

Ch'eng I (1033–1107), *Ching shuo* (Explanations of the Classics), in Ch'eng I and Ch'eng Hao, *Erh-Ch'eng ch'üan-shu.*

———, *I chuan* (Commentary on the *Book of Changes*), *ibid.*

———, and Ch'eng Hao (1032–85), *Erh-Ch'eng ch'üan-shu* (Complete works of the two Ch'engs), *Ssu-pu pei-yao* (Essentials of the four libraries) edition.

———, *I-shu* (Surviving works), *ibid.*

———, *Ts'ui-yen* (Pure words), *ibid.*

Ch'ien-Han shu (History of the Former Han dynasty, 206 B.C.–A.D. 8), by Pan Ku (39–92), *Po-na pen* (Choice works edition).

Chin-kang ching (Diamond cutter scripture).

Chou Tun-i (1017–73), *T'ai-chi-t'u shuo* (Explanation of the diagram of the Great Ultimate), in the *Chou Tzu ch'üan-shu* (Complete works of Master Chou), ch. 1.

Chu Ch'an, *see under Ssu-shih-erh-chang ching.*

Chu Hsi (1130-1200), *Chu Tzu wen-chi* (Collection of literary works by Master Chu), comp. by Chu Tsai (b. 1169) and Yü Shih-lu (fl. 1265), *et al.*, *Ssu-pu pei-yao* ed., entitled *Chu Tzu ta-ch'üan* (Complete literary works of Master Chu).
———, *Chu Tzu yü-lei* (Classified conversations of Master Chu), comp. by Li Ching-te (fl. 1263), 1880 ed.
———, *Chung-yung chang-chü* (Commentary on the *Doctrine of the Mean*).
———, *Djin sï lu* (*Dschu Hsi*), *die sungkonfuzianische Summa mit dem Kommentar des Yä Tsai*, tr. by Olaf Graf, O.S.B., 3 vols. Tokyo: Sophia University, 1953.
———, *The Philosophy of Human Nature, by Chu Hsi*, tr. by J. Percy Bruce. London: Probsthain, 1922.
———, and Lü Tsu-ch'ien (1137–81), *Reflections on Things at Hand, The Neo-Confucian Anthology*, tr. by Wing-tsit Chan. New York: Columbia University Press, 1967.
Chuang Chou (b. 369 B.C.?), *Chuang Tzu*, *Ssu-pu ts'ung k'an* (The four libraries series) ed., entitled *Nan-hua chen-ching* (True classic of Nan-hua).
———, *The Complete Works of Chuang Tzu*, tr. by Burton Watson. New York: Columbia University Press, 1968.
Chuang Tzu, *see under* Chuang Chou.
Chung-yung (*Doctrine of the Mean*), ascribed to Tzu-ssu (492–431 B.C.).
Classic of Filial Piety, see under Hsiao ching.
Confucius (551–479 B.C.), *The Analects of Confucius*, tr. by Arthur Waley. London: Allen and Unwin, 1938.
———, *Confucian Analects*, tr. by James Legge. *The Chinese Classics*, vol 1. Oxford: Clarendon Press, 1893.
Conze, Edward, *Buddhist Wisdom Books*. London: Allen and Unwin, 1958.
Davis, Tenney L., tr., *see under* Ko Hung.
de Bary, Wm. Theodore, ed., *Approaches to Oriental Classics*. New York: Columbia University Press, 1959.
Diamond Scripture, see under Chin-kang ching.
Doctrine of the Mean, see under Chung-yung.
Dubs., H. H., tr., *see under* Hsün Tzu.
Dumoulin, H., S.J., tr., *see under* Tsung-mi.
Fa-tsang (643–712), *Treatise on the Golden Lion*, tr. by Wing-tsit Chan, in his *A Source Book on Chinese Philosophy*, ch. 25.
Fan Chen (fl. 502), *Shen-mieh lun* (Treatise on the destructibility of the soul), *see under* Stefan Balázs.
Fan-wang ching (Brahma-net scripture).
Fan Yeh, *see under Hou-Han shu.*
Feifel, Eugene, tr., *see under* Ko Hung.
Fo-shuo a-mi-t'o ching (Amitābha scripture spoken by the Buddha) *Buddha-bhāsita Amitayūh sūtra*).
Forty-Two Chapters Scripture, see under Ssu-shih-erh-chang ching.
Graf, Olaf, O.S.B., tr., *see under* Chu Hsi.
Great Learning, see under Ta-hsüeh.
Han Fei (d. 233 B.C.), *Han Fei Tzu*, (Works of Master Han Fei).
Han Yü (768–824), *Han Ch'ang-li ch'üan-chi* (Collected works of Han Yü).
History of the Sui Dynasty, see under Sui shu.
History of the Sung Dynasty, see under Sung shih.
Ho-shang Kung (fl. 179–159 B.C.), *Lao Tzu chang-chü* (Commentary on the *Lao Tzu*).
Hou-Han shu (History of the Later Han dynasty, 25–220), by Fan Yeh (398–448).
Hsiao ching, ascribed to Tseng Ts'an (505–c. 436 B.C.), *The Hsiao Ching*, tr. by Mary Leslia Marka. New York: St. John's University Press, 1961.
Hsieh Liang-tso (1050–1103), *Shang-ts'ai yü-lu* (Recorded conversations of Hsieh Liang-tso), *Cheng-i-t'ang ch'üan-shu* (Complete library of the Hall of Rectifying the Way) edition.
Hsien-chieh ching (Scripture of the worthy aeons).
Hsün Tzu (Works of Master Hsün K'uang) by *Hsün K'uang* (313–238 B.C.?), *Ssu-pu ts'ung-k'an* edition.
———, *Hsün Tzu: Basic Writings*, tr. by Burton Watson. New York: Columbia University Press, 1963.
———, *The Works of Hsüntse*, tr. by H. H. Dubs. London: Probsthain, 1928.
Hu Hung (1105–55), *Huang-wang ta-chi* (Great records of emperors and kings).
Hua-yen ching (Flowery splendor scripture).
Huang-t'ing ching (Internal and external scripture).
Hui-neng (638–713), *The Platform Scripture, the Basic Classic of Zen Buddhism*, tr. by Wing-tsit Chan. New York: St. John's University Press, 1963.
Hung-ming chi (Essays spreading and elucidating the doctrine), comp. by Seng-yu (445–518), *Ssu-pu pei-yao* edition.

I ching. The I Ching or Book of Changes, tr. by Cary F. Baynes from the German version of Richard Wilhelm, 2 vols. New York: Pantheon Books, 1953.

Kern, H., tr., *see under Saddharma-puṇḍarīka sūtra.*

Ko Hung (284–363), *Alchemy, Medicine, and Religion in the China of* A.D. 320: *The Nei P'ien of Ku Hung* (*Pao P'u tzu*), tr. by James R. Ware. Cambridge, Mass.: The M. I. T. Press, 1966.

———, "The Inner Chapters of *Pao-p'u-tzu*," tr. by Tenney L. Davis and Ch'en Kuo-fu, *Proceedings of the American Academy of Arts and Sciences*, 74 (1941), 297–325.

———, "Pao-p'u-tzu Nei-p'ien," tr. by Eugene Feifel, *Monumenta Serica*, 6 (1941), 113–213; 9 (1944), 1–33; and 11 (1946), 1–32.

Kuan wu-liang-shou ching (Meditation on the Buddha Amitayūs scripture), *The Amitāyur-Dhyāna-sūtra*, tr. by J. Takakusu, *Sacred Books of the East*, vol. 49, pp. 161–201.

Kuang hung-ming chi (Further essays spreading and elucidating the doctrine), comp. by Tao-hsüan (596–667), *Ssu-pu pei-yao* edition.

Kuo T'ing-tung, *et al.*, *I-kuan Tao i-wen chieh-ta* (Answers to questions on the Way of Pervading Unity).

Kuo-yü (Conversations of the states).

Lao Tzu, *The Way and Its Power*, tr. by Authur Waley. London: Allen and Unwin, 1934.

———, *The Way of Lao Tzu*, tr. by Wing-tsit Chan. Indianapolis: Bobbs-Merrill, 1963.

Lee, Shao Chang, *Popular Buddhism in China*. Shanghai: Commercial Press, 1939.

Legge, James, tr., *see under Mencius; Li chi.*

Li chi. The Li Ki, tr. by James Legge. 2 vols. Oxford: Clarendon Press, 1885.

Liang shu (History of the Liang dynasty, 502–57).

Lieh Tzu (Works of Master Lieh Yü-k'ou), *Ssu-pu ts'ung-k'an edition.*

Liu Hsü, *see under T'ang shu.*

Liu Tsung-yüan (773–819), *Liu Ho-tung ch'üan-chi* (Complete works of Liu Tsung-yüan), *Ssu-pu pei-yao* edition.

Liu Yü-hsi (772–842), *Liu Meng-te wen-chi* (Collection of literary works by Liu Yü-hsi), *Ssu-pu ts'ung-k'an* edition.

Lotus Scripture, see under Saddharma-puṇḍarīka sūtra.

Lun-yü (*Analects*), *see under* Confucius.

Lung-hu ching (Dragon and tiger scripture).

Marka, Mary Leslia, tr., *see under Hsiao ching.*

Mencius (372–289 B.C.?), *The Works of Mencius*, tr. by James Legge. *The Chinese Classics*, vol. 2. Oxford: Clarendon Press, 1895.

Miao-fa lien-hua ching (Wonderful Law lotus scripture), *see under Saddharma-puṇḍarīka sūtra.*

Mou Tzu (2nd century), *Li-huo lun* (Treatise to settle doubts), "Meou Tseou les Doutes Lévés," tr. by P. Pelliot, *T'oung Pao*, 19 (1920), 255–433.

Müller, Max, tr., *see under Wu-liang shou ching.*

Nan-Ch'i shu (History of the Southern Ch'i dynasty, 479–502).

Nan shih (History of the Southern Dynasties, 420–589).

P'an Ku (39–92), *Po Hu T'ung, the Comprehensive Discussions in the White Tiger Hall*, tr. by Tjan Tjoe Som. Leiden: R. J. Brill, 1949.

———, *see under Ch'ien-Han shu.*

Pao-chi scripture (Scripture of the collection of jewels).

Pelliot, P., tr., *see under* Mou Tzu.

Saddharma-puṇḍarīka sūtra. The Lotus of the Wonderful Law, or The Lotus Gospel, tr. by W. S. Soothill. Oxford: Clarendon Press, 1930.

———, *The Saddharma-puṇḍarīka or the Lotus of the True Law*. tr. by H. Kern, *Sacred Books of the East*, vol. 21, 1884.

Scripture in Forty-Two Chapters, see under Ssu-shih-erh-chang ching.

Seng-yu, *see under Hung-ming chi.*

Shao Yung (1011–77), *Huang-chi ching-shih* (Supreme principles governing the world).

Shih chi (Records of the historian), by Ssu-ma Ch'ien (145–86 B.C.), *Po-na pen* edition.

Shih ching, *The Book of Songs*, tr. by Arthur Waley. Boston: Houghton Mifflin, 1937.

Shu ching, *Shoo King*, tr. by James Legge. *The Chinese Classics*, vol. 3. Hong Kong: 1865.

Soothill, W. S., tr., *see under Saddharma-puṇḍarīka sūtra.*

Ssu-ma Ch'ien, *see under Shih chi.*

Ssu-shih-erh-chang ching. The Sutra of 42 Sections, tr. by Chu Ch'an. London: The Buddhist Society, 1947.

Sui shu (History of the Sui dynasty, 581–618).

Sukhāvatī-vyūha (Scripture on Amitayūs spoken by the Buddha). *The Larger Sukhāvatī-vyūha,*

tr. by Max Müller, *Sacred Books of the East*, vol. 49, pt. 2, 10–75.
Sung shih (History of the Sung dynasty 960–1279), by T'o[q]t'o (d. 1328), *Po-na-pen* edition.
Ta-ch'eng ch'i-hsin lun (Treatise on the awakening of faith in the Mahāyāna).
Ta-hsüeh (*Great Learning*), ascribed to Tseng Tzu (505–c. 436 B.C.).
Taishō daizōkyō (Taishō edition of the Buddhist Canon).
T'ai-shang kan-ying p'ien (Treatise of the Most Exalted One on influence and response).
Takakusu, J., tr., *see under Kuan wu-liang-shou ching.*
T'ang shu (History of the T'ang dynasty, 618–907), by Liu Hsü (887–947), *Po-na-pen* edition.
T'ang Yung-t'ung, *Han-Wei Liang-Chin Nan-Pei-ch'ao Fo-chiao shih* (History of Buddhism from 206 B.C. to A.D. 589). Shanghai: Commercial Press, 1938.
Tao-hsüan, *see under Kuang hung-ming chi.*
Tjan Tjoe Som, tr., *see under* Pan Ku.
T'o[q]t'o, *see under Sung shih.*
Ts'an-t'ung-chi (Three ways unified and harmonized), ascribed to Wei Po-yang (fl. 147–67).
Tso Ch'iu-ming, *see under Tso chuan.*
Tso chuan (Tso's commentary on the *Spring and Autumn Annals*), ascribed to Tso Ch'iu-ming (6th century B.C.).
Tsung-mi (780–841), "Tsung-mi's Trakat vom Ursprung des Menschen," tr. by H. Doumoulin, S. J., *Monumenta Nipponica*, 1 (1938), 178–221.
———, *Yüan-jen lun* (An inquiry on man).
Vajracchedikā sūtra, see under Chin-kang ching.
Vimalakīrti-nirdeśa sūtra (Scripture spoken by Vimalakīrti).
Waley, Arthur, tr., *see under* Confucius; Lao Tzu; *Shih ching.*
Wang Shou-jen, *see under* Wang Yang-ming.
Wang Yang-ming (1472–1529), *Instruction for Practical Living and Other Neo-Confucian Writings by Wang Yang-ming*, tr. by Wing-tsit Chan. New York: Columbia University Press, 1963.
Watson, Burton, tr., *see under* Chuang Tzu and Hsün Tzu.
Wei-mo-chieh [*so-shuo*] *ching* (Scripture [spoken by] Vimalakīrti).
Wei Po-yang, *see under Ts'an-t'ung-ch'i.*
Wu-liang-shou ching (Meditation on Amītayūs scripture). *The Larger Sukhāvati-vyūha*, tr. by Max Müller, *Sacred Books of the East*, vol. 49, pt. 2, 1–75.
Yin-chih wen (Silent way of recompense).
Yin-fu ching (Secret accord scripture).

PART THREE: RELIGIONS OF JAPAN

Anesaki, Masaharu, *History of Japanese Religion*. London: Kegan Paul, Trench, Trubner, 1930.
———, *Nichiren, the Buddhist Saint*, Cambridge, Mass.: Harvard University Press, 1916.
Araki, James T., tr., *see under* Muraoka.
Aston, W. G., tr., *Nihongi: Chronicles of Japan from the Earliest Times to A.D. 698* (*Transactions and Proceedings of Japan Society*, London, Supplement). 2 vols., London: 1896; 2 vols. in 1, London: 1956.
Bellah, Robert N., *Tokugawa Religion: The Values of Pre-Industrial Japan*. Glencoe, Ill.: Free Press, 1957.
Bodde, Derk, tr., *see under* Fung Yu-lan.
Brown, Delmer M., tr. *see under* Muraoka.
Chamberlain, Basil Hall, tr., "*Ko-ji-ki*" (*Records of Amcient Matters*), *Transactions of the Asiatic Society of Japan*, 10, (1882), Supplement.
Chan, Wing-tsit, "Chinese Terminology," in Vergilius Ferm, ed., *An Encyclopedia of Religion*, New York: Philosophical Library, 1945.
———, *A Source Book in Chinese Philosophy*. New York: Columbia University Press, 1963.
———, ed., *see under* Takakusu.
Ch'en, Kenneth, *Buddhism in China: A Historical Survey*. Princeton, N.J.: Princeton University Press, 1964.
Classic of Filial Piety, see Part Two.
Coates, Harper H. and Ishizuka Ryūgaku, *Hōnen, the Buddhist Saint*. Kyōto: Society for the Publication of Sacred Books of the World, 1925.
Dai hōshaku kyō (*Maharatnakūta sūtra*, Great scripture of the collection of jewels).
Dainichi kyō (*Mahāvairocana sūtra*, Great sun scripture).
Daishū kyō (Scripture of great assembly).
Dazai Yayemon (1680–1747), *Bendō sho* (Definition of the Way).

Diamond Head Scripture (*Vajrasekhara sūtra.*)
Dōgen (1200–53), *Shōbōgenzō zuimouki* (Eye and treasure of the True Law recorded by his pupils), in the *Nihon koten bungaku taikei* (Japanese classics series), Tokyo: Iwanami Shoten, 1965, vol. 81, pp. 315–438.
Doroumi koki (Ancient accounts of muddy ocean).
Dumoulin, Heinrich, *A History of Zen Buddhism*, tr. by Paul Peachey. New York: Pantheon Books, 1963.
Eliot, Charles, *Japanese Buddhism*. London: Edward Arnold & Co., 1935.
Engi shiki (Institutes of the Engi period), in the *Shintei zōho kokushi taikei* (Revised and supplemented great series of national history), ed. by Kuroita Katsumi. Tokyo: Yoshikawa Kōbunkan, vol. 26, 1937, pp. 9–320.
Florenz, Karl, "Ancient Japanese Rituals," *Transactions of the Asiatic Society of Japan*, 27, pt. 4 (1899), 1–122.
Fugen, Daien, tr., *The Shōshin Ge: The Gatha of True Faith in the Nembutsu*. Kyōto: Ryūkoku University Translation Center, 1961.
Fujiwara, Ryōsetsu, ed., *see under* Shinran.
Fung Yu-lan, *A History of Chinese Philosophy*, tr. by Derk Bodde, vol 2. Princeton, N.J.: Princeton University Press, 1953.
Genshin (942–1017), *Ōjā yōshū* (Essentials of salvation), annot. by Hanayama Shinshō. Tokyo: Koyama Shoten, 1937.
Hakeda, Y. S., "The Religious Novel of Kūkai," *Monumenta Nipponica*, 22, nos. 3–4 (1965), 283–97.
Hanawa Hokiichi, ed., *see under* Ichijō Kanera.
Hanayama Shinshō, annot., *see under* Genshin.
Hirata Atsutane (1776–1843), *Hirata Atsutane zenshū* (Complete works of Hirata Atsutane), ed. by Muromatsu Iwao. Tokyo: Itchi-dō, vol. 1, 1911.
Hitachi-no-kuni fudoki, (Records of customs and land of Hitachi Province), in the *Nihon koten zensho* (A collection of Japanese classics). Tokyo: Asahi Shinbunsha, vol. 1, 1960.
Hokke Scripture (Scripture of the lotus of Law), *see under Saddharma-puṇḍarīka*, Part Two.
Hōnen (1133–1212), *Tozan jō* (Exhortation about mountain climbing), in the *Hōnen-shōnin zenshū* (Complete works of Priest Hōnen), ed. by Ishii Kyōdō. Tokyo: Hōnen-shōnin 750-nen Onki Junbikyoku, 1955.
Hōshaku kyō, see under Dai hōshaku kyō.
Howes, John F., tr., *see under* Kishimoto.
Ichijo Kanera (1402–81), *Bunmei ittōki* (Unification of the nation during the Bunmei period, 1467–89).
———, *Shōdan jiyō* (Principle of good rule) in the *Shinkō gunsho ruijū* (Classified collection of Japanese classics, newly edited edition), ed. by Hanawa Hokiichi. Tokyo: Naigai Shoseki Kabushiki Kaisha, 1930.
Imbe no Hironari (fl. 807), *Kogo shūi* (Gleanings from ancient sources), in Mozume Takami, ed., *Shinshū kōgaku sōsho* (Newly annotated series of works on the imperial tradition). Tokyo: Kobunko Kankōkai, vol. 1, 1927.
Ishii Kyōdō, ed., *see under* Hōnen.
Iwanami Shoten, ed., *The Manyōshū: One Thousand Poems*. Tokyo: Iwanami Shoten, 1940.
Jien (1155–1225), ed., *Gukanshō* (Miscellany of a personal view of an ignorant fool).
Jingi ryō (Law concerning Shintō affairs).
Katō, Genchi and H. Hoshino, tr. & annot., *The Kogoshūi: Gleanings from Ancient Stories*. Tokyo: Meiji Japan Society, 1925.
Kishimoto, Hideo, *Japanese Religion in the Meiji Era*, tr. & adapted by John F. Howes. Tokyo: Ōbun-sha, 1956.
Kitabatake Chikafusa (1293–1354), *Jinnō shōtōki* (Record of the valid succession of divine sovereigns).
Kitagawa, Joseph M., "Japan: Religion," *Encyclopaedia Britannica*, 1967 ed., vol. 12, pp. 882–86.
———, "Master and Saviour," *Studies of Esoteric Buddhism and Tantrism*. Kōyasan, Japan, 1965, pp. 1–26.
———, *Religion in Japanese History*. New York: Columbia University Press, 1966.
———, "Shintō", *Encyclopaedia Britannica*, 1967 ed., vol. 20, pp. 390–93.
Kiyota, Minoru, *The Treasure Key to the Esoteric Store* (unpublished Ph. D. thesis). Tokyo: Tokyo University, 1962.
Kodō taii (Summary of the ancient way).
Kogo shūi, see under Imbe no Hironari.
Kojiki, (Records of ancient matters), in the *Shinshū kōgaku sōsho*, ed. by Mozume Takami, vol. 1, 1927, pp. 1–90.
Kokuzōgunmonji-hō (Rules for seeking to hear [and keep the Law] by means of which the

bodhisattva Ākāśagarbha is able to fulfill all wishes).

Kon kōmyō kyō (*Swarṇa-prabhāsa sūtra*, Scripture of the golden light).

Konjaku monogatari, (Tales of long ago), in the *Nihon koten zensho*, vols. 57–62, 1954–63.

Kōno Shōzō, "The Hitachi-Fudoki or Records of Customs and Lands of Hitachi," tr. by Sakai Atsuharu, *Cultural Nippon*, 8, no. 2 (1940), 154–81.

Kūkai (774–835), *Hizō hōyaku* (Precious key to the esoteric store), in the *Shingon-shū zensho* (Complete works of the Shingon school). Kōyasan: Shingon-shū Zensho Kankōkai, vol. 31, 1936.

———, *Sango shiki* (Arriving at the fundamentals of the Three Teachings) and *Seireishū* (Collection of spiritual stories), in the *Nihon koten bungaku taikei*, vol. 71, 1965.

Kumazawa Banzan (1619–91), *Banzan zenshū* (Collected works of Kumazawa Banzan), ed. by Masamune Atsuo. Tokyo: Banzan Zenshū Kankōkai, vols. 1–2, 1941.

———, *Shūgi gaisho* (Collected essays on public matters).

———, *Shūgi washo* (Collected essays on private matters).

Kuroita Katsumi, ed., *see under Engi shiki, Nihonshoki, Ryō no shūge*, and *Shoku Nihongi.*

Lloyd, Arthur, *The Creed of Half Japan*, London: Smith, Elder & Co., 1911.

———, *Shinran and His Work*. Tokyo: Kyōbunkwan, 1910.

Lotus Scripture, see under Hokke Scripture.

Manyōshū (Collection of a myriad leaves), in the *Nihon koten bungaku taikei*, vol. 1–4, 1957–62.

Masamune Atsuo, ed., *see under* Kumazawa.

Miyagi Eishō, *Engi shiki no kenkyū* (Study of the *Institutes of the Engi period*), 2 vols. Tokyo, 1955 and 1957.

Moore, Charles A., ed., *see under* Takakusu.

Motoori Norinaga (1730–1801), *Kojiki den* (Commentary of the *Kojiki*).

———, *Motoori Norinaga zenshū* (Complete works of Motoori Norinaga). Tokyo: Yoshikawa Hanshichi, vol. 6, 1902.

Mozume Takami, ed., *see under* Imbe no Hironari and Kojiki.

Muraoka, Tsunetsugu, *Studies in Shintō Thought*, tr. by Delmer M. Brown and James T. Araki. Tokyo: Japanese National Commission for UNESCO, Ministry of Education, 1964.

Muromatsu Iwao, ed., *see under* Hirata.

Nakai, Gendō, *Shinran and His Religion of Pure Faith*. Kyōto: Kanao Bunendō, 1946.

Nichiren (1222–82), *Risshō ankoku ron* (The establishment of righteousness and the security of the nation), in the *Nihon Bukkyō shisō shiryōshū* (Collection of source materials on the history of Japanese Buddhist thought). Tokyo: Kokumin Seishinbunka Kenkyūsho, 1941.

Nihon Bukkyō shisō shriyōshū, see under Nichiren and Saicho.

Nihon koten bungaku taikei, see under Dōgen.

Nihon koten zensho, see under Hitachi-no-kuni-fudoki and *Konjaku monogatari.*

Nihongi, see under Nihonshoki.

Nihonshoki (Chronicles of Japan), in Kuroita Katsumi, ed., *Shintei zōho kokushi taikei*, vol. 1, 1952 and 1955.

Ninnō Scripture (Scripture of the benevolent king).

Nirvāṇa Scripture (Scripture on Nirvāṇa).

Peachey, Paul, tr., *see under* Dumoulin.

Philippi, Donald, L., tr., *Kojiki* (unpublished).

———, tr., *Norito* (Ritual prayers). Tokyo: Institute for the Study of Japanese Culture and Classics, 1959.

Rahder, J., tr., "Gukanshō (Miscellany of a personal view of an ignorant fool)," *Acta Orientalia*, 15 (1936), 173–230.

Reischauer, A. K., tr., "Ōjō-yōshū (Collected Essays on Birth into Paradise)," *Transactions of the Asiatic Society of Japan*, 7, 2nd ser., 1930, 16–97.

Ryō no shūge, (Collection of laws), in Kuroita Katsumi, ed., *Shintei zōho kokushi taitei* vol. 23, 1943.

Saicho (767–822), "Ganbun", (Vows) in the *Nihon Bukkyō shisō shiryōshū*. Tokyo: Kokumin Seishinbunka Kenkyūsho, 1941.

Sakai Atsuharu, tr., *see under* Kōno Shōzō.

Sansom, George B., "Early Japanese Law and Administration, pt. 2," *Transactions of the Asiatic Society of Japan*, 11, 2nd ser., 1934, 122–27.

———, *Japan: A Short Cultural History*, rev. ed. New York: Appleton-Century-Crofts, 1962.

Sasaki, Gesshō, *A Study of Shin Buddhism*. Kyōto: Eastern Buddhist Society, 1925.

Satow, Ernest, "Ancient Japanese Rituals, I

Transactions of the Asiatic Society of Japan, 7, pt. 2 (1879), 97–113.

Scripture of Kanzeon (Scripture of Kannon).

Scripture of the Most Excellent King (*Swarṇa-prabhāsottama-raja sūtra*, *Kon kōmyō saishōō kyō*).

Shinran (1173–1262), *The Tanni shō: Notes Lamenting Differences*, tr. and annot. by Ryōsetsu Fujiwara. Kyoto: Ryūkoku University Translation Center, 1962.

Shintō gobusho (Shintō Pentateuch).

Shōbōnen kyō (*Saddharma smrityupasthana sūtra*, Scripture for invoking the aid of the Law).

Shoku Nihongi, (Chronicles of Japan, continued), in Kuroita Katsumi, ed., *Shintei zōho kokushi taikei*, vol. 2, 1935.

Shōman Scripture (*Shrimātādevi-simhanāda sūtra*, Scripture of Lady Malyaśrū spoken by Princess Śrimatā).

Snellen, J. B., tr., "*Shoku Nihongi*," *Transactions of the Asiatic Society of Japan*, 2nd ser., 11 (1934), 15–239; 14 (1937), 209–79.

Sōni-ryō (Law governing monks and nuns), *see under Ryō no shūge*.

Spae, Joseph J., *Itō Jinsai*. Peiping: Catholic University of Peking, 1948.

Straelen, H. van, *The Religion of Divine Wisdom*. Kyōto: Veritas Shoin, 1957.

Sukhavāti-vyūha (Scripture on Amitayūs spoken by the Buddha).

Suzuki, D. T., *A Miscellany of the Shin Teaching of Buddhism*. Kyōto: Shinshū Ōtani-ha Shūmusho, 1946.

Takahashi, Takeichi and Izumida Junjō, *Shinranism in Mahāyāna Buddhism and the Modern World*. Los Angeles: Higashi Honganji, 1932.

Takakusu, Junjirō, *The Essentials of Buddhist Philosophy*, ed. by Wing-tsit Chan and Charles A. Moore. Honolulu: University of Hawaii, 1947.

Takami Mozume, ed. *see under* Imbe no Hironari and *Kojiki*.

Tama katsuma (Jeweled bamboo basket).

Tao-seng ko (Law governing Taoist and Buddhist priests).

Tenri-kyō kyōkai-honbu, ed., *The Doctrine of Tenrikyō* (2nd ed.), Tambaichi, Nara-ken: Tenri-kyō Headquarters, 1958.

———, *Tenri-kyō kyōten* (Doctrinal manual of Tenri-kyō). Tambaichi, Nara-ken: Tenri-kyō Dōyū-sha, 1949.

Tips of the Writing Brush (*Ofudesaki*).

Tsunoda, Ryūsaku *et al.*, comp., *Sources of Japanese Tradition*, New York: Columbia University Press, 1958.

Uraban Scripture (Scripture on offerings to save hungry ghosts).

Vajrasekhara sūtra (Diamond head scripture).

Visser, M. W. de, *Ancient Buddhism in Japan*, vol. 1. Paris: Librairie Orientaliste Paul Geuthner, 1928.

———, *The Bodhisattva Ākāsagarbha* (*Kokuzō*) *in China and Japan*. Amsterdam: Uitgave van de Koninklijke Akademie van Wetenschappen te Amsterdam, 1931.

Vijñapti-mātratā-siddhi (Completion of mere ideation).

Yakushi kyō (Scripture of the divine healer).

Yamamoto, Kōshō, *The Private Letters of Shinran Shōnin*. Tokyo: Okazakiya Shoten, 1956.

———, tr. and annot., *The Kyōgyōshinshō or The "Teaching, Practice, Faith, and Attainment*." Tokyo: Karinbunko, 1958.

Yōrō sōni ryō (Law governing monks and nuns issued during the Yōrō era, 717–24).

Zoku-Shinto taii (Summary of pseudo-Shintō).

PART FOUR: ISLĀM

(The connective *Al* is not alphabetized in Arabic.)

'Abd al Ḥamīd, M. M-d., ed., *see under* Ibn Hishām, and Ibn al Qayyim.

'Abd al Salām Hārūn, *see under* Al Ghazzālī.

'Abduh, Muḥammad (1204–1324 A.H.; 1849–1905), *Risālat al Tawḥīd* (Epistle on the unity of God), 14th ed. Cairo: Al Mu'tamar al Islāmī, 1956.

Abū Ḥanīfah, al Nu'mān ibn Thābit al Kūfī (d. 149 A.H.; 767), *Al Fiqh al Akbar* (Great Islāmic knowledge), in Abū al Muntahā Aḥmad ibn Muḥammad al Maghnisāwī, ed., *Sharḥ al Fiqh al Akbar* (Elaboration of the great Islāmic knowledge). Hyderabad: Dā'irat al Ma'ārif al Niẓāmiyyah 1902.

Abū Yūsuf Ya'qūb ibn Ibrahīm al Kūfī (d. 181 A.H.; 798), *Kitāb al Kharāj* (Book of revenue), 2nd ed. Cairo: Al Maṭba'ah al Salafiyyah, 1932.

Aḥmad 'Ubayd, ed., *see under* Ibn al Qayyim.

Al 'Aqqād, 'Abbās Maḥmūd (d. 1838 A.H.; 1963), *Al Dimuqraṭiyyah fī al Islām* (Democracy in Islām). Cairo: Dar al Ma'ārif, 1952.

———, *Al Falsafah al Qur'āniyyah* (Qur'ānic philosophy). Cairo: Dār al Hilāl, n.d.

Al Ash'arī, Abū al Ḥasan 'Alī ibn Isma'īl (d. 330 A.H.; 942), *Kitāb al Luma' fī al Radd 'Alā Ahl al Zaygh wa al Bida'* (Book of insights in answer to sectarians, deviators, and innovators), ed. by R. J. McCarthy. Beirut: Catholic Press, 1959.

———, *Risālat Istiḥsān al Khawḍ fī 'Ilm al Kalām* (Epistle on the advantages of indulging into theological science). Hyderabad: Dā'irat al Ma'ārif al Niẓāmiyyah, 1925.

Badrān, Muḥammad Fatḥallah, ed., *see under* Al Shahrastānī.

Cureton, William, ed., *see under* Al Nasafī.

Daniels, Norman, *Islam and the West: The Making of an Image*. Edinburgh: The University Press, 1962.

———, *Islam, Europe and Empire*. Edinburgh University Press, 1966.

Darwazah, Muḥammad 'Izzat, *Al Dustūr al Qur'ānī fī Shu'ūn al Ḥayāt* (The Qur'ānic constitution relative to the affairs of life). Cairo: 'Īsā al Bābī al Ḥalabī, 1956.

Dowson, John, ed., *see under* Al Kūfī.

Drāz, M. 'Abdullah, ed., *see under* Al Shāṭibī.

Elliott, A. M., tr., *see under* Al Kūfī.

Al Fārūqī, I. R., *Christian Ethics*. Amsterdam: Djambatan; and Montreal: McGill University Press, 1967.

———, "History of Religions: Its Nature and Significance for Christian Education and the Muslim-Christian Dialogue," *Numen*, 12, Fas. 1, 2 (1965), pp. 35–95.

———, *On Arabism*, vol. 1, *'Urūbah and Religion: A Study of the Fundamental Ideas of Arabism and of Islām as Its Highest Moment of Consciousness*. Amsterdam: Djambatan, 1962.

Frankfort, H., ed., *see under* Wilson.

Al Ghazzālī, Abū Ḥāmid (d. 505 A.H.; 1111), *Iḥyā' 'Ulūm al Dīn* (Vivification of the sciences of religion), selections by 'Abd al Salām Hārūn. Cairo: Dār Sa'd Miṣr, 1951.

———, *Al Munqidh Min al Ḍalāl* (Deliverer from Error), tr. by Montgomery Watt under the title, *The Faith and Practice of Al Ghazzālī*. London: Allen and Unwin, 1953.

Guillaume, A., ed., *see under* Al Shahrastānī.

Hārūn, 'Abd al Salām, ed., *see under* Al Ghazzālī.

Haykal, Muḥammad Ḥusayn, *Al Fārūq 'Umar* ('Umar, the "just separator of justice from injustice"). Cairo: Maṭba'at Miṣr, 1943.

———, *Ḥayāt Muḥammad* (Life of Muḥammad), 14th ed. Cairo: Maktabat al Nahḍah al Miṣriyyah, 1956.

Ibn Abū al Ḥadid, ed., *see under* Ibn Abū Ṭālib.

Ibn Abū Ṭālib, 'Alī (d. 40 A.H.; 661), *Nahj al Balāghah* (Path of eloquence), ed., by Ibn Abū al Ḥadīd and Muḥammad Abū al Faḍl Ibrahīm. Cairo: Dār Iḥyā' al Kutub al 'Arabiyyah, 1961, vol. 10.

Ibn Ḥazm, Abū Muḥammad 'Alī Aḥmad ibn Sa'īd (d. 456 A.H.; 1064), *Al Fiṣal fī al Milal wa al Ahwā' wa al Niḥal* (Book of the branches in sects, schisms, and religious factions), vols. 1–4, Cairo: Mu'assasat al Khānjī, 1898.

———, *Kitāb al Akhlāq wa al Siyar fī Mudāwāt al Nufūs* (Book of ethics and conduct for the curing of souls), ed. by Aḥmad 'Umar al Maḥmaṣānī. Cairo: Maṭba'at al Sa'ādah, n.d.

Ibn Hishām, Abū Muḥammad 'Abd al Malik (d. 218 A.H.; 828), *Sīrat al Nabiyy* (Life of the Prophet), ed. by M. D. 'Abd al Ḥamīd, 7 vols. Cairo: Al Maktabah al Tijāriyyah al Kubrā, 1937.

Ibn al Jawzī, Jamāl al Dīn (d. 597 A.H.; 1201), *Talbīs Iblīs aw Naqd al 'Ilm wa al 'Ulamā'* (Deceit of Satan and criticism of the knowledge of religion and its men). Cairo: Idārat al Ṭibā'ah al Munīriyyah, 1934.

Ibn al Qayyim al Jawziyyah, Shams al Dīn Abū 'Abdullah Muḥammad ibn Abū Bakr (690–750 A.H.; 1292–1350), *I'lām al Muwaqqi'īn 'an Rabb al 'Ālamīn* (Instruction of the convinced in the lessons of the Lord of the universe), ed. by Muḥammad Muḥyī al Dīn 'Abd al Ḥamīd, 2 vols. Cairo: Al Maktabah al Tijāriyyah al Kubrā, 1953.

———, *Rawḍat al Muḥibbīn wa Nuzhat al Mushtāqīn* (Garden of the loving and recreation of the longing), ed. by Aḥmad 'Ubayd. Cairo: Maṭba'at al Sa'ādah, 1956.

Ibn Qutaybah al Dīnawarī (d. 276 A.H.; 889), *Ta'wīl Mukhtalaf al Ḥadīth fī al Radd 'ala A'dā' Ahl al Ḥadīth* (Interpretation of the variants of traditions in answer to the enemies of traditionists), ed. by Isma'īl al Khaṭīb al Salafī al Is'irdī. Cairo: Maṭba'at Kurdistān al 'Ilmiyyah, n.d.

Ibrahīm, M. Abū al Faḍl, ed., *see under* Ibn Abū Ṭālib.

Ikhwān al Ṣafā wa Khillān al Wafā (The Brethren of Purity and Friends of Fidelity, anonymous encyclopaedists and philosophers, 11th and 12th centuries), *Rasā'il Ikhwān al Ṣafā* (Epistles of Ikhwān al Ṣafā), 16 vols. Beirut: Dār Ṣādir Dār Beirut, 1958.

Al Is'irdī, ed., *see under* Ibn Qutaybah.

Al Juwaynī, Abū al Ma'āli 'Abd al Malik ibn 'Abdullah ibn Yūsuf Imām al Ḥaramayn (d. 475 A.H.; 1083), *Al Irshād* (The guidance), ed. by J. D. Luciani. Paris: Librairie Ernest Leroux, 1938.

Al Kūfī, Muḥammad 'Alī bin Ḥāmid bin Abū Bakr (d. 263 A.H.; 878), *Shāh-Nāmah* or *Tārīkh-i-Hind wa Sind* (Book of kings or history of India and of Sind), tr. into English by A. M. Elliott and ed. by John Dowson, from the Persian translation of the Arabic original, in *The History of India as Told by Its Own Historians*. Allahabad: Kitab Mahal Private Ltd., n.d., vol. 1, pp. 184–87.

Luciani, J. D., ed., *see under* Al Juwaynī.

Al Maghnisāwī, Abū al Muntahā Aḥmad Ibn M., *see under* Abū Ḥanīfah.

Al Maḥmaṣānī, Aḥmad 'Umar, ed., *see under* Ibn Ḥazm.

Al Majlis, ed., *see under* Al Muntakhab.

Al Māwardī, Abū al Ḥasan 'Alī ibn Muḥammad (d. 450 A.H.; 1059), *Adab al Duniā wa al Dīn* (Refinement of the world and of religion), ed. by. Musṭafā al Saqqā. Cairo: Musṭafā al Bābī al Ḥalabī, 1955.

McCarthy, R. J., ed., *see under* Al Ash'arī.

Al Muntakhab min al Sunnah (Selections from the *Sunnah*), selected and ed. by Al Majlis al A'lā li al Shu'ūn al Islāmiyyah, 4 vols. so far. Cairo: Dār al Kitāb al 'Arabī, 1961.

Al Nasafī, Najm al Dīn Abū Ḥafṣ 'Umar (d. 709 A.H.; 1310), *'Umdat 'Aqīdat Ahl al Sunnah wa al Jamā'ah* (Basic conviction of the people of the *Sunnah* and the majority of the community), ed. by William Cureton. London: Society for the Publication of Oriental Texts, 1843.

Qur'ān, the Holy.

Riḍā, Muḥammad Rashīd (d. 1354 A.H.; 1935), *Tafsīr al Qur'ān al Karīm* (Exegesis of the Holy Qur'ān), 34 vols. Cairo: Maṭba'at al Manār, n.d.

Al Saqqā, Musṭafā, ed., *see under* Al Māwardi.

Al Shahrastānī, Muḥammad 'Abd al Karīm (d. 548 A.H.; 1153), *Al Milal wa al Niḥal* (Sects and religious factions), ed. by M. Fatḥallah Badrān. Cairo: Al Azhar Press, 1947.

———, *Nihāyat al Iqdām fī 'Ilm al Kalām* (The ultimate in the science of theology), ed. by A. Guillaume. Baghdād: Maktabat al Muthannā, 1951.

Al Shāṭibī, Abū Ishaq Ibrahīm ibn Mūsā al Lakhmī (d. 790 A.H.; 1389), *Al Muwāfaqāt fī Uṣūl al Sharī'ah* (Agreements on the first principles of Islamic law), ed. by Muḥammad 'Abdullah Drāz. 4 vols. Cairo: Al Maktabah al Tijāriyyah al Kubrā, 1939.

Watt, Montgomery, tr., *see under* Al Ghazzālī.

Wilson, John A. "Egypt", in H. Frankfort *et al.*, ed., *Before Philosophy: The Intellectual Adventure of Ancient Man*. Baltimore: Penguin Books, 1964.

———, *The Culture of Ancient Egypt*. Chicago: Chicago University Press, 1951.

Al Zarqānī, Muḥammad 'Abd al 'Aẓīm (d. 1123 A.H.; 1710), *Manāhil al 'Irfān fī 'Ulūm al Qur'ān* (Sources of knowledge in the sciences of the Qur'ān), 6 vols. Cairo: Dār Iḥyā' al Kutub al 'Arabiyyah, 1951.

A Selective Glossary

SANSKRIT, CHINESE, JAPANESE, ARABIC

SANSKRIT

advaita: nondual, nondualism, nonduality, one; monism.
advaitin: nondualist, monist.
advaya: nondual; one.
āgama: the coming down, that which has come down; tradition; name of any of the texts of sectarian religions and philosophies, particularly the Pāñcarātra, the Pāsupata, and the Śākta, also called Tantras; sometimes the Veda; any sacred text.
ahiṁsā: noninjury.
ālaya: "storehouse" from which all levels of consciousness evolve.
Amitābha: literally, "immeasurable light," meaning Infinite Light, the Buddha of Western Paradise. Chinese: A-mi-t'o-fo; Japanese: Amida
Amitāyus: literally, "immeasurable life," meaning Infinite Life. Another name for Amitābha.
ānanda: bliss, freedom.
araṇyaka: forest treatise.
arhat: the worthy or saint, one no longer bound in the chain of birth and rebirth, the ideal man in early Buddhism.
ārya: noble.
asura: demons.
ātman: spirit; self; soul; to be distinguished from *jīva* which strictly means the soul, the ethicospiritual individual. The word has to be interpreted according to context.
Avalokiteśvara: literally, "the Lord who sees," that is, the Lord who sees the sound of the world's suffering. Chinese: Kuan-yin; Japanese: Kannon. See ch. 17, n. 23.
avidyā: same as *ajñāna* (ignorance).
Avyakta: unmanifest, the Unmanifest; used as a synonym for Prakṛti and Māyā also.
bhakti: devotion; love.
bhakti-mārga: way of devotion.
bhāṣya: commentary.
bodhi: wisdom; enlightenment.
bodhisattva: an enlightened being who is about to become a Buddha but postpones his Buddahood and dedicates himself to seek salvation for others as well as for himself; the ideal being in Mahāyāna Buddhism.
Brahman: the ever-growing, the ever-expanding; the Absolute, the Supreme Spirit, God; *brahma* means one of the priests officiating at the sacrifice; *brahmā* generally means the creator god, one of the Hindu Trinity.
Brāhmaṇa: ritual texts.
Brahmin: priest; knower of the Brahman.
cit: knowledge, truth, intelligence.
citta: same as *buddhi.* See *vijñāna.*
dharma: that which supports; nature; the law of nature; virtue, ethical law; merit; the potency of ethical actions; the right action; the law or body of doctrines of any faith; religion; quality, characteristic; element, category; reality. As a technical Buddhist term, it means "that which is held to," connoting all things, with or without form, real or imaginary, the material or principle of an entity, something that holds on to its nature as a particular things.
dharmadhātu: the Realm of Dharma; the universal principle; source of all truth.
dharmakāya: the Law-body; spiritual body; the Buddha-body in its self-nature; the body of the Dharma or truth, the body of reality, the body of principle;

the "body" has no bodily existence; it is identical with truth. In various Buddhist schools, it is identical with *dharmadhātu.*

dhyāna: meditation; concentration of mind.

gītā: song.

guṇa: attribute.

guru: spiritual teacher.

harijan: man of God.

Hīnayāna: Small Vehicle, Lower Vehicle, Lesser Vehicle, referring to the Buddhism of the Theravāda tradition in Southeast Asia whose goal is arhatship. See *Theravāda.*

jīva: soul as ethical personality.

jñana-mārga: way of knowledge.

kāla: time.

karma: activity, action; by mind, mouth, or body; the result, influence, or potency of action in a later stage of life; rites; the moral law of cause and effect.

karma-mārga: way of ethical action.

Kṣatriya: warriors comprising kings and soldiers.

Mahāyāna: literally "larger vehicle" or "larger career"; Large Vehicle, Higher Vehicle, Greater Vehicle, referring to Buddhism in East Asia where the ideal is universal salvation.

Māyā: illusion; a synonym for Prakṛti and Avyakta.

mokṣa: liberation, salvation, emancipation.

neti-neti: "not this, not this."

nirmānakāya: the transformation-body, the body of incarnation, the body in which the Buddha appears among mankind.

nirvāṇa: unagitated, peaceful; the state of peace, of salvation.

pradhāna: a synonym for Prakṛti.

Prajāpati: Lord of living beings.

prajñā: intense knowledge or consciousness; wisdom; intuitive insight; a synonym for *buddhi.*

prājña: the name for the *ātman* in the state of deep sleep.

Prakṛti: Nature; physics; a synonym for *pradhāna*, Māyā, etc.

prāṇa: vital principle that makes life possible.

pratītya-samutpāda: the doctrine of conditioned emergence, or dependent origination.

Pratyeka-buddha: one who attains to his personal enlightenment by his own exertion.

pravṛtti: activity directed towards external objects; opposed to *nivṛtti*, which is actively directed towards the inward self.

purāṇa: epic.

puruṣa: man, person, *ātman*, Brahman.

rajas: the attribute of activity, one of the three attributes of Prakṛti.

ṛṣi: seer, sage.

ṛta: truth, practical truth, right, rite, water, ethical action, the fruit of ethical action.

rūpa: matter; form; color; appearance; phenomenon; thing; etc.

sādhanā: spiritual discipline.

śakti: energy; power; force; the energy aspect of the Godhead; God's consort in popular religion.

Śākyamuni: name of the historical Buddha who lived in India in the 6th century B.C.; literally, "wise man of the Śākya tribe."

samādhi: the placing of oneself in the object concentrated upon; trance, ecstasy, the final stage of meditation.

sambhogakāya: the reward or enjoyment-body, the body in which the Eternal Buddha appears before the bodhisattvas.

saṁghāta: collection, aggregate.

saṁhitā: hymn portion of the Vedas.

saṁsāra: world of becoming.

sannyāsi: ascetic.

sat: existence, being.

sattva: the transparent and pure attribute of Prakṛti.

satya: truth; reality.

skandha: see *saṁghāta.*

smṛti: memory; what is remembered; remembered sacred texts like the epics and ethical codes.

soma: fermented plant juice.

śrāmana: a religious recluse; monk; devotee who has left home life.

śrāvaka: one who has attained to his own salvation by personally hearing the preaching of the Buddha.

śruti: sense of hearing; what is heard; a synonym for the Veda.

Śūdra: laborer of service.

sukhāvatī: pure happy land; Western Paradise; goal of the Pure Land School

(Ching-t'u in China and Jōdo in Japan).

śūnya: void, empty; the Void; that which is devoid of all determinations.

taijasa: of psychic energy; name of the *ātman* in dream.

tamas: one of the attributes of Prakṛti, the dark.

tantra: devotion literature.

Tathāgata: literally, "thus come" or "thus gone," a title of the Buddha, meaning that the Buddha comes as all things come, namely, through causation but in spite of it attains Enlightenment; one who has "thus come" to preach and save all sentient beings.

Tathatā: Thusness or Suchness; truth; truly so; opposed to illusion or falsehood; the Absolute which is eternal, unchangeable, indestructible, without specific character or nature, and not produced by causes; identical with dharmadhātu, dharma-nature, and Perfect Reality.

Theravāda: doctrine or system of the Elders, the elder followers of Gautama Buddha; name of Buddhism in southeast Asia, a name preferable to the people there than Hīnayāna. See *Hīnayāna.*

Vaiṣya: trader.

varṇa: color, caste.

veda: knowledge.

vijñāna: consciousness, knowledge, cognition.

upaniṣad: secret doctrine.

CHINESE

ch'an: meditation; contemplation; Chinese abbreviated pronunciation of *dhyāna*, from which the Japanese word *zen* has been derived.

ch'eng: to complete.

ch'eng: sincerity; truthfulness; realness. Though pronounced the same, the two *ch'engs* are written in two different Chinese characters, the second consisting of the first on the right and the Chinese word for "speech" on the left.

chi: sixth of the Ten Celestial Stems, symbol of the positive element of Earth.

chi: subtle, incipient, activating force; a point at which an activity is about to take place but not yet visible and an opportunity presents itself, and thus an inward spring of movement and an omen of things to come. The word is written in a different character from the preceding *chi* and pronounced in a higher tone.

ch'i: material force; matter; matter-energy; ether; power; breath; vital force; strong, moving power; opposed to *li* (principle), which is the reason or law underlying a thing, whereas *ch'i* gives it concrete substance and form.

chiao: awakening; enlightenment; understanding; consciousness.

chiao: teaching; religion. The two *chiaos* are written and pronounced differently.

ch'ien: name of a trigram and hexagram symbolic of heaven, male, strength, origination, creativity, etc.

Ching-t'u: literally, "pure land," Western Paradise; Chinese translation of *sukhāvatī.* Japanese: Jōdo.

hsü-wu: literally "empty" and "nothing"; not a negative concept but means unobstructed, undifferentiated, etc., that is, pure being.

Hua-yen: Literally "flower splendor," Chinese name for *Avataṁsaka.* Japanese, Kegon.

hun: heavenly component of the soul, the spirit of man's vital force expressed in man's intelligence and power of breathing. See *p'o.*

jen: humanity; human-heartedness; true manhood, goodness; that which makes a man a moral being; the general virtue out of which the various moral virtues have come. The character for it consists of the world for man (*jen*, pronounced the same) on the left and two horizontal strokes on the right suggesting man and society, thus meaning that the perfect virtue includes self-perfection and the realization of a good society. As a particular virtue, it is love, benevolence, altruism, etc.

k'an: name of a trigram and hexagram; literally meaning "pit" and symbol for water, the moon, the northern direction, etc. Cf. *li* (trigram).

Kuan-yin: Chinese translation of the Sanskrit, Avalokiteśvara; literally "see sound," that is, "seeing the sound of (the world's) suffering." Japanese: Kannon.

kuei-shen: literally "ghosts" and "deities." The combined term means spiritual beings in general, often denoting ancestral spirits. In ancient times, *shen* usually refers to heavenly beings whereas *kuei* refers to spirits of deceased human beings. In popular religion *shen* means "gods" (who are good) and *kuei* means "demons" (who are not always good). To the enlightened Chinese, *kuei* and *shen* mean the negative spiritual force of Nature and the positive spiritual force of Nature, respectively. Thus, expansion (pronounced *shen* in a different tone) means *shen* (positive spiritual force) and contraction (or to return, pronounced *kuei* in a different tone) means *kuei* (negative spiritual force).

k'un: name of a trigram and hexagram symbolic of earth, female, weakness, preservation, completion, etc.

kung-an: literally, "public document on the desk," connoting a sense of important decision and the final determination of truth and falsehood. Japanese: *koan.*

li: name of a trigram and hexagram symbolic of fire, brightness, separation, the southern direction, the sun, etc. Cf. *k'an.* The pronunciation of this is different from the following four, which are pronounced the same. The characters for the five *lis* are all different.

li: one third of a mile.

li: a plum tree.

li: the principle, reason, law, order, or pattern of existence. See *ch'i.*

li: principle of conduct; rule of conduct; rules of propriety; good form; good custom; ceremonies; rites; etiquette.

ming: to order; to endow nature in man and things; life; destiny; life span; fate.

p'o: earthly component of the soul, the spirit of man's physical nature expressed in bodily movements. See *hun.*

se: matter; form; color; appearance; phenomenon; thing; etc.; Chinese translation of the Sanskrit, *rūpa.*

Shang-ti: Lord on High; literally "high lord"; the Supreme Being.

shen: see *kuei-shen.*

Tao: the Way; path; the priciple or process of the operation of Nature; moral truth; course of culture. Etymologically the word consists of "head" and "walk," meaning the path along which one walks.

Ti: The Lord. Also means an emperor.

T'ien: heaven; Nature; Shang-ti.

tzu: first of the Twelve Earthly Branches, symbol of fire; the period from 11 p.m. to 1 a.m. In an appellation, like Lao Tzu, it means master, scholar, philosopher, gentleman.

wu: the fifth Celestial Stem, symbol of the yang of Earth.

wu: the seventh Earthly Branch, symbol of water, the period from 11 a.m. to 1 p.m. These two *wus* and the *wu* in *hsü-wu,* are written and pronounced differently.

wu-wei: literally "no action"; taking no artificial or unnatural action; not being engulfed in activity; taking no action with a selfish or impure motive. The same *wu* in *hsü-wu.*

yang: the sun; the sunny side of a slope; male; generally, the positive, male, strong, or active cosmic principle, force, or element.

yin: the moon; the dark side of a slope; female; generally, the negative, female, weak, or passive cosmic principle, force, or element.

yüan: to investigate; source; origin; to inquire into the source.

JAPANESE

Amaterasu: literally, "heavenly illuminating," the name of the mythological ancestress and the tutelary deity of the Japanese imperial family. Referred to as the Sun Goddess for the sake of brevity in this book.

Amida: the Japanese rendering of Amitābha (the Buddha of Infinite Light) or Amitāyus (the Buddha of Infinite Life), whose abode is the Pure Land (Jōdo in Japanese).

Dainichi: the Great Sun Buddha (Mahāvairocana), who is the supreme Buddha of esoteric Buddhism.

Ise: the seat of the Grand Shrine of the

Sun Goddess, situated in the present Miye Prefecture.

Izanagi and Izanami: the parents of the Sun Goddess in Japanese mythology.

Jimmu: the first legendary emperor of Japan; his reign is traditionally dated 660–585 B.C.

Jōdo: the Pure Land, which is Amida's Paradise. It is also the name of the Pure Land school (Jōdo-shū) of Buddhism.

kami: a word of many meanings, such as deity, spirit, or anything that commands the awe and reverence of man. It is the object of worship in Shintō.

kannagara: an adverb that modifies actions of kami; usually translated as "in accordance with the will of the kami."

Kannon: see under the Sanskrit, Avalokiteśvara.

kōan: *see under* the Chinese, *kung-an*.

Kokugaku: national learning which stressed the importance of Japanese cultural tradition before it came under the influence of Chinese civilization and Buddhism.

nembutsu: invocation of the name of Amida, a pious practice followed by the adherents of the Pure Land schools.

Ninigi: the grandson of the Sun Goddess in Japanese mythology, believed to have descended from the Plain of High Heaven to rule Japan.

norito: Shintō ritual prayers.

Ryōbu Shintō: the pattern of Shintō-Buddhist coexistence or almagamation that developed in Japan.

shōgun: the title for the military dictator who was *de facto* ruler of Japan.

ubasoku: the Japanese pronunciation of *upasaka* (Sanskrit), one who is not a member of a monastic community, but who follows the Law of the Buddha. This term, however, was used in Japan to refer to unorthodox, shamanistic Buddhists.

ARABIC

A.H.: after the *Hijrah* (the year of 622).

aflaḥa: to grow fully; to achieve moral and religious felicity.

ahl al ḥadīth: jurists and theologians who presented Islāmic truth in reportative terms concerning the sayings, judgments, and deeds of Muḥammad.

ahl al ḥall wa al 'aqd: literally, "those who bind and loosen," or "make" or "unmake" governments and policies.

ahl al kalām: jurists and theologians who presented Islāmic truth in rational terms.

al ākhirah: the end of all life on earth; the Day of Judgment; the other world.

Allah: proper name of God.

amān: pact between Muslim citizens or State and non-Muslims, granting the latter protection.

'Amr ibn al 'Āṣ: chieftain of the Quraysh tribe and leader of Makkah.

al Anṣār: "helpers" of Muḥammad or the Muslims of Madīnah.

'aql: reason or binding.

'Arafāt, mount of: a hill near Makkah where the pilgrimage prayers are held.

Ash'ariyyah: orthodox theological school founded by al Ash'arī.

Bakkah: another name for Makkah.

Banū 'Auf: Arab tribe.

Banū Fazārah: Arab tribe living between Makkah and Madīnah.

Banū Ghassān: Arab tribe of Ghassān in the south and Palmyra in the north.

Banū al Ḥārith: Arab tribe in Madīnah.

Banū al Layth: Arab tribe that lived southeast of Madīnah.

Banū al Najjār: tribe of Arab Jews in Madīnah.

bay'ah: oath of fealty and obedience given a ruler by the ruled.

caliph: Anglicized form of the Arabic "*Khalifah.*"

dhikr: *du'ā'*, repeated as "remembrance" of God.

du'ā': invocation, or prayer, but not the supreme act of worship.

Fazārah: see *Banū Fazārah.*

Ghassān: see *Banū Ghassān.*

al Ḥadīth: collective name for all *ḥadīths.*

ḥadīth: tradition of Muḥammad.

ḥajj: pilgrimage.

ḥalāl: legally or ethically permissible.

ḥanīf: pre-Islāmic monotheist advocating morality and universalism.

ḥanīfism: religion and morality of the ḥanifs.

hijrah: emigration of the Prophet to

Madīnah on July 16, 622, and hence, the beginning of the Islāmic calendar.

Hudhayl: Arab tribe hostile to Muḥammad.

ḥukm: rule, government, or regime.

Iblīs: Satan.

'Īd al Fiṭr: "feast of the end of the fast."

ijmā': consensus or community of view.

ijtihād: creative interpretation.

imāmate: office of the *imām*, or the theory governing the chief-of-state's assumption and administration of his functions.

īmān: rational certainty or faith by conviction after due critical consideration of alternatives.

al Injīl: the *Evangel*, in the singular form referring to the divine message revealed to Jesus.

'iqāl: that which binds and holds together. See *'aql.*

irādah: God's will as necessary pattern of nature and ideal ought-to-be of moral conduct.

Islām: acquiescence. As a proper name, it denotes the religion revealed to and practiced by the Prophet. Often incorrectly used to mean the culture, thought, civilization, or history of the Muslims.

isti'mān: application for or granting of *amān* to one or many members of the enemy forces.

jihād: exertion, struggle, usually communal, in the cause of God.

jinn: spiritual beings dependent upon divine initiative and efficacy.

jinnī: one member of the class *jinn.*

jizyah: tax levied on the non-Muslim citizens in lieu of *zakāt.*

jumādā I and II: fifth and sixth months of the calendar.

al Ka'bah: the cubicle in the sanctuary of Makkah which all Muslims face in ritual worship and circle in pilgrimage.

khalīfah: successor. Referred to God, it means man in general.

kharāj: proceeds of a land through taxation.

Majūs: pre-Islāmic fire worshipers in Persia.

Makkah: Mecca.

mashī'ah: God's will as divine fiat or decision.

mu'adhdhin: also "Muezzin". The man who calls the Muslims to prayer five times a day.

muhādanah: temporary cessation of hostilities.

Muhājirum: Makkan Muslims who emigrated to Madīnah before the conquest of Makkah in 8 A.H. (630).

al mu'minūm: the believers as convinced of the Islāmic faith.

Muslim: Often erroneously spelled *Moslem* or *Mussulman.* The adherent as acquiescing to God's Lordship and Mastery.

Mu'tazilah: early rationalist school of thought.

muwāda'ah: in Islāmic law, legitimate, friendly intercourse with the enemy.

al Nāmus: literally, "the law" (from the Greek, *nomos*) or the will of God as a synthesis of all values and all oughts.

Negus: royal title of the Kings of Abyssinia.

Prince of Believers: caliphal title first accorded to 'Umar ibn al Khaṭṭāb.

Qur'ān: often erroneously spelled Koran, Coran, or alcoran, it is the scripture of Islām. Though the text is a collection of these verses made under the express order of 'Uthmān between 23 and 28 A.H. (645–650), there is absolutely no doubt that it is the very words which the Prophet conveyed to his companions as the divine revelation.

Quraysh: the Prophet's tribe which dominated Makkah, resisted his call for 18 years.

Rabb: Lord. One of the names of God.

al Raḥman: the Merciful. The most popular name of God.

rajab: the 7th month of the Islāmic lunar calendar.

Ramaḍān: the 9th month and time of fasting.

Ṣalāt: the supreme act of worship in Islām.

ṣawm: fasting, especially during the month of Ramaḍān.

Sha'bān: the 8th month.

shahādah: confession that there is no god but God and Muḥammad is His Prophet.

al Shām: the territories now known as Syria, Lebanon, Palestine, and Jordan.

sharī'ah: the law of Islām.

Shī'ah: the sect that separated itself from the consensus of the community acquiescing to the caliphate of Mu'āwiyah in 161 A.H.

shirk: associationism; the attribution of divine power to beings other than God.

shūrā: Rule by consultation.

sunnah: the Prophet's trodden path or example.

sunnī: follower of the *sunnah.*

sūrah: one of the 114 divisions of the Qur'ānic text.

tawakkul: trust in and dependence upon God.

tawḥīd: "oneness" or "asserting of the unity and uniqueness of God."

ummah: the society of Islām.

zakāt: the legal institution of sharing one's wealth with one's fellows.

zakāt al Fiṭr: charity equivalent to a day's nourishment given at the end of Ramaḍān.

Guide to Pronunciation of Asian Words

The Guide is a nontechnical explanation based on well-established systems of transliteration and pronunciation. Following common practice, diacritical marks are omitted from well-known personal names in history (e.g. Gandhi instead of Gāndhi) and geographical names (Tokyo instead of Tokyō) as well as names of recent and contemporary persons. (It should be pointed out that many traditional authors and most contemporary writers use different diacritical marks or do away with them altogether and that diacritical marks are generally omitted in newspapers, in popular literature, and even sometimes in academic publications, where, when the apostrophe is omitted from Chinese words, one cannot tell whether *chang*, for example, is pronounced *jang* or *ch'ang*.) Useless diacritical marks (like ˘ and ˆ in Chinese), have been omitted.

In accordance with standard transliteration, Sanskrit words such as *Ṛg*, *ṛta*, etc., are used instead of the common renderings of *Rig*, *rita*, etc., and Arabic words like *Qu'rān*, *Madīnha*, *Makkah*, etc., instead of *Koran*, *Medina*, *Mecca*, etc. However, following the general practice in the academic world, widely used, spellings of certain personal and geographical names are used even though they do not conform to the standard transliterations.

SANSKRIT

a as in *particular*
ā as in *father*
i as in *pit*
ī as in the initial *e* in *eve*
ū as in *rude*
ṛ as *ri* in *merrily*
e as in *pet*
ai as in *gait*
ou or *au* as in *house* or German *haus*
o as in *go*
g as in *go*
ṅ as in *sing*
c as *ch* in *chores*
ch as *chh* in *churchhouse*
ñ as in *singe* (pronounced *sinj*)
ṭ as in *true* (uttered with the tip of the tongue turned up and drawn back into the dome of the palate)
ḍ as in *drum* (the same)
ṇ as in *tent* (the same)
t as in *latter*
th as in *latter* with another *h* add (i.e., with a stronger aspirate, as in *anthill*)
d as in *ladder*
dh as *th* in *this* with another *h* added (i.e. with a stronger aspirate as in *madhouse*)
ś as in *sure* (uttered with the flat of the tongue against the forward part of the palatal arch)
ṣ as in *shine* (uttered with the tip of the tongue reverted into the dome of the palate)
s as in *sit*

CHINESE

a as in *father*
e as in *end*
i as the initial *e* in *eve*
o as in *go*
u as in *rude*
ü as in German *grün* or in French *menu*

ai as in *ice*
ao as in *out*
ou as in *obey*
ch is pronounced as *j*
k is pronounced as *g*
p is pronounced as *b*
t is pronounced as *d*
ts or *tz* is pronounced as *tz* or *dz*
hs is pronounced rather like *sh*
j is pronounced like *r*
ch', *k'*, *p'*, *ts'*, or *tz'* is pronounced as in English

JAPANESE

a as in *father*
i as the initial *e* in *eve*
u as in *rude*
e as in *late*; when final usually short as in *end*
o as in *go*
ā as *a*, but held half again as long
ū as *u*, but held half again as long
ō as *o*, but held half again as long
ae as *a* & *e*, but with the *e* half-length
ai as *a* & *i*, but with the *i* half-length
ui as *u* & *i*, but with the *i* half-length
oi as *o* & *i*, but the *i* half-length
ei as *e*, but held half again as long
kk is pronounced as two English *k*'s separated by a hyphen
tt is pronounced as two English *t*'s separated by a hyphen, as *cattail*
tch is pronounced as if hyphenated, *t-ch*
pp is pronounced as two English *p*'s separated by a hyphen
ss is pronounced as English *s*, but held half again as long
nn is pronounced as English *n*, but held half again as long
mm is pronounced English *m*, but held half again as long
r is briefly trilled and made far forward in the mouth
g is pronounced as English *g*, but in the body of a word it is often pronounced *ng*

ARABIC

a as in *chap*
i as in *pit*
u as in *rude*
ā as in *father*
ī as the initial *e* in *eve*.
ū as in *shoot*
dh as in *the*, a voiced dental fricative
th as in *tooth*, a voiceless dental fricative
kh as in Scottish *loch* or German *doch*, a voiceless velar fricative (a fricative is a sound originating in the narrowing of two organs of speech—tongue, teeth, palate, etc.)
ḥ, *ṣ*, *ḍ*, *ṭ*, *ẓ* as in English without the dot, but the sound is intensified in each case and the soft palate is raised to give the sound a laryngeal tone
w always as in *wagon*. It does not make a diphthong when preceded by a vowel.
gh rolled *r*
q laryngeal *k*
' denotes a complete stop before pronouncing the following letter
' a voiceless guttural fricative (tongue and soft palate)

Index

(Arabic surnames preceded by *Al* (the), are indexed under the surnames.)

immortality: in Chinese religions, 100, 103, 144, 163, 170, 185, 190, 195, 224, 266; *see also* everlasting life; in Hinduism, 20, 21, 24, 30, 31, 38, 42, 82
immortals, 100, 156, 160, 162, 163, 170; *see also* immortality
incipient force (*chi*), 171, 172
individual, 2
Indra, 3, 14, 15, 17, 22, 31, 37, 38, 50 n., 59, 75
influence and response, *see* Nature, and man; retribution
Ingen, 284
Injil (the *Evangel*), 323
injustice, 350
Inquiry on Man, 209–212
Institutes of the Engi Period, 262–66
intermarriage, 4, 5, 7–8
'Irāk, 329
Iśāvāsya Upaniṣad, 30
'Isawīs, 327
Ise, 242
Ise Shrine, 234, 240, 246, 264, 271 n., 291, 292, 295
Al Iṣfahānī, Abū 'Īsā, 327
Islām, 7, 90, 307 ff.; Biblical criticism, 327–28; characterized, 307–318; confession, 348–49, 350, 351, 352, 353; ethics, 313, 314, 349–50; *see also* deeds, good and evil; in history, 332–38; compared with Hinduism, 2; in India, 4–6, 10–11; Islāmization of the world, 314–317, 359, 374; model rulers, 367–70; priesthood, 308; rationalism of, 308; *see also* knowledge in Islām, rational; reason; relation with peoples, 337, 355, 375; *see also* Christians; Jews; Makkans; relation with other religions, 307, 328–31; *see also* Christianity; Hinduism; Judaism; on religion, 323–31; sects, 3, 26; society, 314–15, 359–63; *see also ummah*; state of, 366–67, 371; worldliness, 312, 313, 314; *see also* abstinence; charity; faith; family; fasting; Five Pillars; law; man; marriage; pilgrimage; Qur'ān; salvation; state; *sunnah*; *ummah*; war, holy; *zakāt*
Iyeyasu, 305 n.
Izanagi, 232, 271 n., 296, 298, 300
Izanami, 232, 296, 300
Izumo, 233

Jabalah ibn al Ayham, 376
Jaimini, 77
Jainism, 6–7, 9–10, 67–69; action in, 68; *ahiṁsa*, 67; *ātman*, 67, 68; desires, 69; and Hinduism, 1–2; *jīva*, 68; *karma*, 67, 69; knowledge, 68; souls, 67; *mokṣa*, 67, 68; and Śaivism, 85; Supreme Spirit, 64; vows, 67, 68, 69 n.; *yoga*, 68
jen (humanity, love, benevolence), *see* humanity
Jerusalem, 354
Jesus, 323–30, *passim*, 355, 366, 367, 370
Jews, 321, 324, 326, 327, 329, 330, 366, 367, 370
Jimmu, Emperor, 233, 234, 245, 247 n.
Jina, 1, 73
Jingō (Jingū), Empress, 234–35
jinni (spiritual being), 315
jīva (soul), 20, 21, 33, 67, 78, 85 n.; *see also* soul
jizyah (poll tax), 329
Jōdo School, *see* Pure Land School
Jōjitsu School, 256, 269
Joseph, St., 327
Judaism, 77, 323, 324–25, 357
Judgment, Day of, 312
justice, 362, 364, 368, 372, 377
al Juwayni, Abū al Ma āli 'Abd al Malik ibn 'Abdullal ibn Yūsuf Imām al Ḥaramayn, 344–45

Ka, 11 n., 20, 29 n.
Kā, 22
Kabīr, 84, 87 n.
Kada Mabuchi, 291
Kakushin, 283
Kāla, 23
Kāli, 96 n.
Kali Age, 80, *see also* Four Ages
Kami: of Divine Generative Force, 231, 296, 300; of the Eternal Land, 244; of Kashima, 243; of One Word, 243–44; of Thunder, 244; Way of the, 300–301; *see also* kamis, Sun Goddess
kami, 231, 298
kamis, 231–32, 239, 240, 241, 245, 265; birth of, 231–32; Japan as the land of, 294; *see also* kami
k'an (pit) trigram, 164–65
K'an Tse, 220
Kannon, 256, 270; *see also* Kuan-yin
Kao Tzu, 112
Kao Yu, 143
Kara, 249
karma: in Buddhism, 180, 209, 210, 211, 275, 278; in Hinduism, 15, 20, 21, 45, 60, 61, 67; *see also* action
Kāsim, Muḥammad, 4, 328–29
Kasuga Shrine, 271 n.
Kātayavema, 7
Katha Upaniṣad, 31–33
Kātyāyana, 89
Kawabe clan, 244
Kegon School, 256, 270; *see also* Hua-yen School
Kena Upaniṣad, 31
king, 59
Kitabatake Chikafusa, 291
knowledge in Buddhism, 53–74, 79
knowledge in Hinduism: 73, 74, 75, 80; spiritual, 24, 25; two kinds of, 33; way of, 8, 10, 51–53, 61, 68

BL 1035
.G7 ~~290.95~~
~~CH-FA~~
~~KI-RA~~ c.1
Chan, Faruqi, Kitagawa, Rajuc.2

9/26/
4/28 4:
MAY 2
APR
MAY
JAN

BL 1035
.G7
290.95 c.1
CH-FA
KI-RA

AUTHOR
Chan, Faruqi, Kitagawa, Rajuc.3

TITLE
Great Asian Religions

DATE LOANED	BORROWER'S NAME	DATE RETURNED
	RESERVED	
MAY 20 1993	S. Thepsombandith 510237	
May 20 1995	Dan Swenson	NOV 15 1994
331247		

23668

Kansas School of Religion
At the University of Kansas
Smith Hall, Rm. 109, Library
Lawrence, Kansas 66045-2164

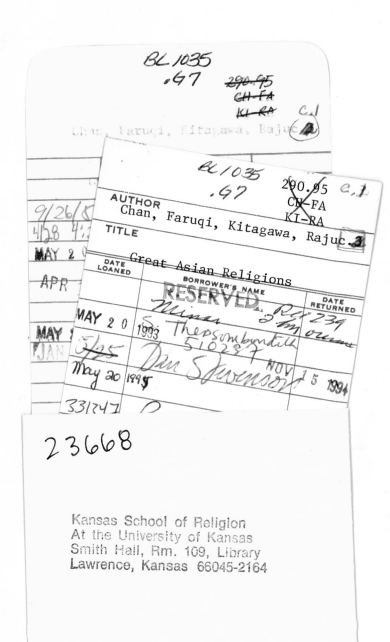